Get Connected.

FEATURES

Interactive Applications

Connect Management's **Interactive Applications** deliver the chapter's content through an engaging and interactive environment that allows students to apply the theory. Students will receive immediate feedback on how they are progressing.

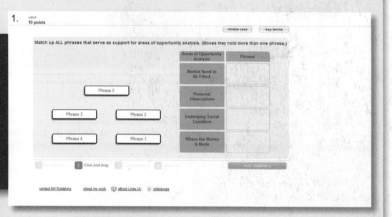

eBooks

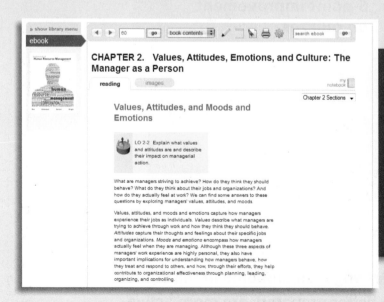

Connect Plus includes an eBook that allows you to share your notes with your students. Your students can insert and review their own notes, highlight the text, search for specific information, and interact with media resources. Using an eBook with *Connect Plus* gives your students a complete digital solution that allows them to access their materials from any computer.

Get Engaged.

Lecture Capture

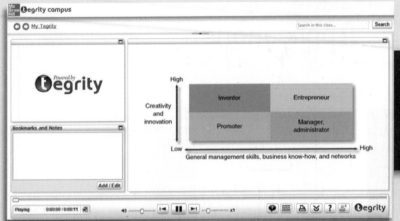

Make your classes available anytime, anywhere. With simple, one-click recording, students can search for a word or phrase and be taken to the exact place in your lecture that they need to review.

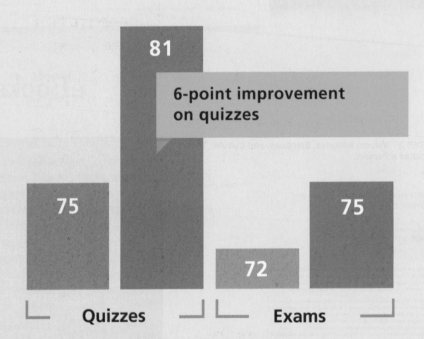

6-point improvement on quizzes

81

75

72

75

Quizzes   Exams

McGraw-Hill Connect engages students in the course content so they are better prepared, are more active in discussion, and achieve better results.

fundamentals of
Human Resource Management

Fifth Edition

Raymond A. Noe
The Ohio State University

John R. Hollenbeck
Michigan State University

Barry Gerhart
University of Wisconsin–Madison

Patrick M. Wright
University of South Carolina

McGraw-Hill Irwin

The McGraw-Hill Companies

FUNDAMENTALS OF HUMAN RESOURCE MANAGEMENT, FIFTH EDITION
International Edition 2014

10 09 08 07 06 05 04 03 02 01
20 15 14 13
CTP   MPM

When ordering this title, use ISBN 978-1-259-07198-0 or MHID 1-259-07198-7

Printed in Singapore

www.mhhe.com

In tribute to the lives of Raymond and Mildred Noe
—R.A.N.

To my parents, Harold and Elizabeth, my wife, Patty, and
my children, Jennifer, Marie, Timothy, and Jeffrey
—J.R.H.

To my parents, Robert and Shirley, my wife, Heather, and
my children, Chris and Annie
—B.G.

To my parents, Patricia and Paul, my wife, Mary, and my
sons, Michael and Matthew
—P.M.W.

About the Authors

Raymond A. Noe is the Robert and Anne Hoyt Designated Professor of Management at The Ohio State University. He was previously a professor in the Department of Management at Michigan State University and the Industrial Relations Center of the Carlson School of Management, University of Minnesota. He received his BS in psychology from The Ohio State University and his MA and PhD in psychology from Michigan State University. Professor Noe conducts research and teaches undergraduate as well as MBA and PhD students in human resource management, managerial skills, quantitative methods, human resource information systems, training, employee development, and organizational behavior. He has published articles in the *Academy of Management Journal*, *Academy of Management Review*, *Journal of Applied Psychology*, *Journal of Vocational Behavior*, and *Personnel Psychology*. Professor Noe is currently on the editorial boards of several journals including *Personnel Psychology*, *Journal of Applied Psychology*, and *Journal of Organizational Behavior*. Professor Noe has received awards for his teaching and research excellence, including the Herbert G. Heneman Distinguished Teaching Award in 1991 and the Ernest J. McCormick Award for Distinguished Early Career Contribution from the Society for Industrial and Organizational Psychology in 1993. He is also a fellow of the Society for Industrial and Organizational Psychology.

John R. Hollenbeck holds the positions of University Distinguished Professor at Michigan State University and Eli Broad Professor of Management at the Eli Broad Graduate School of Business Administration. Dr. Hollenbeck received his PhD in management from New York University in 1984. He served as the acting editor at *Organizational Behavior and Human Decision Processes* in 1995, the associate editor of *Decision Sciences* from 1999 to 2004, and the editor of *Personnel Psychology* from 1996 to 2002. He has published over 80 articles and book chapters on the topics of team decision making and work motivation. According to the Institute for Scientific Information, this body of work has been cited over 2,500 times by other researchers. Dr. Hollenbeck has been awarded over $6 million in external research funding, most of which was granted by the Office of Naval Research and the Air Force Office of Scientific Research. Along with Daniel R. Ilgen, he founded the Michigan State University Team Effectiveness Research Laboratory, and this facility has been dedicated to conducting large sample team research since 1991. Dr. Hollenbeck has been awarded fellowship status in both the Academy of Management and the American Psychological Association, and was recognized with the Career Achievement Award by the HR Division of the Academy of Management (2011) and the Early Career Award by the Society of Industrial and Organizational Psychology (1992). At Michigan State, Dr. Hollenbeck has won several teaching awards, including the Michigan State Distinguished Faculty Award, the Michigan State Teacher-Scholar Award, and the Broad MBA Most Outstanding Faculty Member.

Barry Gerhart is Professor of Management and Human Resources and the Bruce R. Ellig Distinguished Chair in Pay and Organizational Effectiveness, School of Business, University of Wisconsin–Madison. He has also served as department chair or area coordinator at Cornell, Vanderbilt, and Wisconsin. His research interests include compensation, human resource strategy, international human resources, and employee retention. Professor Gerhart received his BS in psychology from Bowling Green State University and his PhD in industrial relations from the University of Wisconsin–Madison. His research has been published in a variety of outlets, including the *Academy of Management Annals, Academy of Management Journal, Annual Review of Psychology, Journal of Applied Psychology,* and *Personnel Psychology.* He has co-authored two books in the area of compensation. He serves on the editorial boards of journals such as the *Academy of Management Journal, Industrial and Labor Relations Review, International Journal of Human Resource Management, Journal of Applied Psychology, Management & Organization Review,* and *Personnel Psychology.* Professor Gerhart is a past recipient of the Scholarly Achievement Award and of the International Human Resource Management Scholarly Research Award, both from the Human Resources Division, Academy of Management. He is a Fellow of the American Psychological Association and the Society for Industrial and Organizational Psychology.

Patrick M. Wright is Thomas C. Vandiver Bicentennial Chair in the Darla Moore School of Business at the University of South Carolina. Prior to joining USC, he served on the faculties at Cornell University, Texas A&M University, and the University of Notre Dame.

Professor Wright teaches, conducts research, and consults in the area of Strategic Human Resource Management (SHRM), particularly focusing on how firms use people as a source of competitive advantage and the changing nature of the Chief HR Officer role. For the past eight years he has been studying the CHRO role through a series of confidential interviews, public podcasts, small discussion groups, and conducting the Cornell/CAHRS Survey of Chief HR Officers. In addition, he is the faculty leader for the Cornell ILR Executive Education/NAHR program, "The Chief HR Officer: Strategies for Success," aimed at developing potential successors to the CHRO role. He served as the lead editor on the recently released book, *The Chief HR Officer: Defining the New Role of Human Resource Leaders*, published by John Wiley and Sons.

He has published more than 60 research articles in journals as well as more than 20 chapters in books and edited volumes. He has co-authored two textbooks titled *Human Resource Management: Gaining Competitive Advantage* (now in its eighth edition) and *Management of Organizations*. He has co-edited a special issue of *Research in Personnel and Human Resources Management* titled "Strategic Human Resource Management in the 21st Century" and guest edited a special issue of *Human Resource Management Review* titled "Research in Strategic HRM for the 21st Century."

He has conducted programs and consulted for a number of large organizations, including Comcast, Royal Dutch Shell, Kennametal, AstraZeneca, BT, and BP. He currently serves as a member on the Board of Directors for the National Academy of Human Resources (NAHR). He is a former board member of HRPS, SHRM Foundation, and World at Work (formerly American Compensation Association). In 2011 he was named by *HRM Magazine* as one of the 20 "Most Influential Thought Leaders in HR."

Preface

Managing human resources is a critical component of any company's overall mission to provide value to customers, shareholders, employees, and the community in which it does business. Value includes profits as well as employee growth and satisfaction, creation of new jobs, contributions to community programs, and protection of the environment. All aspects of human resource management, including acquiring, preparing, developing, and compensating employees, can help companies meet their daily challenges, create value, and provide competitive advantages in the global marketplace. In addition, effective human resource management requires an awareness of broader contextual issues affecting business, such as the economy, legislation, and globalization.

Both the media and academic research show that effective HRM practices result in greater value for shareholders and employees. For example, the human resource practices at companies such as Google, SAS, Wegmans Food Markets, and REI helped them earn recognition on *Fortune* magazine's recent list of "The Top 100 Companies to Work For." This publicity creates a positive vibe for these companies, helping them attract talented new employees, motivate and retain current employees, and make their products and services more desirable to consumers.

Our Approach: Engage, Focus, and Apply

Following graduation, most students will find themselves working in businesses or not-for-profit organizations. Regardless of position or career aspirations, their role in directly managing other employees or understanding human resource management practices is critical for ensuring both company and personal success. As a result, *Fundamentals of Human Resource Management*, Fifth Edition focuses on human resource issues and how HR is used at work. *Fundamentals* is applicable to both HR majors and students from other majors or colleges who are taking an HR course as an elective or a requirement.

Our approach to teaching human resource management involves *engaging* students in learning through the use of real-world examples and best practices; *focusing* them on important HR issues and concepts; and *applying* what they have learned through chapter features and end-of-chapter exercises and cases. Students not only learn about best practices but are actively engaged through the use of cases and decision making. As a result, students will be able to take what they have learned in the course and apply it to solving HRM problems they will encounter on the job.

As described in the guided tour of the book that follows, each chapter includes several different pedagogical features. "Thinking Ethically" confronts students with ethical issues that occur in managing human resources. "HR Oops!" highlights human resource management issues that were handled poorly. "Best Practices" provides examples of companies whose HR activities work well. "Did You Know?" provides interesting statistics about chapter topics and how they play out in real-world companies. For this new edition, we have added a discussion question to this feature to help students evaluate the data presented.

Fundamentals also assists students with "how to" perform HR activities, such as empowering employees to innovate, correcting pay inequity, and identifying high-potential employees, all of which they are likely to encounter as part of their jobs. End-of-chapter cases focus on corporate sustainability ("Taking Responsibility") and managing the workforce ("Managing Talent").

Organization of the Fifth Edition

Part 1 (Chapters 1–4) discusses the environmental forces that companies face in trying to effectively use their human resources. These forces include economic, technological, and social trends; employment laws; and work design. Employers typically have more control over work design than development of equal employment law and economic, technologic, or social trends, but all affect how employers attract, retain, and motivate human resources. Chapter 1 discusses why HRM is a critical component to an organization's overall success. The chapter introduces HRM practices and human resource professionals and managers' roles and responsibilities in managing human resources.

Some of the major trends discussed in Chapter 2 include how workers continue to look for employment as the U.S. economy slowly moves from recession to recovery; greater availability of new and less expensive technologies for human resource management (including social networking); the growth of HRM on a global scale; the types of skills needed for today's jobs; and the importance of aligning HRM with a company's overall strategy to gain competitive advantage. Chapter 3 presents an overview of the major laws affecting employees and the ways that organizations can develop HR practices that comply with the laws. Chapter 4 shows how jobs and work systems determine the knowledge, skills, and abilities that employees need to provide products or services and influence employees' motivation, satisfaction, and safety at work. The process of analyzing and designing jobs is also discussed.

Part 2 (Chapter 5–7) deals with identifying the types of employees needed, recruiting and choosing them, and training them to perform their jobs. Chapter 5 discusses how to develop a human resources plan. The strengths and weaknesses of different employment options for dealing with shortages or excesses of human resources, including outsourcing, use of contract workers, and downsizing, are emphasized. Strategies for recruiting talented employees are highlighted, including use of electronic recruiting sources such as social media and job boards.

Chapter 6 emphasizes that selection is a process that starts with screening applications and résumés and concludes with a job offer. The chapter takes a look at the most widely used methods for minimizing errors in choosing employees, including employment tests and candidate interviews. Selection method standards, such as reliability and validity, are discussed in understandable terms. Chapter 7 covers the features of effective training systems. Effective training includes not only creating a good learning environment but hiring managers who encourage employees to use training content in their jobs and hiring employees who are motivated to learn. Advantages and disadvantages of different training methods, including e-learning and mobile learning, are discussed.

Part 3 (Chapters 8–10) discusses how to assess employees' performance and capitalize on their talents through retention and development. Chapter 8 examines the strengths and weaknesses of different performance management systems including controversial forced distribution or ranking systems. Chapter 9 shows students how assessment, job experiences, formal courses, and mentoring relationships can be used to develop employees for future success. Chapter 10 discusses how to maximize employee engagement and productivity and retain valuable employees as well as how to fairly and humanely separate employees when the need arises because of poor performance or economic conditions.

Part 4 (Chapters 11–13) covers rewarding and compensating human resources, including how to design pay structures, recognize good performers, and provide benefits. Chapter 11 discusses how managers weigh the importance and costs of pay to develop a compensation structure and levels of pay for each job given the worth of the jobs, legal requirements, and employee judgments about the fairness of pay levels. Chapter 12 covers the advantages and disadvantages of different types of incentive pay, including merit pay, gainsharing, and stock ownership. Chapter 13 highlights the contents of employee benefits packages, the ways organizations administer benefits, and what companies can do to help employees understand the value of benefits and control benefits costs.

Part 5 (Chapters 14–16) covers other HR topics including collective bargaining and labor relations; managing human resources globally; and creating and maintaining high-performance organizations. Chapter 14 explores HR activities as they pertain to employees who belong to unions or who are seeking to join unions. Traditional issues in labor–management relations, such as union structure and membership, the labor organizing process, and contract negotiations, are discussed, as well as new ways unions and management are working together in more cooperative relationships. Chapter 15 focuses on HR planning, selection, training, and compensation in international settings. The chapter also shows how global differences among countries affect decisions about human resources. Chapter 16 discusses the important role of human resources in creating an organization that achieves a high level of performance for employees, customers, shareholders, managers, and community. The chapter describes high-performance work systems and the conditions that contribute to high performance. It also introduces students to the ways to measure the effectiveness of human resource management and explores the importance of brand alignment in HR polices, practices, and programs.

New Features and Content Changes

In addition to all new or revised chapter pedagogy, the Fifth Edition of *Fundamentals* contains the following features in each chapter:

- **HRM Social:** Expanding on the importance of technology, these boxes demonstrate how social media and the Internet can be useful in managing HR activities in any organization.

- **Experiencing HR:** These experiential exercises encourage students to explore real-world HR topics and situations in both individual and group settings.

- **Twitter Focus:** Linking students to online business cases that reinforce chapter content, this activity offers students the opportunity to use social media to connect with each other and discuss HR strategies via Twitter.

The following content changes help students and instructors keep current on important HR topics:

- Chapter 1 includes an increased emphasis on the importance of human resources aligning with an organization's overall strategy. A section on workforce analytics has been added and discusses the use of quantitative tools and scientific methods to analyze pertinent information and make evidence-based decisions. Key concepts of talent management and corporate sustainability are also explored.

- Focusing on trends, Chapter 2 includes an updated discussion on how the slowly recovering economy continues to challenge HR professionals to find ways to keep employees working efficiently; to recruit the right people with the right skills; to deal with a multigenerational workforce; and to empower employees. The impact of employee job-hopping is also discussed, along with the increased importance of cloud computing in HR activities.

- Statistics on age discrimination, disability complaints, and safety training have been updated in Chapter 3.

- Discussion of work flow analysis has been expanded in Chapter 4, and a new section on competency models has been added.

- Chapter 5's discussion on recruitment sources has been revised to reflect the increasing importance of online recruiting and the influence of social networks on job hunting and career networking.

- Chapter 6 includes new company examples in the discussion of legal standards for employee selection and the use of references in job applications. The section on background checks for job applicants has been revised, and a new section on the impact of online job applications has been added.

- The discussion of transfer-of-training methodologies in Chapter 7 has been expanded, including how managers must continue to emphasize the importance of training before, during, and after implementation. The strategy of establishing communities of practice is also explored.

- Details on the process of performance management are highlighted in Chapter 8, including a revised illustration that itemizes the six key stages of the process. The importance of an effective performance management process is discussed and how it contributes to a company's overall competitive advantage.

- Chapter 9 provides an updated discussion about the process for developing a succession plan and measuring the plan's effectiveness.

- In Chapter 10, the section on alternative dispute resolution has been expanded and includes a detailed example of how Ford introduced a peer review process that vastly improved handling of complaints and disputes. A new section on employee engagement has also been added.

- New statistics on executive compensation, merit raise increases, and ESOP plans are provided in Chapters 11 and 12.

- In Chapter 13, the discussion on the Affordable Health Care Act has been updated. New statistics on employee compensation and health care costs in other countries are also provided.

- Union statistics have been updated in Chapter 14, including trends, diversity of membership, and a list of the largest unions in the United States.

- In Chapter 15, trends in managing human resources globally have been updated, including a renewed interest in hiring host country nationals in China to manage operations of Western companies.
- Chapter 16 concludes the Fifth Edition with an expanded discussion of job satisfaction and employee engagement. A new section on the importance of brand alignment and the integral part HR plays in this process has been added.

The author team believes that the focused, engaging, and applied approach of *Fundamentals* distinguishes it from other books that have similar coverage of HR topics. The book has timely coverage of important HR issues, is easy to read, has many features that grab the students' attention, and gets students actively involved in learning.

We would like to thank those of you who have adopted previous editions of *Fundamentals,* and we hope that you will continue to use upcoming editions. For those of you considering *Fundamentals* for adoption, we believe that our approach makes *Fundamentals* your text of choice for human resource management.

Acknowledgments

The fifth edition of *Fundamentals of Human Resource Management* would not have been possible without the staff of McGraw-Hill/Irwin. John Weimeister, our former editor, helped us in developing the vision for the book and gave us the resources we needed to develop a top-of-the-line HRM teaching package. Heather Darr's valuable insights and organizational skills kept the author team on deadline and made the book more visually appealing than the authors could have ever done on their own. We would also like to thank Cate Rzasa who worked diligently to make sure that the book was interesting, practical, and readable and remained true to findings of human resource management research. We also thank Elizabeth Trepkowski for her marketing efforts for this new book.

Our supplement authors deserve thanks for helping us create a first-rate teaching package. Julie Gedro of Empire State College wrote the newly custom-designed *Instructor's Manual* and Dr. Connie Sitterly authored the new Power-Point presentation.

We would like to extend our sincere appreciation to all of the professors who gave of their time to offer their suggestions and insightful comments that helped us to develop and shape this new edition:

Michelle Alarcon, Esq.
Hawaii Pacific University

Dr. Minnette A. Bumpus
University of the District of Columbia

Brennan Carr
Long Beach City College/El Camino College

Tom Comstock
Gannon University

Susie S. Cox
McNeese State University

Juan J. DelaCruz
Lehman College—CUNY

AnnMarie DiSienna
Dominican College

Lorrie Ferraro
Northeastern University

Carla Flores
Ball State University

Linette P. Fox
Johnson C. Smith University

Britt Hastey
UCLA, Chapman University, and Los Angeles City College

Kim Hester
Arkansas State University

Samira B. Hussein
Johnson County Community College

Joseph V. Ippolito
Brevard College

Adonis "Sporty" Jeralds
The University of South Carolina–Columbia

Guy Lochiatto
Mass Bay Community College

Liliana Meneses
University of Maryland University College

Kelly Mollica
The University of Memphis

Tami Moser
Southern Oklahoma State University

Richard J. Wagner
University of Wisconsin–Whitewater

Brandon L. Young
Embry-Riddle Aeronautical University

We would also like to thank the professors who gave of their time to review the previous editions through various stages of development.

Cheryl Adkins
Longwood University

Michelle Alarcon
Hawaii Pacific University

Lydia Anderson
Fresno City College

Brenda Anthony
Tallahassee Community College

Barry Armandi
SUNY–Old Westbury

Kristin Backhaus
State University of New York at New Paltz

Charlene Barker
Spokane Falls Community College

Melissa Woodard Barringer
University of Massachusetts at Amherst

Wendy Becker
University of Albany

Jerry Bennett
Western Kentucky University

Tom Bilyeu
Southwestern Illinois College

Genie Black
Arkansas Tech University

Larry Borgen
Normandale Community College

Angela D. Boston
The University of Texas–Arlington

Kay Braguglia
Hampton University

John Brau
Alvin Community College

Jon Bryan
Bridgewater State College

Susan Burroughs
Roosevelt University

Tony Cafarelli
Ursuline College

Jerry Anthony Carbo II
Fairmont State University

Kevin Carlson
Virginia Tech

Xiao-Ping Chen
University of Washington

Sharon Clark
Lebanon Valley College

Gary Corona
Florida Community College

Craig Cowles
Bridgewater State College

Suzanne Crampton
Grand Valley State University

Denise Daniels
Seattle Pacific University

K. Shannon Davis
North Carolina State University

Cedric Dawkins
Ashland University

John Despagna
Nassau Community College

Tom Diamante
Adelphi University

Anita Dickson
Northampton Community College

Robert Ericksen
Craven Community College

Dave Erwin
Athens State University

Philip Ettman
Westfield State College

Elizabeth Evans
Concordia University Wisconsin

Angela Farrar
University of Nevada at Las Vegas

Ronald Faust
University of Evansville

William P. Ferris
Western New England College

David Foote
Middle Tennessee State University

Lucy Ford
Rutgers University

Wanda Foster
Calumet College of St. Joseph

Marty Franklin
Wilkes Community College

Rusty Freed
Tarleton State University

Walter Freytag
University of Washington

Diane Galbraith
Slippery Rock University

Donald Gardner
University of Colorado–Colorado Springs

Michael Gavlik
Vanderbilt University

Jane Whitney Gibson
Nova Southeastern University

Treena Gillespie
California State University–Fullerton

Kris Gossett
Ivy Tech State College

Jean Grube
University of Wisconsin–Madison

Kathy Harris
Northwestern Oklahoma State University

Samuel Hazen
Tarleton State University

Janet Henquinet
Metropolitan State University, St. Paul

James Hess
Ivy Tech State College

Kim Hester
Arkansas State University

Chad Higgins
University of Washington

Nancy Higgins
Montgomery College

Charles Hill
UC Berkeley

Mary Hogue
Kent State University

MaryAnne Hyland
Adelphi University

Linda Isenhour
University of Central Florida

Henry Jackson
Delaware County Community College

Pamela Johnson
California State University–Chico

Coy Jones
The University of Memphis

Gwendolyn Jones
University of Akron

Kathleen Jones
University of North Dakota

Jordan Kaplan
Long Island University

Jim Kennedy
Angelina College

Shawn Komorn
University of Texas Health Sciences Center

Lee W. Lee
Central Connecticut State University

Leo Lennon
Webster University

Beth A. Livingston
Cornell University

Michael Dane Loflin
Limestone College / York Technical College

Dan Lybrook
Purdue University

Cheryl Macon
Butler College

Patricia Martinez
University of Texas at San Antonio

Jalane Meloun
Kent State University

Angela Miles
Old Dominion University

James Morgan
California State University–Chico

Ellen Mullen
Iowa State University

Vicki Mullenex
Davis & Elkins College

Suzy Murray
Piedmont Technical College

Cliff Olson
Southern Adventist University

Laura Paglis
University of Evansville

Teresa Palmer
Illinois State University

Jack Partlow
Northern Virginia Community College

Dana Partridge
University of Southern Indiana

Brooke Quizz
Peirce College

Barbara Rau
University of Wisconsin–Oshkosh

Mike Roberson
Eastern Kentucky University

Foreman Rogers, Jr.
Northwood University

Mary Ellen Rosetti
Hudson Valley Community College

Joseph Salamone
State University of New York at Buffalo

Karen J. Smith
Columbia Southern University

Lucian Spataro
Ohio University

James Tan
University of Wisconsin–Stout

Steven Thomas
Southwest Missouri State University

Alan Tilquist
West Virginia State College

Tom Tudor
University of Arkansas

Linda Turner
Morrisville State College

William Van Lente
Alliant International University

Richard Wagner
University of Wisconsin–Whitewater

Fraya Wagner-Marsh
Eastern Michigan University

Melissa Waite
SUNY Brockport

Nancy Elizabeth Waldeck
University of Toledo

Barbara Warschawski
Schenectady County Community College

Gary Waters
Hawaii Pacific University

Bill Waxman
Edison Community College

Laura Wolfe
Lousiana State University

Steven Wolff
Marist College

John Zietlow
Lee University

John Zummo
York College

Raymond A. Noe
John R. Hollenbeck
Barry Gerhart
Patrick M. Wright

fundamentals of human
resource
management

fundamentals of
Human Resource Management *fifth edition*

Noe   Hollenbeck   Gerhart   Wright

engaging.
focused.
applied.

The fifth edition of *Fundamentals of Human Resource Management* continues to offer students a brief introduction to HRM that is rich with examples and engaging in its application.

Please take a moment to page through some of the highlights of this new edition.

Features

Students who want to learn more about how human resource management is used in the everyday work environment will find that the fifth edition is engaging, focused, and applied, giving them the HRM knowledge they need to succeed.

WHAT DO I NEED TO KNOW?

Assurance of learning:
- Learning objectives open each chapter.
- Learning objectives are referenced in the page margins where the relevant discussion begins.
- The chapter summary is written around the same learning objectives.
- The student quiz on the textbook OLC and instructor testing questions are tagged to the appropriate objective they cover.

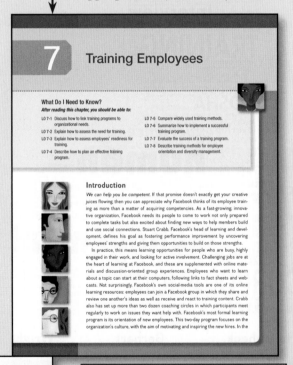

7 Training Employees

What Do I Need to Know?
After reading this chapter, you should be able to:

LO 7-1 Discuss how to link training programs to organizational needs.
LO 7-2 Explain how to assess the need for training.
LO 7-3 Explain how to assess employees' readiness for training.
LO 7-4 Describe how to plan an effective training program.
LO 7-5 Compare widely used training methods.
LO 7-6 Summarize how to implement a successful training program.
LO 7-7 Evaluate the success of a training program.
LO 7-8 Describe training methods for employee orientation and diversity management.

Introduction

We can help you be competent. If that promise doesn't exactly get your creative juices flowing, then you can appreciate why Facebook thinks of its employee training as more than a matter of acquiring competencies. As a fast-growing, innovative organization, Facebook needs its people to come to work not only prepared to complete tasks but also excited about finding new ways to help members build and use social connections. Stuart Crabb, Facebook's head of learning and development, defines his goal as fostering performance improvement by uncovering employees' strengths and giving them opportunities to build on those strengths.

In practice, this means learning opportunities for people who are busy, highly engaged in their work, and looking for active involvement. Challenging jobs are at the heart of learning at Facebook, and these are supplemented with online materials and discussion-oriented group experiences. Employees who want to learn about a topic can start at their computers, following links to fact sheets and webcasts. Not surprisingly, Facebook's own social-media tools are one of its online learning resources: employees can join a Facebook group in which they share and review one another's ideas as well as receive and react to training content. Crabb also has set up more than two dozen coaching circles in which participants meet regularly to work on issues they want help with. Facebook's most formal learning program is its orientation of new employees. This two-day program focuses on the organization's culture, with the aim of motivating and inspiring the new hires. In the

HR Oops!

A Revolving Door for Returning Vets

The president of a manufacturing company had the best of intentions. He was a retired military officer and wanted to provide jobs for some of the many service members ready to make a transition from military to civilian life. He expected that many of them had leadership qualities and would be an asset to his growing business. So he directed his company's human resources department to recruit veterans and track their progress.

A year and a half later, the company president reviewed the numbers and was shocked: many veterans were indeed being hired—and most of them were replacing veterans previously hired. The sad fact was that within months, most of them felt uncomfortable at the company and quit.

Research into this pattern has found a culture clash. Many employers find that their new employees don't know how to function in a civilian environment. What promoted success in the military is not always what works in civilian workplaces.

One solution is to develop orientation programs geared toward veterans. These new employees tend to face particular issues. For example, military organizations tend to emphasize standard processes. In contrast, many businesses want to foster creative thinking, which veterans might interpret as a lack of leadership or failure to communicate. Values such as loyalty and respect are highly prized in the military; veteran employees may be troubled if they perceive a civilian attitude toward values in a civilian workplace. Thus, orientation might need to cover aspects of organizational culture that seem obvious to the civilian trainer. The orientation program might be best supplemented with a mentor who has a military background.

The effort to recruit and train veterans can be worthwhile for many reasons. Many employers prize veterans' strong values, leadership experience, and resourcefulness. The federal government offers guidance and assistance in recruiting and hiring veterans. The wind-down of the wars in Iraq and Afghanistan is creating a huge pool of talented, motivated individuals. And, of course, many employers want to do the right thing for persons who have sacrificed so much for the nation.

Questions

1. In the manufacturing company described here, the president himself was a veteran. Why do you think the newly hired veterans didn't feel at home in a company run by a veteran? What lessons does this suggest about how to plan an orientation program's content?
2. What training methods do you think would be most effective for acquainting retired veterans with civilian business culture?

SOURCES: U.S. Department of Labor, "Hiring Veterans: A Step-by-Step Toolkit for Employers," America's Heroes at Work, http://www.americasheroes atwork.gov, accessed March 15, 2012; Karen Parrish, "Veteran Job Prospects Brighter, Panetta Says," American Forces Press Service, news release, March 15, 2012, http://www.defense. gov; Emily King, "From Boots to Brief-case: Conquering the 18-Month Churn," *T + D*, April 2011, pp. 36–41.

UPDATED!

HR Oops!

Engage students through examples of companies whose HR departments have fallen short. Discussion questions at the end of each example encourage student analysis of the situation. Examples include "Where Merit Pay Has a Failing Grade," "Hiring Clones," and "A Revolving Door for Returning Vets."

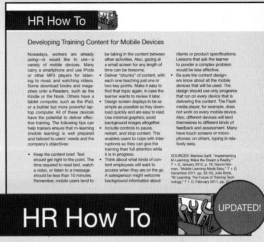

Best Practices — UPDATED!

Engage students through examples of companies whose HR departments are working well. Examples include "How NuStar Energy Keeps Employee Engagement Burning," "Dealing with Dementia at LSI Corporation," and "SeaMicro Designs Work to Stay Onshore."

HR How To — UPDATED!

Engage students through specific steps to create HRM programs and tackle common challenges. Examples include "Aligning HR with the Organization's Strategy," "Developing Training Content for Mobile Devices," and "Responding to Employee Misconduct."

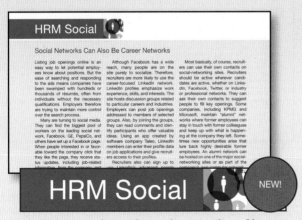

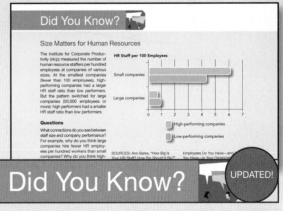

HRM Social — NEW!

Engage students through examples of how HR departments use social media as part of their daily activities. Examples include "Social Networks Can Also Be Career Networks," "Will LinkedIn Make Résumés Obsolete?" and "Inviting Job Hunters to Virtual Career Fairs."

Did You Know? — UPDATED!

Engage students through interesting statistics related to chapter topics. Questions have been added to stimulate student discussions. Examples include "Size Matters for Human Resources," "Top 10 Occupations for Job Growth," and "Fewer Companies Awarding Spot Bonuses."

Features

Focused on ethics. Reviewers indicate that the Thinking Ethically feature, which confronts students in each chapter with an ethical issue regarding managing human resources, is a highlight. This feature has been updated throughout the text.

THINKING ETHICALLY

CAN EMPLOYERS TEACH ETHICS?

Engineering professor Michael Garrett recalls being a new employee at URS Corporation, an engineering and design firm headquartered in San Francisco. On his first day, he was shown around the office on a tour that highlighted safety features such as fire extinguishers, first-aid kits, and emergency escape routes. He also was instructed to complete a safety training course before he began working. During his time on the job, he received monthly newsletters with articles describing safe practices at work and at home. Reflecting on that experience, Garrett asserts that, just as a company can build a culture of safety as URS did, it can also build a culture of ethics with frequent messages affirming the company's commitment to ethical practices. In his view,

making an organization ethical is not a matter of one-time training, but of continual learning, practice, and reinforcement.

Ethical behavior at work is most likely to result from a desire to be ethical combined with skills for ethical reasoning and an organizational context that encourages ethical behavior. Advocates for ethics training suggest that a training program could address all of these. For example, employees can learn the benefits of an ethical workplace. They can learn principles for arriving at ethical choices. And leaders can learn skills for creating an ethical climate by communicating honestly and treating employees with respect. These lessons will be most effective if they are tailored to the specifics of the company and if the messages about

REVIEW AND DISCUSSION QUESTIONS

1. Assume you are the manager of a fast-food restaurant. What are the outputs of your work unit? What are the activities required to produce those outputs? What are the inputs?
2. Based on Question 1, consider the cashier's job in the restaurant. What are the outputs, activities, and inputs for that job?
3. Consider the "job" of college student. Perform a job analysis on this job. What tasks are required in the job? What knowledge, skills, and abilities are necessary to perform those tasks? Prepare a job description based on your analysis.
4. Discuss how the following trends are changing the skill requirements for managerial jobs in the United States:
   a. Increasing use of social media.
   b. Increasing international competition.
   c. Increasing work-family conflicts.
5. Suppose you have taken a job as a trainer in a large bank that has created competency models for all its positions. How could the competency models help you succeed in your career at the bank? How could the competency models help you develop the bank's employees?
6. Consider the job of a customer service representative who fields telephone calls from customers of a retailer that sells online and through catalogs. What measures can an employer take to design this job to

make it efficient? What might be some drawbacks or challenges of designing this job for efficiency?
7. How might the job in Question 6 be designed to make it more motivating? How well would these considerations apply to the cashier's job in Question 2?
8. What ergonomic considerations might apply to each of the following jobs? For each job, what kinds of costs would result from addressing ergonomics? What costs might result from failing to address ergonomics?
   a. A computer programmer.
   b. A UPS delivery person.
   c. A child care worker.
9. Modern electronics have eliminated the need for a store's cashiers to calculate change due on a purchase. How does this development modify the job description for a cashier? If you were a store manager, how would it affect the skills and qualities of job candidates you would want to hire? Does this change in mental processing requirements affect what you would expect from a cashier? How?
10. Consider a job you hold now or have held recently. Would you want this job to be redesigned to place more emphasis on efficiency, motivation, ergonomics, or mental processing? What changes would you want, and why? (Or why do you not want the job to be redesigned?)

Apply the concepts in each chapter through comprehensive review and discussion questions.

EXPERIENCING HR

Divide into groups of four. In your group, develop a job description for your professor's job. Use your knowledge and assumptions about the tasks, duties, and responsibilities you think are involved. If you have been given time for research, review the chapter for additional ideas on where to gather information for your job description, and use it to improve your job description. Then use your completed job description as a basis for listing job specifications for your professor's job.

With the whole class, share which tasks, duties, and responsibilities you included in your job description and which knowledge, skills, abilities, and other

characteristics you included in your job specifications. Discuss what requirements you define as important and what your professor defines as important. Ask your professor how closely your job description and job specifications match the school's actual expectations. Was your professor given a job description? Would professors at your school be more effective if the school used the job descriptions and specifications written by you and your classmates? Why or why not? How would you adjust your team's job description and specifications, based on what you learned from this discussion? Turn in your job description and job specifications for credit on the assignment.

Apply chapter topics to experiential exercises in human relations activities.

MANAGING TALENT: SunTrust Takes Training to the Bank

SunTrust Banks, based in Atlanta, operates the eighth-largest U.S. bank. It also has several subsidiaries offering other financial services such as mortgage banking, insurance, and investment management. The bank serves customers in Florida, Georgia, Maryland, North Carolina, South Carolina, Tennessee, Virginia, West Virginia, and the District of Columbia. As the banking industry struggled to recover from the recent financial crisis and recession (and new regulations) that followed, SunTrust's management decided that the key to the company's future lay with fully engaging employees in serving customers. That approach is consistent with the company's mission of "helping people and institutions prosper."

SunTrust began to restructure its banking business in accordance with three guiding principles: (1) operating as a single team; (2) putting clients first; and (3) focusing on profitable growth. This principle-driven approach to growth requires managers who know how to foster employees' commitment to their work and their clients. To that end, SunTrust has made it a priority to develop managers' leadership skills. First-line

surveys of its customers to learn whether they are satisfied with the bank's products and customer service. It also asks employees whether they have the resources they need to succeed at work and know what the company expects of them. Based on the feedback, the bank's learning team creates training materials for how to meet customer expectations in each line of business. In a program called "Building Solid Relationships," employees learn how to define client needs, explain the bank's financial products and services clearly, and help customers choose which products and services will meet their needs. SunTrust's CEO, Bill Rogers, saw the impact of this training firsthand when he visited a branch and peppered the branch manager and a financial services representative with questions about a new product. They invited Rogers to watch them role-play a scene between a representative and a customer. Rogers was impressed with their confidence and knowledge.

The bank also provides learning support on its SunTrust Learning Portal. This Internet portal gives employees easy access to computer-based training and tools for

Apply concepts in each chapter through two cases that focus on corporate sustainability and talent management. These cases can be used as the basis for class lectures, and the questions provided at the end of each case are suitable for assignments or discussion.

Apply chapter content to ongoing discussions via Twitter. Twitter Focus creates an excellent opportunity for students to use social media to discuss chapter topics and apply them to chapter cases that can be found on the text website at www.mhhe.com/noefund5e.

 TWITTER FOCUS: How Nick's Pizza Delivers Training Results

At first glance, Nick's Pizza & Pub sounds as ordinary as a company can be: a pizza restaurant with two locations, each in one of Chicago's northwest suburbs. But when you take a look at the company's performance measures, something special seems to be going on. In an industry where 200% employee turnover and operating profits around 6 1/2% are normal, Nick's has to replace only 20% of its employees each year and enjoys operating profits of 14% or more. These results are amazing, especially for a business in which 4 out of 10 employees are high school students.

What makes the difference? It could be the culture at Nick's. Rather than hiring expert managers and laying down a lot of rules, Nick's is choosy about who gets hired for every position and then provides them with enough training to operate skillfully and exercise sound judgment. The whole training program emphasizes ways to develop trustworthy, dedicated employees.

Training at Nick's begins with a two-day orientation program. Trainees learn the company's purpose, values, and culture, and they participate in role-playing activities to practice those lessons. Then it's on to skills training, beginning with a course called simply 101. During that four-hour hands-on lesson in the kitchen, all the new employees—regardless of what their future job will be—learn to make a pizza. From there, the trainees divide into work groups for the next level of training. In 201, these groups of trainees embark on longer-term training to be certified in performing a particular job. For example, an employees receive training in communication and leadership and study a book called *Mastery: The Keys to Success and Long-Term Fulfillment* by George Leonard. Employees who complete these requirements receive a Leadership 301 Passport, which includes a checklist of behaviors they are expected to model for the employees they lead. During the weeks that follow, they watch for situations in which they or others are exhibiting each behavior, jotting down descriptions of what they witnessed. When the listed behaviors have all been observed and noted, the participants take a course in training, and they finally are ready to be named trainers themselves.

Along with these formal training programs, Nick's provides further on-the-job learning through coaching by managers and trainers. The goal is to provide feedback in the moment, not waiting for performance appraisal meetings. For example, at the end of each shift, trainers will ask trainees to identify one thing they did well that day and one thing they would like to improve. In addition, managers are taught to observe employees' behavior on the job and ask themselves whether what they see would make them want to hire the employee. If yes, the manager is expected to give immediate positive feedback. If no, the manager is expected to coach the employee on how to do better.

Questions

1. To the extent that you can provide details from the

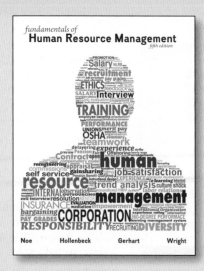

Instructor's Manual

The custom-designed Instructor's Manual includes chapter summaries, learning objectives, an extended chapter outline, key terms, description of text boxes, discussion questions, summary of end-of-chapter cases, and additional activities.

Test Bank

The test bank has been revised and updated to reflect the content of the 5th edition of the book. Each chapter includes multiple choice, true/false, and essay questions.

EZ Test

McGraw-Hill's EZ Test is a flexible and easy-to-use electronic testing program. The program allows instructors to create tests from book-specific items. It accommodates a wide range of question types and instructors may add their own questions. Multiple versions of the test can be created and any test can be exported for use with course management systems such as WebCT, BlackBoard, or PageOut. The program is available for Windows and Macintosh environments.

PowerPoint

The slides include lecture material, additional content to expand concepts in the text, discussion questions, and the PPT also includes detailed teaching notes.

Videos

Human Resource Management Video DVD, volume 3, offers video clips on HRM issues for each chapter of this edition. You'll find a new video produced by the SHRM Foundation, entitled "Once the Deal Is Done: Making Mergers Work." Three new videos specifically address employee benefits: "GM Cuts Benefits and Pay," "Sulphur Springs Teachers," and "Google Employees Perks." Other new videos available for this edition include "E-Learning English" for the chapter on employee development and "Recession Job Growth" for the chapter on HR planning recruitment. Two new videos specifically address recession-related HR issues: "Some Workers Willing to Sacrifice to Avoid Layoffs" and "Stretched Small Business Owners Forced to Lay Off Employees." Other notable videos available for this edition include "Johnson & Johnson eUniversity" for the chapter on training and "Hollywood Labor Unions" for the chapter on collective bargaining and labor relations.

Online Learning Center (OLC)

www.mhhe.com/noefund5e
This text-specific website follows the text chapter by chapter. Instructors and students can access a variety of online teaching and learning tools that are designed to reinforce and build on the text content. Students will have direct access to learning tools such as self-grading quizzes, video clips, Twitter focus cases, and small business cases, while instructor materials are password protected.

Technology

McGRAW-HILL *CONNECT MANAGEMENT*

LESS MANAGING. MORE TEACHING. GREATER LEARNING.

McGraw-Hill *Connect Management* is an online assignment and assessment solution that connects students with the tools and resources they'll need to achieve success.

McGraw-Hill *Connect Management* helps prepare students for their future by enabling faster learning, more efficient studying, and higher retention of knowledge.

MCGRAW-HILL *CONNECT MANAGEMENT* FEATURES

Connect Management offers a number of powerful tools and features to make managing assignments easier, so faculty can spend more time teaching. With *Connect Management*, students can engage with their coursework anytime and anywhere, making the learning process more accessible and efficient. *Connect Management* offers you the features described below.

Simple assignment management

With *Connect Management*, creating assignments is easier than ever, so you can spend more time teaching and less time managing. The assignment management function enables you to

- Create and deliver assignments easily with selectable end-of-chapter questions and Test Bank items.
- Streamline lesson planning, student progress reporting, and assignment grading to make classroom management more efficient than ever.
- Go paperless with the eBook and online submission and grading of student assignments.

Smart grading

When it comes to studying, time is precious. *Connect Management* helps students learn more efficiently by providing feedback and practice material when they need it, where they need it.

When it comes to teaching, your time also is precious. The grading function enables you to

- Have assignments scored automatically, giving students immediate feedback on their work and side-by-side comparisons with correct answers.
- Access and review each response; manually change grades or leave comments for students to review.
- Reinforce classroom concepts with practice tests and instant quizzes.

Instructor library

The *Connect Management* Instructor Library is your repository for additional resources to improve student engagement in and out of class. You can select and use any asset that enhances your lecture. The *Connect Management* Instructor Library includes

- eBook
- Instructor's Manual
- PowerPoint files
- Videos and instructional notes
- Access to interactive study tools

Student study center

The *Connect Management* Student Study Center is the place for students to access additional resources. The Student Study Center

- Offers students quick access to lectures, practice materials, eBooks, and more.
- Provides instant practice material and study questions easily accessible on the go.
- Gives students access to a Personalized Learning Plan.

Student progress tracking

Connect Management keeps instructors informed about how each student, section, and class is performing, allowing for more productive use of lecture and office hours. The progress-tracking function enables you to

- View scored work immediately and track individual or group performance with assignment and grade reports.

- Access an instant view of student or class performance relative to learning objectives.
- Collect data and generate reports required by many accreditation organizations, such as AACSB.

Lecture capture

Increase the attention paid to a lecture discussion by decreasing the attention paid to note-taking. For an additional charge Lecture Capture offers new ways for students to focus on the in-class discussion, knowing they can revisit important topics later. Lecture Capture enables you to

- Record and distribute your lecture with the click of a button.
- Record and index PowerPoint presentations and anything shown on your computer so it is easily searchable, frame by frame.
- Offer access to lectures anytime and anywhere by computer, iPod, or mobile device.
- Increase intent listening and class participation by easing students' concerns about note-taking. Lecture Capture will make it more likely you will see students' faces, not the tops of their heads.

McGraw-Hill *Connect Plus Management*

McGraw-Hill reinvents the textbook learning experience for the modern student with *Connect Plus Management*. A seamless integration of an eBook and *Connect Management*, *Connect Plus Management* provides all the *Connect Management* features plus the following:

- An integrated eBook, allowing for anytime, anywhere access to the textbook.
- Dynamic links between the problems or questions you assign to your students and the location in the eBook where that problem or question is covered.
- A powerful search function to pinpoint and connect key concepts in a snap.

In short, *Connect Management* offers you and your students powerful tools and features that optimize your time and energies, enabling you to focus on course content, teaching, and student learning. *Connect Management* also offers a wealth of

content resources for both instructors and students. This state-of-the-art, thoroughly tested system supports you in preparing students for the world that awaits.

For more information about Connect™ go to www.mcgrawhillconnect.com, or contact your local McGraw-Hill sales representative.

TEGRITY CAMPUS: LECTURES 24/7

 Tegrity Campus is a service that makes class time available 24/7 by automatically capturing every lecture in a searchable format for students to review when they study and complete assignments. With a simple one-click start-and-stop process, you capture all computer screens and corresponding audio. Students can replay any part of any class with easy-to-use browser-based viewing on a PC or Mac.

Educators know that the more students can see, hear, and experience class resources, the better they learn. In fact, studies prove it. With Tegrity Campus, students quickly recall key moments by using Tegrity Campus's unique search feature. This search helps students efficiently find what they need, when they need it, across an entire semester of class recordings. Help turn all your students' study time into learning moments immediately supported by your lecture.

To learn more about Tegrity watch a two-minute Flash demo at http://tegritycampus.mhhe.com.

ASSURANCE OF LEARNING READY

Many educational institutions today are focused on the notion of *assurance of learning*, an important element of some accreditation standards. *Fundamentals of Human Resource Management* is designed specifically to support your assurance of learning initiatives with a simple, yet powerful solution.

Each Test Bank question for *Fundamentals of Human Resource Management* maps to a specific chapter learning outcome/objective listed in the text. You can use our Test Bank software, EZ Test and EZ Test Online, or easily query in *Connect Management* for learning outcomes/objectives that directly relate to the learning objectives for your course. You can then use the reporting features of EZ Test to aggregate student results in a similar fashion, making the collection and presentation of assurance of learning data simple and easy.

MCGRAW-HILL AND BLACKBOARD

McGraw-Hill Higher Education and Blackboard have teamed up. What does this mean for you?

1. **Your life, simplified.** Now you and your students can access McGraw-Hill's Connect™ and Create™ right from within your Blackboard course—all with one single sign-on. Say goodbye to the days of logging in to multiple applications.

2. **Deep integration of content and tools.** Not only do you get single sign-on with Connect™ and Create™, you also get deep integration of McGraw-Hill content and content engines right in Blackboard. Whether you're choosing a book for your course or building Connect™ assignments, all the tools you need are right where you want them—inside Blackboard.

3. **Seamless gradebooks.** Are you tired of keeping multiple gradebooks and manually synchronizing grades into Blackboard? We thought so. When a student completes an integrated Connect™ assignment, the grade for that assignment automatically (and instantly) feeds your Blackboard grade center.

4. **A solution for everyone.** Whether your institution is already using Blackboard or you just want to try Blackboard on your own, we have a solution for you. McGraw-Hill and Blackboard can now offer you easy access to industry-leading technology and content, whether your campus hosts it or we do. Be sure to ask your local McGraw-Hill representative for details.

AACSB STATEMENT

The McGraw-Hill Companies is a proud corporate member of AACSB international. Understanding the importance/and value of AACSB accreditation, *Fundamentals of Human Resource Management*, 5th edition, recognizes the curricula guidelines detailed in the AACSB standards for business accreditation by connecting selected questions in the Test Bank to the six general-knowledge and skill guidelines in the AACSB standards.

The statements contained in *Fundamentals of Human Resource Management*, 5th edition, are provided only as a guide for the users of this textbook. The AACSB leaves content coverage and assessment within the purview of individual schools, the mission of the school, and the faculty. While *Fundamentals of Human Resource Management*, 5th edition, and the teaching package make no claim of any specific AACSB qualification or evaluation, we have within *Fundamentals of Human Resource Management*, 5th edition, labeled selected questions according to the six general-knowledge and skills areas.

MCGRAW-HILL CUSTOMER CARE
CONTACT INFORMATION

At McGraw-Hill, we understand that getting the most from new technology can be challenging. That's why our services don't stop after you purchase our products. You can e-mail our product specialists 24 hours a day to get product-training online. Or you can search our knowledge bank of frequently asked questions on our support website. For customer support, call 800-331-5094, e-mail hmsupport@mcgraw-hill.com, or visit www.mhhe.com/support. One of our technical support analysts will be able to assist you in a timely fashion.

Support Materials

MCGRAW-HILL'S MANAGEMENT ASSET GALLERY!

McGraw-Hill/Irwin Management is excited to now provide a one-stop shop for our wealth of assets, making it quick and easy for instructors to locate specific materials to enhance their courses. All of the following can be accessed within the Management Asset Gallery:

MANAGER'S HOT SEAT

This interactive, video-based application puts students in the manager's hot seat, builds critical thinking and decision-making skills, and allows students to apply concepts to real managerial challenges. Students watch as 15 real managers apply their years of experience when confronting unscripted issues such as bullying in the workplace, cyber loafing, globalization, intergenerational work conflicts, workplace violence, and leadership versus management.

Self-Assessment Gallery

Unique among publisher-provided self-assessments, our 23 self-assessments give students background information to ensure that they understand the purpose of the assessment. Students test their values, beliefs, skills, and interests in a wide variety of areas, allowing them to personally apply chapter content to their own lives and careers.

Every self-assessment is supported with PowerPoints® and an instructor manual in the Management Asset Gallery, making it easy for the instructor to create an engaging classroom discussion surrounding the assessments.

Test Your Knowledge

To help reinforce students' understanding of key management concepts, Test Your Knowledge activities give students a review of the conceptual materials followed by application-based questions to work through. Students can choose practice mode, which gives them detailed feedback after each question, or test mode, which provides feedback after the entire test has been completed. Every Test Your Knowledge activity is supported by instructor notes in the Management Asset Gallery to make it easy for the instructor to create engaging classroom discussions surrounding the materials that students have completed.

Management History Timeline

This web application allows instructors to present and students to learn the history of management in an engaging and interactive way. Management history is presented along an intuitive timeline that can be traveled through sequentially or by selected decade. With the click of a mouse, students learn the important dates, see the people who influenced the field, and understand the general management theories that have molded and shaped management as we know it today.

Video Library DVDs

McGraw-Hill/Irwin offers the most comprehensive video support for the Human Resource Management classroom through course library video DVDs. This discipline has library volume DVDs tailored to integrate and visually reinforce chapter concepts. The library volume DVD contains more than 40 clips! The rich video material, organized by topic, comes from sources such as PBS, NBC, BBC, SHRM, and McGraw-Hill. Video cases and video guides are provided for some clips.

DESTINATION CEO VIDEOS

These video clips feature CEOs on a variety of topics. Accompanying each clip are multiple-choice questions and discussion questions to use in the classroom or assign as a quiz.

Features

CourseSmart eBooks allow students to highlight, take notes, organize notes, and share the notes with other CourseSmart users. Students can also search for terms across all eBooks in their purchased CourseSmart library. CourseSmart eBooks can be printed (five pages at a time).

More info and purchase

Please visit **www.coursesmart.com** for more information and to purchase access to our eBooks. CourseSmart allows students to try one chapter of the eBook, free of charge, before purchase.

Create

Craft your teaching resources to match the way you teach! With McGraw-Hill Create, **www.mcgrawhillcreate.com**, you can easily rearrange chapters, combine material from other content sources, and quickly upload content you have written, like your course syllabus or teaching notes. Find the content you need in Create by searching through thousands of leading McGraw-Hill textbooks. Arrange your book to fit your teaching style. Create even allows you to personalize your book's appearance by selecting the cover and adding your name, school, and course information. Order a Create book and you'll receive a complimentary print review copy in three to five business days or a complimentary electronic review copy (eComp) via e-mail in about one hour. Go to **www.mcgrawhillcreate.com** today and register. Experience how McGraw-Hill Create empowers you to teach *your* students *your* way.

Brief Contents

Contents

The Human Resource Environment

PART ONE

1 Managing Human Resources

What Do I Need to Know?

After reading this chapter, you should be able to:

LO 1-1 Define human resource management, and explain how HRM contributes to an organization's performance.

LO 1-2 Identify the responsibilities of human resource departments.

LO 1-3 Summarize the types of skills needed for human resource management.

LO 1-4 Explain the role of supervisors in human resource management.

LO 1-5 Discuss ethical issues in human resource management.

LO 1-6 Describe typical careers in human resource management.

Introduction

How do you get great performance from employees who don't actually work for you? That was the huge challenge facing Dunkin' Brands when its new chief executive officer, Nigel Travis, came on board. Dunkin' Brands is a franchisor: it sells business owners the right to operate stores under its Dunkin' Donuts and Baskin-Robbins brands in exchange for fees. These franchisees hire hundreds of thousands of employees to manage the stores and serve customers. When the franchise employees keep customers happy, the stores perform well; and when the stores perform well, Dunkin' Brands is successful. So the company's success is in the hands of people who work for the franchisees, not for the company itself.

However, the company *can* use its resources to empower the franchise owners and employees to perform better, and that is what it aimed to do under CEO Travis. Travis determined that the company's success hung on improving the quality of store operations. He hired Christine Deputy as senior vice president of human resources to focus on enabling franchise owners and employees to excel. Deputy started by bringing together corporate managers and a group of franchise owners and managers to learn more about the areas in which they needed help to achieve their goals. She trained her staff to understand franchise as well as corporate needs, rotated them through assignments that taught them more about the business, and encouraged them to consult with one another to benefit from their areas of expertise. She expanded training for franchisees in recruiting, motivating, and retaining excellent frontline workers. Finally, Deputy established performance measures that included customer satisfaction so her group would have an incentive to make sure their efforts were contributing to the corporate goal of improving service quality.[1]

The challenges faced by Dunkin' Brands are important dimensions of **human resource management (HRM),** the policies, practices, and systems that influence employees' behavior, attitudes, and performance. Many companies refer to HRM as involving "people practices." Figure 1.1 emphasizes that there are several important HRM practices that should support the organization's business strategy: analyzing work and designing jobs, determining how many employees with specific knowledge and skills are needed (human resource planning), attracting potential employees (recruiting), choosing employees (selection), teaching employees how to perform their jobs and preparing them for the future (training and development), evaluating their performance (performance management), rewarding employees (compensation), and creating a positive work environment (employee relations). An organization performs best when all of these practices are managed well. At companies with effective HRM, employees and customers tend to be more satisfied, and the companies tend to be more innovative, have greater productivity, and develop a more favorable reputation in the community.[2]

In this chapter, we introduce the scope of human resource management. We begin by discussing why human resource management is an essential element of an organization's success. We then turn to the elements of managing human resources: the roles and skills needed for effective human resource management. Next, the chapter describes how all managers, not just human resource professionals, participate in the activities related to human resource management. The following section of the chapter addresses some of the ethical issues that arise with regard to human resource management. We then provide an overview of careers in human resource management. The chapter concludes by highlighting the HRM practices covered in the remainder of this book.

Human Resource Management (HRM) The policies, practices, and systems that influence employees' behavior, attitudes, and performance.

LO 1-1 Define human resource management, and explain how HRM contributes to an organization's performance.

Human Resources and Company Performance

Managers and economists traditionally have seen human resource management as a necessary expense, rather than as a source of value to their organizations. Economic value is usually associated with *capital*—cash, equipment, technology, and facilities. However, research has demonstrated that HRM practices can be valuable.[3] Decisions such as whom to hire, what to pay, what training to offer, and how to evaluate

Figure 1.1
Human Resource Management Practices

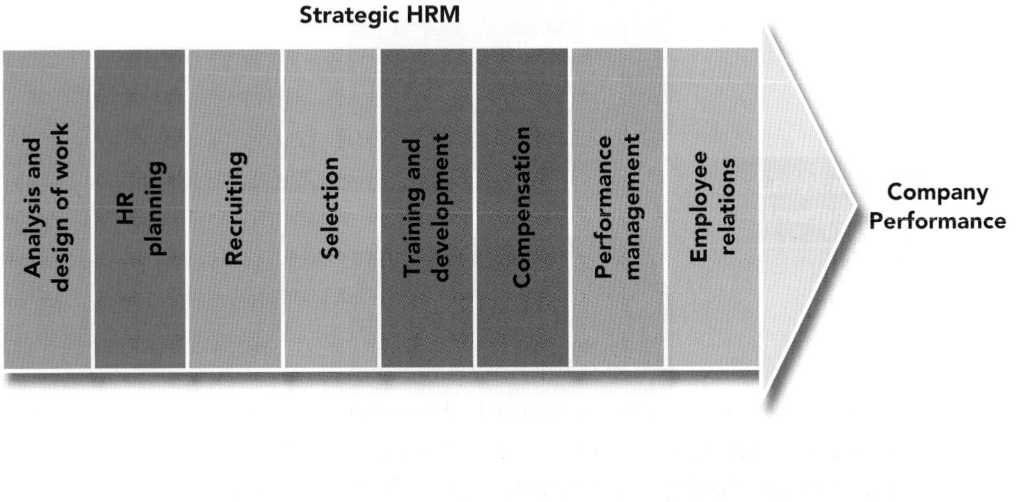

employee performance directly affect employees' motivation and ability to provide goods and services that customers value. Companies that attempt to increase their competitiveness by investing in new technology and promoting quality throughout the organization also invest in state-of-the-art staffing, training, and compensation practices.[4]

Human Capital
An organization's employees, described in terms of their training, experience, judgment, intelligence, relationships, and insight.

The concept of "human resource management" implies that employees are *resources* of the employer. As a type of resource, **human capital** means the organization's employees, described in terms of their training, experience, judgment, intelligence, relationships, and insight—the employee characteristics that can add economic value to the organization. In other words, whether it manufactures automobiles or forecasts the weather, for an organization to succeed at what it does, it needs employees with certain qualities, such as particular kinds of training and experience. This view means employees in today's organizations are not interchangeable, easily replaced parts of a system but the source of the company's success or failure. By influencing *who* works for the organization and *how* those people work, human resource management therefore contributes to basic measures of an organization's performance, such as quality, profitability, and customer satisfaction. Figure 1.2 shows this relationship.

In the United States, low-price retailers are notorious for the ways they keep labor costs down. They pay low wages, limit employees to part-time status (providing little or no employee benefits), and make last-minute adjustments to schedules so staffing is minimal when store traffic is light. Retailing expert Zeynep Ton has studied retailers that invest more in employees—paying higher wages and offering full-time schedules, greater training, and more opportunity for advancement. Ton has found that these stores tend to enjoy higher sales and greater profitability. At Costco, for example, employees earn about 40% more than at the company's main competitor, Sam's Club, and most store managers are promoted from within. Costco's sales per square foot are almost double those of Sam's Club, and its rating in the American Customer Satisfaction Index is comparable to that of the prestigious Nordstrom chain. The QuikTrip chain of convenience stores trains employees to handle a wide variety of tasks, from brewing coffee to ordering merchandise and cleaning restrooms. Instead of sending employees home when traffic is slow, QuikTrip expects them to handle tasks other than selling. Employees have predictable schedules, stay busy throughout

Figure 1.2
Impact of Human Resource Management

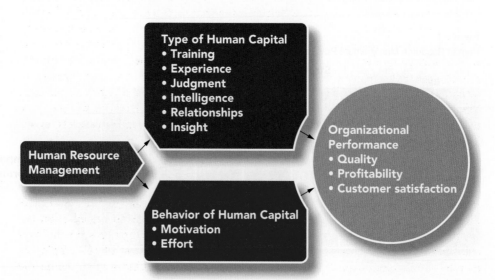

their shift, and sell 66% more per square foot than the average convenience store. In these and other chains that see employees as more than just an expense, retailers are outperforming their competitors.[5]

Human resource management is critical to the success of organizations because human capital has certain qualities that make it valuable. In terms of business strategy, an organization can succeed if it has a *sustainable competitive advantage* (is better than competitors at something and can hold that advantage over a sustained period of time). Therefore, we can conclude that organizations need the kind of resources that will give them such an advantage. Human resources have these necessary qualities:

At Southwest Airlines, the company's focus is on keeping employees loyal, motivated, trained, and compensated. In turn, there is a low turnover rate and a high rate of customer satisfaction.

- Human resources are *valuable*. High-quality employees provide a needed service as they perform many critical functions.
- Human resources are *rare* in the sense that a person with high levels of the needed skills and knowledge is not common. An organization may spend months looking for a talented and experienced manager or technician.
- Human resources *cannot be imitated*. To imitate human resources at a high-performing competitor, you would have to figure out which employees are providing the advantage and how. Then you would have to recruit people who can do precisely the same thing and set up the systems that enable those people to imitate your competitor.
- Human resources have *no good substitutes*. When people are well trained and highly motivated, they learn, develop their abilities, and care about customers. It is difficult to imagine another resource that can match committed and talented employees.

These qualities imply that human resources have enormous potential. An organization realizes this potential through the ways it practices human resource management.

Effective management of human resources can form the foundation of a **high-performance work system**—an organization in which technology, organizational structure, people, and processes work together seamlessly to give an organization an advantage in the competitive environment. As technology changes the ways organizations manufacture, transport, communicate, and keep track of information, human resource management must ensure that the organization has the right kinds of people to meet the new challenges. High-performance work systems also have been essential in making organizations strong enough to weather the storm of the recent recession and remain profitable as the economy slowly begins to expand again. Maintaining a high-performance work system may include development of training programs, recruitment of people with new skill sets, and establishment of rewards for such behaviors as teamwork, flexibility, and learning. In the next chapter, we will see some of the changes that human resource managers are planning for, and Chapter 16 examines high-performance work systems in greater detail.

High-Performance Work System
An organization in which technology, organizational structure, people, and processes work together seamlessly to give an organization an advantage in the competitive environment.

Responsibilities of Human Resource Departments

LO 1-2 Identify the responsibilities of human resource departments.

In all but the smallest organizations, a human resource department is responsible for the functions of human resource management. On average, an organization has roughly two full-time HR staff persons for every hundred employees on the payroll.[6] However, as shown in the "Did You Know?" box, the ratio of HR employees to total employees is much higher in small organizations. One way to define the

Did You Know?

Size Matters for Human Resources

The Institute for Corporate Productivity (i4cp) measured the number of human resource staffers per hundred employees at companies of various sizes. At the smallest companies (fewer than 100 employees), high-performing companies had a larger HR staff ratio than low performers. But the pattern switched for large companies (50,000 employees or more): high performers had a smaller HR staff ratio than low performers.

Questions

What connections do you see between staff size and company performance? For example, why do you think large companies hire fewer HR employees per hundred workers than small companies? Why do you think high-performing small companies have larger HR staffs than low-performing companies of the same size?

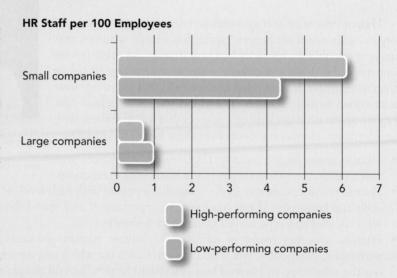

HR Staff per 100 Employees

High-performing companies
Low-performing companies

SOURCES: Ann Bares, "How Big Is Your HR Staff? How Big *Should* It Be?" *Workforce Management,* May 27, 2010, http://www.compensationforce.com; Steve Wexler, "How Many HR Employees Do You Have—and Should You Have—in Your Organization?" Institute for Corporate Productivity, May 21, 2010, http://www.i4cp.com.

---

responsibilities of HR departments is to think of HR as a business within the company with three product lines:[7]

1. *Administrative services and transactions*—Handling administrative tasks (for example, hiring employees and answering questions about benefits) efficiently and with a commitment to quality. This requires expertise in the particular tasks.
2. *Business partner services*—Developing effective HR systems that help the organization meet its goals for attracting, keeping, and developing people with the skills it needs. For the systems to be effective, HR people must understand the business so it can understand what the business needs.
3. *Strategic partner*—Contributing to the company's strategy through an understanding of its existing and needed human resources and ways HR practices can give the company a competitive advantage. For strategic ideas to be effective, HR people must understand the business, its industry, and its competitors.

Another way to think of HR responsibilities is in terms of specific activities. Table 1.1 details the responsibilities of human resource departments. These responsibilities include the practices introduced in Figure 1.1 plus two areas of responsibility that support those practices: (1) establishing and administering personnel policies and (2) ensuring compliance with labor laws.

Although the human resource department has responsibility for these areas, many of the tasks may be performed by supervisors or others inside or outside the organization.

No two human resource departments have precisely the same roles because of differences in organization sizes and characteristics of the workforce, the industry, and management's values. In some companies, the HR department handles all the activities listed in Table 1.1. In others, it may share the roles and duties with managers of other departments such as finance, operations, or information technology. In some companies, the HR department actively advises top management. In others, the department responds to top-level management decisions and implements staffing, training, and compensation activities in light of company strategy and policies.

Let's take an overview of the HR functions and some of the options available for carrying them out. Human resource management involves both the selection of which options to use and the activities involved with using those options. Later chapters of the book will explore each function in greater detail.

Analyzing and Designing Jobs

To produce their given product or service (or set of products or services), companies require that a number of tasks be performed. The tasks are grouped together in various combinations to form jobs. Ideally, the tasks should be grouped in ways that help the organization to operate efficiently and to obtain people with the right qualifications to do the jobs well. This function involves the activities of job analysis and job design. **Job analysis** is the process of getting detailed information about jobs. **Job design** is the process of defining the way work will be performed and the tasks that a given job requires.

In general, jobs can vary from having a narrow range of simple tasks to having a broad array of complex tasks requiring multiple skills. At one extreme is a worker on an assembly line at a poultry-processing facility; at the other extreme is a doctor in an emergency room. In the past, many companies have emphasized the use of narrowly

Job Analysis
The process of getting detailed information about jobs.

Job Design
The process of defining the way work will be performed and the tasks that a given job requires.

Table 1.1

Responsibilities of HR Departments

FUNCTION	RESPONSIBILITIES
Analysis and design of work	Work analysis; job design; job descriptions
Recruitment and selection	Recruiting; job postings; interviewing; testing; coordinating use of temporary labor
Training and development	Orientation; skills training; career development programs
Performance management	Performance measures; preparation and administration of performance appraisals; discipline
Compensation and benefits	Wage and salary administration; incentive pay; insurance; vacation leave administration; retirement plans; profit sharing; stock plans
Employee relations	Attitude surveys; labor relations; employee handbooks; company publications; labor law compliance; relocation and outplacement services
Personnel policies	Policy creation; policy communication
Employee data and information systems	Record keeping; HR information systems; workforce analytics
Compliance with laws	Policies to ensure lawful behavior; reporting; posting information; safety inspections; accessibility accommodations
Support for strategy	Human resource planning and forecasting; talent management; change management

SOURCES: Bureau of Labor Statistics, "Human Resources, Training, and Labor Relations Managers and Specialists," *Occupational Outlook Handbook, 2010–11,* http://data.bls.gov, accessed January 19, 2012; SHRM-BNA Survey No. 66, "Policy and Practice Forum: Human Resource Activities, Budgets, and Staffs, 2000–2001," *Bulletin to Management,* Bureau of National Affairs Policy and Practice Series (Washington, DC: Bureau of National Affairs, June 28, 2001).

Home Depot and other retail stores use in-store kiosks similar to the Career Center shown here to recruit applicants for employment.

defined jobs to increase efficiency. With many simple jobs, a company can easily find workers who can quickly be trained to perform the jobs at relatively low pay. However, greater concern for innovation and quality has shifted the trend to using more broadly defined jobs. Also, as we will see in Chapters 2 and 4, some organizations assign work even more broadly, to teams instead of individuals.

Recruiting and Hiring Employees

Based on job analysis and design, an organization can determine the kinds of employees it needs. With this knowledge, it carries out the function of recruiting and hiring employees. **Recruitment** is the process through which the organization seeks applicants for potential employment. **Selection** refers to the process by which the organization attempts to identify applicants with the necessary knowledge, skills, abilities, and other characteristics that will help the organization achieve its goals. An organization makes selection decisions in order to add employees to its workforce, as well as to transfer existing employees to new positions.

Approaches to recruiting and selection involve a variety of alternatives. Some organizations may actively recruit from many external sources, such as Internet job postings, online social networks, and college recruiting events. Other organizations may rely heavily on promotions from within, applicants referred by current employees, and the availability of in-house people with the necessary skills.

At some organizations the selection process may focus on specific skills, such as experience with a particular programming language or type of equipment. At other organizations, selection may focus on general abilities, such as the ability to work as part of a team or find creative solutions. The focus an organization favors will affect many choices, from the way the organization measures ability, to the questions it asks in interviews, to the places it recruits. Table 1.2 lists the top five qualities that employers say they are looking for in job candidates.

Training and Developing Employees

Although organizations base hiring decisions on candidates' existing qualifications, most organizations provide ways for their employees to broaden or deepen their knowledge, skills, and abilities. To do this, organizations provide for employee training and development. **Training** is a planned effort to enable employees to learn job-related knowledge, skills, and behavior. For example, many organizations offer safety training to teach employees safe work habits. **Development** involves acquiring knowledge, skills, and behaviors that improve employees' ability to meet the challenges of a variety of new or existing jobs, including the client and customer demands of those jobs. Development programs often focus on preparing employees for management responsibility. Likewise, if a company plans to set up teams to manufacture products, it might offer a development program to help employees learn the ins and outs of effective teamwork.

Decisions related to training and development include whether the organization will emphasize enabling employees to perform their current jobs, preparing them for future jobs, or both. An organization may offer programs to a few employees in whom the organization wants to invest, or it may have a philosophy of investing in the training of all its workers. Some organizations, especially large ones, may have

Recruitment
The process through which the organization seeks applicants for potential employment.

Selection
The process by which the organization attempts to identify applicants with the necessary knowledge, skills, abilities, and other characteristics that will help the organization achieve its goals.

Training
A planned effort to enable employees to learn job-related knowledge, skills, and behavior.

Development
The acquisition of knowledge, skills, and behaviors that improve an employee's ability to meet changes in job requirements and in customer demands.

1. Teamwork skills
2. Verbal communication skills
3. Decision making, problem solving
4. Gathering/processing information
5. Planning, prioritizing tasks

SOURCE: Based on National Association of Colleges and Employers, "Job Outlook: The Candidate Skills/ Qualities Employers Want," *Spotlight for Career Services Professionals,* October 26, 2011, http://www .naceweb.org.

Table 1.2

Top Qualities Employers Look For in Employees

extensive formal training programs, including classroom sessions and training programs online. Other organizations may prefer a simpler, more flexible approach of encouraging employees to participate in outside training and development programs as needs are identified. For an example of a company where decisions about training and other HR practices are aimed at providing exceptional customer service, see the "Best Practices" box.

Managing Performance

Managing human resources includes keeping track of how well employees are performing relative to objectives such as job descriptions and goals for a particular position. The process of ensuring that employees' activities and outputs match the organization's goals is called **performance management.** The activities of performance management include specifying the tasks and outcomes of a job that contribute to the organization's success. Then various measures are used to compare the employee's performance over some time period with the desired performance. Often, rewards— the topic of the next section—are developed to encourage good performance.

The human resource department may be responsible for developing or obtaining questionnaires and other devices for measuring performance. The performance measures may emphasize observable behaviors (for example, answering the phone by the second ring), outcomes (number of customer complaints and compliments), or both. When the person evaluating performance is not familiar with the details of the job, outcomes tend to be easier to evaluate than specific behaviors.[8] The evaluation may focus on the short term or long term and on individual employees or groups. Typically, the person who completes the evaluation is the employee's supervisor. Often employees also evaluate their own performance, and in some organizations, peers and subordinates participate, too.

Performance Management
The process of ensuring that employees' activities and outputs match the organization's goals.

Planning and Administering Pay and Benefits

The pay and benefits that employees earn play an important role in motivating them. This is especially true when rewards such as bonuses are linked to the individual's or group's achievements. Decisions about pay and benefits can also support other aspects of an organization's strategy. For example, a company that wants to provide an exceptional level of service or be exceptionally innovative might pay significantly more than competitors in order to attract and keep the best employees. At other companies, a low-cost strategy requires knowledge of industry norms, so that the company does not spend more than it must.

Planning pay and benefits involves many decisions, often complex and based on knowledge of a multitude of legal requirements. An important decision is how

Cooking Up a Service Strategy at Pret a Manger

If the usual fast food isn't fast enough for you, and if you cringe to think of the additives, then you might want to keep an eye out for a British food chain slowly making inroads in the United States. Pret a Manger (the name—pronounced prett-ah-mahn-zhay—is French for "ready to eat") has been selling sandwiches in London since 1986 and opened its first U.S. store in New York in 2000. It has since opened stores in Chicago and Washington, DC, and is gradually expanding as consumers learn to love its thin sandwiches made with natural ingredients.

Besides the food, what sets Pret apart is its customer service. First, the stores aim to take care of customers within 60 seconds. And while moving at this lightning-fast pace, employees are expected to maintain a cheery attitude.

Some New Yorkers, in particular, have been astonished to get a smile along with their quick coffee and sandwich. It seems implausible that employees in a rush can also find the time and energy to display empathy. But Pret's management believes the company has the right methods to maintain the customer-friendly strategy even as the company expands. Those methods lean heavily on human resource practices that include careful hiring, fair pay, and plenty of training.

In hiring, Pret looks for what they term Pret Behaviors: passion, clear but thoughtful communication, and teamwork. A Pret Person is enthusiastic, responsible, hardworking, and committed to quality. The company looks for people who communicate clearly, informally, sincerely, and with respect for others. Also, employees should be friendly, show concern for others, and exude happiness. To ensure it has selected people with these qualities, Pret assigns newly hired employees to work for a six-hour day in one of its shops. The employees then vote on whether to keep the person on the payroll. (Those who aren't kept are paid for the day's work.)

Training, too, emphasizes teamwork and customer service. When employees are hired, they receive a binder full of details on how to behave. For example, they should offer samples and "not hide your true character." They should "bustle around" and avoid "standing around looking bored." After three months, employees take a quiz to assess their knowledge of Pret's performance standards. When they pass the quiz, they are called Team Member Stars, eligible for additional training and promotion to specialized posts such as preparing soup and other hot foods. Although food is prepared in advance, so the "chefs" handling hot foods don't have sophisticated positions, the company's commitment to training and promotions shows employees that they are learning and progressing.

Backing up the careful hiring and extensive training is a system of rewards for delighting customers and contributing to teamwork. Mystery shoppers visit the stores, and when a shop is rated outstanding, all its employees get a bonus. Every three months, the top 10 stores also get a party, and managers have an allowance to spend on treats for workers. The company also sends a silver star made by Tiffany & Co. to an employee whenever a customer contacts Pret to praise the employee's service. Wages, too, are relatively generous for fast-food workers, starting at $9 per hour and rising after 10 weeks of training and experience. The rewards are paying off in low employee turnover and strong sales growth.

SOURCES: Pret A Manger, "About Us," http://www.pret.com, accessed January 31, 2012; Stephanie Clifford, "Would You Like a Smile with That?" *The New York Times,* August 7, 2011, Business & Company Resource Center, http://galenet.galegroup.com.

much to offer in salary or wages, as opposed to bonuses, commissions, and other performance-related pay. Other decisions involve which benefits to offer, from retirement plans to various kinds of insurance to time off with pay. All such decisions have implications for the organization's bottom line, as well as for employee motivation.

Administering pay and benefits is another big responsibility. Organizations need systems for keeping track of each employee's earnings and benefits. Employees need information about their health plan, retirement plan, and other benefits. Keeping track of this involves extensive record keeping and reporting to management, employees, the government, and others.

Maintaining Positive Employee Relations

Organizations often depend on human resource professionals to help them maintain positive relations with employees. This function includes preparing and distributing employee handbooks that detail company policies and, in large organizations, company publications such as a monthly newsletter or a website on the organization's intranet. Preparing these communications may be a regular task for the human resource department.

The human resource department can also expect to handle certain kinds of communications from individual employees. Employees turn to the HR department for answers to questions about benefits and company policy. If employees feel they have been discriminated against, see safety hazards, or have other problems and

One reason W. L. Gore & Associates is repeatedly named one of the 100 Best Companies to Work for in America is their unusual corporate culture where all employees are known as associates and bosses are not to be found. How do you think this boosts morale in the workplace?

are dissatisfied with their supervisor's response, they may turn to the HR department for help. Members of the department should be prepared to address such problems.

In organizations where employees belong to a union, employee relations entail additional responsibilities. The organization periodically conducts collective bargaining to negotiate an employment contract with union members. The HR department maintains communication with union representatives to ensure that problems are resolved as they arise.

Establishing and Administering Personnel Policies

All the human resource activities described so far require fair and consistent decisions, and most require substantial record keeping. Organizations depend on their HR department to help establish policies related to hiring, discipline, promotions, and benefits. For example, with a policy in place that an intoxicated worker will be immediately terminated, the company can handle such a situation more fairly and objectively than if it addressed such incidents on a case-by-case basis. The company depends on its HR professionals to help develop and then communicate the policy to every employee, so that everyone knows its importance. If anyone violates the rule, a supervisor can quickly intervene—confident that the employee knew the consequences and that any other employee would be treated the same way. Not only do such policies promote fair decision making, but they also promote other objectives, such as workplace safety and customer service.

Developing fair and effective policies requires strong decision-making skills, the ability to think ethically, and a broad understanding of business activities that will be covered by the policies. In addition, for employees to comply with policies, they have to know and understand the policies. Therefore, human resource management requires the ability to communicate through a variety of channels. Human resource personnel may teach policies by giving presentations at meetings, posting documents online, writing e-mail messages, setting up social-media pages for employees, and in many other ways.

Managing and Using Human Resource Data

All aspects of human resource management require careful and discreet record keeping, from processing job applications, to performance appraisals, benefits enrollment, and government-mandated reports. Handling records about employees requires accuracy as well as sensitivity to employee privacy. Whether the organization keeps records in file cabinets or on a sophisticated computer information system, it must have methods for ensuring accuracy and for balancing privacy concerns with easy access for those who need information and are authorized to see it.

Thanks to computer tools, employee-related information is not just an administrative responsibility; it also can be the basis for knowledge that gives organizations an edge over their competitors. Data about employees can show, for example, which of the company's talent has the most promise for future leadership, what kinds of employees tend to perform best in particular positions, and in which departments the need for hiring will be most pressing. To use the data for answering questions such as these, many organizations have set up human resource information systems. They may engage in **workforce analytics,** which is the use of quantitative tools and scientific methods to analyze data from human resource databases and other sources to make evidence-based decisions that support business goals. Chapter 2 will take a closer look at how developments in technology are enabling more sophisticated analysis of employee data to support decision making.

Workforce Analytics
The use of quantitative tools and scientific methods to analyze data from human resource databases and other sources to make evidence-based decisions that support business goals.

Ensuring Compliance with Labor Laws

As we will discuss in later chapters, especially Chapter 3, the government has many laws and regulations concerning the treatment of employees. These laws govern such matters as equal employment opportunity, employee safety and health, employee pay and benefits, employee privacy, and job security. Government requirements include filing reports and displaying posters, as well as avoiding unlawful behavior. Most managers depend on human resource professionals to help them keep track of these requirements.

Ensuring compliance with laws requires that human resource personnel keep watch over a rapidly changing legal landscape. For example, the increased use of and access to electronic databases by employees and employers suggest that in the near future legislation will be needed to protect employee privacy rights. Currently, no federal laws outline how to use employee databases in such a way as to protect employees' privacy while also meeting employers' and society's concern for security.

Lawsuits that will continue to influence HRM practices concern job security. Because companies are forced to close facilities and lay off employees because of economic or competitive conditions, cases dealing with the illegal discharge of employees have increased. The issue of "employment at will"—that is, the principle that an employer may terminate employment at any time without notice—will be debated. As the age of the overall workforce increases, as described in the next chapter, the number of cases dealing with age discrimination in layoffs, promotions, and benefits will likely rise. Employers will need to review work rules, recruitment practices, and performance evaluation systems, revising them if necessary to ensure that they do not falsely communicate employment agreements the company does not intend to honor (such as lifetime employment) or discriminate on the basis of age.

Supporting the Organization's Strategy

At one time, human resource management was primarily an administrative function. The HR department focused on filling out forms and processing paperwork. As more organizations have come to appreciate the significance of highly skilled human resources, however, many HR departments have taken on a more active role in supporting the organization's strategy. As a result, today's HR professionals need to understand

Aligning HR with the Organization's Strategy

HR employees often start their careers with a focus on a particular specialty, such as developing training programs or administering payroll. Especially as they move into management roles, they need a broader view of human resource management as supporting the organization's strategy. To think strategically about human resource management, try these ideas:

- Before deciding *how* to complete a project, ask yourself or your team *what* you are supposed to accomplish. For example, don't start with how to present the new benefits package to employees, but with what you want to accomplish by making the presentation. Answering that question might open up new avenues that are more effective and efficient.
- Ask goal-related questions: Where do you envision your team and your company in the next year? The next three years? To meet goals related to human resource management, what in the organization—not just the HR department—would be different?
- In meetings, especially with higher level managers, pay attention to the participants who think strategically. Notice the kinds of questions they ask and the issues they focus on.
- Read about the field of human resources and the industry in which your organization operates. Get involved in professional and industry associations. Keep abreast of the latest research and trends.
- Learn ways to measure the results of human resource management, such as changes in productivity and employee turnover. When communicating with other managers, talk in terms of these results.
- Learn about your own organization's strategy; pay close attention to goals expressed by other managers. For example, when change is afoot in any part of the organization, it will affect the organization's people. Think about how the HR department can support the change—say, by assessing employees' attitudes, communicating with and training employees, and hiring the right talent for new kinds of work. Help the organization anticipate these issues and incorporate them into the plan for the change.
- Seek out work assignments and volunteer opportunities that include planning for an organization's future. These roles offer practical experience in thinking strategically.

SOURCES: Eric Krell, "Change Within," *HR Magazine,* August 2011, pp. 43–50; Jill Fowler and Jeanette Savage, "Ask 'What,' Not 'How,'" *HR Magazine,* August 2011, pp. 85–86.

the organization's business operations, project how business trends might affect the business, reinforce positive aspects of the organization's culture, develop talent for present and future needs, craft effective HR strategies, and make a case for them to top management. Evidence for greater involvement in strategy comes from interviews with finance and HR executives who say they are more interested than ever in collaborating to strengthen their companies.[9] Finance leaders can see that employees are a major budget item, so they want to make sure they are getting the best value for that expense. HR leaders, for their part, are learning to appreciate the importance of using quantitative tools to measure performance. For some practical ideas on how to approach human resource management from a strategic perspective, see "HR How To."

An important element of this responsibility is **human resource planning,** identifying the numbers and types of employees the organization will require in order to meet its objectives. Using these estimates, the human resource department helps the organization forecast its needs for hiring, training, and reassigning employees. Planning also may show that the organization will need fewer employees to meet anticipated needs. In that situation, human resource planning includes how to handle or avoid layoffs. Human resource planning provides important information for

Human Resource Planning
Identifying the numbers and types of employees the organization will require to meet its objectives.

Talent Management
A systematic, planned effort to attract, retain, develop, and motivate highly skilled employees and managers.

talent management—a systematic, planned effort to attract, retain, develop, and motivate highly skilled employees and managers. When managers are clear about the kinds of people they will need to achieve the organization's goals, talent management combines recruiting, selection, training, and motivational practices to meet those needs. Approaching these tasks in terms of talent management is one way HR managers are making the link to organizational strategy. At Zeno Group, a Chicago public relations firm, CFO Tony Blasco has collaborated with the HR manager to identify people to hire as future strategic needs arise. Together, says Blasco, they are planning for how future hires will "further our ambitious growth goals."[10]

Evidence-Based HR
Collecting and using data to show that human resource practices have a positive influence on the company's bottom line or key stakeholders.

As part of its strategic role, one of the key contributions HR can make is to engage in evidence-based HR. **Evidence-based HR** refers to demonstrating that human resource practices have a positive influence on the company's profits or key stakeholders (employees, customers, community, shareholders). This practice helps show that the money invested in HR programs is justified and that HRM is contributing to the company's goals and objectives. For example, data collected on the relationship between HR practices and productivity, turnover, accidents, employee attitudes, and medical costs may show that HR functions are as important to the business as finance, accounting, and marketing.

Often, an organization's strategy requires some type of change—for example, adding, moving, or closing facilities; applying new technology; or entering markets in other regions or countries. Common reactions to change include fear, anger, and confusion. The organization may turn to its human resource department for help in managing the change process. Skilled human resource professionals can apply knowledge of human behavior, along with performance management tools, to help the organization manage change constructively.

Sustainability
An organization's ability to profit without depleting its resources, including employees, natural resources, and the support of the surrounding community.

Stakeholders
The parties with an interest in the company's success (typically, shareholders, the community, customers, and employees).

Another strategic challenge tackled by a growing number of companies is how to seek profits in ways that communities, customers, and suppliers will support over the long run. This concern is called **sustainability**—broadly defined as an organization's ability to profit without depleting its resources, including employees, natural resources, and the support of the surrounding community. Success at sustainability comes from meeting the needs of the organization's **stakeholders,** all the parties who have an interest in the organization's success. Typically, an organization's stakeholders include shareholders, the community, customers, and employees. Sustainable organizations meet their needs by minimizing their environmental impact, providing high-quality products and services, ensuring workplace safety, offering fair compensation, and delivering an adequate return to investors. Sustainability delivers a strategic advantage when it boosts the organization's image with customers, opens access to new markets, and helps attract and retain talented employees. In an organization with a sustainable strategy, HR departments focus on employee development and empowerment rather than short-term costs, on long-term planning rather than smooth turnover and outsourcing, and on justice and fairness over short-term profits.[11] At IBM, human resource management sustainably addresses the company's global presence and drive for innovation in several ways. Diversity training helps people work productively in teams regardless of ethnicity, gender, or other differences. Global Enablement Teams address employee development needs in various regions by sending employees from highly developed nations to mentor employees in developing nations; the mentors teach business skills while learning about these high-potential markets. And IBM's Smarter Planet projects to lower resource use and pollution attract talented innovators; job candidates are excited about the chance to be part of this effort.[12]

Skills of HRM Professionals

LO 1-3 Summarize the types of skills needed for human resource management.

With such varied responsibilities, the human resource department needs to bring together a large pool of skills. These skills fall into the six basic functions shown in Figure 1.3.[13] Members of the HR department need to be:

1. *Credible activists*—are so well respected in the organization that they can influence the positions taken by managers. HR professionals who are competent in this area have the most influence over the organization's success, but to build this competency, they have to gain credibility by mastering all the others.

Figure 1.3
Six Competencies for the HR Profession

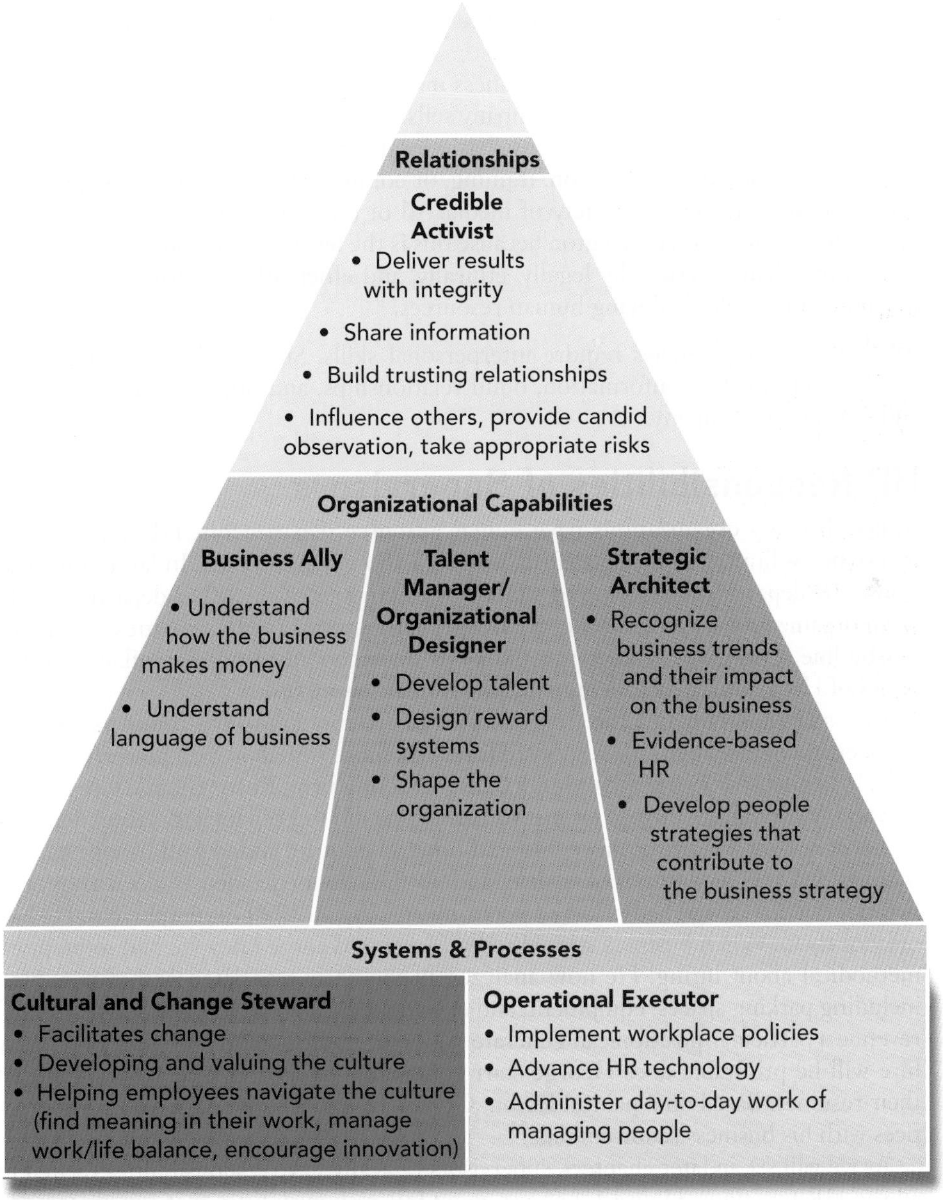

Relationships

Credible Activist
- Deliver results with integrity
- Share information
- Build trusting relationships
- Influence others, provide candid observation, take appropriate risks

Organizational Capabilities

Business Ally
- Understand how the business makes money
- Understand language of business

Talent Manager/ Organizational Designer
- Develop talent
- Design reward systems
- Shape the organization

Strategic Architect
- Recognize business trends and their impact on the business
- Evidence-based HR
- Develop people strategies that contribute to the business strategy

Systems & Processes

Cultural and Change Steward
- Facilitates change
- Developing and valuing the culture
- Helping employees navigate the culture (find meaning in their work, manage work/life balance, encourage innovation)

Operational Executor
- Implement workplace policies
- Advance HR technology
- Administer day-to-day work of managing people

SOURCES: Based on R. Grossman, "New Competencies for HR," *HR Magazine* (June 2007): pp. 58–62; D. Ulrich, W. Bruckbank, D. Johnson, K. Sandholtz, and J. Younger, "HR Competencies; Mastery at the Intersection of People and Business" (Alexandria, VA: Society for Human Resource Management +/RBL Group, 2008).

2. *Cultural and change steward*—understands the organization's culture and helping to build and strengthen or change that culture by identifying and expressing its values through words and actions.

3. *Talent manager/organizational designer*—knows the ways that people join the organization and move to different positions within it. To do this effectively requires knowledge of how the organization is structured and how that structure might be adjusted to help it meet its goals for developing and using employees' talents.

4. *Strategic architect*—requires awareness of business trends and an understanding of how they might affect the business, as well as opportunities and threats they might present. A person with this capability spots ways effective management of human resources can help the company seize opportunities and confront threats to the business.

5. *Business allies*—know how the business makes money, who its customers are, and why customers buy what the company sells.

6. *Operational executors*—at the most basic level carry out particular HR functions such as handling the selection, training, or compensation of employees and communicating through a variety of media. All of the other HR skills require some ability as operational executor, because this is the level at which policies and transactions deliver results by legally, ethically, and efficiently acquiring, developing, motivating, and deploying human resources.

All of these competencies require interpersonal skills. Successful HR professionals must be able to share information, build relationships, and influence persons inside and outside the company.

HR Responsibilities of Supervisors

LO 1-4 Explain the role of supervisors in human resource management.

Although many organizations have human resource departments, HR activities are by no means limited to the specialists who staff those departments. In large organizations, HR departments advise and support the activities of the other departments. In small organizations, there may be an HR specialist, but many HR activities are carried out by line supervisors. Either way, non-HR managers need to be familiar with the basics of HRM and their role in managing human resources.

At a start-up company, the first supervisors are the company's founders. Not all founders recognize their HR responsibilities, but those who do have a powerful advantage. When Rusty George first founded his marketing firm, Rusty George Creative, in Tacoma, Washington, hiring was just something he did to keep up with rising demand. As he signed on law firms, museums, and other clients, he added staff to take care of them. Then the economy took a dive, and all the clients decided to do without the firm's services. George had no way to continue paying all 17 of his employees. He laid off 9 of them. When business started to build again, George knew he had to be more methodical about hiring. He now analyzes all the costs associated with a new hire, including parking spaces, equipment, and even coffee. Then he looks at the additional revenue a particular position can generate. Only when those numbers show that a new hire will be profitable does George start contacting candidates who have submitted their résumés. Based on a painful lesson, George has learned to align his hiring practices with his business requirements.[14]

As we will see in later chapters, supervisors typically have responsibilities related to all the HR functions. Figure 1.4 shows some HR responsibilities that supervisors are likely to be involved in. Organizations depend on supervisors to help them determine what kinds of work need to be done (job analysis and design) and how many employees

are needed (HR planning). Supervisors typically interview job candidates and participate in the decisions about which candidates to hire. Many organizations expect supervisors to train employees in some or all aspects of the employees' jobs. Supervisors
conduct performance appraisals and may recommend pay increases. And, of course,
supervisors play a key role in employee relations because they are most often the voice
of management for their employees, representing the company on a day-to-day basis.
In all these activities, supervisors can participate in HRM by taking into consideration
the ways that decisions and policies will affect their employees. Understanding the
principles of communication, motivation, and other elements of human behavior can
help supervisors inspire the best from the organization's human resources.

Ethics in Human Resource Management

Whenever people's actions affect one another, ethical issues arise, and business decisions are no exception. **Ethics** refers to fundamental principles of right and wrong;
ethical behavior is behavior that is consistent with those principles. Business decisions,
including HRM decisions, should be ethical, but the evidence suggests that is not
always what happens. Recent surveys indicate that the general public and managers do
not have positive perceptions of the ethical conduct of U.S. businesses. For example,
in a Gallup poll on honesty and ethics in 21 professions, only 18% of Americans rated
business executives high or very high; close to twice as many rated them low or very
low. And within organizations, a recent survey of workers found that 45% had witnessed some form of unethical conduct at their workplace.[15]

Many ethical issues in the workplace involve human resource management. The
recent financial crisis, in which the investment bank Lehman Brothers collapsed,
insurance giant AIG survived only with a massive infusion of government funds, and
many observers feared that money for loans would dry up altogether, had many causes.
Among these, some people believe, were ethical lapses related to compensation and
other HR policies.

Employee Rights

In the context of ethical human resource management, HR managers must view
employees as having basic rights. Such a view reflects ethical principles embodied in the
U.S. Constitution and Bill of Rights. A widely adopted understanding of human rights,

LO 1-5 Discuss
ethical issues in human
resource management.

Ethics
The fundamental princi-
ples of right and wrong.

The Case of the Disappearing Potato Chips

At a Walgreens in San Francisco, a cashier who had worked for the store for almost 18 years helped herself to a bag of potato chips and ate them while on duty. When her shift ended, she paid for the chips. Walgreens fired her for violating company policy.

But it wasn't just a case of an employee breaking the rules. The employee has diabetes, and while she was working, she realized her blood sugar was falling dangerously low. She had forgotten to carry her usual piece of candy, so she ate the chips as the best solution she could think of to protect herself. After she was fired, she took her case to the government's Equal Employment Opportunity Commission. The EEOC sued Walgreens for discriminating against her because of her disability.

Questions

1. Which of Kant's human rights do you think should have applied to the employee in this situation? Which of those rights did Walgreens disrespect?
2. How could respect for human rights have shaped a better response from Walgreens?

SOURCES: Nicole Carter, "Bizarre HR of 2011," *Inc.,* December 21, 2011, http://www.inc.com; Equal Employment Opportunity Commission, "Walgreens Sued by EEOC for Disability Discrimination," news release, September 8, 2011, http://www1.eeoc.gov.

based on the work of the philosopher Immanuel Kant, as well as the tradition of the Enlightenment, assumes that in a moral universe, every person has certain basic rights:

- *Right of free consent*—People have the right to be treated only as they knowingly and willingly consent to be treated. An example that applies to employees would be that employees should know the nature of the job they are being hired to do; the employer should not deceive them.
- *Right of privacy*—People have the right to do as they wish in their private lives, and they have the right to control what they reveal about private activities. One way an employer respects this right is by keeping employees' personal records confidential.
- *Right of freedom of conscience*—People have the right to refuse to do what violates their moral beliefs, as long as these beliefs reflect commonly accepted norms. A supervisor who demands that an employee do something that is unsafe or environmentally damaging may be violating this right if the task conflicts with the employee's values. (Such behavior could be illegal as well as unethical.)
- *Right of freedom of speech*—People have the right to criticize an organization's ethics if they do so in good conscience and their criticism does not violate the rights of individuals in the organization. Many organizations address this right by offering hot lines or policies and procedures designed to handle complaints from employees.
- *Right to due process*—If people believe their rights are being violated, they have the right to a fair and impartial hearing. As we will see in Chapter 3, Congress has addressed this right in some circumstances by establishing agencies to hear complaints when employees believe their employer has not provided a fair hearing. For example, the Equal Employment Opportunity Commission may prosecute complaints of discrimination if it believes the employer did not fairly handle the problem.

One way to think about ethics in business is that the morally correct action is the one that minimizes encroachments on and avoids violations of these rights. Consider, for example, whether more careful thought about rights could have prevented the awkward situation described in the "HR Oops!" box.

Organizations often face situations in which the rights of employees are affected. In particular, the right of privacy of health information has received much attention in recent years. Computerized record keeping and computer networks have greatly increased the ways people can gain (authorized or unauthorized) access to records about individuals. Health-related records can be particularly sensitive. HRM responsibilities include the ever growing challenge of maintaining confidentiality and security of employees' health information as required by the Health Insurance Portability and Accountability Act (HIPAA).

Standards for Ethical Behavior

Ethical, successful companies act according to four principles.[16] First, in their relationships with customers, vendors, and clients, ethical and successful companies emphasize mutual benefits. Second, employees assume responsibility for the actions of the company. Third, such companies have a sense of purpose or vision that employees value and use in their day-to-day work. Finally, they emphasize fairness; that is, another person's interests count as much as their own.

Executives at 3M realized the company needed to recommit to principles such as these when the company was trying for a comeback after several difficult years. In an effort to improve profits, past leadership had focused on cutting costs, and 3M's reputation as an innovator suffered from neglect. When George W. Buckley took the chief executive's job, 3M intended to refocus employees on growth and innovation. This would require changes in employees' actions and mind-sets. Angela S. Lalor, 3M's senior vice president of human resources, explained to the leadership team that successful change on that scale would require a high level of employee trust. In particular, employees would need to feel they trusted their immediate supervisors. So the company's HR professionals focused on creating plans to build trusting relationships by ensuring that supervisors treated employees fairly. The company also sought to engage employees by ensuring they were aware of and connected to its efforts to operate sustainably by reducing pollution, providing grants for community projects, and promoting employee health. Since 3M launched the effort, employee surveys have shown higher levels of trust in managers and engagement with the company. The company's financial performance improved as well.[17]

For human resource practices to be considered ethical, they must satisfy the three basic standards summarized in Figure 1.5.[18] First, HRM practices must result in

Figure 1.5

Standards for Identifying Ethical Practices

Greatest good for greatest number

Fair and equitable

Ethical Alternative

Respect for basic human rights

the greatest good for the largest number of people. Second, employment practices must respect basic human rights of privacy, due process, consent, and free speech. Third, managers must treat employees and customers equitably and fairly. At 3M, the human resources department helped supervisors treat employees fairly by educating the supervisors in what kinds of conduct employees consider fair—for example, communicating in ways that are honest, open, and realistic. The training also emphasized the importance of listening carefully to employees and asking questions rather than dictating solutions. HR staffers provided supervisors with information about how 3M establishes pay rates so the supervisors themselves can share the information with employees and demonstrate that the decisions are based on fair criteria.[19]

LO 1-6 Describe typical careers in human resource management.

Careers in Human Resource Management

There are many different types of jobs in the HRM profession. Figure 1.6 shows selected HRM positions and their salaries. The salaries vary depending on education and experience, as well as the type of industry in which the person works. As you can see from Figure 1.6, some positions involve work in specialized areas of HRM such as recruiting, compensation, or employee benefits. Usually, HR generalists make between $50,000 and $80,000, depending on their experience and education level. Generalists usually perform the full range of HRM activities, including recruiting, training, compensation, and employee relations.

The vast majority of HRM professionals have a college degree, and many also have completed postgraduate work. The typical field of study is business (especially human

Figure 1.6

Median Salaries for HRM Positions

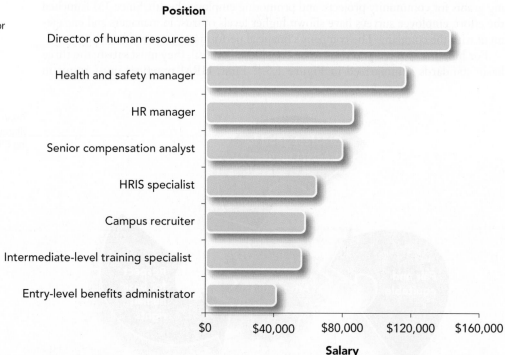

SOURCE: Data from Salary Wizard, Salary.com, http://www1.salary.com, accessed January 24, 2012.

SHRM's Social-Media Presence

Members of the Society of Human Resource Management can connect with the organization's resources and with one another online, thanks to several applications of social media:

- SHRM has a Twitter account (http://twitter.com/#!/shrm), so members can sign up for the group's Twitter feed.
- At the SHRM website, the SHRM Blog (http://blog.shrm.org)

gives members a place to read the organization's latest thoughts and get involved in the conversation by reading and posting comments.

- Also at the website, SHRM has established its own members-only social network called SHRM Connect (http://community.shrm.org). Those who join the network can meet other SHRM members online and trade ideas. SHRM's features include search

capabilities and e-mail alerts so members can look up and be aware of discussions on topics of interest.

- Visitors to SHRM conferences can text questions to presenters. Those who can't make the trip can get updates on what's happening via Twitter.

SOURCE: Based on Henry G. Jackson, "Embracing Social Media," *HR Magazine,* December 2011, p. 10.

---

resources or industrial relations), but some HRM professionals have degrees in the social sciences (economics or psychology), the humanities, and law programs. Those who have completed graduate work have master's degrees in HR management, business management, or a similar field. This is important because to be successful in HR, you need to speak the same language as people in the other business functions. You have to have credibility as a business leader, so you must be able to understand finance and to build a business case for HR activities.

HR professionals can increase their career opportunities by taking advantage of training and development programs. These may include taking courses toward a master's degree, accepting assignments to spend time observing, or "shadowing," a manager in another department, or taking a position in another department to learn more about the business. When Michael Brady was a district HR manager for Walmart, he would travel with the operations manager for his region. Each manager was interested in learning more about the other's perspective on the business, and they eventually learned enough to help one another spot issues to address. Marian M. Graddick-Weir started her HR career as a generalist at AT&T. Her supervisor asked her to serve as chief of staff to the company's vice chairman. The position was heavy on clerical duties but gave Graddick-Weir access to the kinds of decisions and conversations that take place at the highest level of the organization. Graddick-Weir paid attention and then took that knowledge with her when she returned to the HR department. Today she is executive vice president of human resources at Merck & Co.[20]

Some HRM professionals have a professional certification in HRM, but many more are members of professional associations. The primary professional organization for HRM is the Society for Human Resource Management (SHRM). SHRM is the world's largest human resource management association, with more than 250,000 professional and student members throughout the world. SHRM provides education and information services, conferences and seminars, government and media representation, and online services and publications (such as *HR Magazine*). You can visit SHRM's website to see their services at **www.shrm.org**. SHRM also connects with members through various social-media tools, as described in "HRM Social."

Organization of This Book

This chapter has provided an overview of human resource management to give you a sense of its scope. In this book, the topics are organized according to the broad areas of human resource management shown in Table 1.3. The numbers in the table refer to the part and chapter numbers.

The remaining chapters in Part 1 discuss aspects of the human resource environment: trends shaping the field (Chapter 2), legal requirements (Chapter 3), and the work to be done by the organization, which is the basis for designing jobs (Chapter 4). Part 2 explores the responsibilities involved in acquiring and preparing human resources: HR planning and recruiting (Chapter 5), selection and placement of employees (Chapter 6), and training (Chapter 7). Part 3 turns to the assessment and development of human resources through performance management (Chapter 8) and employee development (Chapter 9), as well as appropriate ways to handle employee separation when the organization determines it no longer wants or needs certain employees (Chapter 10). Part 4 addresses topics related to compensation: pay structure (Chapter 11), pay to recognize performance (Chapter 12), and benefits (Chapter 13). Part 5 explores special topics faced by HR managers today: human resource management in organizations where employees have or are seeking union representation (Chapter 14), international human resource management (Chapter 15), and high-performance organizations (Chapter 16).

Along with examples highlighting how HRM helps a company maintain high performance, the chapters offer various other features to help you connect the principles to real-world situations. "Best Practices" boxes tell success stories related to the

Table 1.3

Topics Covered in This Book

I.   The Human Resource Environment
1. Managing Human Resources
2. Trends in Human Resource Management
3. Providing Equal Employment Opportunity and a Safe Workplace
4. Analyzing Work and Designing Jobs

II. Acquiring and Preparing Human Resources
5. Planning For and Recruiting Human Resources
6. Selecting Employees and Placing Them in Jobs
7. Training Employees

III. Assessing Performance and Developing Employees
8. Managing Employees' Performance
9. Developing Employees for Future Success
10. Separating and Retaining Employees

IV. Compensating Human Resources
11. Establishing a Pay Structure
12. Recognizing Employee Contributions with Pay
13. Providing Employee Benefits

V.   Meeting Other HR Goals
14. Collective Bargaining and Labor Relations
15. Managing Human Resources Globally
16. Creating and Maintaining High-Performance Organizations

chapter's topic. "HR Oops!" boxes identify situations gone wrong and invite you to find better alternatives. "HR How To" boxes provide details about how to carry out a practice in each HR area. "Did You Know?" boxes are snapshots of interesting statistics related to chapter topics. Many chapters also include an "HRM Social" box identifying ways that human resource professionals are applying social media to help their organizations excel in the fast-changing modern world.

THINKING ETHICALLY

ARE SMOKING BREAKS AN ETHICAL HR POLICY?

The work environment in U.S. offices has changed considerably from the days when ashtrays decorated desks and smoking was an ordinary workplace ritual. Nowadays, many states ban smoking in some or all workplaces, and many organizations prohibit smoking in most or all of their facilities. The result is a challenge for employees who smoke: if they are unwilling or unable to do without cigarettes until the end of their work shift, they need time and space for breaks. Some employers have union contracts that require breaks. Organizations without such contracts have wide latitude in creating policies for smoking breaks.

Creating such a policy opens up several ethical issues. Some organizations allow smokers to go outside or to a designated area for smoking breaks. Often, at those organizations, nonsmoking employees complain that they get fewer breaks than their colleagues who smoke. The nonsmokers see the policy as unfair.

Another issue relates to the negative health effects of smoking and secondhand smoke. If smoking breaks take place near a doorway, nonsmoking employees may complain that they have to pass through a cloud of smoke every time they enter and leave the building.

Also, some people see employers as having a responsibility to protect the health of all their workers, and they may believe that the smoking breaks make it easier for smoking employees to harm their health.

Some employers see business reasons for forbidding smoking breaks or smoking areas, and these may take precedence over the ethical questions. From this vantage point, allowing any smoking breaks or smoking areas would hurt the organization's image and disrupt the workday, so the organization prohibits all smoking on the premises and during working hours.

Questions

1. Which ethical principles from the chapter do you think are most important to apply to a policy for employee smoking breaks? How would these shape the policy?
2. As a human resource manager developing such a policy, would you create a different policy for a hospital and for the offices of an advertising agency? Why or why not?

SOURCE: Peter Done, "Burning Issue of Smoking Breaks," *Financial Adviser,* October 13, 2011, Business & Company Resource Center, http://galenet.galegroup.com.

SUMMARY

LO 1-1 Define human resource management, and explain how HRM contributes to an organization's performance.

Human resource management consists of an organization's "people practices"—the policies, practices, and systems that influence employees' behavior, attitudes, and performance. HRM influences who works for the organization and how those people work. These human resources,

if well managed, have the potential to be a source of sustainable competitive advantage, contributing to basic objectives such as quality, profits, and customer satisfaction.

LO 1-2 Identify the responsibilities of human resource departments.

By carrying out HR activities or supporting line management, HR departments have responsibility for a variety of functions related to acquiring and managing employees. The HRM process begins with analyzing and designing jobs, then recruiting and selecting employees to fill those jobs. Training and development equip employees to carry out their present jobs and follow a career path in the organization. Performance management ensures that employees' activities and outputs match the organization's goals. Human resource departments also plan and administer the organization's pay and benefits. They carry out activities in support of employee relations, such as communications programs and collective bargaining. Conducting all these activities involves the establishment and administration of personnel policies, as well as careful record keeping and the use of HR information systems. Management also depends on human resource professionals for help in ensuring compliance with labor laws, as well as for support for the organization's strategy—for example, human resource planning and change management.

LO 1-3 Summarize the types of skills needed for human resource management.

Human resource management requires substantial human relations skills, including skill in communicating, negotiating, and team development. Human resource professionals also need decision-making skills based on knowledge of the HR field as well as the organization's line of business. Leadership skills are necessary, especially for managing conflict and change. Technical skills of human resource professionals include knowledge of current techniques, applicable laws, and computer systems.

LO 1-4 Explain the role of supervisors in human resource management.

Although many organizations have human resource departments, non-HR managers must be familiar with the basics of HRM and their own role with regard to managing human resources. Supervisors typically have responsibilities related to all the HR functions. Supervisors help analyze work, interview job candidates, participate in selection decisions, provide training, conduct performance appraisals, and recommend pay increases. On a day-to-day basis, supervisors represent the company to their employees, so they also play an important role in employee relations.

LO 1-5 Discuss ethical issues in human resource management.

Like all managers and employees, HR professionals should make decisions consistent with sound ethical principles. Their decisions should result in the greatest good for the largest number of people; respect basic rights of privacy, due process, consent, and free speech; and treat employees and customers equitably and fairly. Some areas in which ethical issues arise include concerns about employee privacy, protection of employee safety, and fairness in employment practices (for example, avoiding discrimination).

LO 1-6 Describe typical careers in human resource management.

Careers in human resource management may involve specialized work in fields such as recruiting, training, or labor relations. HR professionals may also be generalists, performing the full range of HR activities described in this chapter. People in these positions usually have a college degree in business or the social sciences. Human resource management means enhancing communication with employees and concern for their well-being, but it also involves a great deal of paperwork and a variety of non-people skills, as well as knowledge of business and laws.

KEY TERMS

development, 8
ethics, 17
evidence-based HR, 14
high-performance work system, 5
human capital, 4
human resource management (HRM), 3
human resource planning, 13
job analysis, 7
job design, 7
performance management, 9
recruitment, 8
selection, 8
stakeholders, 14
sustainability, 14
talent management, 14
training, 8
workforce analytics, 12

REVIEW AND DISCUSSION QUESTIONS

1. How can human resource management contribute to a company's success?
2. Imagine that a small manufacturing company decides to invest in a materials resource planning (MRP) system. This is a computerized information system that improves efficiency by automating such work as planning needs for resources, ordering materials, and scheduling work on the shop floor. The company hopes that with the new MRP system, it can grow by quickly and efficiently processing small orders for a variety of products. Which of the human resource functions are likely to be affected by this change? How can human resource management help the organization carry out this change successfully?
3. What skills are important for success in human resource management? Which of these skills are already strengths of yours? Which would you like to develop?
4. Traditionally, human resource management practices were developed and administered by the company's human resource department. Line managers are now playing a major role in developing and implementing HRM practices. Why do you think non-HR managers are becoming more involved?
5. If you were to start a business, which aspects of human resource management would you want to entrust to specialists? Why?
6. Why do all managers and supervisors need knowledge and skills related to human resource management?
7. Federal law requires that employers not discriminate on the basis of a person's race, sex, national origin, or age over 40. Is this also an ethical requirement? A competitive requirement? Explain.
8. When a restaurant employee slipped on spilled soup and fell, requiring the evening off to recover, the owner realized that workplace safety was an issue to which she had not devoted much time. A friend warned the owner that if she started creating a lot of safety rules and procedures, she would lose her focus on customers and might jeopardize the future of the restaurant. The safety problem is beginning to feel like an ethical dilemma. Suggest some ways the restaurant owner might address this dilemma. What aspects of human resource management are involved?
9. Does a career in human resource management, based on this chapter's description, appeal to you? Why or why not?

EXPERIENCING HR

Every year, the Bureau of Labor Statistics publishes a new edition of the *Occupational Outlook Handbook*, a handy—and free—resource for learning basic information about any type of career. In this exercise, you will practice using the handbook as you explore careers in human resource management.

Working alone or in pairs, look up the online edition of the handbook at **http://www.bls.gov/oco/**. Using the Search OOH tool or the link to the Search box, enter "human resources." You should see a list of possible links. Choose the link, Human Resources, Training, and Labor Relations Managers.

At the page for this category, explore the information to learn more about the job and career opportunities, including job descriptions, employment forecasts, and earnings potential. Among the careers described on this page, find the type of work that appeals to you most. Write a paragraph summarizing what you learned about this type of career. Include a sentence or two about what aspects of the career interest you and how well suited you are to this type of work.

TAKING RESPONSIBILITY: Heroes of the Taj Mahal Palace Hotel

In November 2008, the world was shocked when terrorists attacked locations around the Indian city of Mumbai. One of the targets was the prestigious Taj Mahal Palace Hotel. There, terrorists armed with grenades and automatic weapons held hostages for three days and two nights. During the siege, they killed several people and started a fire in the hotel's magnificent dome.

But amid the horrors was an amazing story of bravery. All of the hotel's employees stayed on the job. Rather than escaping to preserve themselves, they remained to help the guests as well as they could. Thinking fast as they heard gunshots, employees rushed guests to safe locations in kitchens and basements. A young manager kept a group of banquet guests quiet and calm through a long night, offering water and checking on their well-being. Employees enabled over a thousand guests to slip away, guiding them to back entries, even though the terrorists might have killed them for doing so. In fact, some *were* killed, including a head waiter who directed kitchen workers to serve as human shields for guests being evacuated. Telephone operators were evacuated, but went back to call guests and offer whatever information they could.

Later, reflecting on what had happened, senior managers of the hotel were simply amazed. They struggled to comprehend what had driven their own employees to put guests' well-being ahead of their own. Certainly, employee conduct far exceeded any company policies that were on the books. Researchers from Harvard were equally intrigued and decided to investigate by reviewing human resource policies and interviewing employees. They concluded that the exceptional conduct resulted largely from the company's recruiting, training, and rewards practices.

The Taj's approach to recruitment is a departure from the norm in India, a fast-developing nation that has not yet developed a business culture of customer service. Because the major schools of the urban areas have focused on preparing technically skilled people who tend to aim for high-paying careers in science and technology companies, the Taj recruits in smaller towns and cities, where there is less competition to pay for the best talent. They work with local schools known for high standards, asking the schools to identify people who stand out for traits such as respect and empathy. These traits are consistent with traditional culture that persists in these communities, including a high value placed on discipline, humility, honesty, respect for one's elders, and consideration of others. The Taj focuses on personal traits on the assumption that these are harder to teach than the skills for running a hotel.

Candidates for entry-level jobs are recruited from high schools and paid a stipend to attend skill certification centers. They live rent-free in the training center dormitories and learn basic skills. Those who do well during this experience are hired by the hotel as trainees. For supervisors, the Taj selects students at India's hotel management and catering institutes, again primarily focusing on candidates' values, such as integrity and conscientiousness rather than strictly hiring for technical skills. The Taj fills its ranks of middle management with graduates from India's second- and third-tier management schools, where it hopes to find candidates who are more customer-centered than money-driven.

Employees undergo an extensive 18-month training program that includes on-the-job training. The effort emphasizes learning to make decisions independently. One training tool is a weekly debriefing session in which the trainee's manager asks, "What did you learn this week?" and "What did you see this week?" These questions offer practice in figuring out how to respond to new situations, especially situations in which employees must listen to guests and respond to their needs. Always, the goal is to put the guests' interests first, on the assumption that when the guests are taken care of, the hotel's needs are protected, not the other way around.

Those who work at the Taj become part of an organization that is relentless in measuring and rewarding superior service. The management of the Taj has determined that in a typical 24-hour period, each guest has an average of 42 interactions with a hotel employee, mostly unseen by supervisors. The Taj considers each of those interactions to be a chance for an employee to delight a customer by being kind. It backs up that belief with a program of rewards. Whenever a guest compliments management about an employee's conduct, the employee is supposed to be rewarded within 48 hours. The rewards are points that employees accumulate to receive a variety of awards delivered at annual celebrations. Perhaps more important, supervisors are expected to thank their employees personally for their efforts to please customers.

Questions

1. In what ways does the Taj meet the criteria for a "sustainable" organization?
2. What would you describe as the Taj's basic strategy as a hotel? How do human resource practices support that strategy?
3. The head researcher who studied Taj has said this case shows that HR practices can ensure that employees will behave ethically. Do you agree? Why or why not?

SOURCES: Alix Spiegel, "Heroes of the Taj Hotel: Why They Risked Their Lives," National Public Radio, December 23, 2011, http://www.npr.org; Rohit Deshpandé and Anjali Raina, "The Ordinary Heroes of the Taj," *Harvard Business Review*, December 2011, pp. 119–123; Taj Hotels corporate website, "About Us—Training Opportunities," http://tajhotels.com/About-Taj/Careers/training-opportunities.html, accessed January 31, 2012.

MANAGING TALENT: Are Employees Golden at Gilt Groupe?

Fashion lovers who also love a great deal are the intended customers of Gilt Groupe. The company runs a flash sales website—an online store offering steep discounts through limited-time sales events. Customers receive e-mail announcements about the day's special deals. When the limited inventory for that deal is gone, the sale ends. The concept of flash sales took off in the late 2000s, when a sudden economic downturn left top-brand companies with huge unsold inventories. Websites like Gilt, HauteLook, and Rue La La formed to offer irresistible deals on prestigious brands, and Gilt soon became the leader in this domain. By one recent count, the company employed 850 people, and the site had registered 3.5 million members.

With several competitors starting at the same time, why did Gilt Groupe take the lead? Gilt's chief executive officer, Kevin Ryan, credits the company's "human talent." He observes that while many companies call their workforce their most important asset, Gilt puts that belief into action. The most important evidence he notes is that he, as the CEO, is personally involved with talent management daily, working directly with the head of human resource management, Melanie Hughes. Ryan has said that getting good people onboard is the most important thing for an organization's CEO to do.

Ryan demonstrates his interest in human resources by making talent a regular topic of conversation, knowing that employees will focus on what their chief cares about. At meetings with his managers, Ryan routinely asks each manager about the employees reporting to him or her. He wants to know how these employees are performing and which have potential to advance—and he wants the managers to be constantly thinking about their talent as well.

If a manager is having difficulties with an employee, Ryan wants to know so he can help resolve the situation. He believes managers tend to avoid asking underperformers to leave, and this limits them from hiring the best talent to fill vacancies. In Ryan's view, it is more honest—and, thus, fairer—to tell employees when they fail to live up to expectations. Conversely, a manager who does not build a team of high performers will not remain on the payroll for long. Ryan will allocate whatever resources are needed to find and hire great people; Gilt has 10 full-time recruiters, a lot for a company of its size, to be on a continual hunt for new talent. And when managers are hiring for a key position, Ryan is available to speak with candidates himself. However, if a manager cannot keep good people in his or her group, the high turnover signals that the manager is leading poorly.

This commitment to talent management helped Gilt grow rapidly when flash sales sites were the hot trend. But tactics that supported the company's expansion are now

being tested by turbulent times. Manufacturers of high-fashion merchandise adjusted to the economic slowdown by trimming inventories, and the growth of flash sales has resulted in more competition to buy a limited amount of goods. Compounding the challenge for companies like Gilt, the recent recovery has enabled high-end shoppers to start buying again at full price. Sites like Gilt can no longer find as much top-tier merchandise, and what they can buy is no longer as steeply discounted. Consequently, the online deals have lost some of their sparkle. Industry analysts say Gilt has yet to turn a profit.

Gilt has tackled the challenge by expanding its offerings beyond fashion apparel to travel, home décor, food, and wine. It also pressed forward with plans to expand into 90 countries beyond the United States. Nevertheless, to achieve profitability, the company recently announced layoff of about 10% of its employees. Two of the layoffs were top managers—John Auerbach, who headed the men's apparel site, and Nathan Richardson, who headed Gilt City, which offers deals tied to the customer's location. According to CEO Ryan, these two managers had talents better suited to running a start-up. The company also announced it would close regional offices in Seattle, Dallas, Atlanta, San Diego, Houston, and Philadelphia.

Questions

1. When Gilt's strategy shifted from fast growth to profitability, which of the responsibilities of human resource management do you think would have been affected?
2. If you were Gilt's director of human resource management, which HR issues would you encourage CEO Kevin Ryan to focus on as the company reorganizes for profitability?
3. What is your opinion of Ryan's heavy involvement in talent management at Gilt? What do you think it would be like to work directly with him as the HR director?

SOURCES: "About Gilt Groupe," http://www.gilt.com, accessed January 25, 2012; Kevin Ryan, "Gilt Groupe's CEO on Building a Team of A Players," *Harvard Business Review*, January–February 2012, pp. 43–46; Tricia Duryee, "Gilt Groupe Cuts Include 10 Percent of Employees and Two Executives," *All Things Digital*, January 23, 2012, http://allthingsd.com; "Daily Deals Doomed? Not So, according to Gilt Groupe," *Inc. Wire*, November 9, 2011, http://www.inc.com; Alistair Barr, "Online Flash Sales Less Flashy as Inventory Shrinks," Reuters, October 17, 2011, http://www.reuters.com; Eric Markowitz, "Gilt CEO: Interviewing Is a Waste of Time," *Inc.*, September 23, 2011, http://www.inc.com; Claire Cain Miller, "Flash-Sale Site Shifts Its Model," *The New York Times*, August 14, 2011, http://www.nytimes.com

 TWITTER FOCUS: Managing HR at a Services Firm

Using Twitter, continue the conversation about how HR helps companies gain competitive advantage by reading the case about managing HR at a services firm at **www.mhhe.com/noefund5e**. Engage with your classmates and instructor via Twitter to chat about the case using the questions posted on the Noe website. Don't have a Twitter account yet? See the instructions for getting started on the Online Learning Center.

NOTES

1. Eric Krell, "Change Within," *HR Magazine*, August 2011, pp. 43–50.
2. A. S. Tsui and L. R. Gomez-Mejia, "Evaluating Human Resource Effectiveness," in *Human Resource Management: Evolving Rules and Responsibilities*, ed. L. Dyer (Washington, DC: BNA Books, 1988), pp. 1187–227; M. A. Hitt, B. W. Keats, and S. M. DeMarie, "Navigating in the New Competitive Landscape: Building Strategic Flexibility and Competitive Advantage in the 21st Century," *Academy of Management Executive* 12, no. 4 (1998), pp. 22–42; J. T. Delaney and M. A. Huselid, "The Impact of Human Resource Management Practices on Perceptions of Organizational Performance," *Academy of Management Journal* 39 (1996), pp. 949–69.
3. W. F. Cascio, *Costing Human Resources: The Financial Impact of Behavior in Organizations*, 3rd ed. (Boston: PWS-Kent, 1991).
4. S. A. Snell and J. W. Dean, "Integrated Manufacturing and Human Resource Management: A Human Capital Perspective," *Academy of Management Journal* 35 (1992), pp. 467–504; M. A. Youndt, S. Snell, J. W. Dean Jr., and D. P. Lepak, "Human Resource Management, Manufacturing Strategy, and Firm Performance," *Academy of Management Journal* 39 (1996), pp. 836–66.
5. Zeynep Ton, "Why Good Jobs Are Good for Retailers," *Harvard Business Review*, January–February 2012, pp. 124–131.
6. Steve Wexler, "How Many HR Employees Do You Have—and Should You Have—in Your Organization?" Institute for Corporate Productivity, May 21, 2010, http://www.i4cp.com.
7. E. E. Lawler, "From Human Resource Management to Organizational Effectiveness," *Human Resource Management* 44 (2005), pp. 165–69.
8. S. Snell, "Control Theory in Strategic Human Resource Management: The Mediating Effect of Administrative Information," *Academy of Management Journal* 35 (1992), pp. 292–327.
9. Joanne Sammer, "A Marriage of Necessity," *HR Magazine*, October 2011, pp. 58–62.
10. Ibid., p. 61.
11. Wendy S. Becker, "Are You Leading a Socially Responsible and Sustainable Human Resource Function?" *People & Strategy*, March 2011, pp. 18–23.
12. Brad Power, "IBM Focuses HR on Change," *Bloomberg Businessweek*, January 10, 2012, http://www.businessweek.com.
13. Robert J. Grossman, "New Competencies for HR," *HR Magazine*, June 2007, pp. 58–62.
14. Wendy Kaufman, "A Single Hire Is a Big Deal to a Small Business," National Public Radio, October 10, 2011, http://www.npr.org.
15. Jeffrey M. Jones, "Record 64% Rate Honesty, Ethics of Members of Congress Low," Gallup, December 12, 2011, http://www.gallup.com; Corruption Currents, "Survey Sees Less Misconduct but More Reporting and Retaliation," *The Wall Street Journal*, January 5, 2012, http://blogs.wsj.com.
16. M. Pastin, *The Hard Problems of Management: Gaining the Ethics Edge* (San Francisco: Jossey-Bass, 1986); and T. Thomas, J. Schermerhorn Jr., and J. Dienhart, "Strategic Leadership of Ethical Behavior in Business," *Academy of Management Executive* 18 (2004), pp. 56–66.
17. Benjamin Schneider and Karen B. Paul, "In the Company We Trust," *HR Magazine*, January 2011, Business & Company Resource Center, http://galenet.galegroup.com.
18. G. F. Cavanaugh, D. Moberg, and M. Velasquez, "The Ethics of Organizational Politics," *Academy of Management Review* 6 (1981), pp. 363–74.
19. Schneider and Paul, "In the Company We Trust."
20. Adrienne Fox, "Paths to the Top," *HR Magazine*, November 2011, pp. 30–35.

2

Trends in Human Resource Management

What Do I Need to Know?

After reading this chapter, you should be able to:

LO 2-1 Describe trends in the labor force composition and how they affect human resource management.

LO 2-2 Summarize areas in which human resource management can support the goal of creating a high-performance work system.

LO 2-3 Define employee empowerment, and explain its role in the modern organization.

LO 2-4 Identify ways HR professionals can support organizational strategies for quality, growth, and efficiency.

LO 2-5 Summarize ways in which human resource management can support organizations expanding internationally.

LO 2-6 Discuss how technological developments are affecting human resource management.

LO 2-7 Explain how the nature of the employment relationship is changing.

LO 2-8 Discuss how the need for flexibility affects human resource management.

Introduction

Line technicians at Duke Energy, an electric-power company based in Charlotte, North Carolina, participate in a stretching program before they start their workday. The company's senior health and safety specialist launched the program to cut down on injuries among the workers, whose average age is between 50 and 55. Duke Energy also has tried to reduce muscle strain by providing line workers with battery-powered wire clippers. It trains them in how to perform job functions such as lifting and climbing in a safe manner. Line worker Barry Poe told a reporter that the safety program should enable him to keep working well into his sixties.[1] That kind of expectation is a major relief to older workers, many of whom saw their retirement savings shrivel during the financial crisis of 2008 and the severe recession that followed.

But from the employer's perspective, why not just replace these older workers with young employees, who might be stronger and less prone to fatigue and injury? Duke Energy appreciates the value of its experienced line technicians. Hiring someone new is not a quick fix, because a line technician typically takes eight years to become expert at the major skills required to repair power lines. In addition, experienced line technicians can serve as role models and mentors for their younger colleagues. Turnover among older workers tends to be lower, so these can be the organization's most loyal employees. Therefore, at companies like Duke Energy, helping older workers stay healthy until they are ready to retire is a worthwhile investment in the value of the workforce.

LO 2-1 Describe trends in the labor force composition and how they affect human resource management.

Over the past few years, the business news has been dominated by stories of persistent high unemployment rates and the need to "create jobs." In that environment, it might seem that employers can downplay the need for effective human resource management. After all, one might think, any employed person should be grateful to have a job, and there seems to be little need to hunt for talent when so many people are desperate for work. But as the Duke Energy example suggests and this chapter will show, the situation for employers is actually much more complex.[2] Although overall growth in hiring has been slow and is expected to remain slow, at least inside the United States, many employers report that recruiting the specific kinds of talent they need is getting harder. The skills required within industries often are changing as technology advances, so current employees need training as much as ever. Rising costs of benefits, especially health insurance, have demanded creativity in planning compensation packages. The difficult economy has made it essential for organizations to find ways for their employees to work more efficiently—getting more done faster and placing lighter demands on natural resources, all without sacrificing quality and customer service. These efficiency improvements can only come from creative thinking by highly motivated and well-trained workers. Addressing all of these challenges and other trends in today's business climate requires more innovative human resource management than ever.

This chapter describes major trends that are affecting human resource management. It begins with an examination of the modern labor force, including trends that are determining who will participate in the workforce of the future. Next is an exploration of the ways HRM can support a number of trends in organizational strategy, from efforts to maintain high-performance work systems to changes in the organization's size and structure. Often, growth includes the use of human resources on a global scale, as more and more organizations hire immigrants or open operations overseas. The chapter then turns to major changes in technology, especially the role of the Internet. As we will explain, the Internet is changing organizations themselves, as well as providing new ways to carry out human resource management. Finally, we explore the changing nature of the employment relationship, in which careers and jobs are becoming more flexible.

Change in the Labor Force

Internal Labor Force
An organization's workers (its employees and the people who have contracts to work at the organization).

External Labor Market
Individuals who are actively seeking employment.

The term *labor force* is a general way to refer to all the people willing and able to work. For an organization, the **internal labor force** consists of the organization's workers—its employees and the people who have contracts to work at the organization. This internal labor force has been drawn from the organization's **external labor market,** that is, individuals who are actively seeking employment. The number and kinds of people in the external labor market determine the kinds of human resources available to an organization (and their cost). Human resource professionals need to be aware of trends in the composition of the external labor market because these trends affect the organization's options for creating a well-skilled, motivated internal labor force.

An Aging Workforce

In the United States, the Bureau of Labor Statistics (BLS), an agency of the Department of Labor, tracks changes in the composition of the U.S. labor force and forecasts employment trends. The BLS has projected that from 2010 to 2020, the total U.S. civilian labor force will grow from 154 million to 164 million workers.[3] This 6.5% increase is noticeably lower than the 13.4% increase experienced during the 1990s.

Some of the expected change involves the distribution of workers by age. From 2010 to 2020, the fastest-growing age group is expected to be workers 55 and older.

The 25- to 44-year-old group will increase its numbers only slightly, so its share of the total workforce will fall. And young workers between the ages of 16 and 24 will actually be fewer in number. This combination of trends will cause the overall workforce to age. Figure 2.1 shows the change in age distribution, as forecast by the Bureau of Labor Statistics between 2010 and 2020. By 2020, all baby boomers will be at least 55 years old, swelling the ranks of workers nearing retirement.[4] Human resource professionals will therefore spend much of their time on concerns related to planning retirement, retraining older workers, and motivating workers whose careers have plateaued. Organizations will struggle with ways to control the rising costs of health care and other benefits, and many of tomorrow's managers will supervise employees much older than themselves. At the same time, organizations will have to find ways to attract, retain, and prepare the youth labor force.

As more and more of the workforce reaches retirement age, some companies have set up mentoring programs between older and younger workers so that knowledge is not lost but passed on. How does the company benefit from these mentoring programs?

Today's older generation includes many people who are in no hurry to retire. They may enjoy making a contribution at work, have ambitious plans for which they want to earn money, or simply be among the many who have inadequate savings for full retirement. Therefore, older workers often want to be allowed to gradually move toward retirement by working part-time or taking temporary assignments. Scripps Health helps its employees gradually transition to full retirement. Employees are allowed to reduce their work hours gradually while maintaining their health insurance. Employees who work at least 16 hours a week are eligible for training programs and flextime. Atlantic Health System allows retirees to take part-time jobs, per diem jobs (billing for each day worked), and temporary assignments. Retired employees have returned to work as consultants and contract workers, and some have telecommuting arrangements (working from home). Many of these assignments give older employees a chance to act as mentors to their younger colleagues.[5]

With older workers continuing to hold jobs at least part-time, today's workplaces often bring together employees representing three or four generations. This creates a need for understanding the values and work habits that tend to characterize each

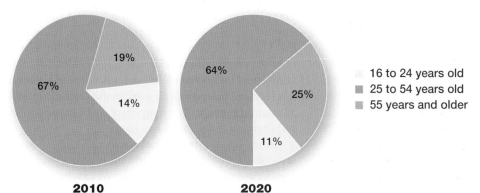

2010 **2020**

Figure 2.1
Age Distribution of U.S. Labor Force, 2010 and 2020

- 16 to 24 years old
- 25 to 54 years old
- 55 years and older

SOURCE: Bureau of Labor Statistics, "Employment Projections, 2010–20," news release, February 1, 2012, http://www.bls.gov/emp.

generation.[6] For example, members of the silent generation (born between 1925 and 1945) tend to value income and employment security and avoid challenging authority. Baby boomers (born between 1946 and 1964) tend to value unexpected rewards, opportunities for learning, and time with management. Members of Generation X (1965–1980) tend to be pragmatic and cynical, and they have well-developed self-management skills. Those born from 1981 to 1995, often called millennials, or Generation Y, are comfortable with the latest technology, and they want to be noticed, respected, and involved. Some say millennials work to live, while baby boomers live to work. Some generational differences can be addressed through effective human resource management. For example, organizations train managers to provide frequent feedback to members of Generation Y, and they show respect for older generations' hard work and respect for authority by asking them to mentor younger workers.

A Diverse Workforce

Another kind of change affecting the U.S. labor force is that it is growing more diverse in racial, ethnic, and gender terms. As Figure 2.2 shows, the 2020 workforce is expected to be 79% white, 12% African American, and 9% Asian and other minorities. The fastest-growing of these categories are Asian and "other groups" because these groups are experiencing immigration and birthrates above the national average. In addition to these racial categories, the ethnic category of Hispanics is growing even faster, and the Hispanic share of the U.S. labor force is expected to near 19% of the total in 2020.[7] Along with greater racial and ethnic diversity, there is also greater gender diversity. More women today, than in the past, are in the paid labor force, and the labor force participation rate for men has been slowly declining. By 2020, the share of women in the civilian labor force is expected to reach 47%.[8]

One important source of racial and ethnic diversity is immigration. The U.S. government establishes procedures for foreign nationals to follow if they wish to live and work permanently in the United States, and it sets limits on the number of immigrants who are admitted through these channels. Of the more than 1 million immigrants who come to the United States legally each year, more than 6 out of 10 are relatives of U.S. citizens. Another 14% come on work-related visas, some of which are set aside for workers with exceptional qualifications in science, business, or the arts. (About half of the work-related visas go to the immediate relatives of those coming to the United States to work, allowing workers to bring their spouse and children.) The U.S. government also grants temporary work visas to a limited number of highly educated workers, permitting them to work in the United States for a set period of time but not to remain as immigrants. U.S. law requires employers to verify that any job candidate who is not a U.S. citizen has received permission to work in the United States as an immigrant or with a temporary work permit. (This requirement is discussed in Chapter 6.)

Other foreign-born workers in the United States arrived to this country without meeting the legal requirements for immigration or asylum. These individuals, known as undocumented or illegal immigrants, likely number in the millions. While government policy toward immigrants is a matter

Figure 2.2
Projected Racial/Ethnic Makeup of the U.S. Workforce, 2020

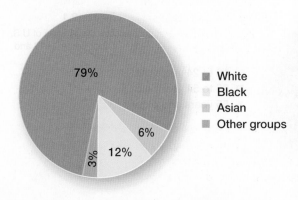

79%
6%
3%
12%

- White
- Black
- Asian
- Other groups

SOURCE: Bureau of Labor Statistics, "Employment Projections, 2010–20," news release, February 1, 2012, http://www.bls.gov/emp.

of heated public debate, the human resource implications have two practical parts. The first involves the supply of and demand for labor. Many U.S. industries, including meatpacking, construction, farming, and services, rely on immigrants to perform demanding work that may be low paid. In other industries, such as computer software development, employers say they have difficulty finding enough qualified U.S. workers to fill technical jobs. These employers are pressing for immigration laws to allow a greater supply of foreign-born workers.

The other HR concern is the need to comply with laws. Recently, Immigration and Customs Enforcement agents have been cracking down on employers who allegedly knew they were employing undocumented immigrants. Businesses that have justified hiring these people on the grounds that they work hard and are needed for the business to continue operating now are facing greater legal risks.[9] Even as some companies are lobbying for changes to immigration laws, the constraints on labor supply force companies to consider a variety of ways to meet their demand for labor, including job redesign (see Chapter 4), higher pay (Chapter 11), and foreign operations (Chapter 15).

The greater diversity of the U.S. labor force challenges employers to create HRM practices that ensure they fully utilize the talents, skills, and values of all employees. As a result, organizations cannot afford to ignore or discount the potential contributions of women and minorities. Employers will have to ensure that employees and HRM systems are free of bias and value the perspectives and experience that women and minorities can contribute to organizational goals such as product quality and customer service. As we will discuss further in the next chapter, managing cultural diversity involves many different activities. These include creating an organizational culture that values diversity, ensuring that HRM systems are bias-free, encouraging career development for women and minorities, promoting knowledge and acceptance of cultural differences, ensuring involvement in education both within and outside the organization, and dealing with employees' resistance to diversity.[10] Figure 2.3 summarizes ways in which HRM can support the management of diversity for organizational success.

Many U.S. companies have already committed themselves to ensuring that they recognize the diversity of their internal labor force and use it to gain a competitive advantage. In a recent survey of executives at large global corporations, 85% said a "diverse and inclusive workforce" is important for encouraging innovation. Majorities of respondents said their companies have a program to recruit a diverse group of employees (65%) and develop an inclusive workforce (53%).[11]

An organization doesn't have to be a huge global enterprise to benefit from valuing diversity. In Poughkeepsie, New York, the Bridgeway Federal Credit Union has realized that it can best serve the groups in its community by ensuring that its employees are representative of that community. About one-fourth of Bridgeway's members are African American, and about 12% are Hispanics. Many of these members come from low-income households where access to banking services has been limited in the past. To attract and include employees from this community, Bridgeway conducts outreach events in neighborhoods and provides diversity training programs for its employees. With ideas from its diverse employees, Bridgeway has come up with helpful products, such as its Drive Up Savings Account, which provides qualified customers with an auto loan that has a payment plan in which a part of the monthly payments is directed into a savings plan. When the loan is paid off, Bridgeway rewards the borrowers by giving them a discount on the interest they paid, and the customers find that they have saved up a tidy sum.[12]

Throughout this book, we will show how diversity affects HRM practices. For example, from a staffing perspective, it is important to ensure that tests used to select

Figure 2.3
HRM Practices That Support Diversity Management

Communication:
Communicate with employees from a variety of backgrounds.

Development:
Provide career development for employees with different backgrounds and abilities.

Performance Appraisal:
Provide feedback based on objective outcomes.

Employee Relations:
Create a work environment that is comfortable for all and fosters creativity.

SOURCE: Based on M. Loden and J. B. Rosener, *Workforce America!* (Homewood, IL: Business One Irwin, 1991).

employees are not unfairly biased against minority groups. From the perspective of work design, employees need flexible schedules that allow them to meet nonwork needs. In terms of training, it is clear that employees must be made aware of the damage that stereotypes can do. With regard to compensation, organizations are providing benefits such as elder care and day care as a way to accommodate the needs of a diverse workforce. As we will see later in the chapter, successfully managing diversity is also critical for companies that compete in international markets.

Skill Deficiencies of the Workforce

The increasing use of computers to do routine tasks has shifted the kinds of skills needed for employees in the U.S. economy. Such qualities as physical strength and mastery of a particular piece of machinery are no longer important for many jobs. More employers are looking for mathematical, verbal, and interpersonal skills, such as the ability to solve math or other problems or reach decisions as part of a team. Often, when organizations are looking for technical skills, they are looking for skills related to computers and using the Internet. Today's employees must be able to handle a variety of responsibilities, interact with customers, and think creatively.

To find such employees, most organizations are looking for educational achievements. A college degree is a basic requirement for many jobs today. Competition for qualified college graduates in many fields is intense. At the other extreme, workers with less education often have to settle for low-paying jobs. Some companies are unable to find qualified employees and instead rely on training to correct skill deficiencies.[13] Other companies team up with universities, community colleges, and high schools to design and teach courses ranging from basic reading to design blueprint reading.

Not all the skills employers want require a college education. The National Association of Manufacturers year after year has reported that the manufacturing companies in the United States have difficulty finding enough people who can operate sophisticated computer-controlled machinery. These jobs rely at least as much on intelligence and teamwork as on physical strength. In some areas, companies and communities have set up apprenticeship and training programs to fix the worker shortage. Some companies are turning to veterans of the wars in Iraq and Afghanistan. These workers have already demonstrated high levels of commitment and teamwork, as well as the ability to make creative use of the resources at hand in difficult situations. Many of them have been trained already by the military in a variety of technical skills. The challenge for employers has been to support these employees in other areas, such as helping them weather the emotional strain of the transition back to civilian life, as well as training them in the technical requirements of their new jobs.[14]

High-Performance Work Systems

Human resource management is playing an important role in helping organizations gain and keep an advantage over competitors by becoming **high-performance work systems.** These are organizations that have the best possible fit between their social system (people and how they interact) and technical system (equipment and processes).[15] As the nature of the workforce and the technology available to organizations have changed, so have the requirements for creating a high-performance work system. Customers are demanding high quality and customized products, employees are seeking flexible work arrangements, and employers are looking for ways to tap people's creativity and interpersonal skills. Such demands require that organizations make full use of their people's knowledge and skill, and skilled human resource management can help organizations do this.

Among the trends that are occurring in today's high-performance work systems are reliance on knowledge workers, empowerment of employees to make decisions, and use of teamwork. The following sections describe those three trends, and Chapter 16 will explore the ways HRM can support the creation and maintenance of a high-performance work system. HR professionals who keep up with change are well positioned to help create high-performance work systems.

LO 2-2 Summarize areas in which human resource management can support the goal of creating a high-performance work system.

High-Performance Work Systems
Organizations that have the best possible fit between their social system (people and how they interact) and technical system (equipment and processes).

Knowledge Workers

The growth in e-commerce, plus the shift from a manufacturing to a service and information economy, has changed the nature of employees who are most in demand. The Bureau of Labor Statistics forecasts that between 2010 and 2020, most new jobs will be in service occupations, especially food preparation, education, and health services.

The number of service jobs has important implications for human resource management. Research shows that if employees have a favorable view of HRM practices—career opportunities, training, pay, and feedback on performance—they are more likely to provide good service to customers. Therefore, quality HRM for service employees can translate into customer satisfaction.

Besides differences among industries, job growth varies according to the type of job. The "Did You Know?" box lists the 10 occupations expected to gain the most jobs between 2010 and 2020. Of the jobs expected to have the greatest percentage increases, most are related to health care. The fastest-growing occupations are expected to be personal care aides and home health aides; biomedical engineers; helpers for brick masons, stonemasons, and tile and marble setters; helpers for carpenters; and veterinary technologists and technicians.[16] These and other fast-growing occupations reflect the steadily growing demand for health care and an expected rebound in the construction industry. While some of these jobs and other fast-growing occupations require a college degree, many of the fast-growing occupations require only on-the-job training. (Exceptions are registered nurses and postsecondary teachers.) This means that many companies' HRM departments will need to provide excellent training as well as hiring.

Top 10 Occupations for Job Growth

The following graph shows the occupations that are expected to add the most new jobs between 2010 and 2020. These jobs require widely different levels of training and responsibility, and pay levels vary considerably.

Question

Which of the positions in this graph would you describe as "knowledge workers"? Why?

SOURCE: Bureau of Labor Statistics, "Employment Projections, 2010–20," news release, February 1, 2012, http://www.bls.gov/emp.

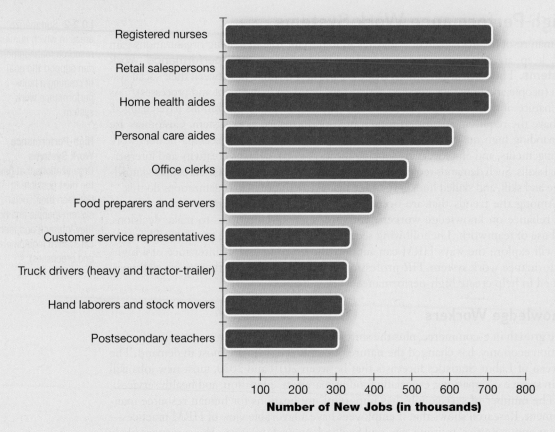

Number of New Jobs (in thousands)

Knowledge Workers
Employees whose main contribution to the organization is specialized knowledge, such as knowledge of customers, a process, or a profession.

These high-growth jobs are evidence of another trend: The future U.S. labor market will be both a knowledge economy and a service economy.[17] Along with low-education jobs in services like health care and food preparation, there will be many high-education professional and managerial jobs. To meet these human capital needs, companies are increasingly trying to attract, develop, and retain knowledge workers. **Knowledge workers** are employees whose main contribution to the organization is specialized knowledge, such as knowledge of customers, a process, or a profession. Further complicating that challenge, many of these knowledge workers will have to be "technoservice" workers who not only know a specialized field such as computer programming or engineering, but also must be able to work directly with customers.

Knowledge workers are in a position of power because they own the knowledge that the company needs in order to produce its products and services, and they must share their knowledge and collaborate with others in order for their employer to succeed. An employer cannot simply order these employees to perform tasks. Managers depend on the employees' willingness to share information. Furthermore, skilled knowledge workers have many job opportunities, even in a slow economy. If they choose, they can leave a company and take their knowledge to another employer. Replacing them may be difficult and time consuming.

Recently, the idea that only some of an organization's workers are knowledge workers has come under criticism.[18] To the critics, this definition is no longer realistic in a day of computerized information systems and computer-controlled production processes. For the company to excel, everyone must know how their work contributes to the organization's success. At the same time, employees—especially younger generations, which grew up with the Internet—will expect to have wide access to information. From this perspective, successful organizations treat *all* their workers as knowledge workers. They let employees know how well the organization is performing, and they invite ideas about how the organization can do better.

Can the "knowledge worker" label really fit everywhere? Think of the expectations organizations have for the typical computer programmer. These high-in-demand employees expect to be valued for their skills, not the hours they put in or the way they dress. Organizations

Knowledge workers are employees whose value to their employers stems primarily from what they know. Engineers such as the ones pictured here have in-depth knowledge of their field and are hard to replace because of their special knowledge.

that successfully recruit and retainer computer programmers give them plenty of freedom to set up their work space and their own schedule. They motivate by assigning tasks that are interesting and challenging and by encouraging friendly collaboration. To some degree, these kinds of measures apply to many employees and many work situations. W. W. Grainger, for example, is not a glamorous company, but it is one that many companies depend on. Grainger distributes an enormous variety of supplies and parts needed by its business customers. Grainger creates an attractive environment for the modern-day version of the knowledge worker by helping to match them up with jobs in which they matter and can excel, even if that means trying out jobs in a variety of departments. Linda Kolbe, the manager of Grainger's e-commerce, started as an administrative assistant and worked her way up, with help from the company's mentoring program. And branch manager Roger Lubert has found that the company is eager to try out his ideas for managing inventory and store operations. The company treats these and other employees as individuals who can both expand their knowledge and apply it to benefit the entire organization.[19]

Employee Empowerment

To completely benefit from employees' knowledge, organizations need a management style that focuses on developing and empowering employees. **Employee empowerment** means giving employees responsibility and authority to make decisions regarding all

LO 2-3 Define employee empowerment, and explain its role in the modern organization.

Employee Empowerment Giving employees responsibility and authority to make decisions regarding all aspects of product development or customer service.

Empowering Employees to Innovate

In most organizations, the employees who work directly with customers, who carry out the organization's operations, and who process its paperwork are in an excellent position to notice when quality, service, and efficiency could be improved. Therefore, many organizations try to empower their employees to come forward with ideas. Human resource departments can help to make these efforts work.

- **Listen with an open mind.** A middle manager at a Charlotte, Virginia company called Meddius once asked company founder and chief executive Jeff Gunther why Meddius kept detailed records of employees' time off but not their late nights of extra work. To some managers, this might sound like mere grumbling, but Gunther considered the manager's main point: employees wanted to be rewarded for their accomplishments, not for their schedules. Meddius now lets employees set their own schedules and focus on their goals.

- **Get employees fully engaged.** Communicate with them about how their jobs support the organization's mission, make sure they have the skills and resources they need to succeed, and be sure reward programs are in place to recognize accomplishments. These efforts create the conditions for employee engagement, and research has shown that fully engaged employees come up with more valuable innovations.

- **Invite all employees to contribute ideas.** Be sure *all* employees are invited to contribute ideas and that ideas are considered without regard for the employee's status in the organization. At the average company, only one-fifth of employees believe their ideas are valued. If the other four-fifths are holding back their ideas, then the company is missing out on many opportunities to innovate.

- **Set up programs to reward innovation.** Typical rewards are public recognition, gifts, and cash. Some companies reward creative ideas with a convenient parking space or a day off with pay. Cash rewards can be tied to the value of the innovation—say, 1% of the savings that comes from implementing the idea.

- **Train managers.** Provide managers with training on how to get employees fully engaged and how to listen respectfully to ideas. Many organizations offer management training; be sure these topics are included in the training program.

- **Be sure the innovation program has a process for responding.** Managers should be evaluated and rewarded for implementing good ideas. Responding quickly to ideas is essential for demonstrating that the organization is serious about innovation.

SOURCE: Based on Tamara Lytle, "Give Employees a Say," *HR Magazine*, October 2011, pp. 68–72.

aspects of product development or customer service.[20] Employees are then held accountable for products and services. In return, they share the resulting losses and rewards. Employee empowerment can also extend to innovation. Employees at all levels are encouraged to share their ideas for satisfying customers better and operating more efficiently and safely. This is empowering if management actually listens to the ideas, implements valuable ones, and rewards employees for their innovations. The "HR How To" box provides ideas for this type of employee empowerment.

HRM practices such as performance management, training, work design, and compensation are important for ensuring the success of employee empowerment. Jobs must be designed to give employees the necessary latitude for making a variety of decisions. Employees must be properly trained to exert their wider authority and use information resources such as the Internet as well as tools for communicating information. Employees also need feedback to help them evaluate their success. Pay and other rewards should reflect employees' authority and be related to successful handling of their responsibility. In addition, for empowerment to succeed, managers must be trained to link employees to resources within and outside the organization, such as customers, co-workers in other departments, and websites with needed information. Managers must also encourage employees to interact with staff throughout the organization, must ensure that employees receive the information they need, and must reward cooperation. Finally, empowered employees deliver the best results if they are fully engaged in their work. *Employee engagement*—full involvement in one's work and commitment to one's job and company—is associated with higher productivity, better customer service, and lower turnover.[21]

As with the need for knowledge workers, use of employee empowerment shifts the recruiting focus away from technical skills and toward general cognitive and interpersonal skills. Employees who have responsibility for a final product or service must be able to listen to customers, adapt to changing needs, and creatively solve a variety of problems.

Teamwork

Modern technology places the information that employees need for improving quality and providing customer service right at the point of sale or production. As a result, the employees engaging in selling and producing must also be able to make decisions about how to do their work. Organizations need to set up work in a way that gives employees the authority and ability to make those decisions. One of the most popular ways to increase employee responsibility and control is to assign work to teams. **Teamwork** is the assignment of work to groups of employees with various skills who interact to assemble a product or provide a service. Work teams often assume many activities traditionally reserved for managers, such as selecting new team members, scheduling work, and coordinating work with customers and other units of the organization. Work teams also contribute to total quality by performing inspection and quality-control activities while the product or service is being completed.

Teamwork
The assignment of work to groups of employees with various skills who interact to assemble a product or provide a service.

In some organizations, technology is enabling teamwork even when workers are at different locations or work at different times. These organizations use *virtual teams*—teams that rely on communications technology such as videoconferences, e-mail, and cell phones to keep in touch and coordinate activities.

Teamwork can motivate employees by making work more interesting and significant. At organizations that rely on teamwork, labor costs may be lower as well. Spurred by such advantages, a number of companies are reorganizing assembly operations—abandoning the assembly line in favor of operations that combine mass production with jobs in which employees perform multiple tasks, use many skills, control the pace of work, and assemble the entire final product.

Witnessing the resulting improvements, companies in the service sector also have moved toward greater use of teamwork. Teamwork is a necessary component of more and more computer programming tasks. Companies that develop software are increasingly using an approach they call *agile*, which involves weaving the development process more tightly into the organization's activities and strategies. In agile software development, self-directed teams of developers and programmers work directly with the business users of the software, using as much face-to-face communication as possible. Rather than devoting endless hours to negotiate contracts and document processes, the teams focus on frequently delivering usable components of the software. Throughout the development process the team is open to changing requirements and computer code as a result of their communication with users. Users of agile software development say it increases customer satisfaction and speeds up the time from concept to usable software.[22]

LO 2-4 Identify ways HR professionals can support organizational strategies for quality, growth, and efficiency.

Focus on Strategy

As we saw in Chapter 1, traditional management thinking treated human resource management primarily as an administrative function, but managers today are beginning to see a more central role for HRM. They are looking at HRM as a means to support a company's *strategy*—its plan for meeting broad goals such as profitability, quality, and market share. This strategic role for HRM has evolved gradually. At many organizations, managers still treat HR professionals primarily as experts in designing and delivering HR systems. But at a growing number of organizations, HR professionals are strategic partners with other managers.

This means they use their knowledge of the business and of human resources to help the organization develop strategies and to align HRM policies and practices with those strategies. To do this, human resource managers must focus on the future as well as the present, and on company goals as well as human resource activities. They may, for example, become experts at analyzing the business impact of HR decisions or at developing and keeping the best talent to support business strategy. Organizations do this, for example, when they integrate all the activities involved in talent management with each other and with the organization's other processes to provide the skills the organization needs to pursue its strategy. An integrated approach to talent management includes acquiring talent (recruiting and selection), providing the right opportunities for training and development, measuring performance, and creating compensation plans that reward the needed behaviors. To choose the right talent, provide the right training, and so on, HR professionals need to be in close, ongoing contact with the members of the organization who need the talent. And when the organization modifies its strategy, HR professionals are part of the planning process so they can modify talent management efforts to support the revised strategy. One organization that does all this is Universal Weather and Aviation, which provides services and support to the owners of private jets. In this market niche, the company does not expect to find people with the precise set of skills it needs; rather, its talent management program emphasizes finding individuals who are a good fit with the organization's culture and then training them in the areas where their skills are weak. Executives are rewarded for achieving talent management objectives that include retaining the best-performing employees and identifying potential successors to fill key positions.[23]

The specific ways in which human resource professionals support the organization's strategy vary according to their level of involvement and the nature of the strategy. Strategic issues include emphasis on quality and decisions about growth and efficiency. Human resource management can support these strategies, including efforts such as quality improvement programs, mergers and acquisitions, and restructuring. Decisions to use reengineering and outsourcing can make an organization more efficient and also give rise to many human resource challenges. International expansion presents a wide variety of HRM challenges and opportunities. Figure 2.4 summarizes these strategic issues facing human resource management.

Total Quality Management (TQM)
A companywide effort to continually improve the ways people, machines, and systems accomplish work.

High Quality Standards

To compete in today's economy, companies need to provide high-quality products and services. If companies do not adhere to quality standards, they will have difficulty selling their product or service to vendors, suppliers, or customers. Therefore, many organizations have adopted some form of **total quality management (TQM)**—a

Figure 2.4
Business Strategy:
Issues Affecting HRM

companywide effort to continually improve the ways people, machines, and systems accomplish work.[24] TQM has several core values:[25]

- Methods and processes are designed to meet the needs of internal and external customers (that is, whomever the process is intended to serve).
- Every employee in the organization receives training in quality.
- Quality is designed into a product or service so that errors are prevented from occurring, rather than being detected and corrected in an error-prone product or service.
- The organization promotes cooperation with vendors, suppliers, and customers to improve quality and hold down costs.
- Managers measure progress with feedback based on data.

Based on these values, the TQM approach provides guidelines for all the organization's activities, including human resource management. To promote quality, organizations need an environment that supports innovation, creativity, and risk taking to meet customer demands. Problem solving should bring together managers, employees, and customers. Employees should communicate with managers about customer needs. For an example of a company that has been learning to engage in such practices, see the "Best Practices" box.

Human resource management also has supported efforts to improve quality of customer service at J.C. Penney. The retailer learned from surveys that fewer than half of customers were highly satisfied with their shopping experience. Penney's responded with a combination of new performance standards and training for employees and their supervisors. The stores had been rewarding salespeople based mainly on how much merchandise they moved onto the floor and then sold. To shift their focus to customers, Penney's added performance standards for helping customers, and they gave

Best Practices

Office Depot Learns to Put Customer Service First

When Kevin Peters became president of Office Depot's North American stores, he knew something had to change, but he wasn't sure what. Office supply stores—and, in fact, most retailers—were suffering from declining sales in a poor economy, but Office Depot's sales were falling faster than its competitors' sales. Yet the company had other data showing it was excelling at customer service: Office Depot had a contract with a company that sent "mystery shoppers" into its stores to grade it on various quality measures, and those measures were soaring.

Peters decided to hunt down the problem in the stores themselves. He dressed casually and began visiting dozens of Office Depots around the country. He wandered through the aisles and chatted with customers, especially those who left the store without buying anything. He soon began to see the source of the company's problem. Employees were doing what the company's evaluation system was measuring, but the system wasn't measuring what customers cared about the most. The mystery shoppers were rating the stores for cleanliness and well-stocked shelves. Customers wanted to find merchandise quickly and obtain helpful answers to their questions. Employees were focused on floors

and shelves, and the shoppers were being ignored.

Office Depot's management began instituting changes aimed at high-quality customer service. They redesigned jobs and work areas to make the process of receiving merchandise and stocking shelves more efficient. This freed up time for employees to focus on customers. They also divided stores into zones and placed employees in charge of a particular zone. This made employees experts in a particular part of the store, so they could be more helpful in that area.

Office Depot also changed the training of store employees. The new training presents a three-step selling process aimed at meeting customers' needs: ask, recommend, and close. Employees practice using this process and focus on asking open-ended questions, such as "What brings you in today?" and "How are you planning to use that?" The training also teaches employees about the products sold in their zones, so they can offer valuable information that leads to purchase decisions.

Finally, management learned that Office Depot needed to modify aspects of its hiring process. The company gave its employees a test of their skills, behaviors, and personal qualities. Management learned that, with the past emphasis on store

appearance, the company had hired a significant number of store employees who preferred stocking merchandise over talking to customers. Office Depot has tried to help these employees develop people skills or move to nonselling positions in the company. In the future, to maintain its drive for quality service, the company must make communication skills a priority in hiring decisions.

Office Depot has rolled out these changes gradually, store by store. At the same time, the company has made marketing changes, such as shrinking the size of stores, placing often-purchased merchandise in more convenient locations, and introducing services, such as copying and shipping. The initial results have been an encouraging rise in sales and positive comments from customers and employees alike. Peters hopes these changes are just the beginning of a full-scale quality-driven turnaround.

SOURCE: Based on Kevin Peters, "Office Depot's President on How 'Mystery Shopping' Helped Spark a Turnaround," *Harvard Business Review,* November 2011, pp. 47–50; Harley Manning, "The Real 'Undercover Boss'—Office Depot's Kevin Peters," July 6, 2011, http://blogs.forrester.com/; and Joan Verdon, "Office Depot's store strategy: Think shrink," *The Record,* January 24, 2012, http://www.northjersey.com.

the salespeople authority to put aside stocking activities whenever a customer wanted assistance, even if the supervisor had assigned the tasks. To prepare salespeople to meet these new requirements, Penney's trained them in how to greet and help customers effectively. The supervisors were nervous about a change that seemed to give them less control over day-to-day activities, so the company also trained them in how to lead a team of empowered workers. Soon the supervisors found that empowered employees and happier customers actually made their own work easier. And within months of making the changes, the customer satisfaction scores were climbing at Penney's.[26]

Mergers and Acquisitions

Often, organizations join forces through mergers (two companies becoming one) and acquisitions (one company buying another). Some mergers and acquisitions result in consolidation within an industry, meaning that two firms in one industry join to hold a greater share of the industry. For example, British Petroleum's acquisition of Amoco Oil represented a consolidation, or a reduction of the number of companies in the oil industry. Other mergers and acquisitions cross industry lines. In a merger to form Citigroup, Citicorp combined its banking business with Traveller's Group's insurance business. Furthermore, these deals more frequently take the form of global megamergers, or mergers of big companies based in different countries (as in the case of BP-Amoco).

HRM should have a significant role in carrying out a merger or acquisition. Differences between the businesses involved in the deal make conflict inevitable. Training efforts should therefore include development of skills in conflict resolution. Also, HR professionals have to sort out differences in the two companies' practices with regard to compensation, performance appraisal, and other HR systems. Settling on a consistent structure to meet the combined organization's goals may help to bring employees together.

Downsizing

As shown in Figure 2.5, the number of employees laid off when organizations downsized soared in 2008 and 2009.[27] Since those years, downsizing has continued, but at a pace more typical of the rest of the decade. The surge in unemployment created a climate of fear for many workers. Even at organizations that were maintaining their workforce, employees tended to worry, and employees who might have otherwise left tended to hold on to their jobs if they could. Therefore, an important challenge

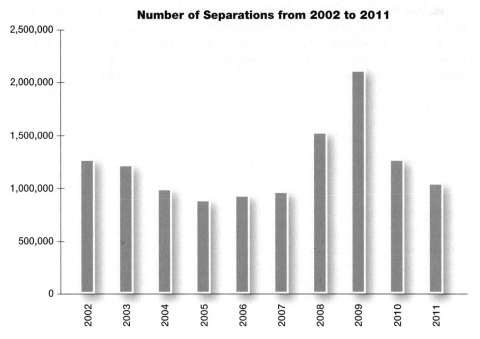

Number of Separations from 2002 to 2011

Figure 2.5
Number of Employees Laid Off during the Past Decade

SOURCE: Bureau of Labor Statistics, "Extended Mass Layoffs: Fourth Quarter 2011, Annual Totals 2011," news release, February 10, 2012, http://www.bls.gov/mls.

for employers was how to maintain a reputation as an employer of choice and how to keep employees engaged in their work and focused on the organization's goals. The way employers meet this challenge will influence how sustainably they can compete, especially as unemployment falls and talented workers see possibilities for work in other organizations.

Downsizing presents a number of challenges and opportunities for HRM. In terms of challenges, the HRM function must "surgically" reduce the workforce by cutting only the workers who are less valuable in their performance. Achieving this is difficult because the best workers are most able (and often willing) to find alternative employment and may leave voluntarily before the organization lays off anyone. Early-retirement programs are humane, but they essentially reduce the workforce with a "grenade" approach—not distinguishing good from poor performers but rather eliminating an entire group of employees. In fact, contrary to popular belief, research has found that downsizing is associated with negative stock returns and lower profitability following the layoffs. One reason may be that although labor costs fall after a downsizing, sales per employee also tend to fall. Circuit City, for example, tried to save money by laying off its highest-paid salespeople. Customers soon found that they preferred other electronics retailers, and Circuit City went out of business. In contrast, Southwest Airlines, which has never laid off employees—not even after air travel plummeted following the terrorist attacks of September 11, 2001—has outperformed its rivals. Like Southwest's managers, Susan Marvin, president of Marvin Windows, thinks it is illogical to call employees the company's "greatest asset" and then lay them off. Although the recent economic recession has been devastating to the construction business and its suppliers, Marvin has avoided layoffs and let employment decline naturally by not replacing employees who have retired during the lean years. Instead, employees have been doing without bonuses and some employee benefits, and the workweek has been shortened, reducing pay to hourly workers. Susan Marvin is convinced that the impact on morale of everyone pulling together during tough times builds a strong commitment to the organization.[28]

Another HRM challenge is to boost the morale of employees who remain after the reduction; this is discussed in greater detail in Chapter 5. HR professionals should maintain open communication with remaining employees to build their trust and commitment, rather than withholding information.[29] All employees should be informed why the downsizing is necessary, what costs are to be cut, how long the downsizing will last, and what strategies the organization intends to pursue. Finally, HRM can provide downsized employees with outplacement services to help them find new jobs. Such services are ways an organization can show that it cares about its employees, even though it cannot afford to keep all of them on the payroll.

Reengineering

Rapidly changing customer needs and technology have caused many organizations to rethink the way they get work done. For example, when an organization adopts new technology, its existing processes may no longer result in acceptable quality levels, meet customer expectations for speed, or keep costs to profitable levels. Therefore, many organizations have undertaken **reengineering**—a complete review of the organization's critical work processes to make them more efficient and able to deliver higher quality.

Ideally, reengineering involves reviewing all the processes performed by all the organization's major functions, including production, sales, accounting, and human

Reengineering
A complete review of the organization's critical work processes to make them more efficient and able to deliver higher quality.

resources. Therefore, reengineering affects human resource management in two ways. First, the way the HR department itself accomplishes its goals may change dramatically. Second, the fundamental change throughout the organization requires the HR department to help design and implement change so that all employees will be committed to the success of the reengineered organization. Employees may need training for their reengineered jobs. The organization may need to redesign the structure of its pay and benefits to make them more appropriate for its new way of operating. It also may need to recruit employees with a new set of skills. Often, reengineering results in employees being laid off or reassigned to new jobs, as the organization's needs change. HR professionals should also help with this transition, as they do for downsizing.

Outsourcing

Many organizations are increasingly outsourcing business activities. **Outsourcing** refers to the practice of having another company (a vendor, third-party provider, or consultant) provide services. For instance, a manufacturing company might outsource its accounting and transportation functions to businesses that specialize in these activities. Outsourcing gives the company access to in-depth expertise and is often more economical as well.

> **Outsourcing**
> The practice of having another company (a vendor, third-party provider, or consultant) provide services.

   Not only do HR departments help with a transition to outsourcing, but many HR functions are being outsourced. According to a recent survey of human resource managers, about 70% of companies had outsourced at least one HR activity. The functions that were most likely to be outsourced were employee assistance, retirement planning, and outplacement.[30] Goodyear Tire and Rubber Company improved its recruiting and hiring practices by outsourcing these activities to a specialist. The recruiting service provider started by learning about Goodyear's history, culture, and experiences with recruiting. It used Internet technology to streamline the hiring process and track the progress of job candidates throughout that process. After outsourcing this function, Goodyear began making quicker hiring decisions, improved the diversity and quality of employees it hired, and reduced employee turnover.[31]

Expanding into Global Markets

Companies are finding that to survive they must compete in international markets as well as fend off foreign competitors' attempts to gain ground in the United States. To meet these challenges, U.S. businesses must develop global markets, keep up with competition from overseas, hire from an international labor pool, and prepare employees for global assignments. As described in the "HR Oops!" box, this global expansion can pose some challenges for human resource management as HR employees learn about the cultural differences that shape the conduct of employees in other parts of the world.

> **LO 2-5** Summarize ways in which human resource management can support organizations expanding internationally.

   Companies that are successful and widely admired not only operate on a multinational scale, but also have workforces and corporate cultures that reflect their global markets. McDonald's opened 165 stores in China in 2010 and laid plans to open 1,000 more by the end of 2013. In support of that strategy, McDonald's built a new Hamburger University near Shanghai. The Shanghai Hamburger University will train future Chinese managers in store operations, leadership, and staff management.[32]

The Global Workforce   For today's and tomorrow's employers, talent comes from a global workforce. Organizations with international operations hire at least

We Thought Everyone Liked Group Projects

When trainers prepare classroom training programs, they often include group exercises and activities as a way to encourage teamwork. They expect that participants will get to know one another and help one another learn. Ideally, these exercises break down cultural barriers.

In some cases, though, trainers haven't taken full account of how people from different cultures will react to these activities. Following one training program that took place in the United States, a Japanese participant noted that she dreaded the times when the instructor asked everyone to break up into teams. This trainee felt uncomfortable inviting herself into a group and even more uncomfortable waiting for others to invite her to join a group after it formed. In another U.S. training program with Asian participants, the trainer held a competition in which the teams were assigned to list major events in the economic history of the United States. Later, an Asian trainee mentioned that the experience felt awful because his lack of knowledge on the subject made him a burden to the team. The team members ignored him while they raced to complete the task.

Questions

1. If you were leading a multicultural group that would divide into teams, how would you ensure that everyone felt equally included?
2. If you were planning team projects for an international group, how would you ensure that everyone was prepared to participate fully?

SOURCE: Based on Wei-Wen Chang, "Is the Group Activity Food or Poison in a Multicultural Classroom?" *T + D*, April 2010, pp. 34–37.

---

some of their employees in the foreign countries where they operate. In fact, regardless of where their customers are located, more and more organizations are looking overseas to hire talented people willing to work for less pay than the U.S. labor market requires. Intel, for example, has projected that most of its future employees will be hired outside U.S. borders. The efforts to hire workers in other countries are common enough that they have spurred the creation of a popular name for the practice: **offshoring.** Just a few years ago, most offshoring involved big manufacturers building factories in countries with lower labor costs. But today it is so easy to send information and software around the world that even start-ups are hiring overseas. For large U.S.-based multinational companies, the overall pattern has been to do most of the organization's hiring outside the United States. During the 2000s, even before the recent recession, these companies' U.S. workforces were shrinking by more than 800,000 workers even as overseas employment was rising by 2.9 million. And during the recession, cuts at home outpaced cuts in the workforce overseas. This trend is driven by more than labor costs: demand for these companies' products is often growing faster in other parts of the world.[33]

Offshoring
Moving operations from the country where a company is headquartered to a country where pay rates are lower but the necessary skills are available.

Hiring in developing nations such as India, Mexico, and Brazil gives employers access to people with potential who are eager to work yet who will accept lower wages than elsewhere in the world. Challenges, however, may include employees' lack of familiarity with technology and corporate practices, as well as political and economic instability in the areas. Important issues that HR experts can help companies weigh include whether workers in the offshore locations can provide the same or better skills, how offshoring will affect motivation and recruitment of employees needed in the United States, and whether managers are well prepared to manage and lead offshore employees. At the same time, as companies based in these parts of the world are developing experienced employees and managers, they are becoming competitors for global talent. Information technology companies based in India, for example, have in recent years increased their hiring of employees in the United States and Europe.[34] This poses a new challenge for U.S. recruiters who may need to improve their tactics and offers if they want to win the war for the best talent.

Even hiring at home may involve selection of employees from other countries. The beginning of the 21st century, like the beginning of the last century, has been a time of significant immigration, with over a million people obtaining permanent resident status in 2010 alone.[35] Figure 2.6 shows the distribution of immigration by continent of origin. The impact of immigration will be especially large in some regions of the United States, with the largest immigrant populations being in the cities and suburbs of New York, Los Angeles, Miami, Chicago, and Houston. About 7 out of 10 foreign-born workers will be Hispanics and Asians.[36] Employers in tight labor markets—such as those seeking experts in computer science, engineering, and information systems—have been especially likely to recruit international students.

International Assignments
Besides hiring an international workforce, organizations must be prepared to send employees to other countries. This requires HR expertise in selecting employees for international assignments and preparing them for those assignments. Employees who take assignments in other countries are called **expatriates.**

U.S. companies must better prepare employees to work in other countries. The failure rate for U.S. expatriates is greater than that for European and Japanese expatriates.[37] To improve in this area, U.S. companies must carefully select employees to work abroad based on their ability to understand and respect the cultural and business norms of the host country. Qualified candidates also need language skills and technical ability. In Chapter 15, we discuss practices for training employees to understand other cultures.

Technological Change in HRM

Advances in computer-related technology have had a major impact on the use of information for managing human resources. Large quantities of employee data (including training records, skills, compensation rates, and benefits usage and cost) can easily be stored on personal computers and manipulated with user-friendly spreadsheets or statistical software. Often these features are combined in a **human resource information system (HRIS),** a computer system used to acquire, store, manipulate, analyze, retrieve, and distribute information related to an organization's human resources.[38] An HRIS can support strategic decision making, help the organization avoid lawsuits, provide data for evaluating programs or policies, and support day-to-day HR decisions. Table 2.1 describes some of the technologies that may be included in an organization's HRIS.

The support of an HRIS can help HR professionals think strategically. As strategies are planned, implemented, and changed, the organization must be constantly prepared to have the right talent in place at all levels. This requires keeping track of an enormous amount of information related to employees' skills, experience, and training needs, as well as the organization's shifting needs for the future. An HRIS can support

Figure 2.6
Where Immigrants to the United States Came from in 2010

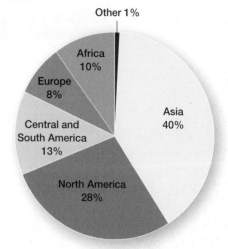

SOURCE: Department of Homeland Security, Office of Immigration Statistics, "U.S. Legal Permanent Residents: 2010," *Annual Flow Report,* March 2011, Table 3, p. 4, www.dhs.gov.

Expatriates
Employees who take assignments in other countries.

LO 2-6 Discuss how technological developments are affecting human resource management.

Human Resource Information System (HRIS)
A computer system used to acquire, store, manipulate, analyze, retrieve, and distribute information related to an organization's human resources.

Table 2.1

New Technologies Influencing HRM

TECHNOLOGY	WHAT IT DOES	EXAMPLE
Internet portal	Combines data from several sources into a single site; lets user customize data without programming skills.	A company's manager can track labor costs by work group.
Shared service centers	Consolidate different HR functions into a single location; eliminate redundancy and reduce administrative costs; process all HR transactions at one time.	AlliedSignal combined more than 75 functions, including finance and HR, into a shared service center.
Cloud computing, such as application service providers (ASPs)	Lets companies rent space on a remote computer system and use the system's software to manage its HR activities, including security and upgrades.	KPMG Consulting uses an ASP to host the company's computerized learning program.
Business intelligence	Provides insight into business trends and patterns and helps businesses improve decisions.	Managers use the system to analyze labor costs and productivity among different employee groups.
Data mining	Uses powerful computers to analyze large amounts of data, such as data about employee traits, pay, and performance.	Managers can identify high-potential employees throughout a large organization and offer them development opportunities.

Electronic Human Resource Management (e-HRM)
The processing and transmission of digitized HR information, especially using computer networking and the Internet.

talent management by integrating data on recruiting, performance management, and training. Integrating the data means, for example, that the HRIS user can see how specific kinds of recruiting, hiring, and training decisions relate to performance success. This helps HR professionals identify how to develop the organization's talent and where to recruit new talent so that an ongoing supply of human resources is available to fill new positions or new openings in existing positions.[39]

Electronic Human Resource Management (e-HRM)

Many HRM activities have moved onto the Internet. Electronic HRM applications let employees enroll in and participate in training programs online. Employees can go online to select from items in a benefits package and enroll in the benefits they choose. They can look up answers to HR-related questions and read company news, perhaps downloading it as a podcast. This processing and transmission of digitized HR information is called **electronic human resource management (e-HRM).**

E-HRM has the potential to change all traditional HRM functions. For example, employees in different geographic areas can work together. Use of the Internet lets companies search for talent without geographic limitations. Recruiting can include online job postings, applications, and candidate screening from the company's website or the websites of companies that specialize in online recruiting, such as Monster.com or CareerBuilder. Employees from different geographic locations can all receive the same training over the company's computer network.

Technology trends that are shaping Internet use are also shaping e-HRM. One example, introduced in Chapter 1, is social networking. Table 2.2 identifies some ways that creative organizations are applying social networking tools to human resource management. And the

The Internet and e-HRM are helpful for employees who work outside the office because they can receive and share information online easily. The benefits of products such as smartphones are enormous, but is it possible to be too accessible?

APPLICATION	PURPOSE
Sites for capturing, sharing, storing knowledge	Preserving knowledge that otherwise could be lost when employees retire
Online surveys to gather employees' opinions	Increasing employees' engagement with the jobs and the organization
Networking tools to create online expert communities	Identifying employee expertise and making it available to those who can apply it
Online discussions, such as commenting tools	Promoting creativity and innovation
Sites where users can post links to articles, webinars, training programs, and other information	Reinforcing lessons learned during training and on-the-job experience
Instant messaging and other communication tools to use with mentors and coaches	Providing employee development through mentoring and coaching
Site where the HR department posts job openings and responds to candidates' questions	Identifying and connecting with promising job candidates

Table 2.2

HRM Applications for Social Networking

SOURCES: P. Brotherson, "Social Networks Enhance Employee Learning," *T + D,* April 2011, pp. 18–19; T. Bingham and M. Connor, *The New Social Learning* (Alexandria, VA: American Society for Training and Development, 2010); M. Derven, "Social Networking: A Frame for Development," *T + D,* July 2009, pp. 58–63; M. Weinstein, "Are You Linked In?" *Training,* September/October 2010, pp. 30–33.

"HRM Social" box offers an example of how MillerCoors set up social networks of employees to improve its retention of female sales representatives.

Another recent technology trend is *cloud computing,* which generally refers to arrangements in which remote server computers do the user's computing tasks. Thus, an organization that once owned a big mainframe computer to process data for payroll and performance data could contract with a service provider to do the data processing on its computer network and make the results available online. Access to cloud computing makes powerful HRIS tools available even to small organizations with limited computer hardware. Some organizations specialize in offering such services. An example is Workday, which hosts software for human resource management, including workforce planning, job design, analysis of compensation to make sure it is aligned with performance, and assessment of the organization's skills and training needs.[40]

Privacy is an important issue in e-HRM. A great deal of HR information is confidential and not suitable for posting on a website for everyone to see. One solution is to set up e-HRM on an *intranet,* which is a network that uses Internet tools but limits access to authorized users in the organization. With any e-HRM application, however, the organization must ensure that it has sufficient security measures in place to protect employees' privacy.

Sharing of Human Resource Information

Information technology is changing the way HR departments handle record keeping and information sharing. Today, HR employees use technology to automate much of their work in managing employee records and giving employees access to information and enrollment forms for training, benefits, and other programs. As a result, HR employees play a smaller role in maintaining records, and employees now get information through **self-service.** This means employees have online access to information about HR issues such as training, benefits, compensation, and contracts; go online to enroll themselves in programs and services; and provide feedback through online surveys. Today, employees routinely look up workplace policies and information about

Self-Service
System in which employees have online access to information about HR issues and go online to enroll themselves in programs and provide feedback through surveys.

MillerCoors Uses Social Media to Support Diversity

MillerCoors wants to promote diversity in the workplace but knows it must improve in the area of hiring and retaining female employees. Overall, the company is about 24% female, and management wants to double that percentage.

To investigate what it might need to do differently, MillerCoors measured employee turnover among its male and female salespeople. The company learned that female sales reps quit at a much higher rate than their male counterparts. Among the reasons was that the female sales reps often felt isolated in jobs that required them to work alone and to make many of their sales calls at nights and on weekends.

As it looked for ways to make work more sociable, MillerCoors turned to social media. Specifically, it expanded its use of a tool called Open Mentoring. This software keeps track of employees' skills and matches them with mentors who already have strengths in desired areas. It lets people connect with their matches and engage in online conversations. Employees who participate in a mentoring network can share ideas, either one-on-one or in a group.

MillerCoors had already used Open Mentoring for one-on-one mentoring to develop employees' skills in other parts of the company. To get its salespeople more engaged, it launched a program

called Women of Sales. The program created three groups of 15 female sales reps, each group with two mentors in leadership positions at the company. Each group uses the Open Mentoring software to keep in touch online wherever they are. Early results show a slowdown in employee turnover as the sales reps are able to encourage one another and learn from people who share their goals and concerns.

SOURCES: Sharon Gaudin, "MillerCoors Turns to Tech to Retain Workers," *Computerworld,* September 12, 2011, p. 12; Triple Creek, "Key Features of Open Mentoring 5," http://www.3creek .com, accessed February 10, 2012.

their benefits online, and they may receive electronic notification when deposits are made directly to their bank accounts.

Self-service is especially convenient when combined with today's use of mobile computing devices such as smartphones and tablet computers. For example, organizations that use the services of ADP can download a free mobile app that enables employees to look up their payroll and benefits information. Employees can use the app to fill out their time sheet or look up their 401(k) (retirement savings plan) contributions and balance. Employers can use the app to deliver company news or offer a directory with employees' contact information.[41]

A growing number of companies are combining employee self-service with management self-service, such as the ability to go online to authorize pay increases, approve expenses, and transfer employees to new positions. More sophisticated systems extend management applications to decision making in areas such as compensation and performance management. To further support management decisions, the company may create an *HR dashboard*, or a display of how the company is performing on specific HR metrics, such as productivity and absenteeism. For example, Cisco Systems helps with talent management by displaying on its HR dashboard how many of its people move and why.[42] The data can help management identify divisions where the managers are successfully developing new talent.

In the age of social networking, information sharing has become far more powerful than simply a means of increasing efficiency through self-service. Creative organizations are enabling information sharing online to permit a free flow of knowledge among the organization's people. Essilor International uses social networking to improve learning in the 40 countries where it makes and sells lenses for use by eye doctors. Trainers share knowledge of what is working best for them: for example, a

Thai lens-processing center came up with a game to teach workers to understand lens shapes and then made it available online.[43] A more dramatic application of social networking to human resource management is the talent management at Morning Star, a California tomato processor. Morning Star has no formal hierarchy or job descriptions. Instead, each employee writes a letter describing his or her responsibilities. As the company has grown to hundreds of full-time employees, it began to use a database of the employees' letters. Employees can go into the database to modify their letters, search for employees with needed experience, or offer one another feedback related to the commitments they made in their letters.[44]

Change in the Employment Relationship

LO 2-7 Explain how the nature of the employment relationship is changing.

Technology and the other trends we have described in this chapter require managers at all levels to make rapid changes in response to new opportunities, competitive challenges, and customer demands. These changes are most likely to succeed in flexible, forward-thinking organizations, and the employees who will thrive in such organizations need to be flexible and open to change as well. In this environment, employers and employees have begun to reshape the employment relationship.[45]

A New Psychological Contract

We can think of that relationship in terms of a **psychological contract,** a description of what an employee expects to contribute in an employment relationship and what the employer will provide the employee in exchange for those contributions.[46] Unlike a written sales contract, the psychological contract is not formally put into words. Instead, it describes unspoken expectations that are widely held by employers and employees. In the traditional version of this psychological contract, organizations expected their employees to contribute time, effort, skills, abilities, and loyalty. In return, the organizations would provide job security and opportunities for promotion.

Psychological Contract A description of what an employee expects to contribute in an employment relationship and what the employer will provide the employee in exchange for those contributions.

However, this arrangement is being replaced with a new type of psychological contract. Companies expect employees to take more responsibility for their own careers, from seeking training to balancing work and family. These expectations result in less job security for employees, who can count on working for several companies over the course of a career. In exchange for top performance and working longer hours without job security, employees want companies to provide flexible work schedules, comfortable working conditions, more control over how they accomplish work, training and development opportunities, and financial incentives based on how the organization performs. (Figure 2.7 provides a humorous look at an employee who seems to have benefited from this modern psychological contract by obtaining a family friendly work arrangement.) Employees realize that companies cannot provide employment security, so they want *employability.* This means they want their company to provide training and job experiences to help ensure that they can find other employment opportunities.

In the federal government's most recent survey of wage and salary, workers age 25 and older report they had been working with their present employer for a median of just 4.4 years.[47] Workers 55 and older tend to have a much longer tenure, and so do workers in government jobs. Still, if four years with a company is typical, this amounts to many employers in the course of one's career. In fact, some employees engage in *job hopping,* the intentional practice of changing jobs frequently—say, every year or two.[48] Job hopping can be appealing to an employee as a way to stave off boredom and win some rapid increases in pay and responsibility. Some employees even are able to pick short-term

Figure 2.7
A Family Friendly Work Arrangement

By permission of Dave Coverly and Creators Syndicate, Inc.

LO 2-8 Discuss how the need for flexibility affects human resource management.

Alternative Work Arrangements
Methods of staffing other than the traditional hiring of full-time employees (for example, use of independent contractors, on-call workers, temporary workers, and contract company workers).

jobs that give them valuable, carefully targeted experiences. However, there are some significant disadvantages. Every time the employee starts with a new employer, the employee needs to learn a new network of contacts and a new set of policies and procedures. This can slow down the employee's ability to learn a career in depth and reduce the employee's value to each employer. Therefore, employers tend to be wary of a job candidate who seems to have a history of job hopping. They may interpret job hopping as evidence of a character flaw such as inability to make a commitment or lack of conscientiousness. Often, employees can enjoy variety, develop skills, and build an interesting career without job hopping by asking for challenging assignments and cultivating a network of professional contacts within their present company.

Flexibility

The new psychological contract largely results from the HRM challenge of building a committed, productive workforce in turbulent economic conditions—conditions that offer opportunity for financial success but can also quickly turn sour, making every employee expendable. From the organization's perspective, the key to survival in a fast-changing environment is flexibility. Organizations want to be able to change as fast as customer needs and economic conditions change. Flexibility in human resource management includes flexible staffing levels and flexible work schedules.

Flexible Staffing Levels   A flexible workforce is one the organization can quickly reshape and resize to meet its changing needs. To be able to do this without massive hiring and firing campaigns, organizations are using more alternative work arrangements. **Alternative work arrangements** are methods of staffing other than the traditional hiring of full-time employees. There are a variety of methods, with the following being most common:

- *Independent contractors* are self-employed individuals with multiple clients.
- *On-call workers* are persons who work for an organization only when they are needed.
- *Temporary workers* are employed by a temporary agency; client organizations pay the agency for the services of these workers.
- *Contract company workers* are employed directly by a company for a specific time specified in a written contract.

However, employers need to use these options with care. In general, if employers direct workers in the details of how and when they do their jobs, these workers are legally defined as employees, not contractors. In that case, employers must meet the legal requirements for paying the employer's share of Social Security, Medicare, and unemployment insurance.

Recent research suggests that the use of contingent workers has been growing and has surpassed 2 million workers in the United States and one-fourth of total work hours.[49] Employers once mainly relied on contingent workers to fill administrative jobs, but now turn to contingent work arrangements for production workers, technical support, and even some professional tasks, such as graphic design, engineering, and finance. A major reason for the popularity of contingent work arrangements is that paying contractors enables an organization to pay only for completion of specific tasks and therefore to control costs.

Doing this is easier than ever with Internet technology. A service called LiveOps contracts for the services of call-center personnel. These individuals work from their homes and are paid by the minute, counting only the time they are actually talking to customers. And for projects that involve many component activities, some organizations get work done through a process known as *crowdsourcing*. To use crowdsourcing, the organization puts out a request on a website such as Mechanical Turk or CrowdFlower, offering to pay anywhere from a few cents to $20 for completion of a task. Individuals who have signed up to provide services at the site then tackle the tiny bits of the project. Because all the recruiting, work submission, and payments are handled electronically, this seemingly complex arrangement is actually extremely efficient. When AOL wanted to determine how to count how many of its web pages contain videos, it decided the most efficient approach would be crowdsourcing. The company paid Mechanical Turk workers to look at the web pages and note whether and where any videos appeared. Completing the project (including verifying the quality of the responses) took about two months—much faster than writing video detection software or hiring a staff of temporary workers.[50]

More workers in alternative employment relationships are choosing these arrangements, but preferences vary. Most independent contractors and contract workers have this type of arrangement by choice. In contrast, temporary agency workers and on-call workers are likely to prefer traditional full-time employment. There is some debate about whether nontraditional employment relationships are good or bad. Some labor analysts argue that alternative work arrangements are substandard jobs featuring low pay, fear of unemployment, poor health insurance and retirement benefits, and dissatisfying work. Additional concerns arise with crowdsourcing because it is difficult or impossible for organizations to know whether these contract workers, located anywhere in the world, have safe working conditions and are not children. Others claim that these jobs provide flexibility for companies and employees alike. With alternative work arrangements, organizations can more easily modify the number of their employees. Continually adjusting staffing levels is especially cost effective for an organization that has fluctuating demand for its products and services. And when an organization downsizes by laying off temporary and part-time employees, the damage to morale among permanent full-time workers is likely to be less severe.

Flexible Work Schedules   The globalization of the world economy and the development of e-commerce have made the notion of a 40-hour workweek obsolete. As a result, companies need to be staffed 24 hours a day, seven days a week. Employees in manufacturing environments and service call centers are being asked to work 12-hour days or to work afternoon or midnight shifts. Similarly, professional employees face long hours and work demands that spill over into their personal lives. E-mail, pagers, and cell phones bombard employees with information and work demands. In the car, on vacation, on planes, and even in the bathroom, employees can be interrupted by work demands. More demanding work results in greater employee stress, less satisfied employees, loss of productivity, and higher turnover—all of which are costly for companies.

Many organizations are taking steps to provide more flexible work schedules, to protect employees' free time, and to more

Multitasking has become a way of life for many employees who need to make the most of every minute. This trend is affecting human resource management and the employees it supports.

productively use employees' work time. Workers consider flexible schedules a valuable way to ease the pressures and conflicts of trying to balance work and nonwork activities. Employers are using flexible schedules to recruit and retain employees and to increase satisfaction and productivity. For Weatherby Healthcare, this kind of flexibility is a good fit with its corporate strategy of providing superior service by "putting people first." Weatherby, a physician staffing company, helps hospitals and other health care institutions find qualified physicians. Weatherby's employees must be skilled at uncovering its clients' culture, needs, and preferences and also be able to identify thousands of top-quality candidates every year, verify their credentials, and discern which clients would be a match for those candidates. To find and keep employees with the necessary level of people skills, Weatherby hires primarily for personal qualities, provides coaching, and works hard to create a positive atmosphere at work. Then they are allowed freedom to get their work done. Eddie Rodriguez, senior marketing coordinator, says, "No one's chained to their desk here." If workers need a break, they are free to go play table tennis or watch the news in the employee lounge. And if they meet their weekly goals by three o'clock on Friday, they are welcome to get an early start on the weekend.[51]

THINKING ETHICALLY

WHAT BOUNDARIES SHOULD EMPLOYERS SET FOR SOCIAL MEDIA?

As more and more millennials enter the labor force, more of an organization's employees will have grown up with the Internet and social media. These employees are unlikely to comprehend being separated from their mobile devices or Internet access. They expect to be able to send a quick text, post a status update (a tweet) on Twitter, or reward themselves with a funny video after wrapping up a report. And as these technologies become mainstream, more of their older colleagues share this attitude.

Employers, in contrast, have tended to greet each new social-media application as a new form of time wasting. Organizations are under intense pressure to improve their performance month after month, and the thought of employees checking out photos on Facebook while at work horrifies many managers. In this view, most uses of social media amount to theft of time from employers, not a reasonable break or a valuable way to stay connected to co-workers and customers as well as family and friends.

Recently, the Ethics Resource Center added to managers' discomfort with a study showing that employees categorized as "active social networkers" are much more likely than their co-workers to say they experience pressure to compromise ethical standards. And when asked about ethically questionable actions, such as taking home company software or keeping personal copies of confidential company information for future career use, the active social networkers are more likely to say these actions are acceptable.

Questions

1. How much time on social media is reasonable at work before it becomes time wasting or a theft of the employer's time? Does your answer depend on whether the employee has met his or her goals? Does it depend on how many hours he or she has worked?

2. Why do you think the heavy social-media users surveyed by the Ethics Resource Center were more likely than other employees to believe employees are justified in making personal use of company software and confidential data? How would you respond to that attitude if you were a human resource manager?

SOURCES: Andrew McIlvaine, "The Word for Today Is . . . ," *Human Resource Executive Online,* January 23, 2012, http://blog.hronline.com; Colleen Taylor, "Study: Social Networkers Have More Ethics Problems at Work," *GigaOM,* January 6, 2012, http://gigaom.com; Liz Ryan, "Five Destructive Company HR Policies," *Bloomberg Businessweek,* April 16, 2010, http://www.businessweek.com; Craig Matsuda, "The Debate over Social Media at the Office," *Entrepreneur,* February 16, 2010, http://www.entrepreneur.com.

SUMMARY

LO 2-1 Describe trends in the labor force composition and how they affect human resource management.

An organization's internal labor force comes from its external labor market—individuals who are actively seeking employment. In the United States, this labor market is aging and becoming more racially and ethnically diverse. The share of women in the U.S. workforce has grown to roughly half of the total. To compete for talent, organizations must be flexible enough to meet the needs of older workers, possibly redesigning jobs. Organizations must recruit from a diverse population, establish bias-free HR systems, and help employees understand and appreciate cultural differences. Organizations also need employees with skills in decision making, customer service, and teamwork, as well as technical skills. The competition for such talent is intense. Organizations facing a skills shortage often hire employees who lack certain skills, then train them for their jobs.

LO 2-2 Summarize areas in which human resource management can support the goal of creating a high-performance work system.

HRM can help organizations find and keep the best possible fit between their social system and technical system. Organizations need employees with broad skills and strong motivation. Recruiting and selection decisions are especially important for organizations that rely on knowledge workers. Job design and appropriate systems for assessment and rewards have a central role in supporting employee empowerment and teamwork.

LO 2-3 Define employee empowerment, and explain its role in the modern organization.

Employee empowerment means giving employees responsibility and authority to make decisions regarding all aspects of product development or customer service. The organization holds employees accountable for products and services, and in exchange, the employees share in the rewards (or losses) that result. Selection decisions should provide to the organization people who have the necessary decision-making and interpersonal skills. HRM must design jobs to give employees latitude for decision making and train employees to handle their broad responsibilities. Feedback and rewards must be appropriate

for the work of empowered employees. HRM can also play a role in giving employees access to the information they need.

LO 2-4 Identify ways HR professionals can support organizational strategies for quality, growth, and efficiency.

HR professionals should be familiar with the organization's strategy and may even play a role in developing the strategy. Specific HR practices vary according to the type of strategy. Job design is essential for empowering employees to practice total quality management. In organizations planning major changes such as a merger or acquisition, downsizing, or reengineering, HRM must provide leadership for managing the change in a way that includes skillful employee relations and meaningful rewards. HR professionals can bring "people issues" to the attention of the managers leading these changes. They can provide training in conflict-resolution skills, as well as knowledge of the other organization involved in a merger or acquisition. HR professionals also must resolve differences between the companies' HR systems, such as benefits packages and performance appraisals. For a downsizing, the HR department can help to develop voluntary programs to reduce the workforce or can help identify the least valuable employees to lay off. Employee relations can help maintain the morale of employees who remain after a downsizing. In reengineering, the HR department can lead in communicating with employees and providing training. It will also have to prepare new approaches for recruiting and appraising employees that are better suited to the reengineered jobs. Outsourcing presents similar issues related to job design and employee selection.

LO 2-5 Summarize ways in which human resource management can support organizations expanding internationally.

Organizations with international operations hire employees in foreign countries where they operate, so they need knowledge of differences in culture and business practices. Even small businesses discover that qualified candidates include immigrants, because they account for a significant and growing share of the U.S. labor market. HRM needs to understand and train employees to deal with differences in cultures.

HRM also must be able to help organizations select and prepare employees for overseas assignments. To support efficiency and growth, HR staff can prepare companies for offshoring, in which operations are moved to countries where wages are lower or demand is growing. HR experts can help organizations determine whether workers in offshore locations can provide the same or better skills, how offshoring will affect motivation and recruitment of employees needed in the United States, and whether managers are prepared to manage offshore employees.

LO 2-6 Discuss how technological developments are affecting human resource management.

Information systems have become a tool for more HR professionals, and often these systems are provided through the Internet. The widespread use of the Internet includes HRM applications. Organizations search for talent globally using online job postings and by screening candidates online. Organizations' websites feature information directed toward potential employees. Employees may receive training online. At many companies, online information sharing enables employee self-service for many HR needs, from application forms to training modules to information about the details of company policies and benefits. Organizations can now structure work that involves collaboration among employees at different times and places. In such situations, HR professionals must ensure that communications remain effective enough to detect and correct problems when they arise.

LO 2-7 Explain how the nature of the employment relationship is changing.

The employment relationship takes the form of a "psychological contract" that describes what employees and employers expect from the employment relationship. It includes unspoken expectations that are widely held. In the traditional version, organizations expected their employees to contribute time, effort, skills, abilities, and loyalty in exchange for job security and opportunities for promotion. Today, modern organizations' needs are constantly changing, so organizations are requiring top performance and longer work hours but cannot provide job security. Instead, employees are looking for flexible work schedules, comfortable working conditions, greater autonomy, opportunities for training and development, and performance-related financial incentives. For HRM, the changes require planning for flexible staffing levels. For employees, the changes may make job hopping look attractive, but this career strategy often backfires.

LO 2-8 Discuss how the need for flexibility affects human resource management.

Organizations seek flexibility in staffing levels through alternatives to the traditional employment relationship. They may use outsourcing as well as temporary and contract workers and even crowdsourcing. The use of such workers can affect job design and also the motivation of the organization's permanent employees. Organizations also may seek flexible work schedules, including shortened workweeks. They may offer flexible schedules as a way for employees to adjust work hours to meet personal and family needs. Organizations also may move employees to different jobs to meet changes in demand.

KEY TERMS

alternative work
   arrangements, 52
electronic human resource
   management (e-HRM), 48
employee empowerment, 37
expatriates, 47
external labor market, 30

high-performance work
   systems, 35
human resource information
   system (HRIS), 47
internal labor force, 30
knowledge workers, 36
offshoring, 46

outsourcing, 45
psychological contract, 51
reengineering, 44
self-service, 49
teamwork, 39
total quality management
   (TQM), 40

REVIEW AND DISCUSSION QUESTIONS

1. How does each of the following labor force trends affect HRM?
   a. Aging of the labor force.
   b. Diversity of the labor force.
   c. Skill deficiencies of the labor force.
2. At many organizations, goals include improving people's performance by relying on knowledge workers, empowering employees, and assigning work to teams. How can HRM support these efforts?
3. Merging, downsizing, and reengineering all can radically change the structure of an organization. Choose one of these changes, and describe HRM's role in making the change succeed. If possible, apply your discussion to an actual merger, downsizing, or reengineering effort that has recently occurred.
4. When an organization decides to operate facilities in other countries, how can HRM practices support this change?
5. Why do organizations outsource HRM functions? How does outsourcing affect the role of human resource professionals? Would you be more attracted to the role of the HR professional in an organization that outsources many HR activities or in the outside firm that has the contract to provide the HR services? Why?
6. Suppose you have been hired to manage human resources for a small company that offers business services including customer service calls and business report preparation. The 20-person company has been preparing to expand from serving a few local clients that are well known to the company's owners. The owners believe that their experience and reputation for quality will help them expand to serve more and larger clients. What challenges will you need to prepare the company to meet? How will you begin?
7. What Internet applications might you use to meet the challenges in Question 4?
8. What HRM functions could an organization provide through self-service? What are some advantages and disadvantages of using self-service for these functions?
9. How is the employment relationship that is typical of modern organizations different from the relationship of a generation ago?

EXPERIENCING HR

This chapter described trends shaping human resource management, including the aging of the workforce and the impact of social media. Alone or with a partner, list three of the trends that interest you. Then select a manager or employee who would be willing to talk about these trends for about 15 minutes—someone in human resource management or in a different field that interests you.

With your partner if you have one, interview the person. Summarize each trend you listed, and ask your interviewee to describe any impact of that trend that he or she has observed at work. Take notes.

In a paragraph, summarize what you learned. In a second paragraph, analyze the impact on human resource management. If your interviewee noted negative impacts, suggest how HR professionals might help the organization cope. If your interviewee noted positive impacts, consider how human resource management might have contributed to, or could enhance, the positives.

TAKING RESPONSIBILITY: P&G's Purposeful Growth

Procter & Gamble is famous for its brands of household products, including Tide, Pampers, Gillette, and Head & Shoulders, sold in more than 180 countries. Since the company's founding in 1837, it has been admired for its marketing creativity. But since Robert McDonald became chief executive officer in 2009, P&G has sought greater success built on a sense of purpose.

McDonald wants P&G's employees to be unified by the company's Purpose Statement: "We will provide branded products and services of superior quality and value that improve the lives of the world's consumers, now and for generations to come." Implied are commitments to quality and sustainability. This purpose assumes that when P&G meets those standards, consumers will see value and buy from P&G, thus rewarding the company and its shareholders for doing the right thing. In a nutshell, P&G is aiming for "purpose-inspired growth."

To get employees dedicated to the vision of purpose-inspired growth, P&G urges them to think about how P&G can "touch and improve more consumers' lives in more parts of the world . . . more completely." The company is especially interested in what this vision can do in high-growth developing nations. When employees think about how consumers' lives can be improved in India or Brazil, they are helping people while opening up huge areas of new growth.

In India, P&G employees noticed that when men needed a shave, about half would go to a local barbershop. Often, a barber would save money by taking double-sided razor blades and breaking them in half, so they could use them for twice as many shaves. Then they would use the same blade on as many customers as they could. As a result, the customers risked infection. P&G responded by analyzing razors to identify their most essential features, creating an ultra-simple razor, and figuring out how to produce it at minimal cost.

In West Africa, P&G established a purpose-related performance measure: Each employee is graded on how many lives P&G has touched. One effort aimed at this kind of performance was creation of Pampers mobile clinics. To improve infant mortality rates and health, these vans, each staffed with a physician and two nurses, travel around the region. At every stop, the professionals offer baby checkups, lessons in postnatal care, and referrals to local hospitals for follow-up care and immunizations. Mothers can sign up for mVillage, a program that sends text messages with health tips and answers to their questions. (In West Africa, even many poor people have cell phones.) Finally, each mother receives two free Pampers diapers. The experience of serving the community gives P&G employees a sense that their work is making life better for families even as West Africa becomes one of P&G's fastest-growing markets.

This goal-directed behavior is not just warm and fuzzy; the company is quite serious about performance management. Each employee has a personalized "cockpit," a display on the employee's computer screen that shows the employee's goals and a range of tolerances for each goal. If the employee's performance veers outside the tolerances, then the computer issues an alert. Employees and their managers are expected to investigate any discrepancy to find out what must change for the employee to meet his or her goals. The constant monitoring and feedback lets the company react quickly, rather than waiting for a quarterly or annual review to find out that, say, the employee lacked necessary resources, or goals were too pessimistic.

A related HR challenge for P&G is to find and keep people with the necessary technical skills. To ensure that the global giant is staying up-to-date on techniques for analyzing data, P&G's chief information officer tracks talent needs in terms of the essential technical skills—for example, knowledge of computer modeling and simulation. Executives also identified the computer and analytic skills required at each level of the organization, so talented people can receive the right training to advance. That's essential for a company that prides itself on promoting from within. All of its CEOs started out as entry-level workers, and management development routinely includes a stint running operations in a foreign nation. Finally, in China, the company established an R&D facility. The goal is to position the company to recruit from China's growing ranks of scientists and engineers, who can provide a close-up perspective on consumers' needs in Asia.

Questions

1. What aspects of P&G's HR practices are positioning the company well for international expansion?
2. How does the company's commitment to sustainability support that effort?
3. What other trends described in this chapter could help P&G meet its goal of purpose-inspired growth? How could they help?

SOURCES: Procter & Gamble, "The Power of Purpose," http://www.pg.com, accessed February 13, 2012; Rosabeth Moss Kanter, "How Great Companies Think Differently," *Harvard Business Review*, November 2011, pp. 66–78; Michael Chui and Thomas Fleming, "Inside P&G's Digital Revolution," *McKinsey Quarterly*, November 2011, https://www.mckinsey.quarterly.com (interview with Robert McDonald); "25 Top Talent Teams," *Fortune*, November 21, 2011, EBSCOhost, http://web.ebscohost.com; "CEO Summit: Cultural Evolution" *WWD*, November 15, 2011, Business & Company Resource Center, http://galenet.galegroup.com; Jennifer Reingold, "Can P&G Make Money in Places Where People Earn $2 a Day?" *Fortune*, January 6, 2011, http://features.blogs.fortune.cnn.com; "The Tussle for Talent," *The Economist*, January 8, 2011, EBSCOhost, http://web.ebscohost.com; Rosabeth Moss Kanter, "Inside Procter & Gamble's New Values-Based Strategy," *Bloomberg Businessweek*, September 15, 2009, http://www.businessweek.com.

MANAGING TALENT: How HR Helps Newell Rubbermaid Navigate Change

Newell Rubbermaid's 22,000 employees produce and market a variety of consumables, including hardware, home furnishings, and office supplies. After the company went through rounds of acquiring and divesting businesses, employees came to think of their employer mainly in terms of its product lines, including Rubbermaid kitchen supplies, Levolor blinds, Goody hair products, and Sharpie markers. The brand focus gave employees no sense of common mission.

Newell Rubbermaid decided to chart a more strategic course. It would become less of a diversified manufacturer and would focus on understanding consumers' everyday frustrations and offering products targeted to unmet needs. It outsourced more of its manufacturing, eventually making only about half of its products. The changes meant that Newell Rubbermaid would need employees with new kinds of skills. Instead of production and marketing experts specializing in particular product lines, Newell Rubbermaid would depend more on people who can learn from consumers and apply what they have learned.

Newell Rubbermaid's HR managers were involved in this strategic change from early on. They decided their role would be "agents of change." In the spirit of the new strategy, they committed themselves to serving the various departments by being part of their everyday planning and operations. For example, when the strategy change was still being planned, leaders of the HR department sat down with the chief marketing officer to identify what processes and roles would need to change. They studied successful companies and interviewed business unit leaders to identify new marketing processes and roles associated with high performance. For example, they learned that the company had been focusing new-product development only on North America, whereas best-in-class companies consider demand globally. They reviewed the results with each business unit leader to identify areas where that group needed to improve most, and this analysis formed the basis of action plans for each group. They also discovered that employees feared the change, so they pressed the leadership to ensure that the change process would build a culture that was ethical and supportive.

Especially given the resistance to change, an essential part of HR's role was to plan how the HR department would communicate the changes to employees. The HR leaders determined that transparency was essential. They not only described what would be different, but also expressed why the changes were important to the company's future. They started with the leaders of marketing and the business units and then delivered this information to every employee. The HR department also prepared all the managers to talk about the change and the company's new cultural values one-on-one with each employee.

The HR department used the information it had gathered about best-in-class companies in other ways. It developed training programs on how to carry out more effective global marketing. Marketing employees were educated about brand strategy, consumer research, pricing strategy, and financial management. Also, the action plans that result from comparing the information against current practices have been used every year as the basis for business unit leaders' performance reviews with the chief executive officer and chief marketing officer.

Within the HR department itself, the company's new strategy meant HR employees had to shift their efforts toward building marketing skills throughout the company. They identified the job capabilities required at each level, rewrote job descriptions, and drew up a career ladder for each position. The career ladder is a kind of flow chart that shows how an individual can take on positions of greater responsibility as he or she gains specific types of skills and experience. They created a training program to teach the skills required for the job descriptions and for progress up the career ladder. The career ladders and training were innovative: in the past, managers often left because they had gone as far as they could within a division and no talent management occurred across divisional lines. When the HR department began training hundreds of Newell Rubbermaid employees, the effort had immediate credibility because everyone could see what was expected and participate in the development programs they needed.

Now a new question facing the company is how it will maintain employees' morale and commitment as it continues to press on toward greater efficiency. Newell Rubbermaid recently announced that it was reorganizing into a simpler structure and would be laying off 500 employees, mostly white-collar workers.

Questions

1. Would you say Newell Rubbermaid is moving toward being a high-performance work system? Why or why not?
2. How well did Newell Rubbermaid empower employees? What else would you recommend? How might the HR department prepare for a strategic shift concerned more with efficiency?

SOURCES: Brian Hults, "Integrate HR with Operating Strategy," *HR Magazine*, October 2011, pp. 64–66; James M. Sweet, "Unifying the Vision at Newell Rubbermaid," *Bloomberg Businessweek*, September 14, 2010, http://www.businessweek.com.

 TWITTER FOCUS: Radio Flyer Rolls Forward

Using Twitter, continue the conversation about strategic HR management by reading the Radio Flyer case at **www.mhhe.com/noefund5e**. Engage with your classmates and instructor via Twitter to chat about Radio Flyer using the case questions posted on the Noe website. Don't have a Twitter account yet? See the instructions for getting started on the Online Learning Center.

NOTES

1. James R. Hagerty, "Keeping Boomers Fit for Work," *The Wall Street Journal*, December 28, 2011, http://online.wsj.com.
2. Jennifer Schramm, "Feels Like Recession, but . . .," *HR Magazine*, HR Trendbook 2012, pp. 54–57.
3. Bureau of Labor Statistics, "Employment Projections, 2010–20," news release, February 1, 2012, http://www.bls.gov/emp.
4. Ibid.
5. AARP, "Best Employers for Workers over 50: 2011 Winners," September 2011, http://www.aarp.org.
6. A. Fox, "Mixing It Up," *HR Magazine*, May 2011, pp. 22–27; B. Hite, "Employers Rethink How They Give Feedback," *The Wall Street Journal*, October 13, 2008, p. B5; E. White, "Age Is as Age Does: Making the Generation Gap Work for You," *The Wall Street Journal*, June 30, 2008, p. B3.
7. Bureau of Labor Statistics, "Employment Projections, 2010–20."
8. Ibid.
9. For background, see Randall Monger and James Yankay, "U.S. Legal Permanent Residents: 2010," *Annual Flow Report*, U.S. Department of Homeland Security, Office of Immigration Statistics, March 2011, http://www.dhs.gov; U.S. Citizenship and Immigration Services, "Green Card (Permanent Residence)," http://www.uscis.gov, last updated May 13, 2011; U.S. Department of State, "Temporary Worker Visas," http://travel.state.gov, accessed February 8, 2012; Miriam Jordan, "Crackdown Resumes on Firms' Illegal Hires," *The Wall Street Journal*, November 15, 2011, http://online.wsj.com; Miriam Jordan, "More Discretion in Deportations," *The Wall Street Journal*, November 18, 2011, http://online.wsj.com.
10. T. H. Cox and S. Blake, "Managing Cultural Diversity: Implications for Organizational Competitiveness," *The Executive* 5 (1991), pp. 45–56.
11. "Global Diversity and Inclusion: Fostering Innovation through a Diverse Workforce," *Forbes Insights*, July 2011, http://www.forbes.com/forbesinsights.
12. Craig Wolf, "Diversity Helps Bridgeway Grow," *Poughkeepsie (N.Y.) Journal*, January 14, 2012, http://www.poughkeepsiejournal.com.
13. "SHRM Poll: Skills Gap Makes Engineering, Medical and Technical Jobs Difficult to Fill," *Investment Weekly News*, November 26, 2011, Business & Company Resource Center, http://galenet.galegroup.com; Lauren Weber, "Fine-Tuning the Perfect Employee," *The Wall Street Journal*, December 5, 2011, http://online.wsj.com.
14. James R. Hagerty, "Industry Puts Heat on Schools to Teach Skills Employers Need," *The Wall Street Journal*, June 6, 2011, http://online.wsj.com; Lucia Mutikani, "Veterans Help Manufacturers Plug Skills Gap," Reuters, February 2, 2012, http://www.reuters.com.
15. J. A. Neal and C. L. Tromley, "From Incremental Change to Retrofit: Creating High-Performance Work Systems," *Academy of Management Executive* 9 (1995), pp. 42–54.
16. Bureau of Labor Statistics, "Employment Projections, 2010–20," Table 7.
17. M. Hilton, "Skills for Work in the 21st Century: What Does the Research Tell Us?" *Academy of Management Executive*, November 2008, pp. 63–78.
18. Evan Rosen, "Every Worker Is a Knowledge Worker," *Bloomberg Businessweek*, January 11, 2011, http://www.businessweek.com; Joe McKendrick, "These Days, Who Is Not a 'Knowledge Worker'?" *SmartPlanet*, April 12, 2010, http://www.smartplanet.com.
19. Corilyn Shropshire, "Grainger Gives Employees Room to Grow," *Chicago Tribune*, November 15, 2011, http://www.chicagotribune.com. See also Jessica Stillman, "The Perpetually Vexing Problem of Hiring Programmers," *Inc.*, January 5, 2012, http://www.inc.com.
20. T. J. Atchison, "The Employment Relationship: Untied or Re-Tied," *Academy of Management Executive* 5 (1991), pp. 52–62.
21. R. Vance, *Employee Engagement and Commitment* (Alexandria, VA: Society for Human Resource Management, 2006); M. Huselid, "The Impact of Human Resource Management Practices on Turnover, Productivity, and Corporate Financial Performance," *Academy of Management Journal* 38 (1995), pp. 635–72; S. Payne and S. Webber, "Effects of Service Provider Attitudes and Employment Status on Citizenship Behaviors and Customers' Attitudes and Loyalty Behavior," *Journal of Applied Psychology* 91 (2006), pp. 365–68; and J. Hartner, F. Schmidt, and T. Hayes, "Business-Unit Level Relationship between Employee Satisfaction, Employee Engagement, and Business Outcomes: A Meta-analysis," *Journal of Applied Psychology* 87 (2002), pp. 268–79.
22. Alex Adamopoulos, "'Agile' Grows Up, Readies to Take Over Your Whole Business," *VentureBeat*, February 9, 2012, http://venturebeat.com; Agile Alliance, "What Is Agile Software Development?" http://www.agilealliance.org, accessed February 10, 2012.

23. Adrienne Fox, "Achieving Integration: Boost Corporate Performance," *HR Magazine*, April 2011, Business & Company Resource Center, http://galenet.galegroup.com.

24. J. R. Jablonski, *Implementing Total Quality Management: An Overview* (San Diego: Pfeiffer, 1991).

25. R. Hodgetts, F. Luthans, and S. Lee, "New Paradigm Organizations: From Total Quality to Learning to World-Class," *Organizational Dynamics*, Winter 1994, pp. 5–19.

26. Bettina Chang, "Learning to Unlearn," *Chief Learning Officer*, January 2011, pp. 32–35.

27. Bureau of Labor Statistics, "Extended Mass Layoffs: Fourth Quarter 2011, Annual Totals 2011," news release, February 10, 2012, http://www.bls.gov/mls.

28. "Lay Off the Layoffs," *Newsweek*, February 4, 2010, http://www.thedailybeast.com/newsweek; Ryan Bakken, "Marvin: A Window on the Economy," *Grand Forks (ND) Herald*, November 21, 2011, Business & Company Resource Center, http://galenet.galegroup.com.

29. A. Church, "Organizational Downsizing: What Is the Role of the Practitioner?" *Industrial-Organizational Psychologist* 33, no. 1 (1995), pp. 63–74.

30. Dori Meinert, "HR Budgets Show Modest Growth," *HR Magazine*, November 2011, p. 24.

31. The Right Thing, "The Goodyear Tire and Rubber Company Discovers Key to Successful Outsourcing Partnerships," *Workforce Management*, March 2011, p. S2.

32. M. Wei, "East Meets West at Hamburger University," *Bloomberg Businessweek*, January 31–February 6, 2011, pp. 22–23.

33. David Wessel, "Big U.S. Firms Shift Hiring Abroad," *The Wall Street Journal*, April 19, 2011, http://online.wsj.com; David Wessel, "U.S. Firms Keen to Add Foreign Jobs," *The Wall Street Journal*, November 22, 2011, http://online.wsj.com.

34. Megha Bahree, "Indian Tech Firms Look to Hire Abroad," *The Wall Street Journal*, November 11, 2011, http://online.wsj.com.

35. Monger and Yankay, "U.S. Legal Permanent Residents: 2010."

36. Audrey Singer, "Immigrants in 2010 Metropolitan America: A Decade of Change," *State of Metropolitan America*, no. 43, Brookings Institution, October 24, 2011, http://www.brookings.edu; Bureau of Labor Statistics, "Foreign-Born Workers: Labor Force Characteristics, 2010," news release, May 27, 2011, http://www.bls.gov/cps.

37. R. L. Tung, "Expatriate Assignments: Enhancing Success and Minimizing Failure," *Academy of Management Executive* 12, no. 4 (1988), pp. 93–106.

38. M. J. Kavanaugh, H. G. Guetal, and S. I. Tannenbaum, *Human Resource Information Systems: Development and Application* (Boston: PWS-Kent, 1990).

39. Dave Zielinski, "HRIS Features Get More Strategic," *HR Magazine*, December 2011, p. 15.

40. Dan Lyons, "Is Workday Silicon Valley's Next Big IPO?" *Newsweek*, February 6, 2012, http://www.thedailybeast.com/newsweek.

41. "Payroll as You Go," *Entrepreneur*, October 2011, p. 45.

42. N. Lockwood, *Maximizing Human Capital: Demonstrating HR Value with Key Performance Indicators* (Alexandria, VA: SHRM Research Quarterly, 2006).

43. "Social Technologies on the Front Line: The Management 2.0 M-Prize Winners," *McKinsey Quarterly*, September 2011, http://www.mckinseyquarterly.com.

44. Ibid.

45. J. O'Toole and E. Lawler III, *The New American Workplace* (New York: Palgrave Macmillan, 2006).

46. D. M. Rousseau, "Psychological and Implied Contracts in Organizations," *Employee Rights and Responsibilities Journal* 2 (1989), pp. 121–29.

47. Bureau of Labor Statistics, "Employee Tenure in 2010," news release, September 14, 2010, http://www.bls.gov/cps.

48. Dan Schawbel, "How Job Hopping Can Hurt Your Career," CNN, January 17, 2012, http://articles.cnn.com; Chrissy Scivicque, "How to Stop Job Hopping Once and for All," *Forbes*, January 23, 2012, http://www.forbes.com; Alina Dizik, "The Pros and Cons of Job-Hopping," CNN, July 4, 2011, http://www.cnn.com.

49. Fast Fact, "Temporary Workforce Stronger than Ever," *T + D*, May 2011, p. 21; Kate Lister, "Freelance Nation," *Entrepreneur*, September 2010, pp. 89–97. See also Thomas Lawrence, "Integrating Contingent Workers," *Baseline*, January 2012, p. 13.

50. Peter Coy, Michelle Conlin, and Moira Herbst, "The Disposable Worker," *Bloomberg Businessweek*, January 18, 2010, pp. 33–39; Rachel Emma Silverman, "Big Firms Try Crowdsourcing," *The Wall Street Journal*, January 17, 2012, http://online.wsj.com.

51. Ed Finkel, "Positive Thinking," *Modern Healthcare*, October 24, 2011, Business & Company Resource Center, http://galenet.galegroup.com; Weatherby Healthcare, "About Us," http://www.weatherbyhealthcare.com, accessed January 25, 2012.

3

Providing Equal Employment Opportunity and a Safe Workplace

What Do I Need to Know?

After reading this chapter, you should be able to:

LO 3-1 Explain how the three branches of government regulate human resource management.

LO 3-2 Summarize the major federal laws requiring equal employment opportunity.

LO 3-3 Identify the federal agencies that enforce equal employment opportunity, and describe the role of each.

LO 3-4 Describe ways employers can avoid illegal discrimination and provide reasonable accommodation.

LO 3-5 Define sexual harassment, and tell how employers can eliminate or minimize it.

LO 3-6 Explain employers' duties under the Occupational Safety and Health Act.

LO 3-7 Describe the role of the Occupational Safety and Health Administration.

LO 3-8 Discuss ways employers promote worker safety and health.

Introduction

Inexperienced workers who assembled Harley-Davidson motorcycles were being injured at a troubling rate. More than 4 out of 10 reported an injury within their first five years on the job. Typically, these were musculoskeletal injuries—a broad category that includes damage to bones, muscles, and joints, usually as a result of strenuous work the body is unprepared to handle safely. Given that the injuries were happening to the company's less-experienced workers, Harley-Davidson considered that it was not accurately matching job applicants' physical abilities to job requirements.

For a solution, Harley-Davidson turned to BTE Technologies, a company with a background in making equipment for physical rehabilitation. BTE has used its expertise in rehabilitation to develop systems for measuring individuals' ability to carry out physical functions. Harley-Davidson hired BTE to analyze the physical requirements of its manufacturing jobs, define the necessary physical job functions, and create a set of tests to measure whether individuals can perform those functions safely.

Harley-Davidson started by using BTE's test at its Milwaukee facility. When Harley-Davidson makes a job offer, that offer is contingent on the employee passing the new physical-abilities test. Almost one-fifth of prospective new hires fail the test, indicating they cannot perform the job safely. By screening out these unqualified workers, Harley-Davidson quickly cut the rate of musculoskeletal injuries among new employees in Milwaukee down to zero. During the same period, at facilities where Harley-Davidson was not yet using the program, workers filed more than

500 injury claims. Seeing the potential to save thousands of dollars in workers' compensation while protecting its workers from injury, Harley-Davidson immediately expanded the program beyond Milwaukee.[1]

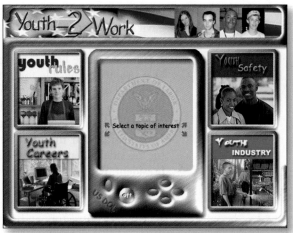

One way the executive branch communicates information about laws is through website like Youth2Work. This site is designed to provide young workers with a safe workplace by making them aware of laws that, for example, restrict the amount of work they can do and the machinery they can operate.

As we saw in Chapter 1, human resource management takes place in the context of the company's goals and society's expectations for how a company should operate. In the United States, the federal government has set some limits on how an organization can practice human resource management. Among these limits are requirements intended to prevent discrimination in hiring and employment practices and to protect the health and safety of workers while they are on the job. Questions about a company's compliance with these requirements can result in lawsuits and negative publicity that often cause serious problems for a company's success and survival. Conversely, a company that skillfully navigates the maze of regulations can gain an advantage over its competitors. A further advantage may go to companies that, like Harley-Davidson, go beyond mere legal compliance to make fair employment and worker safety important components of the company's business strategy. Harley-Davidson schedules physical-ability tests *after* an employment decision is made so it avoids discrimination against individuals who have a disability yet might be able to perform job functions. And it established evidence-based, job-related criteria for measuring the ability to perform jobs. These efforts do not merely keep Harley-Davidson out of legal hot water; they also help it select the most qualified people and operate more efficiently.

This chapter provides an overview of the ways government bodies regulate equal employment opportunity and workplace safety and health. It introduces you to major laws affecting employers in these areas, as well as the agencies charged with enforcing those laws. The chapter also discusses ways organizations can develop practices that ensure they are in compliance with the laws.

One point to make at the outset is that managers often want a list of dos and don'ts that will keep them out of legal trouble. Some managers rely on strict rules such as "Don't ever ask a female applicant if she is married," rather than learning the reasons behind those rules. Clearly, certain practices are illegal or at least inadvisable, and this chapter will provide guidance on avoiding such practices. However, managers who merely focus on how to avoid breaking the law are not thinking about how to be ethical or how to acquire and use human resources in the best way to carry out the company's mission. This chapter introduces ways to think more creatively and constructively about fair employment and workplace safety.

Regulation of Human Resource Management

All three branches of the U.S. government—legislative, executive, and judicial—play an important role in creating a legal environment for human resource management. The legislative branch, which consists of the two houses of Congress, has enacted a number of laws governing human resource activities. Senators and U.S. Representatives generally develop these laws in response to perceived societal needs. For example,

LO 3-1 Explain how the three branches of government regulate human resource management.

during the civil rights movement of the early 1960s, Congress enacted Title VII of the Civil Rights Act to ensure that various minority groups received equal opportunities in many areas of life.

The executive branch, including the many regulatory agencies that the president oversees, is responsible for enforcing the laws passed by Congress. Agencies do this through a variety of actions, from drawing up regulations detailing how to abide by the laws to filing suit against alleged violators. Some federal agencies involved in regulating human resource management include the Equal Employment Opportunity Commission and the Occupational Safety and Health Administration. In addition, the president may issue executive orders, which are directives issued solely by the president, without requiring congressional approval. Some executive orders regulate the activities of organizations that have contracts with the federal government. For example, President Lyndon Johnson signed Executive Order 11246, which requires all federal contractors and subcontractors to engage in affirmative-action programs designed to hire and promote women and minorities. (We will explore the topic of affirmative action later in this chapter.)

The judicial branch, the federal court system, influences employment law by interpreting the law and holding trials concerning violations of the law. The U.S. Supreme Court, at the head of the judicial branch, is the court of final appeal. Decisions made by the Supreme Court are binding; they can be overturned only through laws passed by Congress. The Civil Rights Act of 1991 was partly designed to overturn Supreme Court decisions.

Equal Employment Opportunity

LO 3-2 Summarize the major federal laws requiring equal employment opportunity.

Equal Employment Opportunity (EEO)
The condition in which all individuals have an equal chance for employment, regardless of their race, color, religion, sex, age, disability, or national origin.

Among the most significant efforts to regulate human resource management are those aimed at achieving **equal employment opportunity (EEO)**—the condition in which all individuals have an equal chance for employment, regardless of their race, color, religion, sex, age, disability, or national origin. The federal government's efforts to create equal employment opportunity include constitutional amendments, legislation, and executive orders, as well as court decisions that interpret the laws. Table 3.1 summarizes major EEO laws discussed in this chapter. These are U.S. laws; equal employment laws in other countries may differ.

Constitutional Amendments

Two amendments to the U.S. Constitution—the Thirteenth and Fourteenth—have implications for human resource management. The Thirteenth Amendment abolished slavery in the United States. Though you might be hard-pressed to cite an example of race-based slavery in the United States today, the Thirteenth Amendment has been applied in cases where discrimination involved the "badges" (symbols) and "incidents" of slavery.

The Fourteenth Amendment forbids the states from taking life, liberty, or property without due process of law and prevents the states from denying equal protection of the laws. Recently it has been applied to the protection of whites in charges of reverse discrimination. In a case that marked the early stages of a move away from race-based quotas, Alan Bakke alleged that as a white man he had been discriminated against in the selection of entrants to the University of California at Davis medical school.[2] The university had set aside 16 of the available 100 places for "disadvantaged" applicants who were members of racial minority groups. Under this quota system, Bakke

Table 3.1

Summary of Major EEO Laws and Regulations

ACT	REQUIREMENTS	COVERS	ENFORCEMENT AGENCY
Thirteenth Amendment	Abolished slavery	All individuals	Court system
Fourteenth Amendment	Provides equal protection for all citizens and requires due process in state action	State actions (e.g., decisions of government organizations)	Court system
Civil Rights Acts (CRAs) of 1866 and 1871 (as amended)	Grant all citizens the right to make, perform, modify, and terminate contracts and enjoy all benefits, terms, and conditions of the contractual relationship	All individuals	Court system
Equal Pay Act of 1963	Requires that men and women performing equal jobs receive equal pay	Employers engaged in interstate commerce	EEOC
Title VII of CRA	Forbids discrimination based on race, color, religion, sex, or national origin	Employers with 15 or more employees working 20 or more weeks per year; labor unions; and employment agencies	EEOC
Age Discrimination in Employment Act of 1967	Prohibits discrimination in employment against individuals 40 years of age and older	Employers with 15 or more employees working 20 or more weeks per year; labor unions; employment agencies; federal government	EEOC
Rehabilitation Act of 1973	Requires affirmative action in the employment of individuals with disabilities	Government agencies; federal contractors and subcontractors with contracts greater than $2,500	OFCCP
Pregnancy Discrimination Act of 1978	Treats discrimination based on pregnancy-related conditions as illegal sex discrimination	All employees covered by Title VII	EEOC
Americans with Disabilities Act of 1990	Prohibits discrimination against individuals with disabilities	Employers with more than 15 employees	EEOC
Executive Order 11246	Requires affirmative action in hiring women and minorities	Federal contractors and subcontractors with contracts greater than $10,000	OFCCP
Civil Rights Act of 1991	Prohibits discrimination (same as Title VII)	Same as Title VII, plus applies Section 1981 to employment discrimination cases	EEOC
Uniformed Services Employment and Reemployment Rights Act of 1994	Requires rehiring of employees who are absent for military service, with training and accommodations as needed	Veterans and members of reserve components	Veterans' Employment and Training Service
Genetic Information Nondiscrimination Act of 2008	Prohibits discrimination because of genetic information	Employers with 15 or more employees	EEOC

was able to compete for only 84 positions, whereas a minority applicant was able to compete for all 100. The federal court ruled in favor of Bakke, noting that this quota system had violated white individuals' right to equal protection under the law.

An important point regarding the Fourteenth Amendment is that it applies only to the decisions or actions of the government or of private groups whose activities are deemed government actions. Thus, a person could file a claim under the Fourteenth Amendment if he or she had been fired from a state university (a government organization) but not if the person had been fired by a private employer.

Legislation

The periods following the Civil War and during the civil rights movement of the 1960s were times when many voices in society pressed for equal rights for all without regard to a person's race or sex. In response, Congress passed laws designed to provide for equal opportunity. In later years, Congress has passed additional laws that have extended EEO protection more broadly.

Civil Rights Acts of 1866 and 1871

During Reconstruction, Congress passed two Civil Rights Acts to further the Thirteenth Amendment's goal of abolishing slavery. The Civil Rights Act of 1866 granted all persons the same property rights as white citizens, as well as the right to enter into and enforce contracts. Courts have interpreted the latter right as including employment contracts. The Civil Rights Act of 1871 granted all citizens the right to sue in federal court if they feel they have been deprived of some civil right. Although these laws might seem outdated, they are still used because they allow the plaintiff to recover both compensatory and punitive damages (that is, payment to compensate them for their loss plus additional damages to punish the offender).

Equal Pay Act of 1963

Under the Equal Pay Act of 1963, if men and women in an organization are doing equal work, the employer must pay them equally. The act defines *equal* in terms of skill, effort, responsibility, and working conditions. However, the act allows for reasons why men and women performing the same job might be paid differently. If the pay differences result from differences in seniority, merit, quantity or quality of production, or any factor other than sex (such as participating in a training program or working the night shift), then the differences are legal.

Title VII of the Civil Rights Act of 1964

The major law regulating equal employment opportunity in the United States is Title VII of the Civil Rights Act of 1964. Title VII directly resulted from the civil rights movement of the early 1960s, led by such individuals as Dr. Martin Luther King Jr. To ensure that employment opportunities would be based on character or ability rather than on race, Congress wrote and passed Title VII, and President Lyndon Johnson signed it into law in 1964. The law is enforced by the **Equal Employment Opportunity Commission (EEOC),** an agency of the Department of Justice.

Equal Employment Opportunity Commission (EEOC) Agency of the Department of Justice charged with enforcing Title VII of the Civil Rights Act of 1964 and other antidiscrimination laws.

Title VII prohibits employers from discriminating against individuals because of their race, color, religion, sex, or national origin. An employer may not use these characteristics as the basis for not hiring someone, for firing someone, or for discriminating against them in the terms of their pay, conditions of employment, or privileges of employment. In addition, an employer may not use these characteristics to limit, segregate, or classify employees or job applicants in any way that would deprive any individual of employment opportunities or otherwise adversely affect his or her status as an employee. The act applies to organizations that employ 15 or more persons working 20 or more weeks a year and that are involved in interstate commerce, as well as state and local governments, employment agencies, and labor organizations.

Title VII also states that employers may not retaliate against employees for either "opposing" a perceived illegal employment practice or "participating in a proceeding" related to an alleged illegal employment practice. *Opposition* refers to expressing to someone through proper channels that you believe an illegal employment act has taken place or is taking place. *Participation in a proceeding* refers to testifying in an investigation, hearing, or court proceeding regarding an illegal employment act. The purpose of this provision is to protect employees from employers' threats and other forms of intimidation aimed at discouraging employees from bringing to light acts they believe to be illegal. Companies that violate this prohibition may be liable for punitive damages.

Age Discrimination in Employment Act (ADEA)   One category of employees not covered by Title VII is older workers. Older workers sometimes are concerned that they will be the targets of discrimination, especially when a company is downsizing. Older workers tend to be paid more, so a company that wants to cut labor costs may save by laying off its oldest workers. To counter such discrimination, Congress in 1967 passed the Age Discrimination in Employment Act (ADEA), which prohibits discrimination against workers who are over the age of 40. Similar to Title VII, the ADEA outlaws hiring, firing, setting compensation rates, or other employment decisions based on a person's age being over 40.

Many firms have offered early-retirement incentives as an alternative or supplement to involuntary layoffs. Because this approach to workforce reduction focuses on older employees, who would be eligible for early retirement, it may be in violation of the ADEA. Early-retirement incentives require that participating employees sign an agreement waiving their rights to sue under the ADEA. Courts have tended to uphold the use of early-retirement incentives and waivers as long as the individuals were not coerced into signing the agreements, the agreements were presented in a way the employees could understand (including technical legal requirements such as the ages of discharged and retained employees in the employee's work unit), and the employees had been given enough time to make a decision.[3] Also, these waivers must meet the basic requirements of a contract, so the employer must offer something of value—for example, payment of a percentage of the employee's salary—in exchange for the employee giving up rights under the waiver.

To defend against claims of discrimination, one practical way is to establish performance-related criteria for layoffs, rather than age- or salary-related criteria. Of course, those criteria must be genuinely performance related. The EEOC recently sued a Michigan manufacturer for apparently manipulating its layoff criteria in order to target the oldest engineers for layoffs. In the first round of layoffs at Hutchinson Sealing Systems, the oldest project engineer was the one who met the criteria. Then the company revised its criteria and laid off two more engineers, again the oldest on the payroll. If the criteria had not been changed, younger engineers would have met the layoff criteria, and the EEOC saw that as evidence of age discrimination.[4]

Age discrimination complaints make up a large percentage of the complaints filed with the Equal Employment Opportunity Commission, and whenever the economy is slow, the number of complaints grows. For example, as shown in Figure 3.1, the number of age discrimination cases jumped in 2008 and 2009, when many firms were downsizing. Another increase in age discrimination claims accompanied the economic slowdown at the beginning of the 2000s.

Figure 3.1

Age Discrimination Complaints, 1997–2011

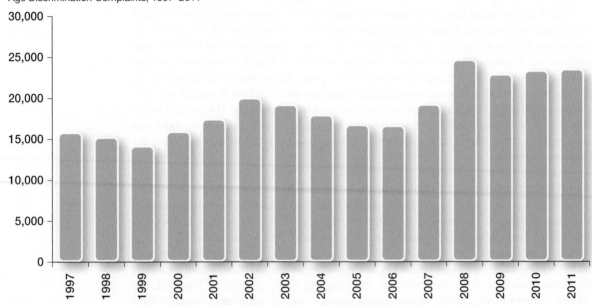

SOURCE: Equal Employment Opportunity Commission, http://www1.eeoc.gov//eeoc/statistics/enforcement/

In today's environment, in which firms are seeking talented individuals to achieve the company's goals, older employees can be a tremendous pool of potential resources. Researchers have found that although muscle power tends to decline with age, older workers tend to offer other important strengths, including conscientiousness and interpersonal skills.[5] Older workers also may have acquired deep knowledge of their work, industry, and employer. Successful companies are finding ways to keep these valuable older workers on the job and contributing. Union Carbide asks retired managers to serve as mentors for its current managers. In Australia, a bank called Westpac has identified knowledgeable older workers, labeled them "sages," and asked them to create a database of what they know about the organization and their work. At Mercy Health Systems, workers approaching retirement are allowed to take leaves of absence with benefits, and retired workers are invited to be part of a temporary workforce that comes back during periods of heavy demand.

Vocational Rehabilitation Act of 1973   In 1973, Congress passed the Vocational Rehabilitation Act to enhance employment opportunity for individuals with disabilities. This act covers executive agencies and contractors and subcontractors that receive more than $2,500 annually from the federal government. These organizations must engage in affirmative action for individuals with disabilities. **Affirmative action** is an organization's active effort to find opportunities to hire or promote people in a particular group. Thus, Congress intended this act to encourage employers to recruit qualified individuals with disabilities and to make reasonable accommodations to all those people to become active members of the labor market. The Department of Labor's Employment Standards Administration enforces this act.

Vietnam Era Veteran's Readjustment Act of 1974   Similar to the Rehabilitation Act, the Vietnam Era Veteran's Readjustment Act of 1974 requires federal

Affirmative Action

An organization's active effort to find opportunities to hire or promote people in a particular group.

contractors and subcontractors to take affirmative action toward employing veterans of the Vietnam War (those serving between August 5, 1964, and May 7, 1975). The Office of Federal Contract Compliance Procedures, discussed later in this chapter, has authority to enforce this act.

Pregnancy Discrimination Act of 1978   An amendment to Title VII of the Civil Rights Act of 1964, the Pregnancy Discrimination Act of 1978 defines discrimination on the basis of pregnancy, childbirth, or related medical conditions to be a form of illegal sex discrimination. According to the EEOC, this means that employers may not treat a female applicant or employee "unfavorably because of pregnancy, childbirth, or a medical condition related to pregnancy or childbirth."[6] For example, an employer may not refuse to hire a woman because she is pregnant. Decisions about work absences or accommodations must be based on the same policies as the organization uses for other disabilities. Benefits, including health insurance, should cover pregnancy and related medical conditions in the same way that it covers other medical conditions.

Americans with Disabilities Act (ADA) of 1990   One of the farthest-reaching acts concerning the management of human resources is the Americans with Disabilities Act. This 1990 law protects individuals with disabilities from being discriminated against in the workplace. It prohibits discrimination based on disability in all employment practices, such as job application procedures, hiring, firing, promotions, compensation, and training. Other employment activities covered by the ADA are employment advertising, recruitment, tenure, layoff, leave, and fringe benefits.

The ADA defines **disability** as a physical or mental impairment that substantially limits one or more major life activities, a record of having such an impairment, or being regarded as having such an impairment. The first part of the definition refers to individuals who have serious disabilities—such as epilepsy, blindness, deafness, or paralysis—that affect their ability to perform major bodily functions and major life activities such as walking, learning, (for example, functions of the brain and immune system) caring for one-self, and working. The second part refers to individuals who have a history of disability, such as someone who has had cancer but is currently in remission, someone with a history of mental illness, and someone with a history of heart disease. The third part of the definition, "being regarded as having a disability," refers to people's subjective reactions, as in the case of someone who is severely disfigured; an employer might hesitate to hire such a person on the grounds that people will react negatively to such an employee.[7]

The ADA covers specific physiological disabilities such as cosmetic disfigurement and anatomical loss affecting the body's systems. In addition, it covers mental and psychological disorders such as mental retardation, organic brain syndrome, emotional or mental illness, and learning disabilities. Conditions not covered include obesity, substance abuse, irritability, and poor judgment.[8] Also, if a person needs ordinary eyeglasses or contact lenses to perform each major life activity with little or no difficulty, the person is not considered disabled under the ADA. (In determining whether an impairment is substantially limiting, mitigating measures, such as medicine, hearing aids, and prosthetics, once could be considered but now must be ignored.) Figure 3.2 shows the types of disabilities associated with complaints filed under the ADA in 2011.

In contrast to other EEO laws, the ADA goes beyond prohibiting discrimination to require that employers take steps to accommodate individuals covered under the act. If a disabled person is selected to perform a job, the employer (perhaps in consultation with the disabled employee) determines what accommodations are necessary for the

Disability
Under the Americans with Disabilities Act, a physical or mental impairment that substantially limits one or more major life activities, a record of having such an impairment, or being regarded as having such an impairment.

Figure 3.2

Disabilities Associated with Complaints Filed under ADA

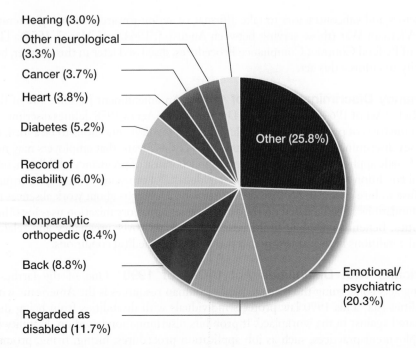

Hearing (3.0%)
Other neurological (3.3%)
Cancer (3.7%)
Heart (3.8%)
Diabetes (5.2%)
Record of disability (6.0%)
Nonparalytic orthopedic (8.4%)
Back (8.8%)
Regarded as disabled (11.7%)
Other (25.8%)
Emotional/ psychiatric (20.3%)

SOURCE: Equal Employment Opportunity Commission, "ADA Charge Data by Impairments/Bases: Receipts, FY1997–FY2011," http://www1.eeoc.gov, accessed February 14, 2012.

employee to perform the job. Examples include using ramps and lifts to make facilities accessible, redesigning job procedures, and providing technology such as TDD lines for hearing-impaired employees. Some employers have feared that accommodations under the ADA would be expensive. As the "Best Practices" box describes, handling the need for accommodations can be a delicate matter in some cases. However, the Department of Labor has found that two-thirds of accommodations cost less than $500, and many of these cost nothing.[9] As technology advances, the cost of many technologies has been falling. In addition, the federal government has created a tax credit, the Work Opportunity Tax Credit, of up to $2,400 for each qualified disabled worker hired. That means accommodating disabled workers can lower an employer's income taxes.

Civil Rights Act of 1991   In 1991 Congress broadened the relief available to victims of discrimination by passing a Civil Rights Act (CRA 1991). CRA 1991 amends Title VII of the Civil Rights Act of 1964, as well as the Civil Rights Act of 1866, the Americans with Disabilities Act, and the Age Discrimination in Employment Act of 1967. One major change in EEO law under CRA 1991 has been the addition of compensatory and punitive damages in cases of discrimination under Title VII and the Americans with Disabilities Act. Before CRA 1991, Title VII limited damage claims to *equitable relief*, which courts have defined to include back pay, lost benefits, front pay in some cases, and attorney's fees and costs. CRA 1991 allows judges to award compensatory and punitive damages when the plaintiff proves the discrimination was intentional or reckless. Compensatory damages include such things as future monetary loss, emotional pain, suffering, and loss of enjoyment of life. Punitive damages are

Best Practices

Dealing with Dementia at LSI Corporation

John McClelland excelled as product marketing manager for LSI Corporation because he understood the company's software, demonstrated to clients how LSI could help them manage their data, and skillfully maintained strong business relationships. But when McClelland was in his mid-fifties, his performance began to suffer. He struggled to keep up and would find himself in the middle of a phone call using the wrong name for the person he was talking to. One day he drove to another LSI office to pick up a colleague, but after parking, he walked right past the colleague waiting at the curb, not recognizing him.

That incident was too much for McClelland. He visited his doctor and learned that he had dementia—possibly Alzheimer's disease, which had already taken the memories and lives of others in his family. McClelland talked to his supervisor about how LSI could accommodate him as long as he could use his skills. He began traveling less and took a co-worker along with him. Within months, however, McClelland could no longer keep up with his job responsibilities, so he took a disability leave—trading his job for volunteer work and receiving benefits from his long-term disability insurance.

Alzheimer's disease is incurable. It and other forms of dementia can devastate an employee's ability to remember even close colleagues and to become confused about performing routine tasks. Given that grim scenario, LSI handled McClelland's disability about as well as an employer could. The company offered him accommodations to see if he could continue to meet his job requirements. And when that wasn't enough, LSI worked with him to transition from employment to disability leave.

All too often, employers grow frustrated with employees who stop meeting standards, and the employees are let go for poor performance. Early signs of dementia may not seem serious—say, a frequently misplaced cell phone and confusion about whether the meeting is today or tomorrow. Only when the employee's disease has progressed so far that the employee forgets where his or her desk is or repeatedly fails to complete a routine task does the employer take action. That happened to engineer Jay Kauphusman, who struggled for two years to stay on the job after a diagnosis of Alzheimer's disease. When his declining performance could no longer be ignored,

his employer, a construction firm, encouraged him to go on disability.

That sad outcome is likely to become more common as the workforce continues to age. As described in Chapter 2, older workers have been delaying retirement, and the share of the population 55 and older is growing. Forecasts suggest that the number of people diagnosed with Alzheimer's will triple, and many of these people will be trying to hold down jobs. Their employers will need to engage in the delicate task of determining how and for how long they can accommodate these workers. An employer has no legal obligation to keep individuals on the payroll if their faded memories and poor judgment prevent them from being able to perform essential tasks. But ethical standards nevertheless require that employers treat their workers with basic dignity and respect.

SOURCES: Diane Stafford, "No More Hiding: Alzheimer's vs. the Workplace," *Kansas City Star,* November 18, 2011, http://www.kansascity.com; "HR in Uncharted Waters as Number of Workers with Alzheimer's Grows," *HR Focus,* June 2011, pp. 1–6; and Pamela Babcock, "Avoid Assumptions about Alzheimer's," Society for Human Resource Management, October 28, 2009, http://www.shrm.org.

a punishment; by requiring violators to pay the plaintiff an amount beyond the actual losses suffered, the courts try to discourage employers from discriminating.

Recognizing that one or a few discrimination cases could put an organization out of business, and so harm many innocent employees, Congress has limited the amount of punitive damages. As shown in Table 3.2, the amount of damages depends on the size of the organization charged with discrimination. The limits range from $50,000 per violation at a small company (14 to 100 employees) to $300,000 at a company with more than 500 employees. A company has to pay punitive damages only if it discriminated intentionally or with malice or reckless indifference to the employee's federally protected rights.

Table 3.2

Maximum Punitive Damages Allowed under the Civil Rights Act of 1991

EMPLOYER SIZE	DAMAGE LIMIT
14 to 100 employees	$ 50,000
101 to 200 employees	100,000
201 to 500 employees	200,000
More than 500 employees	300,000

Uniformed Services Employment and Reemployment Rights Act of 1994   When members of the armed services were called up following the terrorist attacks of September 2001, a 1994 employment law—the Uniformed Services Employment and Reemployment Rights Act (USERRA)—assumed new significance. Under this law, employers must reemploy workers who left jobs to fulfill military duties for up to five years. When service members return from active duty, the employer must reemploy them in the job they would have held if they had not left to serve in the military, providing them with the same seniority, status, and pay rate they would have earned if their employment had not been interrupted. Disabled veterans also have up to two years to recover from injuries received during their service or training, and employers must make reasonable accommodations for a remaining disability.

Service members also have duties under USERRA. Before leaving for duty, they are to give their employers notice, if possible. After their service, the law sets time limits for applying to be reemployed. Depending on the length of service, these limits range from approximately 2 to 90 days. Veterans with complaints under USERRA can obtain assistance from the Veterans' Employment and Training Service of the Department of Labor.

Genetic Information Nondiscrimination Act of 2008   Thanks to the decoding of the human genome and developments in the fields of genetics and medicine, researchers can now identify more and more genes associated with risks for developing particular diseases or disorders. While learning that you are at risk of, say, colon cancer may be a useful motivator to take precautions, the information opens up some risks as well. For example, what if companies began using genetic screening to identify and avoid hiring job candidates who are at risk of developing costly diseases? Concerns such as this prompted Congress to pass the Genetic Information Nondiscrimination Act (GINA) of 2008.

Under GINA's requirements, companies with 15 or more employees may not use genetic information in making decisions related to the terms, conditions, or privileges of employment—for example, decisions to hire, promote, or lay off a worker. This genetic information includes information about a person's genetic tests, genetic tests of the person's family members, and family medical histories. Furthermore, employers may not intentionally obtain this information, except in certain limited situations (such as an employee voluntarily participating in a wellness program or requesting time off to care for a sick relative). If companies do acquire such information, they must keep the information confidential. The law also forbids harassment of any employee because of that person's genetic information.

Executive Orders

Two executive orders that directly affect human resource management are Executive Order 11246, issued by Lyndon Johnson, and Executive Order 11478, issued by Richard Nixon. Executive Order 11246 prohibits federal contractors and subcontractors from discriminating based on race, color, religion, sex, or national origin. In addition, employers whose contracts meet minimum size requirements must engage in affirmative action to ensure against discrimination. Those receiving more than $10,000 from the federal government must take affirmative action, and those with contracts exceeding $50,000 must develop a written affirmative-action plan for each of their establishments. This plan must be in place within 120 days of the beginning of the contract. This executive order is enforced by the Office of Federal Contract Compliance Procedures.

Executive Order 11478 requires the federal government to base all its employment policies on merit and fitness. It specifies that race, color, sex, religion, and national origin may not be considered. Along with the government, the act covers all contractors and subcontractors doing at least $10,000 worth of business with the federal government. The U.S. Office of Personnel Management is in charge of ensuring that the government is in compliance, and the relevant government agencies are responsible for ensuring the compliance of contractors and subcontractors.

Aric Miller, an Army reservist sergeant, was deployed for service with the 363rd military police unit in Iraq for over a year. When he returned to the states, he was able to resume his job as an elementary school teacher thanks to the 1994 Uniformed Services Employment and Reemployment Rights Act. The act requires employers to reemploy service members in the job they would have held if they had not left to serve in the military. Why is this act important?

The Government's Role in Providing for Equal Employment Opportunity

LO 3-3 Identify the federal agencies that enforce equal employment opportunity, and describe the role of each.

At a minimum, equal employment opportunity requires that employers comply with EEO laws. To enforce those laws, the executive branch of the federal government uses the Equal Employment Opportunity Commission and the Office of Federal Contract Compliance Programs.

Equal Employment Opportunity Commission (EEOC)

The Equal Employment Opportunity Commission (EEOC) is responsible for enforcing most of the EEO laws, including Title VII, the Equal Pay Act, and the Americans with Disabilities Act. To do this, the EEOC investigates and resolves complaints about discrimination, gathers information, and issues guidelines.

When individuals believe they have been discriminated against, they may file a complaint with the EEOC or a similar state agency. They must file the complaint within 180 days of the incident. Figure 3.3 illustrates the number of charges filed with the EEOC for different types of discrimination in 2011. Many individuals file more than one type of charge (for instance, both race discrimination and retaliation), so the total number of complaints filed with the EEOC is less than the total of the amounts in each category.

After the EEOC receives a charge of discrimination, it has 60 days to investigate the complaint. If the EEOC either does not believe the complaint to be valid or fails to complete the investigation within 60 days, the individual has the right to sue in federal court. If the EEOC determines that discrimination has taken place, its representatives will attempt to work with the individual and the employer to try to achieve a reconciliation without a lawsuit. Sometimes the EEOC enters into a consent decree with the discriminating organization. This decree is an agreement between the agency and the organization that the organization will cease certain discriminatory practices and possibly institute additional affirmative-action practices to rectify its history of

Figure 3.3

Types of Charges Filed with the EEOC

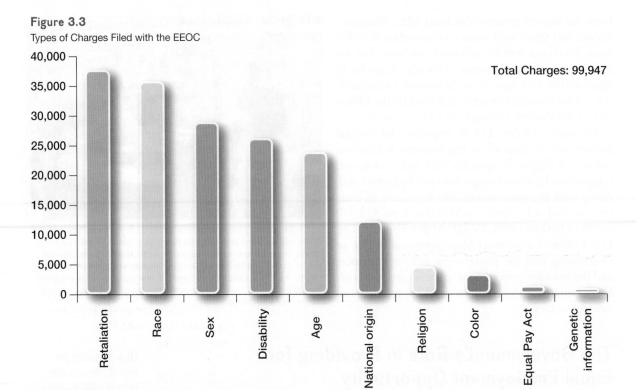

Total Charges: 99,947

SOURCE: Equal Employment Opportunity Commission, "Charge Statistics FY 1997 through FY 2011," http://www1.eeoc.gov, accessed February 14, 2012.

EEO-1 Report
The EEOC's Employer Information Report, which counts employees sorted by job category, sex, ethnicity, and race.

discrimination. A settlement with the EEOC can be costly, including such remedies as back pay, reinstatement of the employee, and promotions.

If the attempt at a settlement fails, the EEOC has two options. It may issue a "right to sue" letter to the alleged victim. This letter certifies that the agency has investigated the victim's allegations and found them to be valid. The EEOC's other option, which it uses less often, is to aid the alleged victim in bringing suit in federal court.

The EEOC also monitors organizations' hiring practices. Each year organizations that are government contractors or subcontractors or have 100 or more employees must file an Employer Information Report (EEO-1) with the EEOC. The **EEO-1 report** is an online questionnaire requesting the number of employees in each job category (such as managers, professionals, and laborers), broken down by their status as male or female, Hispanic or non-Hispanic, and members of various racial groups. The EEOC analyzes those reports to identify patterns of discrimination, which the agency can then attack through class-action lawsuits. Employers must display EEOC posters detailing employment rights. These posters must be in prominent and accessible locations—for example, in a company's cafeteria or near its time clock. Also, employers should retain copies of documents related to employment decisions—recruitment letters, announcements of jobs, completed job applications, selections for training, and so on. Employers must keep these records for at least six months or until a complaint is resolved, whichever is later.

Besides resolving complaints and suing alleged violators, the EEOC issues guidelines designed to help employers determine when their decisions violate the laws enforced by the EEOC. These guidelines are not laws themselves. However, the courts give great consideration to them when hearing employment discrimination cases.

For example, the ***Uniform Guidelines on Employee Selection Procedures*** is a set of guidelines issued by the EEOC and other government agencies. The guidelines identify ways an organization should develop and administer its system for selecting employees so as not to violate Title VII. The courts often refer to the *Uniform Guidelines* to determine whether a company has engaged in discriminatory conduct. Similarly, in the *Federal Register*, the EEOC has published guidelines providing details about what the agency will consider illegal and legal in the treatment of disabled individuals under the Americans with Disabilities Act. Following these guidelines might have prevented some of the costly cases mentioned in the "HR Oops!" box.

Office of Federal Contract Compliance Programs (OFCCP)

The **Office of Federal Contract Compliance Programs (OFCCP)** is the agency responsible for enforcing the executive orders that cover companies doing business with the federal government. As we stated earlier in the chapter, businesses with contracts for more than $50,000 may not discriminate in employment based on race, color, religion, national origin, or sex, and they must have a written affirmative-action plan on file. This plan must include three basic components:

1. *Utilization analysis*—A comparison of the race, sex, and ethnic composition of the employer's workforce with that of the available labor supply. The percentages in the employer's workforce should not be greatly lower than the percentages in the labor supply.
2. *Goals and timetables*—The percentages of women and minorities the organization seeks to employ in each job group, and the dates by which the percentages are to be attained. These are meant to be more flexible than quotas, requiring only that the employer have goals and be seeking to achieve the goals.
3. *Action steps*—A plan for how the organization will meet its goals. Besides working toward its goals for hiring women and minorities, the company must take affirmative steps toward hiring Vietnam veterans and individuals with disabilities.

Each year, the OFCCP audits government contractors to ensure they are actively pursuing the goals in their plans. The OFCCP examines the plan and conducts on-site visits to examine how individual employees perceive the company's affirmative-action policies. If the agency finds that a contractor or subcontractor is not complying with the requirements, it has several options. It may notify the EEOC (if there is evidence of a violation of Title VII), advise the Department of Justice to begin criminal proceedings, request that the Secretary of Labor cancel or suspend any current contracts with the company, and forbid the firm from bidding on future contracts. For a company that depends on the federal government for a sizable share of its business, that last penalty is severe.

Businesses' Role in Providing for Equal Employment Opportunity

Rare is the business owner or manager who wants to wait for the government to identify that the business has failed to provide for equal employment opportunity. Instead, out of motives ranging from concern for fairness to the desire to avoid costly lawsuits and settlements, most companies recognize the importance of complying with these laws. Often, management depends on the expertise of human resource professionals to help in identifying how to comply. These professionals can help organizations take steps to avoid discrimination and provide reasonable accommodation.

Uniform Guidelines on Employee Selection Procedures
Guidelines issued by the EEOC and other agencies to identify how an organization should develop and administer its system for selecting employees so as not to violate antidiscrimination laws.

Office of Federal Contract Compliance Programs (OFCCP)
The agency responsible for enforcing the executive orders that cover companies doing business with the federal government.

LO 3-4 Describe ways employers can avoid illegal discrimination and provide reasonable accommodation.

Record-Breaking Discrimination Charges

In recent years, as businesses and individuals have struggled with an agonizingly slow economic recovery, a growing number of workers have said they faced another kind of agony: discrimination by employers. The Equal Employment Opportunity Commission reported in January 2011 that charges of employment discrimination hit a record the previous year. A year later, the EEOC said charges broke the 2010 record, hitting an all-time high of 99,947 in 2011.

What were employees complaining about? Charges of race and sex discrimination remained the top complaints, although their numbers actually declined. Charges of disability and age discrimination rose, however. Among the cases resolved by the EEOC, disability discrimination charges cost employers $103.4 million in penalties in 2011, up 35.9 percent from the year before.

Questions

1. Why do you think discrimination charges rose when the economy was barely recovering and unemployment was high?

Might it have something to do with the behavior of employers or the options available to employees (or both)?
2. Why does it matter how employers treat employees during a time of high unemployment?

SOURCES: Equal Employment Opportunity Commission, "Private Sector Bias Charges Hit All-Time High," news release, January 25, 2012, http://www1.eeoc.gov; Melanie Trottman, "Charges of Bias at Work Hit Record," *The Wall Street Journal,* January 12, 2011, http://online.wsj.com.

Avoiding Discrimination

How would you know if you had been discriminated against? Decisions about human resources are so complex that discrimination is often difficult to identify and prove. However, legal scholars and court rulings have arrived at some ways to show evidence of discrimination.

Disparate Treatment
Differing treatment of individuals, where the differences are based on the individuals' race, color, religion, sex, national origin, age, or disability status.

Disparate Treatment One potential sign of discrimination is **disparate treatment**—differing treatment of individuals, where the differences are based on the individuals' race, color, religion, sex, national origin, age, or disability status. For example, disparate treatment would include hiring or promoting one person over an equally qualified person because of the individual's race. Or suppose a company fails to hire women with school-age children (claiming the women will be frequently absent) but hires men with school-age children. In that situation, the women are victims of disparate treatment, because they are being treated differently based on their sex. To sustain a claim of discrimination based on disparate treatment, the women would have to prove that the employer intended to discriminate.

To avoid disparate treatment, companies can evaluate the questions and investigations they use in making employment decisions. These should be applied equally. For example, if the company investigates conviction records of job applicants, it should investigate them for all applicants, not just for applicants from certain racial groups. Companies may want to avoid some types of questions altogether. For example, questions about marital status can cause problems, because interviewers may unfairly make different assumptions about men and women. (Common stereotypes about women have been that a married woman is less flexible or more likely to get pregnant than a single woman, in contrast to the assumption that a married man is more stable and committed to his work.)

Evaluating interview questions and decision criteria to make sure they are job related is especially important given that bias is not always intentional or even conscious.

Researchers have conducted studies finding differences between what people *say* about how they evaluate others and how people actually *act* on their attitudes. Duke University business professor Ashleigh Shelby Rosette has found various ways to uncover how individuals evaluate the performance of others.[10] In a recent study, she and colleagues compared the way sports reporters interpreted the performance of college quarterbacks—the leaders of football teams. The researchers found that when teams with a white quarterback performed well, the commentators more often gave credit to the intelligence of the quarterback. When the winning teams had a black quarterback, the announcers were more likely to praise the athletic strengths of the quarterback. When teams with a black quarterback lost, the announcers blamed the quarterback's decision making. In prior research, Rosette has found similar patterns in commentary about the leadership of corporations. In describing successful companies led by black managers, analysts more often credit the managers for their good sense of humor or speaking ability or even point to a favorable market rather than crediting the leaders for their intelligence. Notice that the pattern is not to say people consciously think the black leaders lack intelligence; rather, the association between the leader and intelligence simply is not made. These results suggest that even when we doubt we have biases, it may be helpful to use decision-making tools that keep the focus on the most important criteria.

Is disparate treatment ever legal? The courts have held that in some situations, a factor such as sex or race may be a **bona fide occupational qualification (BFOQ)**, that is, a necessary (not merely preferred) qualification for performing a job. A typical example is a job that includes handing out towels in a locker room. Requiring that employees who perform this job in the women's locker room be female is a BFOQ. However, it is very difficult to think of many jobs where criteria such as sex and race are BFOQs. In a widely publicized case from the 1990s, Johnson Controls, a manufacturer of car batteries, instituted a "fetal protection" policy that excluded women of childbearing age from jobs that would expose them to lead, which can cause birth defects. Johnson Controls argued that the policy was intended to provide a safe workplace and that sex was a BFOQ for jobs that involved exposure to lead. However, the Supreme Court disagreed, ruling that BFOQs are limited to policies directly related to a worker's ability to do the job.[11]

Bona Fide Occupational Qualification (BFOQ)
A necessary (not merely preferred) qualification for performing a job.

Disparate Impact   Another way to assess potential discrimination is by identifying **disparate impact**—a condition in which employment practices are seemingly neutral yet disproportionately exclude a protected group from employment opportunities. In other words, the company's employment practices lack obvious discriminatory content, but they affect one group differently than others. Examples of employment practices that might result in disparate impact include pay, hiring, promotions, or training. In the area of hiring, for example, many companies encourage their employees to refer friends and family members for open positions. These referrals can produce a pool of well-qualified candidates who would be a good fit with the organization's culture and highly motivated to work with people they already know. However, given people's tendency to associate with others like themselves, this practice also can have an unintentional disparate impact on groups not already well represented at the employer. Organizations that encourage employee referrals therefore should combine the program with other kinds of recruitment and make sure that every group in the organization is equally encouraged to participate in the referral program.[12]

A commonly used test of disparate impact is the **four-fifths rule**, which finds evidence of potential discrimination if the hiring rate for a minority group is less than four-fifths the hiring rate for the majority group. Keep in mind that this rule of thumb

Disparate Impact
A condition in which employment practices are seemingly neutral yet disproportionately exclude a protected group from employment opportunities.

Four-Fifths Rule
Rule of thumb that finds evidence of potential discrimination if an organization's hiring rate for a minority group is less than four-fifths the hiring rate for the majority group.

compares *rates* of hiring, not numbers of employees hired. Figure 3.4 illustrates how to apply the four-fifths rule.

If the four-fifths rule is not satisfied, it provides evidence of potential discrimination. To avoid declarations of practicing illegally, an organization must show that the disparate impact caused by the practice is based on a "business necessity." This is accomplished by showing that the employment practice is related to a legitimate business need or goal. In our example, the city could argue that disparate impact of the pay increases between younger and older police officers and dispatchers was necessary to keep pay within the city's budget. Of course, it is ultimately up to the court to decide if the evidence provided by the organization shows a real business necessity or is illegal. The court will also consider if other practices could have been used that would have met the business need or goal but not resulted in discrimination.

An important distinction between disparate treatment and disparate impact is the role of the employer's intent. Proving disparate treatment in court requires showing that the employer intended the disparate treatment, but a plaintiff need not show intent in the case of disparate impact. It is enough to show that the result of the treatment was unequal. For example, the requirements for some jobs, such as firefighters or pilots, have sometimes included a minimum height. Although the intent may be to identify people who can perform the jobs, an unintended result may be disparate impact on groups that are shorter than average. Women tend to be shorter than men, and people of Asian ancestry tend to be shorter than people of European ancestry.

One way employers can avoid disparate impact is to be sure that employment decisions are really based on relevant, valid measurements. If a job requires a certain amount of strength and stamina, the employer would want measures of strength and stamina, not simply individuals' height and weight. The latter numbers are easier to obtain but more likely to result in charges of discrimination. Assessing validity of a measure can be a highly technical exercise requiring the use of statistics. The essence of such an assessment is to show that test scores or other measurements are significantly related

Figure 3.4

Applying the Four-Fifths Rule

Example: A new hotel has to hire employees to fill 100 positions. Out of 300 total applicants, 200 are black and the remaining 100 are white. The hotel hires 40 of the black applicants and 60 of the white applicants.

Step 1: Find the Rates

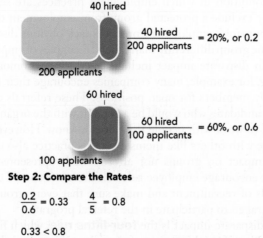

40 hired

$$\frac{40 \text{ hired}}{200 \text{ applicants}} = 20\%, \text{ or } 0.2$$

200 applicants

60 hired

$$\frac{60 \text{ hired}}{100 \text{ applicants}} = 60\%, \text{ or } 0.6$$

100 applicants

Step 2: Compare the Rates

$$\frac{0.2}{0.6} = 0.33 \qquad \frac{4}{5} = 0.8$$

$$0.33 < 0.8$$

The four-fifths requirement is not satisfied, providing evidence of potential discrimination.

Correcting Pay Inequity

Government data show that women are surpassing men in attending and graduating from college, but when it comes to pay, men still outearn women. One reason is that women are more likely than men to hold administrative jobs, which tend to pay less, and men are likelier to hold jobs in engineering and computers, which tend to pay more. But even in similar positions, men continue to earn more than their female co-workers.

This pattern poses a challenge for employers who find pay gaps within their organization. Here are some ways that HR departments are addressing pay inequity to promote fairness, value diversity, and avoid charges of discrimination:

- Increase the lower-paid employees' salaries so they are comparable to the salaries of the higher-paid group. This change may be costly—although perhaps it is a bargain relative to the cost to settle a discrimination lawsuit. If a one-time bump in pay would devastate the bottom line, the employer could phase in the change gradually over a few years.

- Analyze the data carefully, and keep complete records of performance reviews and pay decisions. It is possible that a pay gap really is related to differences in performance. But disparate impact could look suspicious, so relevant performance criteria, fair decisions, and accurate records of both may become essential to protect the employer if a complaint is filed.

- Try to avoid the pay gap from continuing. Make sure the lower-paid employees are getting enough training, strong mentoring, and appropriate assignments to reach their full potential. Keep managers informed of pay gaps that exist in their group, and help them better develop women or other team members who are lagging behind.

SOURCES: Conor Dougherty, "Strides by Women, Still a Wage Gap," *The Wall Street Journal,* March 1, 2011, http://online.wsj .com; "HR Pros Believe Gender Pay Gaps Exist—but What to Do about It?" *Report on Salary Surveys* (Bureau of National Affairs), April 2011, pp. 1–8; Joann S. Lublin, "Coaching Urged for Women," *The Wall Street Journal,* April 4, 2011, http://online.wsj.com.

to job performance. Some employers are also distancing themselves from information that could be seen as producing a disparate impact. For example, many employers are investigating candidates by looking up their social-media profiles. This raises the possibility that candidates for hiring or promotion could say the company passes them over because of information revealed about, say, their religion or ethnic background. Therefore, some companies hire an outside researcher to check profiles and report only information related to the person's job-related qualifications.[13]

Many employers also address the challenge of disparate impact by analyzing their pay data to look for patterns that could signal unintended discrimination. If they find such patterns, they face difficult decisions about how to correct any inequities, as described in "HR How To."

EEO Policy   Employers can also avoid discrimination and defend against claims of discrimination by establishing and enforcing an EEO policy. The policy should define and prohibit unlawful behaviors, as well as provide procedures for making and investigating complaints. The policy also should require that employees at all levels engage in fair conduct and respectful language. Derogatory language can support a court claim of discrimination.

Affirmative Action and Reverse Discrimination   In the search for ways to avoid discrimination, some organizations have used affirmative-action programs, usually to increase the representation of minorities. In its original form, affirmative action was meant as taking extra effort to attract and retain minority employees. These efforts have included extensively recruiting minority candidates on college campuses, advertising in minority-oriented publications, and providing educational and training opportunities to minorities. However, over the years, many organizations have resorted to quotas, or numerical goals for the proportion of certain minority groups, to ensure that their workforce mirrors the proportions of the labor market. Sometimes these organizations act voluntarily; in other cases, the quotas are imposed by the courts or the EEOC.

Whatever the reasons for these hiring programs, by increasing the proportion of minority or female candidates hired or promoted, they necessarily reduce the proportion of white or male candidates hired or promoted. In many cases, white and/or male individuals have fought against affirmative action and quotas, alleging what is called *reverse discrimination*. In other words, the organizations are allegedly discriminating against white males by preferring women and minorities. Affirmative action remains controversial in the United States. Surveys have found that Americans are least likely to favor affirmative action when programs use quotas.[14]

Providing Reasonable Accommodation

Reasonable Accommodation
An employer's obligation to do something to enable an otherwise qualified person to perform a job.

Especially in situations involving religion and individuals with disabilities, equal employment opportunity may require that an employer make **reasonable accommodation**. In employment law, this term refers to an employer's obligation to do something to enable an otherwise qualified person to perform a job. Accommodations for an employee's religion often involve decisions about what kinds of clothing to permit or require. Imperial Security ran afoul of discrimination laws when it would not allow a Muslim security guard to wear a *khimar*, a covering for her hair, ears, and neck. When the employee arrived for her first day on the job, she was asked to remove the *khimar*. When she said she couldn't because her religion required it, the company fired her. In contrast, Belk, a retailer, requested that an employee wear a Santa hat and holiday apron during the weeks leading up to Christmas. The employee, a Jehovah's Witness, explained that her religion does not permit her to celebrate holidays, so she would not wear the items. Her company also fired her for not complying with its dress requirements. In both cases, the EEOC filed a lawsuit against the employer and eventually settled for tens of thousands of dollars.[15]

In the context of religion, this principle recognizes that for some individuals, religious observations and practices may present a conflict with work duties, dress codes, or company practices. For example, some religions require head coverings, or individuals might need time off to observe the sabbath or other holy days, when the company might have them scheduled to work. When the employee has a legitimate religious belief requiring accommodation, the employee should demonstrate this need to the employer. Assuming that it would not present an undue hardship, employers are required to accommodate such religious practices. They may have to adjust schedules so that employees do not have to work on days when their religion forbids it, or they may have to alter dress or grooming requirements.

For employees with disabilities, reasonable accommodations also vary according to the individuals' needs. As shown in Figure 3.5, employers may restructure jobs, make facilities in the workplace more accessible, modify equipment, or reassign an employee to a job that the person can perform. In some situations, a disabled individual may provide his or her own accommodation, which the employer allows, as in the case of a blind worker who brings a guide dog to work.

Figure 3.5

Examples of Reasonable Accommodations under the ADA

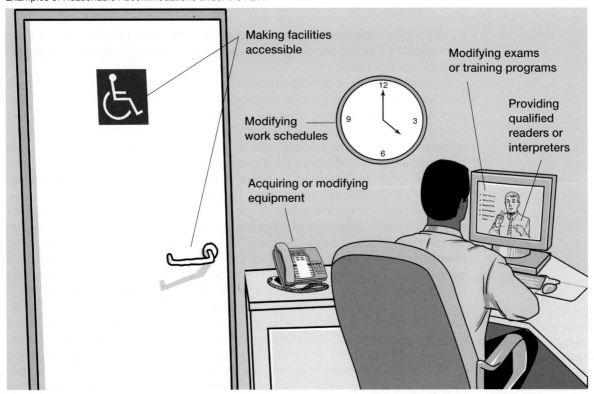

Note: Reasonable accommodations do *not* include hiring an unqualified person, lowering quality standards, or compromising co-workers' safety.

SOURCE: Based on Equal Employment Opportunity Commission, "The ADA: Your Responsibilities as an Employer," modified August 1, 2008, www.eeoc.gov.

If accommodating a disability would require significant expense or difficulty, however, the employer may be exempt from the reasonable accommodation requirement (although the employer may have to defend this position in court). An accommodation is considered "reasonable" if it does not impose an undue hardship on the employer, such as an expense that is large in relation to a company's resources.

Preventing Sexual Harassment

Based on Title VII's prohibition of sex discrimination, the EEOC defines sexual harassment of employees as unlawful employment discrimination. **Sexual harassment** refers to unwelcome sexual advances. The EEOC has defined the types of behavior and the situations under which this behavior constitutes sexual harassment:

> Unwelcome sexual advances, requests for sexual favors, and other verbal or physical contact of a sexual nature constitute sexual harassment when
>
> 1. Submission to such conduct is made either explicitly or implicitly a term or condition of an individual's employment,
> 2. Submission to or rejection of such conduct by an individual is used as the basis for employment decisions affecting such individual, or

LO 3-5 Define sexual harassment, and tell how employers can eliminate or minimize it.

Sexual Harassment
Unwelcome sexual advances as defined by the EEOC.

3. Such conduct has the purpose or effect of unreasonably interfering with an individual's work performance or creating an intimidating, hostile, or offensive working environment.[16]

Under these guidelines, preventing sexual discrimination includes managing the workplace in a way that does not permit anybody to threaten or intimidate employees through sexual behavior.

In general, the most obvious examples of sexual harassment involve *quid pro quo harassment*, meaning that a person makes a benefit (or punishment) contingent on an employee's submitting to (or rejecting) sexual advances. For example, a manager who promises a raise to an employee who will participate in sexual activities is engaging in quid pro quo harassment. Likewise, it would be sexual harassment to threaten to reassign someone to a less-desirable job if that person refuses sexual favors.

A more subtle, and possibly more pervasive, form of sexual harassment is to create or permit a "hostile working environment." This occurs when someone's behavior in the workplace creates an environment in which it is difficult for someone of a particular sex to work. Common complaints in sexual harassment lawsuits include claims that harassers ran their fingers through the plaintiffs' hair, made suggestive remarks, touched intimate body parts, posted pictures with sexual content in the workplace, and used sexually explicit language or told sex-related jokes. The reason that these behaviors are considered discrimination is that they treat individuals differently based on their sex.

Although a large majority of sexual harassment complaints received by the EEOC involve women being harassed by men, a growing share of sexual harassment claims have been filed by men. Some of the men claimed that they were harassed by women, but same-sex harassment also occurs and is illegal. In one case, a teenager working at McDonald's eventually overcame his embarrassment and reported that a male manager was making sexual comments and had started grabbing him. Three other employees also came forward and filed a complaint with the EEOC. The restaurant settled the lawsuit for $90,000.[17]

To ensure a workplace free from sexual harassment, organizations can follow some important steps. First, the organization can develop a policy statement making it very clear that sexual harassment will not be tolerated in the workplace. Second, all employees, new and old, can be trained to identify inappropriate workplace behavior. In addition, the organization can develop a mechanism for reporting sexual harassment in a way that encourages people to speak out. Finally, management can prepare to act promptly to discipline those who engage in sexual harassment, as well as to protect the victims of sexual harassment.

Valuing Diversity

As we mentioned in Chapter 2, the United States is a diverse nation, and becoming more so. In addition, many U.S. companies have customers and operations in more than one country. Managers differ in how they approach the challenges related to this diversity. Some define a diverse workforce as a competitive advantage that brings them a wider pool of talent and greater insight into the needs and behaviors of their diverse customers. These organizations say they have a policy of *valuing diversity*.

The practice of valuing diversity has no single form; it is not written into law or business theory. Organizations that value diversity may practice some form of affirmative action, discussed earlier. They may have policies stating their value of understanding and respecting differences. Organizations may try to hire, reward, and promote employees who demonstrate respect for others. They may sponsor training programs

Organizations that value diversity may try to hire, reward, and promote employees who demonstrate respect for others.

designed to teach employees about differences among groups. Whatever their form, these efforts are intended to make each individual feel respected. Also, these actions can support equal employment opportunity by cultivating an environment in which individuals feel welcome and able to do their best.

Valuing diversity, especially in support of an organization's mission and strategy, need not be limited to the categories protected by law. For example, many organizations see workers struggling to meet the demands of family and career, so they provide family-friendly benefits and policies, as described in Chapter 13. Managers and human resource professionals also are concerned about learning how to treat transgender employees respectfully and appropriately. Transgender individuals who are transitioning to the opposite sex would typically change their names. This change involves administrative decisions for a human resource department. Some of these—for example, changing e-mail addresses and business cards—are a simple matter of calling employees by the names they wish to use. Typically, organizations already do this when, for example, Rebecca Jones wants to be known as Becky or Paul John Smith wants to be known as P. J. If company policies are too rigid to allow this kind of personal decision, the needs of the transgender employee may prompt a review of the policies. Other aspects of the change must meet legal requirements; for example, the name on tax documents must match the name on the employee's social security card, so changing those documents must wait for a legal name change. Even so, employers can respect diversity by demanding no more documentation for name changes in this situation than in other types of name changes (for example, for a woman who wishes to change her name after getting married).[18]

Occupational Safety and Health Act (OSH Act)

Like equal employment opportunity, the protection of employee safety and health is regulated by the government. Through the 1960s, workplace safety was primarily an issue between workers and employers. By 1970, however, roughly 15,000 work-related

LO 3-6 Explain employers' duties under the Occupational Safety and Health Act.

Occupational Safety and Health Act (OSH Act)
U.S. law authorizing the federal government to establish and enforce occupational safety and health standards for all places of employment engaging in interstate commerce.

Occupational Safety and Health Administration (OSHA)
Labor Department agency responsible for inspecting employers, applying safety and health standards, and levying fines for violation.

fatalities occurred every year. That year, Congress enacted the **Occupational Safety and Health Act (OSH Act)**, the most comprehensive U.S. law regarding worker safety. The OSH Act authorized the federal government to establish and enforce occupational safety and health standards for all places of employment engaging in interstate commerce.

The OSH Act divided enforcement responsibilities between the Department of Labor and the Department of Health. Under the Department of Labor, the **Occupational Safety and Health Administration (OSHA)** is responsible for inspecting employers, applying safety and health standards, and levying fines for violation. The Department of Health is responsible for conducting research to determine the criteria for specific operations or occupations and for training employers to comply with the act. Much of the research is conducted by the National Institute for Occupational Safety and Health (NIOSH).

General and Specific Duties

The main provision of the OSH Act states that each employer has a general duty to furnish each employee a place of employment free from recognized hazards that cause or are likely to cause death or serious physical harm. This is called the act's *general-duty clause*. Employers also must keep records of work-related injuries and illnesses and post an annual summary of these records from February 1 to April 30 in the following year. Figure 3.6 shows a sample of OSHA's Form 300A, the annual summary that must be posted, even if no injuries or illnesses occurred.

The act also grants specific rights; for example, employees have the right to:

- Request an inspection.
- Have a representative present at an inspection.
- Have dangerous substances identified.
- Be promptly informed about exposure to hazards and be given access to accurate records regarding exposure.
- Have employer violations posted at the work site.

Although OSHA regulations have a (sometimes justifiable) reputation for being complex, a company can get started in meeting these requirements by visiting OSHA's website (**www.osha .gov**) and looking up resources such as the agency's *Small Business Handbook* and its step-by-step guide called "Compliance Assistance Quick Start."

The Department of Labor recognizes many specific types of hazards, and employers must comply with all the occupational safety and health standards published by NIOSH. With regard to formaldehyde, for example, the agency has determined limits for permissible exposure. It also recommends that workers avoid formaldehyde-containing products when safer alternatives are available, as well as use of ventilation and protective equipment when the formaldehyde cannot be avoided. All of these requirements were not enough, however, when a pattern of injuries led to the discovery that hair salon workers were being exposed to formaldehyde in Brazilian Blowout hair-smoothing solution. Contrary to legal requirements, the manufacturer had not been providing

OSHA is responsible for inspecting businesses, applying safety and health standards, and levying fines for violations. OSHA regulations prohibit notifying employers of inspections in advance.

Figure 3.6

OSHA Form 300A: Summary of Work-Related Injuries and Illnesses

OSHA's Form 300A (Rev. 01/2004)

Summary of Work-Related Injuries and Illnesses

Year 20____

All establishments covered by Part 1904 must complete this Summary page, even if no work-related injuries or illnesses occurred during the year. Remember to review the Log to verify that the entries are complete and accurate before completing this summary.

Using the Log, count the individual entries you made for each category. Then write the totals below, making sure you've added the entries from every page of the Log. If you had no cases, write "0."

Employees, former employees, and their representatives have the right to review the OSHA Form 300 in its entirety. They also have limited access to the OSHA Form 301 or its equivalent. See 29 CFR Part 1904.35, in OSHA's recordkeeping rule, for further details on the access provisions for these forms.

Number of Cases

Total number of deaths	Total number of cases with days away from work	Total number of cases with job transfer or restriction	Total number of other recordable cases
____ (G)	____ (H)	____ (I)	____ (J)

Number of Days

Total number of days away from work	Total number of days of job transfer or restriction
____ (K)	____ (L)

Injury and Illness Types

Total number of . . .
(M)

(1) Injuries ____
(2) Skin disorders ____
(3) Respiratory conditions ____
(4) Poisonings ____
(5) Hearing loss ____
(6) All other illnesses ____

Post this Summary page from February 1 to April 30 of the year following the year covered by the form.

Public reporting burden for this collection of information is estimated to average 58 minutes per response, including time to review the instructions, search and gather the data needed, and complete and review the collection of information. Persons are not required to respond to the collection of information unless it displays a currently valid OMB control number. If you have any comments about these estimates or any other aspects of this data collection, contact: US Department of Labor, OSHA Office of Statistical Analysis, Room N-3644, 200 Constitution Avenue, NW, Washington, DC 20210. Do not send the completed forms to this office.

Establishment information

Your establishment name _____

Street _____

City _____ State ____ ZIP ____

Industry description (e.g., Manufacture of motor truck trailers) _____

Standard Industrial Classification (SIC), if known (e.g., 3715) _____

OR

North American Industrial Classification (NAICS), if known (e.g., 336212) _____

Employment information *(If you don't have these figures, see the Worksheet on the back of this page to estimate.)*

Annual average number of employees _____

Total hours worked by all employees last year _____

Sign here

Knowingly falsifying this document may result in a fine.

I certify that I have examined this document and that to the best of my knowledge the entries are true, accurate, and complete.

_____ Company executive _____ Title _____

(____) Phone _____ Date __/__/__

SOURCE: *The OSHA Recordkeeping Handbook,* U.S. Dept. of Labor, April 1, 2010, http://osha.gov/recordkeeping/new-osha300form1-1-04.pdf.

What NIOSH Wants the Police to Watch on YouTube

As anyone who has ridden a bicycle for more than a few hours knows, those skinny bicycle seats get more than a little uncomfortable. In fact, there is some evidence that the constant pressure on a male rider's groin can restrict blood flow to the genitals and potentially interfere with sexual function. This uncomfortable side effect of an otherwise healthy sport becomes an occupational hazard when police officers are assigned to bicycle patrol units.

The National Institute for Occupational Safety and Health (NIOSH) worked with several police departments to investigate the problem and test bike saddles that would promote better health. As a result, NIOSH has identified a protective measure in the form of "noseless" bicycle seats. These seats omit the "nose" that causes groin pressure. According to NIOSH, the benefits may even extend to making the ride more comfortable for female bicycle users. NIOSH then published its recommendation to use no-nose saddles and made the recommendations available on its website.

Still, many people have never heard of a "noseless" bicycle seat. To explain what this product is, describe how it can benefit users, and encourage bicycle patrol officers to consider using the seats, NIOSH produced a minute-and-a-half-long video called "Safety Check." In the video, Chicago police bicycle officers check their safety equipment, including the "noseless" seats, before going out on patrol. NIOSH has posted it on YouTube. Placing it on social media makes the information available to anyone who might be open to riding more safely.

SOURCES: National Institute for Occupational Safety and Health (NIOSH), "Lights, Camera, Action, Occupational Health Information: NIOSH Uses Social Media to Highlight Police Bike Recommendations," news release, December 20, 2011, http://www.cdc.gov/niosh/; NIOSH, "Bicycle Saddles and Reproductive Health," NIOSH Topics, http://www.cdc.gov/niosh, last updated November 17, 2011; Joe Andruzzi, "Noseless Saddles Provide Protection," International Police Mountain Bike Association, http://www.ipmba.org, accessed February 21, 2012.

the required documentation indicating that the product contains formaldehyde. Stylists using the product were experiencing breathing problems, burning eyes, and other symptoms. Under a settlement with California's attorney general, the maker of Brazilian Blowout paid a fine of $600,000 and began to publish the required disclosures.[19]

Although NIOSH publishes numerous standards, it is impossible for regulators to anticipate all possible hazards that could occur in the workplace. Thus, the general-duty clause requires employers to be constantly alert for potential sources of harm in the workplace (as defined by the standard of what a reasonably prudent person would do) and to correct them. Information about hazards can come from employees or from outside researchers. The union-backed Center for Construction Research and Training sponsored research into the safety problems related to constructing energy-efficient buildings. The study found that workers in "green" construction faced greater risks of falling and were exposed to new risks from building innovations such as rooftop gardens and facilities for treating wastewater. Employers need to make these construction sites safer through measures such as better fall protection and more use of prefabrication.[20] For another example, see the "HRM Social" box, which describes one way NIOSH has been posting online the results of research aimed at promoting worker health and safety.

LO 3-7 Describe the role of the Occupational Safety and Health Administration.

Enforcement of the OSH Act

To enforce the OSH Act, the Occupational Safety and Health Administration conducts inspections. OSHA compliance officers typically arrive at a workplace unannounced; for obvious reasons, OSHA regulations prohibit notifying employers of inspections in advance. After presenting credentials, the compliance officer tells the employer the reasons for the inspection and describes, in a general way, the procedures necessary to conduct the investigation.

An OSHA inspection has four major components. First, the compliance officer reviews the company's records of deaths, injuries, and illnesses. OSHA requires this kind of record keeping at all firms with 11 or more full- or part-time employees. Next, the officer—typically accompanied by a representative of the employer (and perhaps by a representative of the employees)—conducts a "walkaround" tour of the employer's premises. On this tour, the officer notes any conditions that may violate specific published standards or the less specific general-duty clause. The third component of the inspection, employee interviews, may take place during the tour. At this time, anyone who is aware of a violation can bring it to the officer's attention. Finally, in a closing conference, the compliance officer discusses the findings with the employer, noting any violations.

Following an inspection, OSHA gives the employer a reasonable time frame within which to correct the violations identified. If a violation could cause serious injury or death, the officer may seek a restraining order from a U.S. District Court. The restraining order compels the employer to correct the problem immediately. In addition, if an OSHA violation results in citations, the employer must post each citation in a prominent place near the location of the violation.

Besides correcting violations identified during the inspection, employers may have to pay fines. These fines range from $20,000 for violations that result in death of an employee to $1,000 for less-serious violations. Other penalties include criminal charges for falsifying records that are subject to OSHA inspection or for warning an employer of an OSHA inspection without permission from the Department of Labor.

Employee Rights and Responsibilities

Although the OSH Act makes employers responsible for protecting workers from safety and health hazards, employees have responsibilities as well. They have to follow OSHA's safety rules and regulations governing employee behavior. Employees also have a duty to report hazardous conditions.

Along with those responsibilities go certain rights. Employees may file a complaint and request an OSHA inspection of the workplace, and their employers may not retaliate against them for complaining. Employees also have a right to receive information about any hazardous chemicals they handle in the course of their jobs. OSHA's Hazard Communication Standard and many states' **right-to-know laws** require employers to provide employees with information about the health risks associated with exposure to substances considered hazardous. State right-to-know laws may be more stringent than federal standards, so organizations should obtain requirements from their state's health and safety agency, as well as from OSHA.

Under OSHA's Hazard Communication Standard, organizations must have **material safety data sheets (MSDSs)** for chemicals that employees are exposed to. An MSDS is a form that details the hazards associated with a chemical; the chemical's producer or importer is responsible for identifying these hazards and detailing them on the form. Employers must also ensure that all containers of hazardous chemicals are labeled with information about the hazards, and they must train employees in safe handling of the chemicals. Office workers who encounter a chemical infrequently (such as a secretary who occasionally changes the toner in a copier) are not covered by these requirements. In the case of a copy machine, the Hazard Communication Standard would apply to someone whose job involves spending a large part of the day servicing or operating such equipment.

Right-to-Know Laws
State laws that require employers to provide employees with information about the health risks associated with exposure to substances considered hazardous.

Material Safety Data Sheets (MSDSs)
Forms on which chemical manufacturers and importers identify the hazards of their chemicals.

Impact of the OSH Act

The OSH Act has unquestionably succeeded in raising the level of awareness of occupational safety. Yet legislation alone cannot solve all the problems of work site safety. Indeed, the rate of occupational illnesses more than doubled between 1985 and 1990, according to the Bureau of Labor Statistics, while the rate of injuries rose by about 8 percent. However, as depicted in Figure 3.7, both rates have shown an overall downward trend since then.[21]

Many industrial accidents are a product of unsafe behaviors, not unsafe working conditions. Because the act does not directly regulate employee behavior, little behavior change can be expected unless employees are convinced of the standards' importance.[22]

Conforming to the law alone does not necessarily guarantee their employees will be safe, so many employers go beyond the letter of the law. In the next section we examine various kinds of employer-initiated safety awareness programs that comply with OSHA requirements and, in some cases, exceed them.

LO 3-8 Discuss ways employers promote worker safety and health.

Employer-Sponsored Safety and Health Programs

Many employers establish safety awareness programs to go beyond mere compliance with the OSH Act and attempt to instill an emphasis on safety. A safety awareness program has three primary components: identifying and communicating hazards, reinforcing safe practices, and promoting safety internationally.

Figure 3.7

Rates of Occupational Injuries and Illnesses

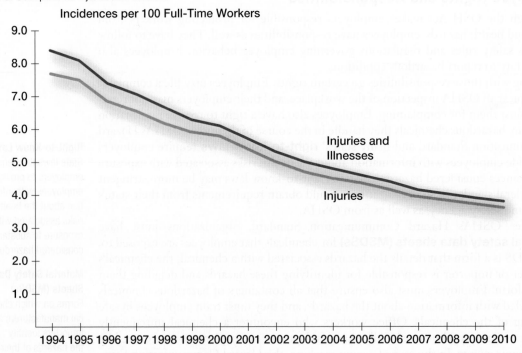

Incidences per 100 Full-Time Workers

Note: Data do not include fatal work-related injuries and illnesses.

SOURCE: Bureau of Labor Statistics, "Industry Injury and Illness Data," www.bls.gov, accessed February 14, 2012.

Identifying and Communicating Job Hazards

Employees, supervisors, and other knowledgeable sources need to sit down and discuss potential problems related to safety. One method for doing this is the **job hazard analysis technique**.[23] With this technique, each job is broken down into basic elements, and each of these is rated for its potential for harm or injury. If there is agreement that some job element has high hazard potential, the group isolates the element and considers possible technological or behavior changes to reduce or eliminate the hazard. This method poses some special challenges for high-tech companies, where workers may be exposed to materials and conditions that are not yet well understood. An example is nanotechnology, which involves applications of extremely tiny products. Masks and other traditional protective equipment do not necessarily prevent nanoparticles from entering the body, and their impact on health is not known. Some exposures may be harmless, but researchers are only beginning to learn their impact.[24]

Another means of isolating unsafe job elements is to study past accidents. The **technic of operations review (TOR)** is an analysis method for determining which specific element of a job led to a past accident.[25] The first step in a TOR analysis is to establish the facts surrounding the incident. To accomplish this, all members of the work group involved in the accident give their initial impressions of what happened. The group must then, through discussion, come to an agreement on the single, systematic failure that most likely contributed to the incident, as well as two or three major secondary factors that contributed to it.

McShane Construction Company combined job analysis with mobile computing technology when it signed on with Field ID to provide the software for its safety inspections. When safety inspectors visit construction sites, they use a mobile device to scan a bar code or read a radio frequency identification (RFID) tag on each piece of equipment. The code calls up a checklist of safety measures for that equipment, and the inspector simply checks off or scores the items one by one. The mobile device then transmits the inspection data to a Field ID database, where information can easily be retrieved if the company ever needs to study the cause of an accident.[26]

To communicate with employees about job hazards, managers should talk directly with their employees about safety. Memos also are important because the written communication helps establish a "paper trail" that can later document a history of the employer's concern regarding the job hazard. Posters, especially if placed near the hazard, serve as a constant reminder, reinforcing other messages.

In communicating risk, managers should recognize that different groups of individuals may constitute different audiences. Safety trainer Michael Topf often encounters workplaces where employees speak more than one language. In those situations, Topf says, it is important to provide bilingual training and signs. But English skills alone do not guarantee that safety messages will be understood. Supervisors and trainers need to use vocabulary and examples that employees will understand, and they need to ask for feedback in a culturally appropriate way. For example, in some cultures, employees will think it is improper to speak up if they see a problem. It is therefore important for managers to promote many opportunities for communication.[27] Human resource managers can support this effort by providing opportunities for supervisors to learn about the values and communication styles of the cultures represented at work.

Safety concerns and safety training needs also vary by age group. According to the Bureau of Labor Statistics, injuries and illnesses requiring time off from work occurred at the highest rate among workers between the ages of 45 and 54; workers aged 55 to 64 were the next highest group. However, patterns vary according to type

Job Hazard Analysis Technique
Safety promotion technique that involves breaking down a job into basic elements, then rating each element for its potential for harm or injury.

Technic of Operations Review (TOR)
Method of promoting safety by determining which specific element of a job led to a past accident.

Did You Know?

Top 10 Causes of Workplace Injuries

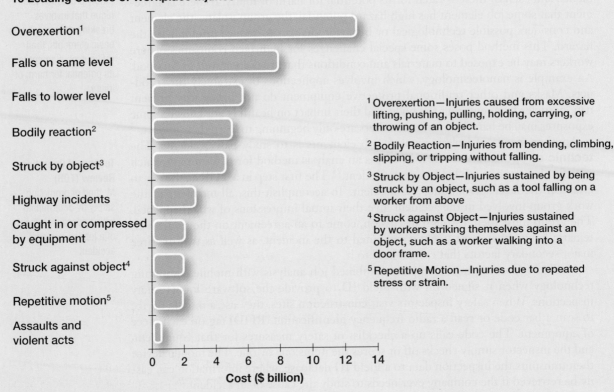

10 Leading Causes of Workplace Injuries in 2009

- Overexertion[1]
- Falls on same level
- Falls to lower level
- Bodily reaction[2]
- Struck by object[3]
- Highway incidents
- Caught in or compressed by equipment
- Struck against object[4]
- Repetitive motion[5]
- Assaults and violent acts

Cost ($ billion) — 0 2 4 6 8 10 12 14

[1] Overexertion—Injuries caused from excessive lifting, pushing, pulling, holding, carrying, or throwing of an object.

[2] Bodily Reaction—Injuries from bending, climbing, slipping, or tripping without falling.

[3] Struck by Object—Injuries sustained by being struck by an object, such as a tool falling on a worker from above

[4] Struck against Object—Injuries sustained by workers striking themselves against an object, such as a worker walking into a door frame.

[5] Repetitive Motion—Injuries due to repeated stress or strain.

Every year, Liberty Mutual conducts research it calls the Workplace Safety Index. In 2009, serious work-related injuries cost employers $50 billion. The leading cause was over-exertion (for example, excessive lifting, pushing, carrying, or throwing), followed by falls on the same level (rather than from a height, such as a ladder), and falls to a lower level.

Question

Think about your current job, your most recent job, or the job you would like to have. Which of the categories of injuries shown in the graph are most likely to occur on that job? (Don't assume injuries never occur in office jobs!)

SOURCES: Liberty Mutual Research Institute for Safety, "2011 Liberty Mutual Workplace Safety Index," http://www.libertymutualgroup.com/researchinstitute, accessed February 21, 2012; Roberto Ceniceros, "Top Five Workplace Injury Causes Make Up 72 Percent of Direct Workers' Comp Costs: Analysis," *Workforce*, January 10, 2012, http://www.workforce.com.

of injury. The Centers for Disease Control and Prevention found the highest rates of falls leading to a doctor visit occurring among people older than 75, with the next highest rate being among teenagers. Thus, safety training needs to address the needs of all age groups. Older workers may have more appreciation of the need for safety, as they have experienced the impact of wear and tear on their bodies and perhaps have seen people injured on the job. Younger workers will expect training to be fast-paced and engaging, and if possible, to incorporate technology. One trainer addressed the needs of multiple generations in a session on fall protection. The group reviewed a few slides of background information, then engaged in discussions of actual workplace conditions and planned how to protect workers. Finally, the group tried on the safety equipment required for their jobs.[28]

Reinforcing Safe Practices

To ensure safe behaviors, employers should not only define how to work safely but reinforce the desired behavior. One common technique for reinforcing safe practices is implementing a safety incentive program to reward workers for their support of and commitment to safety goals. Such programs start by focusing on monthly or quarterly goals or by encouraging suggestions for improving safety. Possible goals might include good housekeeping practices, adherence to safety rules, and proper use of protective equipment. Later, the program expands to include more wide-ranging, long-term goals. Typically, the employer distributes prizes in highly public forums, such as company or department meetings. Surprisingly, one of the most obvious ways to reinforce behavior often does not occur: when employees report unsafe conditions or behavior, the employer should take action to correct the problem. This response signals that the organization is serious when it says it values safety. In a recent survey of employees, most said their organization had a policy that encouraged reporting safety concerns, but many said they did not bother because they had come to expect a negative reaction or no response at all.[29]

Besides focusing on specific jobs, organizations can target particular types of injuries or disabilities, especially those for which employees may be at risk. For example, Prevent Blindness America estimates that more than 2,000 eye injuries occur every day in occupational settings.[30] Organizations can prevent such injuries through a combination of job analysis, written policies, safety training, protective eyewear, rewards and sanctions for safe and unsafe behavior, and management support for the safety effort. Similar practices for preventing other types of injuries are available in trade publications, through the National Safety Council, and on the website of the Occupational Safety and Health Administration (**www.osha.gov**).

Promoting Safety Internationally

Given the increasing focus on international management, organizations also need to consider how to ensure the safety of their employees regardless of the nation in which they operate. Cultural differences may make this more difficult than it seems. For example, a study examined the impact of one standardized corporationwide safety policy on employees in three different countries: the United States, France, and Argentina. The results of this study indicate that employees in the three countries interpreted the policy differently because of cultural differences. The individualistic, control-oriented culture of the United States stressed the role of top management in ensuring safety in a top-down fashion. However, this policy failed to work in Argentina, where the culture is more "collectivist" (emphasizing the group). Argentine employees tend to feel that safety is everyone's joint concern, so the safety programs needed to be defined from the bottom of the organization up.[31]

Another challenge in promoting safety internationally is that laws, enforcement practices, and political climates vary from country to country. With the increasing use of offshoring, described in Chapter 2, more companies have operations in countries where labor standards are far less strict than U.S. standards. Managers and employees in these countries may not think the company is serious about protecting workers' health and safety. In that case, strong communication and oversight will be necessary if the company intends to adhere to the ethical principle of valuing its foreign workers' safety as much as the safety of its U.S. workers. The Gap treats this issue as part of its corporate social responsibility. The company views its supply chain as socially sustainable only when working conditions and factory conditions meet acceptable business practices. According to Eva Sage-Gavin, Gap's executive vice president of human resources and corporate communications, "We know that better factory working conditions lead to better factories, and better factories make better products." In addition, Sage-Gavin notes, Gap employees in the United States care about working for a company they view as socially responsible, so these efforts also matter for corporate performance at home.[32]

THINKING ETHICALLY

IS DISCRIMINATION AGAINST THE UNEMPLOYED ETHICAL?

Following the financial industry's crisis in 2008, unemployment rates in the United States jumped above 7% for the first time in years, and stayed there. As the ranks of the unemployed swelled, workers found themselves unable to find a job month after month. Some could not even seem to get a job interview.

One reason for the difficulty landing an interview, much less a job, may be that some companies have established policies that they will only consider candidates who are currently employed. Companies are flooded with résumés, and considering only employed workers is one way to screen out those who perhaps were not the top performers, who couldn't prevent their former employers from going into decline, or who perhaps will be less stable in the months ahead as they cope with worn-out autos and unpaid bills. Those who held onto jobs during a severe recession might be the workers with exceptional skills and dedication, and they are in the best position to keep up with trends in their industry. Critics of these policies note that organizations could find other ways to identify the best-qualified candidates.

The Equal Employment Opportunity Commission noted that the recession did not affect all categories of workers equally. It held hearings to investigate whether policies to hire only currently employed workers would have a disparate impact on groups that were more likely to be unemployed: minorities and older and disabled persons. As of this writing, however, the EEOC has not completed its analysis or made recommendations.

Questions

1. How are workers affected by employers' policies to hire only those who are already employed? How are employers affected? Their customers? Communities where employers operate? Based on the impact of these policies on these groups, would you say the policies are ethical? Why or why not?
2. Is a policy to hire only employed people fair to workers? Would a law saying employers may not discriminate against the unemployed be fair to employers? Based on fairness, would you say discriminating against the unemployed is ethical? Why or why not?

SOURCES: Richard D. Alaniz, "Is It Legal to Only Hire the Already-Employed?" *Roofing Contractor,* October 2011, Business & Company Resource Center, http://galenet .galegroup.com; Catherine Rampell, "The Help-Wanted Sign Comes with a Frustrating Asterisk," *The New York Times,* July 25, 2011, http://www.nytimes.com; National Employment Law Project, "Hiring Discrimination against the Unemployed," briefing paper, July 12, 2011, http://www.nelp.org.

SUMMARY

LO 3-1 Explain how the three branches of government regulate human resource management.

The legislative branch develops laws such as those governing equal employment opportunity and worker safety and health. The executive branch establishes agencies such as the Equal Employment Opportunity Commission and Occupational Safety and Health Administration to enforce the laws by publishing regulations, filing lawsuits, and performing other activities. The president may also issue executive orders, such as requirements for federal contractors. The judicial branch hears cases related to employment law and interprets the law.

LO 3-2 Summarize the major federal laws requiring equal employment opportunity.

The Civil Rights Acts of 1866 and 1871 grants all persons equal property rights, contract rights, and the right to sue in federal court if they have been deprived of civil rights. The Equal Pay Act of 1963 requires equal pay for men and women who are doing work that is equal in terms of skill, effort, responsibility, and working conditions. Title VII of the Civil Rights Act of 1964 prohibits employment discrimination on the basis of race, color, religion, sex, or national origin. The Age Discrimination in Employment Act prohibits employment discrimination against persons older than 40. The Vocational Rehabilitation Act of 1973 requires that federal contractors engage in affirmative action in the employment of persons with disabilities. The Vietnam Era Veteran's Readjustment Act of 1974 requires affirmative action in employment of veterans who served during the Vietnam War. The Pregnancy Discrimination Act of 1978 treats discrimination based on pregnancy-related conditions as illegal sex discrimination. The Americans with Disabilities Act requires reasonable accommodations for qualified workers with disabilities. The Civil Rights Act of 1991 provides for compensatory and punitive damages in cases of discrimination. The Uniformed Services Employment and Reemployment Rights Act of 1994 requires that employers reemploy service members who left jobs to fulfill military duties. Under the Genetic Information Nondiscrimination Act (GINA) of 2008, employers may not use genetic information in making decisions related to the terms, conditions, or privileges of employment.

LO 3-3 Identify the federal agencies that enforce equal employment opportunity, and describe the role of each.

The Equal Employment Opportunity Commission is responsible for enforcing most of the EEO laws, including Title VII and the Americans with Disabilities Act. It investigates and resolves complaints, gathers information, and issues guidelines. The Office of Federal Contract Compliance Procedures is responsible for enforcing executive orders that call for affirmative action by companies that do business with the federal government. It monitors affirmative-action plans and takes action against companies that fail to comply.

LO 3-4 Describe ways employers can avoid illegal discrimination and provide reasonable accommodation.

Employers can avoid discrimination by avoiding disparate treatment of job applicants and employees, as well as policies that result in disparate impact. Companies can develop and enforce an EEO policy coupled with policies and practices that demonstrate a high value placed on diversity. Affirmative action may correct past discrimination, but quota-based activities can result in charges of reverse discrimination. To provide reasonable accommodation, companies should recognize needs based on individuals' religion or disabilities. Employees may need to make such accommodations as adjusting schedules or dress codes, making the workplace more accessible, or restructuring jobs.

LO 3-5 Define sexual harassment, and tell how employers can eliminate or minimize it.

Sexual harassment is unwelcome sexual advances and related behavior that makes submitting to the conduct a term of employment or the basis for employment decisions or that interferes with an individual's work performance or creates a work environment that is intimidating, hostile, or offensive. Organizations can prevent sexual harassment by developing a policy that defines and forbids it, training employees to recognize and avoid this behavior, and providing a means for employees to complain and be protected.

LO 3-6 Explain employers' duties under the Occupational Safety and Health Act.

Under the Occupational Safety and Health Act, employers have a general duty to provide employees a place of employment free from recognized safety and health hazards. They must inform employees about hazardous substances, maintain and post records of accidents and illnesses, and comply with NIOSH standards about specific occupational hazards.

LO 3-7 Describe the role of the Occupational Safety and Health Administration.

The Occupational Safety and Health Administration publishes regulations and conducts inspections. If OSHA finds violations, it discusses them with the employer and monitors the employer's response in correcting the violation.

LO 3-8 Discuss ways employers promote worker safety and health.

Besides complying with OSHA regulations, employers often establish safety awareness programs designed to instill an emphasis on safety. They may identify and communicate hazards through the job hazard analysis technique or the technic of operations review. They may adapt communications and training to the needs of different employees, such as differences in experience levels or cultural differences from one country to another. Employers may also establish incentive programs to reward safe behavior.

KEY TERMS

affirmative action, 68
bona fide occupational qualification (BFOQ), 77
disability, 69
disparate impact, 77
disparate treatment, 76
EEO-1 report, 74
equal employment opportunity (EEO), 64

Equal Employment Opportunity Commission (EEOC), 66
four-fifths rule, 77
job hazard analysis technique, 89
material safety data sheets (MSDSs), 87
Occupational Safety and Health Act (OSH Act), 84
Occupational Safety and Health Administration (OSHA), 84

Office of Federal Contract Compliance Programs (OFCCP), 75
reasonable accommodation, 80
right-to-know laws, 87
sexual harassment, 81
technic of operations review (TOR), 89
Uniform Guidelines on Employee Selection Procedures, 75

REVIEW AND DISCUSSION QUESTIONS

1. What is the role of each branch of the federal government with regard to equal employment opportunity?
2. For each of the following situations, identify one or more constitutional amendments, laws, or executive orders that might apply.
   a. A veteran of the Vietnam conflict experiences lower-back pain after sitting for extended periods of time. He has applied for promotion to a supervisory position that has traditionally involved spending most of the workday behind a desk.
   b. One of two female workers on a road construction crew complains to her supervisor that she feels uncomfortable during breaks, because the other employees routinely tell off-color jokes.
   c. A manager at an architectural firm receives a call from the local newspaper. The reporter wonders how the firm wishes to respond to calls from two of its employees alleging racial discrimination. About half of the firm's employees

(including all of its partners and most of its architects) are white. One of the firm's clients is the federal government.
3. For each situation in the preceding question, what actions, if any, should the organization take?
4. The Americans with Disabilities Act requires that employers make reasonable accommodations for individuals with disabilities. How might this requirement affect law enforcement officers and firefighters?
5. To identify instances of sexual harassment, the courts may use a "reasonable woman" standard of what constitutes offensive behavior. This standard is based on the idea that women and men have different ideas of what behavior is appropriate. What are the implications of this distinction? Do you think this distinction is helpful or harmful? Why?
6. Given that the "reasonable woman" standard referred to in Question 5 is based on women's ideas of what is appropriate, how might an organization with

mostly male employees identify and avoid behavior that could be found to be sexual harassment?

7. What are an organization's basic duties under the Occupational Safety and Health Act?

8. OSHA penalties are aimed at employers, rather than employees. How does this affect employee safety?

9. How can organizations motivate employees to promote safety and health in the workplace?

10. For each of the following occupations, identify at least one possible hazard and at least one action employers could take to minimize the risk of an injury or illness related to that hazard.
    a. Worker in a fast-food restaurant
    b. Computer programmer
    c. Truck driver
    d. House painter

EXPERIENCING HR

Divide into groups of about six students. Assign three roles for a role-playing exercise: a human resource manager, an office worker in his or her early 60s, and the office worker's supervisor. (If you want to add other roles, others in your group can take on those roles.)

Background: The supervisor is concerned about recently seeing the office worker engage in unsafe behavior. Once, the worker was standing on a chair with wheels in order to retrieve supplies from a high cupboard. In another case, the office worker had decided to rearrange some equipment in a shared workspace, and the supervisor worried that the worker would get back

strain from moving printers or trip over some of the many cords strewn around.

Role-play a meeting in which the supervisor shares these concerns with the HR manager. Then, as a group, decide who should meet with the employee and what should be said. Role-play that meeting. Finally, discuss the outcome of the meetings. Does your group expect the employee will behave more safely? Was the meeting conducted in a way that will avoid accusations of age (or other) discrimination? Write a paragraph to summarize what you learned.

TAKING RESPONSIBILITY: Keeping IHOP Workers Safe

On a February morning in South Charleston, West Virginia, breakfast at IHOP suddenly became hazardous. A kitchen worker was loading the dishwasher and grabbed the wrong cleaning product. Along with a cleaning agent called delimer, used to remove mineral deposits, the employee poured chlorine-based cleanser into the dishwasher. The two chemicals combined to produce a cloud of dangerous fumes with a strong bleach odor.

Minutes later, employees began to feel sick from inhaling the fumes. They began to have difficulty breathing. They called for emergency assistance and evacuated all the customers from the restaurant. Seeing the cloud entering the dining area, the customers quickly left. When police and firefighters arrived, they found that most of the customers had felt well enough to leave the area. However, one employee was semiconscious, and eight others were still having trouble breathing. The nine injured employees were taken to local hospitals.

The first responders directed everyone in the IHOP parking lot to move to a neighboring lot upwind of the fumes. They donned protective equipment, went inside, and determined that the fumes were coming from the dishwasher. At that point, they were able to separate the chemicals and ventilate the restaurant.

Employees at the local poison control center noted that mixing chlorine with other cleaning agents is a frequent cleaning error that produces chlorine gas. Because the gas has such a strong and unpleasant odor, people tend to move away from it quickly, before it can do much damage to the eyes and respiratory system. After the short-term irritation, symptoms subside quickly for most people, unless they already have respiratory conditions such as asthma. To prevent accidents such as the one at the IHOP, the bottle of delimer bore a label with a red-letter warning that it should not be mixed with chlorine-containing products.

IHOP representatives had no immediate public comment on the situation. Most IHOP restaurants operate independently of the main corporation because they are owned by franchisees. However, IHOP tries to instill in all its franchises and employees a set of core values: integrity, excellence, innovation, accountability, inclusion, trust, and commitment to making a difference in their communities.

Restaurant safety is of particular concern because these businesses employ many young workers; almost 30% of employees in eating and drinking establishments are under the age of 20. That means many restaurant workers are inexperienced and may not have the maturity or confidence to speak up when they see a hazard or aren't sure how to work safely. Consequently, young workers are more prone to being injured on the job. Along with the handling of chemicals, restaurants need to train their workers in how to carry food without straining muscles, how to avoid slipping and falling on greasy floors, and how to avoid electrical hazards, especially when outlets are near wet surfaces. Restaurant managers have taken these and other measures to protect their workers, but injury rates among young workers in restaurants remain higher than in other industries.

Questions

1. With the available information, do a simple technic of operations review (TOR) of the chlorine gas incident at IHOP. What should the restaurant's management learn about how to protect employees and customers?

2. How do you think the restaurant's management could have prevented the incident from happening? What could managers do to create a safer kitchen environment?

3. When a business hires teens, rather than only experienced workers, do you think it has a greater obligation to protect their safety and health? Why or why not?

SOURCES: "Chemical Mixture Overcomes Workers," *West Virginia Metro News*, February 17, 2012, http://www.wvmetronews.com; Kathryn Gregory, "Nine Sent to Hospital after Chemical Exposure at IHOP," *Charleston Gazette*, February 17, 2012, http://wvgazette.com; John Raby, "Fumes Injure Nine Workers at West Virginia Restaurant," *Wausau Daily Herald*, February 17, 2012, http://www.wausaudailyherald.com; IHOP, "Jobs@IHOP," http://www.ihop.com, accessed February 17, 2012; Occupational Safety and Health Administration, "Youth Worker Safety in Restaurants," http://www.osha.gov, accessed February 17, 2012; Occupational Safety and Health Administration, "Restaurant Safety for Young Workers," http://www.osha.gov, accessed February 17, 2012.

MANAGING TALENT: General Motors' Commitment to Diversity

Back in the 1980s, valuing diversity was far from the minds of the leadership at General Motors. True, GM had established a program to promote minority-owned dealerships, but there were problems within the company. Women and minorities complained to the Equal Employment Opportunity Commission that the carmaker was discriminating against them. In 1984, the EEOC and GM reached a $42.4 million settlement in which GM promised to promote women and minorities into management positions. Since then, the company has never swerved from that effort at inclusiveness. Today GM garners praise as a company that far exceeds legal standards for equal employment opportunity.

For GM, this commitment to diversity is a way to better serve its customers in the United States and around the world. A diverse workforce, supplier base, and dealer network show GM how to serve a diverse marketplace. And openness to diversity—what GM calls a welcoming Workplace of Choice—gives the company access to the best talent in the world, without regard to such differences as race, sex, and nationality. In the words of Alma Guajardo-Crossley, director of GM's diversity initiatives, recruiting and hiring minorities is "business sense," because in the United States, minority groups "are pretty much going to be the majority here pretty soon." They have an impact because the company does not merely hire minorities, but also develops them, trains all employees to value diversity, and expects all its people to be fully engaged in helping GM "design, build, and sell the world's best vehicles."

Guajardo-Crossley is just one member of a team of managers dedicated to promoting diversity at General Motors. She reports to Eric Peterson, GM's vice president of diversity. Others on the team include managers of diversity communications, diversity advertising, minority dealer development, and supplier diversity. In addition, employees are welcome to form employee resource groups, which bring together employees with shared backgrounds or interests to support one another's career development and be available to consult with others in the company. GM has employee resource groups for women, Asian Indians, Chinese, people of African ancestry, Hispanics, young employees, Native Americans, Mideast and Southeast Asians, people with disabilities, veterans, Vietnamese, and lesbian, gay, bisexual, and transgender (LGBT) employees.

One sign that GM is succeeding in its commitment to diversity is the representation of various groups in leadership positions. Among public companies in Michigan, for example, boards of directors average about 10% women. But at GM, over one-third of the directors are women.

GM managers who have benefited from the company's attitude of inclusiveness assert that this environment frees them to contribute fully. Sabin D. Blake, a dealer organizational manager, said seeing gay and supportive straight employees in the executive ranks gave him the courage to reveal to his colleagues that he is gay. (Courage is necessary because no national laws prohibit discrimination based on sexual orientation.) Coming out, in turn, freed up a lot of energy Blake had spent on hiding his identity at work. Diana Tremblay, GM's vice president of manufacturing and labor relations, is sure that her experiences as labor negotiator, wife, and mother have together shaped her into a woman who succeeds both at work and in family life. For example, after three decades of marriage, she had a deep reservoir of experience in talking out issues rather than letting the conflict drive the couple apart. That same attitude has made her a successful negotiator with the United Auto Workers. In fact, Tremblay has found an advantage of being a woman in a male-dominated industry: when she succeeds, people notice her.

Questions

1. Of the activities and accomplishments described in this case, which does General Motors need to do in order to meet legal requirements? Which go beyond legal requirements?

2. Do you agree with GM's assumption that when employees feel fully accepted for who they are, they will feel free to contribute their talents more fully at work? Why or why not?

3. How might GM measure whether its efforts to promote diversity really are helping it achieve business success?

SOURCES: Broos Campbell, "The Diversity Matrix at GM," *Hispanic Business*, May 2011, pp. 10–11; General Motors, "GM Diversity: Employee Resource Groups," http://www.gm.com, accessed February 15, 2012; General Motors, "Diversity at GM," http://www.gm.com, accessed February 15, 2012; Ellen Mitchell, "Women in Top Jobs Are Still Scarce," *Crain's Detroit Business*, October 17, 2011, Business & Company Resource Center, http://galenet.galegroup.com; Carolyn M. Brown, "Black and Gay in Corporate America," *Black Enterprise*, July 2011, pp. 84–95; "How She Does It: GM's Diana Tremblay," *The Wall Street Journal*, February 28, 2011, http://blogs.wsj.com; Equal Employment Opportunity Commission, "EEOC History: 35th Anniversary, 1965–2000," http://www.eeoc.gov, accessed February 15, 2012.

 TWITTER FOCUS: Company Fails Fair-Employment Test

Using Twitter, continue the conversation about companies complying with federal, state, and local laws by reading the fair-employment case at **www.mhhe.com/noefund5e.** Engage with your classmates and instructor via Twitter to chat about the employee's experience using the case questions posted on the Noe website. Don't have a Twitter account yet? See the instructions for getting started on the Online Learning Center.

NOTES

1. Roberto Ceniceros, "Job Candidate Testing Program Cuts Harley-Davidson's Injuries," *Business Insurance*, August 15, 2011, Business & Company Resource Center, http://galenet.galegroup.com; BTE Technologies, "Employer Payer Services," http://www.btetech.com, accessed February 15, 2012.

2. *Bakke v. Regents of the University of California*, 17 F.E.P.C. 1000 (1978).

3. Equal Employment Opportunity Commission, "Understanding Waivers of Discrimination Claims in Employee Severance Agreements," http://www.eeoc.gov, accessed February 14, 2012; Equal Employment Opportunity Commission, "Age Discrimination," http://www1.eeoc.gov, accessed February 14, 2012.

4. Equal Employment Opportunity Commission, "EEOC Sues Hutchinson Sealing Systems for Age Discrimination," news release, January 20, 2012, http://www1.eeoc.gov.

5. "Age Shall Not Wither Them," *The Economist*, April 9, 2011, EBSCOhost, http://web.ebscohost.com.

6. Equal Employment Opportunity Commission, "Pregnancy Discrimination," http://www1.eeoc.gov, accessed February 14, 2012.

7. Equal Employment Opportunity Commission, "Facts about the Americans with Disabilities Act," http://www1.eeoc.gov//eeoc/publications/, accessed March 3, 2010; Equal Employment Opportunity Commission, "Notice Concerning the Americans with Disabilities Act (ADA) Amendments Act of 2008," http://www1.eeoc.gov, accessed February 14, 2012.

8. Equal Employment Opportunity Commission, "Questions and Answers for Small Businesses: The Final Rule Implementing the ADA Amendments Act of 2008," http://www1.eeoc.gov, accessed February 20, 2012, University of New Hampshire Human Resources, "Americans with Disabilities Act, as Amended 2008 (ADAAA)," http://www.unh.edu/hr/ada.htm, accessed February 20, 2012.

9. Jenell L. S. Wittmer and Leslie Wilson, "Turning Diversity into Dollars: A Business Case for Hiring People with Disabilities," *T + D*, February 2010, pp. 58–61; Office of Disability Employment Policy, "Disability Employment Policy Resources by Topic," http://www.dol.gov/odep/, accessed February 20, 2012.

10. Melissa Korn, "Race Influences How Leaders Are Assessed," *The Wall Street Journal*, January 3, 2012, http://online.wsj.com; Katherine W. Phillips, "Transparent Barriers," *Kellogg Insight* (Kellogg School of Management), November 2008, http://insight.kellogg.northwestern.edu.

11. *UAW v. Johnson Controls, Inc.*, 499 U.S. 187 (1991).

12. Karen Burke, "Referrals and Diversity, Transgender Name Changes, Termination Meeting Pay," *HR Magazine*, November 2011, pp. 27–28.

13. Anne Fisher, "Checking Out Job Applicants on Facebook? Better Ask a Lawyer," *Fortune*, March 2, 2011, http://management.fortune.cnn.com.

14. D. Kravitz and J. Platania, "Attitudes and Beliefs about Affirmative Action: Effects of Target and of Respondent Sex and Ethnicity," *Journal of Applied Psychology* 78 (1993), pp. 928–38.

15. Equal Employment Opportunity Commission, "Imperial Security Will Pay $50,000 to Settle EEOC Religious Discrimination Lawsuit," news release, November 23, 2011, http://www1.eeoc.gov; Equal Employment Opportunity Commission, "Belk, Inc. to Pay $55,000 to Settle EEOC Religious Discrimination Suit," news release, March 16, 2011, http://www1.eeoc.gov.

16. EEOC guideline based on the Civil Rights Act of 1964, Title VII.

17. Dana Mattioli, "More Men Make Harassment Claims," *The Wall Street Journal*, March 23, 2010, http://online.wsj.com; Equal Employment Opportunity Commission, "Sexual Harassment Charges: EEOC and FEPAs Combined, FY1997–FY2011," http://www1.eeoc.gov, accessed February 15, 2012.

18. Burke, "Referrals and Diversity," p. 28.

19. Dede Montgomery, "Hair, Formaldehyde, and Industrial Hygiene," *NIOSH Science Blog*, February 10, 2012, Centers for Disease Control and Prevention, http://blogs.cdc.gov.

20. Laura Walter, "'Green' Construction Workers May Face Additional Safety Risks," *EHS Today*, November 30, 2011, http://www.ehstoday.com.

21. Bureau of Labor Statistics, "Workplace Injuries and Illnesses, 2010," news release, October 20, 2011, http://www.bls.gov/iif/oshsum.htm.

22. J. Roughton, "Managing a Safety Program through Job Hazard Analysis," *Professional Safety* 37 (1992), pp. 28–31.

23. Roughton, "Managing a Safety Program."

24. Duncan Graham-Rowe, "Is Nanotechnology Safe in the Workplace?" *Guardian*, February 13, 2012, http://www.guardian.co.uk.

25. R. G. Hallock and D. A. Weaver, "Controlling Losses and Enhancing Management Systems with TOR Analysis," *Professional Safety* 35 (1990), pp. 24–26.

26. Field ID, "McShane Construction Selects Field ID to Enhance Worksite Safety and Quality Assurance," news release, October 11, 2011, http://www.fieldid.com; Field ID, "What Is Field ID?" http://www.fieldid.com, accessed February 21, 2012.

27. Jill Jusko, "Meeting the Safety Challenge of a Diverse Workforce," *Industry Week*, December 2011, p. 14.

28. Anthony Geise, "The Barriers to Effective Safety Training: Finding Training Techniques That Bridge Generation Gaps," *EHS Today*, October 2011, pp. 72–76; Bureau of Labor Statistics, "Nonfatal Occupational Injuries and Illnesses Requiring Days Away from Work, 2010," news release, November 9, 2011, http://www.bls.gov; Centers for Disease Control and Prevention, "QuickStats: Rate of Nonfatal, Medically Consulted Fall Injury Episodes, by Age Group," *Morbidity and Mortality Weekly*, February 3, 2012, http://www.cdc.gov.

29. Phillip Ragain, Ron Ragain, Michael Allen, and Mike Allen, "A Study of Safety Intervention: The Causes and Consequences of Employees' Silence," *EHS Today*, July 2011, pp. 36–38.

30. Prevent Blindness America, "Eye Safety at Work," http://www.preventblindness.org, accessed February 14, 2012.

31. M. Janssens, J. M. Brett, and F. J. Smith, "Confirmatory Cross-Cultural Research: Testing the Viability of a Corporation-wide Safety Policy," *Academy of Management Journal* 38 (1995), pp. 364–82.

32. E. Sage-Gavin and P. Wright, "Corporate Social Responsibility at Gap, Inc.: An Interview with Eva Sage-Gavin," *Human Resource Planning* 30, mar. 1, (2007), pp. 45–48.

4

Analyzing Work and Designing Jobs

What Do I Need to Know?

After reading this chapter, you should be able to:

LO 4-1 Summarize the elements of work flow analysis.

LO 4-2 Describe how work flow is related to an organization's structure.

LO 4-3 Define the elements of a job analysis, and discuss their significance for human resource management.

LO 4-4 Tell how to obtain information for a job analysis.

LO 4-5 Summarize recent trends in job analysis.

LO 4-6 Describe methods for designing a job so that it can be done efficiently.

LO 4-7 Identify approaches to designing a job to make it motivating.

LO 4-8 Explain how organizations apply ergonomics to design safe jobs.

LO 4-9 Discuss how organizations can plan for the mental demands of a job.

Introduction

Selling shoes online was not exactly an obvious route to business success when Tony Hsieh started **Zappos.com**. Most of us can't tell whether that stylish pair of shoes in a photo will look good on us, much less whether the shoes will pinch our feet. But Hsieh set out to leap that hurdle by making Zappos excel at customer service. To take away the risks of online shoe selection, the company offers free shipping and free returns. And to make sure customers receive their orders as quickly as possible, Zappos maintains a huge inventory. Shoes offered for sale are already in the company's warehouse, waiting to be shipped. This strategy propelled Zappos to the top spot in online shoe retailing, at which point Amazon acquired Zappos for $1.2 billion.

The jobs at Zappos are designed to support the company's service-first strategy. Instead of looking for the cheapest location for customer service, Zappos hires representatives to work at the company's Nevada headquarters. Their job includes helping customers with their requests, however unreasonable. Employees once located a pizzeria for a hungry caller from California. Employees at all levels in every department also are encouraged to promote the Zappos brand on social media. If employees see a shoe they love, for example, Twitter users could send out a tweet about it to their followers. Other companies are more concerned about limiting online messages about their brand, but Zappos focuses on hiring people who embrace its culture and values, and then it trusts them to spread the word.[1]

Commitment to extraordinary customer service, wide latitude in delivering customer satisfaction, and tasks such as answering phone calls and packing shoe orders—all these are elements of employees' jobs with Zappos. These elements give rise to the types of skills and personalities required for success, and they in turn help to narrow the field of people who will succeed at the company. Consideration of such elements is at the heart of analyzing work, whether in a start-up enterprise, a multinational corporation, or a government agency.

This chapter discusses the analysis and design of work and, in doing so, lays out some considerations that go into making informed decisions about how to create and link jobs. The chapter begins with a look at the big-picture issues related to analyzing work flow and organizational structure. The discussion then turns to the more specific issues of analyzing and designing jobs. Traditionally, job analysis has emphasized the study of existing jobs in order to make decisions such as employee selection, training, and compensation. In contrast, job design has emphasized making jobs more efficient or more motivating. However, as this chapter shows, the two activities are interrelated.

Work Flow in Organizations

LO 4-1 Summarize the elements of work flow analysis.

Work Flow Design
The process of analyzing the tasks necessary for the production of a product or service.

Job
A set of related duties.

Position
The set of duties (job) performed by a particular person.

Informed decisions about jobs take place in the context of the organization's overall work flow. Through the process of **work flow design**, managers analyze the tasks needed to produce a product or service. With this information, they assign these tasks to specific jobs and positions. (A **job** is a set of related duties. A **position** is the set of duties performed by one person. A school has many teaching *positions;* the person filling each of those positions is performing the *job* of teacher.) Basing these decisions on work flow design can lead to better results than the more traditional practice of looking at jobs individually.

Work Flow Analysis

Before designing its work flow, the organization's planners need to analyze what work needs to be done. Figure 4.1 shows the elements of a work flow analysis. For each type of work, such as producing a product line or providing a support service (accounting, legal support, and so on), the analysis identifies the output of the process, the activities involved, and the three categories of inputs (materials and information, equipment, and human resources).

Outputs are the products of any work unit, say, a department or team. Outputs may be tangible, as in the case of a restaurant meal or finished part. They may be intangible, such as building security or an answered question about employee benefits. In identifying the outputs of particular work units, work flow analysis considers both quantity and quality. Thinking in terms of these outputs gives HRM professionals a clearer view of how to increase each work unit's effectiveness.

Work flow analysis next considers the *work processes* used to generate the outputs identified. Work processes are the activities that a work unit's members engage in to produce a given output. They are described in terms of operating procedures for every task performed by each employee at each stage of the process. Specifying the processes helps HRM professionals design efficient work systems by clarifying which tasks are necessary. Knowledge of work processes also can guide staffing changes when work is automated, outsourced, or restructured.

Finally, work flow analysis identifies the *inputs* required to carry out the work processes. As shown in Figure 4.1, inputs fall into three categories: raw inputs (materials

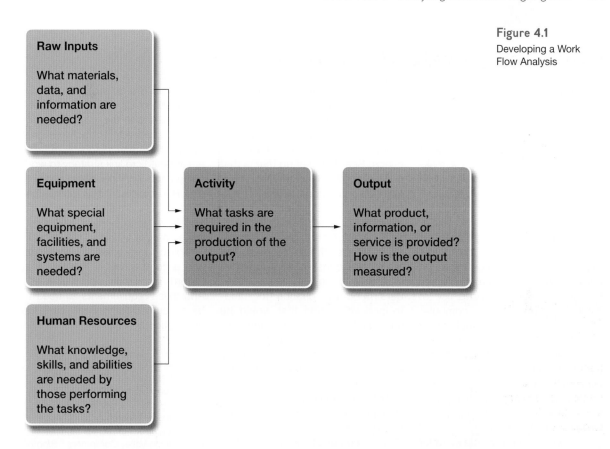

Figure 4.1
Developing a Work
Flow Analysis

and information), equipment, and human resources (knowledge, skills, and abilities). At manufacturing companies in the United States, there has been a shift in the kinds of inputs needed for success. Most low-wage, low-skill manufacturing processes have been moved to parts of the world where the cost of labor is low. In the United States, successful manufacturers now emphasize innovation and short runs of specialized products. This kind of work calls for greater use of comput- erized equipment, which is run by lean workforces of highly skilled technicians.[2]

LO 4-2 Describe how work flow is related to an organization's structure.

Work Flow Design and an Organization's Structure

Work flow takes place in the context of an organization's struc- ture. It requires the cooperation of individuals and groups. Ide- ally, the organization's structure brings together the people who must collaborate to create the desired outputs efficiently. The structure may do this in a way that is highly centralized (that is, with authority concentrated in a few people at the top of the organization) or decentralized (with authority spread among many people). The organization may group jobs according to functions (for example, welding, painting, packaging), or it may set up divisions to focus on products or customer groups.

Firefighters work as a team. They and their equipment are the "inputs" (they do the work), and the "output" is an extinguished fire and the rescue of people and pets. In any organization or team, workers need to be cross- trained in several skills to create an effective team. If all of these firefighters are trained to do any part of the job, the chief can deploy them rapidly as needed.

SeaMicro Designs Work to Stay Onshore

As we saw in Chapter 2, many U.S. manufacturers have been doing a majority of their hiring overseas in recent years. Although California's famous Silicon Valley is named after a primary ingredient used for making microchips, the fact is that when it comes to computer hardware, very little manufacturing has taken place in California since the 1980s. One notable exception is SeaMicro, which builds servers (computers that do the data processing for a network) in Santa Clara, California. SeaMicro's specialty is the use of small, energy-efficient computer chips, such as those that might operate a smartphone or notebook computer. These processors are combined with custom-made hardware and software that enable them to deliver plenty of computing power for today's web-based applications while using far less energy. Customers are willing to pay a little extra for these servers in exchange for the savings on energy to power them.

With a strategy based on innovation, SeaMicro needs an organizational structure and work design that support creative thinking and rapid response to customers' needs. SeaMicro set up teams that bring together employees from different functions. The cross-functional teams work on the combination of hardware, software, and manufacturing processes needed for each new product. The teams are constantly engaged in experimentation, so team members need the chance for face-to-face interaction that would be impossible if the company offshored manufacturing to Asia. And when a customer calls for a change or an engineer thinks of a way to improve efficiency, all the needed expertise at headquarters is just two miles from the manufacturing floor.

This combination of innovation and environmental sustainability has attracted favorable attention, with *The Wall Street Journal* identifying SeaMicro as one of the "green" companies with the greatest potential to succeed. To achieve that potential, human resource managers at SeaMicro link strategy to work design and work design to a variety of HR practices: They must identify and hire creative thinkers who also have good skills at collaborating as part of a team. They need to establish performance measures and a compensation structure that reward innovation and teamwork. And these requirements all need to be accounted for in SeaMicro's job descriptions.

SOURCES: Cade Metz, "As Apple Toils in China, Others Make It in America," *Wired,* February 13, 2012, http://www.wired.com; Colleen DeBaise, "The Top 10 Clean-Tech Companies," *The Wall Street Journal,* March 4, 2011, http://online.wsj.com; Ashlee Vance, "SeaMicro's Silicon Valley Computers," *Bloomberg Businessweek,* February 24, 2011, http://www.businessweek.com.

Although there are an infinite number of ways to combine the elements of an organization's structure, we can make some general observations about structure and work design. If the structure is strongly based on function, workers tend to have low authority and to work alone at highly specialized jobs. Jobs that involve teamwork or broad responsibility tend to require a structure based on divisions other than functions. When the goal is to empower employees, companies then need to set up structures and jobs that enable broad responsibility, such as jobs that involve employees in serving a particular group of customers or producing a particular product, rather than performing a narrowly defined function. The organization's structure also affects managers' jobs. Managing a division responsible for a product or customer group tends to require more experience and cognitive (thinking) ability than managing a department that handles a particular function.[3]

Work design often emphasizes the analysis and design of jobs, as described in the remainder of this chapter. Although all of these approaches can succeed, each focuses on one isolated job at a time. These approaches do not necessarily consider how that single job fits into the overall work flow or structure of the organization. To use these techniques effectively, human resource personnel should also understand their organization as a whole. The "Best Practices" box offers an example of how a high-tech company matched its job design to its structure and strategy for manufacturing in the United States.

Job Analysis

To achieve high-quality performance, organizations have to understand and match job requirements and people. This understanding requires **job analysis**, the process of getting detailed information about jobs. Analyzing jobs and understanding what is required to carry out a job provide essential knowledge for staffing, training, performance appraisal, and many other HR activities. For instance, a supervisor's evaluation of an employee's work should be based on performance relative to job requirements. In very small organizations, line managers may perform a job analysis, but usually the work is done by a human resource professional. A large company may have a compensation management department that includes job analysts (also called personnel analysts). Organizations may also contract with firms that provide this service.

LO 4-3 Define the elements of a job analysis, and discuss their significance for human resource management.

Job Analysis
The process of getting detailed information about jobs.

Job Descriptions

An essential part of job analysis is the creation of job descriptions. A **job description** is a list of the tasks, duties, and responsibilities (TDRs) that a job entails. TDRs are observable actions. For example, a news photographer's job requires the jobholder to use a camera to take photographs. If you were to observe someone in that position for a day, you would almost certainly see some pictures being taken. When a manager attempts to evaluate job performance, it is most important to have detailed information about the work performed in the job (that is, the TDRs). This information makes it possible to determine how well an individual is meeting each job requirement.

A job description typically has the format shown in Figure 4.2. It includes the job title, a brief description of the TDRs, and a list of the essential duties with detailed specifications of the tasks involved in carrying out each duty. Although organizations may modify this format according to their particular needs, all job descriptions within an organization should follow the same format. This helps the organization make consistent decisions about such matters as pay and promotions. It also helps the organization show that it makes human resource decisions fairly.

Whenever the organization creates a new job, it needs a new job description. Preparation of a job description begins with gathering information about the job from people already performing the task, the position's supervisor, or the managers creating the position. Based on that information, the writer of the job description identifies the essential duties of the job, including mental and physical tasks and any methods and resources required. Job descriptions should then be reviewed periodically (say, once a year) and updated if necessary. Performance appraisals can provide a good opportunity for updating job descriptions, as the employee and supervisor compare what the employee has been doing against the details of the job description.

Organizations should give each newly hired employee a copy of his or her job description. This helps the employee to understand what is expected, but it shouldn't be presented as limiting the employee's commitment to quality and customer satisfaction. Ideally, employees will want to go above and beyond the listed duties when the situation and their abilities call for that. Many job descriptions include the phrase *and other duties as requested* as a way to remind employees not to tell their supervisor, "But that's not part of my job."

Job Description
A list of the tasks, duties, and responsibilities (TDRs) that a particular job entails.

Job Specifications

Whereas the job description focuses on the activities involved in carrying out a job, a **job specification** looks at the qualities or requirements the person performing the job must possess. It is a list of the knowledge, skills, abilities, and other characteristics

Job Specification
A list of the knowledge, skills, abilities, and other characteristics (KSAOs) that an individual must have to perform a particular job.

Figure 4.2

Sample Job Description

TRAIN CREW/SERVICE AT UNION PACIFIC

OVERVIEW

When you work on a Union Pacific train crew, you're working at the very heart of our railroad. Moving trains. Driving trains. Making sure our customers' freight gets delivered safely and on time.

JOB DESCRIPTION

In this entry-level position, you'll start as a Switchperson or Brakeperson, working as on-the-ground traffic control. You don't need any previous railroad experience; we provide all training. These jobs directly lead to becoming a Conductor and a Locomotive Engineer, where you will have a rare opportunity to work on board a moving locomotive. The Conductor is responsible for the train, the freight and the crew. The Locomotive Engineer actually operates the locomotive.

DUTIES

As a Switchperson or Brakeperson, you'll learn to move trains safely in the yards and over the road. You'll be climbing ladders, boarding freight cars, operating track switches, inspecting cars, and using radio communications to control train movement.

MAJOR TASKS AND RESPONSIBILITIES

You won't work a standard 40-hour workweek. Train crews are always on call, even on weekends and holidays. You'll travel with our trains, sometimes spending a day or more away from your home terminal.

SOURCE: Union Pacific website, www.unionpacific.jobs/careers/explore/train/train_service.shtml, accessed February 28, 2012. Reprinted with permission of Union Pacific Railroad.

(KSAOs) that an individual must have to perform the job. *Knowledge* refers to factual or procedural information that is necessary for successfully performing a task. For example, this course is providing you with knowledge in how to manage human resources. A *skill* is an individual's level of proficiency at performing a particular task—that is, the capability to perform it well. With knowledge and experience, you could acquire skill in the task of preparing job specifications. *Ability*, in contrast to skill, refers to a more general enduring capability that an individual possesses. A person might have the ability to cooperate with others or to write clearly and precisely. Finally, *other characteristics* might be personality traits such as someone's persistence or motivation to achieve. Some jobs also have legal requirements, such as licensing or certification. Figure 4.3 is a set of sample job specifications for the job description in Figure 4.2.

In developing job specifications, it is important to consider all of the elements of KSAOs. As with writing a job description, the information can come from a combination of people performing the job, people supervising or planning for the job, and trained job analysts. A study by ACT's Workforce Development Division interviewed manufacturing supervisors to learn what they do each day and what skills they rely on. The researchers learned that the supervisors spend much of their day monitoring their employees to make sure the workplace is safe, product quality is maintained, and

---

TRAIN CREW/SERVICE AT UNION PACIFIC

REQUIREMENTS

You must be at least 18 years old. You must speak and read English because you'll be asked to follow posted bulletins, regulations, rule books, timetables, switch lists, etc. You must pass a reading comprehension test (see sample) to be considered for an interview.

JOB REQUIREMENTS

You must be able to use a computer keyboard, and you must be able to count and compare numbers. (You might, for example, be asked to count the cars on a train during switching.) You must be able to solve problems quickly and react to changing conditions on the job.

You must have strong vision and hearing, including the ability to: see and read hand signals from near and far; distinguish between colors; visually judge the speed and distance of moving objects; see at night; and recognize changes in sounds.

You must also be physically strong: able to push, pull, lift and carry up to 25 pounds frequently; up to 50 pounds occasionally; and up to 83 pounds infrequently. You'll need good balance to regularly step on and off equipment and work from ladders to perform various tasks. And you must be able to walk, sit, stand and stoop comfortably.

You'll be working outdoors in all weather conditions—including snow, ice, rain, cold, and heat—and frequently at elevations more than 12 feet above the ground.

Figure 4.3
Sample Job Specifications

SOURCE: Union Pacific website, www.unionpacific.jobs/careers/explore/train/train_service.shtml, accessed February 28, 2012. Reprinted with permission of Union Pacific Railroad.

work processes are optimal. Also, they rely heavily on their technical knowledge of the work processes they supervise.[4] Based on this information, job specifications for a manufacturing supervisor would include skill in observing how people work, as well as in-depth knowledge of manufacturing processes and tools.

In contrast to tasks, duties, and responsibilities, KSAOs are characteristics of people and are not directly observable. They are observable only when individuals are carrying out the TDRs of the job—and afterward, if they can show the product of their labor. Thus, if someone applied for a job as a news photographer, you could not simply look at the individual to determine whether he or she can spot and take effective photographs. However, you could draw conclusions later about the person's skills by looking at examples of his or her photographs. Similarly, as illustrated in the "Did You Know?" box, many employers specify educational requirements. Meeting these requirements is treated as an indication that a person has some desired level of knowledge and skills.

Accurate information about KSAOs is especially important for making decisions about who will fill a job. A manager attempting to fill a position needs information about the characteristics required and about the characteristics of each applicant. Interviews and selection decisions should therefore focus on KSAOs.

About One in Three High School Grads Hold Middle-Class Jobs

Companies filling jobs that place earners in the middle class tend to require at least an associate's degree, according to research by the Georgetown University Center on Education and the Workforce. (The center defined middle-class earnings as starting at $35,000 per year, which would place a family of four at 150% above the poverty level.) However, 36% of high school graduates with no college education land jobs paying at least $35,000 per year. These jobs are most often in the fields of manufacturing, construction, and transportation and distribution.

Question

Positions such as supervisors, office administrators, and office machine repair technicians tend to require some college education. What KSAOs do you think employers are trying to obtain with this requirement? Can you think of a better way to identify people with those KSAOs?

SOURCES: Georgetown University Center on Education and the Workforce, "Career Clusters: Forecasting Demand for High School through College Jobs, 2008–2018," executive summary, November 2011, http://cew .georgetown.edu/Clusters/; Georgetown University Center on Education and the Workforce, "New Report Finds the Best Education Pathways out of Jobless Recovery," news release, November 14, 2011, http://www9.georgetown.edu; Jennifer Gonzalez, "Bachelor's Degree Is Still Best Path to Middle-Class Jobs and Earnings, Report Says," *Chronicle of Higher Education,* November 14, 2011, http://chronicle.com.

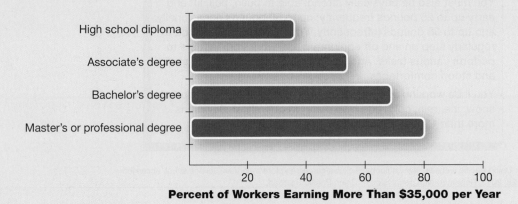

Percent of Workers Earning More Than $35,000 per Year

LO 4-4 Tell how to obtain information for a job analysis.

Sources of Job Information

Information for analyzing an existing job often comes from incumbents, that is, people who currently hold that position in the organization. They are a logical source of information because they are most acquainted with the details of the job. Incumbents should be able to provide very accurate information.

A drawback of relying solely on incumbents' information is that they may have an incentive to exaggerate what they do in order to appear more valuable to the organization. Information from incumbents should therefore be supplemented with information from observers, such as supervisors, who look for a match between what incumbents are doing and what they are supposed to do. Research suggests that supervisors may provide the most accurate estimates of the importance of job duties, while incumbents may be more accurate in reporting information about the actual time spent performing job tasks and safety-related risk factors.[5] For analyzing skill levels, the best source may be external job analysts who have more experience rating a wide range of jobs.[6]

The government also provides background information for analyzing jobs. In the 1930s, the U.S. Department of Labor created the *Dictionary of Occupational Titles (DOT)* as a vehicle for helping the new public employment system link the demand for skills and the supply of skills in the U.S. workforce. The *DOT* described over 12,000 jobs, as well as some of the requirements of successful job holders. This system served the United States well for over 60 years, but it became clear to Labor Department officials that jobs in the new economy were so different that the *DOT* no longer served its purpose. The Labor Department therefore introduced a new system, called the Occupational Information Network (O*NET).

Instead of relying on fixed job titles and narrow task descriptions, the O*NET uses a common language that generalizes across jobs to describe the abilities, work styles, work activities, and work context required for 1,000 broadly defined occupations. Users can visit O*NET OnLine (**http://www.onetonline .org**) to review jobs' tasks, work styles and context, and require-

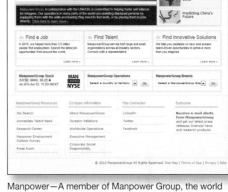

Manpower—A member of Manpower Group, the world leader in innovative workforce solutions—uses the O*Net to classify its jobs and track demand nationwide.

ments including skills, training, and experience. ManpowerGroup, a staffing services agency, uses O*NET's information on skills to match individuals more precisely to jobs it has been hired to fill. Piedmont Natural Gas uses O*NET to conduct job analyses and match job applicants' skills and preferences to the requirements of available positions. The effort has helped reduce turnover among Piedmont's entry-level workers.[7] Furthermore, although the O*NET was developed to analyze jobs in the U.S. economy, research suggests that its ratings tend to be the same for jobs located in other countries.[8]

Position Analysis Questionnaire

After gathering information, the job analyst uses the information to analyze the job. One of the broadest and best-researched instruments for analyzing jobs is the **Position Analysis Questionnaire (PAQ)**. This is a standardized job analysis questionnaire containing 194 items that represent work behaviors, work conditions, and job characteristics that apply to a wide variety of jobs. The questionnaire organizes these items into six sections concerning different aspects of the job:

1. *Information input*—Where and how a worker gets information needed to perform the job.
2. *Mental processes*—The reasoning, decision making, planning, and information-processing activities involved in performing the job.
3. *Work output*—The physical activities, tools, and devices used by the worker to perform the job.
4. *Relationships with other persons*—The relationships with other people required in performing the job.
5. *Job context*—The physical and social contexts where the work is performed.
6. *Other characteristics*—The activities, conditions, and characteristics other than those previously described that are relevant to the job.

The person analyzing a job determines whether each item on the questionnaire applies to the job being analyzed. The analyst rates each item on six scales: extent of

Position Analysis Questionnaire (PAQ)
A standardized job analysis questionnaire containing 194 questions about work behaviors, work conditions, and job characteristics that apply to a wide variety of jobs.

use, amount of time, importance to the job, possibility of occurrence, applicability, and special code (special rating scales used with a particular item). The PAQ headquarters uses a computer to score the questionnaire and generate a report that describes the scores on the job dimensions.

Using the PAQ provides an organization with information that helps in comparing jobs, even when they are dissimilar. The PAQ also has the advantage that it considers the whole work process, from inputs through outputs. However, the person who fills out the questionnaire must have college-level reading skills, and the PAQ is meant to be completed only by job analysts trained in this method. In fact, the ratings of job incumbents tend to be less reliable than ratings by supervisors and trained analysts.[9] Also, the descriptions in the PAQ reports are rather abstract, so the reports may not be useful for writing job descriptions or redesigning jobs.

Fleishman Job Analysis System

Fleishman Job Analysis System
Job analysis technique that asks subject-matter experts to evaluate a job in terms of the abilities required to perform the job.

To gather information about worker requirements, the **Fleishman Job Analysis System** asks subject-matter experts (typically job incumbents) to evaluate a job in terms of the abilities required to perform the job.[10] The survey is based on 52 categories of abilities, ranging from written comprehension to deductive reasoning, manual dexterity, stamina, and originality. As in the example in Figure 4.4, the survey items are arranged into a scale for each ability. Each begins with a description of the ability and a comparison to related abilities. Below this is a seven-point scale with phrases describing extemely high and low levels of the ability. The person completing the survey indicates which point on the scale represents the level of the ability required for performing the job being analyzed.

When the survey has been completed in all 52 categories, the results provide a picture of the ability requirements of a job. Such information is especially useful for employee selection, training, and career development.

Importance of Job Analysis

Job analysis is so important to HR managers that it has been called the building block of everything that personnel does.[11] The fact is that almost every human resource management program requires some type of information that is gleaned from job analysis:[12]

- *Work redesign*—Often an organization seeks to redesign work to make it more efficient or to improve quality. The redesign requires detailed information about the existing job(s). In addition, preparing the redesign is similar to analyzing a job that does not yet exist.
- *Human resource planning*—As planners analyze human resource needs and how to meet those needs, they must have accurate information about the levels of skill required in various jobs, so that they can tell what kinds of human resources will be needed.
- *Selection*—To identify the most qualified applicants for various positions, decision makers need to know what tasks the individuals must perform, as well as the necessary knowledge, skills, and abilities.
- *Training*—Almost every employee hired by an organization will require training. Any training program requires knowledge of the tasks performed in a job so that the training is related to the necessary knowledge and skills.

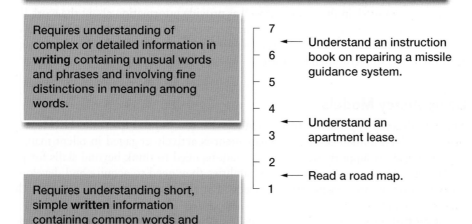

Written Comprehension

This is the ability to understand written sentences and paragraphs. How written comprehension is different from other abilities:

This Ability	Other Abilities
Understand written English words, sentences, and paragraphs.	vs. *Oral comprehension (1): Listen and understand spoken* English words and sentences.
	vs. *Oral expression (3) and written expression (4): Speak or write* English words and sentences so others will understand.

Requires understanding of complex or detailed information in **writing** containing unusual words and phrases and involving fine distinctions in meaning among words.

7

6 ← Understand an instruction book on repairing a missile guidance system.

5

4

3 ← Understand an apartment lease.

2

1 ← Read a road map.

Requires understanding short, simple **written** information containing common words and phrases.

Figure 4.4

Example of an Ability from the Fleishman Job Analysis System

SOURCE: From E. A. Fleishman and M. D. Mumford, "Evaluating Classifications of Job Behavior: A Construct Validation of the Ability Requirements Scales," *Personnel Psychology* 44 (1991), pp. 523–575. Copyright © 1991. Reproduced with permission of Blackwell Publishing Ltd.

- *Performance appraisal*—An accurate performance appraisal requires information about how well each employee is performing in order to reward employees who perform well and to improve their performance if it is below standard. Job analysis helps in identifying the behaviors and the results associated with effective performance.
- *Career planning*—Matching an individual's skills and aspirations with career opportunities requires that those in charge of career planning know the skill requirements of the various jobs. This allows them to guide individuals into jobs in which they will succeed and be satisfied.
- *Job evaluation*—The process of job evaluation involves assessing the relative dollar value of each job to the organization in order to set up fair pay structures. If employees do not believe pay structures are fair, they will become dissatisfied and may quit, or they will not see much benefit in striving for promotions. To put dollar values on jobs, it is necessary to get information about different jobs and compare them.

Job analysis is also important from a legal standpoint. As we saw in Chapter 3, the government imposes requirements related to equal employment opportunity. Detailed, accurate, objective job specifications help decision makers comply with these regulations by keeping the focus on tasks and abilities. These documents also provide evidence of efforts made to engage in fair employment practices. For example, to enforce the Americans with Disabilities Act, the Equal Employment Opportunity Commission may look at job descriptions to identify the essential functions of a job and determine whether a disabled person could have performed those functions with reasonable accommodations. Likewise, lists of duties in different jobs could be compared to evaluate claims under the Equal Pay Act. However, job descriptions and job specifications are not a substitute for fair employment practices.

Besides helping human resource professionals, job analysis helps supervisors and other managers carry out their duties. Data from job analysis can help managers identify the types of work in their units, as well as provide information about the work flow process, so that managers can evaluate whether work is done in the most efficient way. Job analysis information also supports managers as they make hiring decisions, review performance, and recommend rewards.

LO 4-5 Summarize recent trends in job analysis.

Competency Models

These traditional approaches to job analysis are too limited for some HRM needs, however. When human resource management is actively engaged in talent management as a way to support strategy, organizations need to think beyond skills for particular jobs. They must identify the capabilities they need to acquire and develop in order to promote the organization's success. For this purpose, organizations develop competency models.

Competency
An area of personal capability that enables employees to perform their work successfully.

A **competency** is an area of personal capability that enables employees to perform their work successfully.[13] For example, success in a job or career path might require leadership strength, skill in coaching others, and the ability to bring out the best in each member of a diverse team of employees. A competency model identifies and describes all the competencies required for success in a particular occupation or set of jobs. Organizations may create competency models for occupational groups, levels of the organization, or even the entire organization. A competency model might require that all middle managers or all members of the organization be able to act with integrity, value diversity, and commit themselves to delighting customers. Table 4.1 shows an example of a competency model for a project manager. The left side of the table lists competencies required for a project manager (organizational & planning skills; communications; and financial & quantitative skills). The right side of the table shows behaviors that might be used to determine a project manager's level of proficiency for each competency. As in these examples, competency models focus more on how people work, whereas job analysis focuses more on work tasks and outcomes.

Competency models help HR professionals ensure that all aspects of talent management are aligned with the organization's strategy. Looking at the competencies needed for a particular occupational group, department, or the organization as a whole shows which candidates will be the best to fill open positions. Not only can the organization select those who can carry out a particular job today, but it can spot those with competencies they can develop further to assume greater responsibility in the future. Competency models for a career path or for success

Table 4.1

Example of Competencies and a Competency Model

PROJECT MANAGER COMPETENCIES	PROFICIENCY RATINGS
Organizational & Planning Skills Ability to establish priorities on projects and schedule activities to achieve results.	**1—Below Expectations:** Unable to perform basic tasks. **2—Meets Expectations:** Understands basic principles and performs routine tasks with reliable results; works with minimal supervision or assistance. **3—Exceeds Expectations:** Performs complex and multiple tasks; can coach, teach, or lead others.
Communications Ability to build credibility and trust through open and direct communications with internal and external customers.	**1—Below Expectations:** Unable to perform basic tasks. **2—Meets Expectations:** Understands basic principles and performs routine tasks with reliable results; works with minimal supervision or assistance. **3—Exceeds Expectations:** Performs complex and multiple tasks; can coach, teach, or lead others.
Financial & Quantitative Skills Ability to analyze financial information accurately and set financial goals that have a positive impact on company's bottom line and fiscal objectives.	**1—Below Expectations:** Unable to perform basic tasks. **2—Meets Expectations:** Understands basic principles and performs routine tasks with reliable results; works with minimal supervision or assistance. **3—Exceeds Expectations:** Performs complex and multiple tasks; can coach, teach, or lead others.

SOURCE: Based on R. J. Mirabile, "Everything You Wanted to Know about Competency Modeling," *Training and Development* (August 1997): pp. 73–77.

in management show the organization which competencies to emphasize in plans for development of high-potential employees. And competency models identify the important capabilities to measure in performance evaluations and to reward with pay and promotions.

Trends in Job Analysis

As we noted in the earlier discussion of work flow analysis, organizations have been appreciating the need to analyze jobs in the context of the organization's structure and strategy. In addition, organizations are recognizing that today's workplace must be adaptable and is constantly subject to change. Thus, although we tend to think of "jobs" as something stable, they actually tend to change and evolve over time. Those who occupy or manage jobs often make minor adjustments to match personal preferences or changing conditions.[14] Indeed, although errors in job analysis can have many sources, most inaccuracy is likely to result from job descriptions being outdated. For this reason, job analysis must not only define jobs when they are created, but also detect changes in jobs as time passes.

With global competitive pressure and economic downturns, one corporate change that has affected many organizations is downsizing. Research suggests that successful downsizing efforts almost always entail changes in the nature of jobs, not just their number. Jobs that have survived the downsizing of the most recent recession tend to have a broader scope of responsibilities coupled with less supervision.[15]

These changes in the nature of work and the expanded use of "project-based" organizational structures require the type of broader understanding that comes from an analysis of work flows. Because the work can change rapidly and it is impossible to rewrite job descriptions every week, job descriptions and specifications need to be flexible. At the same time, legal requirements (as discussed in Chapter 3) may discourage organizations from writing flexible job descriptions. This means organizations must balance the need for flexibility with the need for legal documentation. This presents one of the major challenges to be faced by HRM departments in the next decade. Many professionals are meeting this challenge with a greater emphasis on careful job design.

Job Design

LO 4-6 Describe methods for designing a job so that it can be done efficiently.

Although job analysis, as just described, is important for an understanding of existing jobs, organizations also must plan for new jobs and periodically consider whether they should revise existing jobs. When an organization is expanding, supervisors and human resource professionals must help plan for new or growing work units. When an organization is trying to improve quality or efficiency, a review of work units and processes may require a fresh look at how jobs are designed.

Job Design
The process of defining how work will be performed and what tasks will be required in a given job.

These situations call for **job design**, the process of defining how work will be performed and what tasks will be required in a given job, or *job redesign*, a similar process that involves changing an existing job design. To design jobs effectively, a person must thoroughly understand the job itself (through job analysis) and its place in the larger work unit's work flow process (through work flow analysis). Having a detailed knowledge of the tasks performed in the work unit and in the job, a manager then has many alternative ways to design a job. As shown in Figure 4.5, the available approaches emphasize different aspects of the job: the mechanics of doing a job efficiently, the job's impact on motivation, the use of safe work practices, and the mental demands of the job.

Designing Efficient Jobs

Industrial Engineering
The study of jobs to find the simplest way to structure work in order to maximize efficiency.

If workers perform tasks as efficiently as possible, not only does the organization benefit from lower costs and greater output per worker, but workers should be less fatigued. This point of view has for years formed the basis of classical **industrial engineering**, which looks for the simplest way to structure work in order to maximize efficiency. Typically, applying industrial engineering to a job reduces the complexity of the work, making it so simple that almost anyone can be trained quickly and easily to perform the job. Such jobs tend to be highly specialized and repetitive.

Figure 4.5
Approaches to Job Design

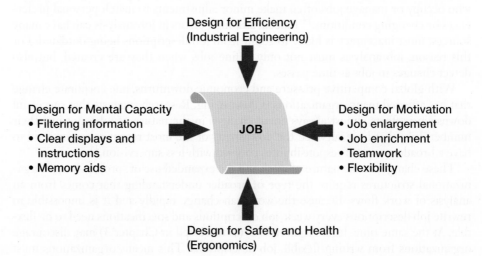

Design for Efficiency
(Industrial Engineering)

Design for Mental Capacity
• Filtering information
• Clear displays and
  instructions
• Memory aids

JOB

Design for Motivation
• Job enlargement
• Job enrichment
• Teamwork
• Flexibility

Design for Safety and Health
(Ergonomics)

In practice, the scientific method traditionally seeks the "one best way" to perform a job by performing time-and-motion studies to identify the most efficient movements for workers to make. Once the engineers have identified the most efficient sequence of motions, the organization should select workers based on their ability to do the job, then train them in the details of the "one best way" to perform that job. The company also should offer pay structured to motivate workers to do their best. (Chapters 11 and 12 discuss pay and pay structures.)

Industrial engineering provides measurable and practical benefits. However, a focus on efficiency alone can create jobs that are so simple and repetitive that workers get bored. Workers performing these jobs may feel their work is meaningless. Hence, most organizations combine industrial engineering with other approaches to job design.

Designing Jobs That Motivate

Especially when organizations must compete for employees, depend on skilled knowledge workers, or need a workforce that cares about customer satisfaction, a pure focus on efficiency will not achieve human resource objectives. Employers also need to ensure that workers have a positive attitude toward their jobs so that they show up at work with enthusiasm, commitment, and creativity. To improve job satisfaction, organizations need to design jobs that take into account factors that make jobs motivating and satisfying for employees.

A model that shows how to make jobs more motivating is the Job Characteristics Model, developed by Richard Hackman and Greg Oldham. This model describes jobs in terms of five characteristics:[16]

LO 4-7 Identify approaches to designing a job to make it motivating.

1. *Skill variety*—The extent to which a job requires a variety of skills to carry out the tasks involved.
2. *Task identity*—The degree to which a job requires completing a "whole" piece of work from beginning to end (for example, building an entire component or resolving a customer's complaint).
3. *Task significance*—The extent to which the job has an important impact on the lives of other people.
4. *Autonomy*—The degree to which the job allows an individual to make decisions about the way the work will be carried out.
5. *Feedback*—The extent to which a person receives clear information about performance effectiveness from the work itself.

As shown in Figure 4.6, the more of each of these characteristics a job has, the more motivating the job will be, according to the Job Characteristics Model. The model predicts that a person with such a job will be more satisfied and will produce more and better work. Some of these factors are behind the satisfaction of workers at Continuum Practical Nursing, which assigns nurses to provide at-home care to children who have been discharged from the hospital. Offering nursing care to children who are disabled or suffer from severe illnesses enables them to stay at home instead of in an institution. Although the nurses tend to earn less than they could in a hospital job, they enjoy flexible schedules and, even more, appreciate the privilege to improve children's quality of life. Continuum's operations director told a reporter, "I have a purpose every day." Jane Bocek, assistant director of nursing, echoed that sentiment: "I've helped change lives."[17] In contrast to their experience, employees in a job that rates low on these characteristics would not find it very motivating. At the extreme are jobs like those described in the "HR Oops!" box.

Figure 4.6

Characteristics of a Motivating Job

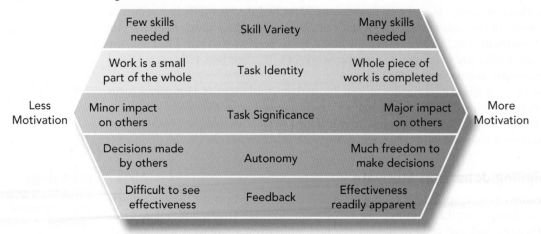

Applications of the job characteristics approach to job design include job enlargement, job enrichment, self-managing work teams, flexible work schedules, and telework.

Job Enlargement

Broadening the types of tasks performed in a job.

Job Enlargement   In a job design, **job enlargement** refers to broadening the types of tasks performed. The objective of job enlargement is to make jobs less repetitive and more interesting. Jobs also become enlarged when organizations add new goals or ask fewer workers to accomplish work that had been spread among more people. In those situations, the challenge is to avoid crossing the line from interesting jobs into jobs that burn out employees. In Minnesota, school principals have been asked to stretch beyond their administrative tasks such as staffing, budgeting, and ensuring building security to take responsibility for student success and teacher development. These goals emphasize the basic purpose that likely drew many principals to careers in education. However, the new goals require many additional hours to observe and evaluate teachers. Schools that can afford it are adding behavior specialists and administration managers to help principals keep schools running as they focus on their new priorities.[18]

Job Extension

Enlarging jobs by combining several relatively simple jobs to form a job with a wider range of tasks.

Organizations that use job enlargement to make jobs more motivational employ techniques such as job extension and job rotation. **Job extension** is enlarging jobs by combining several relatively simple jobs to form a job with a wider range of tasks. An example might be combining the jobs of receptionist, typist, and file clerk into jobs containing all three kinds of work. This approach to job enlargement is relatively simple, but if all the tasks are dull, workers will not necessarily be more motivated by the redesigned job.

Job Rotation

Enlarging jobs by moving employees among several different jobs.

Job rotation does not actually redesign the jobs themselves, but moves employees among several different jobs. This approach to job enlargement is common among production teams. During the course of a week, a team member may carry out each of the jobs handled by the team. Team members might assemble components one day and pack products into cases another day. As with job extension, the enlarged jobs may still consist of repetitive activities, but with greater variation among those activities.

HR Oops!

Jobs That Literally Make People Sick

While effective human resource management aims to create motivating jobs, poor leadership coupled with difficult circumstances can result in jobs that are so unpleasant that workers' mental health begins to suffer. Researchers at the Australian National University analyzed data about working conditions and mental health in more than 7,000 adults over a seven-year period. They found that the mental health of workers in the worst of these jobs was no better than—and sometimes worse than—the mental health of unemployed adults.

The job characteristics that were mostly strongly associated with mental health were the job's complexity and demands, job security, the perceived fairness of pay, and control over the job (for example, ability to decide how to perform tasks). In highly demanding jobs with low security, unfair pay, and little control, workers experienced declining mental health. Unemployment also had an impact on mental health, but it was not as severe.

People differ in what kinds of work they consider unbearable, but many would have that attitude toward working in an Alabama fish-processing plant. The rooms have to be kept cold, and they are wet as well. Some people would likely object to smelling fish all day long. Workers stand for at least 10 hours a day, making repetitive cuts. For all this, they earn minimum wage and limited benefits. In spite of these conditions, employers were able until recently to fill these positions with immigrant workers. But after Alabama passed a law requiring police to question individuals who they believe could be in the United States illegally, many of those workers left the state. Employers report difficulty filling jobs such as these with U.S. workers.

Questions

1. What would be the consequences to an employer of having highly demanding jobs with low security, unfair pay, and little control?
2. How could fish-processing plants like the one described here improve jobs so they can fill vacant positions profitably?

SOURCES: Elizabeth Dwoskin, "Do You Want This Job?" *Bloomberg Businessweek,* November 14, 2011, pp. 70–78; Stephen Long, "Bad Job Worse for Your Mental State than No Job at All," *PM,* June 9, 2011, http://www.abc.net.au/pm/; "When a Job Is So Bad It Hurts," *The Wall Street Journal,* March 29, 2011, http://blogs.wsj.com; Matt McMillen, "For Mental Health, Bad Job Worse than No Job," *Health,* March 14, 2011, http://www.cnn.com.

Job Enrichment   The idea of **job enrichment**, or empowering workers by adding more decision-making authority to their jobs, comes from the work of Frederick Herzberg. According to Herzberg's two-factor theory, individuals are motivated more by the intrinsic aspects of work (for example, the meaningfulness of a job) than by extrinsic rewards, such as pay. Herzberg identified five factors he associated with motivating jobs: achievement, recognition, growth, responsibility, and performance of the entire job. Thus, ways to enrich a manufacturing job might include giving employees authority to stop production when quality standards are not being met and having each employee perform several tasks to complete a particular stage of the process, rather than dividing up the tasks among the employees. For a salesperson in a store, job enrichment might involve the authority to resolve customer problems, including the authority to decide whether to issue refunds or replace merchandise.

In practice, however, it is important to note that not every worker responds positively to enriched jobs. These jobs are best suited to workers who are flexible and responsive to others; for these workers, enriched jobs can dramatically improve motivation.[19]

Job Enrichment
Empowering workers by adding more decision-making authority to jobs.

Nordstrom empowers its employees to resolve customer problems, which can enhance their job experience.

115

Self-Managing Work Teams

Instead of merely enriching individual jobs, some organizations empower employees by designing work to be done by self-managing work teams. As described in Chapter 2, these teams have authority for an entire work process or segment. Team members typically have authority to schedule work, hire team members, resolve problems related to the team's performance, and perform other duties traditionally handled by management. Teamwork can give a job such motivating characteristics as autonomy, skill variety, and task identity.

Because team members' responsibilities are great, their jobs usually are defined broadly and include sharing of work assignments. Team members may, at one time or another, perform every duty of the team. The challenge for the organization is to provide enough training so that the team members can learn the necessary skills. Another approach, when teams are responsible for particular work processes or customers, is to assign the team responsibility for the process or customer, then let the team decide which members will carry out which tasks.

A study of work teams at a large financial services company found that the right job design was associated with effective teamwork.[20] In particular, when teams are self-managed and team members are highly involved in decision making, teams are more productive, employees more satisfied, and managers are more pleased with performance. Teams also tend to do better when each team member performs a variety of tasks and when team members view their effort as significant.

Flexible Work Schedules

One way in which an organization can give employees some say in how their work is structured is to offer flexible work schedules. Depending on the requirements of the organization and the individual jobs, organizations may be able to be flexible about when employees work. As introduced in Chapter 2, types of flexibility include flextime and job sharing. Figure 4.7 illustrates alternatives to the traditional 40-hour workweek.

Flextime

A scheduling policy in which full-time employees may choose starting and ending times within guidelines specified by the organization.

Flextime is a scheduling policy in which full-time employees may choose starting and ending times within guidelines specified by the organization. The flextime policy may require that employees be at work between certain hours, say, 10:00 am and 3:00 pm. Employees work additional hours before or after this period in order to work the full day. One employee might arrive early in the morning in order to leave at 3:00 pm to pick up children after school. Another employee might be a night owl who prefers to arrive at 10:00 am and work until 6:00, 7:00, or even later in the evening. A flextime policy also may enable workers to adjust a particular day's hours in order to make time for doctor's appointments, children's activities, hobbies, or volunteer work. A work schedule that allows time for community and family interests can be extremely motivating for some employees.

Job Sharing

A work option in which two part-time employees carry out the tasks associated with a single job.

Job sharing is a work option in which two part-time employees carry out the tasks associated with a single job. Such arrangements can enable an organization to attract or retain valued employees who want more time to attend school or to care for family members. The job requirements in such an arrangement include the ability to work cooperatively and coordinate the details of one's job with another person. The "HR How To" box offers ideas for using job sharing and other flexible work arrangements and career paths to make work more motivational.

Although not strictly a form of flexibility for all individual employees, another scheduling alternative is the *compressed workweek*. A compressed workweek is a schedule in which full-time workers complete their weekly hours in fewer than five days. For example, instead of working eight hours a day for five days, the employees could complete 40 hours of work in four 10-hour days. This alternative is most common,

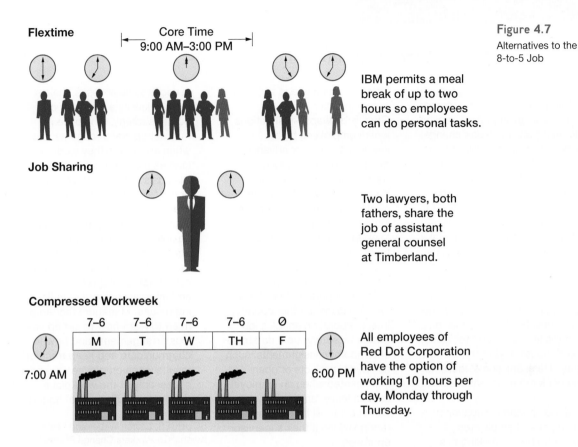

Figure 4.7
Alternatives to the
8-to-5 Job

Flextime

Core Time
9:00 AM–3:00 PM

IBM permits a meal
break of up to two
hours so employees
can do personal tasks.

Job Sharing

Two lawyers, both
fathers, share the
job of assistant
general counsel
at Timberland.

Compressed Workweek

| 7–6 | 7–6 | 7–6 | 7–6 | Ø |
| M | T | W | TH | F |

7:00 AM   6:00 PM

All employees of
Red Dot Corporation
have the option of
working 10 hours per
day, Monday through
Thursday.

but some companies use other alternatives, such as scheduling 80 hours over nine days (with a three-day weekend every other week) or reducing the workweek from 40 to 38 or 36 hours. Employees may appreciate the extra days available for leisure, family, or volunteer activities. An organization might even use this schedule to offer a kind of flexibility—for example, letting workers vote whether they want a compressed workweek during the summer months. This type of schedule has a couple of drawbacks, however. One is that employees may become exhausted on the longer workdays. Another is that if the arrangement involves working more than 40 hours during a week, the Fair Labor Standards Act requires the payment of overtime wages to nonsupervisory employees.

Telework   Flexibility can extend to work locations as well as work schedules. Before the Industrial Revolution, most people worked either close to or inside their own homes. Mass production technologies changed all this, separating work life from home life, as people began to travel to centrally located factories and offices. Today, however, skyrocketing prices for office space, combined with drastically reduced prices for portable communication and computing devices, seem ready to reverse this trend. The broad term for doing one's work away from a centrally located office is *telework*, or telecommuting.

For employers, advantages of telework include less need for office space and the ability to offer greater flexibility to employees who are disabled or need to be available for children or elderly relatives. The employees using telework arrangements may have less absences from work than employees with similar demands who must

Job Flexibility Makes Work Motivational

The old-fashioned static approach to defining rigid jobs and career paths misses an important reality: people aren't static. Needs change, interests changes, and skills change. Workers reach points in their lives when they need more time to care for elderly parents or young children. Workers pursue their educations and discover new passions. Workers gain maturity and long to take on new responsibilities. Because of these and other changes, some employees leave organizations to job-hop or to stay home and meet family obligations. In contrast, workers are motivated by jobs that give them flexibility to learn, to adjust their work hours, and to try out new interests. Here are some ideas for making work more motivational:

- Offer job sharing in situations where pairs of employees are committed to making this arrangement work. Job sharing is not simply a matter of dividing one full-time job into two part-time jobs. The job sharers must work together seamlessly to meet the requirements of a single job, so they must have a strong work ethic and excellent communication skills.

- Offer "job swaps" in situations where employees highly value learning and career advancement. Such employees may be inclined to engage in job hopping as a way to earn promotions and make work more interesting. Organizations can keep these talented and ambitious people onboard by allowing qualified employees to trade places with an employee in a different department or different location (even another country). Intel Corporation enables job swaps by setting up a database of temporary assignments, such as special projects or openings created when an employee takes a leave, and employees can apply to fill those temporary positions if their supervisor approves.

- Consider making flexibility a policy, rather than a menu of programs. To be truly flexible, an organization is open to ideas coming from employees themselves. BDO USA, which offers tax, financial, and consulting services to businesses, makes work flexibility a matter of corporate strategy. Employees may set up any arrangement for when and where they work, as long as that arrangement meets the goals of the employee, his or her team, the firm, and its clients.

- Train managers in managing a flexible workplace. Older managers especially may not be used to the idea that employers can adapt to employees' needs and interests without sacrificing results. Managers therefore need to learn how to set up various arrangements and how to communicate and keep track of results when employees are not necessarily at the workplace during a specified set of hours.

SOURCES: Lauren Weber and Leslie Kwoh, "Co-Workers Change Places," *The Wall Street Journal,* February 21, 2012, http://online.wsj.com; Ellen Weinreb, "How Job Sharing May Be the Secret to Work-Life Balance," *Forbes,* October 24, 2011, http://www.forbes.com; "Employers Embracing Programs as Morale Booster, Business Strategy," *HR Focus,* September 2011, pp. 1–4.

commute to work. Telecommuting can also support a strategy of corporate social responsibility because these employees do not produce the greenhouse gas emissions that result from commuting by car. Telework is easiest to implement for people in managerial, professional, or sales jobs, especially those that involve working and communicating on a computer. A telework arrangement is generally difficult to set up for manufacturing workers. A recent survey by WorldatWork found that more than half of teleworkers were men, their median age was 40, and three-quarters had at least some college education. WorldatWork sees in the demographic data evidence that teleworkers tend to be knowledge workers taking advantage of the ability to work wherever they have Internet and computer access.[21]

Given the possible benefits, it is not surprising that telework has been a growing trend. WorldatWork has found growth in the number of teleworkers every year between 2001 and 2008. The number dipped in 2010, but this partly reflected a decline in the total number of employed workers. In a 2011 survey by Telework Exchange, 60% of employees said their employers are more positive toward telework than they were the year before. Survey respondents also offered a practical reason for that support: three-quarters of those who teleworked said they accomplished more than when they were at the workplace.[22]

Designing Ergonomic Jobs

The way people use their bodies when they work—whether toting heavy furniture onto a moving van or sitting quietly before a computer screen—affects their physical well-being and may affect how well and how long they can work. The study of the interface between individuals' physiology and the characteristics of the physical work environment is called **ergonomics**. The goal of ergonomics is to minimize physical strain on the worker by structuring the physical work environment around the way the human body works. Ergonomics therefore focuses on outcomes such as reducing physical fatigue, aches and pains, and health complaints. Ergonomic research includes the context in which work takes place, such as the lighting, space, and hours worked.[23]

Ergonomic job design has been applied in redesigning equipment used in jobs that are physically demanding. Such redesign is often aimed at reducing the physical demands of certain jobs so that anyone can perform them. In addition, many interventions focus on redesigning machines and technology—for instance, adjusting the height of a computer keyboard to minimize occupational illnesses, such as carpal tunnel syndrome. The design of chairs and desks to fit posture requirements is very important in many office jobs. One study found that having employees participate in an ergonomic redesign effort significantly reduced the number and severity of cumulative trauma disorders (injuries that result from performing the same movement over and over), lost production time, and restricted-duty days.[24]

A recent ergonomic challenge comes from the popularity of mobile devices. As workers find more and more uses for these devices, they are at risk from repetitive-stress injuries (RSIs). Typing with one's thumbs to send frequent text messages on a smartphone can result in inflammation of the tendons that move the thumbs. Laptop and notebook computers are handy to carry, but because the screen and keyboard are attached in a single device, the computer can't be positioned to the ergonomically correct standards of screen at eye level and keyboard low enough to type with arms bent at a 90-degree angle. Heavy users of these devices must therefore trade off eyestrain against physical strain to wrists, unless they can hook up their device to an extra, properly positioned keyboard or monitor. Touchscreens pose their own risks. They are typically part of a flat device such as a smartphone or tablet computer, and these are difficult to position for optimal viewing and typing. Using vertically oriented touchscreens causes even more muscle strain than tapping on a screen lying flat. In addition, because touchscreens usually lack the tactile feedback of pressing keys on a keyboard, users tend to strike them with more force than they use on real keys. Attaching a supplemental keyboard addresses this potential source of

LO 4-8 Explain how organizations apply ergonomics to design safe jobs.

Ergonomics
The study of the interface between individuals' physiology and the characteristics of the physical work environment.

Although employers in all industries are supposed to protect workers under the "general duty" clause, shipyards, nursing homes, grocery stores, and poultry-processing plants are the only four industries for which OSHA has published ergonomic standards.

strain. When using mobile devices or any computer, workers can protect themselves by taking frequent breaks and paying attention to their posture while they work.[25]

The Occupational Safety and Health Administration has a "four-pronged" strategy for encouraging ergonomic job design. The first prong is to issue guidelines (rather than regulations) for specific industries. As of 2012, these guidelines have been issued for the nursing home, grocery store, poultry-processing industries, and shipyards. Second, OSHA enforces violations of its requirement that employers have a general duty to protect workers from hazards, including ergonomic hazards. Third, OSHA works with industry groups to advise employers in those industries. And finally, OSHA established a National Advisory Committee on Ergonomics to define needs for further research. You can learn more about OSHA's guidelines at the agency's website, **www.osha.gov**.

LO 4-9 Discuss how organizations can plan for the mental demands of a job.

Designing Jobs That Meet Mental Capabilities and Limitations

Just as the human body has capabilities and limitations, addressed by ergonomics, the mind, too, has capabilities and limitations. Besides hiring people with certain mental skills, organizations can design jobs so that they can be accurately and safely performed given the way the brain processes information. Generally, this means reducing the information-processing requirements of a job. In these simpler jobs, workers may be less likely to make mistakes or have accidents. Of course, the simpler jobs also may be less motivating. Research has found that challenging jobs tend to fatigue and dissatisfy workers when they feel little control over their situation, lack social support, and feel motivated mainly to avoid errors. In contrast, they may enjoy the challenges of a difficult job where they have some control and social support, especially if they enjoy learning and are unafraid of making mistakes.[26] Because of this drawback to simplifying jobs, it can be most beneficial to simplify jobs where employees will most appreciate having the mental demands reduced (as in a job that is extremely challenging) or where the costs of errors are severe (as in the job of a surgeon or air-traffic controller).

There are several ways to simplify a job's mental demands. One is to limit the amount of information and memorization that the job requires. Organizations can also provide adequate lighting, easy-to-understand gauges and displays, simple-to-operate equipment, and clear instructions. For project management, teamwork, and work done by employees in different locations, organizations may provide social-media tools to simplify information sharing, as described in the "HRM Social" box. Often, employees try to simplify some of the mental demands of their own jobs by creating checklists, charts, or other aids. Finally, every job requires some degree of thinking, remembering, and paying attention, so for every job, organizations need to evaluate whether their employees can handle the job's mental demands.

Changes in technology sometimes reduce job demands and errors, but in some cases, technology has made the problem worse. Some employees try to juggle information from several sources at once—say, talking on a cell phone while typing, surfing the web for information during a team member's business presentation, or repeatedly stopping work on a project to check e-mail or Twitter feeds. In these cases, the cell phone, handheld computer, and e-mail or tweets are distracting the employees from their primary task. They may convey important information, but they also break the employee's train of thought, reducing performance and increasing the likelihood of errors. Research by a firm called Basex, which specializes in the knowledge economy, found that a big part of the information overload problem is recovery time, that is,

Status Updates Help West Wing Writers Stay on the Same Page

West Wing Writers is a speech-writing firm founded by partners who had worked together writing speeches for Bill Clinton. Today they and the associates they hired write speeches for leaders in business, entertainment, politics, and private charities. They research topics, help generate and refine ideas, and prepare polished speeches for their clients to deliver.

To complete these projects, the members of the firm work together closely, contributing ideas to one another's projects and editing one another's work. Yet the work of writing also requires focused thinking without constant interruptions.

That makes it tricky for each writer and project leader to know when is a good time to bring in others to discuss a project, when someone might be available to assist with a new job, and how well current projects are progressing.

The tools of social media have given West Wing Writers an easy way to address all those challenges. The organization bought a time-tracking system called Harvest from a company of the same name. Harvest is basically an online time-sheet with social-media features. Users keep track of their hours by clicking on Start and Stop buttons that time their work on each project. They post status updates to indicate when they are starting and finishing projects. The system is online, so writers can use it from any computer or mobile device with Internet access. Project leaders can quickly check the system to see who is in the middle of a project, who is finishing up, and how long each project is taking.

SOURCES: Harvest, "Time Tracking Made Easy," http://www.getharvest.com, accessed February 23, 2012; West Wing Writers, "About Us," http://www.westwingwriters.com, accessed February 23, 2012; Alina Dizik, "It's 10 A.M. Here's How to Find Your Workers," *The Wall Street Journal,* November 14, 2011, http://online.wsj.com.

the time it takes a person's thinking to switch back from an interruption to the task at hand. The Basex researchers found that recovery time is from 10 to 20 times the length of the interruption. For example, after a 30-second pause to check a Twitter feed, the recovery time could be five minutes or longer.[27]

Organizations probably can't design interruption-free jobs, and few employees would want to isolate themselves entirely from the information and relationships available online. But employers can design jobs that empower workers to manage their time—for example, allowing them to schedule blocks of time when they concentrate on work and do not answer phone calls, e-mails, or text messages. Some employees set aside one or two periods during the day when they will open their e-mail programs, read messages, and respond to the messages immediately. Employers also may provide training in communicating efficiently online—for example, writing informative subject lines and avoiding the "Reply All" option in e-mail.[28]

Information-processing errors also are greater in situations in which one person hands off information to another. Such transmission problems have become a major concern in the field of medicine because critical information is routinely shared among nurses, doctors, and medical technicians, as well as between hospital employees changing shifts. Problems during shift changes are especially likely as a result of fatigue and burnout among employees with stressful jobs.[29] A study of handoffs at Yale–New Haven Hospital found that the information conveyed was often informal, incomplete, and vague. One-fourth of the studied hand-offs led to errors in the care given to patients afterward. Pediatrician Ted Sectish has conducted a pilot program to improve information-sharing during hand-offs. After he trained young doctors in teamwork, set up computerized summaries of patients, and established a structure for what information to convey, medical errors fell by 40%.[30]

don't assume employees know what to do or how to behave—they need training

THINKING ETHICALLY

SHOULD EMPLOYERS FRET ABOUT MAKING EMPLOYEES HAPPY?

One consideration in job design is to increase job satisfaction. The expectation is that employees with high job satisfaction will be motivated to do their best. Some managers are interested in taking this idea a step further. They are applying research into what conditions are associated with happiness. By using our knowledge about what makes people happy, the thinking goes, organizations can try to establish the conditions for a happy workforce.

During the past two decades, psychologists have become much more involved in the study of emotions, especially happiness. As one would expect, they have learned that happiness is greater under conditions such as good health and strong relationships. But the difference that comes from any single condition is not large or long lasting. People do, however, sustain happiness when they experience frequent positive events, even minor ones. Therefore, people can add to their happiness with positive activities such as meditation, exercise, good deeds for others, and social interaction. This logic suggests that organizations could add to employees' happiness by building positive experiences into each day—praise from supervisors, for example, or a time for employees to describe where they have seen acts of kindness at work.

But should employers even take on employee happiness as another project? Time for feel-good activities could take away time from productive activities. And managers might worry that if employees are *too* comfortable, they won't be motivated to try hard. Psychology professor Daniel Gilbert has one response to those concerns: "people are happiest when they're appropriately challenged." People who aren't challenge get bored, and boredom reduces happiness. Former Verizon CEO Denny Strigl would agree. He notes, "Good results make happy employees—and not the other way around."

Questions

1. What ethical responsibilities do organizations have with regard to employees' health? To their happiness?
2. If designing work so that employees will be happier will also make employees more engaged in challenging assignments, should employers address happiness in job design? Should they address happiness if it will instead distract employees from their work? Why or why not?

SOURCES: Gardiner Morse, "The Science behind the Smile," *Harvard Business Review,* January–February 2012, pp. 85–90 (interview with Daniel Gilbert); Denny Strigl, "Results Drive Happiness," *HR Magazine,* October 2011, p. 113.

SUMMARY

LO 4-1 Summarize the elements of work flow analysis.

The analysis identifies the amount and quality of a work unit's outputs (products, parts of products, or services). Next, the analyst determines the work processes required to produce the outputs, breaking down tasks into those performed by each person. Finally, the work flow analysis identifies the inputs used to carry out the processes.

LO 4-2 Describe how work flow is related to an organization's structure.

Within an organization, units and individuals must cooperate to create outputs, and the organization's structure brings people together for this purpose. The structure may be centralized or decentralized, and people may be grouped according to function or into divisions focusing on particular products or customer groups. A

functional structure is most appropriate for people who perform highly specialized jobs and hold relatively little authority. Employee empowerment and teamwork succeed best in a divisional structure.

LO 4-3 Define the elements of a job analysis, and discuss their significance for human resource management.

Job analysis is the process of getting detailed information about jobs. It includes preparation of job descriptions and job specifications. A job description lists the tasks, duties, and responsibilities of a job. Job specifications look at the qualities needed in a person performing the job. They list the knowledge, skills, abilities, and other characteristics that are required for successful performance of a job. Job analysis provides a foundation for carrying out many HRM responsibilities, including work redesign, human resource planning, employee selection and training, performance appraisal, career planning, and job evaluation to determine pay scales.

LO 4-4 Tell how to obtain information for a job analysis.

Information for analyzing an existing job often comes from incumbents and their supervisors. The Labor Department publishes general background information about jobs in the *Dictionary of Occupational Titles* and Occupational Information Network (O*NET). Job analysts, employees, and managers may complete a Position Analysis Questionnaire or fill out a survey for the Fleishman Job Analysis System.

LO 4-5 Summarize recent trends in job analysis.

To broaden traditional approaches to job analysis in support of talent management, organizations develop competency models. A competency model identifies and describes all the competencies, or personal capabilities, required for success in a particular occupation or set of jobs. Because today's workplace requires a high degree of adaptability, job tasks and requirements are subject to constant change. For example, as some organizations downsize, they are defining jobs more broadly, with less supervision of people in those positions. Organizations are also adopting project-based structures and teamwork, which also require flexibility and the ability to handle broad responsibilities.

LO 4-6 Describe methods for designing a job so that it can be done efficiently.

The basic technique for designing efficient jobs is industrial engineering, which looks for the simplest way to structure work to maximize efficiency. Through methods such as time-and-motion studies, the industrial engineer creates jobs that are relatively simple and typically repetitive. These jobs may bore workers because they are so simple.

LO 4-7 Identify approaches to designing a job to make it motivating.

According to the Job Characteristics Model, jobs are more motivating if they have greater skill variety, task identity, task significance, autonomy, and feedback about performance effectiveness. Ways to create such jobs include job enlargement (through job extension or job rotation) and job enrichment. In addition, self-managing work teams offer greater skill variety and task identity. Flexible work schedules and telework offer greater autonomy.

LO 4-8 Explain how organizations apply ergonomics to design safe jobs.

The goal of ergonomics is to minimize physical strain on the worker by structuring the physical work environment around the way the human body works. Ergonomic design may involve modifying equipment to reduce the physical demands of performing certain jobs or redesigning the jobs themselves to reduce strain. Ergonomic design may target work practices associated with injuries.

LO 4-9 Discuss how organizations can plan for the mental demands of a job.

Employers may seek to reduce mental as well as physical strain. The job design may limit the amount of information and memorization involved. Adequate lighting, easy-to-read gauges and displays, simple-to-operate equipment, and clear instructions also can minimize mental strain. Computer software can simplify jobs—for example, by performing calculations or filtering out spam from important e-mail. Finally, organizations can select employees with the necessary abilities to handle a job's mental demands.

KEY TERMS

competency, 110
ergonomics, 119
Fleishman Job Analysis System, 108
flextime, 116
industrial engineering, 112
job, 100
job analysis, 103

job description, 103
job design, 112
job enlargement, 114
job enrichment, 115
job extension, 114
job rotation, 114
job sharing, 116

job specification, 103
position, 100
Position Analysis Questionnaire (PAQ), 107
work flow design, 100

REVIEW AND DISCUSSION QUESTIONS

1. Assume you are the manager of a fast-food restaurant. What are the outputs of your work unit? What are the activities required to produce those outputs? What are the inputs?

2. Based on Question 1, consider the cashier's job in the restaurant. What are the outputs, activities, and inputs for that job?

3. Consider the "job" of college student. Perform a job analysis on this job. What tasks are required in the job? What knowledge, skills, and abilities are necessary to perform those tasks? Prepare a job description based on your analysis.

4. Discuss how the following trends are changing the skill requirements for managerial jobs in the United States:
   a. Increasing use of social media.
   b. Increasing international competition.
   c. Increasing work-family conflicts.

5. Suppose you have taken a job as a trainer in a large bank that has created competency models for all its positions. How could the competency models help you succeed in your career at the bank? How could the competency models help you develop the bank's employees?

6. Consider the job of a customer service representative who fields telephone calls from customers of a retailer that sells online and through catalogs. What measures can an employer take to design this job to make it efficient? What might be some drawbacks or challenges of designing this job for efficiency?

7. How might the job in Question 6 be designed to make it more motivating? How well would these considerations apply to the cashier's job in Question 2?

8. What ergonomic considerations might apply to each of the following jobs? For each job, what kinds of costs would result from addressing ergonomics? What costs might result from failing to address ergonomics?
   a. A computer programmer.
   b. A UPS delivery person.
   c. A child care worker.

9. Modern electronics have eliminated the need for a store's cashiers to calculate change due on a purchase. How does this development modify the job description for a cashier? If you were a store manager, how would it affect the skills and qualities of job candidates you would want to hire? Does this change in mental processing requirements affect what you would expect from a cashier? How?

10. Consider a job you hold now or have held recently. Would you want this job to be redesigned to place more emphasis on efficiency, motivation, ergonomics, or mental processing? What changes would you want, and why? (Or why do you not want the job to be redesigned?)

EXPERIENCING HR

Divide into groups of four. In your group, develop a job description for your professor's job. Use your knowledge and assumptions about the tasks, duties, and responsibilities you think are involved. If you have been given time for research, review the chapter for additional ideas on where to gather information for your job description, and use it to improve your job description. Then use your completed job description as a basis for listing job specifications for your professor's job.

With the whole class, share which tasks, duties, and responsibilities you included in your job description and which knowledge, skills, abilities, and other characteristics you included in your job specifications. Discuss what requirements you define as important and what your professor defines as important. Ask your professor how closely your job description and job specifications match the school's actual expectations. Was your professor given a job description? Would professors at your school be more effective if the school used the job descriptions and specifications written by you and your classmates? Why or why not? How would you adjust your team's job description and specifications, based on what you learned from this discussion? Turn in your job description and job specifications for credit on the assignment.

TAKING RESPONSIBILITY: Job Design for Drivers Keeps UPS on the Road to Energy Efficiency

United Parcel Service is famous for its brown-uniformed drivers behind the wheel of brown delivery trucks. But when it comes to energy consumption, UPS is all green. The company is constantly looking for better fuel-efficient vehicles. Its fleet includes electric, hybrid, and natural-gas vehicles, as well as its standard gasoline-powered trucks. Recently, for example, UPS ordered all-electric vans to deliver packages in Southern California and the Central Valley. Because each van travels the same limited route each day, drivers don't have to worry about running out of electricity between charges. Between 2000 and 2009, UPS recorded a 10% improvement in the miles per gallon it gets from its delivery vehicles.

UPS drivers are expected to follow very specific guidelines for how to deliver packages. These aim to complete each route in the fastest, most efficient way possible. The company details the route that each vehicle is to follow; the routes avoid left turns, which require time and gas to idle while the driver waits for oncoming traffic to clear. At each stop, drivers are supposed to walk at a "brisk pace" of 2.5 paces per second as they move to and from their truck. They keep this up as they make an average of up to 20 stops an hour to deliver about 500 packages a day.

Until recently, drivers were supposed to carry their key ring on their ring finger, so they would never need to spend time fumbling around in pockets. Now the company has improved on that method: Drivers no longer need to waste time pulling keys out of the ignition and using them to unlock the door to the packages. Instead, UPS is giving drivers a digital-remote fob to wear on their belts. With the new keyless system, drivers stop the truck and press a button to turn off the engine and unlock the bulkhead door. The changes will save 1.75 seconds at each stop. That's equivalent to an average of 6.5 minutes per driver per day. Besides saving time, the changes save motions by the driver, thus reducing fatigue.

Specific requirements such as these are the result of relentless efforts to improve efficiency. Throughout each day, computers installed in each truck gather data about the truck's activities: how long it idled, how often it backed up, how far it traveled when it was time for the driver's break. The computers also record whether drivers wore their seat belts. At the end of each delivery day, industrial engineers analyze the day's data and look for ways they can save more time, fuel, and money.

The demand to maintain a "brisk pace" is only one reason why jobs for drivers and other workers at UPS can be physically taxing. Besides being able to move quickly, workers are expected to be able to lift packages weighing up to 70 pounds without assistance. Joe Korziuk told a reporter that in more than two decades with UPS, he has enjoyed his jobs driving and washing trucks, but it has taken a toll. He says the surgeries he has had on both knees and a shoulder and the bulging disks in his back are all results of working conditions: "They're always harping on you and pushing you to go faster and faster." As a result, he said, he also was injured when boxes fell on his head, causing a concussion. Responding to complaints such as these, the union representing UPS workers in the Chicago area demanded that UPS reduce workloads and take more responsibility for workers' safety. According to workers, UPS promoted safety and higher efficiency at the same time. Workers trying to keep up with the pace were unable to meet the safety goals. UPS's response has been that safety is a top priority and injury rates are low for the messenger and courier industry. Officials note that when employees experience even minor on-the-job injuries, they receive training in how to prevent similar injuries in the future.

Despite the safety complaints, UPS is a good employer in the opinion of many workers. Drivers appreciate what they consider to be good wages and benefits.

Questions

1. How do UPS's goals for environmental sustainability affect its job design?
2. How well does UPS take worker safety into account in its job design? How could the company better incorporate safety into job design in a way that is consistent with the company's business strategy?
3. Based on the information given, what role would you say motivation plays in the design of drivers' jobs at UPS? How could the company make its jobs more motivational?

SOURCES: Jennifer Levitz, "Deliver Drivers to Pick Up Pace by Surrendering Keys," *The Wall Street Journal*, September 16, 2011, http://online.wsj.com; Kari Lydersen, "UPS Workers Demand New Approach to Safety," *The New York Times*, May 6, 2011, Business & Company Resource Center, http://galenet.galegroup.com; Seth Skydel, "Makes Good Sense," *Fleet Equipment*, July 2011, Business & Company Resource Center, http://galenet.galegroup.com; David R. Baker, "100 Brown UPS Trucks Going Greener on Inside," *San Francisco Chronicle*, August 25, 2011, Business & Company Resource Center, http://galenet.galegroup.com.

MANAGING TALENT: Why Employees Are Loyal to Bon Secours Health System

Unemployment may persist in other industries, but even through the recent recession, hospitals have struggled to find and keep enough qualified medical professionals on their staffs. The need to provide care 24 hours a day, seven days a week intensifies the problem. Shortages of nurses and other health care workers have been a constant challenge. Therefore, any hospital's approach to talent management has to include ways to reduce employee turnover.

In Virginia, the Bon Secours Health System meets the challenge with flexible scheduling. The organization runs four hospitals, a separate emergency department, a health center, and a college of nursing. To staff all these facilities, Bon Secours is open to a variety of schedules. Employees may choose to work compressed workweeks of four 10-hour shifts or three 12-hour shifts. They have other choices as well: weekends only (at higher pay), four- or eight-hour shifts, and seven-day workweeks followed by seven-day breaks. Employees who want to work part-time may do so and receive full benefits if they work at least 16 hours a week. These part-time workers are especially important when managers are looking for extra help on busy days.

The scheduling options are popular. In a recent analysis, most Bon Secours employees chose one of these flexible work schedules, with one-fourth opting for temporary or part-time work. In addition, 10% of Bon Secours employees are in job-sharing arrangements, and 3% are engaged in telework.

The variety of schedules reflects management's recognition that employees have a variety of needs. Newly hired employees fresh out of college may welcome a full-time schedule and be willing to rotate shifts. Employees with children want a schedule that is the same each week and corresponds to times when child care is available. The option of part-time status lets employees adjust their total work hours as family or other needs require. Without that option, some employees would likely quit when full-time work becomes too demanding.

Bon Secours tracks measures that show real benefits from flexible work arrangements. Surveys of employee engagement show that it has risen from 3.6 points out of 5 in 2005 to 4.55 in 2010. During the same period, employee turnover fell dramatically. At 10% per year, turnover among first-year employees is far below the median for hospitals (28.3%). The cost of hiring and training a nurse is estimated to be three times the nurse's annual salary. At that rate, reducing turnover has a real impact on a hospital's financial performance.

Another way Bon Secours retains employees is by offering a comprehensive set of benefits. After financial meltdown of 2008, many workers were devastated by the plummeting value of their homes, followed by tight lending standards that shrank the options of people looking for a way out of the mess. Bon Secours responded by offering financial assistance. It set up financial education programs, seminars to help out unemployed family members, an option to receive cash in exchange for working instead of taking time off, and a crisis fund to help out employees experiencing financial difficulties. Other benefits that help Bon Secours employees make ends meet during lean times include college tuition assistance (for employees and family members) and discounts arranged with local businesses.

Employee turnover is not the only area in which job design is linked to the organization's performance. Bon Secours participates in the Hospital Quality Incentive Demonstration Project, run by the federal government's Centers for Medicare and Medicaid Services as part of a drive to slow rising costs of health care and improve health care outcomes. The project has identified best practices associated with superior results, and it pays a financial award to participating institutions that can demonstrate they have followed these best practices.

Participating in the program means that designated employees monitor the care given to groups of patients, to make sure practices follow established guidelines. For example, when patients undergo knee or hip replacement surgery, a program coordinator visits them to verify that each has received a set of treatments to prevent blood clots. The hospital also set up measures to ensure that these patients stop receiving antibiotics within 24 hours after the surgery to prevent resistance to the drugs. Such measures are a change from days when hospitals left it up to doctors to ensure that the proper care was delivered to each patient. The more structured approach is associated with lower rates of complications, readmissions, and deaths.

Questions

1. How does Bon Secours make work more motivating?
2. How does Bon Secours address the mental demands of providing quality patient care?
3. How might Bon Secours use competency modeling to improve employee engagement and retention?

SOURCES: Dori Meinert, "The Gift of Time," *HR Magazine*, November 2011, pp. 37–41; Amy Jeter, "Bon Secours Health System Earns Bragging Rights," *HamptonRoads.com*, February 27, 2011, http://hamptonroads.com; Ellen Galinsky, Tyler Wigton, and Lois Backon, "Creative Management Practices for Making Work Work," *Bloomberg Businessweek*, August 28, 2009, http://www.businessweek.com.

TWITTER FOCUS: Inclusivity Defines BraunAbility's Products and Its Jobs

Using Twitter, continue the conversation about job analysis and design by reading the BraunAbility case at **www.mhhe.com/noefund5e.** Engage with your classmates and instructor via Twitter to chat about Ralph Braun and his company using the case questions posed on the Noe website. Don't have a Twitter account yet? See the instructions for getting started on the Online Learning Center.

NOTES

1. Karen J. Bannan, "Fancy Footwork," *Adweek,* September 13, 2010, EBSCOhost, http://web .ebscohost.com.
2. Bill Gregar, "Midwest Firms: Jobs Exist, Skills Scarce," *Plastics News,* October 17, 2011, Business & Company Resource Center, http:// galenet.galegroup.com; Timothy Aeppel, "Man vs. Machine, a Jobless Recovery," *The Wall Street Journal,* January 17, 2012, http://online.wsj.com.
3. J. R. Hollenbeck, H. Moon, A. Ellis, et al., "Structural Contingency Theory and Individual Differences: Examination of External and Internal Person-Team Fit," *Journal of Applied Psychology* 87 (2002), pp. 599–606.
4. Oliver W. Cummings, "What Do Manufacturing Supervisors Really Do on the Job?" *Industry Week,* February 2010, p. 53.
5. A. O'Reilly, "Skill Requirements: Supervisor-Subordinate Conflict," *Personnel Psychology* 26 (1973), pp. 75–80; J. Hazel, J. Madden, and R. Christal, "Agreement between Worker-Supervisor Descriptions of the Worker's Job," *Journal of Industrial Psychology* 2 (1964), pp. 71–79; and A. K. Weyman, "Investigating the Influence of Organizational Role on Perceptions of Risk in Deep Coal Mines," *Journal of Applied Psychology* 88 (2003), pp. 404–12.
6. L. E. Baranowski and L. E. Anderson, "Examining Rater Source Variation in Work Behavior to KSA Linkages," *Personnel Psychology* 58 (2005), pp. 1041–54.
7. National Center for O*NET Development, "O*NET Products at Work," Spring 2011, http:// www.onetcenter.org.
8. P. J. Taylor, W. D. Li, K. Shi, and W. C. Borman, "The Transportability of Job Information across Countries," *Personnel Psychology* 61 (2008), pp. 69–111.
9. *PAQ Newsletter,* August 1989; and E. C. Dierdorff and M. A. Wilson, "A Meta-analysis of Job Analysis Reliability," *Journal of Applied Psychology* 88 (2003), pp. 635–46.
10. E. Fleishman and M. Reilly, *Handbook of Human Abilities* (Palo Alto, CA: Consulting Psychologists Press, 1992); E. Fleishman and M. Mumford, "Ability Requirements Scales," in *The Job Analysis Handbook for Business, Industry, and Government,* ed. S. Gael (New York: Wiley, 1988), pp. 917–35.
11. W. Cascio, *Applied Psychology in Personnel Management,* 4th ed. (Englewood Cliffs, NJ: Prentice Hall, 1991).
12. P. Wright and K. Wexley, "How to Choose the Kind of Job Analysis You Really Need," *Personnel,* May 1985, pp. 51–55.
13. M. Campion, A. Fink, B. Ruggeberg, L. Carr, G. Phillips, and R. Odman, "Doing Competencies Well: Best Practices in Competency Modeling," *Personnel Psychology* 64 (2011): 225–262; R. A. Noe, *Employee Training and Development,* 5e (New York: McGraw-Hill Irwin, 2010); J. Shippmann, R. Ash, M. Battista, L. Carr, L. Eyde, B. Hesketh, J. Kehow, K. Pearlman, and J. Sanchez, "The Practice of Competency Modeling," *Personnel Psychology* 53 (2000): 703–740; A. Lucia and R. Lepsinger, *The Art and Science of Competency Models* (San Francisco: Jossey-Bass, 1999).
14. M. K. Lindell, C. S. Clause, C. J. Brandt, and R. S. Landis, "Relationship between Organizational Context and Job Analysis Ratings," *Journal of Applied Psychology* 83 (1998), pp. 769–76.
15. D. S. DeRue, J. R. Hollenbeck, M. D. Johnson, D. R. Ilgen, and D. K. Jundt, "How Different Team Downsizing Approaches Influence Team-Level Adaptation and Performance," *Academy of Management Journal* 51 (2008), pp. 182–96; Anne Kadet, "'Superjobs': Why You Work More, Enjoy It Less," *The Wall Street Journal,* May 8, 2011, http://online .wsj.com.
16. R. Hackman and G. Oldham, *Work Redesign* (Boston: Addison-Wesley, 1980).
17. Janet Kidd Stewart, "Support for Nurses, Chance to Change Lives Put Continuum Pediatric Nursing in Good Company," *Chicago Tribune,* November 15, 2011, http://www.chicagotribune.com.
18. Alleen Brown, "Twin Cities Principals See Expanding Job Descriptions and Longer Work Hours,"

Twin Cities (MN) Daily Planet, October 30, 2011, http://www.tcdailyplanet.net.

19. F. W. Bond, P. E. Flaxman, and D. Bunce, "The Influence of Psychological Flexibility on Work Redesign: Mediated Moderation of a Work Reorganization Intervention," *Journal of Applied Psychology* 93 (2008), pp. 645–54.

20. M. A. Campion, G. J. Medsker, and A. C. Higgs, "Relations between Work Group Characteristics and Effectiveness: Implications for Designing Effective Work Groups," *Personnel Psychology* 46 (1993), pp. 823–50.

21. Andrea Ozias, ed., "Telework 2011: A Worldat-Work Special Report," WorldatWork, July 2011, http://www.worldatwork.org.

22. Ozias, "Telework 2011"; "What Are Some of the Current Best Practices in Telecommuting?" *HR Focus*, July 2011, Business & Company Resource Center, http://galenet.galegroup.com.

23. See, for example, S. Sonnentag and F. R. H. Zijistra, "Job Characteristics and Off-the-Job Activities as Predictors of Need for Recovery, Well-Being, and Fatigue," *Journal of Applied Psychology* 91 (2006), pp. 330–50.

24. D. May and C. Schwoerer, "Employee Health by Design: Using Employee Involvement Teams in Ergonomic Job Redesign," *Personnel Psychology* 47 (1994), pp. 861–86.

25. Franklin Tessler, "The Hidden Danger of Touch-screens," *InfoWorld.com*, January 11, 2012, Business & Company Resource Center, http://galenet .galegroup.com.

26. N. W. Van Yperen and M. Hagerdoorn, "Do High Job Demands Increase Intrinsic Motivation or Fatigue or Both? The Role of Job Support and Social Control," *Academy of Management Journal* 46 (2003), pp. 339–48; and N. W. Van Yperen and O. Janssen, "Fatigued and Dissatisfied or Fatigued but Satisfied? Goal Orientations and Responses to High Job Demands," *Academy of Management Journal* 45 (2002), pp. 1161–71.

27. Jonathan Spira, "Information Overload: None Are Immune," *Information Management*, September/October 2011, p. 32.

28. Ibid.; Sharon Ann Holgate, "Conquering Information Overload," *Science Careers*, November 4, 2011, http://sciencecareers.sciencemag.org.

29. L. E. LaBlanc, J. J. Hox, W. B. Schaufell, T. W. Taris, and M. C. W. Peters, "Take Care! The Evaluation of a Team-Based Burnout Intervention Program for Oncology Health Care Providers," *Journal of Applied Psychology* 92 (2007), pp. 213–27.

30. Darshak Sanghavi, "The Last of the All-Nighters," *The New York Times Magazine*, August 7, 2011, Business & Company Resource Center, http://galenet .galegroup.com.

Acquiring and Preparing Human Resources

PART TWO

5 Planning for and Recruiting Human Resources

What Do I Need to Know?

After reading this chapter, you should be able to:

LO 5-1 Discuss how to plan for human resources needed to carry out the organization's strategy.

LO 5-2 Determine the labor demand for workers in various job categories.

LO 5-3 Summarize the advantages and disadvantages of ways to eliminate a labor surplus and avoid a labor shortage.

LO 5-4 Describe recruitment policies organizations use to make job vacancies more attractive.

LO 5-5 List and compare sources of job applicants.

LO 5-6 Describe the recruiter's role in the recruitment process, including limits and opportunities.

Introduction

For anyone with a smartphone or other mobile device, apps are such a normal part of life that it's easy to forget they have been around just a few years. Apple launched its App Store in 2008, and it was followed later by Google's Android Market. Software companies are scrambling to come out with new programs and extensions of existing programs that can run on mobile devices. That means they need programmers and software engineers who know the operating systems of iPhones, BlackBerries, and Android phones, even as programmers are only beginning to develop the necessary skills. Many companies are overlooking a lack of experience and training of both new hires and existing software engineers so they can write code for mobile apps.[1]

The story has been far different in the manufacturing sector. Between 1997 and 2009, the number of manufacturing jobs in the United States declined every year. A modest turnaround finally came in 2010, making up for some of the losses that followed the financial crisis and severe recession of the prior years.[2] Skilled jobs, such as precision machining and operating computer-controlled equipment, are in high demand. But for unskilled manufacturing work, U.S. companies have found ways to apply robotics and efficient work design so they can make more goods with fewer workers. Therefore, as manufacturing companies respond to growing demand, they are hiring cautiously. And when employers post an opening, they tend to be flooded with applications.

As these two examples show, trends in technology and the economy also create opportunities and problems in obtaining human resources. When customer demand rises (or falls), organizations may need more (or fewer) employees. When the labor market changes—say, when more people go to college or when a sizable share of the population retires—the supply of qualified workers may grow, shrink, or change in nature. Organizations recently have had difficulty filling information technology jobs because the demand for people with these skills outstrips the supply. To prepare for and respond to these challenges, organizations engage in *human resource planning*—defined in Chapter 1 as identifying the numbers and types of employees the organization will require to meet its objectives.

This chapter describes how organizations carry out human resource planning. In the first part of the chapter, we lay out the steps that go into developing and implementing a human resource plan. Throughout each section, we focus especially on recent trends and practices, including downsizing, employing temporary workers, and outsourcing. The remainder of the chapter explores the process of recruiting. We describe the process by which organizations look for people to fill job vacancies and the usual sources of job candidates. Finally, we discuss the role of recruiters.

The Process of Human Resource Planning

Organizations should carry out human resource planning so as to meet business objectives and gain an advantage over competitors. To do this, organizations need a clear idea of the strengths and weaknesses of their existing internal labor force. They also must know what they want to be doing in the future—what size they want the organization to be, what products and services it should be producing, and so on. This knowledge helps them define the number and kinds of employees they will need. Human resource planning compares the present state of the organization with its goals for the future, then identifies what changes it must make in its human resources to meet those goals. The changes may include downsizing, training existing employees in new skills, or hiring new employees.

These activities give a general view of HR planning. They take place in the human resource planning process shown in Figure 5.1. The process consists of three stages: forecasting, goal setting and strategic planning, and program implementation and evaluation.

LO 5-1 Discuss how to plan for human resources needed to carry out the organization's strategy.

Forecasting

The first step in human resource planning is **forecasting**, as shown in the top portion of Figure 5.1. In personnel forecasting, the HR professional tries to determine the supply of and demand for various types of human resources. The primary goal is to predict which areas of the organization will experience labor shortages or surpluses.

Forecasting supply and demand can use statistical methods or judgment. Statistical methods capture historic trends in a company's demand for labor. Under the right conditions, these methods predict demand and supply more precisely than a human forecaster can using subjective judgment. But many important events in the labor market have no precedent. When such events occur, statistical methods are of little use. To prepare for these situations, the organization must rely on the subjective judgments of experts. Pooling their "best guesses" is an important source of ideas about the future.

Forecasting
The attempts to determine the supply of and demand for various types of human resources to predict areas within the organization where there will be labor shortages or surpluses.

Figure 5.1
Overview of the Human
Resource Planning
Process

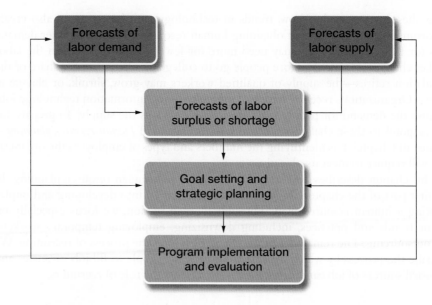

LO 5-2 Determine
the labor demand for
workers in various job
categories.

Trend Analysis
Constructing and apply-
ing statistical models
that predict labor
demand for the next
year, given relatively
objective statistics from
the previous year.

Leading Indicators
Objective measures that
accurately predict future
labor demand.

Forecasting the Demand for Labor

Usually, an organization forecasts demand for specific job categories or skill areas. After identifying the relevant job categories or skills, the planner investigates the likely demand for each. The planner must forecast whether the need for people with the necessary skills and experience will increase or decrease. There are several ways of making such forecasts.

At the most sophisticated level, an organization might use **trend analysis**, constructing and applying statistical models that predict labor demand for the next year, given relatively objective statistics from the previous year. These statistics are called **leading indicators**—objective measures that accurately predict future labor demand. They might include measures of the economy (such as sales or inventory levels), actions of competitors, changes in technology, and trends in the composition of the workforce and overall population. For example, hospitals need to be aware of trends that may shape the demand for medical care because that demand will drive their need for nursing staff. During the recent recession, many workers lost their health insurance along with their jobs, and the value of homes and investments plunged. With fewer resources to draw on, people postponed elective surgeries and tests, so hospitals' current staffing levels were sufficient. But looking ahead, many hospitals foresee a return to nursing shortages. The recovering economy is enabling people to afford procedures they had postponed. And hospitals must plan for the impact of the federal health care reform law. If it is fully implemented, it may add 30 million more people to the ranks of those with health insurance. Hospitals expect that some of them will need medical procedures and nursing care, so they are gearing up for a surge in hiring.[3]

Statistical planning models are useful when there is a long, stable history that can be used to reliably detect relationships among variables. However, these models almost always have to be complemented with subjective judgments of experts. There are simply too many "once-in-a-lifetime" changes to consider, and statistical models cannot capture them.

Determining Labor Supply   Once a company has forecast the demand for labor, it needs an indication of the firm's labor supply. Determining the internal labor supply calls for a detailed analysis of how many people are currently in various job categories or have specific skills within the organization. The planner then modifies this analysis to reflect changes expected in the near future as a result of retirements, promotions, transfers, voluntary turnover, and terminations.

One type of statistical procedure that can be used for this purpose is the analysis of a **transitional matrix**. This is a chart that lists job categories held in one period and shows the proportion of employees in each of those job categories in a future period. It answers two questions: "Where did people who were in each job category go?" and "Where did people now in each job category come from?" Table 5.1 is an example of a transitional matrix.

This example lists job categories for an auto parts manufacturer. The jobs listed at the left were held in 2009; the numbers at the right show what happened

As the average age of many workers in skilled trades grows, the coming demand for workers in many trades is expected to outstrip supply in the United States. There is a potential for employers in some areas to experience a labor shortage because of this. How can HR prepare for this reality? What should be done now to avoid the shortage?

to the people in 2012. The numbers represent proportions. For example, .95 means 95% of the people represented by a row in the matrix. The column headings under 2012 refer to the row numbers. The first row is sales managers, so the numbers under column (1) represent people who became sales managers. Reading across the first row, we see that 95 of the people who were sales managers in 2009 are still sales managers in 2012. The other 5% correspond to position (8), "Not in organization," meaning the 5% of employees who are not still sales managers have left the organization. In the second row are sales representatives. Of those who were sales reps in 2009, 5% were promoted to sales manager, 60% are still sales reps, and 35% have left the organization. In row (3), half (50%) of sales apprentices are still in that job, but 20% are now sales reps and 30% have left the organization. This pattern of jobs shows a career path from sales apprentice to sales representative to sales manager. Of course, not everyone is promoted, and some of the people leave instead.

Reading down the columns provides another kind of information: the sources of employees holding the positions in 2012. In the first column, we see that most sales managers (95%) held that same job three years earlier. The other 5% were promoted from sales representative positions. Skipping over to column (3), half the sales apprentices on the payroll in 2012 held the same job three years before, and the other half were hired from outside the organization. This suggests that the organization fills

Transitional Matrix
A chart that lists job categories held in one period and shows the proportion of employees in each of those job categories in a future period.

2009	2012							
	(1)	**(2)**	**(3)**	**(4)**	**(5)**	**(6)**	**(7)**	**(8)**
(1) Sales manager	.95							.05
(2) Sales representative	.05	.60						.35
(3) Sales apprentice		.20	.50					.30
(4) Assistant plant manager				.90	.05			.05
(5) Production manager				.10	.75			.15
(6) Production assembler					.10	.80		.10
(7) Clerical							.70	.30
(8) Not in organization	.00	.20	.50	.00	.10	.20	.30	

Table 5.1

Transitional Matrix: Example for an Auto Parts Manufacturer

sales manager positions primarily through promotions, so planning for this job would focus on preparing sales representatives. In contrast, planning to meet the organization's needs for sales apprentices would emphasize recruitment and selection of new employees.

Matrices such as this one are extremely useful for charting historical trends in the company's supply of labor. More important, if conditions remain somewhat constant, they can also be used to plan for the future. For example, if we believe that we are going to have a surplus of labor in the production assembler job category in the next three years, we can plan to avoid layoffs. Still, historical data may not always reliably indicate future trends. Planners need to combine statistical forecasts of labor supply with expert judgments. For example, managers in the organization may see that a new training program will likely increase the number of employees qualified for new openings. Forecasts of labor supply also should take into account the organization's pool of skills. Many organizations include inventories of employees' skills in an HR database. When the organization forecasts that it will need new skills in the future, planners can consult the database to see how many existing employees have those skills.

Besides looking at the labor supply within the organization, the planner should examine trends in the external labor market. The planner should keep abreast of labor market forecasts, including the size of the labor market, the unemployment rate, and the kinds of people who will be in the labor market. For example, we saw in Chapter 2 that the U.S. labor market is aging and that immigration is an important source of new workers. Important sources of data on the external labor market include the *Occupational Outlook Quarterly* and the *Monthly Labor Review*, published by the Labor Department's Bureau of Labor Statistics. Details and news releases are available at the website of the Bureau of Labor Statistics (**www.bls.gov**).

Determining Labor Surplus or Shortage

LO 5-3 Summarize the advantages and disadvantages of ways to eliminate a labor surplus and avoid a labor shortage.

Based on the forecasts for labor demand and supply, the planner can compare the figures to determine whether there will be a shortage or surplus of labor for each job category. Determining expected shortages and surpluses allows the organization to plan how to address these challenges.

Issues related to a labor surplus or shortage can pose serious challenges for the organization. As businesses increasingly compete on a global scale, one challenge is to find U.S. workers who can communicate in the parts of the world where companies see the greatest potential for growth. U.S. companies are especially interested in finding employees who speak Spanish and Chinese. However, college enrollment in Spanish and Chinese classes is not growing fast enough to meet that demand.[4]

Goal Setting and Strategic Planning

The second step in human resource planning is goal setting and strategic planning, as shown in the middle of Figure 5.1. The purpose of setting specific numerical goals is to focus attention on the problem and provide a basis for measuring the organization's success in addressing labor shortages and surpluses. The goals should come directly from the analysis of labor supply and demand. They should include a specific figure indicating what should happen with the job category or skill area and a specific timetable for when the results should be achieved.

For each goal, the organization must choose one or more human resource strategies. A variety of strategies is available for handling expected shortages and surpluses of labor. The top of Table 5.2 shows major options for reducing an expected

OPTIONS FOR REDUCING A SURPLUS		
OPTION	**SPEED OF RESULTS**	**AMOUNT OF SUFFERING CAUSED**
Downsizing	Fast	High
Pay reductions	Fast	High
Demotions	Fast	High
Transfers	Fast	Moderate
Work sharing	Fast	Moderate
Hiring freeze	Slow	Low
Natural attrition	Slow	Low
Early retirement	Slow	Low
Retraining	Slow	Low
OPTIONS FOR AVOIDING A SHORTAGE		
OPTION	**SPEED OF RESULTS**	**ABILITY TO CHANGE LATER**
Overtime	Fast	High
Temporary employees	Fast	High
Outsourcing	Fast	High
Retrained transfers	Slow	High
Turnover reductions	Slow	Moderate
New external hires	Slow	Low
Technological innovation	Slow	Low

Table 5.2

HR Strategies for Addressing a Labor Shortage or Surplus

Core Competency
A set of knowledge and skills that make the organization superior to competitors and create value for customers.

labor surplus, and the bottom of the table lists options for avoiding an expected labor shortage.

This planning stage is critical. The options differ widely in their expense, speed, and effectiveness. Options for reducing a labor surplus cause differing amounts of human suffering. The options for avoiding a labor shortage differ in terms of how easily the organization can undo the change if it no longer faces a labor shortage. For example, an organization probably would not want to handle every expected labor shortage by hiring new employees. The process is relatively slow and involves expenses to find and train new employees. Also, if the shortage becomes a surplus, the organization will have to consider laying off some of the employees. Layoffs involve another set of expenses, such as severance pay, and they are costly in terms of human suffering.

Another consideration in choosing an HR strategy is whether the employees needed will contribute directly to the organization's success. Organizations are most likely to benefit from hiring and retaining employees who provide a **core competency**—that is, a set of knowledge and skills that make the organization superior to competitors and create value for customers. At a store, for example, core competencies include choosing merchandise that shoppers want and providing shoppers with excellent service. For other work that is not a core competency—say, cleaning the store and providing security—the organization may benefit from using HR strategies other than hiring full-time employees.

Organizations try to anticipate labor surpluses far enough ahead that they can freeze hiring and let natural attrition (people leaving on their own) reduce the labor force. Unfortunately for many workers, organizations often stay competitive in a fast-changing environment by responding to a labor surplus with downsizing, which delivers fast results. The impact

Cold Stone Creamery employees give their company the competitive advantage with their "entertainment factor." The company is known to seek out employees who like to perform and then "audition" rather than interview potential employees.

is painful for those who lose jobs, as well as those left behind to carry on without them. To handle a labor shortage, organizations typically hire temporary employees or use outsourcing. Because downsizing, using temporary employees, and outsourcing are most common, we will look at each of these in greater detail in the following sections.

Downsizing
The planned elimination of large numbers of personnel with the goal of enhancing the organization's competitiveness.

Downsizing   As we discussed in Chapter 2, **downsizing** is the planned elimination of large numbers of personnel with the goal of enhancing the organization's competitiveness. The primary reason organizations engage in downsizing is to promote future competitiveness. According to surveys, they do this by meeting four objectives:

1. *Reducing costs*—Labor is a large part of a company's total costs, so downsizing is an attractive place to start cutting costs.
2. *Replacing labor with technology*—Closing outdated factories, automating, or introducing other technological changes reduces the need for labor. Often, the labor savings outweigh the cost of the new technology.
3. *Mergers and acquisitions*—When organizations combine, they often need less bureaucratic overhead, so they lay off managers and some professional staff members.
4. *Moving to more economical locations*—Some organizations move from one area of the United States to another, especially from the Northeast and Midwest to the South and the mountain regions of the West. Although the recent recession hit California, Florida, and Texas particularly hard in terms of the number of job losses, strong job growth in those states supports expectations that the longer-term pattern of job movement to the South and West will continue in the future.[5] Other moves have shifted jobs to other countries, including Mexico, India, and China, where wages are lower. In some cases, however, the United States can be a relatively low-cost location. Electrolux recently closed its vacuum cleaner factories in Vastervik, Sweden, and L'Assomption, Quebec. It replaced them with facilities in the lower-cost locations of Hungary (to serve the European market) and Memphis, Tennessee (to serve North America).[6]

Although downsizing has an immediate effect on costs, much of the evidence suggests that it hurts long-term organizational effectiveness. This is especially true for certain kinds of companies, such as those that emphasize research and development and where employees have extensive contact with customers.[7] The negative effect of downsizing was especially high among firms that engaged in high-involvement work practices, such as the use of teams and performance-related pay incentives. As a result, the more a company tries to compete through its human resources, the more layoffs hurt productivity.[8]

Why do so many downsizing efforts fail to meet expectations? There seem to be several reasons. First, although the initial cost savings give a temporary boost to profits, the long-term effects of an improperly managed downsizing effort can be negative. Downsizing leads to a loss of talent, and it often disrupts the social networks through which people are creative and flexible.[9] Unless the downsizing is managed well, employees feel confused, demoralized, and even less willing to stay with the organization. Organizations may not take (or even know) the steps that can counter these reactions—for example, demonstrating how they are treating employees fairly, building confidence in the company's plans for a stronger future, and showing the organization's commitment to behaving responsibly with regard to all its stakeholders, including employees, customers, and the community.[10] The "HR Oops!" box illustrates consequences of not taking those steps.

Trimming More Than the Fat

Getting lean improves an organization's efficiency and makes it stronger for the long haul. But some organizations are so desperate to cut costs that they don't just get lean, they starve themselves of important human resources.

That happened at a technology company in Texas. The company kept laying off employees in its design department until one interactive designer who remained was handling what she saw as the work of three designers. She also managed many of the company's web projects.

The employee was afraid to quit during a slow economy, but she was burning out from the strain of falling behind in spite of constant overtime and taking work home. Eventually she could no longer keep quiet, so she gave her supervisor the choice between promoting her to art director or dividing up the work among more people. The supervisor gave her the promotion (with a small raise) and began authorizing the employee to contract for help from a freelancer.

Companies that downsized during the recent recession may find themselves making more such bargains. Employees who feel exhausted and unappreciated are beginning to indicate that they want to leave their employers to find better jobs. The ones with the best chance to get a better offer are likely to be an organization's most valuable people.

Questions

1. In what ways do you think the downsizing in the technology company's design department was ineffective at improving the company's performance?
2. Besides layoffs, how else might the design department respond to a decline in demand?

SOURCES: Judy Martin, "This Could Be the Year Fed Up Employees Have Had It," *Forbes,* January 16, 2012, http://www.msnbc.msn.com; Vickie Elmer, "The Invisible Promotion," *Fortune,* February 7, 2011, EBSCOhost, http://web.ebscohost.com; CareerBuilder, "Nearly One-Third of Employers Willing to Negotiate Salary Increases for Current Employees for 2011, CareerBuilder Survey Finds," news release, November 10, 2010, http://www.careerbuilder.com.

Also, many companies wind up rehiring. Downsizing campaigns often eliminate people who turn out to be irreplaceable. In one survey, 80% of the firms that had downsized later replaced some of the very people they had laid off. In one Fortune 100 firm, a bookkeeper making $9 an hour was let go. Later, the company realized she knew many things about the company that no one else knew, so she was hired back as a consultant—for $42 an hour.[11] However, recent trends in employment suggest that companies will not rehire employees for many of the jobs eliminated when they restructure; introduce automation, or move work to lower-cost regions.[12]

Finally, downsizing efforts often fail because employees who survive the purge become self-absorbed and afraid to take risks. Motivation drops because any hope of future promotions—or any future—with the company dies. Many employees start looking for other employment opportunities. The negative publicity associated with a downsizing campaign can also hurt the company's image in the labor market, so it is harder to recruit employees later.

Many problems with downsizing can be reduced with better planning. Instead of slashing jobs across the board, successful downsizing makes surgical strategic cuts that improve the company's competitive position, and management addresses the problem of employees becoming demoralized. During the housing boom of the previous decade, landscaping companies struggled to find enough talented, motivated workers, especially at the supervisory level. When bust followed boom, well-managed landscapers used downsizing as an opportunity to improve quality. Bill Davids of Clarence Davids & Co. was one landscaping manager who selected the least productive employees for layoffs. He then rallied the remaining employees to focus on how to operate more efficiently and keep the business afloat during lean times. Davids told a reporter, "Once [employees] see you're serious and several people have exited, you get the buy-in pretty quick."[13] In fact, for good workers, it can be motivating to be part of a higher-quality, if smaller, team.

Reducing Hours   Given the limitations of downsizing, many organizations are more carefully considering other avenues for eliminating a labor surplus. Among the alternatives listed in Table 5.2, one that is seen as a way to spread the burden more fairly is cutting work hours, generally with a corresponding reduction in pay. Besides the thought that this is a more equitable way to weather a slump in demand, companies choose a reduction in work hours because it is less costly than layoffs requiring severance pay, and it is easier to restore the work hours than to hire new employees after a downsizing effort. When American Airlines scaled back its flights, it initially planned to lay off 500 flight attendants. However, it worked with the attendants' union to save jobs by giving flight attendants the option to share jobs or take voluntary leaves of absence. Enough employees volunteered for job sharing and leaves that American canceled the layoffs. This plan was based on the expectation that demand would improve over the next few years, ending the need for job sharing and leaves of absence.[14]

Early-Retirement Programs   Another popular way to reduce a labor surplus is with an early-retirement program. As we discussed in Chapter 2, the average age of the U.S. workforce is increasing. But even though many baby boomers are reaching traditional retirement age, indications are that this group has no intention of leaving the workforce soon.[15] Reasons include improved health of older people, jobs becoming less physically demanding, concerns about the long-term viability of social security and pensions, the recent drop in the value of older workers' retirement assets (especially stock funds and home values), and laws against age discrimination. Under the pressures associated with an aging labor force, many employers try to encourage older workers to leave voluntarily by offering a variety of early-retirement incentives. The more lucrative of these programs succeed by some measures. Research suggests that these programs encourage lower-performing older workers to retire.[16] Sometimes they work so well that too many workers retire.

Many organizations are moving from early-retirement programs to phased-retirement programs. In a *phased-retirement program*, the organization can continue to enjoy the experience of older workers while reducing the number of hours that these employees work, as well as the cost of those employees. This option also can give older employees the economic and psychological benefits of easing into retirement, rather than being thrust entirely into a new way of life.[17]

Employing Temporary and Contract Workers   While downsizing has been a popular way to reduce a labor surplus, the most widespread methods for eliminating a labor shortage are hiring temporary and contract workers and outsourcing work. Employers may arrange to hire a temporary worker through an agency that specializes in linking employers with people who have the necessary skills. The employer pays the agency, which in turn pays the temporary worker. Employers also may contract directly with individuals, often professionals, to provide a particular service.

To use this source of labor effectively, employers need to overcome some disadvantages. In particular, temporary and contract workers may not be as committed to the organization, so if they work directly with customers, that attitude may spill over and affect customer loyalty. Therefore, many organizations try to use permanent employees in key jobs and use temporary and contract workers in ways that clearly supplement—and do not potentially replace—the permanent employees.[18]

Temporary Workers As we saw in Chapter 2, the federal government estimated that organizations are using over a million temporary workers. Temporary employment is popular with employers because it gives them flexibility they need to operate efficiently when demand for their products changes rapidly. If an employer believes a higher level of demand will persist, it often can hire the temps as permanent workers. Siemens contracts with a temporary employment agency to provide production and warehouse workers for its Rail Systems Division in Sacramento. If Siemens determines a long-term need for additional workers, it selects high-performing temporary employees to put on its payroll.[19]

In addition to flexibility, temporary employment offers lower costs. Using temporary workers frees the employer from many administrative tasks and financial burdens associated with being the "employer of record." The cost of employee benefits, including health care, pension, life insurance, workers' compensation, and unemployment insurance, can account for 40% of payroll expenses for permanent employees. Assuming the agency pays for these benefits, a company using temporary workers may save money even if it pays the agency a higher rate for that worker than the usual wage paid to a permanent employee.

Agencies that provide temporary employees also may handle some of the tasks associated with hiring. Small companies that cannot afford their own testing programs often get employees who have been tested by a temporary agency. Many temporary agencies also train employees before sending them to employers. This reduces employers' training costs and eases the transition for the temporary worker and employer.

Finally, temporary workers may offer value not available from permanent employees. Because the temporary worker has little experience at the employer's organization, this person brings an objective point of view to the organization's problems and procedures. Also, a temporary worker may have a great deal of experience in other organizations that can be applied to the current assignment.

To obtain these benefits, organizations need to overcome the disadvantages associated with temporary workers. For example, tension can develop between temporary and permanent employees. Employers can minimize resentment and ensure that all workers feel valued by not bringing in temporary or contract workers immediately after downsizing and by hiring temporary workers from agencies that provide benefits. In addition, employers must avoid the legal pitfalls associated with temporary employees and contract workers, as described in "HR How To."

Employee or Contractor? Besides using a temporary employment agency, a company can obtain workers for limited assignments by entering into contracts with them. If the person providing the services is an independent contractor, rather than an employee, the company does not pay employee benefits, such as health insurance and vacations. As with using temporary employees, the savings can be significant, even if the contractor works at a higher rate of pay.

This strategy carries risks, however. If the person providing the service is a contractor and not an employee, the company is not supposed to directly supervise the worker. The company can tell the contractor what criteria the finished assignment should meet but not, for example, where or what hours to work. This distinction is significant, because under federal law, if the company treats the contractor as an employee, the company has certain legal obligations, described in Part 4, related to matters such as overtime pay and withholding taxes.

HR How To

Using Temporary Employees and Contractors

When a company lands a big order, needs to catch up on administrative work, or isn't sure demand will continue at present levels, contingent workers look like the ideal solution. The company can hire workers from a temp agency or negotiate contracts for short-term projects, and when the project ends or demand falls, the company doesn't have to figure out what to do with the workers. In addition, the company may be able to save money because it doesn't have to provide employee benefits or withhold taxes from contract workers' pay.

However, it is not up to the company to decide whether its workers are really independent contractors. The Internal Revenue Service has guidelines for what constitutes an employee and an independent contractor. Here are some tips for how to classify workers:

- Companies can specify what they want a contractor to accomplish. But if the employer tells the workers how to do the work and controls the workers' activities, then the workers are employees, not independent contractors.
- Providing the workers with supplies or tools and reimbursing the workers for the expenses associated with their work tend to be signs that the workers are employees.
- Providing the workers with benefits such as insurance and paid vacation time is a sign that the workers are employees. Usually, temporary workers receive these benefits from an agency that employs them, not from the company that pays the agency for the workers' services.
- If a company hires workers from a temp agency to do work for a long period of time, directly controls what these workers do, and uses them to perform key roles, the government may see the company as an employer or "joint employer" with the temp agency. A company that is a joint employer has to follow labor laws, including those against discrimination (see Chapter 3) and legal requirements for pay (see Chapter 11).
- If a company is not sure whether its workers are employees or independent contractors, it should get professional advice. Companies and workers may ask the IRS to decide. The way to do this is to file a Form SS-8 requesting a determination from the IRS. The form is available at the IRS website (http://www.irs.gov).

SOURCES: Internal Revenue Service, "Independent Contractor (Self-Employed) or Employee?" last updated February 23, 2012, http://www.irs.gov; Internal Revenue Service, "Employee vs. Independent Contractor: Seven Tips for Business Owners," IRS Summertime Tax Tip 2010–20, last updated October 6, 2011, http://www.irs.gov; "Review of Hiring Policies Urged as Misclassification Issues Heat Up," *HR Focus,* January 2011, Business & Company Resource Center, http://galenet.galegroup.com.

When an organization wants to consider using independent contractors as a way to expand its labor force temporarily, human resource professionals can help by alerting the company to the need to verify that the arrangement will meet the legal requirements. A good place to start is with the advice to small businesses at the Internal Revenue Service website (**www.irs.gov**); search for "independent contractor" to find links to information and guidance. In addition, the organization may need to obtain professional legal advice.

Outsourcing

Contracting with another organization to perform a broad set of services.

Outsourcing   Instead of using a temporary or contract employee to fill a single job, an organization might want a broader set of services. Contracting with another organization to perform a broad set of services is called **outsourcing**. Organizations use outsourcing as a way to operate more efficiently and save money. They choose outsourcing firms that promise to deliver the same or better quality at a lower cost. One reason they can do this is that the outside company specializes in the service and can benefit from economies of scale (the economic principle that producing something in large volume tends to cost less for each additional unit than producing in small volume). This efficiency is often the attraction for outsourcing human resource functions such as payroll. Costs also are lower when the outsourcing firm is located in a part of the world where wages are relatively low. The labor forces of countries such as China, India, Jamaica, and those in Eastern Europe have been creating an abundant supply of labor for unskilled and low-skilled work.

The first uses of outsourcing emphasized manufacturing and routine tasks. However, technological advances in computer networks and transmission have speeded up the outsourcing process and have helped it spread beyond manufacturing areas and low-skilled jobs. For example, newspapers outsource ad creation to Outsourcing USA, a small business in Dallas, Pennsylvania. At Outsourcing USA, employees design advertisements for print, web, and mobile editions of their clients' newspapers. The company offers low costs by specializing in a niche market, focusing relentlessly on efficiency, and hiring recent graduates. Careful supervision and a one-month training program ensure that Outsourcing USA delivers quality work.[20]

Using outsourcing may be a necessary way to operate as efficiently as competitors, but it does pose challenges. Quality-control problems, security violations, and poor customer service have sometimes wiped out the cost savings attributed to lower wages. To ensure success with an outsourcing strategy, companies should follow these guidelines:

- Learn about what the provider can do for the company, not just the costs. Make sure the company has the necessary skills, including an environment that can meet standards for clear communication, on-time shipping, contract enforcement, fair labor practices, and environmental protection. Outsourcing USA finds that its clients prefer buying ad production services from a local company rather than going overseas for potentially lower prices. The Pennsylvania company can offer newspapers in the region faster communications (by being in the same time zone) and greater familiarity with the nuances of American English.[21]
- Do not offshore any work that is proprietary or requires tight security.[22]
- Start small and monitor the work closely, especially in the beginning, when problems are most likely. Boeing offers a cautionary tale with its ambitious plan to have a worldwide network of suppliers build all the components for its 787 Dreamliner. The project eventually fell three years behind schedule and went billions of dollars over budget as various subcontractors fell behind and failed to meet exacting quality standards. Along the way, Boeing went so far as to acquire some of the suppliers to gain more control over the production process.[23]
- Look for opportunities to outsource work in areas that promote growth, for example, by partnering with experts who can help the organization tap new markets. Mansfield Sales Partners offers this type of advantage to companies that have a limited sales force or want to test a new market. Such companies can use Mansfield's team of experienced salespeople to introduce their products in markets around the world.[24]

Overtime and Expanded Hours   Organizations facing a labor shortage may be reluctant to hire employees, even temporary workers, or to commit to an outsourcing arrangement. Especially if the organization expects the shortage to be temporary, it may prefer an arrangement that is simpler and less costly. Under some conditions, these organizations may try to garner more hours from the existing labor force, asking them to go from part-time to full-time status or to work overtime.

A major downside of overtime is that the employer must pay nonmanagement employees one-and-a-half times their normal wages for work done overtime. Even so, employers see overtime pay as preferable to the costs of hiring and training new employees. The preference is especially strong if the organization doubts that the current higher level of demand for its products will last long.

For a short time at least, many workers appreciate the added compensation for working overtime. Over extended periods, however, employees feel stress and frustration from working long hours. Overtime therefore is best suited for short-term labor shortages.

Implementing and Evaluating the HR Plan

For whatever HR strategies are selected, the final stage of human resource planning involves implementing the strategies and evaluating the outcomes. This stage is represented by the bottom part of Figure 5.1. When implementing the HR strategy, the organization must hold some individual accountable for achieving the goals. That person also must have the authority and resources needed to accomplish those goals. It is also important that this person issue regular progress reports, so the organization can be sure that all activities occur on schedule and that the early results are as expected.

Implementation that ties planning and recruiting to the organization's strategy and to its efforts to develop employees becomes a complete program of talent management. Today's computer systems have made talent management more practical. For example, companies can tap into databases and use analytic tools to keep track of which skills and knowledge they need, which needs have already been filled, which employees are developing experiences to help them meet future needs, and which sources of talent have met talent needs most efficiently.

In evaluating the results, the most obvious step is checking whether the organization has succeeded in avoiding labor shortages or surpluses. Along with measuring these numbers, the evaluation should identify which parts of the planning process contributed to success or failure. For example, consider a company where meeting human resource needs requires that employees continually learn new skills. If there is a gap between needed skills and current skill levels, the evaluation should consider whether the problem lies with failure to forecast the needed skills or with implementation. Are employees signing up for training, and is the right kind of training available?

Applying HR Planning to Affirmative Action

As we discussed in Chapter 3, many organizations have a human resource strategy that includes affirmative action to manage diversity or meet government requirements. Meeting affirmative-action goals requires that employers carry out an additional level of human resource planning aimed at those goals. In other words, besides looking at its overall workforce and needs, the organization looks at the representation of subgroups in its labor force—for example, the proportion of women and minorities.

Affirmative-action plans forecast and monitor the proportion of employees who are members of various protected groups (typically, women and racial or ethnic minorities). The planning looks at the representation of these employees in the organization's job categories and career tracks. The planner can compare the proportion of employees who are in each group with the proportion each group represents in the labor market. For example, the organization might note that in a labor market that is 25% Hispanic, 60% of its customer service personnel are Hispanic. This type of comparison is called a **workforce utilization review**. The organization can use this process to determine whether there is any subgroup whose proportion in the relevant labor market differs substantially from the proportion in the job category.

Workforce Utilization Review
A comparison of the proportion of employees in protected groups with the proportion that each group represents in the relevant labor market.

If the workforce utilization review indicates that some group—for example, African Americans—makes up 35% of the relevant labor market for a job category but that this same group constitutes only 5% of the employees actually in the job category at the organization, this is evidence of underutilization. That situation could result from problems in selection or from problems in internal movement (promotions or other movement along a career path). One way to diagnose the situation would be to use transitional matrices, such as the matrix shown in Table 5.1 earlier in this chapter.

The steps in a workforce utilization review are identical to the steps in the HR planning process that were shown in Figure 5.1. The organization must assess current utilization patterns, then forecast how they are likely to change in the near future. If these analyses suggest the organization is underutilizing certain groups and if forecasts suggest this pattern is likely to continue, the organization may need to set goals and timetables for changing. The planning process may identify new strategies for recruitment or selection. The organization carries out these HR strategies and evaluates their success.

Recruiting Human Resources

As the first part of this chapter shows, it is difficult to always predict exactly how many (if any) new employees the organization will have to hire in a given year in a given job category. The role of human resource recruitment is to build a supply of potential new hires that the organization can draw on if the need arises. In human resource management, **recruiting** consists of any practice or activity carried on by the organization with the primary purpose of identifying and attracting potential employees.[25] It thus creates a buffer between planning and the actual selection of new employees (the topic of the next chapter). The goals of recruiting (encouraging qualified people to apply for jobs) and selection (deciding which candidates would be the best fit) are different enough that they are most effective when performed separately, rather than combined as in a job interview that also involves selling candidates on the company.[26]

Because of differences in companies' strategies, they may assign different degrees of importance to recruiting.[27] In general, however, all companies have to make decisions in three areas of recruiting: personnel policies, recruitment sources, and the characteristics and behavior of the recruiter. As shown in Figure 5.2, these aspects of recruiting have

LO 5-4 Describe recruitment policies organizations use to make job vacancies more attractive.

Recruiting
Any activity carried on by the organization with the primary purpose of identifying and attracting potential employees.

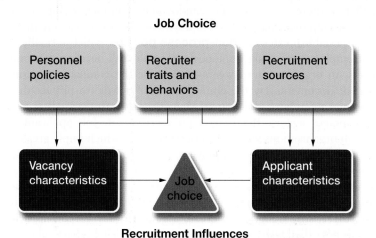

Job Choice

Recruitment Influences

Figure 5.2
Three Aspects of Recruiting

different effects on whom the organization ultimately hires. Personnel policies influence the characteristics of the positions to be filled. Recruitment sources influence the kinds of job applicants an organization reaches. And the nature and behavior of the recruiter affect the characteristics of both the vacancies and the applicants. Ultimately, an applicant's decision to accept a job offer—and the organization's decision to make the offer—depend on the match between vacancy characteristics and applicant characteristics.

The remainder of this chapter explores these three aspects of recruiting: personnel policies, recruitment sources, and recruiter traits and behaviors.

Personnel Policies

An organization's *personnel policies* are its decisions about how it will carry out human resource management, including how it will fill job vacancies. These policies influence the nature of the positions that are vacant. According to the research on recruitment, it is clear that characteristics of the vacancy are more important than recruiters or recruiting sources for predicting job choice. Several personnel policies are especially relevant to recruitment:

- *Internal versus external recruiting*—Organizations with policies to "promote from within" try to fill upper-level vacancies by recruiting candidates internally—that is, finding candidates who already work for the organization. Opportunities for advancement make a job more attractive to applicants and employees. Decisions about internal versus external recruiting affect the nature of jobs, recruitment sources, and the nature of applicants, as we will describe later in the chapter.
- *Lead-the-market pay strategies*—Pay is an important job characteristic for almost all applicants. Organizations have a recruiting advantage if their policy is to take a "lead-the-market" approach to pay—that is, pay more than the current market wages for a job. Higher pay can also make up for a job's less desirable features, such as working on a night shift or in dangerous conditions. Organizations that compete for applicants based on pay may use bonuses, stock options, and other forms of pay besides wages and salaries. Chapters 11 and 12 will take a closer look at these and other decisions about pay.
- *Employment-at-will policies*—Within the laws of the state where they are operating, employers have latitude to set polices about their rights in an employment relationship. A widespread policy follows the principle of **employment at will**, which holds that if there is no specific employment contract saying otherwise, the employer or employee may end an employment relationship at any time. An alternative is to establish extensive **due-process policies**, which formally lay out the steps an employee may take to appeal an employer's decision to terminate that employee. An organization's lawyers may advise the company to ensure that all recruitment documents say the employment is "at will" to protect the company from lawsuits about wrongful charge. Management must decide how to weigh any legal advantages against the impact on recruitment. Job applicants are more attracted to organizations with due-process policies, which imply greater job security and concern for protecting employees, than to organizations with employment-at-will policies.[28]
- *Image advertising*—Besides advertising specific job openings, as discussed in the next section, organizations may advertise themselves as a good place to work in general. Advertising designed to create a generally favorable impression of the organization is called *image advertising*. Image advertising is particularly important

Employment at Will
Employment principle that if there is no specific employment contract saying otherwise, the employer or employee may end an employment relationship at any time, regardless of cause.

Due-Process Policies
Policies that formally lay out the steps an employee may take to appeal the employer's decision to terminate that employee.

for organizations in highly competitive labor markets that perceive themselves as having a bad image.[29] Research suggests that the image of an organization's brand—for example, innovative, dynamic, or fun—influences the degree to which a person feels attracted to the organization.[30] This attraction is especially true if the person's own traits seem to match those of the organization. Also, job applicants seem to be particularly sensitive to issues of diversity and inclusion in image advertising, so organizations should ensure that their image advertisements reflect the broad nature of the labor market from which they intend to recruit.[31]

Image advertising, such as in this campaign to recruit nurses, promotes a whole profession or organization as opposed to a specific job opening. This ad is designed to create a positive impression of the profession, which is now facing a shortage of workers.

Recruitment Sources

Another critical element of an organization's recruitment strategy is its decisions about where to look for applicants. The total labor market is enormous and spread over the entire globe. As a practical matter, an organization will draw from a small fraction of that total market. The methods the organization chooses for communicating its labor needs and the audiences it targets will determine the size and nature of the labor market the organization taps to fill its vacant positions.[32] A person who responds to a job advertisement on the Internet is likely to be different from a person responding to a sign hanging outside a factory. The "Did You Know?" box presents some data on sources of recruitment. Each of the major sources from which organizations draw recruits has advantages and disadvantages.

Internal Sources

As we discussed with regard to personnel policies, an organization may emphasize internal or external sources of job applicants. Internal sources are employees who currently hold other positions in the organization. Organizations recruit existing employees through **job posting**, or communicating information about the vacancy on company bulletin boards, in employee publications, on corporate intranets, and anywhere else the organization communicates with employees. Managers also may identify candidates to recommend for vacancies. Policies that emphasize promotions and even lateral moves to achieve broader career experience can give applicants a favorable impression of the organization's jobs. The use of internal sources also affects what kinds of people the organization recruits.

For the employer, relying on internal sources offers several advantages.[33] First, it generates applicants who are well known to the organization. In addition, these applicants are relatively knowledgeable about the organization's vacancies, which minimizes the possibility they will have unrealistic expectations about the job. Finally, filling vacancies through internal recruiting is generally cheaper and faster than looking outside the organization.

One company that has benefited from a strong internal hiring system is Intercontinental Hotels Group. Intercontinental has been opening about one new hotel every day. These expansion plans are driving a need for hundreds of thousands of new employees, but the company wants to fill as many positions as possible from inside the organization. Internal recruiting supports the organization's strategy of

LO 5-5 List and compare sources of job applicants.

Job Posting
The process of communicating information about a job vacancy on company bulletin boards, in employee publications, on corporate intranets, and anywhere else the organization communicates with employees.

Four in Ten Positions Are Filled with Insiders

In a survey of large, well-known businesses, respondents said over 40% of positions are filled with people who already work for the company and accept a promotion or transfer.

During the recent recession, hiring from within accounted for about half of all positions filled. As companies have begun to grow again, the greater demand for talent is requiring more external recruiting.

Question

Could a growing company fill more than half its open positions with internal recruiting? Why or why not?

SOURCES: Steven Rothberg, "Job Boards Are 2nd Largest Source of Hire: College Is 5th," *ResumeBear,* February 29, 2012, http://blog.resumebear.com; Tony Rosato, "What We Can Learn from the 2012 CareerXroads Sources of Hire Survey," Alstin Communications, February 24, 2012, http://blog .alstin.com; Gerry Crispin and Mark Mehler, "2012 Sources of Hire: Channels That Influence," CareerXroads, posted February 16, 2012, http://www .slideshare.net.

Sources of Hire

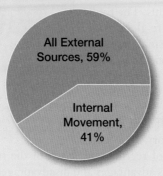

All External Sources, 59%

Internal Movement, 41%

Note: "Internal movement" refers to jobs filled from employees currently in the company who are referred by managers or receive promotions or transfers; "all external sources" refers to employees found using sources outside the company such as electronic recruiting from company or job websites, employment agencies, colleges and universities, walk-in applicants, print ads, and referrals.

staffing with people who are so dedicated to the brand that this attitude shows up in exceptional customer service. People already working at the company are most likely to have developed the desired level of commitment. To match employees with open positions, the company runs a Careers Week twice a year. During Careers Week, Intercontinental encourages its employees to create a profile in the company's online talent management system. So far, 5,000 employees in 89 countries have created profiles that include preferences for the locations and functions in which they would like to work. When Intercontinental has an opening, it can easily search the profiles to find candidates who might be interested and well qualified. Using the talent management system, Intercontinental is filling 84% of general manager positions and 26% of corporate jobs with current employees. The initiative has lowered recruiting costs, increased employee loyalty, and boosted productivity and profitability.[34]

External Sources

Despite the advantages of internal recruitment, organizations often have good reasons to recruit externally.[35] For entry-level positions and perhaps for specialized upper-level positions, the organization has no internal recruits from which to draw. Also, bringing in outsiders may expose the organization to new ideas or new ways of doing business. An organization that uses only internal recruitment can wind up with a workforce whose members all think alike and therefore may be poorly suited to innovation.[36] And finally, companies that are able to grow during a slow economy can gain a competitive edge by hiring the best talent when other organizations are forced to avoid hiring, freeze pay increases, or even lay off talented people. So organizations often recruit through direct applicants and referrals, advertisements, employment agencies, schools, and websites. Figure 5.3 shows which of these sources are used most among large companies surveyed.

Direct Applicants and Referrals   Even without a formal effort to reach job applicants, an organization may hear from candidates through direct applicants and referrals. **Direct applicants** are people who apply for a vacancy without prompting from the organization. **Referrals** are people who apply because someone in the organization prompted them to do so. According to the survey results shown in Figure 5.3, the largest share (over one-fourth) of new employees hired by large companies came

Direct Applicants
People who apply for a vacancy without prompting from the organization.

Referrals
People who apply for a vacancy because someone in the organization prompted them to do so.

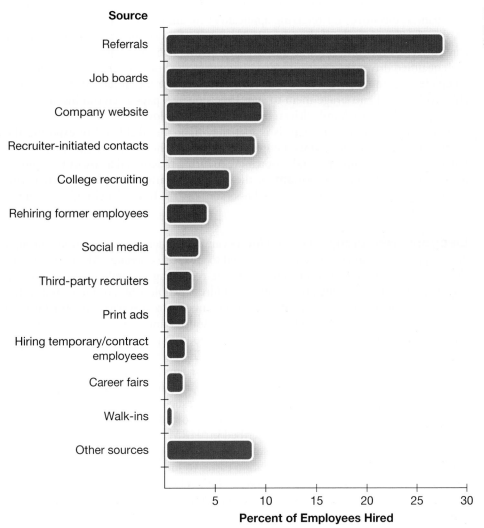

Figure 5.3
External Recruiting Sources

SOURCE: Based on Gerry Crispin and Mark Mehler, "2012 Sources of Hire: Channels That Influence," CareerXroads, posted February 16, 2012, http://www.slideshare.net.

from referrals, and the third-largest share (almost 10%) came from direct applications made at the employer's website.[37] These two sources of recruits share some characteristics that make them excellent pools from which to draw.

One advantage is that many direct applicants are to some extent already "sold" on the organization. Most have done some research and concluded there is enough fit between themselves and the vacant position to warrant submitting an application, a process called *self-selection*, which, when it works, eases the pressure on the organization's recruiting and selection systems. A form of aided self-selection occurs with referrals. Many job seekers look to friends, relatives, and acquaintances to help find employment. Using these social networks not only helps the job seeker but also simplifies recruitment for employers.[38] Current employees (who are familiar with the vacancy as well as the person they are referring) decide that there is a fit between the person and the vacancy, so they convince the person to apply for the job.

An additional benefit of using such sources is that it costs much less than formal recruiting efforts. Considering these combined benefits, referrals and direct applications are among the best sources of new hires. Some employers offer current employees financial incentives for referring applicants who are hired and perform acceptably on the job (for example, if they stay 180 days). To fill dozens of open positions for truck drivers, Precision Motor Transport Group offers a $100 bonus to employees for each qualified driver they refer. The company pays the bonus after the new employee completes a training program. As an additional incentive for employees to refer reliable workers and encourage them to stay, Precision also pays a referral incentive of a penny per mile for each mile driven by the referred employee.[39]

The major downside of referrals is that they limit the likelihood of exposing the organization to fresh viewpoints. People tend to refer others who are like themselves. Furthermore, sometimes referrals contribute to hiring practices that are or that appear unfair, an example being **nepotism**, or the hiring of relatives. Employees may resent the hiring and rapid promotion of "the boss's son" or "the boss's daughter," or even the boss's friend.

Nepotism
The practice of hiring relatives.

Electronic Recruiting
Few employers can fill all their vacant positions through direct applications and referrals, so most need to advertise openings. Most often today, that means posting information online. Online recruiting generally involves posting career information at company websites to address people who are interested in the particular company and posting paid advertisements at career services to attract people who are searching for jobs. Job boards such as Monster and CareerBuilder are widely used, but they can generate an unmanageable flood of applications from unqualified workers. Ads on a company's careers web page, in contrast, may generate too little notice, especially at a company that is not large or famous. Employers therefore are looking for alternatives.[40] They may advertise on an industry or professional group's website, or they may select specialized niche boards, such as Dice.com's job listings for information technology professionals. In addition, companies are increasingly finding candidates through social media, as described in "HRM Social."

Most large companies and many smaller ones make career information available at their websites. To make that information easier to find, they may register a domain name with a ".jobs" extension, such as **www.starbucks.jobs** for a link to information about careers at Starbucks and **www.unionpacific.jobs** for information about careers at Union Pacific. To be an effective recruiting tool, corporate career information should move beyond generalities, offering descriptions of open positions and an easy way to submit a résumé. One of the best features of this kind of electronic recruiting

Social Networks Can Also Be Career Networks

Listing job openings online is an easy way to let potential employees know about positions. But the ease of searching and responding to the ads means companies have been swamped with hundreds or thousands of résumés, often from individuals without the necessary qualifications. Employers therefore are trying to maintain more control over the search process.

Many are turning to social media. They can find the biggest pool of workers on the leading social network, Facebook. GE, PepsiCo, and others have set up a Facebook page. When people interested in or favorable toward the company click that they like the page, they receive status updates, including job-related information, from the company, and they can post comments on the company's page, perhaps leading to job-related communications. Some Facebook apps let users create résumés that are searchable by recruiters that pay for access to the data; other apps let companies post job openings. Also, employers sometimes encourage employees to tell their Facebook friends about jobs. They generally offer rewards when employees recruit a friend who gets hired.

Although Facebook has a wide reach, many people are on the site purely to socialize. Therefore, recruiters are more likely to use the career-focused LinkedIn network. LinkedIn profiles emphasize work experience, skills, and interests. The site hosts discussion groups related to particular careers and industries. Employers can post job openings addressed to members of selected groups. Also, by joining the groups, they can read comments and identify participants who offer valuable ideas. Using an app created by software company Taleo, LinkedIn members can enter their profile data on job applications and give recruiters access to their profiles.

Recruiters also can sign up to use LinkedIn's advanced people search. With this tool, the recruiter can search on job titles, employers, specialties, and other credentials. After finding candidates that seem to match job requirements, the recruiter can send each of them an invitation to connect and discuss the open position. Organizations also may create a company page on LinkedIn to describe themselves using keywords that candidates could use in a job search.

Most basically, of course, recruiters can use their own contacts on social-networking sites. Recruiters should be active wherever candidates are active, whether on LinkedIn, Facebook, Twitter, or industry or professional networks. They can ask their own contacts to suggest people to fill key openings. Some companies, including KPMG and Microsoft, maintain "alumni" networks where former employees can stay in touch with former colleagues and keep up with what is happening at the company they left. Sometimes new opportunities arise that lure back highly desirable former employees. An alumni network can be hosted on one of the major social-networking sites or as part of the company's own computer network.

SOURCES: Jon Gelberg, "Hiring? Up Your Game with LinkedIn," *Inc.,* December 26, 2011, http://www.inc.com; Shayndi Raice, "Friend—and Possible Employee," *The Wall Street Journal,* October 23, 2011, http://online.wsj.com; Francine Russo, "The New Online Job Hunt," *Time,* October 3, 2011, EBSCOhost, http://web.ebscohost.com; Michael A. Tucker, "Don't Say Goodbye," *HR Magazine,* August 2011, pp. 71–72; Elizabeth Sile, "Eight Tips for Recruiting Using Social Media," *Inc. Technology,* July 27, 2011, http://technology.inc.com.

is the ability to target and attract job candidates whose values match the organization's values and whose skills match the job requirements.[41] Candidates also appreciate an e-mail response that the company has received the résumé—especially a response that gives a timetable about further communications from the company.

Accepting applications at the company website is not so successful for smaller and less well-known organizations because fewer people are likely to visit the website. These organizations may get better results by going to the websites that are set up to attract job seekers, such as Monster, Yahoo HotJobs, and CareerBuilder, which attract a vast array of applicants. At these sites, job seekers submit standardized résumés. Employers can search the site's database for résumés that include specified key terms, and they can also submit information about their job opportunities, so that job seekers can search that information by key term. With both employers and job seekers submitting information to and conducting searches on them, these sites offer an efficient way to find matches between job seekers and job vacancies. However, a drawback is that the big job websites can provide too many leads of inferior quality because they are so huge and serve all job seekers and employers, not a select segment.

Because of this limitation of the large websites, smaller, more tailored websites called "niche boards" focus on certain industries, occupations, or geographic areas. **Telecommcareers.net**, for example, is a site devoted to, as the name implies, the telecommunications industry. **CIO.com**, a companion site to *CIO Magazine*, specializes in openings for chief information officers.

Advertisements in Newspapers and Magazines   Although computer search tools have made electronic job listings the most popular way to advertise a job opening, some recruiters still follow the traditional route and advertise open positions in newspapers or magazines. When the goal is to find people who know the local community, advertising in a local newspaper can reach that audience. Similarly, when the goal is to find people in a specialized field, advertising in a trade, professional, or industry publication can reach the right subset of job candidates.

Advertising can be expensive, so it is especially important that the ads be well written. The person designing a job advertisement needs to answer two questions:

What do we need to say?
To whom do we need to say it?

With respect to the first question, an ad should give readers enough information to evaluate the job and its requirements, so they can make a well-informed judgment about their qualifications. Providing enough information may require long advertisements, which cost more. The employer should evaluate the additional costs against the costs of providing too little information: Vague ads generate a huge number of applicants, including many who are not reasonably qualified or would not accept the job if they learned more about it. Reviewing all these applications to eliminate unsuitable applicants is expensive. In practice, the people who write job advertisements tend to overstate the skills and experience required, perhaps generating too few qualified candidates.

Specifying whom to reach with the message helps the advertiser decide where to place the ad. Ads placed in the classified section of local newspapers are relatively inexpensive yet reach many people in a specific geographic area who are currently looking for work (or at least interested enough to be reading the classifieds). On the downside, this medium offers little ability to target skill levels. Typically, many of the people reading classified ads are either over- or underqualified for the position. Also, people who are not looking for work rarely read the classifieds. These people may include candidates the organization could lure from their current employers. For reaching a specific part of the labor market, including certain skill levels and more people who are employed, the organization may get better results from advertising in professional or industry journals. Some employers also advertise on television— particularly cable television.[42]

Public Employment Agencies   The Social Security Act of 1935 requires that everyone receiving unemployment compensation be registered with a local state employment office. These state employment offices work with the U.S. Employment Service (USES) to try to ensure that unemployed individuals eventually get off state aid and back on employer payrolls. To accomplish this, agencies collect information from the unemployed people about their skills and experience.

Employers can register their job vacancies with their local state employment office, and the agency will try to find someone suitable, using its computerized inventory of local unemployed individuals. The agency refers candidates to the employer at no charge. The organization can interview or test them to see if they are suitable for its vacancies. Besides offering access to job candidates at low cost, public employment agencies can be a useful resource for meeting certain diversity objectives. Laws often mandate that the agencies maintain specialized "desks" for minorities, disabled individuals, and war veterans. Employers that feel they currently are underutilizing any of these subgroups of the labor force may find the agencies to be an excellent source.

Government-run employment agencies also may partner with nonprofit groups to meet the needs of a community. In California's Alameda and Contra Costa Counties, several agencies have cooperated to form EastBay Works. This organization is dedicated to bringing together employers and workers in the two counties. EastBay Works offers a variety of recruiting tools at its website. Employers can post job openings, research the local labor market, and set up a search tool to identify candidates with have skills the employer is looking for. Job seekers can visit the site to hunt for jobs, set up a search tool that finds jobs related to the skills in their profile, assess their existing skills, and arrange for training in skills that employers want.[43]

Private Employment Agencies   In contrast to public employment agencies, which primarily serve the blue-collar labor market, private employment agencies provide much the same service for the white-collar labor market. Workers interested in finding a job can sign up with a private employment agency whether or not they are currently unemployed. Another difference between the two types of agencies is that private agencies charge the employers for providing referrals. Therefore, using a private employment agency is more expensive than using a public agency, but the private agency is a more suitable source for certain kinds of applicants.

For managers or professionals, an employer may use the services of a type of private agency called an *executive search firm (ESF)*. People often call these agencies "headhunters" because, unlike other employment agencies, they find new jobs for people almost exclusively already employed. For job candidates, dealing with executive search firms can be sensitive. Typically, executives do not want to advertise their availability, because it could trigger a negative reaction from their current employer. ESFs serve as a buffer, providing confidentiality between the employer and the recruit. That benefit may give an employer access to candidates it cannot recruit in other, more direct ways.

Colleges and Universities   Most colleges and universities have placement services that seek to help their graduates obtain employment. On-campus interviewing is the most important source of recruits for entry-level professional and managerial vacancies. Organizations tend to focus especially on colleges that have strong reputations in areas for which they have critical needs—say, chemical engineering or public accounting. Bain & Co., a consulting firm, recruits on about 15 U.S. campuses each year and may hire up to 40 students at one school for positions and interns and full-time employees. It chooses schools to visit based on their size, reputation, and whether it has succeeded in finding good employees at the school in the past.[44]

Many employers have found that successfully competing for the best students requires more than just signing up prospective

One of the best ways for a company to establish a stronger presence on a campus is with a college internship program. Embassy Suites is one company that participates in such a program. How does this benefit the company and the students at the same time?

graduates for interview slots. One of the best ways to establish a stronger presence on a campus is with a college internship program. Internship programs give an organization early access to potential applicants and let the organization assess their capabilities directly. Internships also give applicants firsthand experience with the employer, so both parties can make well-informed choices about fit when it comes time to consider long-term commitment.[45] Google calls internships "one of the primary ways we find full-time hires." In a recent year, the company hired 1,000 engineering interns.[46]

Another way of increasing the employer's presence on campus is to participate in university job fairs. In general, a job fair is an event where many employers gather for a short time to meet large numbers of potential job applicants. Although job fairs can be held anywhere (such as at a hotel or convention center), campuses are ideal locations because of the many well-educated, yet unemployed, individuals who are there. Job fairs are an inexpensive means of generating an on-campus presence. They can even provide one-on-one dialogue with potential recruits—dialogue that would be impossible through less interactive media, such as newspaper ads.

Evaluating the Quality of a Source

Yield Ratio
A ratio that expresses the percentage of applicants who successfully move from one stage of the recruitment and selection process to the next.

In general, there are few rules that say what recruitment source is best for a given job vacancy. Therefore, it is wise for employers to monitor the quality of all their recruitment sources. One way to do this is to develop and compare **yield ratios** for each source.[47] A yield ratio expresses the percentage of applicants who successfully move from one stage of the recruitment and selection process to the next. For example, the organization could find the number of candidates interviewed as a percentage of the total number of résumés generated by a given source (that is, number of interviews divided by number of résumés). A high yield ratio (large percentage) means that the source is an effective way to find candidates to interview. By comparing the yield ratios of different recruitment sources, HR professionals can determine which source is the best or most efficient for the type of vacancy.

Another measure of recruitment success is the *cost per hire*. To compute this amount, find the cost of using a particular recruitment source for a particular type of vacancy. Then divide that cost by the number of people hired to fill that type of vacancy. A low cost per hire means that the recruitment source is efficient; it delivers qualified candidates at minimal cost.

To see how HR professionals use these measures, look at the examples in Table 5.3. This table shows the results for a hypothetical organization that used six kinds of recruitment sources to fill a number of vacancies. For each recruitment source, the table shows four yield ratios and the cost per hire. To fill these jobs, the best two sources of recruits were local universities and employee referral programs. Online job board ads generated the largest number of recruits (7,000 résumés). However, only 350 were judged acceptable, of which a little more than half accepted employment offers, for a cumulative yield ratio of 200/7,000, or 3%. Recruiting at renowned universities generated highly qualified applicants, but relatively few of them ultimately accepted positions with the organization. Executive search firms produced the highest cumulative yield ratio. These generated only 20 applicants, but all of them accepted interview offers, most were judged acceptable, and 79% of these acceptable candidates took jobs with the organization. However, notice the cost per hire. The executive search firms charged $90,000 for finding these 15 employees, resulting in the largest cost per hire. In contrast, local universities provided modest yield ratios at the lowest cost per hire. Employee referrals provided excellent yield ratios at a slightly higher cost.

Table 5.3

Results of a Hypothetical Recruiting Effort

	RECRUITING SOURCE					
	LOCAL UNIVERSITY	**RENOWNED UNIVERSITY**	**EMPLOYEE REFERRALS**	**NEWSPAPER AD**	**ONLINE JOB BOARD AD**	**EXECUTIVE SEARCH FIRMS**
Résumés generated	200	400	50	500	7,000	20
Interview offers accepted	175	100	45	400	500	20
Yield ratio	**87%**	**25%**	**90%**	**80%**	**7%**	**100%**
Applicants judged acceptable	100	95	40	50	350	19
Yield ratio	**57%**	**95%**	**89%**	**12%**	**70%**	**95%**
Accept employment offers	90	10	35	25	200	15
Yield ratio	**90%**	**11%**	**88%**	**50%**	**57%**	**79%**
Cumulative yield ratio	**90/200**	**10/400**	**35/50**	**25/500**	**200/7,000**	**15/20**
	45%	3%	70%	5%	3%	75%
Cost	$30,000	$50,000	$15,000	$20,000	$5,000	$90,000
Cost per hire	**$333**	**$5,000**	**$428**	**$800**	**$25**	**$6,000**

Would be interesting to measure retention rates @ ea. method.

The cost per hire is not simply related to the type of recruiting method. These costs also tend to vary by industry and organization size. A recent survey found that the median cost per hire at companies with more than 10,000 employees was $1,949; small companies paid far more for each hire, a median of $3,665. One reason for this difference is that small companies have fewer recruiters in-house, so they are likelier to hire outsiders at a higher cost. Comparing industries, manufacturers paid the highest cost per hire, because finding individuals with knowledge of the relevant equipment or software is more difficult than finding employees with standard kinds of certification, as in the case of nurses.[48] At any employer, however, recruiters' challenge is to identify the particular methods that will yield the best candidates as efficiently as possible.

Recruiter Traits and Behaviors

As we showed in Figure 5.2, the third influence on recruitment outcomes is the recruiter, including this person's characteristics and the way he or she behaves. The recruiter affects the nature of both the job vacancy and the applicants generated. However, the recruiter often becomes involved late in the recruitment process. In many cases, by the time a recruiter meets some applicants, they have already made up their minds about what they desire in a job, what the vacant job has to offer, and their likelihood of receiving a job offer.[49]

Many applicants approach the recruiter with some skepticism. Knowing it is the recruiter's job to sell them on a vacancy, some applicants discount what the recruiter says in light of what they have heard from other sources, such as friends, magazine articles, and professors. When candidates are already familiar with the company through knowing about its products, the recruiter's impact is especially weak.[50] For these and other reasons, recruiters' characteristics and behaviors seem to have limited impact on applicants' job choices.

LO 5-6 Describe the recruiter's role in the recruitment process, including limits and opportunities.

Best Practices

How Teach for America Aces the Recruiting Project

Teach for America is a nonprofit organization that recruits recent college graduates to serve as teachers for two years in a low-income community. They may be assigned to any grade from prekindergarten through high school. Although many do not start as certified teachers, they are expected to do teachers' jobs, including lesson planning, instruction, and assessment of students' progress. They earn the same starting salary as an entry-level teacher in the community they serve. As tough as those teaching positions are, Teach for America's recruiters manage to go to the nation's most prestigious colleges, speak to students, and obtain tens of thousands of job applications for about one-tenth as many open positions.

One secret of the organization's success in attracting so many excellent job applicants is its 140 recruiters. Every year, these recruiters travel to hundreds colleges and universities, where they meet one-on-one with tens of thousands of students. In these personal conversations, the recruiters aim to convey Teach for America's sense of mission. The organization seeks to do nothing less than help "eliminate educational inequity." Speaking to young recruits who have been enjoying the privilege of a great college education, these recruiters have a message with a significance that will capture the imagination.

About three-quarters of the recruiters formerly taught in the Teach for America program. That means they, too, were excited to make a difference and they, too, believe in the agency's mission. The recruiters also can give a realistic, specific, and detailed picture of what the work is like. This experience goes to the top of the recruiting team, with Elissa Kim, executive vice president of recruitment. Kim started out with Teach for America as a high school English teacher in the New Orleans area. From there, she moved to the organization's headquarters and led the recruiting effort.

One member of Kim's team is Melissa Gregson, a recruiter who used to teach in New York. Gregson knows that when she describes Teach for America to college students, they will ask her what the experience was like and what the biggest challenges were—and she will be able to give honest answers. Her enthusiasm makes an emotional connection with some members of her audience, and those are the kinds of candidates the agency wants to consider hiring.

SOURCES: Teach for America, "Our Organization," http://www.teachforamerica.org, accessed March 5, 2012; Jennifer C. Berkshire, "How Charities Can Recruit the Top New Graduates," *Chronicle of Philanthropy,* April 3, 2011, Business & Company Resource Center, http://galenet.galegroup.com; Dennis Vilorio, "Serving, Learning, and Earning: An Overview of Three Organizations," *Occupational Outlook Quarterly,* Summer 2011, pp. 2–15; Bob Lavigna, "Teach for America: A Model for Attracting and Developing Talent," *PA Times* (American Society for Public Administration), February 2, 2010, http://patimes.eznuz.com.

Characteristics of the Recruiter

Most organizations must choose whether their recruiters are specialists in human resources or are experts at particular jobs (that is, those who currently hold the same kinds of jobs or supervise people who hold the jobs). According to some studies, applicants perceive HR specialists as less credible and are less attracted to jobs when recruiters are HR specialists.[51] The evidence does not completely discount a positive role for personnel specialists in recruiting. It does indicate, however, that these specialists need to take extra steps to ensure that applicants perceive them as knowledgeable and credible. As the "Best Practices" box describes, Teach for America's use of former teachers to recruit new teachers helps the organization lure exceptional graduates to apply for jobs.

In general, applicants respond positively to recruiters whom they perceive as warm and informative. "Warm" means the recruiter seems to care about the applicant and to be enthusiastic about the applicant's potential to contribute to the organization. "Informative" means the recruiter provides the kind of information the applicant is seeking. The evidence of impact of other characteristics of recruiters—including their age, sex, and race—is complex and inconsistent.[52]

Behavior of the Recruiter

Recruiters affect results not only by providing plenty of information, but by providing the right kind of information. Perhaps the most-researched aspect of recruiting is the level of realism in the recruiter's message. Because the recruiter's job is to attract candidates, recruiters may feel pressure to exaggerate the positive qualities of the vacancy and to downplay its negative qualities. Applicants are highly sensitive to negative information. The highest-quality applicants may be less willing to pursue jobs when this type of information comes out.[53] But if the recruiter goes too far in a positive direction, the candidate can be misled and lured into taking a job that has been misrepresented. Then unmet expectations can contribute to a high turnover rate. When recruiters describe jobs unrealistically, people who take those jobs may come to believe that the employer is deceitful.[54]

Many studies have looked at how well **realistic job previews**—background information about jobs' positive and negative qualities—can get around this problem and help organizations minimize turnover among new employees. On the whole, the research suggests that realistic job previews have a weak and inconsistent effect on turnover.[55] Although recruiters can go overboard in selling applicants on the desirability of a job vacancy, there is little support for the belief that informing people about the negative characteristics of a job will "inoculate" them so that the negative features don't cause them to quit.[56]

Finally, for affecting whether people choose to take a job, but even more so, whether they stick with a job, the recruiter seems less important than an organization's personnel policies that directly affect the job's features (pay, security, advancement opportunities, and so on).

Realistic Job Preview
Background information about a job's positive and negative qualities.

Enhancing the Recruiter's Impact

Nevertheless, although recruiters are probably not the most important influence on people's job choices, this does not mean recruiters cannot have an impact. Most recruiters receive little training.[57] If we were to determine what does matter to job candidates, perhaps recruiters could be trained in those areas.

Researchers have tried to find the conditions in which recruiters do make a difference. Such research suggests that an organization can take several steps to increase the positive impact that recruiters have on job candidates:

- Recruiters should provide timely feedback. Applicants dislike delays in feedback. They may draw negative conclusions about the organization (for starters, that the organization doesn't care about their application).
- Recruiters should avoid offensive behavior. They should avoid behaving in ways that might convey the wrong impression about the organization.[58] Figure 5.4 quotes applicants who felt they had extremely bad experiences with recruiters. Their statements provide examples of behaviors to avoid.
- The organization can recruit with teams rather than individual recruiters. Applicants view job experts as more credible than HR specialists, and a team can include both kinds of recruiters. HR specialists on the team provide knowledge about company policies and procedures.

Through such positive behavior, recruiters can give organizations a better chance of competing for talented human resources. In the next chapter, we will describe how an organization selects the candidates who best meet its needs.

Figure 5.4

Recruits Who Were Offended by Recruiters

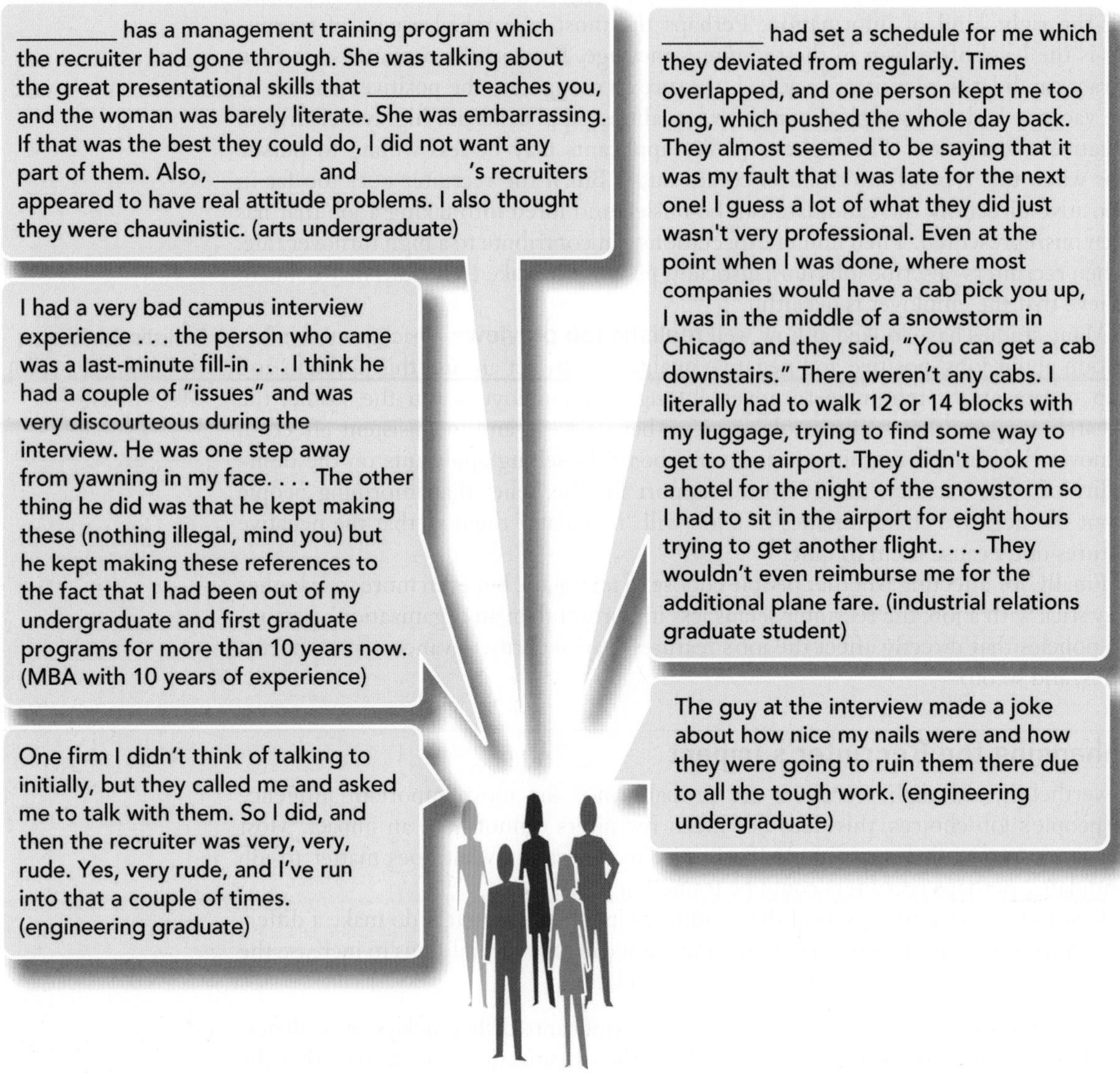

_____ has a management training program which the recruiter had gone through. She was talking about the great presentational skills that _____ teaches you, and the woman was barely literate. She was embarrassing. If that was the best they could do, I did not want any part of them. Also, _____ and _____ 's recruiters appeared to have real attitude problems. I also thought they were chauvinistic. (arts undergraduate)

I had a very bad campus interview experience . . . the person who came was a last-minute fill-in . . . I think he had a couple of "issues" and was very discourteous during the interview. He was one step away from yawning in my face. . . . The other thing he did was that he kept making these (nothing illegal, mind you) but he kept making these references to the fact that I had been out of my undergraduate and first graduate programs for more than 10 years now. (MBA with 10 years of experience)

One firm I didn't think of talking to initially, but they called me and asked me to talk with them. So I did, and then the recruiter was very, very, rude. Yes, very rude, and I've run into that a couple of times. (engineering graduate)

_____ had set a schedule for me which they deviated from regularly. Times overlapped, and one person kept me too long, which pushed the whole day back. They almost seemed to be saying that it was my fault that I was late for the next one! I guess a lot of what they did just wasn't very professional. Even at the point when I was done, where most companies would have a cab pick you up, I was in the middle of a snowstorm in Chicago and they said, "You can get a cab downstairs." There weren't any cabs. I literally had to walk 12 or 14 blocks with my luggage, trying to find some way to get to the airport. They didn't book me a hotel for the night of the snowstorm so I had to sit in the airport for eight hours trying to get another flight. . . . They wouldn't even reimburse me for the additional plane fare. (industrial relations graduate student)

The guy at the interview made a joke about how nice my nails were and how they were going to ruin them there due to all the tough work. (engineering undergraduate)

THINKING ETHICALLY

IS SOCIALSCORE MIXING BUSINESS AND PLEASURE?

Until recently, Facebook was mainly a place to keep up with the personal lives of family and friends. But after LinkedIn began to build a network of people focused on career development, Facebook wanted in on the career networking, too. It found a way in with a website called BranchOut, which offers a job board and job-hunting database. BranchOut users link to their Facebook account, and BranchOut pulls their information on education and work history from Facebook to create a BranchOut career profile. BranchOut also collects the user's connections to his or her Facebook friends.

To get people more engaged with the site, BranchOut came up with a quiz game called SocialScore. The game displays pairs of randomly selected Facebook friends and asks the player to choose which of those friends he or she would rather work with. BranchOut keeps score, notifies the winners, and saves the data. It can then combine the scores with, say, job title to create rankings. For example, at least in theory, a recruiter could buy rankings of accountants or waitresses based on their ratings by their friends.

Some people see the SocialScore game as a kind of middle-school-style popularity contest, not at all professional. Others can envision that the results would be a useful way to identify prospective hires who get along well with others.

Questions

1. If a BranchOut user plays SocialScore, who is affected by the scores? Does it seem ethical to you that a recruiter could evaluate a candidate based on a score over which the candidate has no control? Why or why not?

2. If you were to play SocialScore with random pairs of people in your own Facebook network (or in other social networks you belong to), how well do you think your scores would represent these people's actual performance of a job? Would the scores be more fair or less fair to them than what you would say if a recruiter directly asked you to evaluate them as a possible employee? Is it ethical to ask people to play a game and then use the scores for hiring decisions? Why or why not?

SOURCES: Susan Berfield, "Dueling Your Facebook Friends for a New Job," *Bloomberg Businessweek,* March 3, 2011, http://www.businessweek.com; "LinkedIn Competitor Branches Out to 300 Million Users," *The Wall Street Journal,* February 8, 2012, http://blogs.wsj.com; BranchOut, "BranchOut Wins 'Top HR Product' Award," news release, October 3, 2011, http://branchout.com.

SUMMARY

LO 5-1 Discuss how to plan for human resources needed to carry out the organization's strategy.

The first step in human resource planning is personnel forecasting. Through trend analysis and good judgment, the planner tries to determine the supply of and demand for various human resources. Based on whether a surplus or a shortage is expected, the planner sets goals and creates a strategy for achieving those goals. The organization then implements its HR strategy and evaluates the results.

LO 5-2 Determine the labor demand for workers in various job categories.

The planner can look at leading indicators, assuming trends will continue in the future. Multiple regression can convert several leading indicators into a single prediction of labor needs. Analysis of a transitional matrix can help the planner identify which job categories can be filled internally and where high turnover is likely.

LO 5-3 Summarize the advantages and disadvantages of ways to eliminate a labor surplus and avoid a labor shortage.

To reduce a surplus, downsizing, pay reductions, and demotions deliver fast results but at a high cost in human suffering that may hurt surviving employees' motivation and future recruiting. Also, the organization may lose some of its best employees. Transferring employees and requiring them to share work are also fast methods and the consequences in human suffering are less severe. A hiring freeze or natural attrition is slow to take effect, but avoids the pain of layoffs. Early-retirement packages may unfortunately induce the best employees to leave and may be slow to implement; however, they, too, are less painful than layoffs. Retraining can improve the organization's overall pool of human resources and maintain high morale, but it is relatively slow and costly.

To avoid a labor shortage, requiring overtime is the easiest and fastest strategy, which can easily be changed if conditions change. However, overtime may exhaust workers and can hurt morale. Using temporary employees and outsourcing do not build an in-house pool of talent, but by these means staffing levels can be quickly and easily modified. Transferring and retraining employees require investment of time and money, but can enhance the quality of the organization's human resources; however, this may backfire if a labor surplus develops. Hiring new employees is slow and expensive, but strengthens the organization if labor needs are expected to expand for the long term. Using technology as a substitute for labor can be slow to implement and costly, but it may improve the organization's long-term performance. New technology and hiring are difficult to reverse if conditions change.

LO 5-4 Describe recruitment policies organizations use to make job vacancies more attractive.

Internal recruiting (promotions from within) generally makes job vacancies more attractive because candidates see opportunities for growth and advancement. Lead-the-market pay strategies make jobs economically desirable. Due-process policies signal that employers are concerned about employee rights. Image advertising can give candidates the impression that the organization is a good place to work.

LO 5-5 List and compare sources of job applicants.

Internal sources, promoted through job postings, generate applicants who are familiar to the organization and motivate other employees by demonstrating opportunities for advancement. However, internal sources are usually insufficient for all of an organization's labor needs. Direct applicants and referrals tend to be inexpensive and to generate applicants who have self-selected; this source risks charges of unfairness, especially in cases of nepotism. Electronic recruiting gives organizations access to a global labor market, tends to be inexpensive, and allows

convenient searching of databases. Newspaper and magazine advertising reach a wide audience and may generate many applications, although many are likely to be unsuitable. Public employment agencies are inexpensive and typically have screened applicants. Private employment agencies charge fees, but may provide many services. Another inexpensive channel is schools and colleges, which may give the employer access to top-notch entrants to the labor market.

LO 5-6 Describe the recruiter's role in the recruitment process, including limits and opportunities.

Through their behavior and other characteristics, recruiters influence the nature of the job vacancy and the kinds of applicants generated. Applicants tend to perceive job experts as more credible than recruiters who are HR specialists. They tend to react more favorably to recruiters who are warm and informative. Recruiters should not mislead candidates. Realistic job previews are helpful but have a weak and inconsistent effect on job turnover compared with personnel policies and actual job conditions. Recruiters can improve their impact by providing timely feedback, avoiding behavior that contributes to a negative impression of the organization, and teaming up with job experts.

KEY TERMS

core competency, 135
direct applicants, 147
downsizing, 136
due-process policies, 144
employment at will, 144
forecasting, 131

job posting, 145
leading indicators, 132
nepotism, 148
outsourcing, 140
realistic job preview, 155
recruiting, 143

referrals, 147
transitional matrix, 133
trend analysis, 132
workforce utilization review, 142
yield ratio, 152

REVIEW AND DISCUSSION QUESTIONS

1. Suppose an organization expects a labor shortage to develop in key job areas over the next few years. Recommend general responses the organization could make in each of the following areas:
   a. Recruitment
   b. Training
   c. Compensation (pay and employee benefits)
2. Review the sample transitional matrix shown in Table 5.1. What jobs experience the greatest turnover (employees leaving the organization)? How

might an organization with this combination of jobs reduce the turnover?
3. In the same transitional matrix, which jobs seem to rely the most on internal recruitment? Which seem to rely most on external recruitment? Why?
4. Why do organizations combine statistical and judgmental forecasts of labor demand, rather than relying on statistics or judgment alone? Give an example of a situation in which each type of forecast would be inaccurate.

5. Some organizations have detailed affirmative-action plans, complete with goals and timetables, for women and minorities, yet have no formal human resource plan for the organization as a whole. Why might this be the case? What does this practice suggest about the role of human resource management in these organizations?

6. Give an example of a personnel policy that would help attract a larger pool of job candidates. Give an example of a personnel policy that would likely reduce the pool of candidates. Would you expect these policies to influence the quality as well as the number of applicants? Why or why not?

7. Discuss the relative merits of internal versus external recruitment. Give an example of a situation in which each of these approaches might be particularly effective.

8. List the jobs you have held. How were you recruited for each of these? From the organization's perspective, what were some pros and cons of recruiting you through these methods?

9. Recruiting people for jobs that require international assignments is increasingly important for many organizations. Where might an organization go to recruit people interested in such assignments?

10. A large share of HR professionals have rated e-cruiting as their best source of new talent. What qualities of electronic recruiting do you think contribute to this opinion?

11. How can organizations improve the effectiveness of their recruiters?

EXPERIENCING HR

Imagine you work in the HR department of a heating, cooling, and plumbing services contractor. The company installs and repairs these systems in new construction and existing buildings. Management has noted an uptick in demand for plumbing services over the past few months and believes it is time to add a few plumbers to the workforce.

Visit the website of the Bureau of Labor Statistics to learn more about the expected supply and demand for plumbers. Use the search box for the site and follow the links under Publications to find current information. Write a paragraph summarizing what you learned.

Next, consider the kinds of sources employers use to find job applicants. Choose three for your company to use. (To see where other employers find plumbers, you might do an Internet search on "plumbing jobs." But you don't have to use the same sources if you think another source would better meet your objectives.) List the sources you chose, and next to each, tell why you think this source would be effective. Finally, explain how you could measure the performance of the sources you chose.

TAKING RESPONSIBILITY: Can Chipotle Source Employees as Ethically as It Sources Food?

With a strategy to sell "food with integrity," Chipotle Mexican Grill has pleased the taste of Americans and turned into a fast-food success story. In contrast to the typical fast-food chain, where recipes and menus are driven by marketing goals, Chipotle starts with the goal of selling delicious, fresh, sustainably grown foods. As hungry customers snap up its burritos and tacos, Chipotle is scheduling the addition of more than a hundred new outlets per year. Keeping up with growth is a major challenge for human resource management in the restaurant business. At fast-food restaurants, triple-digit turnover is normal, so restaurant managers are constantly in hiring mode. Thus, while Chipotle has 30,000 employees, it forecasts a need to hire 100,000 workers over three years.

The pace of growth has also challenged the company to hire enough managers. Under the leadership of co-CEO Monty Moran, the company has emphasized promoting managers from within. The goal is to retain the best performers by giving them raises and promotions. Chipotle's talent management efforts include career paths along which crew members become general managers with the potential to earn $100,000 or more. In fact, most of Chipotle's store managers started out making and serving the food.

Along the way, however, Chipotle has hit some bumps in recruitment. About half of Chipotle's employees are Hispanic, which the company sees as a plus because Chipotle sees this ethnic group as an important source of customers as well as employees. However, in hiring these workers, it needs to distinguish between those who are permitted to work in the United States (because they are citizens or immigrants with the necessary government documents) and those who are immigrants without authorization to work. Federal agents for Immigration and Customs Enforcement inspected the company's records in Minnesota, Virginia, and Washington, D.C., and determined that Chipotle had hired more than 500 undocumented immigrants. As a result, the company had to lay off hundreds of employees. At the affected restaurants, managers scrambled to keep operating while hiring and training replacement workers as fast as they could. In addition, Chipotle has spent more than $1 million in legal fees and risks being fined.

Meanwhile, to avoid further legal embarrassments, the company signed on to the government's E-Verify screening program, which uses a database to spot illegal workers. One practical result of compliance has been that workers who lacked documents no longer apply to Chipotle. That helps the company stay on the right side of the law but also has reduced the company's pool of applicants. Those who still apply do not always have the necessary skills and experience. In some markets, managers report interviewing up to 40 candidates to fill each job opening. And at a job fair in the state of Washington, Chipotle recruiters interviewed 100 people but found only eight of them to be qualified. Employee turnover has suffered as well, rising from 125% annually, in contrast to 100% turnover before the immigration enforcement. Moran suspects that many of the employees who quit were worried their documents would not stand up to government scrutiny, so they left to avoid trouble. Many immigrant workers in restaurants are in the United States on temporary visas that expire after a year, so even if hiring them is legal, they may not be able to stay legally employed for long.

In Moran's view, Chipotle's struggle to fill jobs is a by-product of overly harsh immigration laws. Moran has been urging the federal government to improve the process for legal immigration and hiring of immigrants. He wants good workers to be allowed to stay in the United States for the long term, so the company can let them build careers, as its strategy requires, rather than return to their country of origin after a year or two. Replacing and training workers with temporary visas every year is expensive and disrupts the development of teamwork in a work crew. So far, however, Moran's message has failed to sway politicians, so Chipotle must continue to staff its restaurants with workers who can prove they have the necessary documents under current law.

Questions

1. What factors can you identify that affect the supply of and demand for labor at Chipotle?
2. Immigrant workers have been an important part of the labor pool for Chipotle (and many other restaurants). If you worked in Chipotle's HR department, would you recommend that it continue to recruit immigrant workers or target another group of workers for hiring? Why? Which other groups, if any, would you target?
3. Suggest two or three recruiting methods Chipotle could use to locate qualified, legal workers who would be likely to stay with Chipotle for the long term. What are the advantages and drawbacks of the methods you chose?

SOURCES: Danielle Sacks, "Chipotle: For Exploding All the Rules of Fast Food," *Fast Company*, February 14, 2012, http://www.fastcompany.com; Miriam Jordan, "A CEO's Demand: Fix Immigration," *The Wall Street Journal*, December 19, 2011, http://online.wsj.com; Jack Nicas, Miriam Jordan, and Julie Jargon, "After the Audit: Chipotle Faces Higher Turnover," *The Wall Street Journal*, August 15, 2011, http://online.wsj.com; Steve Coomes, "Crackdown Costs," *Nation's Restaurant News*, May 2, 2011, Business & Company Resource Center, http://galenet.galegroup.com.

MANAGING TALENT: Can Yahoo Still Attract Tech Workers?

In many fields, workers are practically begging employers to hire them, but in information technology, the demand for talent often outstrips the supply. Employers struggle to attract and keep software experts, always concerned about the risk that their best people will leave for a better offer somewhere else. For a high-tech worker, what often amounts to a better offer is a chance to be a part of the exciting new thing, whatever that is.

That presents a challenge for Yahoo. A couple of decades ago, the web search company (now an advertising, news, and e-mail company) was one of the hot businesses of the Internet age. Today Yahoo's sites attract 700 million visitors a month, and the company's 14,000 employees are well paid, but the excitement is no longer there. To the industry, Yahoo is part of the old Internet. The best and brightest want to be part of the new Internet, especially social media, cloud computing, and mobile apps.

In that environment, Yahoo is seeking pathways for growth even as some of its best talent is slipping out the doors. Greg Cohn, who worked his way up from business strategist to senior director responsible for new initiatives, admires Yahoo's management but left to start his own business. A vice president of Yahoo's operations in Latin America also left, and so has the company's chief trust officer, who moved to a position at Google. In another sign of employee dissatisfaction, a recruiter told a reporter, "If you call nine people at Yahoo, you'll get nine calls back." In other words, leaving sounds like an option for just about everyone. Executives are preparing for a faster exodus as job growth heats up elsewhere in Silicon Valley.

Because of these trends, Yahoo forecasts that it will need to do intensive recruiting. But how do you get people to think about working for a company that many believe has passed its prime? Yahoo definitely has work to do. Software engineers who look up employee reviews on Glassdoor.com would notice that employees rate Yahoo just 3.2 on a scale of 1 to 5, trailing Facebook (4.2), Google (3.9), and Apple (3.6). Seeing that, an engineer probably wouldn't bother to look up a Yahoo careers page.

One person who contributes to a solution is Susan Burnett, Yahoo's senior vice president of talent and organization development. Burnett aims to create an environment in which employees learn the skills they need to take on greater responsibilities. Burnett first established a development program for 2,000 high-potential employees. The program, called Leading Yahoos, teaches leadership, goal setting, and measurement of results. By helping these new leaders align their work with the company's overall strategy, it supports Yahoo's effort to make goals more visible to employees at all levels.

More directly, Yahoo is seeking to find highly skilled software experts by recruiting away from Silicon Valley, where the competition for talent is intense. For example, it worked with the Champaign County Economic Development Corporation to announce that it wanted to hire software developers to work at the University of Illinois Research Park. Yahoo said it had six to nine open positions but would consider hiring more if it received enough good applications. The company's publicity noted that it paid above-average salaries for the research park and that the Champaign facility was innovative, having applied for patents on 25 ideas.

Observers note that Yahoo still earns most of its money by employing reporters to write stories and salespeople to sell ads, an old-media kind of operation that is hard to run at a profit. Yahoo outsourced web search to Microsoft's Bing, and in spite of its leadership role in advertising, it has yet to offer much in the hot young market of mobile ads. Shifting from unprofitable, low-growth activities to activities with more potential could lead to significant staff cuts in some areas even as a hiring push continues in others. Still, one former employee sees hope. Geoff Ralston, who worked on Yahoo Mail, notes that EBay and Apple both survived periods when they seemed to be fading away. Ralston believes the solution is to buy or build "consumer experiences that are unbelievably great." That's a mission a tech worker would choose to accept.

Questions

1. What conclusions can you draw about the supply of and demand for labor at Yahoo?
2. What actions might Yahoo take to strengthen its internal recruiting? How might these efforts support Yahoo's corporate strategy?
3. If you were responsible for college recruiting at Yahoo, where would you recruit, and what would you say? Why?

SOURCES: Kara Swisher, "Yahoo's New CEO Preps Major Restructuring, including Significant Layoffs," *All Things Digital*, March 5, 2012, http://allthingsd.com; Don Dodson, "Yahoo in Market for a Few Good Engineers," *America's Intelligence Wire*, December 15, 2011, Business & Company Resource Center, http://galenet.galegroup.com; Amir Efrati, "Yahoo Battles Brain Drain," *The Wall Street Journal*, December 5, 2011, http://online.wsj.com; Ladan Nikravan, "An Engine for Growth," *Chief Learning Officer*, September 2011, pp. 22–24; Peter Burrows, "The Web's Walking Dead," *Bloomberg Businessweek*, September 19, 2011, pp. 41–42.

 TWITTER FOCUS: For Personal Financial Advisors, a Small Staffing Plan with a Big Impact

Using Twitter, continue the conversation about HR planning and recruitment by reading the Personal Advisors case at **www.mhhe.com/noefund5e**. Engage with your classmates and instructor via Twitter to chat about the company's recruitment strategy using the case questions posted on the Noe website. Don't have a Twitter account yet? See the instructions for getting started on the Online Learning Center.

NOTES

1. Joe Light, "Mobile App Talent Pool Is Shallow," *The Wall Street Journal*, April 15, 2011, http://online.wsj.com.

2. James R. Hagerty, "U.S. Factories Buck Decline," *The Wall Street Journal*, January 19, 2011, http://online.wsj.com.

3. Marc D. Allan, "Nursing a Shortage," *Indianapolis Business Journal*, October 3, 2011, pp. 1, 24–25.

4. Joe Light, "Languages Needed, but No Plans to Learn," *The Wall Street Journal*, January 18, 2011, http://online.wsj.com.

5. Bureau of Labor Statistics, "Regional and State Employment and Unemployment, December 2011," news release, January 24, 2012, http://www.bls.gov.

6. Daniel Connolly, "Straberg's Strategy," *Commercial Appeal (Memphis, TN)*, September 18, 2011, Business & Company Resource Center, http://galenet.galegroup.com.

7. J. P. Guthrie, "Dumb and Dumber: The Impact of Downsizing on Firm Performance as Moderated by Industry Conditions," *Organization Science* 19 (2008), pp. 108–23; "Lay Off the Layoffs," *Newsweek*, February 4, 2010, http://www.thedailybeast.com/newsweek/.

8. C. D. Zatzick and R. D. Iverson, "High-Involvement Management and Workforce Reduction: Competitive Advantage or Disadvantage?" *Academy of Management Journal* 49 (2006), pp. 999–1015.

9. P. P. Shaw, "Network Destruction: The Structural Implications of Downsizing," *Academy of Management Journal* 43 (2000), pp. 101–12.

10. Brenda Kowske, Kyle Lundby, and Rena Rasch, "Turning 'Survive' into 'Thrive': Managing Survivor Engagement in a Downsized Organization," *People & Strategy* 32, no. (4), (2009), pp. 48–56.

11. W. F. Cascio, "Downsizing: What Do We Know? What Have We Learned?" *Academy of Management Executive* 7 (1993), pp. 95–104.

12. Hagerty, "U.S. Factories Buck Decline"; Scott Kirsner, "The Tech Bust: 10 Years After," *Boston Globe*, February 20, 2011, http://www.boston.com; Bill Saporito and Deirdre Van Dyk, "Where the Jobs Are," *Time*, January 17, 2011, EBSCOhost, http://web.ebscohost.com.

13. Dan Jacobs, "Lessons from the Recession," *Landscape Management*, June 2011, pp. S21–S23.

14. Associated Press, "American Airlines to Reduce Jobs without Layoffs," *Seattle Times*, February 22, 2012, http://seattletimes.nwsource.com.

15. CareerBuilder, "Retirement May Be a Thing of the Past, New CareerBuilder Survey Finds," news release, February 16, 2012, http://www.careerbuilder.com.

16. S. Kim and D. Feldman, "Healthy, Wealthy, or Wise: Predicting Actual Acceptances of Early Retirement Incentives at Three Points in Time," *Personnel Psychology* 51 (1998), pp. 623–42.

17. Donna Rosato, "Ease Your Way into Retirement," *Money*, February 2012, EBSCOhost, http://web.ebscohost.com.

18. S. A. Johnson and B. E. Ashforth, "Externalization of Employment in a Service Environment: The Role of Organizational and Customer Identification," *Journal of Organizational Behavior* 29 (2008), pp. 287–309; and M. Vidal and L. M. Tigges, "Temporary Employment and Strategic Staffing in the Manufacturing Sector," *Industrial Relations* 48 (2009), pp. 55–72.

19. "Where Do You Find New Talent?" *Mass Transit*, September/October 2011, pp. 102–103.

20. Tim Sohn, "Don't Go It Alone," *Editor & Publisher*, April 2011, EBSCOhost, http://web.ebscohost.com.

21. Ibid.

22. A. Tiwana, "Does Firm Modularity Complement Ignorance? A Field Study of Software Outsourcing Alliances," *Strategic Management Journal* 29 (2008), pp. 1241–52.

23. Kelley Hunsberger, "The Risk of Outsourcing," *PM Network*, November 2011, EBSCOhost, http://web.ebscohost.com; "The Trouble with Outsourcing," *The Economist*, July 30, 2011, EBSCOhost, http://web.ebscohost.com.

24. Mansfield Sales Partners, "Sales Outsourcing: Expand Rapidly into New Markets," http://www.mansfieldsp.com, accessed March 3, 2012.

25. A. E. Barber, *Recruiting Employees* (Thousand Oaks, CA: Sage, 1998).

26. C. K. Stevens, "Antecedents of Interview Interactions, Interviewers' Ratings, and Applicants' Reactions," *Personnel Psychology* 51 (1998), pp. 55–85; A. E. Barber, J. R. Hollenbeck, S. L. Tower, and J. M. Phillips, "The Effects of Interview Focus on Recruitment Effectiveness: A Field Experiment," *Journal of Applied Psychology* 79 (1994), pp. 886–96; and D. S. Chapman and D. I. Zweig, "Developing a Nomological Network for Interview Structure: Antecedents and Consequences of the Structured Selection Interview," *Personnel Psychology* 58 (2005), pp. 673–702.

27. J. D. Olian and S. L. Rynes, "Organizational Staffing: Integrating Practice with Strategy," *Industrial Relations* 23 (1984), pp. 170–83.

28. M. Leonard, "Challenges to the Termination-at-Will Doctrine," *Personnel Administrator* 28 (1983), pp. 49–56; C. Schowerer and B. Rosen, "Effects of Employment-at-Will Policies and Compensation Policies on Corporate Image and Job Pursuit Intentions," *Journal of Applied Psychology* 74 (1989), pp. 653–56.

29. S. L. Rynes and A. E. Barber, "Applicant Attraction Strategies: An Organizational Perspective," *Academy of Management Review* 15 (1990), pp. 286–310; and J. A. Breaugh, *Recruitment: Science and Practice* (Boston: PWS-Kent, 1992), p. 34.

30. J. E. Slaughter, M. J. Zickar, S. Highhouse, and D. C. Mohr, "Personality Trait Inferences about Organizations: Development of a Measure and Assessment of Construct Validity," *Journal of Applied Psychology* 89 (2004), pp. 85–103; and D. S. Chapman, K. L. Uggerslev, S. A. Carroll, K. A. Piasentin, and D. A. Jones, "Applicant Attraction to Organizations and Job Choice: A Meta-analytic Review of the Correlates of Recruiting Outcomes," *Journal of Applied Psychology* 90 (2005), pp. 928–44.

31. D. R. Avery, "Reactions to Diversity in Recruitment Advertising—Are Differences in Black and White?" *Journal of Applied Psychology* 88 (2003), pp. 672–79.

32. M. A. Conrad and S. D. Ashworth, "Recruiting Source Effectiveness: A Meta-Analysis and Re-examination of Two Rival Hypotheses," paper presented at the annual meeting of the Society of Industrial/Organizational Psychology, Chicago, 1986.

33. Breaugh, *Recruitment*.

34. Taleo Corporation, "Intercontinental Hotels Group Mobilizes Internal Talent with Taleo in Biggest Ever Recruitment Drive," news release, February 6, 2012, http://ir.taleo.com.

35. Breaugh, *Recruitment*, pp. 113–14.

36. R. S. Schuler and S. E. Jackson, "Linking Competitive Strategies with Human Resource Management Practices," *Academy of Management Executive* 1 (1987), pp. 207–19.

37. Gerry Crispin and Mark Mehler, "2012 Sources of Hire: Channels That Influence," CareerXroads, posted February 16, 2012, http://www.slideshare.net.

38. C. R. Wanberg, R. Kanfer, and J. T. Banas, "Predictors and Outcomes of Networking Intensity among Job Seekers," *Journal of Applied Psychology* 85 (2000), pp. 491–503.

39. Precision Motor Transport Group, "Employee Referral Bonus for All Qualified Drivers," news release, August 25, 2011, http://www.pmtghome.com.

40. Joe Light, "Recruiters Rethink Online Playbook," *The Wall Street Journal*, January 18, 2011, http://online.wsj.com.

41. B. Dineen and R. A. Noe, "Effects of Customization on Applicant Decisions and Applicant Pool Characteristics in a Web-Based Recruiting Context," *Journal of Applied Psychology* 94 (2009), pp. 224–34.

42. Breaugh, *Recruitment*, p. 87.

43. EastBay Works, "What Is EastBay Works?" http://www.eastbayworks.com, accessed March 3, 2012.

44. Melissa Korn, "Companies Size Up Options at Small Schools," *The Wall Street Journal*, March 1, 2012, http://online.wsj.com.

45. Hao Zhao and Robert C. Liden, "Internship: A Recruitment and Selection Perspective," *Journal of Applied Psychology* 96 (2011): 221–229.

46. Jessica E. Vascellaro, "Interns Are Largest Target in Battle for Tech Talent," *The Wall Street Journal*, December 22, 2011, http://online.wsj.com.

47. R. Hawk, *The Recruitment Function* (New York: American Management Association, 1967).

48. Lauren Weber, "For Smaller Firms, Recruiting Costs Add Up," *The Wall Street Journal*, November 28, 2011, http://online.wsj.com.

49. C. K. Stevens, "Effects of Preinterview Beliefs on Applicants' Reactions to Campus Interviews," *Academy of Management Journal* 40 (1997), pp. 947–66.

50. C. Collins, "The Interactive Effects of Recruitment Practices and Product Awareness on Job Seekers' Employer Knowledge and Application Behaviors," *Journal of Applied Psychology* 92 (2007), pp. 180–90.

51. M. S. Taylor and T. J. Bergman, "Organizational Recruitment Activities and Applicants' Reactions at Different Stages of the Recruitment Process," *Personnel Psychology* 40 (1984), pp. 261–85; and C. D. Fisher, D. R. Ilgen, and W. D. Hoyer, "Source Credibility, Information Favorability, and Job Offer Acceptance," *Academy of Management Journal* 22 (1979), pp. 94–103.

52. L. M. Graves and G. N. Powell, "The Effect of Sex Similarity on Recruiters' Evaluation of Actual Applicants: A Test of the Similarity-Attraction Paradigm," *Personnel Psychology* 48 (1995), pp. 85–98.

53. R. D. Tretz and T. A. Judge, "Realistic Job Previews: A Test of the Adverse Self-Selection Hypothesis," *Journal of Applied Psychology* 83 (1998), pp. 330–37.

54. P. Hom, R. W. Griffeth, L. E. Palich, and J. S. Bracker, "An Exploratory Investigation into Theoretical Mechanisms Underlying Realistic Job Previews," *Personnel Psychology* 51 (1998), pp. 421–51.

55. G. M. McEvoy and W. F. Cascio, "Strategies for Reducing Employee Turnover: A Meta-Analysis," *Journal of Applied Psychology* 70 (1985), pp. 342–53; and S. L. Premack and J. P. Wanous, "A Meta-Analysis of Realistic Job Preview Experiments," *Journal of Applied Psychology* 70 (1985), pp. 706–19.

56. P. G. Irving and J. P. Meyer, "Reexamination of the Met-Expectations Hypothesis: A Longitudinal Analysis," *Journal of Applied Psychology* 79 (1995), pp. 937–49.

57. R. W. Walters, "It's Time We Become Pros," *Journal of College Placement* 12 (1985), pp. 30–33.

58. S. L. Rynes, R. D. Bretz, and B. Gerhart, "The Importance of Recruitment in Job Choice: A Different Way of Looking," *Personnel Psychology* 44 (1991), pp. 487–522.

Selecting Employees and Placing Them in Jobs

Introduction

Groupon, the daily-deals website, is leading the way into a new kind of marketing. With a strategy based on innovation, the company puts creativity and flexibility at the top of its list of job requirements. From that perspective, it makes sense that Groupon's vice president of human resources (or "head of people strategy"), Dan Jessup, also leads improv workshops at Second City Communications. A successful improv performance has to be creative, nimble, and clever—just like an Internet start-up.

Jessup believes that finding this kind of talent requires a fast-moving, flexible process. Groupon's recruiters partner with hiring managers to evaluate candidates based on what Jessup calls "relevance and character"—a personality that fits in well with the company's free-spirited, high-energy culture. Interviewers identify these individuals based on behaviors such as speaking freely and asking intelligent questions. The process has to move fast because the company is growing rapidly; some months Groupon has added 200 new employees. Typically, recruiters start by contacting individuals who applied and screening them in a phone interview. For some positions, candidates who pass the screening take skills tests, often available to them online. Most candidates also participate in a face-to-face interview before the company offers them a job. Up to three people conduct the interviews, so that if one person misses an important quality in a candidate, another interviewer may notice it.[1]

Hiring decisions are about finding the people who will be a good fit with the job and the organization. Any organization that appreciates the competitive edge provided by good people must take the utmost care in choosing its members. The organization's decisions about selecting personnel are central to its ability to survive, adapt, and grow. Selection decisions become especially critical when organizations face tight labor markets or must compete for talent with other organizations in the same industry. If a competitor keeps getting the best applicants, the remaining companies must make do with who is left.

This chapter will familiarize you with ways to minimize errors in employee selection and placement. The chapter starts by describing the selection process and how to evaluate possible methods for carrying out that process. It then takes an in-depth look at the most widely used methods: applications and résumés, employment tests, and interviews. The chapter ends by describing the process by which organizations arrive at a final selection decision.

Selection Process

Through **personnel selection,** organizations make decisions about who will or will not be allowed to join the organization. Selection begins with the candidates identified through recruitment and with attempts to reduce their number to the individuals best qualified to perform the available jobs. At the end of the process, the selected individuals are placed in jobs with the organization.

The process of selecting employees varies considerably from organization to organization and from job to job. At most organizations, however, selection includes the steps illustrated in Figure 6.1. First, a human resource professional reviews the applications received to see which meet the basic requirements of the job. For candidates who meet the basic requirements, the organization administers tests and reviews work samples to rate the candidates' abilities. Those with the best abilities are invited to the organization for one or more interviews. Often, supervisors and team members are involved in this stage of the process. By this point, the decision makers are beginning to form opinions about which candidates are most desirable. For the top few candidates, the organization should check references and conduct background checks to verify that the organization's information is correct. Then supervisors, teams, and other decision makers select a person to receive a job offer. In some cases, the candidate may negotiate with the organization regarding salary, benefits, and the like. If the candidate accepts the job, the organization places him or her in that job.

LO 6-1 Identify the elements of the selection process.

Personnel Selection
The process through which organizations make decisions about who will or will not be allowed to join the organization.

Figure 6.1
Steps in the Selection Process

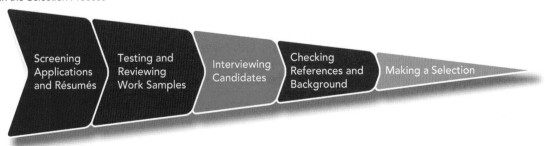

Screening Applications and Résumés | Testing and Reviewing Work Samples | Interviewing Candidates | Checking References and Background | Making a Selection

Nowadays, the ease of applying online coupled with the high unemployment rates of the past few years have made this processing overwhelming for many recruiters. A simple job posting online could generate hundreds of résumés in one day. Many employers are coping by automating much of the selection process with an applicant-tracking system. Typically, the system starts by receiving the data provided in electronically submitted résumés and matching it against the company's selection criteria. The system might find that half the résumés lack necessary keywords, so it sends those applicants a polite "no thank you" e-mail. The applications that survive the automated screening go to a hiring manager, often ranked by how well they meet preset criteria. The manager reviews these applications and selects candidates to contact for a telephone or face-to-face interview and/or testing.

Critics point out that these automated systems may arbitrarily reject highly qualified people who submit a creatively worded résumé rather than simply mimicking the wording of the job posting. Moreover, a recent study by the Talent Board suggests that rejected job applicants have the potential to hurt a company's bottom line. More than 8% of the study's participants said that their job rejection would affect their relationship as customers with the company, the sentiment being "if I'm not good enough to work here I probably don't want to be a customer." Nevertheless, automated systems can make the application process more efficient by speeding up the steps and perhaps allowing applicants to check the status of their applications.[2]

How does an organization decide which of these steps to use and in what order? Some organizations simply repeat a selection process that is familiar. If members of the organization underwent job interviews, *they* conduct job interviews, asking familiar questions. However, what organizations *should* do is to create a selection process in support of its job descriptions. In Chapter 3, we explained that a job description identifies the knowledge, skills, abilities, and other characteristics required for successfully performing a job. The selection process should be set up in such a way that it lets the organization identify people who have the necessary KSAOs. In Winston-Salem, North Carolina, a mortgage company called BB&T bases its growth strategy on excellent customer service. BB&T hires customer-focused loan officers by seeking a combination of cultural fit with the organization and skill in "relationship selling" (selling that builds long-term customer relationships by identifying and meeting customers' needs). First, the BB&T recruiter and hiring manager assess cultural fit by talking to candidates about how they work with customers. If candidates focus on their earnings or express little interest in customers' well-being, BB&T screens them out no matter how skillful they are at closing a deal. Candidates with the necessary attitude are invited to continue with an assessment of their technical skills. Candidates who pass both steps of the initial screening are invited to interview with branch managers. If all the interviewers agree that the candidate is a good fit, BB&T makes an offer. This careful approach to hiring has built a workforce characterized by exceptionally high productivity and low turnover.[3] For another example of a well-planned selection process, see the "Best Practices" box.

This kind of strategic approach to selection requires ways to measure the effectiveness of selection tools. From science, we have basic standards for this:

- The method provides *reliable* information.
- The method provides *valid* information.
- The information can be *generalized* to apply to the candidates.
- The method offers *high utility* (practical value).
- The selection criteria are *legal*.

Best Practices

How Associated Bank Selects the Best, Even in Lean Times

Hiring tellers is always a challenge for a bank. Workers who can handle money, have great people skills, and are willing to work on their feet for hours at a stretch in exchange for modest pay generally have a lot of options in the labor market. Teller positions therefore have high turnover, so banks are constantly looking for replacements, whether or not they are expanding their business. This is true of Associated Bank, which is headquartered in Green Bay, Wisconsin. To fill teller positions in more than 250 branches in Wisconsin, Illinois, and Minnesota, Associated's recruiters need to hire about 700 tellers every year.

The challenge was at least as hard during the financial crisis that started in 2008. Associated borrowed hundreds of millions of dollars from the federal government's Troubled Asset Relief Program, which it needed to repay during the most serious economic recession since the 1930s. Attracting valuable employees during such a bleak time for banks was an added challenge. And Associated would have to do so with extreme efficiency.

To streamline the process, Associated purchased new technology called Voice Advantage—a phone system for conducting the first round of candidate interviews automatically. Associated places an "Interview Now!" link on careers sites, or if the bank comes across individuals it wants to invite to apply, it sends them an e-mail with the link included in the message. Candidates who click on the link are taken to a web page that collects basic information including a phone number where the candidate can be reached directly. Then the Voice Advantage system calls the candidate and delivers a series of prerecorded questions. As the candidate answers each question, the system records the answers. Each interview is available for the recruiter to review and comment on online.

In contrast to the basic data of a résumé or job application, the phone interviews are a chance for the candidates to describe how they handle specific situations. For example, candidates are asked to describe how they have reconciled a cash drawer that is short. Recruiters listen for candidates who describe a logical process and sound pleasant to deal with. Because the recruiters don't have to spend time scheduling interviews and delivering questions, they can process many more interviews per day than they could before Associated began using Voice Advantage. Thus, Voice Advantage enables Associated's recruiters to quickly move to the stages of selection that are most relevant for teller positions: methods in which they can gauge candidates' interpersonal skills.

Since Associated started using Voice Advantage, the company has been able to save money by reducing its recruiting staff from 11 recruiters to 6. At least as important, the new selection process moves much more quickly. The recruiters used to need 6 to 10 days to identify candidates who met basic requirements and send them for an interview with a hiring manager. With Voice Advantage, they have cut that step down to 3 days. This reduces the number of qualified candidates—usually the best qualified—who find another job while they are waiting to interview with Associated Bank.

SOURCES: Voice Advantage, "Tour," http://www.voiceadvantage.com, accessed March 9, 2012; Associated Banc-Corp, "Who We Are," http://careers.associatedbank.com, accessed March 8, 2012; Shane Kite, "Prescreening Teller Candidates," *Bank Technology News,* March 1, 2012, Business & Company Resource Center, http://galenet.galegroup.com.

Reliability

The **reliability** of a type of measurement indicates how free that measurement is from random error.[4] A reliable measurement therefore generates consistent results. Assuming that a person's intelligence is fairly stable over time, a reliable test of intelligence should generate consistent results if the same person takes the test several times. Organizations that construct intelligence tests should be able to provide (and explain) information about the reliability of their tests.

Usually, this information involves statistics such as *correlation coefficients*. These statistics measure the degree to which two sets of numbers are related. A higher

LO 6-2 Define ways to measure the success of a selection method.

Reliability
The extent to which a measurement is free from random error.

correlation coefficient signifies a stronger relationship. At one extreme, a correlation coefficient of 1.0 means a perfect positive relationship—as one set of numbers goes up, so does the other. If you took the same vision test three days in a row, those scores would probably have nearly a perfect correlation. At the other extreme, a correlation of −1.0 means a perfect negative correlation—when one set of numbers goes up, the other goes down. In the middle, a correlation of 0 means there is no correlation at all. For example, the correlation (or relationship) between weather and intelligence would be at or near 0. A reliable test would be one for which scores by the same person (or people with similar attributes) have a correlation close to 1.0.

Reliability answers one important question—whether you are measuring something accurately—but ignores another question that is as important: Are you measuring something that matters? Consider what happened to Chroma Technologies when it needed to hire customer service representatives. The company makes and sells optical filters for scientific equipment, so most of its customers are scientists. To get representatives who communicate effectively with these customers, management decided to specify that candidates have a degree in biology or at least five years' experience in selling optical filters. Chroma posted the ad and waited for applications, but almost no one applied. As it turns out, there is not a huge pool of workers with biology degrees who want to sell optical filters. Furthermore, the managers hadn't really thought about how important that degree would be. The company's own founder had no scientific training but had learned through his own selling experiences, and other scientists on the company's payroll would be available to help with technical questions. Chroma's managers rethought the selection criteria and decided that although a biology degree was a reliable measure of scientific training, it wasn't necessarily important. Chroma relaxed the hiring criteria and found a pair of sales reps who succeeded very well without a biology degree.[5] As in this example, employers need to consider both the reliability of their selection methods and their validity, defined next.

Validity

For a selection measure, **validity** describes the extent to which performance on the measure (such as a test score) is related to what the measure is designed to assess (such as job performance). Although we can reliably measure such characteristics as weight and height, these measurements do not provide much information about how a person will perform most kinds of jobs. Thus, for most jobs height and weight provide little validity as selection criteria. One way to determine whether a measure is valid is to compare many people's scores on that measure with their job performance. For example, suppose people who score above 60 words per minute on a keyboarding test consistently get high marks for their performance in data-entry jobs. This observation suggests the keyboarding test is valid for predicting success in that job. In contrast, "HR Oops!" describes a situation in which a manager made hiring decisions based on criteria that were not valid for predicting job performance.

As with reliability, information about the validity of selection methods often uses correlation coefficients. A strong positive (or negative) correlation between a measure and job performance means the measure should be a valid basis for selecting (or rejecting) a candidate. This information is important not only because it helps organizations identify the best employees, but also because organizations can demonstrate fair employment practices by showing that their selection process is valid. The federal government's *Uniform Guidelines on Employee Selection Procedures* accept three ways of measuring validity: criterion-related, content, and construct validity.

Hiring Clones

Entrepreneur Todd Morris made an all-too-common hiring mistake. As BrickHouse Security began to grow, he brought in individuals who pressed hard to get results and worked independently. Morris possesses the same qualities, and they enabled him to get his company off the ground. But as Morris hired more and more people, they needed to be able to collaborate. Instead, they were overly competitive and began complaining about one another.

Morris hired a consulting firm to help him figure out what was making the work environment so poisonous. The consultants gave all the employees a personality test, which showed that Morris had been hiring people who tended to lack the kinds of human relations skills that are related to cooperating and listening.

Morris now makes personality testing part of the selection process at BrickHouse, and he looks for people who are less like himself—the independent entrepreneur—and more like team players.

Morris's lesson is one that many companies could benefit from applying. A recent survey found that when an employee doesn't live up to expectations, the most common reason is that the employer failed to match the candidate's skills to the actual job requirements. Effective hiring decisions are not like making friends at a party. Instead of simply picking the individuals they feel most comfortable around, careful decision makers first establish the qualities they are seeking and then choose methods that consistently identify those qualities.

Questions

1. Morris felt he needed to be hard-driving and independent to get a business off the ground, so he looked for the same kinds of people to carry out the business. How would you rate the validity of his approach to choosing employees? How would you rate its reliability?
2. Besides the addition of personality tests, what other steps of Morris's hiring process might benefit from change?

SOURCES: April Joyner, "Are You a Narcissistic Boss?" *Inc.*, November 2011, http://www.inc.com; Robert Half Finance & Accounting, "Bad Match," news release, September 29, 2011, http://rhfa.mediaroom.com.

Criterion-Related Validity The first category, **criterion-related validity,** is a measure of validity based on showing a substantial correlation between test scores and job performance scores. In the example in Figure 6.2, a company compares two measures—an intelligence test and college grade point average—with performance as sales representative. In the left graph, which shows the relationship between the intelligence test scores and job performance, the points for the 20 sales reps fall near the 45-degree line. The correlation coefficient is near .90 (for a perfect 1.0, all the points would be on the 45-degree line). In the graph at the right, the points are scattered more widely. The correlation between college GPA and sales reps' performance is much lower. In this hypothetical example, the intelligence test is more valid than GPA for predicting success at this job.

Two kinds of research are possible for arriving at criterion-related validity:

1. **Predictive validation**—This research uses the test scores of all applicants and looks for a relationship between the scores and future performance. The researcher administers the tests, waits a set period of time, and then measures the performance of the applicants who were hired.
2. **Concurrent validation**—This type of research administers a test to people who currently hold a job, then compares their scores to existing measures of job performance. If the people who score highest on the test also do better on the job, the test is assumed to be valid.

Predictive validation is more time consuming and difficult, but it is the best measure of validity. Job applicants tend to be more motivated to do well on the tests, and

Criterion-Related Validity
A measure of validity based on showing a substantial correlation between test scores and job performance scores.

Predictive Validation
Research that uses the test scores of all applicants and looks for a relationship between the scores and future performance of the applicants who were hired.

Concurrent Validation
Research that consists of administering a test to people who currently hold a job, then comparing their scores to existing measures of job performance.

Figure 6.2

Criterion-Related Measurements of a Student's Aptitude

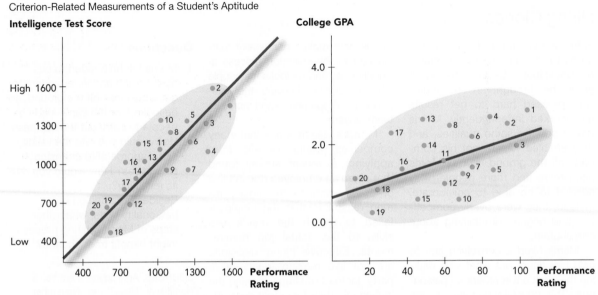

their performance on the tests is not influenced by their firsthand experience with the job. Also, the group studied is more likely to include people who perform poorly on the test—a necessary ingredient to accurately validate a test.[6]

Content and Construct Validity

Content Validity
Consistency between the test items or problems and the kinds of situations or problems that occur on the job.

Content and Construct Validity   Another way to show validity is to establish **content validity**—that is, consistency between the test items or problems and the kinds of situations or problems that occur on the job. A test that is "content valid" exposes the job applicant to situations that are likely to occur on the job. It tests whether the applicant has the knowledge, skills, or ability to handle such situations. In the case of a company using tests for selecting a construction superintendent, tests with content validity included organizing a random list of subcontractors into the order they would appear at a construction site and entering a shed to identify construction errors that had intentionally been made for testing purposes.[7] More commonly today, employers use computer role-playing games in which software is created to include situations that occur on the job. The game measures how the candidate reacts to the situations, and then it computes a score based on how closely the candidate's responses match those of an ideal employee.[8]

The usual basis for deciding that a test has content validity is through expert judgment. Experts can rate the test items according to whether they mirror essential functions of the job. Because establishing validity is based on the experts' subjective judgments, content validity is most suitable for measuring behavior that is concrete and observable.

Construct Validity
Consistency between a high score on a test and high level of a construct such as intelligence or leadership ability, as well as between mastery of this construct and successful performance of the job.

For tests that measure abstract qualities such as intelligence or leadership ability, establishment of validity may have to rely on **construct validity.** This involves establishing that tests really do measure intelligence, leadership ability, or other such "constructs," as well as showing that mastery of this construct is associated with successful performance of the job. For example, if you could show that a test measures something called "mechanical ability," and that people with superior mechanical ability perform well as assemblers, then the test has construct validity for the assembler job. Tests that measure a construct usually measure a combination of behaviors thought to be associated with the construct.

Ability to Generalize

Along with validity in general, we need to know whether a selection method is valid in the context in which the organization wants to use it. A **generalizable** method applies not only to the conditions in which the method was originally developed—job, organization, people, time period, and so on. It also applies to other organizations, jobs, applicants, and so on. In other words, is a selection method that was valid in one context also valid in other contexts?

Researchers have studied whether tests of intelligence and thinking skills (called *cognitive ability*) can be generalized. The research has supported the idea that these tests are generalizable across many jobs. However, as jobs become more complex, the validity of many of these tests increases. In other words, they are most valid for complex jobs.[9]

Generalizable
Valid in other contexts beyond the context in which the selection method was developed.

Practical Value

Not only should selection methods such as tests and interview responses accurately predict how well individuals will perform, but they should also produce information that actually benefits the organization. Being valid, reliable, and generalizable adds value to a method. Another consideration is the cost of using the selection method. Selection procedures such as testing and interviewing cost money. They should cost significantly less than the benefits of hiring the new employees. Methods that provide economic value greater than the cost of using them are said to have **utility.**

The choice of a selection method may differ according to the job being filled. If the job involves providing a product or service of high value to the organization, it is worthwhile to spend more to find a top performer. At a company where salespeople are responsible for closing million-dollar deals, the company will be willing to invest more in selection decisions. At a fast-food restaurant, such an investment will not be worthwhile; the employer will prefer faster, simpler ways to select workers who ring up orders, prepare food, and keep the facility clean.

Utility
The extent to which something provides economic value greater than its cost.

LO 6-3 Summarize the government's requirements for employee selection.

Legal Standards for Selection

As we discussed in Chapter 3, the U.S. government imposes legal limits on selection decisions. The government requires that the selection process be conducted in a way that avoids discrimination and provides access to employees with disabilities. The laws described in Chapter 3 have many applications to the selection process:

- The Civil Rights Act of 1991 and the Age Discrimination in Employment Act of 1967 place requirements on the choice of selection methods. An employer that uses a neutral-appearing selection method that damages a protected group is obligated to show that there is a business necessity for using that method. For example, if an organization uses a test that eliminates many candidates from minority groups, the organization must show that the test is valid for predicting performance of

NFL teams have been using cognitive tests to select players, assuming that intelligence can be generalized to the job requirements of football teams, especially on teams that compete using complex offensive and defensive schemes. What other things, in addition to intelligence, would teams need to look for?

that job. In this context, good performance does not include "customer preference" or "brand image" as a justification for adverse impact. As we saw in Chapter 3, the courts may view a discriminatory pattern of hiring as evidence that the company is engaged in illegal discrimination. For example, Mavis Discount Tire over three years hired no women among its 800 tire installers, mechanics, assistant managers, and managers. Other evidence suggested that some female applicants held superior credentials for such positions. The Equal Employment Opportunity Commission therefore filed a lawsuit against Mavis, charging it with sex discrimination.[10]

- The Civil Rights Act of 1991 also prohibits preferential treatment in favor of minority groups. In the case of an organization using a test that tends to reject members of minority groups, the organization may not simply adjust minority applicants' scores upward. Such practices can create an environment that is demotivating to all employees and can lead to government sanctions. In Buffalo, New York, minority firefighters scored poorly on civil service exams, so the city let its list of candidates for promotion expire rather than promote only white firefighters. White firefighters who had been on the list filed a lawsuit claiming they were discriminated against, and they won back pay, benefits, and damages for emotional distress. Their attorney said the situation had created morale problems among firefighters who saw the discriminatory treatment as unfair.[11]

- Equal employment opportunity laws affect the kinds of information an organization may gather on application forms and in interviews. As summarized in Table 6.1, the organization may not ask questions that gather information about a person's protected status, even indirectly. For example, requesting the dates a person attended high school and college could indirectly gather information about an applicant's age.

- The Americans with Disabilities Act (ADA) of 1991 requires employers to make "reasonable accommodation" to disabled individuals and restricts many kinds of questions during the selection process. Under the ADA, preemployment questions may not investigate disabilities, but must focus on job performance. An interviewer may ask, "Can you meet the attendance requirements for this job?" but may not ask, "How many days did you miss work last year because you were sick?" Also, the employer may not, in making hiring decisions, use employment physical exams or other tests that could reveal a psychological or physical disability.

Along with equal employment opportunity, organizations must be concerned about candidates' privacy rights. The information gathered during the selection process may include information that employees consider confidential. Confidentiality is a particular concern when job applicants provide information online. Employers should collect data only at secure websites, and they may have to be understanding if online applicants are reluctant to provide data such as Social Security numbers, which hackers could use for identity theft. For some jobs, background checks look at candidates' credit history. The Fair Credit Reporting Act requires employers to obtain a candidate's consent before using a third party to check the candidate's credit history or references. If the employer then decides to take an adverse action (such as not hiring) based on the report, the employer must give the applicant a copy of the report and summary of the applicant's rights *before* taking the action.

Immigration Reform and Control Act of 1986
Federal law requiring employers to verify and maintain records on applicants' legal rights to work in the United States.

Another legal requirement is that employers hiring people to work in the United States must ensure that anyone they hire is eligible for employment in this country. Under the **Immigration Reform and Control Act of 1986,** employers must verify and maintain records on the legal rights of applicants to work in the United States. They do this by having applicants fill out the U.S. Citizenship and Immigration

PERMISSIBLE QUESTIONS	IMPERMISSIBLE QUESTIONS
What is your full name? Have you ever worked under a different name? [Ask all candidates.]	What was your maiden name? What's the nationality of your name?
If you are hired, can you show proof of age (to meet a legal age requirement)?	How old are you? How would you feel about working for someone younger than you?
Will you need any reasonable accommodation for this hiring process? Are you able to perform this job, with or without reasonable accommodation?	What is your height? Your weight? Do you have any disabilities? Have you been seriously ill? Please provide a photograph of yourself.
What languages do you speak? [Statement that employment is subject to verification of applicant's identity and employment eligibility under immigration laws]	What is your ancestry? Are you a citizen of the United States? Where were you born? How did you learn to speak that language?
What schools have you attended? What degrees have you earned? What was your major?	Is that school affiliated with [religious group]?When did you attend high school? [to learn applicant's age]
Can you meet the requirements of the work schedule? [Ask all candidates.]	What is your religion? What religious holidays do you observe?
Please provide the names of any relatives currently employed by this employer.	What is your marital status? Would you like to be addressed as Mrs., Ms., or Miss? Do you have any children?
Have you ever been convicted of a crime?	Have you ever been arrested?
What organizations or groups do you belong to that you consider relevant to being able to perform this job?	What organizations or groups do you belong to?

Table 6.1

Permissible and Impermissible Questions for Applications and Interviews

Note: This table provides examples and is not intended as a complete listing of permissible and impermissible questions. The examples are based on federal requirements; state laws vary and may affect these examples.

SOURCES: Equal Employment Opportunity Commission, "Prohibited Employment Policies/Practices: Pre-Employment Inquiries," http://eeoc.gov, accessed March 8, 2012; Lilly Garcia, "How to Interview: Improper Questions," *The Washington Post,* http://www.washingtonpost.com, accessed March 8, 2012; Alison Green, "Is That Interview Question Legal?" *U.S. News and World Report,* January 10, 2011, http://money.usnews.com.

Services' Form I-9 and present documents showing their identity and eligibility to work. Employers must complete their portion of each Form I-9, check the applicant's documents, and retain the Form I-9 for at least three years. Employers may (and in some cases must) also use the federal government's electronic system for verifying eligibility to work. To use the system, called E-Verify, employers go online (**https://e-verify.uscis.gov**) to submit information on the applicant's I-9. The system compares it against information in databases of the Social Security Administration and Department of Homeland Security. It then notifies the employer of the candidate's eligibility, usually within 24 hours. At the same time, assuming a person is eligible to work under the Immigration Reform and Control Act, the law prohibits the employer from discriminating against the person on the basis of national origin or citizenship status.

An important principle of selection is to combine several sources of information about candidates, rather than relying solely on interviews or a single type of testing. The sources should be chosen carefully to relate to the characteristics identified in the job description. When organizations do this, they are increasing the validity of the decision criteria. They are more likely to make hiring decisions that are fair and unbiased. They also are more likely to choose the best candidates.

Visit the text website www.mhhe.com/noefund5e for tips on writing an effective résumé.

LO 6-4 Compare the common methods used for selecting human resources.

Job Applications and Résumés

Nearly all employers gather background information on applicants at the beginning of the selection process. The usual ways of gathering background information are by asking applicants to fill out application forms and provide résumés. Organizations also verify the information by checking references and conducting background checks.

Asking job candidates to provide background information is inexpensive. The organization can get reasonably accurate information by combining applications and résumés with background checks and well-designed interviews.[12] A major challenge with applications and résumés is the sheer volume of work they generate for the organization. Human resource departments often are swamped with far more résumés than they can carefully review.

Application Forms

Asking each applicant to fill out an employment application is a low-cost way to gather basic data from many applicants. It also ensures that the organization has certain standard categories of information, such as mailing address and employment history, from each. Figure 6.3 is an example of an application form.

Employers can buy general-purpose application forms from an office supply store, or they can create their own forms to meet unique needs. Either way, employment applications include areas for applicants to provide several types of information:

- *Contact information*—The applicant's name, address, phone number, and e-mail address.
- *Work experience*—Companies the applicant worked for, job titles, and dates of employment.
- *Educational background*—High school, college, and universities attended and degree(s) awarded.
- *Applicant's signature*—Signature following a statement that the applicant has provided true and complete information.

The application form may include other areas for the applicant to provide additional information, such as specific work experiences, technical skills, or memberships in professional or trade groups. Also, including the date on an application is useful for keeping up-to-date records of job applicants. The application form should not request information that could violate equal employment opportunity standards. For example, questions about an applicant's race, marital status, or number of children would be inappropriate.

By reviewing application forms, HR personnel can identify which candidates meet minimum requirements for education and experience. They may be able to rank applicants—for example, giving applicants with 10 years of experience a higher ranking than applicants with 2 years of experience. In this way, the applications enable the organization to narrow the pool of candidates to a number it can afford to test and interview.

Résumés

The usual way that applicants introduce themselves to a potential employer is to submit a résumé. An obvious drawback of this information source is that applicants control the content of the information as well as the way it is presented. This type of

Figure 6.3

Sample Job Application Form

APPLICATION FOR EMPLOYMENT
An Equal Opportunity Employer

FIRST NAME	MIDDLE NAME	LAST NAME	SOCIAL SECURITY NUMBER

LOCAL	STREET ADDRESS	CITY AND STATE	ZIP CODE	TELEPHONE

PERMANENT	STREET ADDRESS	CITY AND STATE	ZIP CODE	TELEPHONE

ELECTRONIC MAIL ADDRESS

PLEASE ANSWER ALL ITEMS. IF NOT APPLICABLE, WRITE N/A.

ARE YOU A U.S. CITIZEN OR AUTHORIZED TO BE LEGALLY EMPLOYED ON AN ONGOING BASIS IN THE U.S. BASED ON YOUR VISA OR IMMIGRATION STATUS? ☐ YES ☐ NO

ARE YOU OVER 18 YEARS OF AGE? YES☐ NO☐

DO YOU CURRENTLY HAVE A NONIMMIGRANT U.S. VISA? ☐ YES ☐ NO IF YES, PLEASE SPECIFY:

DO YOU HAVE ANY RELATIVES EMPLOYED HERE? ☐ NO ☐ YES
IF YES, GIVE NAME, RELATIONSHIP AND LOCATION WHERE THEY WORK

DO YOU HAVE ANY RELATIVES EMPLOYED BY THE COMPETITION? ☐ NO ☐ YES WHAT COMPANY?

ARE YOU ABLE TO TRAVEL AS REQUIRED FOR THE POSITION SOUGHT? ☐ YES ☐ NO

ARE YOU WILLING TO RELOCATE? ☐ YES ☐ NO

ARE THERE GEOGRAPHICAL AREAS WHICH YOU WOULD PREFER OR REFUSE? ☐ NO ☐ YES IF YES, PLEASE SPECIFY:

HAVE YOU EVER BEEN CONVICTED OR PLED GUILTY TO ANY FELONY OR MISDEMEANOR OTHER THAN FOR A MINOR TRAFFIC VIOLATION? ☐ NO ☐ YES
IF YES, STATE THE DATE(S) AND LOCATION(S):

WHEN	WHERE	NATURE OF OFFENSE(S)

WORK PREFERENCE

SPECIFIC POSITION FOR WHICH YOU ARE APPLYING

NUMBER OF YEARS OF RELATED EXPERIENCE

LIST COMPUTER SOFTWARE PACKAGES OR PROGRAMMING LANGUAGE SKILLS

STARTING SALARY EXPECTED	DATE AVAILABLE TO START WORK	HOW DID YOU HAPPEN TO APPLY FOR A POSITION HERE?

HAVE YOU EVER WORKED AT, OR APPLIED FOR WORK HERE BEFORE? ☐ NO ☐ YES
IF YES: WHEN? WHERE?

LIST EMPLOYMENT REFERENCES HERE, IF NOT INCLUDED ON ATTACHED RESUME

TURN OVER

COMPLETE THIS SECTION IF INFORMATION IS NOT INCLUDED ON ATTACHED RESUME

EDUCATION (CIRCLE THE HIGHEST GRADE COMPLETED: ELEMENTARY 6 7 8 HIGH SCHOOL 1 2 3 4 COLLEGE 1 2 3 4 5 6 7 8)

	NAME(S)	LOCATION(S)	GRADUATED ☐ YES ☐ NO	MAJOR FIELD(S) OF STUDY AND PRINCIPAL PROFESSOR (OR ADVISOR)	DEGREE(S) RECEIVED	GRADE AVERAGE	CLASS RANK ___ OUT OF
HIGH SCHOOL							
COLLEGE							OVERALL AND MAJOR GPA'S

ACADEMIC HONORS OR OTHER SPECIAL RECOGNITION

FOREIGN LANGUAGES READ

FOREIGN LANGUAGES SPOKEN

HAVE YOU TAKEN THE GMAT, GRE, SAT OR OTHER ACADEMIC ENTRANCE TEST(S) WITHIN THE LAST TEN YEARS? ☐ YES ☐ NO
IF YES, LIST TEST(S), DATE(S) AND HIGHEST SCORE(S).

	DATE TAKEN		SCORE(S)		
SAT		TOTAL:	VERBAL:		MATHEMATICAL:
ACT		TOTAL:	ENGLISH:	MATHEMATICS:	READING: SCIENCE:
GRE (GENERAL TEST)		TOTAL:	VERBAL:	QUANTITATIVE:	ANALYTICAL:
GMAT		TOTAL:	VERBAL:	MATH:	AWA:
OTHER		TOTAL:			

EMPLOYMENT AND MILITARY RECORD

LIST MOST RECENT FIRST. I AGREE TO FURNISH VERIFICATION IF REQUESTED. ATTACH RESUME. RESPOND BELOW IF INFORMATION IS NOT INCLUDED ON RESUME.

NAME AND ADDRESS OF EMPLOYER	POSITION HELD	PRIMARY RESPONSIBILITIES AND ACCOUNTABILITIES	SALARY START	SALARY FINISH	DATES FROM	DATES TO	REASON FOR LEAVING

ENCIRCLE THOSE EMPLOYERS YOU DO NOT WANT US TO CONTACT

TURN OVER

information is therefore biased in favor of the applicant and (although this is unethical) may not even be accurate. Some employers today see social media as an alternative source of information that is more relevant or more accurate, as described in "HRM Social." However, résumés are an inexpensive way to gather information and provide employers with a starting point. Organizations typically use résumés as a basis for deciding which candidates to investigate further.

As with employment applications, an HR staff member reviews the résumés to identify candidates meeting such basic requirements as educational background, related work performed, and types of equipment the person has used. Because résumés are created by the job applicants (or the applicants have at least approved résumés created by someone they hire), they also may provide some insight into how candidates communicate and present themselves. Employers tend to decide against applicants whose résumés are unclear, sloppy, or full of mistakes. On the positive side, résumés may enable applicants to highlight accomplishments that might not show up in the format of an employment application. Review of résumés is most valid when the content of the résumés is evaluated in terms of the elements of a job description.

References

Application forms often ask that applicants provide the names of several references. Applicants provide the names and phone numbers of former employers or others who can vouch for their abilities and past job performance. In some situations, the applicant may provide letters of reference written by those people. It is then up to the organization to have someone contact the references to gather information or verify the accuracy of the information provided by the applicant.

As you might expect, references are not an unbiased source of information. Most applicants are careful to choose references who will say something positive. In addition, former employers and others may be afraid that if they express negative opinions, they will be sued. Their fear is understandable. In a recent case, a former U.S. Marine and recipient of the Medal of Honor sued his former employer, BAE Systems, for telling a prospective employer that he had mental health and drinking problems. The former employee alleged that BAE was retaliating against him for objecting to BAE's plans to sell advanced thermal optic scopes to Pakistan and that the company was defaming him by making untrue statements about him.[13] Whether or not BAE successfully defends the lawsuit, it was an embarrassing and expensive situation for the company to be in.

Usually the organization checks references after it has determined that the applicant is a finalist for the job. Contacting references for all applicants would be time consuming, and it does pose some burden on the people contacted. Part of that burden is the risk of giving information that is seen as too negative or too positive. If the person who is a reference gives negative information, there is a chance the candidate will claim *defamation*, meaning the person damaged the applicant's reputation by making statements that cannot be proved truthful.[14] At the other extreme, if the person gives a glowing statement about a candidate, and the new employer later learns of misdeeds such as sexual misconduct or workplace violence, the new employer might sue the former employer for misrepresentation.[15]

Because such situations occasionally arise, often with much publicity, people who give references tend to give as little information as possible. Most organizations have policies that the human resource department will handle all requests for references and that they will only verify employment dates and sometimes the employee's final

Will LinkedIn Make the Résumé Obsolete?

Job application forms and résumés are still the norm, but managers at more companies are starting to think they can find a more realistic assessment of candidates by looking at their online presence. One of those companies is Union Square Ventures, a venture capital firm (a company that invests in start-up businesses). Union Square has invested in social-media companies including Foursquare, Zynga, and Twitter, so it needs employees who are at home with that technology. The firm asks job applicants to submit links that demonstrate their "web presence." Union Square hired Christina Cacioppo after reviewing her personal blog, Twitter feed, LinkedIn profile, and travel stories on Delicious and Dopplr. This selection approach makes perfect sense to Cacioppo because, she says, Union Square primarily considers how people think and how they will fit in at the company.

Such intangibles tend to be hard to detect from a résumé.

Seeking to build its own business on recruiters' interest in social media, LinkedIn is offering a tool to increase job applications through its site. The tool is called Apply with LinkedIn. Recruiters can post job openings on their company's LinkedIn page. If they include an "Apply with LinkedIn" button, job seekers can click on the button to send their profile to the company. The user's profile includes not only a résumé but also recommendations and contact information. It also can contain links to examples of or information about the user's accomplishments. The tool also lets the user type a short introduction (in place of a cover letter with a mailed résumé). When users apply, the recruiter receives e-mail containing links to each applicant's profile.

Recruiters also use social media later in the selection process to check whether candidates of interest

meet the company's standards in their online conduct. Roughly 7 in 10 recruiters in the United States have acknowledged rejecting candidates because of something learned during a check of social media. That's a word of warning to users of LinkedIn and other social media. Present and future job seekers should be sure that their online comments are as courteous and professional as they would be in a meeting at the company they would most like to work for.

SOURCES: Rachel Emma Silverman, "No More Résumés, Say Some Firms," *The Wall Street Journal,* January 24, 2012, http://online.wsj.com; Benny Evangelista, "LinkedIn Initiates Job Application Click Feature," *San Francisco Chronicle,* July 26, 2011, Business & Company Resource Center, http://galenet.galegroup.com; Virginia Matthews, "Social Media Background Checks: A Minefield for Recruiters," *Employers Law,* October 2011, EBSCOhost, http://web.ebscohost.com.

---

salary. In organizations without such a policy, HR professionals should be careful—and train managers to be careful—to stick to observable, job-related behaviors and to avoid broad opinions that may be misinterpreted. In spite of these drawbacks of references, the risks of not learning about significant problems in a candidate's past outweigh the possibility of getting only a little information. Potential employers should check references. In general, the results of this effort will be most valid if the employer contacts many references (if possible, going beyond the list of names provided by the applicant), speaks with them directly by phone, and listens carefully for clues such as tone of voice.[16]

Background Checks

A background check is a way to verify that applicants are as they represent themselves to be. Unfortunately, not all candidates are open and honest. Liz Crawford, who is responsible for hiring employees at Factory VFX, has seen some notable attempts to deceive her. One candidate handed her a résumé including employment experience at a company Crawford knows well. When she commented on this, the candidate gave her a different résumé and tried to explain that the first one was a "wish résumé" of positions she wished she had held. Another candidate announced at his interview that he had been recommended by a Factory VFX artist. At the end of the interview, Crawford picked up the phone and dialed the artist so they could greet one another—and the embarrassed candidate admitted he didn't actually know the artist.[17]

Besides checking employment references, many employers also conduct criminal background checks. Some positions are so sensitive that the law may even limit hiring a person with certain kinds of convictions: for example, a person convicted of domestic violence may not hold positions that involve shipping firearms. The use of criminal background checks is a sensitive issue in the United States, however, especially since crackdowns on crime have resulted in many arrests. Recent statistics show that 1 in 100 U.S. adults is imprisoned, and 92 million people in the United States have a criminal record (with many of those crimes being nonviolent).[18] An additional concern is the disparate impact of considering criminal history. Men are far more likely to have a criminal record than women, and arrests and convictions are far more common among African Americans than whites. The Equal Employment Opportunity Commission has published guidelines that employers who check criminal histories consider the nature and gravity of the offense, the time that has passed since conviction or completion of sentence, and the nature of the job the candidate is applying for.

Another type of background check that has recently drawn greater scrutiny is the use of credit checks. Employers in certain situations, such as processes that involve handling money, are concerned that employees with credit problems will behave less honestly. To avoid hiring such employees, these employers conduct a background check. Also, some employers see good credit as an indicator that a person is responsible. For reasons such as these, 60% of employers report that they conduct credit checks.[19] But in a time of high unemployment and many home foreclosures, some people see this type of investigation as unfair to people who are desperately trying to find work: the worse their financial situation, the harder the job search becomes. Under federal law, conducting a credit check is legal if the person consents, but some states ban or are considering bans on the practice.

Employment Tests and Work Samples

LO 6-5 Describe major types of employment tests.

When the organization has identified candidates whose applications or résumés indicate they meet basic requirements, the organization continues the selection process with this narrower pool of candidates. Often, the next step is to gather objective data through one or more employment tests. These tests fall into two broad categories:

1. **Aptitude tests** assess how well a person can learn or acquire skills and abilities. In the realm of employment testing, the best-known aptitude test is the General Aptitude Test Battery (GATB), used by the U.S. Employment Service.
2. **Achievement tests** measure a person's existing knowledge and skills. For example, government agencies conduct civil service examinations to see whether applicants are qualified to perform certain jobs.

Aptitude Tests
Tests that assess how well a person can learn or acquire skills and abilities.

Achievement Tests
Tests that measure a person's existing knowledge and skills.

Before using any test, organizations should investigate the test's validity and reliability. Besides asking the testing service to provide this information, it is wise to consult more impartial sources of information, such as the ones identified in Table 6.2.

Physical Ability Tests

Physical strength and endurance play less of a role in the modern workplace than in the past, thanks to the use of automation and modern technology. Even so, many jobs

Mental Measurements Yearbook	Descriptions and reviews of tests that are commercially available	**Table 6.2** **Sources of Information about Employment Tests**
Principles for the Validation and Use of Personnel Selection Procedures (Society for Industrial and Organizational Psychology)	Guide to help organizations evaluate tests	
Standards for Educational and Psychological Tests (American Psychological Association)	Description of standards for testing programs	
Tests: A Comprehensive Reference for Assessments in Psychology, Education, and Business	Descriptions of thousands of tests	
Test Critiques	Reviews of tests, written by professionals in the field	

still require certain physical abilities or psychomotor abilities (those connecting brain and body, as in the case of eye-hand coordination). When these abilities are essential to job performance or avoidance of injury, the organization may use physical ability tests. These evaluate one or more of the following areas of physical ability: muscular tension, muscular power, muscular endurance, cardiovascular endurance, flexibility, balance, and coordination.[20]

Although these tests can accurately predict success at certain kinds of jobs, they also tend to exclude women and people with disabilities. As a result, use of physical ability tests can make the organization vulnerable to charges of discrimination. It is therefore important to be certain that the abilities tested for really are essential to job performance or that the absence of these abilities really does create a safety hazard.

Cognitive Ability Tests

Although fewer jobs require muscle power today, brainpower is essential for most jobs. Organizations therefore benefit from people who have strong mental abilities. **Cognitive ability tests**—sometimes called "intelligence tests"—are designed to measure such mental abilities as verbal skills (skill in using written and spoken language), quantitative skills (skill in working with numbers), and reasoning ability (skill in thinking through the answer to a problem). Many jobs require all of these cognitive skills, so employers often get valid information from general tests. Many reliable tests are commercially available. The tests are especially valid for complex jobs and for those requiring adaptability in changing circumstances.[21]

Cognitive Ability Tests Tests designed to measure such mental abilities as verbal skills, quantitative skills, and reasoning ability.

The evidence of validity, coupled with the relatively low cost of these tests, makes them appealing, except for one problem: concern about legal issues. These concerns arise from a historical pattern in which use of the tests has had an adverse impact on African Americans. Some organizations responded with *race norming*, establishing different norms for hiring members of different racial groups. Race norming poses its own problems, not the least of which is the negative reputation it bestows on the minority employees selected using a lower standard. In addition, the Civil Rights Act of 1991 forbids the use of race or sex norming. As a result, organizations that want to base selection decisions on cognitive ability must make difficult decisions about how to measure this ability while avoiding legal problems. One possibility is a concept called *banding*. This concept treats a range of scores as being similar, as when an instructor gives the grade of A to any student whose average test score is at least 90. All applicants within a range of scores, or band, are treated as having the same score. Then within the set of "tied" scores, employers give preference to underrepresented groups. This is a controversial practice, and some have questioned its legality.[22]

Job Performance Tests and Work Samples

Many kinds of jobs require candidates who excel at performing specialized tasks, such as operating a certain machine, handling phone calls from customers, or designing advertising materials. To evaluate candidates for such jobs, the organization may administer tests of the necessary skills. Sometimes the candidates take tests that involve a sample of work, or they may show existing samples of their work. Testing may involve a simulated work environment, a difficult team project, or a complex computer programming puzzle.[23] Examples of job performance tests include tests of keyboarding speed and *in-basket tests*. An in-basket test measures the ability to juggle a variety of demands, as in a manager's job. The candidate is presented with simulated memos and phone messages describing the kinds of problems that confront a person in the job. The candidate has to decide how to respond to these messages and in what order. Examples of jobs for which candidates provide work samples include graphic designers and writers.

Assessment Center
A wide variety of specific selection programs that use multiple selection methods to rate applicants or job incumbents on their management potential.

Tests for selecting managers may take the form of an **assessment center**—a wide variety of specific selection programs that use multiple selection methods to rate applicants or job incumbents on their management potential. An assessment center typically includes in-basket tests, tests of more general abilities, and personality tests. Combining several assessment methods increases the validity of this approach.

Job performance tests have the advantage of giving applicants a chance to show what they can do, which leads them to feel that the evaluation was fair.[24] The tests also are job specific—that is, tailored to the kind of work done in a specific job. So they have a high level of validity, especially when combined with cognitive ability tests and a highly structured interview.[25] This advantage can become a disadvantage, however, if the organization wants to generalize the results of a test for one job to candidates for other jobs. The tests are more appropriate for identifying candidates who are generally able to solve the problems associated with a job, rather than for identifying which particular skills or traits the individual possesses.[26] Developing different tests for different jobs can become expensive. One way to save money is to prepare computerized tests that can be delivered online to various locations.

Personality Inventories

In some situations, employers may also want to know about candidates' personalities. For example, one way that psychologists think about personality is in terms of the "Big Five" traits: extroversion, adjustment, agreeableness, conscientiousness, and inquisitiveness (explained in Table 6.3). There is evidence that people who score high on conscientiousness tend to excel at work, especially when they also have high cognitive ability.[27] For people-related jobs like sales and management, extroversion and agreeableness also seem to be associated with success.[28] Strong social skills help conscientious people ensure that they get positive recognition for their hard work.[29] However, high scores are less than ideal for some traits in some situations. For example, the best performers often score in the middle of the range on emotional stability. In other words, an employee can be either too nervous or too calm to do the best work.[30]

Table 6.3

Five Major Personality Dimensions Measured by Personality Inventories

1. Extroversion	Sociable, gregarious, assertive, talkative, expressive
2. Adjustment	Emotionally stable, nondepressed, secure, content
3. Agreeableness	Courteous, trusting, good-natured, tolerant, cooperative, forgiving
4. Conscientiousness	Dependable, organized, persevering, thorough, achievement-oriented
5. Inquisitiveness	Curious, imaginative, artistically sensitive, broad-minded, playful

To test tech workers' programming and problem-solving skills, Google sponsors contests called Code Jams at locations around the world. The winners gain fame as well as visibility with Google recruiters. The Code Jams also cement Google's reputation for hiring the best thinkers and offering them exciting challenges.

The usual way to identify a candidate's personality traits is to administer one of the personality tests that are commercially available. The employer pays for the use of the test, and the organization that owns the test then scores the responses and provides a report about the test taker's personality. An organization that provides such tests should be able to discuss the test's validity and reliability. Assuming the tests are valid for the organization's jobs, they have advantages. Administering commercially available personality tests is simple, and these tests have generally not violated equal opportunity employment requirements.[31] On the downside, compared with intelligence tests, people are better at "faking" their answers to a personality test to score higher on desirable traits.[32] For example, people tend to score higher on conscientiousness when filling out job-related personality tests than when participating in research projects.[33] Ways to address this problem include using trained interviewers rather than surveys, collecting information about the applicant from several sources, and letting applicants know that several sources will be used.[34]

A recent study found that 18% of U.S. organizations use personality tests when selecting personnel.[35] One reason is organizations' greater use of teamwork, where personality conflicts can be a significant problem. Traits such as agreeableness and conscientiousness have been associated with effective teamwork.[36] In addition, an organization might try to select team members with similar traits and values in order to promote a strong culture where people work together harmoniously, or they instead might look for a diversity of personalities and values as a way to promote debate and creativity.

Honesty Tests and Drug Tests

No matter what employees' personalities may be like, organizations want employees to be honest and to behave safely. Some organizations are satisfied to assess these qualities based on judgments from reference checks and interviews. Others investigate these characteristics more directly through the use of honesty tests and drug tests.

Did You Know?

Drug Tests Are Becoming the Norm

Extent of Drug Testing (percent of companies)

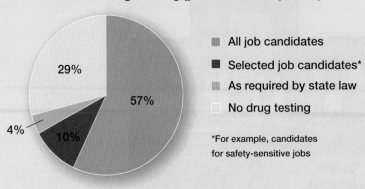

- 29%
- 4%
- 10%
- 57%

■ All job candidates

■ Selected job candidates*

■ As required by state law

□ No drug testing

*For example, candidates for safety-sensitive jobs

A majority of companies conduct preemployment drug tests, according to a study by the Drug and Alcohol Testing Industry Association. (Other studies have found similar results.) Employers say that after they implemented testing programs, productivity improved. The tests are most common at large companies, and most companies that use them test all of their candidates.

Question

What would be the advantages and drawbacks of testing all job candidates, rather than just the ones being considered for safety-sensitive jobs, such as truck driver or electrician?

SOURCES: Bill Leonard, "Poll: Majority Favors Drug Testing Applicants," *HR Magazine,* November 2011, p. 87; Neil A. Fortner, David M. Martin, S. Evren Esen, and Laura Shelton, "Employee Drug Testing: Study Shows Improved Productivity and Attendance and Decreased Workers' Compensation and Turnover," *Journal of Global Drug Policy and Practice,* Winter 2011, accessed at Drug and Alcohol Testing Industry Association, http://www.datia.org; "Current Practices and Issues in Workplace Drug Testing," *Security Director's Report,* November 2011, pp. 4–5.

The most famous kind of honesty test is the polygraph, the so-called lie detector test. However, in 1988 the passage of the Polygraph Act banned the use of polygraphs for screening job candidates. As a result, testing services have developed paper-and-pencil honesty (or integrity) tests. Generally these tests ask applicants directly about their attitudes toward theft and their own experiences with theft. Most of the research into the validity of these tests has been conducted by the testing companies, but evidence suggests they do have some ability to predict such behavior as theft of the employer's property.[37]

As concerns about substance abuse have grown during recent decades, so has the use of drug testing (see the "Did You Know?" box). As a measure of a person's exposure to drugs, chemical testing has high reliability and validity. However, these tests are controversial for several reasons. Some people are concerned that they invade individuals' privacy. Others object from a legal perspective. When all applicants or employees are subject to testing, whether or not they have shown evidence of drug use, the tests might be an unreasonable search and seizure or a violation of due process. Taking urine and blood samples involves invasive procedures, and accusing someone of drug use is a serious matter.

Employers considering the use of drug tests should ensure that their drug-testing programs conform to some general rules:[38]

- Administer the tests systematically to all applicants for the same job.
- Use drug testing for jobs that involve safety hazards.

- Have a report of the results sent to the applicant, along with information about how to appeal the results and be retested if appropriate.
- Respect applicants' privacy by conducting tests in an environment that is not intrusive and keeping results confidential.

Even at an organization with these best practices, employers have to keep in mind that drug testing will not uncover all problems with impairment. One recent concern is that much drug abuse today involves legal prescription painkillers rather than substances traditionally tested for. Boeing ran into this problem a few years ago at its facility near Philadelphia. When management became suspicious of the problem, it realized that, as a defense contractor, it would have to involve the federal government. The company notified authorities, and the government sent in undercover investigators, who discovered several Boeing employees selling and possessing prescription drugs.[39] An undercover investigation is difficult and expensive, but routine testing for prescription drugs would be a tricky alternative because the employer has to be careful not to discriminate on the basis of disabilities.

Medical Examinations

Especially for physically demanding jobs, organizations may wish to conduct medical examinations to see that the applicant can meet the job's requirements. Employers may also wish to establish an employee's physical condition at the beginning of employment, so that there is a basis for measuring whether the employee has suffered a work-related disability later on. At the same time, as described in Chapter 3, organizations may not discriminate against individuals with disabilities who could perform a job with reasonable accommodations. Likewise, they may not use a measure of size or strength that discriminates against women, unless those requirements are valid in predicting the ability to perform a job. Furthermore, to protect candidates' privacy, medical exams must be related to job requirements and may not be given until the candidate has received a job offer. Therefore, organizations must be careful in how they use medical examinations. Many organizations make selection decisions first and then conduct the exams to confirm that the employee can handle the job with any reasonable accommodations required. Limiting the use of medical exams in this way also holds down the cost of what tends to be an expensive process.

Interviews

LO 6-6 Discuss how to conduct effective interviews.

Supervisors and team members most often get involved in the selection process at the stage of employment interviews. These interviews bring together job applicants and representatives of the employer to obtain information and evaluate the applicant's qualifications. While the applicant is providing information, he or she is also forming opinions about what it is like to work for the organization. Most organizations use interviewing as part of the selection process. In fact, this method is used more than any other.

Interviewing Techniques

Interview techniques include choices about the type of questions to ask and the number of people who conduct the interview. Several question types are possible:

Nondirective Interview
A selection interview in which the interviewer has great discretion in choosing questions to ask each candidate.

- In a **nondirective interview,** the interviewer has great discretion in choosing questions. The candidate's reply to one question may suggest other questions to ask. Nondirective interviews typically include open-ended questions about

When interviewing candidates, it's valid to ask about willingness to travel if that is part of the job. Interviewers might ask questions about previous business travel experiences and/or how interviewees handled situations requiring flexibility and self-motivation (qualities that would be an asset in someone who is traveling alone and solving business problems on the road).

Structured Interview
A selection interview that consists of a predetermined set of questions for the interviewer to ask.

Situational Interview
A structured interview in which the interviewer describes a situation likely to arise on the job, then asks the candidate what he or she would do in that situation.

Behavior Description Interview (BDI)
A structured interview in which the interviewer asks the candidate to describe how he or she handled a type of situation in the past.

Panel Interview
Selection interview in which several members of the organization meet to interview each candidate.

the candidate's strengths, weaknesses, career goals, and work experience. Because these interviews give the interviewer wide latitude, their reliability is not great, and some interviewers ask questions that are not valid or even legal.

- A **structured interview** establishes a set of questions for the interviewer to ask. Ideally, the questions are related to job requirements and cover relevant knowledge, skills, and experiences. The interviewer is supposed to avoid asking questions that are not on the list. Although interviewers may object to being restricted, the results may be more valid and reliable than with a nondirective interview.
- A **situational interview** is a structured interview in which the interviewer describes a situation likely to arise on the job and asks the candidate what he or she would do in that situation. This type of interview may have high validity in predicting job performance.[40]
- A **behavior description interview (BDI)** is a situational interview in which the interviewer asks the candidate to describe how he or she handled a type of situation in the past. Questions about candidates' actual experiences tend to have the highest validity.[41]

The common setup for either a nondirected or structured interview is for an individual (an HR professional or the supervisor for the vacant position) to interview each candidate face to face. However, variations on this approach are possible. In a **panel interview,** several members of the organization meet to interview each candidate. A panel interview gives the candidate a chance to meet more people and see how people interact in that organization. It provides the organization with the judgments of more than one person, to reduce the effect of personal biases in selection decisions. Panel interviews can be especially appropriate in organizations that use teamwork. At the other extreme, some organizations conduct interviews without any interviewers; they use a computerized interviewing process. The candidate sits at a computer and enters replies to the questions presented by the computer. Such a format eliminates a lot of personal bias—along with the opportunity to see how people interact. Therefore, computer interviews are useful for gathering objective data, rather than assessing people skills.

For suggestions on how to apply these techniques to conduct effective job interviews, see "HR How To."

Advantages and Disadvantages of Interviewing

The wide use of interviewing is not surprising. People naturally want to see prospective employees firsthand. As we noted in Chapter 1, the top qualities that employers seek in new hires include communication skills and interpersonal skills. Talking face to face can provide evidence of these skills. Interviews can give insights into candidates' personalities and interpersonal styles. They are more valid, however, when they focus on job knowledge and skill. Interviews also provide a means to check the accuracy of information on the applicant's résumé or job application. Asking applicants to elaborate about their experiences and offer details reduces the likelihood of a candidate being able to invent a work history.[42]

Despite these benefits, interviewing is not necessarily the most accurate basis for making a selection decision. Research has shown that interviews can be unreliable,

HR How To

Interviewing Effectively

Interviewing job candidates is time consuming, and unfortunately, many companies waste that time with highly subjective, unplanned interviews that fail to reveal much relevant information. Here are some ideas for making the most of the interview process:

- Plan questions that are specific, invite detailed responses, and zero in on what you don't yet know but should know about the candidate. Questions should relate to skills and personal qualities that are relevant to success on the job. If some job candidates already hold other positions at the company, don't assume you have nothing to learn. Instead, review the job requirements, and identify the areas where you should learn more about how the candidate would handle job-related situations.
- Ahead of time, develop ideas about the kind of personality needed in the open position. Without this preparation, it will

be too easy simply to hire the individual you feel most comfortable with. For example, one team might already have many members who hold lively debates and generate ideas, so it needs a quiet thinker with an analytical outlook. One work unit might need people who are serious and dependable; another might need someone who readily strikes up a conversation in order to uncover customers' desires. In the interview, ask about situations that would reveal whether candidates have these desired qualities. If you ask how candidates would handle conflict in a meeting or what candidates would do if they arrive at a meeting early, listen for examples of the kinds of behaviors needed.

- As much as possible, keep questions consistent across candidates. You might have to adapt some questions to make them equally relevant to internal and external candidates, or to more or less experienced

workers. But try to ask all applicants the same basic set of questions to demonstrate that the hiring process is fair and to avoid discrimination.

- A candidate's strengths and skills are valuable only if the candidate makes the effort to apply them in the organization. While résumés and tests can show what candidates' skills are, the interview should ask candidates how they have applied their skills and what they have accomplished as a result. Interviewers should probe for specific examples: "You say you are a team player. Tell me about a time when your teamwork skills helped you make your current employer better or stronger."

SOURCES: Geil Browning, "How to Spot Innovative Hires," *Inc.,* February 23, 2012, http://www.inc.com; Matthew Beecher, "Only Assets Need Apply," *HR Magazine,* November 2011, pp. 84–85; Amy Gallo, "How to Conduct an Internal Interview," *Bloomberg Businessweek,* July 13, 2010, http://www.businessweek.com.

low in validity,[43] and biased against a number of different groups.[44] Interviews are also costly. They require that at least one person devote time to interviewing each candidate, and the applicants typically have to be brought to one geographic location. Interviews are also subjective, so they place the organization at greater risk of discrimination complaints by applicants who were not hired, especially if those individuals were asked questions not entirely related to the job. The Supreme Court has held that subjective selection methods like interviews must be validated, using methods that provide criterion-related or content validation.[45]

Organizations can avoid some of these pitfalls.[46] Human resource staff should keep the interviews narrow, structured, and standardized. The interview should focus on accomplishing a few goals, so that at the end of the interview, the organization has ratings on several observable measures, such as ability to express ideas. The interview should not try to measure abilities and skills—for example, intelligence—that tests can measure better. As noted earlier, situational interviews are especially effective for doing this. Organizations can prevent problems related to subjectivity by training interviewers and using more than one person to conduct interviews. Training typically includes focusing on the recording of observable facts, rather than on making subjective judgments, as well as developing interviewers' awareness of their biases.[47] Using a structured system for taking notes or scoring responses may help limit subjectivity and help the interviewer remember and justify an evaluation later.[48] Finally, to address costs of interviewing, many organizations videotape interviews and send the tapes (rather than the applicants) from department to department.

Preparing to Interview

Organizations can reap the greatest benefits from interviewing if they prepare carefully. A well-planned interview should be standardized, comfortable for the participants, and focused on the job and the organization. The interviewer should have a quiet place in which to conduct interviews without interruption. This person should be trained in how to ask objective questions, what subject matter to avoid, and how to detect and handle his or her own personal biases or other distractions in order to fairly evaluate candidates.

The interviewer should have enough documents to conduct a complete interview. These should include a list of the questions to be asked in a structured interview, with plenty of space for recording the responses. When the questions are prepared, it is also helpful to determine how the answers will be scored. For example, if questions ask how interviewees would handle certain situations, consider what responses are best in terms of meeting job requirements. If the job requires someone who motivates others, then a response that shows motivating behavior would receive a higher score. The interviewer also should have a copy of the interviewee's employment application and résumé to review before the interview and refer to during the interview. If possible, the interviewer should also have printed information about the organization and the job. Near the beginning of the interview, it is a good idea to go over the job specifications, organizational policies, and so on, so that the interviewee has a clearer understanding of the organization's needs.

The interviewer should schedule enough time to review the job requirements, discuss the interview questions, and give the interviewee a chance to ask questions. To close, the interviewer should thank the candidate for coming and provide information about what to expect—for example, that the organization will contact a few finalists within the next two weeks or that a decision will be made by the end of the week.

Selection Decisions

LO 6-7 Explain how employers carry out the process of making a selection decision.

After reviewing applications, scoring tests, conducting interviews, and checking references, the organization needs to make decisions about which candidates to place in which jobs. In practice, most organizations find more than one qualified candidate to fill an open position. The selection decision typically combines ranking based on objective criteria along with subjective judgments about which candidate will make the greatest contribution.

How Organizations Select Employees

The selection decision should not be a simple matter of whom the supervisor likes best or which candidate will take the lowest offer. Also, observing confidence in job candidates does not necessarily mean they are competent. Rather, the people making the selection should look for the best fit between candidate and position. In general, the person's performance will result from a combination of ability and motivation. Often, the selection is a choice among a few people who possess the basic qualifications. The decision makers therefore have to decide which of those people have the best combination of ability and motivation to fit in the position and in the organization as a whole.

The usual process for arriving at a selection decision is to gradually narrow the pool of candidates for each job. This approach, called the **multiple-hurdle model,** is based on a process such as the one shown earlier in Figure 6.1. Each stage of the process is a hurdle, and candidates who overcome a hurdle continue to the next stage of the process. For example, the organization reviews applications and/or résumés of all candidates, conducts some tests on those who meet minimum requirements, conducts initial interviews with those who had the highest test scores, follows up with additional interviews or testing, and then selects a candidate from the few who survived this process. Another, more expensive alternative is to take most applicants through all steps of the process and then to review all the scores to find the most desirable candidates. With this alternative, decision makers may use a **compensatory model,** in which a very high score on one type of assessment can make up for a low score on another.

Whether the organization uses a multiple-hurdle model or conducts the same assessments on all candidates, the decision maker or makers need criteria for choosing among qualified candidates. An obvious strategy is to select the candidates who score highest on tests and interviews. However, employee performance depends on motivation as well as ability. It is possible that a candidate who scores very high on an ability test might be "overqualified"—that is, the employee might be bored by the job the organization needs to fill, and a less-able employee might actually be a better fit. Similarly, a highly motivated person might learn some kinds of jobs very quickly, potentially outperforming someone who has the necessary skills. Furthermore, some organizations have policies of developing employees for career paths in the organization. Such organizations might place less emphasis on the skills needed for a particular job and more emphasis on hiring candidates who share the organization's values, show that they have the people skills to work with others in the organization, and are able to learn the skills needed for advancement.

Finally, organizations have choices about who will make the decision. Usually a supervisor makes the final decision, often alone. This person may couple knowledge of the job with a judgment about who will fit in best with others in the department. The decision could also be made by a human resource professional using standardized, objective criteria. Especially in organizations that use teamwork, selection decisions may be made by a work team or other panel of decision makers.

Multiple-Hurdle Model
Process of arriving at a selection decision by eliminating some candidates at each stage of the selection process.

Compensatory Model
Process of arriving at a selection decision in which a very high score on one type of assessment can make up for a low score on another.

Communicating the Decision

The human resource department is often responsible for notifying applicants about the results of the selection process. When a candidate has been selected, the organization should communicate the offer to the candidate. The offer should include the job responsibilities, work schedule, rate of pay, starting date, and other relevant details. If placement in a job requires that the applicant pass a physical examination, the offer should state that contingency. The person communicating the offer should also indicate a date by which the candidate should reply with an acceptance or rejection of the offer. For some jobs, such as management and professional positions, the candidate and organization may negotiate pay, benefits, and work arrangements before they arrive at a final employment agreement.

The person who communicates this decision should keep accurate records of who was contacted, when, and for which position, as well as of the candidate's reply. The HR department and the supervisor also should be in close communication about the job offer. When an applicant accepts a job offer, the HR department must notify the supervisor so that he or she can be prepared for the new employee's arrival.

THINKING ETHICALLY

SELECTING ETHICAL EMPLOYEES

Many companies publish a code of ethics to inform their employees and others about the standards of behavior the company expects from its people. But there is always a risk that employees will ignore ethical standards and try to hide unethical activities. So companies also need to select employees who value and follow ethical principles.

One way to select ethical employees is to look for evidence that a candidate has behaved ethically in the past. Résumés should identify situations in which employees took responsibility and were accountable for their actions. Volunteer activities can be signs of a person who cares about others.

Reference checks should seek information about how well the candidate has lived up to ethical standards. Evidence of criminal activity would, of course, raise a red flag that the employer should ask about. Public information online could also offer evidence of how the person behaves in a variety of situations.

Interviews provide an opportunity for the employer to explore all of these sources of information. The interviewer can ask, for example, about how the candidate responds to difficult customers, whether information found online is true, and why a former supervisor hesitated when asked to provide a reference. Generally, candidates will avoid saying they would make an unethical choices. Therefore, it is usually most effective to ask candidates to describe when they have faced ethical issues, how they thought about the issues, and how they responded. Another approach is to ask broad questions, such as "Have you ever worked for a company that had a code of ethics, and if so, what was your experience there like?" This type of question avoids suggesting an answer that is obviously correct.

Of course, it is also important to model ethical behavior. Human resource professionals and hiring managers should communicate honestly with every candidate, from the job advertisement through the job offer.

Questions

1. Imagine that you work in the human resources department of a company that is hiring a project manager for its information technology department. The hiring manager in the IT department is excited about a candidate who has held similar positions in two top companies and who demonstrates deep knowledge of the field. But you did a background check online and found that someone with this candidate's name frequently posts comments on news sites, and his tone is often crude and nasty. This raises questions in your mind about the candidate's personal ethics. How should you handle this situation?

2. Suppose your company hires this candidate in spite of your concerns. What might be the consequences to the company? How can you communicate the hiring decision in a way that promotes future ethical conduct?

SOURCES: Dona DeZube, "How to Interview to Uncover a Candidate's Ethical Standards," Monster, Recruiting and Hiring Advice, http://hiring.monster.com, accessed March 8, 2012; Society for Human Resource Management, "Ethical Dilemmas," April 28, 2011, http://www.shrm.org; Denis Collins, "Here's How to Hire Ethical Employees," *Inside Business (Norfolk, VA)*, January 21, 2011, http://insidebiz.com.

SUMMARY

LO 6-1 Identify the elements of the selection process.

Selection typically begins with a review of candidates' employment applications and résumés. The organization administers tests to candidates who meet basic requirements, and qualified candidates undergo one or more interviews. Organizations check references and conduct background checks to verify the accuracy of information provided by candidates. A candidate is selected to fill each vacant position. Candidates who accept offers are placed in the positions for which they were selected.

LO 6-2 Define ways to measure the success of a selection method.

One criterion is reliability, which indicates the method is free from random error, so that measurements are consistent. A selection method should also be valid, meaning that performance on the measure (such as a test score) is related to what the measure is designed to assess (such as job performance). Criterion-related validity shows a correlation between test scores and job performance scores. Content validity shows consistency between the test items or problems and the kinds of situations or problems that occur on the job. Construct validity establishes that the test actually measures a specified construct, such as intelligence or leadership ability, which is presumed to be associated with success on the job. A selection method also should be generalizable, so that it applies to more than one specific situation. Each selection method should have utility, meaning it provides economic value greater than its cost. Finally, selection methods should meet the legal requirements for employment decisions.

LO 6-3 Summarize the government's requirements for employee selection.

The selection process must be conducted in a way that avoids discrimination and provides access to persons with disabilities. This means selection methods must be valid for job performance, and scores may not be adjusted to discriminate against or give preference to any group. Questions may not gather information about a person's membership in a protected class, such as race, sex, or religion, nor may the employer investigate a person's disability status. Employers must respect candidates' privacy rights and ensure that they keep personal information confidential. They must obtain consent before conducting background checks and notify candidates about adverse decisions made as a result of background checks.

LO 6-4 Compare the common methods used for selecting human resources.

Nearly all organizations gather information through employment applications and résumés. These methods are inexpensive, and an application form standardizes basic information received from all applicants. The information is not necessarily reliable, because each applicant provides the information. These methods are most valid when evaluated in terms of the criteria in a job description. References and background checks help to verify the accuracy of the information. Employment tests and work samples are more objective. To be legal, any test must measure abilities that actually are associated with successful job performance. Employment tests range from general to specific. General-purpose tests are relatively inexpensive and simple to administer. Tests should be selected to be related to successful job performance and avoid charges of discrimination. Interviews are widely used to obtain information about a candidate's interpersonal and communication skills and to gather more detailed information about a candidate's background. Structured interviews are more valid than unstructured ones. Situational interviews provide greater validity than general questions. Interviews are costly and may introduce bias into the selection process. Organizations can minimize the drawbacks through preparation and training.

LO 6-5 Describe major types of employment tests.

Physical ability tests measure strength, endurance, psychomotor abilities, and other physical abilities. They can be accurate but can discriminate and are not always job related. Cognitive ability tests, or intelligence tests, tend to be valid, especially for complex jobs and those requiring adaptability. They are a relatively low-cost way to predict job performance but have been challenged as discriminatory. Job performance tests tend to be valid but are not always generalizable. Using a wide variety of job performance tests can be expensive. Personality tests measure personality traits such as extroversion and adjustment. Research supports their validity for appropriate job situations, especially for individuals who score high on conscientiousness, extroversion, and agreeableness. These tests are relatively simple to administer and generally meet legal requirements. Organizations may use paper-and-pencil honesty tests, which can predict certain behaviors, including employee theft. Organizations may not use polygraphs to screen job candidates. Organizations may also administer drug tests (if all candidates are tested and drug use can be an on-the-job safety hazard). Passing a medical examination may be a condition of employment, but to avoid discrimination against persons with disabilities, organizations usually administer a medical exam only after making a job offer.

LO 6-6 Discuss how to conduct effective interviews.

Interviews should be narrow, structured, and standardized. Interviewers should identify job requirements and create a list of questions related to the requirements. Interviewers should be trained to recognize their own personal biases and conduct objective interviews. Panel interviews can reduce problems related to interviewer bias. Interviewers should put candidates at ease in a comfortable place that is free of distractions. Questions should ask for descriptions of relevant experiences and job-related behaviors. The interviewers also should be prepared to provide information about the job and the organization.

LO 6-7 Explain how employers carry out the process of making a selection decision.

The organization should focus on the objective of finding the person who will be the best fit with the job and organization. This includes an assessment of ability and motivation. Decision makers may use a multiple-hurdle model in which each stage of the selection process eliminates some of the candidates from consideration at the following stages. At the final stage, only a few candidates remain, and the selection decision determines which of these few is the best fit. An alternative is a compensatory model, in which all candidates are evaluated with all methods. A candidate who scores poorly with one method may be selected if he or she scores very high on another measure.

KEY TERMS

achievement tests, 178

aptitude tests, 178

assessment center, 180

behavior description
   interview (BDI), 184

cognitive ability tests, 179

compensatory model, 187

concurrent validation, 169

construct validity, 170

content validity, 170

criterion-related validity, 169

generalizable, 171

Immigration Reform and
   Control Act of 1986, 172

multiple-hurdle model, 187

nondirective interview, 183

panel interview, 184

personnel selection, 165

predictive validation, 169

reliability, 167

situational interview, 184

structured interview, 184

utility, 171

validity, 168

REVIEW AND DISCUSSION QUESTIONS

1. What activities are involved in the selection process? Think of the last time you were hired for a job. Which of those activities were used in selecting you? Should the organization that hired you have used other methods as well?

2. Why should the selection process be adapted to fit the organization's job descriptions?

3. Choose two of the selection methods identified in this chapter. Describe how you can compare them in terms of reliability, validity, ability to generalize, utility, and compliance with the law.

4. Why does predictive validation provide better information than concurrent validation? Why is this type of validation more difficult?

5. How do U.S. laws affect organizations' use of each of the employment tests? Interviews?

6. Suppose your organization needs to hire several computer programmers, and you are reviewing résumés you obtained from an online service. What kinds of information will you want to gather from the "work experience" portion of these résumés? What kinds of information will you want to gather from the "education" portion of these résumés? What methods would you use for verifying or exploring this information? Why would you use those methods?

7. For each of the following jobs, select the two kinds of tests you think would be most important to include in the selection process. Explain why you chose those tests.
   a. City bus driver
   b. Insurance salesperson
   c. Member of a team that sells complex high-tech equipment to manufacturers
   d. Member of a team that makes a component of the equipment in (c)

8. Suppose you are a human resource professional at a large retail chain. You want to improve the company's hiring process by creating standard designs for interviews, so that every time someone is interviewed for a particular job category, that person answers the same questions. You also want to make sure the questions asked are relevant to the job and maintain equal employment opportunity. Think of three questions to include in interviews for each of the following jobs. For each question, state why you think it should be included.
   a. Cashier at one of the company's stores
   b. Buyer of the stores' teen clothing line
   c. Accounts payable clerk at company headquarters

9. How can organizations improve the quality of their interviewing so that interviews provide valid information?

10. Some organizations set up a selection process that is long and complex. In some people's opinion,

this kind of selection process not only is more valid but also has symbolic value. What can the use of a long, complex selection process symbolize to job seekers? How do you think this would affect the organization's ability to attract the best employees?

EXPERIENCING HR

Print out a copy of your résumé. If you don't already have a résumé, create one summarizing your education, work history, and accomplishments. (For guidelines, visit **www.mhhe.com/noefund5e** or get help at your school's library or career center.)

Find a job listing for a career or company that interests you. You could visit a job board, such as Monster, and search for jobs by company. Or visit careers pages of companies you'd like to work for.

Compare your résumé with the details in the job advertisement. What qualities on your résumé match what the company is looking for? What words and phrases does the company use in its job ad and on its website that you could use (truthfully) to show you are a good fit with the company? What additional experiences and skills do you need before you would be considered for a job at this company?

Write a one-page paper summarizing your comparison. Attach your résumé, and turn it in for credit on the assignment. Keep a copy of your summary to refer to later when planning the next step in your career.

TAKING RESPONSIBILITY: Customer-First Values Shape Hiring Decisions at Zappos

The original idea for online retailer Zappos was to offer the biggest selection of shoes. But it turned out that this strategy didn't really make the company stand out from the competition. There are plenty of places, online and off, where consumers can find shoes. So chief executive officer Tony Hsieh switched the mission to one of offering the best customer service of any shoe retailer. That got customers' attention, but Hsieh saw that he still had not tapped the heart of what makes a company great. So he made one more switch: Zappos would maintain a dynamic, fulfilling company culture. The company would be a great place to work, and in that environment, employees would delight customers, and loyal customers would provide the income needed to please shareholders.

That mission affects every function at Zappos, including employee selection. The hiring process aims to find and keep employees who share the company's values, such as "Deliver Wow through service" and "Create fun and a little weirdness." To identify 30 new hires a month from tens of thousands of applicants, Zappos focuses on finding a good fit with the company culture, along with basic job skills. Candidates initially apply at the company's website, where a prominent message urges them to read the company's values first. Successful candidates undergo two interviews. In the first, which may be a phone interview, the interviewer talks to each candidate about his or her skills and experience. About half the candidates are invited to a second interview, held in a room set up to look like the set of a television talk show. There, candidates answer questions about Zappos' core values. For example, interviewers try to evaluate whether candidates value honesty, are committed to learning, and have a sense of fun.

Learning candidates' values through an interview can be tricky, since many candidates simply want to say the right thing to please the interviewer. Senior human resources manager Christa Foley says one of her favorite questions is "What's the biggest misperception people typically have about you?" She uses the question to identify candidates who are sincere and honest.

Besides traditional interview questions, Zappos has some unconventional ways to learn about candidates. One of the company's values is "Be humble." To gauge humility, HR directors talk to someone candidates didn't know they were supposed to impress: the drivers of the shuttle buses that bring candidates to the company's offices. The HR directors find out whether the candidates treated the driver with respect; if not, the candidate is eliminated from consideration. Another value is creativity and open-mindedness. To test for this, the interviewer gives candidates a mockup of a newspaper and asks how many photos it contains. On one page of the newspaper, a headline states the answer. The assumption is that people who are open-minded will be paying attention and notice the headline. The recruiting team also goes to lunch with the candidates and observes how they interact with other people. The Zappos environment is loud, lively, and sociable, so candidates who are a good cultural fit are likely to be engaged with others during the meal.

After this process is over, about one-tenth of the candidates receive a job offer from Zappos. As one final check of cultural fit, these new employees are offered $3,000 to leave at the end of the initial training if they conclude they won't actually fit in.

Creating a lively, affirmative culture has given Zappos a positive reputation that attracts superior job candidates. They are excited to work for a company that shares their values, empowers them to please customers, and encourages them to have fun. Despite modest pay, employees are loyal and highly engaged in their work.

Questions

1. What are the steps in the selection process at Zappos? Does this seem like a complete selection process? If not, what steps would you add?

2. Review the criteria for a successful selection method: reliable, valid, generalizable, practical, and legal. How well does Zappos meet those criteria? How can it measure the success of its selection methods?

3. Would you recommend that decision makers at Zappos use highly structured job interviews? Why or why not?

SOURCES: Zappos, "Jobs.Zappos.com," http://about.zappos.com/jobs, accessed March 8, 2012; Steven Greenberg, "Who Zappos Is Hiring," *CNNMoney*, October 19, 2011, http://money.cnn.com (interview with Christa Foley); Kathleen Koster, "Zappos CEO Uses Company Culture to Boost Bottom Line," *Employee Benefit News*, September 1, 2011, Business & Company Resource Center, http://galenet.galegroup.com; Kathy Gurchiek, "Delivering HR at Zappos," *HR Magazine*, June 2011, pp. 44–45; Wendy S. Becker, "Are You Leading a Socially Responsible and Sustainable Human Resource Function?" *People & Strategy*, March 2011, Business & Company Resource Center, http://galenet.galegroup.com.

MANAGING TALENT: Cutting Hiring Red Tape at the Office of Personnel Management

When people think of agile, efficient processes, they rarely think of government bureaucracy. But if Angela Bailey has her way, that perception could start to change. Bailey is the chief human capital officer for the federal government's Office of Personnel Management (OPM). OPM receives over 59,000 applications *every day* from people hoping to land a job in the federal government, which employs more than two million civilians just in the executive branch.

Processing so many applications and making good selection decisions is a daunting task. What made it even worse until May 2010, OPM had such a cumbersome application and selection process that it would astonish hiring managers in the private sector. Applicants were expected to fill out several forms and write as many as five essays describing their work experience. These 500- to 1,000-word essays—called knowledge, skills, and abilities statements—were intended to find good matches between candidates and jobs. However, reading them was an endless process. On average, OPM needed four and a half months to complete the process of filling a position. Worse, applicants had difficulty learning how far along in the process they were. Many candidates, including some of the best, gave up and took jobs elsewhere.

In May 2010, President Obama directed OPM and other federal agencies to make the hiring process more efficient. The directive requires plain language for job announcements; the ability to accept applicants' résumés, rather than requiring the use of complex forms created for government computer systems; and the expansion of the number of candidates a hiring manager may consider. One early step has been to improve the federal government's jobs board (**www .usajobs.gov**). The database management software has been upgraded, and the links to job announcements were improved. But perhaps the most dramatic change to the application process was the elimination of the essays, which were considered too subjective as well as too time consuming. They also were seen by some as an inaccurate assessment because some applicants paid writers to compose them.

To replace the essays, OPM officials have had to review the skills requirements for every job and identify the kinds of assessments that best measure those skills. The goal is to decide which selection tools every agency will use, based on the requirements of positions being filled. For example, online tests are being created in which applicants read about situations and identify how they would act in each situation. The tests are interactive: the way a candidate answers one question determines which additional questions will be given to the candidate. The applicant's final score is associated with a particular skill level; accurate answers to the hardest questions would yield a score placing the applicant at the top level for skills.

Efforts to improve the selection process are continuing. Within agencies, managers are evaluating their processes by breaking each process down into steps and deciding which steps are actually necessary. Many are discovering that some of their steps and tools are unnecessary or irrelevant.

The effort to improve efficiency has made measurable progress. A recent analysis found that the time to hire had fallen from 122 days to 105. (Critics say the process must become must faster still; agencies are striving to trim the process to 80 days.) Job announcements that once ran as long as 35 pages are now an almost-digestible 3 to 5 pages. Surveys by agency managers show that their satisfaction with the hiring process is increasing. Creating the system is expected to cost millions of dollars, but Bailey predicts that the savings from greater efficiency will exceed the costs.

Questions

1. Review the criteria for a successful selection method: reliable, valid, generalizable, practical, and legal. How well did the Office of Personnel Management meet those criteria both before and after the reform effort?

2. What types of selection methods are described in this case? What other selection methods do you think federal agencies should use? Why?

3. In general, how can an organization's employee selection process support a strategy aimed at improving efficiency and lowering costs? How would you rate OPM's efforts to support this type of strategy? What else could it do?

SOURCES: Bill Leonard, "Wanted: Shorter Time-to-Hire," *HR Magazine*, November 2011, pp. 49–52; Tim McManus, "We Want You: Recruiters Target Mission-Critical Talent," *Public Manager*, Fall 2011, pp. 26–29; Emily Long, "Smarter Hiring," *Government Executive*, May 1, 2011, Business & Company Resource Center, http://galenet.galegroup.com; Office of Personnel Management, "OPM and OMB Announce Unprecedented Hiring Reforms," news release, May 11, 2010, http://www.opm.gov.

 TWITTER FOCUS: Kinaxis Chooses Sales Reps with Personality

Using Twitter, continue the conversation about personnel selection and placement by reading the Kinaxis case at **www.mhhe.com/noefund5e.**

Engage your classmates and instructor via Twitter to chat about Kinaxis's hiring strategy using the case questions posed on the Noe website. Don't have a Twitter account yet? See the instructions for getting started on the Online Learning Center.

NOTES

1. Vickie Elmer, "Hiring without a Net: Groupon's Recruiter Speaks," *Fortune*, July 25, 2011, EBSCO-host, http://web.ebscohost.com; Vickie Elmer, "Groupon's Hiring Team: Improv, Humor, Skills Tests and Hurry to Hire," *Working Kind*, July 12, 2011, http://workingkind.com.

2. Lauren Weber, "Angry Job Applicants Can Hurt Bottom Line," *The Wall Street Journal*, March 13, 2012, http://online.wsj.com; Lauren Weber, "Your Résumé vs. Oblivion," *The Wall Street Journal*, January 24, 2012, http://online.wsj.com.

3. Patricia M. Sherlock, "Walking the Walk," *Mortgage Banking*, May 2011, Business & Company Resource Center, http://galenet.galegroup.com.

4. J. C. Nunnally, *Psychometric Theory* (New York: McGraw-Hill, 1978).

5. April Joyner, "Are You a Perfectionist Boss?" *Inc.*, November 2011, http://www.inc.com.

6. N. Schmitt, R. Z. Gooding, R. A. Noe, and M. Kirsch, "Meta-Analysis of Validity Studies Published between 1964 and 1982 and the Investigation of Study Characteristics," *Personnel Psychology* 37 (1984), pp. 407–22.

7. D. D. Robinson, "Content-Oriented Personnel Selection in a Small Business Setting," *Personnel Psychology* 34 (1981), pp. 77–87.

8. George Anders, "Work: The Games They Make You Play," *Guardian (London)*, October 29, 2011, Business & Company Resource Center, http://galenet.galegroup.com.

9. F. L. Schmidt and J. E. Hunter, "The Future of Criterion-Related Validity," *Personnel Psychology* 33 (1980), pp. 41–60; F. L. Schmidt, J. E. Hunter, and K. Pearlman, "Task Differences as Moderators of Aptitude Test Validity: A Red Herring," *Journal of Applied Psychology* 66 (1982), pp. 166–85; and R. L. Gutenberg, R. D. Arvey, H. G. Osburn, and R. P. Jeanneret, "Moderating Effects of Decision-Making/Information Processing Dimensions on Test Validities," *Journal of Applied Psychology* 68 (1983), pp. 600–8.

10. Equal Employment Opportunity Commission, "Mavis Discount Tire Sued by EEOC for Sex Discrimination in Hiring," news release, January 31, 2012, http://www1.eeoc.gov.

11. Dan Herbeck, "Firefighters Are Awarded $2.7 Million in Bias Case," *Buffalo (NY) News*, February 9, 2012, Business & Company Resource Center, http://galenet.galegroup.com.

12. T. W. Dougherty, D. B. Turban, and J. C. Callender, "Confirming First Impressions in the Employment Interview: A Field Study of Interviewer

Behavior," *Journal of Applied Psychology* 79 (1994), pp. 659–65.

13. Julian E. Barnes, "Decorated Marine Sues Contractor," *The Wall Street Journal*, November 29, 2011, http://online.wsj.com; Andrew Chow, "Medal of Honor Lawsuit Serves Lessons in Law," *Free Enterrprise* (FindLaw), November 30, 2011, http://blogs.findlaw.com.

14. A. Ryan and M. Lasek, "Negligent Hiring and Defamation: Areas of Liability Related to Preemployment Inquiries," *Personnel Psychology* 44 (1991), pp. 293–319.

15. A. Long, "Addressing the Cloud over Employee References: A Survey of Recently Enacted State Legislation," *William and Mary Law Review* 39 (October 1997), pp. 177–228.

16. Dori Meinert, "Seeing behind the Mask," *HR Magazine*, February 2011, pp. 31–37; Jay Goltz, "Why Checking References Isn't a Waste of Time," *The New York Times*, March 10, 2011, http://boss.blogs.nytimes.com.

17. Sarah E. Needleman, "Big Blunders Job Hunters Make," *The Wall Street Journal*, June 28, 2010, http://online.wsj.com.

18. "EEOC Examines Employer Use of Criminal Records When Hiring," *HR Focus*, September 2011, Business & Company Resource Center, http://galenet.galegroup.com.

19. Annamaria Andriotis, "For Job-Seekers, a New Push to Keep Financial Skeletons Buried," *The Wall Street Journal*, January 31, 2012, http://online.wsj.com.

20. L. C. Buffardi, E. A. Fleishman, R. A. Morath, and P. M. McCarthy, "Relationships between Ability Requirements and Human Errors in Job Tasks," *Journal of Applied Psychology* 85 (2000), pp. 551–64; J. Hogan, "Structure of Physical Performance in Occupational Tasks," *Journal of Applied Psychology* 76 (1991), pp. 495–507.

21. J. F. Salagado, N. Anderson, S. Moscoso, C. Bertuas, and F. De Fruyt, "International Validity Generalization of GMA and Cognitive Abilities: A European Community Meta-analysis," *Personnel Psychology* 56 (2003), pp. 573–605; M. J. Ree, J. A. Earles, and M. S. Teachout, "Predicting Job Performance: Not Much More than *g*," *Journal of Applied Psychology* 79 (1994), pp. 518–24; L. S. Gottfredson, "The *g* Factor in Employment," *Journal of Vocational Behavior* 29 (1986), pp. 293–96; J. E. Hunter and R. H. Hunter, "Validity and Utility of Alternative Predictors of Job Performance," *Psychological Bulletin* 96 (1984), pp. 72–98; Gutenberg et al., "Moderating Effects of Decision-Making/Information Processing Dimensions on Test Validities";

F. L. Schmidt, J. G. Berner, and J. E. Hunter, "Racial Differences in Validity of Employment Tests: Reality or Illusion," *Journal of Applied Psychology* 58 (1974), pp. 5–6; and J. A. LePine, J. A. Colquitt, and A. Erez, "Adaptability to Changing Task Contexts: Effects of General Cognitive Ability, Conscientiousness, and Openness to Experience," *Personnel Psychology* 53 (2000), pp. 563–93.

22. D. A. Kravitz and S. L. Klineberg, "Reactions to Versions of Affirmative Action among Whites, Blacks, and Hispanics," *Journal of Applied Psychology* (2000), pp. 597–611.

23. George Anders, "The Rare Find," *Bloomberg Businessweek*, October 17, 2011, EBSCOhost, http://web.ebscohost.com.

24. D. J. Schleiger, V. Venkataramani, F. P. Morgeson, and M. A. Campion, "So You Didn't Get the Job . . . Now What Do You Think? Examining Opportunity to Perform Fairness Perceptions," *Personnel Psychology* 59 (2006), pp. 559–90.

25. F. L. Schmidt and J. E. Hunter, "The Validity and Utility of Selection Methods in Personnel Psychology: Practical and Theoretical Implications of 85 Years of Research Findings," *Psychological Bulletin* 124 (1998), pp. 262–74.

26. W. Arthur, E. A. Day, T. L. McNelly, and P. S. Edens, "Meta-Analysis of the Criterion-Related Validity of Assessment Center Dimensions," *Personnel Psychology* 56 (2003), pp. 125–54; and C. E. Lance, T. A. Lambert, A. G. Gewin, F. Lievens, and J. M. Conway, "Revised Estimates of Dimension and Exercise Variance Components in Assessment Center Postexercise Dimension Ratings," *Journal of Applied Psychology* 89 (2004), pp. 377–85.

27. N. M. Dudley, K. A. Orvis, J. E. Lebieki, and J. M. Cortina, "A Meta-analytic Investigation of Conscientiousness in the Prediction of Job Performance: Examining the Intercorrelation and the Incremental Validity of Narrow Traits," *Journal of Applied Psychology* 91 (2006), pp. 40–57; W. S. Dunn, M. K. Mount, M. R. Barrick, and D. S. Ones, "Relative Importance of Personality and General Mental Ability on Managers' Judgments of Applicant Qualifications," *Journal of Applied Psychology* 79 (1995), pp. 500–9; P. M. Wright, K. M. Kacmar, G. C. McMahan, and K. Deleeuw, "$P = f(M \times A)$: Cognitive Ability as a Moderator of the Relationship between Personality and Job Performance," *Journal of Management* 21 (1995), pp. 1129–39.

28. M. Mount, M. R. Barrick, and J. P. Strauss, "Validity of Observer Ratings of the Big Five Personality Factors," *Journal of Applied Psychology* 79 (1994), pp. 272–80.

29. L. A. Witt and G. R. Ferris, "Social Skill as Moderator of the Conscientiousness–Performance Relationship: Convergent Results across Four Studies," *Journal of Applied Psychology* 88 (2003), pp. 809–20.

30. H. Le, I. S. Oh, S. B. Robbins, R. Ilies, E. Holland, and P. Westrick, "Too Much of a Good Thing? Curvilinear Relationship between Personality Traits and Job Performance," *Journal of Applied Psychology* 96 (2011): 113–33.

31. L. Joel, *Every Employee's Guide to the Law* (New York: Pantheon, 1993).

32. N. Schmitt and F. L. Oswald, "The Impact of Corrections for Faking on the Validity of Noncognitive Measures in Selection Contexts," *Journal of Applied Psychology* (2006), pp. 613–21.

33. S. A. Birkland, T. M. Manson, J. L. Kisamore, M. T. Brannick, and M. A. Smith, "Faking on Personality Measures," *International Journal of Selection and Assessment* 14 (December 2006), pp. 317–35.

34. C. H. Van Iddekinge, P. H. Raymark, and P. L. Roth, "Assessing Personality with a Structured Employment Interview: Construct-Related Validity and Susceptibility to Response Inflation," *Journal of Applied Psychology* 90 (2005), pp. 536–52; R. Mueller-Hanson, E. D. Heggestad, and G. C. Thornton, "Faking and Selection: Considering the Use of Personality from Select-In and Select-Out Perspectives," *Journal of Applied Psychology* 88 (2003), pp. 348–55; and N. L. Vasilopoulos, J. M. Cucina, and J. M. McElreath, "Do Warnings of Response Verification Moderate the Relationship between Personality and Cognitive Ability?" *Journal of Applied Psychology* 90 (2005), pp. 306–22.

35. "Poll: Most Organizations Don't Use Personality Tests," *HR Magazine*, February 2012, Business & Company Resource Center, http://galenet.galegroup.com.

36. V. Knight, "Personality Tests as Hiring Tools," *The Wall Street Journal*, March 15, 2006, p. B1; G. L. Steward, I. S. Fulmer, and M. R. Barrick, "An Exploration of Member Roles as a Multilevel Linking Mechanism for Individual Traits and Team Outcomes," *Personnel Psychology* 58 (2005), pp. 343–65; and M. Mount, R. Ilies, and E. Johnson, "Relationship of Personality Traits and Counterproductive Work Behaviors: The Mediation Effects of Job Satisfaction," *Personnel Psychology* 59 (2006), pp. 591–622.

37. D. S. Ones, C. Viswesvaran, and F. L. Schmidt, "Comprehensive Meta-analysis of Integrity Test Validities: Findings and Implications for Personnel Selection and Theories of Job Performance," *Journal of Applied Psychology* 78 (1993), pp. 679–703; and H. J. Bernardin and D. K. Cooke, "Validity of an Honesty Test in Predicting Theft among Convenience Store Employees," *Academy of Management Journal* 36 (1993), pp. 1079–1106.

38. K. R. Murphy, G. C. Thornton, and D. H. Reynolds, "College Students' Attitudes toward Drug Test Programs," *Personnel Psychology* 43 (1990), pp. 615–31; and M. E. Paronto, D. M. Truxillo, T. N. Bauer, and M. C. Leo, "Drug Testing, Drug Treatment, and Marijuana Use: A Fairness Perspective," *Journal of Applied Psychology* 87 (2002), pp. 1159–66.

39. "What Can You Learn from the Drug Raid at Boeing," *Security Director's Report*, December 2011, pp. 1, 13–15.

40. M. A. McDaniel, F. P. Morgeson, E. G. Finnegan, M. A. Campion, and E. P. Braverman, "Use of Situational Judgment Tests to Predict Job Performance: A Clarification of the Literature," *Journal of Applied Psychology* 86 (2001), pp. 730–40; and J. Clavenger, G. M. Perreira, D. Weichmann, N. Schmitt, and V. S. Harvey, "Incremental Validity of Situational Judgment Tests," *Journal of Applied Psychology* 86 (2001), pp. 410–17.

41. M. A. Campion, J. E. Campion, and J. P. Hudson, "Structured Interviewing: A Note of Incremental Validity and Alternative Question Types," *Journal of Applied Psychology* 79 (1994), pp. 998–1002; E. D. Pulakos and N. Schmitt, "Experience-Based and Situational Interview Questions: Studies of Validity," *Personnel Psychology* 48 (1995), pp. 289–308; and A. P. J. Ellis, B. J. West, A. M. Ryan, and R. P. DeShon, "The Use of Impression Management Tactics in Structured Interviews: A Function of Question Type?" *Journal of Applied Psychology* 87 (2002), pp. 1200–8.

42. N. Schmitt, F. L. Oswald, B. H. Kim, M. A. Gillespie, L. J. Ramsey, and T. Y Yoo, "The Impact of Elaboration on Socially Desirable Responding and the Validity of Biodata Measures," *Journal of Applied Psychology* 88 (2003), pp. 979–88; and N. Schmitt and C. Kunce, "The Effects of Required Elaboration of Answers to Biodata Questions," *Personnel Psychology* 55 (2002), pp. 569–87.

43. Hunter and Hunter, "Validity and Utility of Alternative Predictors of Job Performance."

44. R. Pingitore, B. L. Dugoni, R. S. Tindale, and B. Spring, "Bias against Overweight Job Applicants in a Simulated Interview," *Journal of Applied Psychology* 79 (1994), pp. 184–90.

45. *Watson v. Fort Worth Bank and Trust*, 108 Supreme Court 2791 (1988).

46. M. A. McDaniel, D. L. Whetzel, F. L. Schmidt, and S. D. Maurer, "The Validity of Employment Interviews: A Comprehensive Review and Meta-Analysis," *Journal of Applied Psychology* 79 (1994),

pp. 599–616; and A. I. Huffcutt and W. A. Arthur, "Hunter and Hunter (1984) Revisited: Interview Validity for Entry-Level Jobs," *Journal of Applied Psychology* 79 (1994), pp. 184–90.

47. Y. Ganzach, A. N. Kluger, and N. Klayman, "Making Decisions from an Interview: Expert Measurement and Mechanical Combination," *Personnel Psychology* 53 (2000), pp. 1–21; and G. Stasser and W. Titus, "Effects of Information Load and Percentage of Shared Information on the Dissemination of Unshared Information during Group Discussion," *Journal of Personality and Social Psychology* 53 (1987), pp. 81–93.

48. C. H. Middendorf and T. H. Macan, "Note-Taking in the Interview: Effects on Recall and Judgments," *Journal of Applied Psychology* 87 (2002), pp. 293–303. K. G. Melchers, N. Lienhardt, M. Von Aartburg, and M. Kleinmann, "Is More Structure Really Better? A Comparison of Frame of Reference Training and Descriptively Anchored Rating Scales to Improve Interviewers' Rating Quality," *Personnel Psychology* 64 (2011): 53–87.

Training Employees

What Do I Need to Know?

After reading this chapter, you should be able to:

LO 7-1 Discuss how to link training programs to organizational needs.

LO 7-2 Explain how to assess the need for training.

LO 7-3 Explain how to assess employees' readiness for training.

LO 7-4 Describe how to plan an effective training program.

LO 7-5 Compare widely used training methods.

LO 7-6 Summarize how to implement a successful training program.

LO 7-7 Evaluate the success of a training program.

LO 7-8 Describe training methods for employee orientation and diversity management.

Introduction

We can help you be competent. If that promise doesn't exactly get your creative juices flowing, then you can appreciate why Facebook thinks of its employee training as more than a matter of acquiring competencies. As a fast-growing, innovative organization, Facebook needs its people to come to work not only prepared to complete tasks but also excited about finding new ways to help members build and use social connections. Stuart Crabb, Facebook's head of learning and development, defines his goal as fostering performance improvement by uncovering employees' strengths and giving them opportunities to build on those strengths.

In practice, this means learning opportunities for people who are busy, highly engaged in their work, and looking for active involvement. Challenging jobs are at the heart of learning at Facebook, and these are supplemented with online materials and discussion-oriented group experiences. Employees who want to learn about a topic can start at their computers, following links to fact sheets and webcasts. Not surprisingly, Facebook's own social-media tools are one of its online learning resources: employees can join a Facebook group in which they share and review one another's ideas as well as receive and react to training content. Crabb also has set up more than two dozen coaching circles in which participants meet regularly to work on issues they want help with. Facebook's most formal learning program is its orientation of new employees. This two-day program focuses on the organization's culture, with the aim of motivating and inspiring the new hires. In the hundred days that follow, new employees are given access to learning tools related to job skills.[1]

Training
An organization's planned efforts to help employees acquire job-related knowledge, skills, abilities, and behaviors, with the goal of applying these on the job.

So that employees can increase their ability to contribute to successful growth, Facebook provides them with the right kind of training. **Training** consists of an organization's planned efforts to help employees acquire job-related knowledge, skills, abilities, and behaviors, with the goal of applying these on the job. A training program may range from formal classes to one-on-one mentoring, and it may take place on the job or at remote locations. No matter what its form, training can benefit the organization when it is linked to organizational needs and when it motivates employees.

This chapter describes how to plan and carry out an effective training program. We begin by discussing how to develop effective training in the context of the organization's strategy. Next, we discuss how organizations assess employees' training needs. We then review training methods and the process of evaluating a training program. The chapter concludes by discussing some special applications of training: orientation of new employees and the management of diversity.

LO 7-1 Discuss how to link training programs to organizational needs.

Instructional Design
A process of systematically developing training to meet specified needs.

Training Linked to Organizational Needs

The nature of the modern business environment makes training more important today than it ever has been. Rapid change, especially in the area of technology, requires that employees continually learn new skills. The new psychological contract, described in Chapter 2, has created the expectation that employees invest in their own career development, which requires learning opportunities. Growing reliance on teamwork creates a demand for the ability to solve problems in teams, an ability that often requires formal training. Finally, the diversity of the U.S. population, coupled with the globalization of business, requires that employees be able to work well with people who are different from them. Successful organizations often take the lead in developing this ability.

With training so essential in modern organizations, it is important to provide training that is effective. An effective training program actually teaches what it is designed to teach, and it teaches skills and behaviors that will help the organization achieve its goals. To achieve those goals, HR professionals approach training through **instructional design**—a process of systematically developing training to meet specified needs.[2]

A complete instructional design process includes the steps shown in Figure 7.1. It begins with an assessment of the needs for training—what the organization requires that its people learn. Next, the organization ensures that employees are ready for training in terms of their attitudes, motivation, basic skills, and work environment. The third step is to plan the training program, including the program's objectives, instructors, and methods. The organization then implements the program. Finally, evaluating the results of the training provides feedback for planning future training programs. For an example of a company that effectively uses this process, see the "Best Practices" box.

Figure 7.1
Stages of Instructional Design

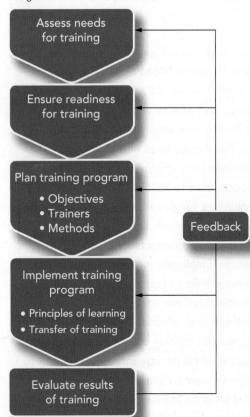

Best Practices

Training Is a Well-Oiled Machine for Jiffy Lube

Most car owners know that regular oil changes are an essential part of their vehicle's maintenance, but if they aren't do-it-yourselfers, where should they take the car? Jiffy Lube tries to be the top choice by combining convenient locations with a reputation for professional service. Its 2,000 service centers are owned by franchisees, so Jiffy Lube could leave the employees' qualifications up to the service center owners. Instead, the company has developed a training program aimed at ensuring that all its technicians are skilled in preventive maintenance. Franchise owners must ensure that all their technicians complete the training.

Jiffy Lube employs a staff of training experts in what it calls Jiffy Lube University (JLU). JLU has prepared 60 courses on subjects such as customer service, technical procedures, and service standards. It also offers training in management skills such as leading, setting goals, and managing time, finances, and people. Together, these courses lead to 10 different certifications. Each employee, depending on his or her position, is assigned to a training path requiring the completion of certain certifications within a specified time frame. For example, every new technician has 30 days to earn certifications in safety and product knowledge. Each training path defines the competencies the employee is supposed to learn, so that employees and their supervisors can readily see whether the employees are meeting expectations.

To develop the content of the training program, the JLU staff works with a Franchise Training Committee, which includes eight franchise managers. The committee reviews what the franchises are doing, identifies areas where changes are needed, and sets priorities for what training should emphasize. JLU also had the National Institute for Automotive Service Excellence (ASE) audit the training program to certify that the training materials and methods meet its quality standards.

Most of the training material is delivered to employees online. Employees view the presentations on a computer and then take an online test to show they have learned the material. Their supervisors supplement the training by observing and coaching the employees on the job and noting their progress in guides created for that purpose. In addition, six full-time trainers travel around North America to deliver face-to-face management training. New supervisors receive a combination of computer-based and classroom training.

Franchise owners welcome the training program because it helps them succeed in meeting real-world challenges such as customer satisfaction and employee turnover. The technical training itself also helps to retain technicians. Seeing the training as part of a career path gives them a reason to stay and improve their earnings and status in the organization.

Although the program has so much going for it—employee satisfaction and ASE certification—the training team is serious about evaluation. It recently conducted an extensive evaluation of the entire program, updated the materials, and asked ASE to recertify the program. The company also surveyed franchise owners to make sure they remain satisfied that the program ensures they have qualified people. Also, since the update, customer satisfaction with employees' training has risen from 87.9% to 94%.

SOURCES: Jiffy Lube, "About Jiffy Lube," http://www.jiffylube.com, accessed March 15, 2012; Jennifer J. Salopek, "Keeping Learning Well-Oiled," *T + D*, October 2011, pp. 32–35; "Best Practices and Outstanding Initiatives," *Training*, January/February 2011, EBSCOhost, http://web.ebscohost.com.

To carry out this process more efficiently and effectively, a growing number of organizations are using a **learning management system (LMS)**, a computer application that automates the administration, development, and delivery of a company's training programs.[3] Managers and employees can use the LMS to identify training needs and enroll in courses. LMSs can make training programs more widely available and help companies reduce travel and other costs by providing online training. Administrative tools let managers track course enrollments and program completion. The system can be linked to the organization's performance management system to plan for and manage training needs, training outcomes, and associated rewards together.

Learning Management System (LMS)
A computer application that automates the administration, development, and delivery of training programs.

LO 7-2 Explain how to assess the need for training.

Needs Assessment

Instructional design logically should begin with a **needs assessment**, the process of evaluating the organization, individual employees, and employees' tasks to determine what kinds of training, if any, are necessary. As this definition indicates, the needs assessment answers questions in three broad areas:[4]

1. *Organization*—What is the context in which training will occur?
2. *Person*—Who needs training?
3. *Task*—What subjects should the training cover?

The answers to these questions provide the basis for planning an effective training program.

A variety of conditions may prompt an organization to conduct a needs assessment. Management may observe that some employees lack basic skills or are performing poorly. Decisions to produce new products, apply new technology, or design new jobs should prompt a needs assessment because these changes tend to require new skills. The decision to conduct a needs assessment also may be prompted by outside forces, such as customer requests or legal requirements.

The outcome of the needs assessment is a set of decisions about how to address the issues that prompted the needs assessment. These decisions do not necessarily include a training program, because some issues should be resolved through methods other than training. For example, suppose a company uses delivery trucks to transport anesthetic gases to medical facilities, and a driver of one of these trucks mistakenly hooks up the supply line of a mild anesthetic from the truck to the hospital's oxygen system, contaminating the hospital's oxygen supply. This performance problem prompts a needs assessment. Whether or not the hospital decides to provide more training will depend partly on the reasons the driver erred. The driver may have hooked up the supply lines incorrectly because of a lack of knowledge about the appropriate line hookup, anger over a request for a pay raise being denied, or mislabeled valves for connecting the supply lines. Out of these three possibilities, only the lack of knowledge can be corrected through training. Other outcomes of a needs assessment might include plans for better rewards to improve motivation, better hiring decisions, and better safety precautions.

The remainder of this chapter discusses needs assessment and then what the organization should do when assessment indicates a need for training. The possibilities for action include offering existing training programs to more employees; buying or developing new training programs; and improving existing training programs. Before we consider the available training options, let's examine the elements of the needs assessment in more detail.

Organization Analysis

Usually, the needs assessment begins with the **organization analysis**. This is a process for determining the appropriateness of training by evaluating the characteristics of the organization. The organization analysis looks at training needs in light of the organization's strategy, resources available for training, and management's support for training activities.

Training needs will vary depending on whether the organization's strategy is based on growing or shrinking its personnel, whether it is seeking to serve a broad customer

Needs Assessment
The process of evaluating the organization, individual employees, and employees' tasks to determine what kinds of training, if any, are necessary.

Organization Analysis
A process for determining the appropriateness of training by evaluating the characteristics of the organization.

Pfizer employees go through a representative training phase which teaches them about different Pfizer products and how to market them. Success at a drug company such as Pfizer depends on the frequent introduction of new medicines and the expertise of sales representatives who tell health care professionals about those products.

base or focusing on the specific needs of a narrow market segment, and various other strategic scenarios. An organization that concentrates on serving a niche market may need to continually update its workforce on a specialized skills set. A company that is cutting costs with a downsizing strategy may need to train employees who will be laid off in job search skills. The employees who remain following the downsizing may need cross-training so that they can handle a wider variety of responsibilities.

Anyone planning a training program must consider whether the organization has the budget, time, and expertise for training. For example, if the company is installing computer-based manufacturing equipment in one of its plants, it can ensure that it has the necessary computer-literate employees in one of three ways. If it has the technical experts on its staff, they can train the employees affected by the change. Or the company may use testing to determine which of its employees are already computer literate and then replace or reassign employees who lack the necessary skills. The third choice is to purchase training from an outside individual or organization.

Even if training fits the organization's strategy and budget, it can be viable only if the organization is willing to support the investment in training. Managers increase the success of training when they support it through such actions as helping trainees see how they can use their newly learned knowledge, skills, and behaviors on the job.[5] Conversely, the managers will be most likely to support training if the people planning it can show that it will solve a significant problem or result in a significant improvement, relative to its cost. Managers appreciate training proposals with specific goals, timetables, budgets, and methods for measuring success.

Person Analysis

Person Analysis
A process of determining individuals' needs and readiness for training.

Following the organizational assessment, needs assessment turns to the remaining areas of analysis: person and task. The **person analysis** is a process for determining individuals' needs and readiness for training. It involves answering several questions:

- Do performance deficiencies result from a lack of knowledge, skill, or ability? (If so, training is appropriate; if not, other solutions are more relevant.)
- Who needs training?
- Are these employees ready for training?

The answers to these questions help the manager identify whether training is appropriate and which employees need training. In certain situations, such as the introduction of a new technology or service, all employees may need training. However, when needs assessment is conducted in response to a performance problem, training is not always the best solution.

The person analysis is therefore critical when training is considered in response to a performance problem. In assessing the need for training, the manager should identify all the variables that can influence performance. The primary variables are the person's ability and skills, his or her attitudes and motivation, the organization's input (including clear directions, necessary resources, and freedom from interference and distractions), performance feedback (including praise and performance standards), and positive consequences to motivate good performance. Of these variables, only ability and skills can be affected by training. Therefore, before planning a training program, it is important to be sure that any performance problem results from a deficiency in knowledge and skills. Otherwise, training dollars will be wasted, because the training is unlikely to have much effect on performance.

The person analysis also should determine whether employees are ready to undergo training. In other words, the employees to receive training not only should require additional knowledge and skill, but must be willing and able to learn. (After our discussion of the needs assessment, we will explore the topic of employee readiness in greater detail.)

Task Analysis

Task Analysis
The process of identifying and analyzing tasks to be trained for.

The third area of needs assessment is **task analysis**, the process of identifying the tasks, knowledge, skills, and behaviors that training should emphasize. Usually, task analysis is conducted along with person analysis. Understanding shortcomings in performance usually requires knowledge about the tasks and work environment as well as the employee.

To carry out the task analysis, the HR professional looks at the conditions in which tasks are performed. These conditions include the equipment and environment of the job, time constraints (for example, deadlines), safety considerations, and performance standards. These observations form the basis for a description of work activities, or the tasks required by the person's job. For a selected job, the analyst interviews employees and their supervisors to prepare a list of tasks performed in that job. Then the analyst validates the list by showing it to employees, supervisors, and other subject-matter experts and asking them to complete a questionnaire about the importance, frequency, and difficulty of the tasks. For each task listed, the subject-matter expert uses a sliding scale (for example, 0 = task never performed to 5 = task often performed) to rate the task's importance, frequency, and difficulty.[6]

The information from these questionnaires is the basis for determining which tasks will be the focus of the training. The person or committee conducting the needs assessment must decide what levels of importance, frequency, and difficulty signal a need for training. Logically, training is most needed for tasks that are important, frequent, and at least moderately difficult. For each of these tasks, the analysts must identify the knowledge, skills, and abilities required to perform the task. This information usually comes from interviews with subject-matter experts, such as employees who currently hold the job.

Readiness for Training

Effective training requires not only a program that addresses real needs, but also a condition of employee readiness. **Readiness for training** is a combination of employee characteristics and positive work environment that permit training. It exists when employees are able and eager to learn and when their organizations encourage learning.

Employee Readiness Characteristics

To be ready to learn, employees need basic learning skills, especially *cognitive ability*, which includes being able to use written and spoken language, solve math problems, and use logic to solve problems. Ideally, the selection process identified job candidates with enough cognitive ability to handle not only the requirements for doing a job, but also the training associated with that job. However, recent forecasts of the skill levels of the U.S. workforce indicate that many companies will have to work with employees who lack basic skills.[7] For example, they may have to provide literacy training or access to classes teaching math skills before some employees can participate in job-related training.

Employees learn more from training programs when they are highly motivated to learn—that is, when they really want to learn the content of the training program.[8] Employees tend to feel this way if they believe they are able to learn, see potential benefits from the training program, are aware of their need to learn, see a fit between the training and their career goals, and have the basic skills needed for participating in the program. Managers can influence a ready attitude in a variety of ways—for example, by providing feedback that encourages employees, establishing rewards for learning, and communicating with employees about the organization's career paths and future needs.

Work Environment

Readiness for training also depends on two broad characteristics of the work environment: situational constraints and social support.[9] *Situational constraints* are the limits on training's effectiveness that arise from the situation or the conditions within the organization. Constraints can include a lack of money for training, lack of time for training or practicing, and failure to provide proper tools and materials for learning or applying the lessons of training. Conversely, trainees are likely to apply what they learn if the organization gives them opportunities to use their new skills and if it rewards them for doing so.[10]

Social support refers to the ways the organization's people encourage training, including giving trainees praise and encouraging words, sharing information about participating in training programs, and expressing positive attitudes toward the organization's training programs. Table 7.1 summarizes some ways in which managers can support training.

LO 7-3 Explain how to assess employees' readiness for training.

Readiness for Training A combination of employee characteristics and positive work environment that permit training.

Table 7.1

What Managers Should Do to Support Training

Understand the content of the training.
Know how training relates to what you need employees to do.
In performance appraisals, evaluate employees on how they apply training to their jobs.
Support employees' use of training when they return to work.
Ensure that employees have the equipment and technology needed to use training.
Prior to training, discuss with employees how they plan to use training.
Recognize newly trained employees who use training content.
Give employees release time from their work to attend training.
Explain to employees why they have been asked to attend training.
Give employees feedback related to skills or behavior they are trying to develop.
If possible, be a trainer.

SOURCES: Based on A. Rossett, "That Was a Great Class, but . . ." *Training and Development,* July 1977, p. 21; R. Bates, "Managers as Transfer Agents," In E. Hotiton III and T. Baldwin (eds.), *Improving Learning Transfer in Organizations* (San Francisco: Jossey-Bass, 2003): pp. 243–270.

Support can also come from employees' peers. Readiness for training is greater in an organization where employees share knowledge, encourage one another to learn, and have a positive attitude about carrying the extra load when co-workers are attending classes. Employers foster such attitudes and behavior when they reward learning.

LO 7-4 Describe how to plan an effective training program.

Planning the Training Program

Decisions about training are often the responsibility of a specialist in the organization's training or human resources department. When the needs assessment indicates a need for training and employees are ready to learn, the person responsible for training should plan a training program that directly relates to the needs identified. Planning begins with establishing objectives for the training program. Based on those objectives, the planner decides who will provide the training, what topics the training will cover, what training methods to use, and how to evaluate the training.

Objectives of the Program

Formally establishing objectives for the training program has several benefits. First, a training program based on clear objectives will be more focused and more likely to succeed. In addition, when trainers know the objectives, they can communicate them to the employees participating in the program. Employees learn best when they know what the training is supposed to accomplish. Finally, down the road, establishing objectives provides a basis for measuring whether the program succeeded, as we will discuss later in this chapter.

Effective training objectives have several characteristics:

- They include a statement of what the employee is expected to do, the quality or level of performance that is acceptable, and the conditions under which the employee is to apply what he or she learned (for instance, physical conditions, mental stresses, or equipment failure).[11]
- They include performance standards that are measurable.
- They identify the resources needed to carry out the desired performance or outcome. Successful training requires employees to learn but also employers to provide the necessary resources.

A related issue at the outset is who will participate in the training program. Some training programs are developed for all employees of the organization or all members

Many Companies Outsource Training Tasks

A recent survey of U.S.-based corporations found that over half were outsourcing the instruction of training courses. Almost half use contractors to develop custom content, and 40% use them to operate or host a learning management system. All together, 23% of companies' training budgets went to contractors.

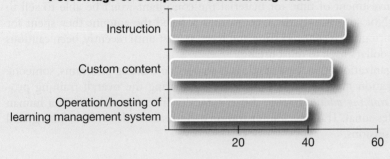

Percentage of Companies Outsourcing Task

Question

Suppose you need to train office workers on how to use social media without risking your company's reputation or data security. What are some advantages of company employees developing the course content? What are some advantages of using a firm that specializes in training about information technology?

SOURCE: "2011 Training Industry Report," *Training,* November/December 2011, pp. 22–35.

of a team. Other training programs identify individuals who lack desirable skills or have potential to be promoted, then provide training in the areas of need that are identified for the particular employees. When deciding whom to include in training, the organization has to avoid illegal discrimination. The organization should not—intentionally or unintentionally—exclude members of protected groups, such as women, minorities, and older employees. During the training, all participants should receive equal treatment, such as equal opportunities for practice. In addition, the training program should provide reasonable accommodation for trainees with disabilities. The kinds of accommodations that are appropriate will vary according to the type of training and type of disability. One employee might need an interpreter, whereas another might need to have classroom instruction provided in a location accessible to wheelchairs.

In-House or Contracted Out?

An organization can provide an effective training program, even if it lacks expertise in training. As shown in the "Did You Know?" box, many organizations use outside experts to develop and instruct training courses. Many companies and consultants provide training services to organizations. Community colleges often work with employers to train employees in a variety of skills.

To select a training service, an organization can mail several vendors a *request for proposal (RFP)*, which is a document outlining the type of service needed, the type and number of references needed, the number of employees to be trained, the date by which the training is to be completed, and the date by which proposals should be received. A complete RFP also indicates funding for the project and the process by which the organization will determine its level of satisfaction. Putting together a request for proposal is time consuming but worthwhile because it helps the organization clarify its objectives, compare vendors, and measure results.

Vendors that believe they are able to provide the services outlined in the RFP submit proposals that provide the types of information requested. The organization reviews the proposals to eliminate any vendors that do not meet requirements and to compare the vendors that do qualify. They check references and select a candidate, based on the proposal and the vendor's answers to questions about its experience, work samples, and evidence that its training programs meet objectives.

The cost of purchasing training from a contractor can vary substantially. In general, it is much costlier to purchase specialized training that is tailored to the organization's unique requirements than to participate in a seminar or training course that teaches general skills or knowledge. Preparing a specialized training program can require a significant investment of time for material the consultant won't be able to sell to other clients. Not surprisingly then, companies reduced the amount they spent for outsourcing during the recent recession and have, at least until recently, been cautious about shifting dollars back to outsourcing.[12]

Even in organizations that send employees to outside training programs, someone in the organization may be responsible for coordinating the overall training program. Called *training administration*, this is typically the responsibility of a human resources professional. Training administration includes activities before, during, and after training sessions.

Choice of Training Methods

Whether the organization prepares its own training programs or buys training from other organizations, it is important to verify that the content of the training relates directly to the training objectives. Relevance to the organization's needs and objectives ensures that training money is well spent. Tying training content closely to objectives also improves trainees' learning, because it increases the likelihood that the training will be meaningful and helpful.

After deciding on the goals and content of the training program, planners must decide how the training will be conducted. As we will describe in the next section, a wide variety of methods is available. Training methods fall into the broad categories described in Table 7.2: presentation, hands-on, and group-building methods.

Training programs may use these methods alone or in combination. In general, the methods used should be suitable for the course content and the learning abilities of the participants. The following section explores the options in greater detail.

Table 7.2

Categories of Training Methods

METHOD	TECHNIQUES	APPLICATIONS
Presentation methods: trainees receive information provided by others	Lectures, workbooks, video clips, podcasts, websites	Conveying facts or comparing alternatives
Hands-on methods: trainees are actively involved in trying out skills	On-the-job training, simulations, role-plays, computer games	Teaching specific skills; showing how skills are related to job or how to handle interpersonal issues
Group-building methods: trainees share ideas and experiences, build group identities, learn about interpersonal relationships and the group	Group discussions, experiential programs, team training	Establishing teams or work groups; managing performance of teams or work groups

Training Methods

LO 7-5 Compare widely used training methods.

A wide variety of methods is available for conducting training. Figure 7.2 shows the percentage of learner hours delivered to employees by each of several methods: instructor-led classrooms, online self-study, virtual classrooms, social media and mobile devices, and combinations of these methods. Although the share of instruction provided online is growing, classroom training remains the most popular of these methods.[13]

Classroom Instruction

At school, we tend to associate learning with classroom instruction, and that type of training is most widely used in the workplace, too. Classroom instruction typically involves a trainer lecturing a group. Trainers often supplement lectures with slides, discussions, case studies, question-and-answer sessions, and role playing. Actively involving trainees enhances learning.

When the course objectives call for presenting information on a specific topic to many trainees, classroom instruction is one of the least expensive and least time-consuming ways to accomplish that goal. Learning will be more effective if trainers enhance lectures with job-related examples and opportunities for hands-on learning.

Modern technology has expanded the notion of the classroom to classes of trainees scattered in various locations. With *distance learning*, trainees at different locations attend programs online, using their computers to view lectures, participate in discussions, and share documents. Technology applications in distance learning may include videoconferencing, e-mail, instant messaging, document-sharing software, and web cameras. When Steelcase was ready to begin selling its Node chair, a flexible classroom chair with a swivel seat, storage for backpacks, and a customizable work surface, it needed to show its global sales force how adaptable it was to today's classrooms and teaching methods. Steelcase also had to deliver the training fast, so that the sales reps would be prepared before schools were making their annual purchases for the next academic year. The solution was a virtual classroom, which allowed trainees to see the chair as well as hear the training.[14]

Distance learning provides many of the benefits of classroom training without the cost and time of travel to a shared classroom. The major disadvantage of distance learning is that interaction between the trainer and audience may be limited. To overcome this hurdle, distance learning usually provides a communications link between trainees and trainer. Also, on-site instructors or facilitators should be available to answer questions and moderate question-and-answer sessions.

Percentage of Student Hours Delivered by Each Training Method

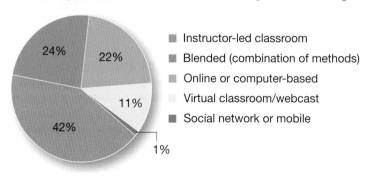

Figure 7.2

Use of Instructional Methods

- Instructor-led classroom
- Blended (combination of methods)
- Online or computer-based
- Virtual classroom/webcast
- Social network or mobile

SOURCE: "2011 Training Industry Report," *Training*, November/December 2011, pp. 22–35.

Mobile technology not only is useful for entertainment, but also can be used for employees who travel and need to be in touch with the office. Smartphones, iPods, and tablet computers also give employees the ability to listen to and participate in training programs at their own leisure.

Audiovisual Training

Presentation methods need not require trainees to attend a class. Trainees can also work independently, using course material in workbooks, on DVDs, or on the Internet. Audiovisual techniques such as overhead transparencies, PowerPoint or other presentation software, and video or audio clips can also supplement classroom instruction.

With modern technology, audiovisual materials can easily be made available on a variety of devices, from desktop computers to the tiny screens of smartphones and MP3 players. Today's mobile devices can display charts, play audio podcasts, and link to video clips. The DoubleTree by Hilton in Bloomington, Illinois, has placed two iPads loaded with training material at its front desk so employees can use them to complete training programs during slow periods. DoubleTree's training lessons are available in a choice of English or Spanish.[15] To keep the attention of its young workers, a restaurant chain called Flippin' Pizza provides training via an iPad app. The app gives trainees links to a series of two-minute videos, each with a lesson in cooking or customer service.[16] The "HR How To" box offers ideas for effectively delivering training on iPads and other mobile devices.

Users of audiovisual training often have some control over the presentation. They can review material and may be able to slow down or speed up the lesson. Videos can show situations and equipment that cannot be easily demonstrated in a classroom. Another advantage of audiovisual presentations is that they give trainees a consistent presentation, not affected by an individual trainer's goals and skills. The problems associated with these methods may include their trying to present too much material, poorly written dialogue, overuse of features such as humor or music, and drama that distracts from the key points. A well-written and carefully produced video can overcome these problems.

Computer-Based Training

Although almost all organizations use classroom training, new technologies are gaining in popularity as technology improves and becomes cheaper. With computer-based training, participants receive course materials and instruction distributed over the Internet or on CD-ROM. Often, these materials are interactive, so participants can answer questions and try out techniques, with course materials adjusted according to participants' responses. Online training programs may allow trainees to submit questions via e-mail and to participate in online discussions. Multimedia capabilities enable computers to provide sounds, images, and video presentations, along with text.

Computer-based training is generally less expensive than putting an instructor in a classroom of trainees. The low cost to deliver information gives the company flexibility in scheduling training so that it can fit around work requirements. Training can be delivered in smaller doses so material is easier to remember. Trainees often appreciate the multimedia capabilities, which appeal to several senses, and the chance to learn from experts anywhere in the world. Finally, it is easier to customize computer-based training for individual learners.

Current applications of computer-based training can extend its benefits:

E-Learning
Receiving training via the Internet or the organization's intranet.

- **E-learning** involves receiving training via the Internet or the organization's intranet, typically through some combination of web-based training modules, distance learning, and virtual classrooms. E-learning uses electronic networks for delivering and

HR How To

Developing Training Content for Mobile Devices

Nowadays, workers are already using—or would like to use—a variety of mobile devices. Many carry a smartphone and use iPods or other MP3 players for listening to music and watching videos. Some download books and magazines onto e-Readers, such as the Kindle or the Nook. Others have a tablet computer, such as the iPad, or a bulkier but more powerful laptop computer. All of these devices have the potential to deliver effective training. The following tips can help trainers ensure that m-learning (mobile learning) is well prepared and tailored to users' needs and the company's objectives:

- Keep the content brief. Text should get right to the point. The time required to read text, watch a video, or listen to a message should be less than 10 minutes. Remember, mobile users tend to be taking in the content between other activities. Also, gazing at a small screen for any length of time can be tiresome.

- Deliver "chunks" of content, with each one teaching just one or two key points. Make it easy to find that topic again, in case the learner wants to review it later.

- Design screen displays to be as simple as possible so they download quickly and are easy to read. Use minimal graphics; avoid background images altogether.

- Include controls to pause, restart, and stop content. This enables users to cope with interruptions so they can give the training their full attention while it is in progress.

- Think about what kinds of content employees will want to access when they are on the go. A salesperson might welcome background information about clients or product specifications. Lessons that ask the learner to ponder a complex problem would be less effective.

- Be sure the content designers know about all the mobile devices that will be used. The design should use only programs that run on every device that is delivering the content. The Flash media player, for example, does not work on every mobile device. Also, different devices will lend themselves to different kinds of feedback and assessment. Many have touch screens or microphones; on others, typing is relatively easy.

sharing information, and it offers tools and information for helping trainees improve performance. Training programs may include links to other online information resources and to trainees and experts for collaboration on problem solving. The e-learning system may also process enrollments, test and evaluate participants, and monitor progress. Quicken Loans uses e-learning to motivate employees to learn from their peers' best practices in customer service. It created an online contest called "Quicken's Got Talent." Employees who serve customers over the phone can submit recordings of calls they handled well. Trainers pick one submission per day to post on the game. Employees listen to the recordings and rate their co-worker's performance on a scale of 1 to 5. Each month the employee who submitted the top-scoring call receives a prize worth up to $200; winners of the monthly round are eligible for a competition with a $1,000 prize. The e-learning program tracks participation and creates a library of best-practices clips that are available for future learning.[17]

- **Electronic performance support systems (EPSSs)** are computer applications that provide access to skills training, information, and expert advice when a problem occurs on the job.[18] Employees needing guidance can use the EPSS to look up the particular information they need, such as detailed instructions on how to perform an unfamiliar task. Using an EPSS is faster and more relevant than attending classes, even classes offered online.

Electronic Performance Support System (EPSS)
Computer application that provides access to skills training, information, and expert advice as needed.

The best e-learning combines the advantages of the Internet with the principles of a good learning environment. It takes advantage of the web's dynamic nature and ability to use many positive learning features, including hyperlinks to other training sites and content, control by the trainee, and ability for trainees to collaborate.

On-the-Job Training

On-the-job Training (OJT)
Training methods in which a person with job experience and skill guides trainees in practicing job skills at the workplace.

Although people often associate training with classrooms, much learning occurs while employees are performing their jobs. **On-the-job training (OJT)** refers to training methods in which a person with job experience and skill guides trainees in practicing job skills at the workplace. This type of training takes various forms, including apprenticeships and internships.

An **apprenticeship** is a work-study training method that teaches job skills through a combination of structured on-the-job training and classroom training. The OJT component of an apprenticeship involves the apprentice assisting a certified tradesperson (a journeyman) at the work site. Typically, the classroom training is provided by local trade schools, high schools, and community colleges. Government requirements for an apprenticeship program vary by occupation, but programs generally range from one to six years. Requirements may be based on a minimum amount of time (often at least 2,000 hours of on-the-job learning), mastery of specified skills following classroom or online instruction plus on-the-job learning, or some combination of the two measures.[19] Some apprenticeship programs are sponsored by individual companies, others by employee unions. As shown in the left column of Table 7.3, most apprenticeship programs are in the skilled trades, such as plumbing, carpentry, and electrical work.

Apprenticeship
A work-study training method that teaches job skills through a combination of on-the-job training and classroom training.

For trainees, a major advantage of apprenticeship is the ability to earn an income while learning a trade. In addition, training through an apprenticeship is usually effective because it involves hands-on learning and extensive practice. Building a car today requires skilled labor, so in Tennessee, Volkswagen partnered with the Tennessee Technology Center of Chattanooga State Community College to create an apprenticeship program in automotive mechatronics. In this three-year program, apprentices receive classroom instruction and on-the-job training in machining, electricity, pneumatics, robotics, automation, programmable logic controls, and computer numeric controls. Volkswagen pays the apprentices for their on-the-job training time, and in return it acquires a workforce with hard-to-find skills in fixing problems in an automated manufacturing facility.[20]

Internship
On-the-job learning sponsored by an educational institution as a component of an academic program.

An **internship** is on-the-job learning sponsored by an educational institution as a component of an academic program. The sponsoring school works with local employers to place students in positions where they can gain experience related to their area of study. Ernst & Young hires interns to prepare them for possible permanent jobs as consultants and accountants if they demonstrate they can lead a project and work with a diverse team. Whirlpool hires interns to test their skills as it prepares them for positions in sales, technology, and human resource management.[21] Many internships prepare students for professions such as those listed in the right column of Table 7.3.

To be effective, OJT programs should include several characteristics:

- The organization should issue a policy statement describing the purpose of OJT and emphasizing the organization's support for it.
- The organization should specify who is accountable for conducting OJT. This accountability should be included in the relevant job descriptions.
- The organization should review OJT practices at companies in similar industries.
- Managers and peers should be trained in OJT principles.

APPRENTICESHIP	INTERNSHIP
Bricklayer	Accountant
Carpenter	Doctor
Electrician	Journalist
Plumber	Lawyer
Printer	Nurse
Welder	

Table 7.3

Typical Jobs for Apprentices and Interns

- Employees who conduct OJT should have access to lesson plans, checklists, procedure manuals, training manuals, learning contracts, and progress report forms.
- Before conducting OJT with an employee, the organization should assess the employee's level of basic skills.[22]

Simulations

A **simulation** is a training method that represents a real-life situation, with trainees making decisions resulting in outcomes that mirror what would happen on the job. Simulations enable trainees to see the impact of their decisions in an artificial, risk-free environment. They are used for teaching production and process skills as well as management and interpersonal skills. Simulations used in training include call centers stocked with phones and reference materials, as well as mockups of houses used for training cable installers. Airlines purchasing Boeing's latest-model passenger jet, the 787 Dreamliner, are using simulators to train the pilots who will fly it. Although the 787 flight deck is designed with the same layout as the familiar 777, it has a new feature called the head-up display (HUD). When flying conditions are poor, this small see-through screen drops down in pilots' line of vision to provide information to help them navigate. Pilots need to practice with the simulator until they are accustomed to landing the jet while using the HUD.[23]

Simulators must have elements identical to those found in the work environment. The simulator needs to respond exactly as equipment would under the conditions and response given by the trainee. For this reason, simulators are expensive to develop and need constant updating as new information about the work environment becomes available. Still, they are an excellent training method when the risks of a mistake on the job are great. Trainees do not have to be afraid of the impact of wrong decisions when using the simulator, as they would be with on-the-job training. Also, trainees tend to be enthusiastic about this type of learning and to learn quickly, and the lessons are generally related very closely to job performance. Given these benefits, this training method is likely to become more widespread as its development costs fall into a range more companies can afford.[24]

When simulations are conducted online, trainees often participate by creating **avatars**, or computer depictions of themselves, which they manipulate onscreen to play roles as workers or other participants in a job-related situation. Another way to enhance the simulation experience is to use **virtual reality**, a computer-based technology that provides an interactive, three-dimensional learning experience. Using specialized equipment or viewing the virtual model on a computer screen, trainees move through the simulated environment and interact with its components. Devices relay information from the environment to the trainees' senses. For example, audio interfaces, gloves that provide a sense of touch, treadmills, or motion platforms create a

Simulation
A training method that represents a real-life situation, with trainees making decisions resulting in outcomes that mirror what would happen on the job.

Avatars
Computer depictions of trainees, which the trainees manipulate in an online role-play.

Virtual Reality
A computer-based technology that provides an interactive, three-dimensional learning experience.

realistic but artificial environment. Devices also communicate information about the trainee's movements to a computer.

The Centers for Disease Control and Prevention (CDC) is using a virtual-reality program to prepare professionals for disaster response. Survivors of a disease outbreak, terrorist attack, hurricane, or earthquake are in desperate need of medical help, but the professionals who arrive on the scene can become overwhelmed by destroyed medical facilities, intense sights and smells, and barriers such as language differences. Typically, medical training does not prepare them for these situations, so the CDC wanted a training program that would mimic as much as possible the conditions of disaster response, enabling the professionals to practice their responses without compromising anyone's safety. The training contractor, Virtually Better Inc. (VBI), used content provided by the CDC to develop stories and present them in a virtual reality environment that exposes trainees to the sounds, sights, and scents of an African village where the people speak Swahili. (VBI also has begun preparing simulations of a coastal town after an earthquake strikes.) Trainees wearing head-mounted displays and headphones can move around the scene and interact with characters in the environment as they complete assigned tasks and encounter hazards. The environment offers different levels of difficulty, which increase the stressors presented. Trainees who complete the three-session program have improved their scores on safety skills and resiliency.[25]

Business Games and Case Studies

Training programs use business games and case studies to develop employees' management skills. A case study is a detailed description of a situation that trainees study and discuss. Cases are designed to develop higher-order thinking skills, such as the ability to analyze and evaluate information. They also can be a safe way to encourage trainees to take appropriate risks, by giving them practice in weighing and acting on uncertain outcomes. There are many sources of case studies, including Harvard Business School, the Darden Business School at the University of Virginia, and McGraw-Hill publishing company.

With business games, trainees gather information, analyze it, and make decisions that influence the outcome of the game. To train salespeople in its Winning Major program, Humana assembles teams of five trainees and has each team imagine it is a salesperson for a robotics company. Each team plays three rounds of simulations in which it handles issues from three imaginary clients. The team that generates the most revenue is declared the winner.[26] Games stimulate learning because they actively involve participants and mimic the competitive nature of business. A realistic game may be more meaningful to trainees than presentation techniques such as classroom instruction.

Training with case studies and games requires that participants come together to discuss the cases or the progress of the game. This requires face-to-face or electronic meetings. Also, participants must be willing to be actively involved in analyzing the situation and defending their decisions.

Behavior Modeling

Research suggests that one of the most effective ways to teach interpersonal skills is through behavior modeling.[27] This involves training sessions in which participants observe other people demonstrating the desired behavior, then have opportunities to practice the behavior themselves. For example, a training program could involve several days of four-hour sessions, each focusing on one interpersonal skill, such as communicating or coaching. At the beginning of each session, participants hear the reasons for using the key behaviors; then they watch a video of a model performing the key behaviors. They practice through role-playing and receive feedback about their performance. In addition, they evaluate the performance of the model in the video and discuss how they can apply the behavior on the job.

Experiential Programs

To develop teamwork and leadership skills, some organizations enroll their employees in a form of training called **experiential programs**. In experiential programs, participants learn concepts and then apply them by simulating the behaviors involved and analyzing the activity, connecting it with real-life situations.[28] Tyson Foods incorporates experiential learning into its two-year program for preparing managers to fill executive slots. After a year of self-assessments and meetings with executives, the managers participate in an experiential learning event designed to be intense. It tests how well the managers can use their skills to handle an experience in which the odds are stacked against them. Reviewing what they have learned from the experience prepares the managers to tackle a challenging new job at Tyson they will take on during the second year of the training program.[29]

Experiential training programs should follow several guidelines. A program should be related to a specific business problem. Participants should feel challenged and move outside their comfort zones but within limits that keep their motivation strong and help them understand the purpose of the program.

One form of experiential program, called **adventure learning**, uses challenging, structured outdoor activities, which may include difficult sports such as dogsledding

Experiential Programs
Training programs in which participants learn concepts and apply them by simulating behaviors involved and analyzing the activity, connecting it with real-life situations.

Adventure Learning
A teamwork and leadership training program based on the use of challenging, structured outdoor activities.

One of the most important features of organizations today is teamwork. Experiential programs include team-building exercises like wall climbing and rafting to help build trust and cooperation among employees.

or mountain climbing. Other activities may be structured tasks like climbing walls, completing rope courses, climbing ladders, or making "trust falls" (in which each trainee stands on a table and falls backward into the arms of other group members).

The impact of adventure learning programs has not been rigorously tested, but participants report they gained a greater understanding of themselves and the ways they interact with their co-workers. One key to the success of such programs may be that the organization needs to insist that entire work groups participate together. This encourages people to see, discuss, and correct the kinds of behavior that keep the group from performing well.

Before requiring employees to participate in experiential programs, the organization should consider the possible drawbacks. Because these programs are usually physically demanding and often require participants to touch each other, companies face certain risks. Some employees may be injured or may feel that they were sexually harassed or that their privacy was invaded. Also, the Americans with Disabilities Act (discussed in Chapter 3) raises questions about requiring employees with disabilities to participate in physically demanding training experiences.

Team Training

A possible alternative to experiential programs is team training, which coordinates the performance of individuals who work together to achieve a common goal. An organization may benefit from providing such training to groups when group members must share information and group performance depends on the performance of the individual group members. Examples include the military, nuclear power plants, and commercial airlines. In those work settings, much work is performed by crews, groups, or teams. Success depends on individuals' coordinating their activities to make decisions, perhaps in dangerous situations.

Cross-Training
Team training in which team members understand and practice each other's skills so that they are prepared to step in and take another member's place.

Coordination Training
Team training that teaches the team how to share information and make decisions to obtain the best team performance.

Ways to conduct team training include cross-training and coordination training.[30] In **cross-training**, team members understand and practice each other's skills so that they are prepared to step in and take another member's place. In a factory, for example, production workers could be cross-trained to handle all phases of assembly. This enables the company to move them to the positions where they are most needed to complete an order on time.

Coordination training trains the team in how to share information and decisions to obtain the best team performance. This type of training is especially important for commercial aviation and surgical teams. Both of these kinds of teams must monitor different aspects of equipment and the environment at the same time sharing information to make the most effective decisions regarding patient care or aircraft safety and performance.

At S&ME, an engineering services firm, branch manager Keith Brown tried team training when he saw that the need for downsizing had drained his employees. His smaller staff was struggling to be creative as these few people were forced to complete more projects with limited resources. Brown decided that better teamwork could help his people accomplish goals more efficiently. He devoted one day to a training program run by Discovery Learning. The participants pretended to be the production team of a paper-plane manufacturer trying to sell more and more under increasingly difficult circumstances. The employees were initially doubtful that the program would be meaningful, but they soon became engrossed in the challenge. They discovered barriers to success and identified ways they can work more creatively together—for example, by communicating more.[31]

Training may also target the skills needed by the teams' leaders. **Team leader training** refers to training people in the skills necessary for team leadership. For example, the training may be aimed at helping team leaders learn to resolve conflicts or coordinate activities.

Team Leader Training Training in the skills necessary for effectively leading the organization's teams.

Action Learning

Another form of group building is **action learning**. In this type of training, teams or work groups get an actual problem, work on solving it and commit to an action plan, and are accountable for carrying out the plan. Ideally, the project is one for which the efforts and results will be visible not only to participants but also to others in the organization. The visibility and impact of the task are intended to make participation exciting, relevant, and engaging. At Automatic Data Processing, action learning assigns teams of 10 managers to study a real business problem or opportunity facing the company and present recommendations to senior executives.[32] To heighten learning, organizations can get their best leaders involved as mentors and coaches to the participants.

Action Learning Training in which teams get an actual problem, work on solving it and commit to an action plan, and are accountable for carrying it out.

The effectiveness of action learning has not been formally evaluated. This type of training seems to result in a great deal of learning, however, and employees are able to apply what they learn because action learning involves actual problems the organization is facing. The group approach also helps teams identify behaviors that interfere with problem solving.

Implementing the Training Program

Learning permanently changes behavior. For employees to acquire knowledge and skills in the training program, the training program must be implemented in a way that applies what is known about how people learn. Equally important, implementation of a training program should enable employees to transfer what they have learned to the workplace—in other words, employees should behave differently as a result of the training.

LO 7-6 Summarize how to implement a successful training program.

Principles of Learning

Researchers have identified a number of ways employees learn best.[33] Table 7.4 summarizes ways that training can best encourage learning. In general, effective training communicates learning objectives clearly, presents information in distinctive and memorable ways, and helps trainees link the subject matter to their jobs.

Employees are most likely to learn when training is linked to their current job experiences and tasks.[34] There are a number of ways trainers can make this link. Training sessions should present material using familiar concepts, terms, and examples. As far as possible, the training context—such as the physical setting or the images presented on a computer—should mirror the work environment. Along with physical elements, the context should include emotional elements. In the earlier example of store personnel training to handle upset customers, the physical context is more relevant if it includes trainees acting out scenarios of personnel dealing with unhappy customers. The role-play interaction between trainees adds emotional realism and further enhances learning.

To fully understand and remember the content of the training, employees need a chance to demonstrate and practice what they have learned. Trainers should provide ways to actively involve the trainees, have them practice repeatedly, and have them complete tasks within a time that is appropriate in light of the learning objectives. Practice

Table 7.4

Ways That Training Helps Employees Learn

TRAINING ACTIVITY	WAYS TO PROVIDE TRAINING ACTIVITY
Communicate the learning objective.	Demonstrate the performance to be expected. Give examples of questions to be answered.
Use distinctive, attention-getting messages.	Emphasize key points. Use pictures, not just words.
Limit the content of training.	Group lengthy material into chunks. Provide a visual image of the course material. Provide opportunities to repeat and practice material.
Guide trainees as they learn.	Use words as reminders about sequence of activities. Use words and pictures to relate concepts to one another and to their context. Prompt trainees to evaluate whether they understand and are using effective tactics to learn the material.
Elaborate on the subject.	Present the material in different contexts and settings. Relate new ideas to previously learned concepts. Practice in a variety of contexts and settings.
Provide memory cues.	Suggest memory aids. Use familiar sounds or rhymes as memory cues.
Transfer course content to the workplace.	Design the learning environment so that it has elements in common with the workplace. Require learners to develop action plans that apply training content to their jobs. Use words that link the course to the workplace.
Provide feedback about performance.	Tell trainees how accurately and quickly they are performing their new skill. Show how trainees have met the objectives of the training.

SOURCES: Adapted from R. M. Gagne, "Learning Processes and Instruction," *Training Research Journal 1* (1995/96), pp. 17–28; and Traci Sitzmann, "Self-Regulating Online Course Engagement," *T&D,* March 2010, Business & Company Resource Center, http://galenet.galegroup.com.

requires physically carrying out the desired behaviors, not just describing them. Practice sessions could include role-playing interactions, filling out relevant forms, or operating machinery or equipment to be used on the job. The more the trainee practices these activities, the more comfortable he or she will be in applying the skills on the job. People tend to benefit most from practice that occurs over several sessions, rather than one long practice session.[35] For complex tasks, it may be most effective to practice a few skills or behaviors at a time, then combine them in later practice sessions.

Trainees need to understand whether or not they are succeeding. Therefore, training sessions should offer feedback. Effective feedback focuses on specific behaviors and is delivered as soon as possible after the trainees practice or demonstrate what they have learned.[36] One way to do this is to videotape trainees, then show the video while indicating specific behaviors that do or do not match the desired outcomes of the training. Feedback should include praise when trainees show they have learned material, as well as guidance on how to improve.

Well-designed training helps people remember the content. Training programs need to break information into chunks that people can remember. Research suggests that people can attend to no more than four to five items at a time. If a concept or procedure involves more than five items, the training program should deliver information in shorter sessions or chunks.[37] Other ways to make information more memorable include presenting it with visual images and practicing some tasks enough that they become automatic.

Written materials should have an appropriate reading level. A simple way to assess **readability**—the difficulty level of written materials—is to look at the words being used and at the length of sentences. In general, it is easiest to read short sentences and simple, standard words. If training materials are too difficult to understand, several adjustments can help. The basic approach is to rewrite the material looking for ways to simplify it.

Readability
The difficulty level of written materials.

- Substitute simple, concrete words for unfamiliar or abstract words.
- Divide long sentences into two or more short sentences.
- Divide long paragraphs into two or more short paragraphs.
- Add checklists (like this one) and illustrations to clarify the text.

Another approach is to substitute video, hands-on learning, or other nonwritten methods for some of the written material. A longer-term solution is to use tests to identify employees who need training to improve their reading levels and to provide that training first.

Transfer of Training

Ultimately, the goal of implementation is **transfer of training**, or on-the-job use of knowledge, skills, and behaviors learned in training. Transfer of training requires that employees actually learn the content of the training program. Then, for employees to apply what they learned, certain conditions must be in place: social support, technical support, and self-management.

Transfer of Training
On-the-job use of knowledge, skills, and behaviors learned in training.

Social support, as we saw in the discussion of readiness for training, includes support from the organization and from trainees' peers. Before, during, and after implementation, the organization's managers need to emphasize the importance of training, encourage their employees to attend training programs, and point out connections between training content and employees' job requirements. The organization can formally provide peer support by establishing **communities of practice**—groups of employees who work together, learn from each other, and develop a common understanding of how to get work accomplished. It also may assign experienced employees to act as mentors, who provide advice and support to the trainees. Social support has been essential for transfer of training at hospitals teaching doctors to use electronic medical records, which can reduce errors and costs. For example, Good Samaritan Hospital in Vincennes, Indiana, had a tech-savvy radiologist conduct the training. At Deaconess Health System in Evansville, Indiana, the most effective motivation for reluctant physicians came from the doctors who received training early on and who would prod their colleagues to catch up.[38]

Communities of Practice
Groups of employees who work together, learn from each other, and develop a common understanding of how to get work accomplished.

Transfer of training is greater when organizations also provide technical resources that help people acquire and share information. Technical support may come from electronic performance support systems (EPSS), described earlier as a type of computer-based training. Knowledge management systems including online and database tools also make it easy for employees to look up information they want to review or consult later. Mohawk Industries set up a human resources information system by creating a web page called myMohawk, which is the default home page on each employee's computer. The training team uses it to post announcements of training opportunities, blog about the benefits of learning, and provide links to training materials. Employees also are encouraged to use myMohawk to post their own blogs and share what they have learned.[39]

Organizations are beginning to provide a strong combination of social and technical support for transfer of training by setting up social media applications that promote learning. To learn more, see the "HRM Social" box.

Social Learning

Young workers entering the workforce grew up with the Internet and have been using social media all of their adult lives. Older workers may see social media as a new development, but many of them, too, are quick to embrace the technology. Thus, when employees today want information or encouragement, they often start by reaching out to their online community. Informal learning through social networks has always been a part of human interaction; what is new is that it takes place online, unconstrained by physical location. Some innovative employers are taking an active role in promoting informal learning that is aligned with the organization's strategy. These approaches to training are often called *social learning*.

A primary use of social learning, of course, is to provide the peer support that fosters transfer of training. These peer networks can also be a means for individual employees to share their own expertise, not limited by what the formal trainer has conveyed. On a social networking site such as Facebook or Google+, for example, a trainer

or employee might post links to videos, blogs, training lessons, or other content that provides information other employees need. Users of the network can add comments that add to learning, or they can request information from others in the network. A formal training program could be supplemented with a Facebook page where participants later can trade comments about their experiences in applying the training lessons, perhaps encouraging one another and reminding one another of key points they learned.

Social learning can also emphasize the delivery of information. The trainer might set up a wiki, an online joint project that is quickly created by the submissions of many contributors (most people are familiar with one famous example, Wikipedia). Suppose the organization wants its salespeople to learn more about customers' needs. Perhaps the training department would identify several people with relevant knowledge, and they would start by posting reports on their areas of specialty. Someone else would have a firsthand experience with a

customer and write about that. Yet another employee would read a report and think of another aspect of customer service to report on. And in this way, the wiki would become a source of customer information offering greater depth than any trainer could develop on his or her own.

Intercontinental Hotels Group benefited from both uses of social learning when it set up its Leaders Lounge, a social learning community for its top managers and hotel general managers. The site offers links to leadership tips, articles, and videos, as well as 15-minute e-learning materials designed for executives to share with their teams. Managers also visit the Leaders Lounge to build connections with their colleagues, who often are located far apart.

SOURCES: Aaron Silvers, "The Blueprint for Social Learning," *T + D*, January 2012, pp. 34–39; Matt Allen and Jennifer Naughton, "Social Learning: A Call to Action for Learning Professionals," *T + D*, August 2011, pp. 50–55; "Best Practices and Outstanding Initiatives," *Training*, January/February 2011, EBSCOhost, http://web.ebscohost.com.

Finally, to ensure transfer of training, an organization's training programs should prepare employees to self-manage their use of new skills and behaviors on the job.[40] To that end, the trainer should have trainees set goals for using skills or behaviors on the job, identify conditions under which they might fail to use the skills and behaviors, and identify the consequences (positive and negative) of using them. Employees should practice monitoring their use of the new skills and behaviors. The trainer should stress that learning to use new skills on the job is naturally difficult and will not necessarily proceed perfectly, but that employees should keep trying. Trainers also should support managers and peers in finding ways to reward employees for applying what they learned.

Measuring Results of Training

LO 7-7 Evaluate the success of a training program.

After a training program ends, or at intervals during an ongoing training program, organizations should ensure that the training is meeting objectives. The stage to prepare for evaluating a training program is when the program is being developed. Along with designing course objectives and content, the planner should identify how to measure achievement of objectives. Depending on the objectives, the evaluation can use one or more of the measures shown in Figure 7.3: trainee satisfaction with the program, knowledge or abilities gained, use of new skills and behavior on the job (transfer of training), and improvements in individual and organizational performance. The usual way to measure whether participants have acquired information is to administer tests on paper or electronically. Trainers or supervisors can observe whether participants demonstrate the desired skills and behaviors. Surveys measure changes in attitude. Changes in company performance have a variety of measures, many of which organizations keep track of for preparing performance appraisals, annual reports, and other routine documents in order to demonstrate the final measure of success shown in Figure 7.3: return on investment.

Figure 7.3
Measures of Training Success

Evaluation Methods

To measure whether the conditions are in place for transfer of training, the organization can ask employees three questions about specific training-related tasks:

1. Do you perform the task?
2. How many times do you perform the task?
3. To what extent do you perform difficult and challenging learned tasks?

Frequent performance of difficult training-related tasks would signal great opportunity to perform. If there is low opportunity to perform, the organization should conduct further needs assessment and reevaluate readiness to learn. Perhaps the organization does not fully support the training activities in general or the employee's supervisor does not provide opportunities to apply new skills. Lack of transfer can also mean that employees have not learned the course material. The organization might offer a refresher course to give trainees more practice. Another reason for poor transfer of training is that the content of the training may not be important for the employee's job.

Assessment of training also should evaluate training *outcomes*, that is, what (if anything) has changed as a result of the training. The relevant training outcomes are the ones related to the organization's goals for the training and its overall performance. Possible outcomes include the following:

- Information such as facts, techniques, and procedures that trainees can recall after the training.
- Skills that trainees can demonstrate in tests or on the job.
- Trainee and supervisor satisfaction with the training program.
- Changes in attitude related to the content of the training (for example, concern for safety or tolerance of diversity).
- Improvements in individual, group, or company performance (for example, greater customer satisfaction, more sales, fewer defects).

Training is a significant part of many organizations' budgets. Therefore, economic measures are an important way to evaluate the success of a training program. Businesses that invest in training want to achieve a high *return on investment*—the monetary benefits of the investment compared to the amount invested, expressed as a percentage. For example, Mayo Clinic provided training for its managers after it discovered that employees were quitting because of dissatisfaction with their managers. After the training, employee turnover rates improved. To determine the return on the investment in the training, Mayo's human resource department calculated that one-third of the employees retained (29 employees) would have left if the training had not occurred. The department calculated the cost of an employee leaving as 75% of average total compensation, or $42,000 per employee. Multiplied by the number of employees ($42,000 times 29), that is equivalent to lowering costs by $609,000. The training cost $125,000, so the company saved $484,000 by providing it. The return on investment would be $484,000 divided by $125,000, or an impressive 387%.[41] Even if some of the estimates were wrong, Mayo's HR department could feel confident in making a case that the training was beneficial.

For any of these methods, the most accurate but most costly way to evaluate the training program is to measure performance, knowledge, or attitudes among all employees before the training and then train only part of the employees. After the training is complete, the performance, knowledge, or attitudes are again measured, and the trained group is compared with the untrained group. A simpler but less accurate way to assess the training is to conduct the pretest and posttest on all trainees, comparing their performance, knowledge, or attitudes before and after the training. This form of measurement does not rule out the possibility that change resulted from something other than training (for example, a change in the compensation system). The simplest approach is to use only a posttest. Use of only a posttest can show if trainees have reached a specified level of competency, knowledge, or skill. Of course, this type of measurement does not enable accurate comparisons, but it may be sufficient, depending on the cost and purpose of the training.

Applying the Evaluation

The purpose of evaluating training is to help with future decisions about the organization's training programs. Using the evaluation, the organization may identify a need to modify the training and gain information about the kinds of changes needed. The organization may decide to expand on successful areas of training and cut back on training that has not delivered significant benefits.

A major producer of packaged foods has identified both successes and needs for improvement after analyzing its training programs. The company began conducting management training for supervisors and treated the first 12 months as a test of the program. After a year, the company determined that turnover rates were much lower among supervisors who had received training. That difference was strongest among more recently hired supervisors and persisted even after the company made statistical adjustments for other possible influences on turnover. The company therefore recommitted to its training goals for supervisors, especially targeting those hired most recently. In contrast, training had a minimal impact on safety performance at the company's facilities. The training department concluded it would have to improve the safety component of the training program or replace it with a new approach to safety training.[42]

LO 7-8 Describe training methods for employee orientation and diversity management.

Applications of Training

Two training applications that have become widespread among U.S. companies are orientation of new employees and training in how to manage workforce diversity.

Orientation of New Employees

Many employees receive their first training during their first days on the job. This training is the organization's **orientation** program—its training designed to prepare employees to perform their job effectively, learn about the organization, and establish work relationships. Organizations provide for orientation because, no matter how realistic the information provided during employment interviews and site visits, people feel shock and surprise when they start a new job.[43] Also, employees need to become familiar with job tasks and learn the details of the organization's practices, policies, and procedures.

The objectives of orientation programs include making new employees familiar with the organization's rules, policies, and procedures. Table 7.5 summarizes the content of a typical orientation program. Such a program provides information about the overall company and about the department in which the new employee will be working. The topics include social as well as technical aspects of the job. Miscellaneous information helps employees from out of town learn about the surrounding community.

Orientation for servers at restaurant chains includes how to look for clues to the kind of service diners are expecting and the actions that could boost sales and satisfaction. Blue Smoke's orientation program includes seven days of formal training, five days of following an experienced waiter, and two days of working under the observation of an experienced waiter. Each day's training focuses on one area of learning, such as how to greet guests, and ends with a quiz on the day's lesson. At Cheesecake Factory, new employees spend slow periods discussing how to interact with diners who are with children or having a celebration. They learn to look each customer in the eye when moving through the dining room and to notice behavior that signals disappointment with the food—for example, pushing food around the plate or removing an ingredient from a dish.[44]

Orientation
Training designed to prepare employees to perform their jobs effectively, learn about their organization, and establish work relationships.

Company-level information
Company overview (e.g., values, history, mission)
Key policies and procedures
Compensation
Employee benefits and services
Safety and accident prevention
Employee and union relations
Physical facilities
Economic factors
Customer relations
Department-level information
Department functions and philosophy
Job duties and responsibilities
Policies, procedures, rules, and regulations
Performance expectations
Tour of department
Introduction to department employees
Miscellaneous
Community
Housing
Family adjustment

Table 7.5

Content of a Typical Orientation Program

SOURCE: J. L. Schwarz and M. A. Weslowski, "Employee Orientation: What Employers Should Know," *Journal of Contemporary Business Issues,* Fall 1995, p. 48. Used with permission.

A Revolving Door for Returning Vets

The president of a manufacturing company had the best of intentions. He was a retired military officer and wanted to provide jobs for some of the many service members ready to make a transition from military to civilian life. He expected that many of them had leadership qualities and would be an asset to his growing business. So he directed his company's human resources department to recruit veterans and track their progress.

A year and a half later, the company president reviewed the numbers and was shocked: many veterans were indeed being hired—and most of them were replacing veterans previously hired. The sad fact was that within months, most of them felt uncomfortable at the company and quit.

Research into this pattern has found a culture clash. Many employers find that their new employees don't know how to function in a civilian environment. What promoted success in the military is not always what works in civilian workplaces.

One solution is to develop orientation programs geared toward veterans. These new employees tend to face particular issues. For example, military organizations tend to emphasize standard processes. In contrast, many businesses want to foster creative thinking, which veterans might interpret as a lack of leadership or failure to communicate. Values such as loyalty and respect are highly prized in the military; veteran employees may be troubled if they perceive a lax attitude toward values in a civilian workplace. Thus, orientation might need to cover aspects of organizational culture that seem obvious to the civilian trainer. The orientation program might be best supplemented with a mentor who has a military background.

The effort to recruit and train veterans can be worthwhile for many reasons. Many employers prize veterans' strong values, leadership experience, and resourcefulness. The federal government offers guidance and assistance in recruiting and hiring veterans. The wind-down of the wars in Iraq and Afghanistan is creating a huge pool of talented, motivated individuals. And, of course, many employers want to do the right thing for persons who have sacrificed so much for the nation.

Questions

1. In the manufacturing company described here, the president himself was a veteran. Why do you think the newly hired veterans didn't feel at home in a company run by a veteran? What lessons does this suggest about how to plan an orientation program's content?
2. What training methods do you think would be most effective for acquainting retired veterans with civilian business culture?

SOURCES: U.S. Department of Labor, "Hiring Veterans: A Step-by-Step Toolkit for Employers," *America's Heroes at Work,* http://www.americasheroes atwork.gov, accessed March 15, 2012; Karen Parrish, "Veteran Job Prospects Brighter, Panetta Says," American Forces Press Service, news release, March 15, 2012, http://www.defense .gov; Emily King, "From Boots to Briefcase: Conquering the 18-Month Churn," *T + D,* April 2011, pp. 36–41.

Orientation programs may combine various training methods, such as printed and audiovisual materials, classroom instruction, on-the-job training, and e-learning. Decisions about how to conduct the orientation depend on the type of material to be covered and the number of new employees, among other factors. To learn how the needs of veterans entering the civilian workforce shape the kind of orientation needed, see "HR Oops!"

Diversity Training

In response to Equal Employment Opportunity laws and market forces, many organizations today are concerned about managing diversity—creating an environment that allows all employees to contribute to organizational goals and experience personal growth. This kind of environment includes access to jobs as well as fair and positive treatment of all employees. Chapter 3 described how organizations manage diversity by complying with the law. Besides these efforts, many organizations provide training designed to teach employees attitudes and behaviors that support the management of diversity, such as appreciation of cultural differences and avoidance of behaviors that isolate or intimidate others.

Training designed to change employee attitudes about diversity and/or develop skills needed to work with a diverse workforce is called **diversity training**. These programs generally emphasize either attitude awareness and change or behavior change.

Programs that focus on attitudes have objectives to increase participants' awareness of cultural and ethnic differences, as well as differences in personal characteristics and physical characteristics (such as disabilities). These programs are based on the assumption that people who become aware of differences and their stereotypes about those differences will be able to avoid letting stereotypes influence their interactions with people. Many of these programs use video and experiential exercises to increase employees' awareness of the negative emotional and performance effects of stereotypes and resulting behaviors on members of minority groups. A risk of these programs—especially when they define diversity mainly in terms of race, ethnicity, and sex—is that they may alienate white male employees, who conclude that if the company values diversity more, it values them less.[45] Diversity training is more likely to get everyone onboard if it emphasizes respecting and valuing all the organization's employees in order to bring out the best work from everyone to open up the best opportunities for everyone.

Diversity training programs, like the one conducted by Harvard Pilgrim Health Care, are designed to teach employees attitudes and behaviors that support the management of diversity. Why is it important for companies to provide this type of training?

Diversity Training Training designed to change employee attitudes about diversity and/or develop skills needed to work with a diverse workforce.

Programs that focus on behavior aim at changing the organizational policies and individual behaviors that inhibit employees' personal growth and productivity. Sometimes these programs identify incidents that discourage employees from working up to their potential. Employees work in groups to discuss specific promotion opportunities or management practices that they believe were handled unfairly. Another approach starts with the assumption that all individuals differ in various ways and teaches skills for constructively handling the communication barriers, conflicts, and misunderstandings that necessarily arise when different people try to work together.[46] Trainees may be more positive about receiving this type of training than other kinds of diversity training. Finally, some organizations provide diversity training in the form of *cultural immersion*, sending employees directly into communities where they have to interact with persons from different cultures, races, and nationalities. Participants might talk with community members, work in community organizations, or learn about events that are significant to the community they visit. Sometimes cultural immersion comes with the job. At a large Japanese automaker, Japanese, U.S., and Mexican employees often had to interact but frequently fell victim to misunderstandings. The company hired a training consultant to develop a different classroom training program for each group, focusing on the other groups' cultural expectations and ways to communicate effectively. She also coached employees before they went on international assignments. The training program was well received because it helped employees avoid conflict.[47]

Although many organizations have used diversity training, few have provided programs lasting more than a day, and few have researched their long-term effectiveness.[48] The little research that exists on the subject has provided no support for a direct link between diversity programs and business success, but there is evidence that some characteristics make diversity training more effective.[49] Most important, the training should be tied to business objectives, such as understanding customers. The support and involvement of top management, and the involvement of managers at all levels, also are important. Diversity training should emphasize learning behaviors and skills, not blaming employees. Finally, the program should help employees see how they can apply their new skills on the job, deliver rewards for performance, be tied to organizational policies and practices that value diversity, and include a way to measure the success of the training.

Some organizations are getting it right. At the Oregon Center for Nursing, many of the nurses are eager to learn how to provide better care to patients who come from different cultures. The organization hosts online seminars on cultural backgrounds represented in the area, including Latino, Burmese, and Somali/Bantu people. The training also provides general guidelines for identifying relevant cultural differences so that nurses can apply the principles to cultural groups they haven't specifically studied. In contrast, at a big-box retail chain, diversity training had to start by convincing employees of the need for training. The store had launched a strategy calling for improved customer service, and employees were demonstrating that they were learning the lessons taught in sales training programs, but sales were not improving. Research showed that the problem lay with the assumptions salespeople were making: they were operating according to stereotypes about which types of customers would make a purchase, and they were ignoring customers who didn't fit the right profile. The retailer studied purchase data and was able to show salespeople that their assumptions were false. The company developed new training that focused on confronting and correcting the stereotypes. Salespeople began to apply these new lessons, and sales soon began to climb.[50]

THINKING ETHICALLY

CAN EMPLOYERS TEACH ETHICS?

Engineering professor Michael Garrett recalls being a new employee at URS Corporation, an engineering and design firm headquartered in San Francisco. On his first day, he was shown around the office on a tour that highlighted safety features such as fire extinguishers, first-aid kits, and emergency escape routes. He also was instructed to complete a safety training course before he began working. During his time on the job, he received monthly newsletters with articles describing safe practices at work and at home. Reflecting on that experience, Garrett asserts that, just as a company can build a culture of safety as URS did, it can also build a culture of ethics with frequent messages affirming the company's commitment to ethical practices. In his view, making an organization ethical is not a matter of one-time training, but of continual learning, practice, and reinforcement.

Ethical behavior at work is most likely to result from a desire to be ethical combined with skills for ethical reasoning and an organizational context that encourages ethical behavior. Advocates for ethics training suggest that a training program could address all of these. For example, employees can learn the benefits of an ethical workplace. They can learn principles for arriving at ethical choices. And leaders can learn skills for creating an ethical climate by communicating honestly and treating employees with respect. These lessons will be most effective if they are tailored to the specifics of the company and if the messages about ethics are delivered by respected people from within the organization. Also, because the choice to behave ethically is a personal choice, the lessons are most powerful coming from sincere individuals, delivered face-to-face.

Questions

1. Imagine you have been asked to prepare an ethics training program for the credit union where you work. The program is supposed to reinforce your organization's commitment to integrity as an employer and member of the community. What training methods do you think would be most effective for this training program? Why?
2. Continuing the same example, what steps can you take to encourage transfer of training?

SOURCES: Andrew S. Hubbard, "Five Essentials for Ethics Training (OK, Four and a Half)," *Mortgage Banking,* December 2011, p. 110; Ross Tartell, "Can Leadership Ethics Be Learned?" *Training,* May/June 2011, EBSCOhost, http://web.ebscohost.com; Michael Garrett, "The Importance of Regular Ethical Exercise," *Leadership and Management in Engineering,* January 2010, pp. 49–51.

SUMMARY

LO 7-1 Discuss how to link training programs to organizational needs.

Organizations need to establish training programs that are effective. In other words, they teach what they are designed to teach, and they teach skills and behaviors that will help the organization achieve its goals. Organizations create such programs through instructional design. This process begins with a needs assessment. The organization then ensures readiness for training, including employee characteristics and organizational support. Next, the organization plans a training program, implements the program, and evaluates the results.

LO 7-2 Explain how to assess the need for training.

Needs assessment consists of an organization analysis, person analysis, and task analysis. The organization analysis determines the appropriateness of training by evaluating the characteristics of the organization, including its strategy, resources, and management support. The person analysis determines individuals' needs and readiness for training. The task analysis identifies the tasks, knowledge, skills, and behaviors that training should emphasize. It is based on examination of the conditions in which tasks are performed, including equipment and environment of the job, time constraints, safety considerations, and performance standards.

LO 7-3 Explain how to assess employees' readiness for training.

Readiness for training is a combination of employee characteristics and positive work environment that permit training. The necessary employee characteristics include ability to learn the subject matter, favorable attitudes toward the training, and motivation to learn. A positive work environment avoids situational constraints such as lack of money and time. In a positive environment, both peers and management support training.

LO 7-4 Describe how to plan an effective training program.

Planning begins with establishing objectives for the training program. These should define an expected performance or outcome, the desired level of performance, and the conditions under which the performance should occur. Based on the objectives, the planner decides who will provide the training, what topics the training will cover, what training methods to use, and how to evaluate the training. Even when organizations purchase outside training, someone in the organization, usually a member of the HR department, often is responsible for training administration. The training methods selected should be related to the objectives and content of the training program. Training methods may include presentation methods, hands-on methods, or group-building methods.

LO 7-5 Compare widely used training methods.

Classroom instruction is most widely used and is one of the least expensive and least time-consuming ways to present information on a specific topic to many trainees. It also allows for group interaction and may include hands-on practice. Audiovisual and computer-based training need not require that trainees attend a class, so organizations can reduce time and money spent on training. Computer-based training may be interactive and may provide for group interaction. On-the-job training methods such as apprenticeships and internships give trainees firsthand experiences. A simulation represents a real-life situation, enabling trainees to see the effects of their decisions without dangerous or expensive consequences. Business games and case studies are other methods for practicing decision-making skills. Participants need to come together in one location or collaborate online. Behavior modeling gives trainees a chance to observe desired behaviors, so this technique can be effective for teaching interpersonal skills. Experiential and adventure learning programs provide an opportunity for group members to interact in challenging circumstances but may exclude members with disabilities. Team training focuses a team on achievement of a common goal. Action learning offers relevance, because the training focuses on an actual work-related problem.

LO 7-6 Summarize how to implement a successful training program.

Implementation should apply principles of learning and seek transfer of training. In general, effective training communicates learning objectives, presents information in distinctive and memorable ways, and helps trainees link the subject matter to their jobs. Employees are most likely to learn when training is linked to job experiences and tasks. Employees learn best when they demonstrate or practice what they have learned and when they receive feedback that helps them improve. Trainees remember information better when it is broken into small chunks, presented with visual images, and practiced many times. Written materials should be easily readable by trainees. Transfer of training is most likely when there is social support (from

managers and peers), technical support, and self-management.

LO 7-7 Evaluate the success of a training program.

Evaluation of training should look for transfer of training by measuring whether employees are performing the tasks taught in the training program. Assessment of training also should evaluate training outcomes, such as change in attitude, ability to perform a new skill, and recall of facts or behaviors taught in the training program. Training should result in improvement in the group's or organization's outcomes, such as customer satisfaction or sales. An economic measure of training success is return on investment.

LO 7-8 Describe training methods for employee orientation and diversity management.

Employee orientation is training designed to prepare employees to perform their job effectively, learn about the organization, and establish work relationships. Organizations provide for orientation because, no matter how realistic the information provided during employment interviews and site visits, people feel shock and surprise when they start a new job, and they need to learn the details of how to perform the job. A typical orientation program includes information about the overall company and the department in which the new employee will be working, covering social as well as technical aspects of the job. Orientation programs may combine several training methods, from printed materials to on-the-job training to e-learning. Diversity training is designed to change employee attitudes about diversity and/or develop skills needed to work with a diverse workforce. Evidence regarding these programs suggests that diversity training is most effective if it is tied to business objectives, has management support, emphasizes behaviors and skills, and is tied to organizational policies and practices that value diversity, including a way to measure success.

KEY TERMS

action learning, 215
adventure learning, 213
apprenticeship, 210
avatars, 211
communities of practice, 217
coordination training, 214

cross-training, 214
diversity training, 223
e-learning, 208
electronic performance support
    system, 209
experiential programs, 213

instructional design, 198
internship, 210
learning management system
    (LMS), 199
needs assessment, 200
on-the-job training (OJT), 210

REVIEW AND DISCUSSION QUESTIONS

1. "Melinda!" bellowed Toran to the company's HR specialist, "I've got a problem, and you've got to solve it. I can't get people in this plant to work together as a team. As if I don't have enough trouble with our competitors and our past-due accounts, now I have to put up with running a zoo. You're responsible for seeing that the staff gets along. I want a training proposal on my desk by Monday." Assume you are Melinda.
   a. Is training the solution to this problem? How can you determine the need for training?
   b. Summarize how you would conduct a needs assessment.

2. How should an organization assess readiness for learning? In Question 1, how do Toran's comments suggest readiness (or lack of readiness) for learning?

3. Assume you are the human resource manager of a small seafood company. The general manager has told you that customers have begun complaining about the quality of your company's fresh fish. Currently, training consists of senior fish cleaners showing new employees how to perform the job. Assuming your needs assessment indicates a need for training, how would you plan a training program? What steps should you take in planning the program?

4. Many organizations turn to e-learning as a less-expensive alternative to classroom training. What are some other advantages of substituting e-learning for classroom training? What are some disadvantages?

5. Suppose the managers in your organization tend to avoid delegating projects to the people in their groups. As a result, they rarely meet their goals. A training needs analysis indicates that an appropriate solution is training in management skills. You have identified two outside training programs that are consistent with your goals. One program involves experiential programs, and the other is an inter-active computer program. What are the strengths and weaknesses of each technique? Which would you choose? Why?

6. Consider your current job or a job you recently held. What types of training did you receive for the job? What types of training would you like to receive? Why?

7. A manufacturing company employs several maintenance employees. When a problem occurs with the equipment, a maintenance employee receives a description of the symptoms and is supposed to locate and fix the source of the problem. The company recently installed a new, complex electronics system. To prepare its maintenance workers, the company provided classroom training. The trainer displayed electrical drawings of system components and posed problems about the system. The trainer would point to a component in a drawing and ask, "What would happen if this component were faulty?" Trainees would study the diagrams, describe the likely symptoms, and discuss how to repair the problem. If you were responsible for this company's training, how would you evaluate the success of this training program?

8. In Question 7, suppose the maintenance supervisor has complained that trainees are having difficulty trouble-shooting problems with the new electronics system. They are spending a great deal of time on problems with the system and coming to the supervisor with frequent questions that show a lack of understanding. The supervisor is convinced that the employees are motivated to learn the system, and they are well qualified. What do you think might be the problems with the current training program? What recommendations can you make for improving the program?

9. Who should be involved in orientation of new employees? Why would it not be appropriate to provide employee orientation purely online?

10. Why do organizations provide diversity training? What kinds of goals are most suitable for such training?

EXPERIENCING HR

Go online and visit eHow (**http://www.ehow.com**), YouTube (**http://www.youtube.com**), or another site recommended by your instructor. Use the site's search function to look up a lesson on how to do one of the following tasks:

- Conduct an interview
- Dress business casual
- Give a presentation
- Clean a laptop computer
- Handle an angry customer

View the presentation you selected, taking notes to help you recall its content and methods. Then write a one-page review of the presentation. Rate the presentation's content (was it relevant and understandable?) and methods (was it engaging and effective?). Also, note whether the presentation provided a means for assessing what was learned. Finally, suggest how the presentation could have been improved. What could make it more effective as part of an employer's training program?

TAKING RESPONSIBILITY: How Barnes-Jewish Hospital Trains Nurses to Cope

Barnes-Jewish Hospital has been ranked by *U.S. News and World Report* as one of the best hospitals in the United States and as its top-rated hospital for St. Louis, Missouri. The 1,258-bed not-for-profit hospital is part of the BJC HealthCare chain, which serves patients in the St. Louis metropolitan area. A big part of the Barnes-Jewish staff is its more than 2,500 full-time and 800 part-time registered nurses.

A registered nurse comes to Barnes-Jewish (or any other) hospital after extensive training in human health and patient care. But one of the major challenges facing a nurse is not a matter of deploying technical skills; it is how to cope with the day-in, day-out experience of witnessing patients' suffering and sometimes death. Especially during periods when several of their patients have poor outcomes, nurses can feel worn down by the stress. They can suffer "compassion fatigue," experienced as sadness, despair, and reduced empathy. At worst, nurses' health suffers, and they find themselves avoiding certain patients and perhaps failing to deliver quality care when they fail to notice or correctly interpret patients' needs.

A commitment to high-quality care and concern for its nurses' well-being has led Barnes-Jewish to offer training in how to cope with stress and avoid or recover from compassion fatigue. The issue first received attention when three nurse managers agreed they had a problem with high turnover and poor patient satisfaction with nursing care in the oncology unit. Because patients with cancer can become very ill, caring for them can pose a heavy emotional and physical strain. Nurses seemed to be coping by detaching themselves emotionally, which patients experienced in a negative way. With this evidence of a problem, the nurse managers asked Barnes-Jewish's director of research for patient care services and the head of its patient and family counseling program to help. They interviewed nurses and concluded that the

issue was compassion fatigue, so they suggested a program to help the nurses cope.

The hospital contracted with Eric Gentry, a psychotherapist with a specialty in teaching disaster responders and emergency physicians how to manage stress. He developed a program suitable for use with the nurses and other staff members at the hospital. The course describes symptoms of compassion fatigue and activities that promote resiliency in the face of stress. According to the course, caregivers will be more resilient if they take five steps: (1) self-regulation, or simple exercises such as deep breathing to lower the physical response when they perceive a threat; (2) intentionality, which means reminding themselves to follow their values and original motivation, rather than being overwhelmed by other people's endless demands; (3) self-validation, in which they keep in mind the positive impact they have on patients; (4) formation of a support network; and (5) self-care so they do not burn out.

The hospital first tried the program in a pilot test with 14 oncology nurses. After five weeks of 90-minute sessions once a week, the nurses saw an improvement in their coping ability. The hospital decided to make the program available to all the oncology nurses. Gentry trained 25 hospital staffers—including physician assistants, psychologists, chaplains, and social workers—to deliver the course. Seeing the impact on the oncology department, others in the hospital became interested in the training, so Barnes-Jewish recently made it available to the entire staff, including doctors, nurses, and support personnel.

Nurses who have participated in the training say parts of it have felt strange. Not everyone was eager to gaze into a partner's eyes and state affirmations, and male employees were sometimes mystified by an exercise that involved relaxing pelvic-floor muscles (a muscle group that tends to tighten under stress). However, after completing the program, nurses have reported feeling more positive about their profession and better able to cope with the stress that goes with it.

Questions

1. How did Barnes-Jewish Hospital assess the need for training? Do you think training was the appropriate solution to its problem? Why or why not?
2. How did the hospital go about planning its training to combat compassion fatigue? How well did the plans align with the organization's needs?
3. How could Barnes-Jewish assess the effectiveness of its training program?

SOURCES: "U.S. News Best Hospitals 2011–12: Barnes-Jewish Hospital/Washington University," *U.S. News & World Report*, http://health.usnews.com, accessed March 15, 2012; BJC HealthCare, home page, http://www.bjc.org, accessed March 15, 2012; Cynthia Billhartz Gregorian, "Nurses Take Steps to Battle Compassion Fatigue," *St. Louis Post-Dispatch*, January 12, 2012, Business & Company Resource Center, http://galenet.galegroup.com; Laura Landro, "When Nurses Catch Compassion Fatigue, Patients Suffer," *The Wall Street Journal*, January 3, 2012, http://online.wsj.com.

MANAGING TALENT: SunTrust Takes Training to the Bank

SunTrust Banks, based in Atlanta, operates the eighth-largest U.S. bank. It also has several subsidiaries offering other financial services such as mortgage banking, insurance, and investment management. The bank serves customers in Florida, Georgia, Maryland, North Carolina, South Carolina, Tennessee, Virginia, West Virginia, and the District of Columbia. As the banking industry struggled to recover from the recent financial crisis and recession (and new regulations) that followed, SunTrust's management decided that the key to the company's future lay with fully engaging employees in serving customers. That approach is consistent with the company's mission of "helping people and institutions prosper."

SunTrust began to restructure its banking business in accordance with three guiding principles: (1) operating as a single team; (2) putting clients first; and (3) focusing on profitable growth. This principle-driven approach to growth requires managers who know how to foster employees' commitment to their work and their clients. To that end, SunTrust has made it a priority to develop managers' leadership skills. First-line managers receive training in how to coach and lead others. Middle managers work with mentors on their leadership skills. Upper-level managers use assessments by peers, subordinates, and others to identify areas for growth and, with coaching, develop leadership skills taught during a three-week training program.

SunTrust also selects its top 3,500 managers to receive training in employee engagement. Managers learn not only to assess employees' performance in terms of numbers (a natural approach in a bank), but also to consider ways to build positive feelings about meeting goals and serving customers.

For training aimed at emotions to be relevant, it must enable better job performance. To meet the principle of putting customers first, SunTrust conducts surveys of its customers to learn whether they are satisfied with the bank's products and customer service. It also asks employees whether they have the resources they need to succeed at work and know what the company expects of them. Based on the feedback, the bank's learning team creates training materials for how to meet customer expectations in each line of business. In a program called "Building Solid Relationships," employees learn how to define client needs, explain the bank's financial products and services clearly, and help customers choose which products and services will meet their needs. SunTrust's CEO, Bill Rogers, saw the impact of this training firsthand when he visited a branch and peppered the branch manager and a financial services representative with questions about a new product. They invited Rogers to watch them role-play a scene between a representative and a customer. Rogers was impressed with their confidence and knowledge.

The bank also provides learning support on its SunTrust Learning Portal. This Internet portal gives employees easy access to computer-based training and tools for collaboration that can support informal learning.

Since SunTrust initiated the new training programs, it has seen evidence of improved performance. The bank has enjoyed a record pace of growth in deposits and top scores for the industry in client loyalty. Such feedback has given SunTrust's executives the necessary justification for increasing training budgets regardless of economic recession.

This is all taking place at a delicate time for the banking industry. Many citizens are irate about the government's "bank bailouts," question why banks are now very cautious about lending, and object to the fees many banks have charged to make up for revenue that has shrunk elsewhere. SunTrust, for example, tried imposing a monthly fee for unlimited debit card transactions, but reversed the decision after a public outcry. Still, there are signs that banks are emerging from the worst times. Recent examinations by the Federal Reserve show that the amount of capital on hand at SunTrust and other major banks is approaching a level the Fed considers adequate for sustaining another economic downturn. As conditions improve, SunTrust hopes its strategic investment in training will position it at the forefront of the next round of growth.

Questions

1. What training needs did SunTrust have in the broad areas of organization, person, and tasks? How does its training address those needs?

2. For SunTrust's "Building Solid Relationships" training, what training methods do you think would be most effective? Why?

3. How should SunTrust measure the success of its training program?

SOURCES: Dan Fitzpatrick and Victoria McGrane, "Stress Tests Buoy U.S. Banks," *The Wall Street Journal*, March 14, 2012, http://online.wsj.com; SunTrust Banks, "Company Profile," https://www.suntrust.com, accessed March 14, 2012; Mary Slaughter, "Success at SunTrust Begins and Ends with Talent," *T + D*, November 2011, pp. 38–42; Tony Bingham and Pat Galagan, "A Banker's Trust in Training," *T + D*, November 2011, pp. 33–37 (interview with Bill Rogers); Laura Marcinek, "SunTrust Ends Card Fee, Plans Refund of Previous Charges," *Bloomberg Businessweek*, October 31, 2011, http://www.businessweek.com.

 TWITTER FOCUS: How Nick's Pizza Delivers Training Results

Using Twitter, continue the conversation about training after reading the Nick's Pizza & Pub case at **www.mhhe.com/noefund5e**. Engage with your classmates and instructor via Twittter to chat about Nick's training program using the case questions posted on the Noe website. Don't have a Twitter account yet? See the instructions for getting started on the Online Learning Center.

NOTES

1. Justin Brusino, "The Long View: Stuart Crabb," *T + D*, January 2012, pp. 64–65; Kellye Whitney, "Facebook 'Likes' Learning," *Chief Learning Officer*, November 2011, pp. 22–25.
2. R. Noe, *Employee Training and Development*, 5th ed. (New York: Irwin/McGraw-Hill, 2010).
3. Ryann K. Ellis, *A Field Guide to Learning Management Systems*, Learning Circuits (American Society for Training & Development, 2009), accessed at http://www.astd.org.
4. I. L. Goldstein, E. P. Braverman, and H. Goldstein, "Needs Assessment," in *Developing Human Resources*, ed. K. N. Wexley (Washington, DC: Bureau of National Affairs, 1991), pp. 5-35–5-75.
5. J. Z. Rouillier and I. L. Goldstein, "Determinants of the Climate for Transfer of Training" (presented at Society of Industrial/Organizational Psychology meetings, St. Louis, MO, 1991); J. S. Russell, J. R. Terborg, and M. L. Powers, "Organizational Performance and Organizational Level Training and Support," *Personnel Psychology* 38 (1985), pp. 849–63; and H. Baumgartel, G. J. Sullivan, and L. E. Dunn, "How Organizational Climate and Personality Affect the Payoff from Advanced Management Training Sessions," *Kansas Business Review* 5 (1978), pp. 1–10.
6. E. F. Holton III and C. Bailey, "Top-to-Bottom Curriculum Redesign," *Training and Development*, March 1995, pp. 40–44.
7. Eric Spiegel, "Making Science and Math a Priority," *Boston Globe*, December 9, 2011, http://www.boston.com; Lucia Mutikani, "So Many U.S. Manufacturing Jobs, So Few Skilled Workers," Reuters, October 13, 2011, http://www.reuters.com; Elizabeth G. Olson, "Confronting the Coming American Worker Shortage," *Fortune*, May 20, 2011, http://management.fortune.cnn.com.
8. R. A. Noe, "Trainees' Attributes and Attitudes: Neglected Influences on Training Effectiveness," *Academy of Management Review* 11 (1986), pp. 736–49; T. T. Baldwin, R. T. Magjuka, and B. T. Loher, "The Perils of Participation: Effects of Choice on Trainee Motivation and Learning," *Personnel Psychology* 44 (1991), pp. 51–66; and S. I. Tannenbaum, J. E. Mathieu, E. Salas, and J. A. Cannon-Bowers, "Meeting Trainees' Expectations: The Influence of Training Fulfillment on the Development of Commitment, Self-Efficacy, and Motivation," *Journal of Applied Psychology* 76 (1991), pp. 759–69.
9. L. H. Peters, E. J. O'Connor, and J. R. Eulberg, "Situational Constraints: Sources, Consequences, and Future Considerations," in *Research in Personnel and*

Human Resource Management, eds. K. M. Rowland and G. R. Ferris (Greenwich, CT: JAI Press, 1985), vol. 3, pp. 79–114; E. J. O'Connor, L. H. Peters, A. Pooyan, J. Weekley, B. Frank, and B. Erenkranz, "Situational Constraints' Effects on Performance, Affective Reactions, and Turnover: A Field Replication and Extension," *Journal of Applied Psychology* 69 (1984), pp. 663–72; D. J. Cohen, "What Motivates Trainees?" *Training and Development Journal*, November 1990, pp. 91–93; and Russell, Terborg, and Powers, "Organizational Performance."

10. J. B. Tracey, S. I. Trannenbaum, and M. J. Kavanaugh, "Applying Trade Skills on the Job: The Importance of the Work Environment," *Journal of Applied Psychology* 80 (1995), pp. 239–52; P. E. Tesluk, J. L. Farr, J. E. Mathieu, and R. J. Vance, "Generalization of Employee Involvement Training to the Job Setting: Individuals and Situational Effects," *Personnel Psychology* 48 (1995), pp. 607–32; and J. K. Ford, M. A. Quinones, D. J. Sego, and J. S. Sorra, "Factors Affecting the Opportunity to Perform Trained Tasks on the Job," *Personnel Psychology* 45 (1992), pp. 511–27.

11. B. Mager, *Preparing Instructional Objectives*, 2nd ed. (Belmont, CA: Lake, 1984); and B. J. Smith and B. L. Delahaye, *How to Be an Effective Trainer*, 2nd ed. (New York: Wiley, 1987).

12. "2011 Training Industry Report," *Training*, November/December 2011, pp. 22–35.

13. Ibid.; Michael Green and Erin McGill, "The 2011 State of the Industry: Increased Commitment to Workplace Learning," *T + D*, November 2011, http://www.astd.org.

14. Jennifer J. Salopek, "Learning Has a Seat at the Table," *T + D*, October 2011, pp. 49–50.

15. Karina Gonzalez, "iPad a Training Tool at Twin City Hotel," *Pantagraph.com* (Bloomington, IL), March 7, 2012, http://www.pantagraph.com.

16. "Flippin' Pizza Training Staff with New iPad App," *Pizza Market Place*, February 29, 2012, http://www.pizzamarketplace.com.

17. "Best Practices and Outstanding Initiatives," *Training*, January/February 2011, EBSCOhost, http://web.ebscohost.com.

18. American Society for Training and Development, *Learning Circuits: Glossary*, http://www.astd.org/LC/glossary.htm, accessed March 16, 2012.

19. U.S. Department of Labor, Employment and Training Administration (ETA), "At-a-Glance: Three Approaches to Apprenticeship Program Completion, Apprenticeship Final Rule, 29 CFR Part 29," http://www.doleta.gov, accessed March 16, 2012; ETA, "Apprenticeship Final Rule Fact Sheet," http://www.doleta.gov, accessed March

16, 2012; ETA, "At-a-Glance: Electronic Media in Related Instruction, Apprenticeship Final Rule, 29 CFR Part 29," http://www.doleta.gov, accessed March 16, 2012.

20. "Apprenticeships Multiply at Volkswagen," *Chattanooga (TN) Times/Free Press*, February 22, 2012, Business & Company Resource Center, http://galenet.galegroup.com; Chattanooga State Community College, "Automotive Mechatronics Program (AMP)," last modified February 17, 2012, http://www.chattanoogastate.edu.

21. Richard Rothschild, "Basic Chemistry? Paid Internships Tend to Yield Full-Time Jobs," *Workforce Management*, August 2011, Business & Company Resource Center, http://galenet.galegroup.com.

22. W. J. Rothwell and H. C. Kanzanas, "Planned OJT Is Productive OJT," *Training and Development Journal*, October 1990, pp. 53–56.

23. Doug Cameron, "Dreamliner's Here: Now Learn to Fly It," *The Wall Street Journal*, November 1, 2011, http://online.wsj.com.

24. T. Sitzmann, "A Meta-analytic Examination of the Instructional Effectiveness of Computer-Based Simulation Games," *Personnel Psychology* 64 (2011): 489–528; C. Cornell, "Better than the Real Thing?" *Human Resource Executive*, August 2005, pp. 34–37; and S. Boehle, "Simulations: The Next Generation of E-Learning," *Training*, January 2005, pp. 22–31.

25. Richard W. Klomp, Josh S. Spitalnick, and Dori B. Reissman, "Virtual Classroom Immersion Training," *T + D*, January 2011, pp. 38–43.

26. Ladan Nikravan, "More than Fun and Games," *Chief Learning Officer*, January 2012, pp. 20–21.

27. G. P. Latham and L. M. Saari, "Application of Social Learning Theory to Training Supervisors through Behavior Modeling," *Journal of Applied Psychology* 64 (1979), pp. 239–46.

28. D. Brown and D. Harvey, *An Experiential Approach to Organizational Development* (Englewood Cliffs, NJ: Prentice Hall, 2000); and Larissa Jõgi, review of *The Handbook of Experiential Learning and Management Education*, eds. Michael Reynolds and Russ Vince, *Studies in the Education of Adults* 40, no. 2 (Autumn 2008): pp. 232–234, accessed at OCLC FirstSearch, http://newfirstsearch.oclc.org.

29. Mike Thompson, "What Makes Tyson's High-Potential Leadership Program Critical to Company Success?" *T + D*, April 2011, pp. 98–100.

30. J. Cannon-Bowers and C. Bowers, "Team Development and Functioning," in *A Handbook of Industrial and Organizational Psychology*, ed. S. Zedeck, 1: 597–650 (Washington, DC: American Psychological Association, 2011); L. Delise, C. Gorman, A. Brooks, J. Rentsch, and D. Steele-Johnson, "The

Effects of Team Training on Team Outcomes: A Meta-analysis," *Performance Improvement Quarterly* 22 (2010): 53–80.

31. Tracy C. F. Brown, "In Practice: Learning by Doing," *Chief Learning Officer*, October 2011, p. 46.

32. "Best Practices and Outstanding Initiatives."

33. C. E. Schneier, "Training and Development Programs: What Learning Theory and Research Have to Offer," *Personnel Journal*, April 1974, pp. 288–93; M. Knowles, "Adult Learning," in *Training and Development Handbook*, 3rd ed., ed. R. L. Craig (New York: McGraw-Hill, 1987), pp. 168–79; B. J. Smith and B. L. Delahaye, *How to Be an Effective Trainer*, 2nd ed. (New York: Wiley, 1987); and Traci Sitzmann, "Self-Regulating Online Course Engagement," *T&D*, March 2010, Business & Company Resource Center, http://galenet.galegroup.com.

34. K. A. Smith-Jentsch, F. G. Jentsch, S. C. Payne, and E. Salas, "Can Pretraining Experiences Explain Individual Differences in Learning?" *Journal of Applied Psychology* 81 (1996), pp. 110–16.

35. W. McGehee and P. W. Thayer, *Training in Business and Industry* (New York: Wiley, 1961).

36. R. M. Gagne and K. L. Medsker, *The Condition of Learning* (Fort Worth, TX: Harcourt-Brace, 1996).

37. J. C. Naylor and G. D. Briggs, "The Effects of Task Complexity and Task Organization on the Relative Efficiency of Part and Whole Training Methods," *Journal of Experimental Psychology* 65 (1963), pp. 217–24.

38. Katherine Hobson, "Getting Docs to Use PCs," *The Wall Street Journal*, March 15, 2011, http://online.wsj.com.

39. Margery Weinstein, "Mohawk Maximizes Learning," *Training*, January/February 2012, EBSCOhost, http://web.ebscohost.com.

40. R. D. Marx, "Relapse Prevention for Managerial Training: A Model for Maintenance of Behavior Change," *Academy of Management Review* 7 (1982): 433–41; G. P. Latham and C. A. Frayne, "Self-Management Training for Increasing Job Attendance: A Follow-Up and Replication," *Journal of Applied Psychology* 74 (1989): 411–16.

41. D. Sussman, "Strong Medicine Required," *T&D*, November 2005, pp. 34–38.

42. Karie Willyerd and Gene A. Pease, "How Does Social Learning Measure Up?" *T + D*, January 2011, pp. 32–37.

43. M. R. Louis, "Surprise and Sense Making: What Newcomers Experience in Entering Unfamiliar Organizational Settings," *Administrative Science Quarterly* 25 (1980), pp. 226–51.

44. Sarah Nassauer, "How Waiters Read Your Table," *The Wall Street Journal*, February 22, 2012, http://online.wsj.com.

45. Peter Bregman, "Diversity Training Doesn't Work," *Forbes*, March 12, 2012, http://www.forbes.com.

46. Todd Henneman, "Making the Pieces Fit," *Workforce Management*, August 2011, Business & Company Resource Center, http://galenet.galegroup.com.

47. Mary Beauregard, "Culturally Canny," *T + D*, September 2011, p. 88.

48. S. Rynes and B. Rosen, "A Field Study of Factors Affecting the Adoption and Perceived Success of Diversity Training," *Personnel Psychology* 48 (1995), pp. 247–70.

49. Bregman, "Diversity Training Doesn't Work"; Henneman, "Making the Pieces Fit"; and Aparna Nancherta, "Nobody's Perfect: Diversity Training Study Finds Common Flaws," *T&D*, May 2008, OCLC FirstSearch, http://newfirstsearch.oclc.org.

50. Christen McCurdy, "Cultural Competency Training Offered by Oregon Center for Nursing," *The Lund Report*, March 8, 2012, http://www.thelundreport.org; Aaron DeSmet, Monica McGurk, and Elizabeth Schwartz, "Getting More from Your Training Programs," *McKinsey Quarterly*, October 2010, http://www.mckinseyquarterly.com.

Assessing Performance and Developing Employees

PART THREE

8   Managing Employees' Performance

What Do I Need to Know?

After reading this chapter, you should be able to:

LO 8-1 Identify the activities involved in performance management.

LO 8-2 Discuss the purposes of performance management systems.

LO 8-3 Define five criteria for measuring the effectiveness of a performance management system.

LO 8-4 Compare the major methods for measuring performance.

LO 8-5 Describe major sources of performance information in terms of their advantages and disadvantages.

LO 8-6 Define types of rating errors, and explain how to minimize them.

LO 8-7 Explain how to provide performance feedback effectively.

LO 8-8 Summarize ways to produce improvement in unsatisfactory performance.

LO 8-9 Discuss legal and ethical issues that affect performance management.

Introduction

Zions First National Bank, headquartered in Salt Lake City, wanted to get its employees to focus more on the activities that directly contribute to the bank's success. So Zions defined the results it is seeking from the organization as a whole, from each department, and from each employee. The bank sorted these goals into two categories: wildly important goals (WIGs) and pretty important goals (PIGs). WIGs are the results that are most critical, and PIGs are necessary activities but not at the heart of the bank's overall mission.

Once a week, managers meet with their group to review the group's progress on its WIGs. Also, once a month, managers meet one-on-one with each of their employees to discuss the employee's progress toward meeting his or her individual WIGs. The weekly meetings provide an opportunity to see what resources employees need and what skills they must develop if they aren't making enough progress. The emphasis is on the goals ahead rather than on past incidents. In a recent assessment of this system, Zions learned that it not only aligns employees' efforts with company strategy but also is personally satisfying to employees. Most said it helped them develop their knowledge and skills, and most said their supervisors were providing ongoing support and recognition.[1]

Setting goals and holding regular meetings to discuss performance, as managers and employees do at Zions First National Bank, are elements of performance management. **Performance management** is the process through which managers ensure that employees' activities and outputs contribute to the organization's goals. This process requires knowing what activities and outputs are desired, observing whether they occur, and providing feedback to help employees meet expectations. In the course of providing feedback, managers and employees may identify performance problems and establish ways to resolve those problems.

Performance Management
The process through which managers ensure that employees' activities and outputs contribute to the organization's goals.

In this chapter we examine a variety of approaches to performance management. We begin by describing the activities involved in managing performance, then discuss the purpose of carrying out this process. Next, we discuss specific approaches to performance management, including the strengths and weaknesses of each approach. We also look at various sources of performance information. The next section explores the kinds of errors that commonly occur during the assessment of performance, as well as ways to reduce those errors. Then we describe ways of giving performance feedback effectively and intervening when performance must improve. Finally, we summarize legal and ethical issues affecting performance management.

The Process of Performance Management

LO 8-1 Identify the activities involved in performance management.

Although many employees dread the annual performance appraisal meeting at which a boss picks apart the employee's behaviors from the past year, performance management can potentially deliver many benefits—to individual employees as well as to the organization as a whole. Effective performance management can tell top performers they are valued, encourage communication between managers and their employees, establish consistent standards for evaluating employees, and help the organization identify its strongest and weakest employees. To meet these objectives, companies must think of effective performance management as a process, not an event.

Figure 8.1 shows the six steps in the performance management process. As shown in the model, feedback and formal performance evaluation are important parts of the process; however, they are not the only critical components. An effective performance management process contributes to the company's overall competitive advantage and must be given visible support by the CEO and other senior managers. This support ensures that the process is consistently used across the company, appraisals are completed on time, and giving and receiving ongoing performance feedback is recognized as an accepted part of the company's culture.

The first two steps of the process involve identifying what the company is trying to accomplish (its goals or objectives) and developing employee goals and actions to achieve these outcomes. Typically the outcomes benefit customers, the employee's peers or team members, and the organization itself. The goals, behaviors, and activities should be measurable and become part of the employee's job description.

Step three in the process—organizational support—involves providing employees with training, necessary resources and tools, and ongoing feedback between the employee and manager, which focuses on accomplishments as well as issues and challenges that influence performance. For effective performance management, both the manager and the employee have to value feedback and exchange it on a regular basis—not just once or twice a year. Also, the manager needs to make time to provide ongoing feedback to the employee and learn how to give and receive it.

Step four involves evaluating performance; that is, when the manager and employee discuss and compare targeted goals and supporting behavior with actual results. This step includes the annual formal performance review.

Figure 8.1

Steps in the Performance Management Process

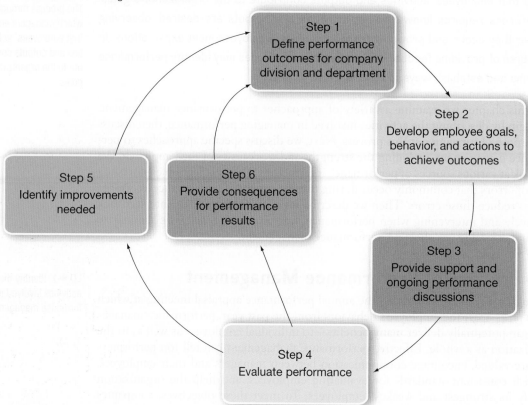

SOURCE: Based on E. Pulakos, *Performance Management* (Oxford, England: Wiley-Blackwell, 2009); H. Aguinis, "An Expanded View of Performance Management," in J. W. Smith and M. London (eds.), *Performance Management* (San Francisco: Jossey-Bass, 2009), pp. 1–43; and J. Russell and L. Russell, "Talk Me Through It: The Next Level of Performance Management," *T + D,* April 2010, pp. 42–48.

The final steps of the performance management process involve both the employee and manager identifying what the employee can do to capitalize on performance strengths and address weaknesses (step 5) and providing consequences for achieving (or failing to achieve) performance outcomes (such as pay increases, bonuses, or action plans) (step 6). This includes identifying training needs; adjusting the type or frequency of feedback the manager provides to the employee; clarifying, adjusting, or modifying performance outcomes; and discussing behaviors or activities that need improvement.

To be effective, the entire performance management process should be reviewed each year to ensure that what is being measured at the employee level aligns strategically with company, division, and departmental goals and objectives.[2]

LO 8-2 Discuss the purposes of performance management systems.

Purposes of Performance Management

Organizations establish performance management systems to meet three broad purposes: strategic, administrative, and developmental. As you read the "HR Oops!" box and the rest of this section, think about which purposes of performance management the airline in that example should have met more effectively.

Strategic purpose means effective performance management helps the organization achieve its business objectives. It does this by helping to link employees' behavior

HR Oops!

When the Rules Don't Fly

Was performance management to blame when a major U.S. airline failed to give a friendly welcome home to a U.S. Army unit returning from Afghanistan? When the 34-member unit arrived in Baltimore for an 18-hour layover, the airline transporting them informed two staff sergeants that they needed to pay $200 for each soldier carrying a fourth bag. The military orders for the unit stated that the bags would be covered by the ticket price, but the sergeants could not persuade the airline's agents. These employees insisted that they had to follow company policy, and according to that policy, checking a fourth bag costs $200.

Airlines impose the fees as a way to keep up with rising transportation costs even as fliers shop around for the lowest airfare. This airline's policy was in line with similar fees at other air carriers. Like other kinds of companies, airlines make their employees responsible for following the rules. Following rules is often the most basic kind of performance standard.

In this case, however, the employees' attempts to follow the rules led the airline into an embarrassing situation. The frustrated sergeants videotaped their reaction at the airport and posted the video on YouTube. Before long, the airline was publicly humiliated for its treatment of soldiers who had been away serving the country. Shortly afterward, the airline announced that it would refund the $2,800 it had charged the soldiers for excess-baggage fees. It noted that the normal procedure is for traveling service members—who fly at a reduced rate—to be reimbursed by the military for any excess-baggage fees. Apparently, the agents had not explained the procedure clearly. Also, carrying an unlimited amount of baggage for free would put airlines at a disadvantage in serving their most profitable customer segment, business customers. These customers place a high value on reliable transportation of their bags and on-time arrivals.

Questions

1. If a company measures performance in terms of rules such as charging customers full price according to company policy, what kinds of strategic objectives does that performance standard help the company meet? What kinds of strategic objectives does that performance standard *not* contribute to (or even interfere with)?
2. To avoid this kind of embarrassment, what kinds of performance standards do you think an airline should establish for employees working at ticket counters?

SOURCES: Adrian C. Ott, "When Scorecards and Metrics Kill Employee Engagement," *Bloomberg Businessweek,* July 12, 2011, http://www.businessweek.com; Raven L. Hill, "Soldiers Returning through BWI Decry Delta Baggage Fees," *Baltimore Sun,* June 8, 2011, http://articles.baltimoresun.com; Jay Boehmer, "Air Service Basics Still Paramount: Arrive on Time, with Bags in Tow," *Business Travel News,* May 2011, EBSCOhost, http://web.ebscohost.com.

with the organization's goals. Performance management starts with defining what the organization expects from each employee. It measures each employee's performance to identify where those expectations are and are not being met. This enables the organization to take corrective action, such as training, incentives, or discipline. Performance management can achieve its strategic purpose only when measurements are truly linked to the organization's goals and when the goals and feedback about performance are communicated to employees. At wireless provider Sprint, employees are appraised in terms of three to five criteria, each linked to one of the company's strategic objectives for improving the customer experience, strengthening the brand, or increasing profits. Employees in Sprint's call centers and retail stores can go online to review their individual objectives and check their progress toward achieving them.[3]

The *administrative purpose* of a performance management system refers to the ways in which organizations use the system to provide information for day-to-day decisions about salary, benefits, and recognition programs. Performance management can also support decision making related to employee retention, termination for poor behavior, and hiring or layoffs. Because performance management supports these administrative decisions, the information in a performance appraisal can have a great impact on the future of individual employees. Managers recognize this, which is the reason they may feel uncomfortable conducting performance appraisals when the appraisal information is negative and, therefore, likely to lead to a layoff, disappointing pay increase, or other negative outcome.

Finally, performance management has a *developmental purpose*, meaning that it serves as a basis for developing employees' knowledge and skills. Even employees who are meeting expectations can become more valuable when they hear and discuss performance feedback. Effective performance feedback makes employees aware of their strengths and of the areas in which they can improve. Discussing areas in which employees fall short can help the employees and their manager uncover the source of problems and identify steps for improvement. Although discussing weaknesses may feel uncomfortable, it is necessary when performance management has a developmental purpose.

Criteria for Effective Performance Management

LO 8-3 Define five criteria for measuring the effectiveness of a performance management system.

In Chapter 6, we saw that there are many ways to predict performance of a job candidate. Similarly, there are many ways to measure the performance of an employee. For performance management to achieve its goals, its methods for measuring performance must be good. Selecting these measures is a critical part of planning a performance management system. Several criteria determine the effectiveness of performance measures:

- *Fit with strategy*—A performance management system should aim at achieving employee behavior and attitudes that support the organization's strategy, goals, and culture. If a company emphasizes customer service, then its performance management system should define the kinds of behavior that contribute to good customer service. Performance appraisals should measure whether employees are engaging in those behaviors. Feedback should help employees improve in those areas. When an organization's strategy changes, human resource personnel should help managers assess how the performance management system should change to serve the new strategy.
- *Validity*—As we discussed in Chapter 6, *validity* is the extent to which a measurement tool actually measures what it is intended to measure. In the case of performance appraisal, validity refers to whether the appraisal measures all the relevant aspects of performance and omits irrelevant aspects of performance. Figure 8.2

Figure 8.2

Contamination and Deficiency of a Job Performance Measure

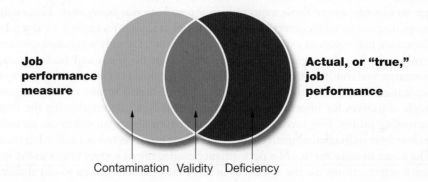

Job performance measure

Actual, or "true," job performance

Contamination   Validity   Deficiency

shows two sets of information. The circle on the left represents all the information in a performance appraisal; the circle on the right represents all relevant measures of job performance. The overlap of the circles contains the valid information. Information that is gathered but irrelevant is "contamination." Comparing salespeople based on how many calls they make to customers could be a contaminated measure. Making a lot of calls does not necessarily improve sales or customer satisfaction, unless every salesperson makes only well-planned calls. Information that is not gathered but is relevant represents a deficiency of the performance measure. For example, suppose a company measures whether employees have good attendance records but not whether they work efficiently. This limited performance appraisal is unlikely to provide a full picture of employees' contribution to the company. Performance measures should minimize both contamination and deficiency.

- *Reliability*—With regard to a performance measure, reliability describes the consistency of the results that the performance measure will deliver. *Interrater reliability* is consistency of results when more than one person measures performance. Simply asking a supervisor to rate an employee's performance on a scale of 1 to 5 would likely have low interrater reliability; the rating will differ depending on who is scoring the employees. *Test-retest reliability* refers to consistency of results over time. If a performance measure lacks test-retest reliability, determining whether an employee's performance has truly changed over time will be impossible.

- *Acceptability*—Whether or not a measure is valid and reliable, it must meet the practical standard of being acceptable to the people who use it. For example, the people who use a performance measure must believe that it is not too time consuming. Likewise, if employees believe the measure is unfair, they will not use the feedback as a basis for improving their performance.

- *Specific feedback*—A performance measure should specifically tell employees what is expected of them and how they can meet those expectations. Being specific helps performance management meet the goals of supporting strategy and developing employees. If a measure does not specify what an employee must do to help the organization achieve its goals, it does not support the strategy. If the measure fails to point out employees' performance problems, they will not know how to improve.

For an example of a company that sets effective standards for performance management, see the "Best Practices" box.

Methods for Measuring Performance

LO 8-4 Compare the major methods for measuring performance.

Organizations have developed a wide variety of methods for measuring performance. Some methods rank each employee to compare employees' performance. Other methods break down the evaluation into ratings of individual attributes, behaviors, or results. Many organizations use a measurement system that includes a variety of the preceding measures, as in the case of applying total quality management to performance management. Table 8.1 compares these methods in terms of our criteria for effective performance management.

Making Comparisons

The performance appraisal method may require the rater to compare one individual's performance with that of others. This method involves some form of ranking, in

How Connecticut Health Foundation Sets Effective Performance Standards

The Connecticut Health Foundation (CHF) is a nonprofit organization with a mission to ensure that groups and individuals are not cut off from access to health care. It provides funding for programs to improve health systems in Connecticut and helps Connecticut residents make informed decisions about health care and advocate for their health. It focuses on three needs it has defined as priorities: children's mental health, oral health, and health disparities that put racial and ethnic groups at a disadvantage. For each need, the organization's leaders establish yearly objectives the agency should attain to fulfill its mission.

Making progress on these difficult challenges requires a dedicated staff of employees who are clear about what they are expected to do. The person responsible for performance management of these employees is Carol Pollack, CHF's vice president of finance and operations. Her broad responsibilities include accounting, technology, and human resource management. Pollack established a performance management system

with the assistance of an HR consulting firm called Kardas Larson.

At CHF, each employee collaborates with his or her supervisor to define the employee's performance objectives. The goal is to establish objectives that are specific, measurable, involve doable but difficult actions, are related to job content, and have an established time frame. Because the organization has already established and published yearly organization-level objectives, the supervisor has a sense of what his or her group needs to accomplish to support those objectives. This information enables the manager to support the employee in identifying goals that will contribute to achieving the group's effort.

In practice, meeting these ideals can be challenging. Some accomplishments are difficult to measure, and some appear unrelated to promoting health. For example, attitudes are not easy for a supervisor to measure. CHF addresses this by gathering performance information from an employee's peers, customers, and subordinates. They can indicate whether, for example, they

feel that the employee has treated them with respect. Likewise, measurements of an employee group's morale gauge whether the group's manager is leading effectively. With regard to connecting goals to the organization's mission, it can be easier for employees in the accounting department to think about paying bills on time than to focus on a broader purpose such as "maintaining the integrity of the foundation's financial information." Still, the goal-setting process ensures that people are doing the things that contribute to the organization's overall success.

SOURCES: Carol Pollack, "Measuring Employee Performance: Easier Said than Done!" Connecticut Health Foundation blog, January 3, 2012, http://www.cthealth.org; Carol Pollack, "Employee Performance: From Both an Inside and Outside View," Connecticut Health Foundation blog, January 5, 2012, http://www.cthealth.org; Connecticut Health Foundation, "About Us: What We Do," http://www.cthealth.org, accessed March 23, 2012.

which some employees are best, some are average, and others are worst. The usual techniques for making comparisons are simple ranking, forced distribution, and paired comparison.

Simple ranking requires managers to rank employees in their group from the highest performer to the poorest performer. In a variation of this approach, *alternation ranking*, the manager works from a list of employees. First, the manager decides which employee is best and crosses that person's name off the list. From the remaining names, the manager selects the worst employee and crosses off that name. The process continues with the manager selecting the second best, second worst, third best, and so on, until all the employees have been ranked. The major downside of ranking involves validity. To state a performance measure as broadly as "best" or "worst" doesn't define what exactly is good or bad about the person's contribution to the organization. Ranking therefore raises questions about fairness.

Simple Ranking
Method of performance measurement that requires managers to rank employees in their group from the highest performer to the poorest performer.

Table 8.1

Basic Approaches to Performance Measurement

APPROACH	FIT WITH STRATEGY	VALIDITY	RELIABILITY	ACCEPTABILITY	SPECIFICITY
			CRITERIA		
Comparative	Poor, unless manager takes time to make link	Can be high if ratings are done carefully	Depends on rater, but usually no measure of agreement used	Moderate; easy to develop and use but resistant to normative standard	Very low
Attribute	Usually low; requires manager to make link	Usually low; can be fine if developed carefully	Usually low; can be improved by specific definitions of attributes	High; easy to develop and use	Very low
Behavioral	Can be quite high	Usually high; minimizes contamination and deficiency	Usually high	Moderate; difficult to develop, but accepted well for use	Very high
Results	Very high	Usually high; can be both contaminated and deficient	High; main problem can be test–retest—depends on timing of measure	High; usually developed with input from those to be evaluated	High regarding results, but low regarding behaviors necessary to achieve them
Quality	Very high	High, but can be both contaminated and deficient	High	High; usually developed with input from those to be evaluated	High regarding results, but low regarding behaviors necessary to achieve them

Another way to compare employees' performance is with the **forced-distribution method.** This type of performance measurement assigns a certain percentage of employees to each category in a set of categories. For example, the organization might establish the following percentages and categories:

- Exceptional—5%
- Exceeds standards—25%
- Meets standards—55%
- Room for improvement—10%
- Not acceptable—5%

Forced-Distribution Method
Method of performance measurement that assigns a certain percentage of employees to each category in a set of categories.

The manager completing the performance appraisal would rate 5% of his or her employees as exceptional, 25% as exceeding standards, and so on. A forced-distribution approach works best if the members of a group really do vary this much in terms of their performance. It overcomes the temptation to rate everyone high in order to avoid conflict. Research simulating some features of forced rankings found that they improved performance when combined with goals and rewards, especially in the first few years, when the system eliminated the poorest performers.[4] However, a manager who does very well at selecting, motivating, and training employees will have a group of high performers. This manager would have difficulty assigning employees to the bottom categories. In that situation, saying that some employees require improvement or are "not acceptable" not only will be inaccurate, but will hurt morale.

Paired-Comparison Method
Method of performance measurement that compares each employee with each other employee to establish rankings.

Another variation on rankings is the **paired-comparison method.** This approach involves comparing each employee with each other employee to establish rankings. Suppose a manager has five employees, Allen, Barbara, Caitlin, David, and Edgar. The manager compares Allen's performance to Barbara's and assigns one point to whichever employee is the higher performer. Then the manager compares Allen's performance to Caitlin's, then to David's, and finally to Edgar's. The manager repeats this process with Barbara, comparing her performance to Caitlin's, David's, and Edgar's. When the manager has compared every pair of employees, the manager counts the number of points for each employee. The employee with the most points is considered the top-ranked employee. Clearly, this method is time consuming if a group has more than a handful of employees. For a group of 15, the manager must make 105 comparisons.

In spite of the drawbacks, ranking employees offers some benefits. It counteracts the tendency to avoid controversy by rating everyone favorably or near the center of the scale. Also, if some managers tend to evaluate behavior more strictly (or more leniently) than others, a ranking system can erase that tendency from performance scores. Therefore, ranking systems can be useful for supporting decisions about how to distribute pay raises or layoffs. Some ranking systems are easy to use, which makes them acceptable to the managers who use them. A major drawback of rankings is that they often are not linked to the organization's goals. Also, a simple ranking system leaves the basis for the ranking open to interpretation. In that case, the rankings are not helpful for employee development and may hurt morale or result in legal challenges.

Rating Individuals

Instead of focusing on arranging a group of employees from best to worst, performance measurement can look at each employee's performance relative to a uniform set of standards. The measurement may evaluate employees in terms of attributes (characteristics or traits) believed desirable. Or the measurements may identify whether employees have *behaved* in desirable ways, such as closing sales or completing assignments. For both approaches, the performance management system must identify the desired attributes or behaviors, then provide a form on which the manager can rate the employee in terms of those attributes or behaviors. Typically, the form includes a rating scale, such as a scale from 1 to 5, where 1 is the worst performance and 5 is the best.

Graphic Rating Scale
Method of performance measurement that lists traits and provides a rating scale for each trait; the employer uses the scale to indicate the extent to which an employee displays each trait.

Rating Attributes   The most widely used method for rating attributes is the **graphic rating scale**. This method lists traits and provides a rating scale for each trait. The employer uses the scale to indicate the extent to which the employee being rated displays the traits. The rating scale may provide points to circle (as on a scale going from 1 for poor to 5 for excellent), or it may provide a line representing a range of scores, with the manager marking a place along the line. Figure 8.3 shows an example of a graphic rating scale that uses a set of ratings from 1 to 5. A drawback of this approach is that it leaves to the particular manager the decisions about what is "excellent knowledge" or "commendable judgment" or "poor interpersonal skills." The result is low reliability because managers are likely to arrive at different judgments.

Figure 8.3

Example of a Graphic Rating Scale

The following areas of performance are significant to most positions. Indicate your assessment of performance on each dimension by circling the appropriate rating.

PERFORMANCE DIMENSION	RATING				
	DISTINGUISHED	EXCELLENT	COMMENDABLE	ADEQUATE	POOR
Knowledge	5	4	3	2	1
Communication	5	4	3	2	1
Judgment	5	4	3	2	1
Managerial skill	5	4	3	2	1
Quality performance	5	4	3	2	1
Teamwork	5	4	3	2	1
Interpersonal skills	5	4	3	2	1
Initiative	5	4	3	2	1
Creativity	5	4	3	2	1
Problem solving	5	4	3	2	1

To get around this problem, some organizations use **mixed-standard scales,** which use several statements describing each trait to produce a final score for that trait. The manager scores the employee in terms of how the employee compares to each statement. Consider the sample mixed-standard scale in Figure 8.4. To create this scale, the organization determined that the relevant traits are initiative, intelligence, and relations with others. For each trait, sentences were written to describe a person having a high level of that trait, a medium level, and a low level. The sentences for the traits were rearranged so that the nine statements about the three traits are mixed together. The manager who uses this scale reads each sentence, then indicates whether the employee performs above (+), at (0), or below (−) the level described. The key in the middle section of Figure 8.4 tells how to use the pluses, zeros, and minuses to score performance. Someone who excels at every level of performance (pluses for high, medium, and low performance) receives a score of 7 for that trait. Someone who fails to live up to every description of performance (minuses for high, medium, and low) receives a score of 1 for that trait. The bottom of Figure 8.4 calculates the scores for the ratings used in this example.

Mixed-Standard Scales Method of performance measurement that uses several statements describing each trait to produce a final score for that trait.

Rating attributes is the most popular way to measure performance in organizations. In general, attribute-based performance methods are easy to develop and can be applied to a wide variety of jobs and organizations. If the organization is careful to identify which attributes are associated with high performance, and to define them carefully on the appraisal form, these methods can be reliable and valid. However, appraisal forms often fail to meet this standard. In addition, measurement of attributes is rarely linked to the organization's strategy. Furthermore, employees tend perhaps rightly to be defensive about receiving a mere numerical rating on some attribute. How would you feel if you were told you scored 2 on a 5-point scale of initiative or communication skill? The number might seem arbitrary, and it doesn't tell you how to improve.

An employee's performance measurement differs from job to job. For example, a car dealer's performance is measured by the dollar amount of sales, the number of new customers, and customer satisfaction surveys. How would the performance measurements of a car dealer differ from those of an auto mechanic?

Figure 8.4

Example of a Mixed-Standard Scale

Three traits being assessed:	Levels of performance in statements:
Initiative (INTV)	High (H)
Intelligence (INTG)	Medium (M)
Relations with others (RWO)	Low (L)

Instructions: Please indicate next to each statement whether the employee's performance is above (+), equal to (0), or below (−) the statement.

INTV	H	1. This employee is a real self-starter. The employee always takes the initiative and his/her superior never has to prod this individual.	+
INTG	M	2. While perhaps this employee is not a genius, s/he is a lot more intelligent than many people I know.	+
RWO	L	3. This employee has a tendency to get into unnecessary conflicts with other people.	0
INTV	M	4. While generally this employee shows initiative, occasionally his/her superior must prod him/her to complete work.	±
INTG	L	5. Although this employee is slower than some in understanding things, and may take a bit longer in learning new things, s/he is of average intelligence.	+
RWO	H	6. This employee is on good terms with everyone. S/he can get along with people even when s/he does not agree with them.	−
INTV	L	7. This employee has a bit of a tendency to sit around and wait for directions.	+
INTG	H	8. This employee is extremely intelligent, and s/he learns very rapidly.	−
RWO	M	9. This employee gets along with most people. Only very occasionally does s/he have conflicts with others on the job, and these are likely to be minor.	−

Scoring Key:

STATEMENTS			SCORE
HIGH	MEDIUM	LOW	
+	+	+	7
0	+	+	6
−	+	+	5
−	0	+	4
−	−	+	3
−	−	0	2
−	−	−	1

Example score from preceding ratings:

	STATEMENTS			SCORE
	HIGH	MEDIUM	LOW	
Initiative	+	+	+	7
Intelligence	0	+	+	6
Relations with others	−	−	0	2

Rating Behaviors One way to overcome the drawbacks of rating attributes is to measure employees' behavior. To rate behaviors, the organization begins by defining which behaviors are associated with success on the job. Which kinds of employee behavior help the organization achieve its goals? The appraisal form asks the manager to rate an employee in terms of each of the identified behaviors.

One way to rate behaviors is with the **critical-incident method**. This approach requires managers to keep a record of specific examples of the employee acting in ways that are either effective or ineffective. Here's an example of a critical incident in the performance evaluation of an appliance repairperson:

> A customer called in about a refrigerator that was not cooling and was making a clicking noise every few minutes. The technician prediagnosed the cause of the problem and checked his truck for the necessary parts. When he found he did not have them, he checked the parts out from inventory so that the customer's refrigerator would be repaired on his first visit and the customer would be satisfied promptly.

This incident provides evidence of the employee's knowledge of refrigerator repair and concern for efficiency and customer satisfaction. Evaluating performance in this specific way gives employees feedback about what they do well and what they do poorly. The manager can also relate the incidents to how the employee is helping the company achieve its goals. Keeping a daily or weekly log of critical incidents requires significant effort, however, and managers may resist this requirement. Also, critical incidents may be unique, so they may not support comparisons among employees.

A **behaviorally anchored rating scale (BARS)** builds on the critical-incidents approach. The BARS method is intended to define performance dimensions specifically using statements of behavior that describe different levels of performance.[5] (The statements are "anchors" of the performance levels.) The scale in Figure 8.5 shows various performance levels for the behavior of "preparing for duty." The statement at the top (rating 7) describes the highest level of preparing for duty. The statement at the bottom describes behavior associated with poor performance. These statements are based on data about past performance. The organization gathers many critical incidents representing effective and ineffective performance, then classifies them from most to least effective. When experts about the job agree the statements clearly represent levels of performance, they are used as anchors to guide the rater. Although BARS can improve interrater reliability, this method can bias the manager's memory. The statements used as anchors can help managers remember similar behaviors, at the expense of other critical incidents.[6]

A **behavioral observation scale (BOS)** is a variation of a BARS. Like a BARS, a BOS is developed from critical incidents.[7] However, while a BARS discards many examples in creating the rating scale, a BOS uses many of them to define all behaviors necessary for effective performance (or behaviors that signal ineffective performance). As a result, a BOS may use 15 behaviors to define levels of performance. Also, a BOS asks the manager to rate the frequency with which the employee has exhibited the behavior during the rating period. These ratings are averaged to compute an overall performance rating. Figure 8.6 provides a simplified example of a BOS for measuring the behavior "overcoming resistance to change."

A major drawback of this method is the amount of information required. A BOS can have 80 or more behaviors, and the manager must remember how often the employee exhibited each behavior in a 6- to 12-month rating period. This is taxing enough for one employee, but managers often must rate 10 or more employees. Even so, compared to BARS and graphic rating scales, managers and employees have said they prefer BOS for ease of use, providing feedback, maintaining objectivity, and suggesting training needs.[8]

Critical-Incident Method
Method of performance measurement based on managers' records of specific examples of the employee acting in ways that are either effective or ineffective.

Behaviorally Anchored Rating Scale (BARS)
Method of performance measurement that rates behavior in terms of a scale showing specific statements of behavior that describe different levels of performance.

Behavioral Observation Scale (BOS)
A variation of a BARS which uses all behaviors necessary for effective performance to rate performance at a task.

Figure 8.5
Task-BARS Rating
Dimension: Patrol
Officer

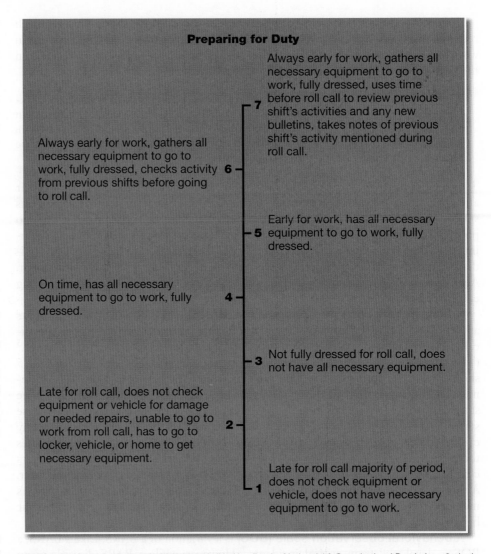

Preparing for Duty

7 — Always early for work, gathers all necessary equipment to go to work, fully dressed, uses time before roll call to review previous shift's activities and any new bulletins, takes notes of previous shift's activity mentioned during roll call.

6 — Always early for work, gathers all necessary equipment to go to work, fully dressed, checks activity from previous shifts before going to roll call.

5 — Early for work, has all necessary equipment to go to work, fully dressed.

4 — On time, has all necessary equipment to go to work, fully dressed.

3 — Not fully dressed for roll call, does not have all necessary equipment.

2 — Late for roll call, does not check equipment or vehicle for damage or needed repairs, unable to go to work from roll call, has to go to locker, vehicle, or home to get necessary equipment.

1 — Late for roll call majority of period, does not check equipment or vehicle, does not have necessary equipment to go to work.

SOURCE: Adapted from R. Harvey, "Job Analysis," in *Handbook of Industrial & Organizational Psychology,* 2nd ed., eds, M. Dunnette and L. Hough (Palo Alto, CA: Consulting Psychologists Press, 1991), p. 138.

Organizational Behavior Modification (OBM)
A plan for managing the behavior of employees through a formal system of feedback and reinforcement.

Another approach to assessment builds directly on a branch of psychology called *behaviorism,* which holds that individuals' future behavior is determined by their past experiences—specifically, the ways in which past behaviors have been reinforced. People tend to repeat behaviors that have been rewarded in the past. Providing feedback and reinforcement can therefore modify individuals' future behavior. Applied to behavior in organizations, **organizational behavior modification (OBM)** is a plan for managing the behavior of employees through a formal system of feedback and reinforcement. Specific OBM techniques vary, but most have four components:[9]

1. Define a set of key behaviors necessary for job performance.
2. Use a measurement system to assess whether the employee exhibits the key behaviors.

Figure 8.6

Example of a Behavioral Observation Scale

Overcoming Resistance to Change

Directions: Rate the frequency of each behavior from 1 (Almost Never) to 5 (Almost Always).

	Almost Never				Almost Always
1. Describes the details of the change to employees.	1	2	3	4	5
2. Explains why the change is necessary.	1	2	3	4	5
3. Discusses how the change will affect the employee.	1	2	3	4	5
4. Listens to the employee's concerns.	1	2	3	4	5
5. Asks the employee for help in making the change work.	1	2	3	4	5
6. If necessary, specifies the date for a follow-up meeting to respond to the employee's concerns.	1	2	3	4	5

Score: Total number of points = _____

Performance

Points	*Performance Rating*
6–10	Below adequate
11–15	Adequate
16–20	Full
21–25	Excellent
26–30	Superior

Scores are set by management.

3. Inform employees of the key behaviors, perhaps in terms of goals for how often to exhibit the behaviors.
4. Provide feedback and reinforcement based on employees' behavior.

OBM techniques have been used in a variety of settings. For example, a community mental health agency used OBM to increase the rates and timeliness of critical job behaviors by showing employees the connection between job behaviors and the agency's accomplishments.[10] This process identified job behaviors related to administration, record keeping, and service provided to clients. Feedback and reinforcement improved staff performance. OBM also increased the frequency of safety behaviors in a processing plant.[11]

Behavioral approaches such as organizational behavior modification and rating scales can be very effective. These methods can link the company's goals to the specific behavior required to achieve those goals. Behavioral methods also can generate specific feedback, along with guidance in areas requiring improvements. As a result, these methods tend to be valid. The people to be measured often help in developing the measures, so acceptance tends to be high as well. When raters are well trained, reliability also tends to be high. However, behavioral methods do not work as well for complex jobs in which it is difficult to see a link between behavior and results or there is more than one good way to achieve success.[12]

Measuring Results

Performance measurement can focus on managing the objective, measurable results of a job or work group. Results might include sales, costs, or productivity (output per worker or per dollar spent on production), among many possible measures. Two of the most popular methods for measuring results are measurement of productivity and management by objectives.

Productivity is an important measure of success because getting more done with a smaller amount of resources (money or people) increases the company's profits. Productivity usually refers to the output of production workers, but it can be used more generally as a performance measure. To do this, the organization identifies the products—set of activities or objectives—it expects a group or individual to accomplish. At a repair shop, for instance, a product might be something like "quality of repair." The next step is to define how to measure production of these products. For quality of repair, the repair shop could track the percentage of items returned because they still do not work after a repair and the percentage of quality-control inspections passed. For each measure, the organization decides what level of performance is desired. Finally, the organization sets up a system for tracking these measures and giving employees feedback about their performance in terms of these measures. This type of performance measurement can be time consuming to set up, but research suggests it can improve productivity.[13]

Management by objectives (MBO) is a system in which people at each level of the organization set goals in a process that flows from top to bottom, so employees at all levels are contributing to the organization's overall goals. These goals become the standards for evaluating each employee's performance. An MBO system has three components:[14]

Management by Objectives (MBO)
A system in which people at each level of the organization set goals in a process that flows from top to bottom, so employees at all levels are contributing to the organization's overall goals; these goals become the standards for evaluating each employee's performance.

1. Goals are specific, difficult, and objective. The goals listed in the second column of Table 8.2 provide two examples for a bank.
2. Managers and their employees work together to set the goals.
3. The manager gives objective feedback through the rating period to monitor progress toward the goals. The two right-hand columns in Table 8.2 are examples of feedback given after one year.

MBO can have a very positive effect on an organization's performance. In 70 studies of MBO's performance, 68 showed that productivity improved.[15] The productivity gains tended to be greatest when top management was highly committed to MBO. Also, because staff members are involved in setting goals, it is likely that MBO systems effectively link individual employees' performance with the organization's overall goals.

Table 8.2

Management by Objectives: Two Objectives for a Bank

KEY RESULT AREA	OBJECTIVE	% COMPLETE	ACTUAL PERFORMANCE
Loan portfolio management	Increase portfolio value by 10% over the next 12 months	90	Increased portfolio value by 9% over the past 12 months
Sales	Generate fee income of $30,000 over the next 12 months	150	Generated fee income of $45,000 over the past 12 months

In general, evaluation of results can be less subjective than other kinds of performance measurement. This makes measuring results highly acceptable to employees and managers alike. Results-oriented performance measurement is also relatively easy to link to the organization's goals. However, measuring results has problems with validity because results may be affected by circumstances beyond each employee's performance. Also, if the organization measures only final results, it may fail to measure significant aspects of performance that are not directly related to those results. If individuals focus only on aspects of performance that are measured, they may neglect significant skills or behaviors. For example, if the organization measures only productivity, employees may not be concerned enough with customer service. The outcome may be high efficiency (costs are low) but low effectiveness (sales are low, too).[16] Finally, focusing strictly on results does not provide guidance on how to improve.

Total Quality Management

The principles of *total quality management*, introduced in Chapter 2, provide methods for performance measurement and management. Total quality management (TQM) differs from traditional performance measurement in that it assesses both individual performance and the system within which the individual works. This assessment is a process through which employees and their customers work together to set standards and measure performance, with the overall goal being to improve customer satisfaction. In this sense, an employee's customers may be inside or outside the organization; a "customer" is whoever uses the goods or services produced by the employee. The feedback aims at helping employees continuously improve the satisfaction of their customers. The focus on continuously improving customer satisfaction is intended to avoid the pitfall of rating individuals on outcomes, such as sales or profits, over which they do not have complete control.

Coaches provide feedback to their team just as managers provide feedback to their employees. Feedback is important so that individuals know what they are doing well and what areas they may need to work on.

With TQM, performance measurement essentially combines measurements of attributes and results. The feedback in TQM is of two kinds: (1) subjective feedback from managers, peers, and customers about the employee's personal qualities such as cooperation and initiative; and (2) objective feedback based on the work process. The second kind of feedback comes from a variety of methods called *statistical quality control*. These methods use charts to detail causes of problems, measures of performance, or relationships between work-related variables. Employees are responsible for tracking these measures to identify areas where they can avoid or correct problems. Because of the focus on systems, this feedback may result in changes to a work process, rather than assuming that a performance problem is the fault of an employee. The TQM system's focus has practical benefits, but it does not serve as well to support decisions about work assignments, training, or compensation.

Sources of Performance Information

LO 8-5 Describe major sources of performance information in terms of their advantages and disadvantages.

360-Degree Performance Appraisal Performance measurement that combines information from the employee's managers, peers, subordinates, self, and customers.

All the methods of performance measurement require decisions about who will collect and analyze the performance information. To qualify for this task, a person should have an understanding of the job requirements and the opportunity to see the employee doing the job. The traditional approach is for managers to gather information about their employees' performances and arrive at performance ratings. However, many sources are possible. In fact, as described in the "Did You Know?" box, many employees welcome feedback from multiple sources. Possibilities of information sources include managers, peers, subordinates, self, and customers.

Using just one person as a source of information poses certain problems. People tend to like some people more than others, and those feelings can bias how an employee's efforts are perceived. Also, one person is likely to see an employee in a limited number of situations. A supervisor, for example, cannot see how an employee behaves when the supervisor is not watching—for example, when a service technician is at the customer's facility. To get as complete an assessment as possible, some organizations combine information from most or all of the possible sources, in what is called a **360-degree performance appraisal**.

Performance management is critical for executing a talent management system and involves one-on-one contact with managers to ensure that proper training and development are taking place.

Managers

The most-used source of performance information is the employee's manager. For example, at online retailer Zappos, managers give their employees two main kinds of performance feedback. They provide regular status reports of routine measures for the position, such as the percentage of time a customer service representative spends on the phone with customers. Managers also are expected to keep track of situations in which they see employees demonstrating the company's core values, including determination, creativity, and openness to change. In formal performance evaluations, managers score employees for exhibiting those values, providing specific examples to back up the scores.[17]

Employees Want More Feedback

A majority of employees (53%) say their only performance feedback comes from their supervisors. But many would appreciate feedback from other sources as well. This may help to explain why barely more than one-third (37%) said they have received useful performance feedback and less than half (45%) said their feedback was fair and accurate.

Question

How might obtaining performance feedback from multiple sources help to make the information more fair, accurate, and useful?

SOURCES: "U.S. Employees Desire More Sources of Feedback for Performance Reviews," *T + D*, February 2012, p. 18; Cornerstone OnDemand, "Stopping the Exodus: Findings from the Cornerstone OnDemand/Harris Employee Performance Management Study," news release, December 6, 2011, http://www.cornerstoneondemand.com; John Hollon, "Tired of Poor Performance Appraisals? Survey Shows Most Workers Are, Too," *TLNT,* December 8, 2011, http://www.tlnt.com.

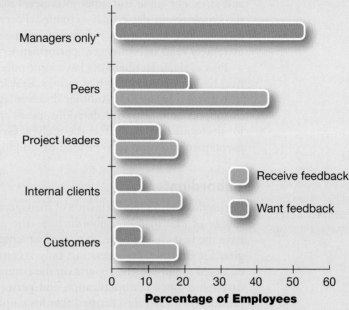

Feedback Source

Categories: Managers only*, Peers, Project leaders, Internal clients, Customers

Percentage of Employees

Legend: Receive feedback, Want feedback

* Percentage of employees wanting feedback from managers not given.

It is usually safe for organizations to assume that supervisors have extensive knowledge of the job requirements and that they have enough opportunity to observe their employees. In other words, managers possess the basic qualifications for this responsibility. Another advantage of using managers to evaluate performance is that they have an incentive to provide accurate and helpful feedback because their own success depends so much on their employees' performance.[18] Finally, when managers try to observe employee behavior or discuss performance issues in the feedback session, their feedback can improve performance, and employees tend to perceive the appraisal as accurate.[19]

Still, in some situations, problems can occur with using supervisors as the source of performance information. For employees in some jobs, the supervisor does not have enough opportunity to observe the employee performing job duties. A sales manager with many outside salespeople cannot be with the salespeople on many visits to customers. Even if the sales manager does make a point of traveling with salespeople for a few days, they are likely to be on their best behavior while the manager is there. The manager cannot observe how they perform at other times.

Peers

Another source of performance information is the employee's peers or co-workers. Peers are an excellent source of information about performance in a job where the supervisor does not often observe the employee. Examples include law enforcement and sales. For these and other jobs, peers may have the most opportunity to observe the employee in day-to-day activities. Peers have expert knowledge of job requirements. They also bring a different perspective to the evaluation and can provide extremely valid assessments of performance.[20]

Peer evaluations obviously have some potential disadvantages. Friendships (or rivalries) have the potential to bias ratings. Research, however, has provided little evidence that this is a problem.[21] Another disadvantage is that when the evaluations are done to support administrative decisions, peers are uncomfortable with rating employees for decisions that may affect themselves. Generally, peers are more favorable toward participating in reviews to be used for employee development.[22]

Subordinates

For evaluating the performance of managers, subordinates are an especially valuable source of information. Subordinates—the people reporting to the manager—often have the best chance to see how well a manager treats employees. At HCL Technologies, for example, managers not only receive reviews from their employees but are expected to publish the reports on the company's internal website to create a climate that values open communication and personal development. Sanjeev Nikore, a vice president who did this, learned that his employees found him resistant to delegating. He acknowledged he needed to improve his people skills, made some changes, and earned a key promotion.[23]

Subordinate evaluations have some potential problems because of the power relationships involved. Subordinates are reluctant to say negative things about the person to whom they report; they prefer to provide feedback anonymously. Managers, however, have a more positive reaction to this type of feedback when the subordinates are identified. When feedback forms require that the subordinates identify themselves, they tend to give the manager higher ratings.[24] Another problem is that when managers receive ratings from their subordinates, the employees have more power, so managers tend to emphasize employee satisfaction, even at the expense of productivity. This issue arises primarily when the evaluations are used for administrative decisions. Therefore, as with peer evaluations, subordinate evaluations are most appropriate for developmental purposes. To protect employees, the process should be anonymous and use at least three employees to rate each manager.

Despite these challenges, subordinate ratings of managers could become even more widespread for the simple reason that individuals are growing used to the experience of using social media to publish online ratings of everything from movies and restaurants to professors and doctors. For more on this phenomenon and how it might affect performance management, see the "HRM Social" box.

Self

No one has a greater chance to observe the employee's behavior on the job than does the employee himself or herself. Self-ratings are rarely used alone, but they can contribute valuable information. A common approach is to have employees evaluate their

Crowdsourcing: The Future of Appraisals?

The collaborative tools of social media can allow individuals to work together by contributing small pieces to a bigger project. Especially when this is done on a large scale, it is known as *crowdsourcing*. An employer might conduct a research project quickly by inviting many people to complete small portions of it simultaneously. Or a travel website might invite travelers to post reviews of hotels and airlines to create an online travel guide.

With regard to performance management, Harvard professor Linda Hill and executive coach Kent Lineback propose that performance appraisals be "crowdsourced" to all of a manager's employees—or perhaps to anyone a manager or employee works with. Hill and Lineback predict that such reviewing will surely take place: reviews of workplaces are already popping up online, alongside websites where customers and students evaluate their experiences. The question, rather, is whether employers will operate these websites as part of an official performance management system or leave the operation of review sites to outsiders.

Hill and Lineback say crowdsourcing management reviews can offer real benefits. The evaluations easily provide managers with much more information than they typically can get from a traditional review process. Also, when employees are asked to give their opinions and management responds to feedback, employees feel engaged, and the process tends to build trust.

Certainly, these systems also have drawbacks. Anyone who has read online comments knows many are neither relevant nor appropriate, to put it politely. This is especially true when comments are posted anonymously, yet employees would be reluctant to post anything negative (no matter how true or significant) if their names would appear with their comments. Anonymous employees might use crowdsourcing as a chance to get even with a boss they dislike.

Weighing the concerns against the potential advantages, employers need to establish appropriate guidelines for accepting performance reviews on social media and applying them to performance evaluation or management development. One approach is to have all responses "curated," or edited to be sure all comments are relevant and appropriate. The employer also can invite individual reviews but report them as a group evaluation. The employer can, for example, determine areas of performance that are important for success (say, delegating, communicating, and giving directions clearly) and ask reviewers to rate a manager or employee on each dimension. Then it presents the person with the group's average score on each dimension. These results could show employees how their work is perceived throughout the organization. Of course, for this process to succeed, the criteria rated must actually be related to success, and employees must be given the training and other resources they need to perform well on each dimension. The organization also would have to train all employees, not just managers, in how to give constructive feedback.

SOURCES: Linda A. Hill and Kent Lineback, "Crowdsource Management Reviews," *Harvard Business Review*, January–February 2012, pp. 60–61; Linda Hill and Kent Lineback, "Crowdsourcing Management Reviews for Better Management," *Harvard Business Review*, January 13, 2012, http://blogs.hbr.org; Amanda Seidler, "Crowdsourcing and Curating the Performance Evaluation Process," viaPeople, July 22, 2011, http://web.viapeople.com.

own performance before the feedback session. This activity gets employees thinking about their performance. Areas of disagreement between the self-appraisal and other evaluations can be fruitful topics for the feedback session. At an Australia-based software company called Atlassian, self-appraisals are part of weekly performance feedback. Employees use an online app that displays performance-related questions such as, "How often have you stretched yourself?" and lets employees move a dot along a scale with a range of possible answers. The responses then serve as a catalyst for discussion in meetings between each employee and his or her supervisor.[25]

The obvious problem with self-ratings is that individuals have a tendency to inflate assessments of their performance. Especially if the ratings will be used for administrative decisions, exaggerating one's contributions has practical benefits. Also, social psychologists have found that, in general, people tend to blame outside circumstances for their failures while taking a large part of the credit for their successes. Supervisors can soften this tendency by providing frequent feedback, but because people tend to perceive situations this way, self-appraisals are not appropriate as the basis for administrative decisions.[26]

Customers

Services are often produced and consumed on the spot, so the customer is often the only person who directly observes the service performance and may be the best source of performance information. Many companies in service industries have introduced customer evaluations of employee performance. Marriott Corporation provides a customer satisfaction card in every room and mails surveys to a random sample of its hotel customers. Whirlpool's Consumer Services Division conducts mail and telephone surveys of customers after factory technicians have serviced their appliances. These surveys allow the company to evaluate an individual technician's customer-service behaviors while in the customer's home.

Using customer evaluations of employee performance is appropriate in two situations.[27] The first is when an employee's job requires direct service to the customer or linking the customer to other services within the organization. Second, customer evaluations are appropriate when the organization is interested in gathering information to determine what products and services the customer wants. That is, customer evaluations contribute to the organization's goals by enabling HRM to support the organization's marketing activities. In this regard, customer evaluations are useful both for evaluating an employee's performance and for helping to determine whether the organization can improve customer service by making changes in HRM activities such as training or compensation.

The weakness of customer surveys for performance measurement is their expense. The expenses of a traditional survey can add up to hundreds of dollars to evaluate one individual. Many organizations therefore limit the information gathering to short periods once a year.

LO 8-6 Define types of rating errors, and explain how to minimize them.

Errors in Performance Measurement

As we noted in the previous section, one reason for gathering information from several sources is that performance measurements are not completely objective and errors can occur. People observe behavior, and they have no practical way of knowing all the circumstances, intentions, and outcomes related to that behavior, so they interpret what they see. In doing so, observers make a number of judgment calls and in some situations may even distort information on purpose. Therefore, fairness in rating performance and interpreting performance appraisals requires that managers understand the kinds of distortions that commonly occur.

Types of Rating Errors

Several kinds of errors and biases commonly influence performance measurements:

- People often tend to give a higher evaluation to people they consider similar to themselves. Most of us think of ourselves as effective, so if others are like us, they must be effective, too. Research has demonstrated that this effect is strong.

Unfortunately, it is sometimes wrong, and when similarity is based on characteristics such as race or sex, the decisions may be discriminatory.[28]

- If the rater compares an individual, not against an objective standard, but against other employees, *contrast errors* occur. A competent performer who works with exceptional people may be rated lower than competent simply because of the contrast.
- Raters make *distributional errors* when they tend to use only one part of a rating scale. The error is called *leniency* when the reviewer rates everyone near the top, *strictness* when the rater favors lower rankings, and *central tendency* when the rater puts everyone near the middle of the scale. Distributional errors make it difficult to compare employees rated by the same person. Also, if different raters make different kinds of distributional errors, scores by these raters cannot be compared.
- Raters often let their opinion of one quality color their opinion of others. For example, someone who speaks well might be seen as helpful or talented in other areas simply because of the overall good impression created by this one quality. Or someone who is occasionally tardy might be seen as lacking in motivation. When the bias is in a favorable direction, this is called the *halo error*. When it involves negative ratings, it is called the *horns error*. Halo error can mistakenly tell employees they don't need to improve in any area, while horns error can cause employees to feel frustrated and defensive.

Ways to Reduce Errors

Usually people make these errors unintentionally, especially when the criteria for measuring performance are not very specific. Raters can be trained how to avoid rating errors.[29] Prospective raters watch videos whose scripts or storylines are designed to lead them to make specific rating errors. After rating the fictional employees in the videos, raters discuss their rating decisions and how such errors affected their rating decisions. Training programs offer tips for avoiding the errors in the future.

Another training method for raters focuses on the complex nature of employee performance.[30] Raters learn to look at many aspects of performance that deserve their attention. Actual examples of performance are studied to bring out various performance dimensions and the standards for those dimensions. This training aims to help raters evaluate employees' performance more thoroughly and accurately.

Political Behavior in Performance Appraisals

Unintentional errors are not the only cause of inaccurate performance measurement. Sometimes the people rating performance distort an evaluation on purpose to advance their personal goals. This kind of appraisal politics is unhealthy especially because the resulting feedback does not focus on helping employees contribute to the organization's goals. High-performing employees who are rated unfairly will become frustrated, and low-performing employees who are overrated will be rewarded rather than encouraged to improve. Therefore, organizations try to identify and discourage appraisal politics.

Several characteristics of appraisal systems and company culture tend to encourage appraisal politics. Appraisal politics are most likely to occur when raters are accountable to the employee being rated, the goals of rating are not compatible with one another, performance appraisal is directly linked to highly desirable rewards, top executives tolerate or ignore distorted ratings, and senior employees tell newcomers company "folklore" that includes stories about distorted ratings.

Political behavior occurs in every organization. Organizations can minimize appraisal politics by establishing an appraisal system that is fair. One technique is to hold a **calibration meeting,** a gathering at which managers discuss employee performance ratings and provide evidence supporting their ratings with the goal of eliminating the influence of rating errors. As they discuss ratings and the ways they arrive at ratings, managers may identify undervalued employees, notice whether they are much harsher or more lenient than other managers, and help each other focus on how well ratings are associated with relevant performance outcomes. In a survey by the Society for Human Resource Management, 35% of companies holding calibration meetings changed evaluations regularly, and another 63% reported making infrequent changes. The biggest reasons for a change were that managers discovered they weren't rating their employees consistently or learned new information about employees.[31] The organization can also help managers give accurate and fair appraisals by training them to use the appraisal process, encouraging them to recognize accomplishments that the employees themselves have not identified, and fostering a climate of openness in which employees feel they can be honest about their weaknesses.[32]

Calibration Meeting
Meeting at which managers discuss employee performance ratings and provide evidence supporting their ratings with the goal of eliminating the influence of rating errors.

LO 8-7 Explain how to provide performance feedback effectively.

Giving Performance Feedback

Once the manager and others have measured an employee's performance, this information must be given to the employee. Only after the employee has received feedback can he or she begin to plan how to correct any shortcomings. Although the feedback stage of performance management is essential, it is uncomfortable to managers and employees. Delivering feedback feels to the manager as if he or she is standing in judgment of others—a role few people enjoy. Receiving criticism feels even worse. Fortunately, managers can do much to smooth the feedback process and make it effective.

Scheduling Performance Feedback

Performance feedback should be a regular, expected management activity. The custom or policy at many organizations is to give formal performance feedback once a year. But annual feedback is not enough. One reason is that managers are responsible for correcting performance deficiencies as soon as they occur. If the manager notices a problem with an employee's behavior in June, but the annual appraisal is scheduled for November, the employee will miss months of opportunities for improvement.

Another reason for frequent performance feedback is that feedback is most effective when the information does not surprise the employee. If an employee has to wait for up to a year to learn what the manager thinks of his work, the employee will wonder whether he is meeting expectations.

When giving performance feedback, do it in an appropriate meeting place. Meet in a setting that is neutral and free of distractions. What other factors are important for a feedback session?

Employees should instead receive feedback so often that they know what the manager will say during their annual performance review.

Finally, employees have indicated that they are motivated and directed by regular feedback; they want to know if they are on the right track. Managers have found that young employees in particular are looking for frequent and candid performance feedback from their managers. In response, Sibson Consulting combines several kinds of performance reviews: project reviews at the completion of each project (usually after one and a half to six months), reviews of the employee's key strengths twice a year, and a formal performance appraisal at the end of each year. Besides requiring these reviews, Sibson recommends that its managers meet with employees at least once a quarter to discuss progress.[33]

Preparing for a Feedback Session

Managers should be well prepared for each formal feedback session. The manager should create the right context for the meeting. The location should be neutral. If the manager's office is the site of unpleasant conversations, a conference room may be more appropriate. In announcing the meeting to an employee, the manager should describe it as a chance to discuss the role of the employee, the role of the manager, and the relationship between them. Managers should also say (and believe) that they would like the meeting to be an open dialogue. The content of the feedback session and the type of language used can determine the success of this meeting.

Managers should also enable the employee to be well prepared. The manager should ask the employee to complete a self-assessment ahead of time. The self-assessment requires employees to think about their performance over the past rating period and to be aware of their strengths and weaknesses so they can participate more fully in the discussion. Even though employees may tend to overstate their accomplishments, the self-assessment can help the manager and employee identify areas for discussion. When the purpose of the assessment is to define areas for development, employees may actually understate their performance. Also, differences between the manager's and the employee's rating may be fruitful areas for discussion.

Conducting the Feedback Session

During the feedback session, managers can take any of three approaches. In the "tell-and-sell" approach, managers tell the employees their ratings and then justify those ratings. In the "tell-and-listen" approach, managers tell employees their ratings and then let the employees explain their side of the story. In the "problem-solving" approach, managers and employees work together to solve performance problems in an atmosphere of respect and encouragement. Not surprisingly, research demonstrates that the problem-solving approach is superior. Perhaps surprisingly, most managers rely on the tell-and-sell approach.[34] Managers can improve employee satisfaction with the feedback process by letting employees voice their opinions and discuss performance goals.[35]

The content of the feedback should emphasize behavior, not personalities. For example, "You did not meet the deadline" can open a conversation about what needs to change, but "You're not motivated" may make the employee feel defensive and angry. The feedback session should end with goal setting and a decision about when to follow up. The "HR How To" box provides additional guidance on delivering performance feedback.

Discussing Employee Performance

Employees and managers often dread feedback sessions, because they expect some level of criticism, and criticism feels uncomfortable. However, there are ways to structure communication about employee performance so that it feels more constructive. Here are some ideas for talking about employee performance in a way that comes across as clear, honest, and fair:

- **Prevent surprises.** Employees should have clear job descriptions and receive clear directions. Supervisors should be communicating regularly with employees about expectations and how well they are performing. Then when the formal feedback is delivered to an employee, it should be consistent with what the employee has been hearing since the previous review.
- **Use specific, concrete examples.** Statements about "attitude" or "commitment" require some mind-reading, and employees may feel misunderstood. In contrast, references to specific accomplishments and examples of behavior are more neutral. Even if the supervisor is concerned about attitude, talking about behaviors can open a discussion of the real changes

that might be needed: "Several customers commented that you seemed angry when you spoke to them. Let's talk about what's happening in those conversations so you can find a way to come across to customers as pleasant." Specific comments are especially important to back up negative feedback; employees will ask for examples if they don't hear any.

- **Focus on goals.** If in a prior review, the employee and supervisor planned for the employee to complete more projects on time, they should compare the previous on-time performance with the most recent measure to look for improvement.
- **Listen as well as talk.** Especially when the reviewer is nervous, the instinct is to fill up the interview time with comments. However, this interview is a valuable opportunity for the supervisor to learn about the employee's expectations and hopes for learning and advancement. Employees who feel heard are more likely to believe that the review is fair and that their contributions are valued.
- **Be honest.** If performance is not acceptable, don't pretend that it is. Pretending is disrespectful of the employee and could get

the organization in legal trouble if the employee is later let go and believes the company discriminated. If the employee asks a question and the supervisor is unsure of the answer, honesty is again the wisest course. Guessing at an answer related to an employee's future is another way to create problems for the organization, as well as for the supervisor's relationship with the employee.

- **Treat employees with respect.** Besides careful listening and honesty, ways to show respect include using polite language and looking for solutions rather than simply placing blame on employees when performance is less than desired. Treating mistakes as a chance to learn encourages employees to do their best and continue improving. In a respectful climate, conversations about performance can be, if not enjoyable, as least positive and productive.

SOURCES: Jeff Haden, "Nine Ways to Ruin a Performance Review," *Inc.*, January 10, 2012, http://www.inc.com; T. L. Stanley, "Creating a No-Blame Culture," *Supervision,* October 2011, pp. 3–6; C. Anne Pontius, "Addressing Management Issues: Performance-Evaluation Anxiety," *Medical Laboratory Observer,* February 2011, p. 6.

LO 8-8 Summarize ways to produce improvement in unsatisfactory performance.

Finding Solutions to Performance Problems

When performance evaluation indicates that an employee's performance is below standard, the feedback process should launch an effort to correct the problem. Even when the employee is meeting current standards, the feedback session may identify areas in which the employee can improve in order to contribute more to the organization in a current or future job. In sum, the final feedback stage of performance management involves identifying areas for improvement and ways to improve performance in those areas.

Figure 8.7
Improving Performance

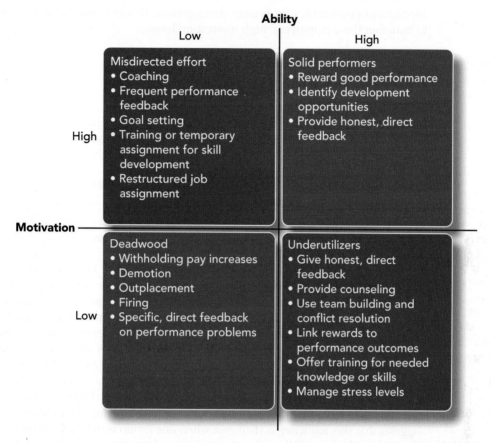

SOURCE: Based on M. London, *Job Feedback* (Mahwah, NJ: Lawrence Erlbaum Associates, 1997), pp. 96–97. Used with permission.

As shown in Figure 8.7, the most effective way to improve performance varies according to the employee's ability and motivation. In general, when employees have high levels of ability and motivation, they perform at or above standards. But when they lack ability, motivation, or both, corrective action is needed. The type of action called for depends on what the employee lacks:

- *Lack of ability*—When a motivated employee lacks knowledge, skills, or abilities in some area, the manager may offer coaching, training, and more detailed feedback. Sometimes it is appropriate to restructure the job so the employee can handle it.
- *Lack of motivation*—Managers with an unmotivated employee can explore ways to demonstrate that the employee is being treated fairly and rewarded adequately. The solution may be as simple as more positive feedback (praise). Employees may need a referral for counseling or help with stress management.
- *Lack of both*—Performance may improve if the manager directs the employee's attention to the significance of the problem by withholding rewards or providing specific feedback. If the employee does not respond, the manager may have to demote or terminate the employee.

As a rule, employees who combine high ability with high motivation are solid performers. As Figure 8.7 indicates, managers should by no means ignore these employees on the grounds of leaving well enough alone. Rather, such employees are likely to appreciate opportunities for further development. Rewards and direct feedback help to maintain these employees' high motivation levels.

LO 8-9 Discuss legal and ethical issues that affect performance management.

Legal and Ethical Issues in Performance Management

In developing and using performance management systems, human resource professionals need to ensure that these systems meet legal requirements, such as the avoidance of discrimination. In addition, performance management systems should meet ethical standards, such as protection of employees' privacy.

Legal Requirements for Performance Management

Because performance measures play a central role in decisions about pay, promotions, and discipline, employment-related lawsuits often challenge an organization's performance management system. Lawsuits related to performance management usually involve charges of discrimination or unjust dismissal.

Discrimination claims often allege that the performance management system discriminated against employees on the basis of their race or sex. Many performance measures are subjective, and measurement errors, such as those described earlier in the chapter, can easily occur. The Supreme Court has held that the selection guidelines in the federal government's *Uniform Guidelines on Employee Selection Procedures* also apply to performance measurement.[36] In general, these guidelines (discussed in Chapters 3 and 6) require that organizations avoid using criteria such as race and age as a basis for employment decisions. This requires overcoming widespread rating errors. A substantial body of evidence has shown that white and black raters tend to give higher ratings to members of their own racial group, even after rater training.[37] In addition, evidence suggests that this tendency is strongest when one group is only a small percentage of the total work group. When the vast majority of the group is male, females receive lower ratings; when the minority is male, males receive lower ratings.[38]

With regard to lawsuits filed on the grounds of unjust dismissal, the usual claim is that the person was dismissed for reasons besides the ones that the employer states. Suppose an employee who works for a defense contractor discloses that the company defrauded the government. If the company fires the employee, the employee might argue that the firing was a way to punish the employee for blowing the whistle. In this type of situation, courts generally focus on the employer's performance management system, looking to see whether the firing could have been based on poor performance. To defend itself, the employer would need a performance management system that provides evidence to support its employment decisions.

To protect against both kinds of lawsuits, it is important to have a legally defensible performance management system.[39] Such a system would be based on valid job analyses, as described in Chapter 4, with the requirements for job success clearly communicated to employees. Performance measurement should evaluate behaviors or results rather than traits. The organization should use multiple raters (including self-appraisals) and train raters in how to use the system. The organization should provide for a review of all performance ratings by upper-level managers and set up a system for employees to appeal when they believe they were evaluated unfairly. Along with feedback, the system should include a process for coaching or training employees to help them improve, rather than simply dismissing poor performers.

Electronic Monitoring and Employee Privacy

Computer technology now supports many performance management systems. Organizations often store records of employees' performance ratings, disciplinary actions, and work-rule violations in electronic databases. Many companies use computers to monitor productivity and other performance measures electronically. A company called E22 Alloy has developed a service that collects data about employees' activities on their computers, smartphones, and other devices and stores the data in the "cloud" (using computer servers accessed online). Employees can visit the service to review the data collected about themselves and delete any data they believe to be inaccurate or irrelevant. Employers can review the data—including information about what data were erased and by whom—to identify employees' activities. They can combine this information with data on business results (say, projects completed or sales closed) to inform decisions about which employees are delivering the most value.[40]

Although electronic monitoring can improve productivity, it also generates privacy concerns. Critics point out that an employer should not monitor employees when it has no reason to believe anything is wrong. They complain that monitoring systems threaten to make the workplace an electronic sweatshop in which employees are treated as robots, robbing them of dignity. Some note that employees' performances should be measured by accomplishments, not just time spent at a desks or workbenches. Electronic systems should not be a substitute for careful management. When monitoring is necessary, managers should communicate the reasons for using it. Monitoring may be used more positively to gather information for coaching employees and helping them develop their skills. Finally, organizations must protect the privacy of performance measurements, as they must do with other employee records.

THINKING ETHICALLY

ARE FORCED RANKINGS FAIR?

Emotions can run high when it comes to the performance management practice of using forced rankings to identify the top performers to retain and the bottom performers to let go. When Jack Welch was chief executive officer of General Electric, he introduced and later championed this method. At GE, managers were ranked according to their performance against goals and sorted into the top 20% (who were richly rewarded), the middle 70%, and the bottom 10% (who often were asked to leave). Today LendingTree follows a similar approach, ranking managers as 1s (the top 15%), 2s (the middle 75%), and 3s (the bottom 10%). The idea is that if the organization lays off the 3s, it can later replace them with people who have the potential to become 1s, improving the overall performance. American International Group (AIG) recently began ranking employees on a scale of 1 to 5, with the biggest bonuses awarded to the top categories and no bonuses to the worst performers.

Critics deride the method, which they call "rank and yank," as ruthless and even demotivating. In their view, organizations should hire and develop good talent, so if the organization is well run, it shouldn't have any underperformers. In addition, they say, the practice tempts managers to compete against one another and perhaps undermine one another when they should be cooperating to help the organization attain its goals. If the organization wants teamwork but being a team player means you help your colleague meet more goals than you did and earn a higher ranking, would you want to be a team player?

Jack Welch insists that forced ranking is actually the fairest approach if done well. Assuming that the organization has made its goals clear, every manager knows where he or she stands. If the organization dismisses someone for being one of the lowest performers, the decision is fairly based on performance rather than personalities or other irrelevant criteria. People who have underperformed their colleagues know it and respect the reasons for the decisions. In addition, forced rankings can correct for any unfairness that results from the common error of a manager tending to be harsh or lenient compared with peers evaluating other employees. Nevertheless, surveys suggest that many organizations are uncomfortable with the method. A study by the Institute for Corporate Productivity, for example, found that use of forced ranking fell from 42% in 2009 to just 14% in 2011.

Questions

1. Based on the description of forced rankings here and in text of the chapter, how fair would you say this method is to employees being ranked? How relevant to the organization's strategy? How useful for employee development?

2. How fair are forced rankings relative to the other methods of measuring performance described in this chapter?

3. At an organization that wants to use forced rankings because it supports this strategy, what measures can it take to make sure the process is as ethical as possible?

SOURCES: Leslie Kwoh, "'Rank and Yank' Retains Vocal Fans," *The Wall Street Journal,* January 31, 2012, http://online.wsj.com; Liz Ryan, "Ten Management Practices to Throw Overboard in 2012," *Bloomberg Businessweek,* January 23, 2012, EBSCOhost, http://web.ebscohost.com; Jonathan A. Segal, "The Dirty Dozen Appraisal Errors," *Bloomberg Businessweek,* January 17, 2011, EBSCOhost, http://web.ebscohost.com.

SUMMARY

LO 8-1 Identify the activities involved in performance management.

Performance management is the process through which managers ensure that employees' activities and outputs contribute to the organization's goals. The organization begins by specifying which aspects of performance are relevant to the organization. Next, the organization measures the relevant aspects of performance through performance appraisal. Finally, in performance feedback sessions, managers provide employees with information about their performance so they can adjust their behavior to meet the organization's goals. Feedback includes efforts to identify and solve problems.

LO 8-2 Discuss the purposes of performance management systems.

Organizations establish performance management systems to meet three broad purposes. Effective performance management helps the organization with strategic purposes, that is, meeting business objectives. It does this by helping to link employees' behavior with the organization's goals. The administrative purpose of performance management is to provide information for day-to-day decisions about salary, benefits, recognition, and retention or termination. The developmental purpose of performance management is using the system as a basis for developing employees' knowledge and skills.

LO 8-3 Define five criteria for measuring the effectiveness of a performance management system.

Performance measures should fit with the organization's strategy by supporting its goals and culture. Performance measures should be valid, so they measure all the relevant aspects of performance and do not measure irrelevant aspects of performance. These measures should also provide interrater and test-retest reliability, so that appraisals are consistent among raters and over time. Performance measurement systems should be acceptable to the people who use them or receive feedback from them. Finally, a performance measure should specifically tell employees what is expected of them and how they can meet those expectations.

LO 8-4 Compare the major methods for measuring performance.

Performance measurement may use ranking systems such as simple ranking, forced distribution, or paired comparisons to compare one individual's performance with that of other employees. These methods may be time consuming, and they will be seen as unfair if actual performance is not distributed in the same way as the ranking system requires. However, ranking counteracts some forms of rater bias and helps distinguish employees for administrative decisions. Other approaches involve rating employees' attributes, behaviors, or outcomes. Rating attributes is relatively simple but not always valid, unless attributes are specifically defined. Rating behaviors requires a great deal of information, but these methods can be very effective. They can link behaviors to goals, and ratings by trained raters may be highly reliable. Rating results, such as productivity or achievement of objectives, tends to be less subjective than other kinds of rating, making this approach highly acceptable. Validity may be a problem because of factors outside the employee's control. This method also tends not to provide much basis for determining how to improve. Focusing on quality can provide practical benefits, but is not as useful for administrative and developmental decisions.

LO 8-5 Describe major sources of performance information in terms of their advantages and disadvantages.

Performance information may come from an employee's self-appraisal and from appraisals by the employee's supervisor, employees, peers, and customers. Using only one source makes the appraisal more subjective. Organizations may combine many sources into a 360-degree performance appraisal. Gathering information from each employee's manager may produce accurate information, unless the supervisor has little opportunity to observe the employee. Peers are an excellent source of information about performance in a job where the supervisor does not often observe the employee. Disadvantages are that friendships (or rivalries) may bias ratings and peers may be uncomfortable with the role of rating a friend. Subordinates often have the best chance to see how a manager treats employees. Employees may be reluctant to contribute honest opinions about a supervisor unless they can provide information anonymously. Self-appraisals may be biased, but they do come from the person with the most knowledge of the employee's behavior on the job, and they provide a basis for discussion in feedback sessions, opening up fruitful comparisons and areas of disagreement between the self-appraisal and other appraisals. Customers may be an excellent source of performance information, although obtaining customer feedback tends to be expensive.

LO 8-6 Define types of rating errors, and explain how to minimize them.

People observe behavior often without a practical way of knowing all the relevant circumstances and outcomes, so they necessarily interpret what they see. A common tendency is to give higher evaluations to people we consider similar to ourselves. Other errors involve using only part of the rating scale: Giving all employees ratings at the high end of the scale is called leniency error. Rating everyone at the low end of the scale is called strictness error. Rating all employees at or near the middle is called central tendency. The halo error refers to rating employees positively in all areas because of strong performance observed in one area. The horns error is rating employees negatively in all areas because of weak performance observed in one area. Ways to reduce rater error are training raters to be aware of their tendencies to make rating errors and training them to be sensitive to the complex nature of employee performance so they will consider many aspects of performance in greater depth. Politics also may influence ratings. Organizations can minimize appraisal politics by establishing a fair appraisal system and bringing managers together to discuss ratings in calibration meetings.

LO 8-7 Explain how to provide performance feedback effectively.

Performance feedback should be a regular, scheduled management activity so that employees can correct problems as soon as they occur. Managers should prepare by establishing a neutral location, emphasizing that the feedback session will be a chance for discussion, and asking the employee to prepare a self-assessment. During the feedback session, managers should strive for a problem-solving approach and encourage employees to voice their opinions and discuss performance goals. The manager should look for opportunities to praise and should limit criticism. The discussion should focus on behavior and results rather than on personalities.

LO 8-8 Summarize ways to produce improvement in unsatisfactory performance.

For an employee who is motivated but lacks ability, the manager should provide coaching and training, give detailed feedback about performance, and consider restructuring the job. For an employee who has ability but lacks motivation, the manager should investigate whether outside problems are a distraction and if so, refer the employee for help. If the problem has to do with the employee's not feeling appreciated or rewarded, the manager should try to deliver more praise and evaluate whether additional pay and other rewards are appropriate. For an employee lacking both ability and motivation, the manager should consider whether the employee is a good fit for the position. Specific feedback or withholding rewards may spur improvement, or the employee may have to be demoted or terminated. Solid employees who are high in ability and motivation will continue so and may be able to contribute even more if the manager provides appropriate direct feedback, rewards, and opportunities for development.

LO 8-9 Discuss legal and ethical issues that affect performance management.

Lawsuits related to performance management usually involve charges of discrimination or unjust dismissal. Managers must make sure that performance management systems and decisions treat employees equally, without regard to

their race, sex, or other protected status. Organizations can do this by establishing and using valid performance measures and by training raters to evaluate performance accurately. A system is more likely to be legally defensible if it is based on behaviors and results, rather than on traits, and if multiple raters evaluate each person's performance. The system should include a process for coaching or training employees to help them improve, rather than simply dismissing poor performers. An ethical issue of performance management is the use of electronic monitoring. This type of performance measurement provides detailed, accurate information, but employees may find it demoralizing, degrading, and stressful. They are more likely to accept it if the organization explains its purpose, links it to help in improving performance, and keeps the performance data private.

KEY TERMS

360-degree performance
 appraisal, 250
behavioral observation scale
 (BOS), 245
behaviorally anchored rating scale
 (BARS), 245
calibration meeting, 256

critical-incident method, 245
forced-distribution method, 241
graphic rating scale, 242
management by objectives
 (MBO), 248
mixed-standard scales, 243

organizational behavior
 modification (OBM), 246
paired-comparison method, 242
performance management, 235
simple ranking, 240

REVIEW AND DISCUSSION QUESTIONS

1. How does a complete performance management system differ from the use of annual performance appraisals?
2. Give two examples of an administrative decision that would be based on performance management information. Give two examples of developmental decisions based on this type of information.
3. How can involving employees in the creation of performance standards improve the effectiveness of a performance management system? (Consider the criteria for effectiveness listed in the chapter.)
4. Consider how you might rate the performance of three instructors from whom you are currently taking a course. (If you are currently taking only one or two courses, consider this course and two you recently completed.)
   a. Would it be harder to *rate* the instructors' performance or to *rank* their performance? Why?

   b. Write three items to use in rating the instructors—one each to rate them in terms of an attribute, a behavior, and an outcome.
   c. Which measure in (*b*) do you think is most valid? Most reliable? Why?
   d. Many colleges use questionnaires to gather data from students about their instructors' performance. Would it be appropriate to use the data for administrative decisions? Developmental decisions? Other decisions? Why or why not?

5. Imagine that a pet supply store is establishing a new performance management system to help employees provide better customer service. Management needs to decide who should participate in measuring the performance of each of the store's salespeople. From what sources should the store gather information? Why?

6. Would the same sources be appropriate if the store in Question 5 used the performance appraisals to support decisions about which employees to promote? Explain.

7. Suppose you were recently promoted to a supervisory job in a company where you have worked for two years. You genuinely like almost all your co-workers, who now report to you. The only exception is one employee, who dresses more formally than the others and frequently tells jokes that embarrass you and the other workers. Given your preexisting feelings for the employees, how can you measure their performance fairly and effectively?

8. Continuing the example in Question 7, imagine that you are preparing for your first performance feedback session. You want the feedback to be effective—that is, you want the feedback to result in improved performance. List five or six steps you can take to achieve your goal.

9. Besides giving employees feedback, what steps can a manager take to improve employees' performance?

10. Suppose you are a human resource professional helping to improve the performance management system of a company that sells and services office equipment. The company operates a call center that takes calls from customers who are having problems with their equipment. Call center employees are supposed to verify that the problem is not one the customer can easily handle (for example, equipment that will not operate because it has come unplugged). Then, if the problem is not resolved over the phone, the employees arrange for service technicians to visit the customer. The company can charge the customer only if a service technician visits, so performance management of the call center employees focuses on productivity—how quickly they can complete a call and move on to the next caller. To measure this performance efficiently and accurately, the company uses electronic monitoring.

   a. How would you expect the employees to react to the electronic monitoring? How might the organization address the employees' concerns?

   b. Besides productivity in terms of number of calls, what other performance measures should the performance management system include?

   c. How should the organization gather information about the other performance measures?

EXPERIENCING HR

If your school publishes student reviews of instructors, look up and read some of these reviews, taking notes on the kinds of comments students make. If your school does not publish reviews, do the same at a public website such as Rate My Professors (**www.ratemyprofessors.com**), Professor Performance (**www.professorperformance.com**), or another site suggested by your instructor.

Consider how, if at all, a professor and school might make use of reviews such as these. Review the criteria for effective performance management, and consider the following questions: Do the reviews suggest relevant areas of improvement? Do they address the qualities or behavior that could enable a school to accomplish its mission? Do the ratings seem thoughtful or just like a place for students to complain if they struggle in a class?

Imagine you are a consultant invited to a small private college that has a mission to provide excellent teaching. You have been asked to advise the school on how it might use student appraisals as part of a 360-degree review process to support the development of professors' teaching skills. Based on what you have learned about performance management and seen of your school's or online reviews, write a one- or two-page recommendation to the school. Consider possible uses of student reviews as well as any steps the school should take to keep the process fair and legal.

TAKING RESPONSIBILITY: Performance Measurement for Public School Teachers

Public schools have a major responsibility to their communities: preparing children to become good citizens, productive employees, and smart consumers. Unfortunately, trends such as test scores, dropout rates, readiness for work and college, and persistent differences between ethnic and economic groups suggest that schools often fail to deliver.

Meeting the goals requires talented, motivated teachers who understand what behaviors are associated with successful instruction and have the necessary resources. A basic tool for achieving this should be a school's performance management system. However, efforts to design measures for teacher performance suggest that it is complicated. Certainly, politics plays a role, but performance measurement for schools is challenging even from a strictly HR point of view.

The traditional approach has been to identify the teachers with the longest tenure and greatest education, then to reward these teachers with job retention and pay. The rationale is that the measures are objective (a teacher has a master's degree or doesn't and has clearly worked for some number of years), so they can be applied equitably. In addition, an experienced, highly educated teacher logically would have skills that a new college graduate has yet to learn. Still, former students would say the teachers who inspired them most are not always the oldest ones.

An approach to measuring performance that has recently been emphasized is students' performance on standardized tests. This measure focuses on results, but test scores have their drawbacks. First, they raise the question of how much control a teacher has over scores. If a teacher's class contains many students with behavioral problems, learning disabilities, or poor preparation in previous grades, should the teacher's evaluation take that into account—and if so, how? Standardized tests also need to measure the outcomes that matter most. Should the school only be preparing students to recall facts on a multiple-choice test—or also to express their reasoning in writing? Further, standardized tests usually are relevant only to certain teachers. Most states test only reading and math skills. A few states test students in science and social studies. Some subjects, including music and physical education, lack standardized tests. Even where a test exists in a subject area, should a science teacher be penalized if students don't read well enough to perform well on a science test? Furthermore, as a school superintendent in New York pointed out, it is expensive to create or buy a rubric specifying learning goals in each subject area for every grade.

Despite these challenges, some school districts have pursued more comprehensive testing, with results influencing bonuses paid to teachers. In Florida, Hillsborough County Public Schools developed tests for every subject in every grade level. Tennessee relies only on math and reading scores but ties those scores to evaluations of teachers in all subject areas. However, the Memphis school district allows music, drama, and dance teachers to compile portfolios showing the progress of their students. North Carolina has been developing standardized tests for all subjects, but in Charlotte-Mecklenburg Schools, parents revolted when they learned that much classroom time in kindergarten was being devoted to one-on-one tests of the young students.

Iowa has considered yet another approach. The state had required that, every three years, a supervisor would evaluate experienced teachers (those who have been working more than two years). The state's education director proposed a policy that these reviews be supplemented with peer reviews each year in between, so teachers receive more timely feedback, enabling them to identify and work on areas of improvement.

Bill Gates, Microsoft's founder, has yet another idea. Gates suggests that researchers investigate why some teachers get better outcomes than others. He proposes observing teachers with practical skills such as bringing order to a classroom and engaging a student who is lagging behind, to identify exactly what these teachers are doing. Then those behaviors could be measured in other teachers and taught to those who lack the skills. Teachers can be trained to give peer reviews based on this type of model. The Bill & Melinda Gates Foundation funded a survey of teachers, to get their perspective on what would help them perform better. According to that survey, teachers want to receive more evaluations, from more sources. Most agree that the best measure of their success should be the progress students make during the school year.

Questions

1. How well do the performance management ideas described in this case meet the three purposes of performance management (strategic, administrative, and developmental)?
2. How well do the ideas meet the five criteria for effective performance management?
3. From a human resource management perspective, what additional principles do you think school systems should apply to managing teachers' performance?

SOURCES: Harold McNeil, "Superintendent Describes Difficulty in Implementing Teacher Evaluations," *Buffalo (NY) News*, March 21, 2012, Business & Company Resource Center, http://galenet.galegroup.com; Amanda Paulson, "Surprise: Teachers Crave Evaluation," *Christian Science Monitor*, March 16, 2012, http://www.csmonitor.com; Stephanie Banchero, "Teacher Evaluations Pose Test for States," *The Wall Street Journal*, March 8, 2012, http://online.wsj.com; Mary Stegmeir, "Iowa Officials Rework Plan on Teacher Reviews," *Des Moines Register*, February 29, 2012, http://www.desmoinesregister.com; Alan Hughes, "Can Bill Gates Save Our Schools?" *Black Enterprise*, October 2011, EBSCOhost, http://web.ebscohost.com.

MANAGING TALENT: How Google Searches for Performance Measures

If there's one thing Google knows, it's how to use software to wade through massive amounts of data and find what is most relevant. So it should come as no surprise that when the information technology powerhouse

wanted to develop better managers, it started by looking at the data. As it turns out, Google found plenty to learn.

Like most businesses, Google had files of data about managers—results of performance reviews, surveys measuring employee attitudes, and nominations for management awards. Unlike most businesses, Google figured out how to analyze all that data to come up with a profile of the kind of manager whose team is most successful. The company's people analytics group (which brings together psychologists, MBAs, and data-mining experts) analyzed 10,000 observations about managers in terms of more than 100 variables, looking for patterns. The initial finding was a surprise to some at a company that had once operated without managers: teams with good managers outperform teams with bad managers. But what makes a good manager? Under the leadership of Google's HR vice president, Laszlo Bock, the company distilled its findings into a list of the behaviors that get results:

1. Be a good coach.
2. Empower your team, and don't micromanage.
3. Express interest in team members' success and personal well-being.
4. Don't be a sissy: Be productive and results-oriented.
5. Be a good communicator, and listen to your team.
6. Help your employees with career development.
7. Have a clear vision and strategy for the team.
8. Have key technical skills so you can help advise the team.

Perhaps those points sound obvious. But keep in mind that someone hired as a programming or analytic whiz and later promoted to a managerial role might not have given much thought to, say, cultivating the ability to express interest in team members' success, which ranks far above technical skills. Seeing this on a list identifies the behavior as something statistically related to superior performance not just in general, but at Google specifically. Furthermore, this is a behavior that can be measured (for example, by asking employees if their supervisor expresses interest in them), and it can be learned by managers who want to improve.

By building performance measures in the eight key areas, Google was able to evaluate its managers' performance and identify those who needed to improve in particular areas. It developed training programs in the eight types of desired behavior. Before and after providing performance appraisals, training, and coaching, Google conducted surveys to gauge managers' performance. It measured a significant improvement in manager quality for 75% of its lowest-performing managers. But Bock isn't resting on that success. Google intends to keep crunching the data, in case the criteria for a successful Google manager change at some point in the future. One thing is for sure: Google will continue to follow the data.

Questions

1. How well does Google's approach to performance management meet the five criteria for effectiveness of a performance management system? How well does it fit with the company's mission to organize information and make it universally accessible and useful?
2. What errors could arise in the way Google collects performance data on managers? How could it minimize these errors?
3. Suppose you are responsible for delivering performance feedback to managers at Google. How would you present the information so as to promote the managers' success at the company?

SOURCES: Adam Bryant, "Google's Quest to Build a Better Boss," *The New York Times*, March 12, 2011, http://www.nytimes.com; Clara Byrne, "People Analytics: How Google Does HR by the Numbers," *VentureBeat*, September 20, 2011, http://venturebeat.com; Pat Galagan, "Measure for Measure," *T + D*, May 2011, pp. 28–30.

 TWITTER FOCUS: Appraisals Matter at Meadow Hills Veterinary Center

Using Twitter, continue the conversation about performance management by reading the Meadow Hills Veterinary Center case at **www.mhhe.com/noefund5e**. Engage your classmates and instructor via Twitter to chat about Meadow Hills' performance appraisal process using the case questions posted on the Noe website. Don't have a Twitter account yet? See the instructions for getting started on the Online Learning Center.

NOTES

1. Jathan Janove, "Reviews—Good for Anything?" *HR Magazine*, June 2011, pp. 121–26.
2. Discussion based on E. Pulakos, *Performance Management* (Oxford, England: Wiley-Blackwell, 2009); H. Aguinis, "An Expanded View of Performance Management," " in J. W. Smith and M. London (eds.), *Performance Management* (San Francisco: Jossey-Bass, 2009), pp. 1–43; and J. Russell and L. Russell, "Talk Me Through It: The Next Level of Performance Management," *T + D*, April 2010, pp. 42–48.

3. E. Krell, "All for Incentives, Incentives for All," *HR Magazine*, January 2011, pp. 35–38.

4. S. Scullen, P. Bergey, and L. Aiman-Smith, "Forced Choice Distribution Systems and the Improvement of Workforce Potential: A Baseline Simulation," *Personnel Psychology* 58 (2005), pp. 1–32.

5. P. Smith and L. Kendall, "Retranslation of Expectations: An Approach to the Construction of Unambiguous Anchors for Rating Scales," *Journal of Applied Psychology* 47 (1963), pp. 149–55.

6. K. Murphy and J. Constans, "Behavioral Anchors as a Source of Bias in Rating," *Journal of Applied Psychology* 72 (1987), pp. 573–77; M. Piotrowski, J. Barnes-Farrel, and F. Estig, "Behaviorally Anchored Bias: A Replication and Extension of Murphy and Constans," *Journal of Applied Psychology* 74 (1989), pp. 823–26.

7. G. Latham and K. Wexley, *Increasing Productivity through Performance Appraisal* (Boston: Addison-Wesley, 1981).

8. U. Wiersma and G. Latham, "The Practicality of Behavioral Observation Scales, Behavioral Expectation Scales, and Trait Scales," *Personnel Psychology* 39 (1986), pp. 619–28.

9. D. C. Anderson, C. Crowell, J. Sucec, K. Gilligan, and M. Wikoff, "Behavior Management of Client Contacts in a Real Estate Brokerage: Getting Agents to Sell More," *Journal of Organizational Behavior Management* 4 (2001), pp. 580–90; and F. Luthans and R. Kreitner, *Organizational Behavior Modification and Beyond* (Glenview, IL: Scott-Foresman, 1975).

10. K. L. Langeland, C. M. Jones, and T. C. Mawhinney, "Improving Staff Performance in a Community Mental Health Setting: Job Analysis, Training, Goal Setting, Feedback, and Years of Data," *Journal of Organizational Behavior Management* 18 (1998), pp. 21–43.

11. J. Komaki, R. Collins, and P. Penn, "The Role of Performance Antecedents and Consequences in Work Motivation," *Journal of Applied Psychology* 67 (1982), pp. 334–40.

12. S. Snell, "Control Theory in Strategic Human Resource Management: The Mediating Effect of Administrative Information," *Academy of Management Journal* 35 (1992), pp. 292–327.

13. R. Pritchard, S. Jones, P. Roth, K. Stuebing, and S. Ekeberg, "The Evaluation of an Integrated Approach to Measuring Organizational Productivity," *Personnel Psychology* 42 (1989), pp. 69–115.

14. G. Odiorne, *MOBII: A System of Managerial Leadership for the 80s* (Belmont, CA: Pitman, 1986).

15. R. Rodgers and J. Hunter, "Impact of Management by Objectives on Organizational Productivity," *Journal of Applied Psychology* 76 (1991), pp. 322–26.

16. P. Wright, J. George, S. Farnsworth, and G. McMahan, "Productivity and Extra-role Behavior: The Effects of Goals and Incentives on Spontaneous Helping," *Journal of Applied Psychology* 78, no. 3 (1993), pp. 374–81.

17. Rita Pyrillis, "The Reviews Are In," *Workforce Management*, May 2011, Business & Company Resource Center, http://galenet.galegroup.com.

18. R. Heneman, K. Wexley, and M. Moore, "Performance Rating Accuracy: A Critical Review," *Journal of Business Research* 15 (1987), pp. 431–48.

19. T. Becker and R. Klimoski, "A Field Study of the Relationship between the Organizational Feedback Environment and Performance," *Personnel Psychology* 42 (1989), pp. 343–58; H. M. Findley, W. F. Giles, and K. W. Mossholder, "Performance Appraisal and Systems Facets: Relationships with Contextual Performance," *Journal of Applied Psychology* 85 (2000), pp. 634–40.

20. K. Wexley and R. Klimoski, "Performance Appraisal: An Update," in *Research in Personnel and Human Resource Management*, vol. 2, ed. K. Rowland and G. Ferris (Greenwich, CT: JAI Press, 1984).

21. F. Landy and J. Farr, *The Measurement of Work Performance: Methods, Theory, and Applications* (New York: Academic Press, 1983).

22. G. McEvoy and P. Buller, "User Acceptance of Peer Appraisals in an Industrial Setting," *Personnel Psychology* 40 (1987), pp. 785–97.

23. Joann S. Lublin, "Transparency Pays Off in 360-Degree Reviews," *The Wall Street Journal*, December 8, 2011, http://online.wsj.com.

24. D. Antonioni, "The Effects of Feedback Accountability on Upward Appraisal Ratings," *Personnel Psychology* 47 (1994), pp. 349–56.

25. Rachel Emma Silverman, "Performance Reviews Lose Steam," *The Wall Street Journal*, December 19, 2011, http://online.wsj.com.

26. H. Heidemeier and K. Moser, "Self-Other Agreement in Job Performance Rating: A Meta-Analytic Test of a Process Model," *Journal of Applied Psychology* 94 (2008), pp. 353–70.

27. J. Bernardin, C. Hagan, J. Kane, and P. Villanova, "Effective Performance Management: A Focus on Precision, Customers, and Situational Constraints," in *Performance Appraisal: State of the Art in Practice*, ed. J. W. Smither (San Francisco: Jossey-Bass, 1998), pp. 3–48.

28. K. Wexley and W. Nemeroff, "Effects of Racial Prejudice, Race of Applicant, and Biographical Similarity on Interviewer Evaluations of Job Applicants," *Journal of Social and Behavioral Sciences* 20 (1974), pp. 66–78.
29. D. Smith, "Training Programs for Performance Appraisal: A Review," *Academy of Management Review* 11 (1986), pp. 22–40; and G. Latham, K. Wexley, and E. Pursell, "Training Managers to Minimize Rating Errors in the Observation of Behavior," *Journal of Applied Psychology* 60 (1975), pp. 550–55.
30. E. Pulakos, "A Comparison of Rater Training Programs: Error Training and Accuracy Training," *Journal of Applied Psychology* 69 (1984), pp. 581–88.
31. Claudine Kapel, "Addressing Consistency in Performance Reviews," *HR Reporter*, March 5, 2012, http://www.hrreporter.com.
32. S. W. J. Kozlowski, G. T. Chao, and R. F. Morrison, "Games Raters Play: Politics, Strategies, and Impression Management in Performance Appraisal," in *Performance Appraisal: State of the Art in Practice*, pp. 163–205; and C. Rosen, P. Levy, and R. Hall, "Placing Perceptions of Politics in the Context of the Feedback Environment, Employee Attitudes, and Job Performance," *Journal of Applied Psychology* 91 (2006), pp. 211–20.
33. "Should Performance Reviews Be Fired?" *Knowledge@Wharton* (Wharton School, University of Pennsylvania), April 27, 2011, http://knowledge.wharton.upenn.edu.
34. K. Wexley, V. Singh, and G. Yukl, "Subordinate Participation in Three Types of Appraisal Interviews," *Journal of Applied Psychology* 58 (1973), pp. 54–57; K. Wexley, "Appraisal Interview," in *Performance Assessment*, ed. R. A. Berk (Baltimore: Johns Hopkins University Press, 1986), pp. 167–85; B. D. Cawley, L. M. Keeping, and P. E. Levy, "Participation in the Performance Appraisal Process and Employee Reactions: A Meta-analytic Review of Field Investigations," *Journal of Applied Psychology* 83, no. 3 (1998), pp. 615–63; H. Aguinis, *Performance Management* (Upper Saddle River, NJ:
Pearson Prentice-Hall, 2007); and C. Lee, "Feedback, Not Appraisal," *HR Magazine*, November 2006, pp. 111–14.
35. D. Cederblom, "The Performance Appraisal Interview: A Review, Implications, and Suggestions," *Academy of Management Review* 7 (1982), pp. 219–27; B. D. Cawley, L. M. Keeping, and P. E. Levy, "Participation in the Performance Appraisal Process and Employee Reactions: A Meta-analytic Review of Field Investigations," *Journal of Applied Psychology* 83, no. 3 (1998), pp. 615–63; and W. Giles and K. Mossholder, "Employee Reactions to Contextual and Session Components of Performance Appraisal," *Journal of Applied Psychology* 75 (1990), pp. 371–77.
36. *Brito v. Zia Co.*, 478 F.2d 1200 (10th Cir. 1973).
37. K. Kraiger and J. Ford, "A Meta-Analysis of Ratee Race Effects in Performance Rating," *Journal of Applied Psychology* 70 (1985), pp. 56–65.
38. P. Sackett, C. DuBois, and A. Noe, "Tokenism in Performance Evaluation: The Effects of Work Group Representation on Male-Female and White-Black Differences in Performance Ratings," *Journal of Applied Psychology* 76 (1991), pp. 263–67.
39. G. Barrett and M. Kernan, "Performance Appraisal and Terminations: A Review of Court Decisions since *Brito v. Zia* with Implications for Personnel Practices," *Personnel Psychology* 40 (1987), pp. 489–503; H. Feild and W. Holley, "The Relationship of Performance Appraisal System Characteristics to Verdicts in Selected Employment Discrimination Cases," *Academy of Management Journal* 25 (1982), pp. 392–406; J. M. Werner and M. C. Bolino, "Explaining U.S. Courts of Appeals Decisions Involving Performance Appraisal: Accuracy, Fairness, and Validation," *Personnel Psychology* 50 (1997), pp. 1–24; J. Segal, "Performance Management Blunders," *HR Magazine*, November 2010, pp. 75–77; Janove, "Reviews—Good for Anything?"
40. Michael Hugos, "Monitoring Employee Performance in Real Time," *CIO*, February 29, 2012, http://blogs.cio.com.

9 Developing Employees for Future Success

What Do I Need to Know?

After reading this chapter, you should be able to:

LO 9-1 Discuss how development is related to training and careers.

LO 9-2 Identify the methods organizations use for employee development.

LO 9-3 Describe how organizations use assessment of personality type, work behaviors, and job performance to plan employee development.

LO 9-4 Explain how job experiences can be used for developing skills.

LO 9-5 Summarize principles of successful mentoring programs.

LO 9-6 Tell how managers and peers develop employees through coaching.

LO 9-7 Identify the steps in the process of career management.

LO 9-8 Discuss how organizations are meeting the challenges of the "glass ceiling," succession planning, and dysfunctional managers.

Introduction

LiquidAgents Healthcare recently found itself in the top spot for small companies in *Modern Healthcare* magazine's ranking of the 100 Best Places to Work in Healthcare. One reason the Plano, Texas, staffing firm is so well regarded is that it is committed to helping its employees grow into the positions they have the best potential to fill. Sometimes those aren't the positions employees originally see themselves holding. Javier Llevada, for example, had a college degree and experience in accounting when he was hired. He expected those credentials would define his career at LiquidAgents. But managers soon noticed that he was an excellent communicator who worked well with others. They encouraged him to go outside his comfort zone and try working as a territory manager, a job that would require him to work directly with the firm's clients.

Llevada says of his new position at LiquidAgents, "I love what I'm doing." And his manager, Oren Lavi, expects that Llevada will continue to advance at the firm as it gives him more opportunities to build on his strengths. That kind of effort is part of the firm's approach to talent management. Twice-yearly performance appraisals and 360-degree feedback are applied to helping managers and their employees pinpoint the employees' strengths, goals, and areas to improve. Then LiquidAgents uses training programs and stretch assignments that prepare employees to meet new challenges.[1]

As LiquidAgents realizes and as we noted in Chapter 1, employees' commitment to their organization depends on how their managers treat them. To "win the war for talent" managers must be able to identify high-potential employees, make sure the organization uses the talents of these people, and reassure them of their value so that they do not become dissatisfied and leave the organization. Managers also must be able to listen. Although new employees need strong direction, they expect to be able to think independently and be treated with respect. In all these ways, managers provide for **employee development**—the combination of formal education, job experiences, relationships, and assessment of personality and abilities to help employees prepare for the future of their careers. Human resource management establishes a process for employee development that prepares employees to help the organization meet its goals.

This chapter explores the purpose and activities of employee development. We begin by discussing the relationships among development, training, and career management. Next, we look at development approaches, including formal education, assessment, job experiences, and interpersonal relationships. The chapter emphasizes the types of skills, knowledge, and behaviors that are strengthened by each development method, so employees and their managers can choose appropriate methods when planning for development. The third section of the chapter describes the steps of the career management process, emphasizing the responsibilities of employee and employer at each step of the process. The chapter concludes with a discussion of special challenges related to employee development—the so-called glass ceiling, succession planning, and dysfunctional managers.

> **Employee Development**
> The combination of formal education, job experiences, relationships, and assessment of personality and abilities to help employees prepare for the future of their careers.

Training, Development, and Career Management

> **LO 9-1** Discuss how development is related to training and careers.

Organizations and their employees must constantly expand their knowledge, skills, and behavior to meet customer needs and compete in today's demanding and rapidly changing business environment. More and more companies operate internationally, requiring that employees understand different cultures and customs. More companies organize work in terms of projects or customers, rather than specialized functions, so employees need to acquire a broad range of technical and interpersonal skills. Many companies expect employees at all levels to perform roles once reserved for management. Modern organizations are expected to provide development opportunities to employees without regard to their sex, race, ethnic background, or age so that they have equal opportunity for advancement. In this climate, organizations are placing greater emphasis on training and development. To do this, organizations must understand development's relationship to training and career management.

Development and Training

The definition of development indicates that it is future oriented. Development implies learning that is not necessarily related to the employee's current job.[2] Instead, it prepares employees for other jobs or positions in the organization and increases their ability to move into jobs that may not yet exist.[3] Development also may help employees prepare for changes in responsibilities and requirements in their current jobs, such as changes resulting from new technology, work designs, or customers.

In contrast, training traditionally focuses on helping employees improve performance of their current jobs. Many organizations have focused on linking training programs to business goals. In these organizations, the distinction between training and development is more blurred. Table 9.1 summarizes the traditional differences.

	TRAINING	DEVELOPMENT
Focus	Current	Future
Use of work experiences	Low	High
Goal	Preparation for current job	Preparation for changes
Participation	Required	Voluntary

Development for Careers

The concept of a career has changed in recent years. In the traditional view, a career consists of a sequence of positions within an occupation or organization.[4] For example, an academic career might begin with a position as a university's adjunct professor. It continues with appointment to faculty positions as assistant professor, then associate professor, and finally full professor. An engineer might start as a staff engineer, then with greater experience earn promotions to the positions of advisory engineer, senior engineer, and vice president of engineering. In these examples, the career resembles a set of stairs from the bottom of a profession or organization to the top. Especially at organizations where careers progress in this way, development programs need to ensure that employees are prepared to ascend to each new level. Unfortunately, as described in the "HR Oops!" box, some don't.

Recently, however, changes such as downsizing and restructuring have become the norm, so the concept of a career has become more fluid. Today's employees are more likely to have a **protean career,** one that frequently changes based on changes in the person's interests, abilities, and values and in the work environment. For example, an engineer might decide to take a sabbatical from her job to become a manager with Engineers without Borders, so she can develop managerial skills and decide whether she likes managing. As in this example, employees in protean careers take responsibility for managing their careers. This practice is consistent with the modern *psychological contract* described in Chapter 2. Employees look for organizations to provide not job security and a career ladder to climb, but instead development opportunities and flexible work arrangements.

To remain marketable, employees must continually develop new skills. Fewer of today's careers involve repetitive tasks, and more rely on an expanding base of knowledge.[5] Jobs are less likely to last a lifetime, so employees have to prepare for newly created positions. Beyond knowing job requirements, employees need to understand the business in which they are working and be able to cultivate valuable relationships with co-workers, managers, suppliers, and customers. They also need to follow trends in their field and industry, so they can apply technology and knowledge that will match emerging priorities and needs. Learning such skills requires useful job experiences as well as effective training programs.

These relationships and experiences often take an employee along a career path that is far different from the traditional steps upward through an organization or profession. Although such careers will not disappear, more employees will follow a spiral career path in which they cross the boundaries between specialties and organizations. As organizations provide for employee development (and as employees take control of their own careers), they will need to (1) determine their interests, skills, and weaknesses and (2) seek development experiences involving jobs, relationships, and formal courses. As discussed later in the chapter, organizations can meet these needs through a system for *career management* or *development planning*. Career

Protean Career
A career that frequently changes based on changes in the person's interests, abilities, and values and in the work environment.

Ignoring Middle Management

Research by Development Dimensions International (DDI) finds that many of today's middle managers feel unprepared to handle their responsibilities. Middle managers are the layer of an organization's hierarchy that translates the top executives' vision into the projects and plans carried out by departments and teams. The middle managers oversee the supervisors and first-line managers who oversee those departments and teams. That means they have to be able to put a vision into practice, understand the financial impact of their performance, lead and motivate the people who report to them, and cultivate relationships throughout the organization with the people who can advance or interfere with their group's performance.

The middle managers surveyed by DDI said their most important challenges are leading change, executing strategic priorities, and making complex decisions. Asked about their preparation for handling those challenges, however, only 11% rated themselves well prepared.

Tacy M. Byham, DDI's vice president of executive development, says the problem is that many organizations focus on preparing employees to be first-line supervisors and developing successful managers to move into top-level positions. That dual focus ignores the organization's needs for well-developed managers in the middle. Byham notes an additional consequence of ignoring development of middle managers: loss of talent. Managers tend to be more engaged in their work when they feel competent and valued. Lack of preparation translates into lack of trust in middle managers to make good decision. Midlevel managers stuck in that situation indicate that they expect to move on to another employer before long.

Questions

1. Why do you think many organizations focus their development efforts primarily on top management and new (first-line) managers?
2. Imagine you are moving in your career from supervisor to middle manager. What changes would you hope for in your company's employee development program?

SOURCES: Development Dimensions International, "Reshaping the Middle of Organizations," news release, February 29, 2012, http://www.ddiworld.com; Roberta Matuson, "Leadership Starts in the Middle, Not at the Top," *Fast Company*, October 24, 2011, http://www.fastcompany.com; Ann Pace, "The Weary Middle," *T + D*, January 2011, p. 22.

management helps employees select development activities that prepare them to meet their career goals. It helps employers select development activities in line with their human resource needs.

Approaches to Employee Development

LO 9-2 Identify the methods organizations use for employee development.

The many approaches to employee development fall into four broad categories: formal education, assessment, job experiences, and interpersonal relationships.[6] Figure 9.1 summarizes these four methods. Many organizations combine these approaches.

Formal Education

Organizations may support employee development through a variety of formal educational programs, either at the workplace or off-site. These may include workshops designed specifically for the organization's employees, short courses offered by consultants or universities, university programs offered to employees who live on campus during the program, and executive MBA programs (which enroll managers to meet on weekends or evenings to earn a master's degree in business administration). These programs may involve lectures by business experts, business games and simulations, experiential programs, and meetings with customers. Chapter 7 described most of these training methods, including their pros and cons.

Figure 9.1
Four Approaches to Employee Development

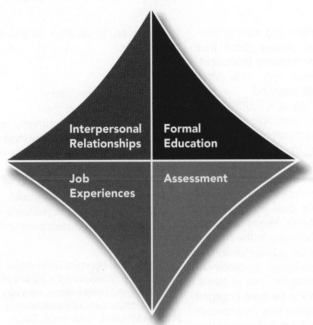

Interpersonal Relationships

Formal Education

Job Experiences

Assessment

Many companies operate training and development centers that offer seminars and longer-term programs. Among the most famous are General Electric's John F. Welch Leadership Center in Crotonville, New York, and McDonald's Hamburger University in Oak Brook, Illinois. The thousands of restaurant managers and owner-operators who attend Hamburger U each year get classroom training and simulations on how to run a business that delivers consistent service, quality, and cleanliness. They also receive coaching and peer support face-to-face and online. The company's highest-performing executives participate in a nine-month leadership institute at Hamburger U, where they tackle major issues facing the company.[7]

Independent institutions offering executive education include Harvard, the Wharton School of Business, the University of Michigan, and the Center for Creative Leadership. At the University of Virginia, the Darden School of Business offers an executive MBA program in which students attend classes on campus once a month on Thursday through Saturday. The on-campus time provides opportunities for students to collaborate on presentations, simulations, and case studies. The school also brings executive MBA students to campus four times for leadership residencies. During each weeklong residency, the students use workshops, coaching, and reflection to get better at handling their everyday management challenges. Between the times on campus, the students continue their education with independent study, online classes, and tools for virtual meetings and online exams.[8]

LO 9-3 Describe how organizations use assessment of personality type, work behaviors, and job performance to plan employee development.

Another trend in executive education is for employers and the education provider to create short courses with content designed specifically for the audience. Hasbro worked with Dartmouth's Tuck School of Business to create the Hasbro Global Leadership Program. This annual weeklong program covers areas where the toy company's managers needed greater strength: global strategy, emerging markets, personal leadership, ethics, and brand building.[9]

Assessment

assessment
Collecting information and providing feedback to employees about their behavior, communication style, or skills.

Another way to provide for employee development is **assessment**—collecting information and providing feedback to employees about their behavior, communication style, or skills.[10] Information for assessment may come from the employees, their peers, managers, and customers. The most frequent uses of assessment are to identify employees with managerial potential to measure current managers' strengths and weaknesses. Organizations also use assessment to identify managers with potential to move into higher-level executive positions. Organizations that assign work to teams may use assessment to identify the strengths and weaknesses of individual team members and the effects of the team members' decision-making and communication styles on the team's productivity.

For assessment to support development, the information must be shared with the employee being assessed. Along with that assessment information, the employee needs suggestions for correcting skill weaknesses and for using skills already learned. The suggestions might be to participate in training courses or develop skills through new job experiences. Based on the assessment information and available development opportunities, employees should develop action plans to guide their efforts at self-improvement.

Organizations vary in the methods and sources of information they use in developmental assessment. Many organizations appraise performance. Organizations with sophisticated development systems use psychological tests to measure employees' skills, personality types, and communication styles. They may collect self, peer, and manager ratings of employees' behavior and style of working with others. The tools used for these assessment methods include the Myers-Briggs Type Indicator, assessment centers, the Benchmarks assessment, performance appraisal, and 360-degree feedback. CareSource, a Dayton, Ohio, provider of managed care for Medicaid, identifies employees' personal preferences and strengths with the Myers-Briggs Type Indicator and the Gallup Strength Finder. It also uses the Leadership Practices Inventory, a kind of 360-degree appraisal of managers' leadership skills, to build a personal plan for leadership development.[11]

One way to develop employees is to begin with an assessment that may consist of assigning an activity to a team and seeing who brings what skills and strengths to the team. How can this assessment help employees?

Myers-Briggs Type Indicator   The most popular psychological inventory for employee development is the **Myers-Briggs Type Indicator (MBTI).** This assessment identifies individuals' preferences for source of energy, means of information gathering, way of decision making, and lifestyle. The assessment consists of more than 100 questions about how the person feels or prefers to behave in different situations (such as "Are you usually a good 'mixer' or rather quiet and reserved?"). The assessment describes these individuals' preferences in the four areas:

1. The *energy* dichotomy indicates where individuals gain interpersonal strength and vitality, measured as their degree of introversion or extroversion. Extroverted types (E) gain energy through interpersonal relationships. Introverted types (I) gain energy by focusing on inner thoughts and feelings.
2. The *information-gathering* dichotomy relates to the preparations individuals make before making decisions. Individuals with a Sensing (S) preference tend to gather the facts and details to prepare for a decision. Intuitive types (N) tend to focus less on the facts and more on possibilities and relationships among them.
3. In *decision making,* individuals differ in the amount of consideration they give to their own and others' values and feelings, as opposed to the hard facts of a situation. Individuals with a Thinking (T) preference try always to be objective in making decisions. Individuals with a Feeling (F) preference tend to evaluate the impact of the alternatives on others, as well as their own feelings; they are more subjective.

Myers-Briggs Type Indicator (MBTI)
Psychological test that identifies individuals' preferences for source of energy, means of information gathering, way of decision making, and lifestyle, providing information for team building and leadership development.

4. The *lifestyle* dichotomy describes an individual's tendency to be either flexible or structured. Individuals with a Judging (J) preference focus on goals, establish deadlines, and prefer to be conclusive. Individuals with a Perceiving (P) preference enjoy surprises, are comfortable with changing a decision, and dislike deadlines.

The alternatives for each of the four dichotomies result in 16 possible combinations. Of course people are likely to be mixtures of these types, but the point of the assessment is that certain types predominate in individuals.

As a result of their psychological types, people develop strengths and weaknesses. For example, individuals who are Introverted, Sensing, Thinking, and Judging (known as ISTJs) tend to be serious, quiet, practical, orderly, and logical. They can organize tasks, be decisive, and follow through on plans and goals. But because they do not have the opposite preferences (Extroversion, Intuition, Feeling, and Perceiving), ISTJs have several weaknesses. They may have difficulty responding to unexpected opportunities, appear to their colleagues to be too task-oriented or impersonal, and make decisions too fast.

Applying this kind of information about employees' preferences or tendencies helps organizations understand the communication, motivation, teamwork, work styles, and leadership of the people in their groups. For example, salespeople or executives who want to communicate better can apply what they learn about their own personality styles and the way other people perceive them. For team development, the MBTI can help teams match team members with assignments based on their preferences and thus improve problem solving.[12] The team could assign brainstorming (idea-generating) tasks to employees with an Intuitive preference and evaluation of the ideas to employees with a Sensing preference.

Research on the validity, reliability, and effectiveness of the MBTI is inconclusive.[13] People who take the MBTI find it a positive experience and say it helps them change their behavior. However, MBTI scores are not necessarily stable over time. Studies in which the MBTI was administered at two different times found that as few as one-fourth of those who took the assessment were classified as exactly the same type the second time. Still, the MBTI is a valuable tool for understanding communication styles and the ways people prefer to interact with others. It is not appropriate for measuring job performance, however, or as the only means of evaluating promotion potential.

Assessment Center
An assessment process in which multiple raters or evaluators (assessors) evaluate employees' performance on a number of exercises, usually as they work in a group at an off-site location.

Leaderless Group Discussion
An assessment center exercise in which a team of five to seven employees is assigned a problem and must work together to solve it within a certain time period.

Assessment Centers   At an **assessment center,** multiple raters or evaluators (assessors) evaluate employees' performance on a number of exercises.[14] An assessment center is usually an off-site location such as a conference center. Usually 6 to 12 employees participate at one time. The primary use of assessment centers is to identify whether employees have the personality characteristics, administrative skills, and interpersonal skills needed for managerial jobs. Organizations also use them to determine whether employees have the skills needed for working in teams.

The types of exercises used in assessment centers include leaderless group discussions, interviews, in-baskets, and role-plays.[15] In a **leaderless group discussion,** a team of five to seven employees is assigned a problem and must work together to solve it within a certain time period. The problem may involve buying and selling supplies, nominating a subordinate for an award, or assembling a product. Interview questions typically cover each employee's work and personal experiences, skill strengths and weaknesses, and career plans. In-basket exercises, discussed as a selection method in Chapter 6, simulate the administrative tasks of a manager's job, using a pile of documents for the employee to handle. In role-plays, the participant takes the part of a manager or employee in a situation involving the skills to be assessed. For example, a participant might be given the role of a manager who must discuss performance problems with an employee, played by someone who works for the assessment center. Other exercises in assessment centers might include interest and aptitude tests to evaluate an employee's vocabulary, general mental ability, and reasoning skills. Personality tests may be used to determine employees' ability to get along with others, tolerance for uncertainty, and other traits related to success as a manager or team member.

The assessors are usually managers who have been trained to look for employee behaviors that are related to the skills being assessed. Typically, each assessor observes and records one or two employees' behaviors in each exercise. The assessors review their notes and rate each employee's level of skills (for example, 5 = high level of leadership skills, 1 = low level of leadership skills). After all the employees have completed the exercises, the assessors discuss their observations of each employee. They compare their ratings and try to agree on each employee's rating for each of the skills.

As we mentioned in Chapter 6, research suggests that assessment center ratings are valid for predicting performance, salary level, and career advancement.[16] Assessment centers may also be useful for development because of the feedback that participants receive about their attitudes, skill strengths, and weaknesses.[17]

Benchmarks   A development method that focuses on measuring management skills is an instrument called **Benchmarks.** This measurement tool gathers ratings of a manager's use of skills associated with success in managing. The items measured by Benchmarks are based on research into the lessons that executives learn in critical events of their careers.[18] Items measure the 16 skills and perspectives listed in Table 9.2, including how well managers deal with subordinates, acquire resources, and create a productive work climate. Research has found that managers who have these skills are more likely to receive positive performance evaluations, be considered promotable, and be promoted.[19]

> **Benchmarks**
> A measurement tool that gathers ratings of a manager's use of skills associated with success in managing.

To provide a complete picture of managers' skills, the managers' supervisors, their peers, and the managers themselves all complete the instrument. The results include a summary report, which the organization provides to the manager so he or she can see the self-ratings in comparison to the ratings by others. Also available with this method is a development guide containing examples of experiences that enhance each skill and ways successful managers use the skill.

Performance Appraisals and 360-Degree Feedback   As we stated in Chapter 8, *performance appraisal* is the process of measuring employees' performance. This information can be useful for employee development under certain conditions.[20] The appraisal system must tell employees specifically about their performance problems and ways to improve their performance. Employees must gain a clear understanding of the differences between current performance and expected performance. The appraisal process must identify causes of the performance discrepancy and develop plans for improving performance. Managers must be trained to deliver frequent performance feedback and must monitor employees' progress in carrying out their action plans.

A recent trend in performance appraisals, also discussed in Chapter 8, is *360-degree feedback*—performance measurement by the employee's supervisor, peers, employees, and customers. Often the feedback involves rating the individual in terms of work-related behaviors. For development purposes, the rater would identify an area of behavior as a strength of that employee or an area requiring further development.

Table 9.2

Skills Related to Success as a Manager

Resourcefulness	Can think strategically, engage in flexible problem solving, and work effectively with higher management.
Doing whatever it takes	Has perseverance and focus in the face of obstacles.
Being a quick study	Quickly masters new technical and business knowledge.
Building and mending relationships	Knows how to build and maintain working relationships with co-workers and external parties.
Leading subordinates	Delegates to subordinates effectively, broadens their opportunities, and acts with fairness toward them.
Compassion and sensitivity	Shows genuine interest in others and sensitivity to subordinates' needs.
Straightforwardness and composure	Is honorable and steadfast.
Setting a developmental climate	Provides a challenging climate to encourage subordinates' development.
Confronting problem subordinates	Acts decisively and fairly when dealing with problem subordinates.
Team orientation	Accomplishes tasks through managing others.
Balance between personal life and work	Balances work priorities with personal life so that neither is neglected.
Decisiveness	Prefers quick and approximate actions to slow and precise ones in many management situations.
Self-awareness	Has an accurate picture of strengths and weaknesses and is willing to improve.
Hiring talented staff	Hires talented people for the team.
Putting people at ease	Displays warmth and a good sense of humor.
Acting with flexibility	Can behave in ways that are often seen as opposites.

SOURCE: Adapted with permission from C. D. McCauley, M. M. Lombardo, and C. J. Usher, "Diagnosing Management Development Needs: An Instrument Based on How Managers Develop," *Journal of Management* 15 (1989), pp. 389–403. Reproduced with permission of Sage Publications, Inc. via Copyright Clearance Center.

The results presented to the employee show how he or she was rated on each item and how self-evaluations differ from other raters' evaluations. The individual reviews the results, seeks clarification from the raters, and sets specific development goals based on the strengths and weaknesses identified.[21] PepsiCo provides 360-degree feedback to all of its managers as a way to build self-awareness and plan for their development. The feedback process requires that each manager meet with a certified professional to discuss the results.[22]

There are several benefits of 360-degree feedback. Organizations collect multiple perspectives of managers' performance, allowing employees to compare their own personal evaluations with the views of others. This method also establishes formal communications about behaviors and skill ratings between employees and their internal and external customers. Several studies have shown that performance improves and behavior changes as a result of participating in upward feedback and 360-degree feedback systems.[23] The change is greatest in people who received lower ratings from others than what they gave themselves. The 360-degree feedback system is most likely to be effective if the rating instrument enables reliable or consistent ratings, assesses behaviors or skills that are job related, and is easy to use. Other ways the organization can make it more likely that 360-degree feedback will yield benefits are to have the assessment results delivered by a trained person and to hold the employees accountable in follow-up meetings with their manager or a coach.[24]

There are potential limitations of 360-degree feedback. This method demands a significant amount of time for raters to complete the evaluations. If raters, especially subordinates or peers, provide negative feedback, some managers might try to identify and punish them. A facilitator is needed to help interpret results. Finally, simply delivering ratings to a manager does not provide ways for the manager to act on the feedback (for example, development planning, meeting with raters, or taking courses). As noted earlier, any form of assessment should be accompanied by suggestions for improvement and development of an action plan.

Job Experiences

Most employee development occurs through **job experiences**[25]—the combination of relationships, problems, demands, tasks, and other features of an employee's jobs. Using job experiences for employee development assumes that development is most likely to occur when the employee's skills and experiences do not entirely match the skills required for the employee's current job. To succeed, employees must stretch their skills. In other words, they must learn new skills, apply their skills and knowledge in new ways, and master new experiences.[26] For example, companies that want to prepare employees to expand overseas markets are assigning them to a variety of international jobs. To learn how a health care company successfully uses job experiences to develop employees, see the "Best Practices" box.

Most of what we know about development through job experiences comes from a series of studies conducted by the Center for Creative Leadership.[27] These studies asked executives to identify key career events that made a difference in their managerial styles and the lessons they learned from these experiences. The key events included job assignments (such as fixing a failed operation), interpersonal relationships (getting along with supervisors), and types of transitions (situations in which the manager at first lacked the necessary background). Through job experiences like these, managers learn how to handle common challenges, prove themselves, lead change, handle pressure, and influence others.

The usefulness of job experiences for employee development varies depending on whether the employee views the experiences as positive or negative sources of stress. When employees view job experiences as positive stressors, the experiences challenge them and stimulate learning. When they view job experiences as negative stressors, employees may suffer from high levels of harmful stress. Of the job demands studied, managers were most likely to experience negative stress from creating change and overcoming obstacles (adverse business conditions, lack of management support, lack of personal support, or a difficult boss). Research suggests that all of the job demands except obstacles are related to learning.[28] Organizations should offer job experiences that are most likely to increase learning, and they should consider the consequences of situations that involve negative stress.

Although the research on development through job experiences has focused on managers, line employees also can learn through job experiences. Organizations may, for example, use job experiences to develop skills needed for teamwork, including conflict resolution, data analysis, and customer service. These experiences may occur when forming a team and when employees switch roles within a team.

Various job assignments can provide for employee development. The organization may enlarge the employee's current job or move the employee to different jobs. Lateral moves include job rotation, transfer, or temporary assignment to another organization. The organization may also use downward moves or promotions as a source of job experience. Figure 9.2 summarizes these alternatives.

Job Enlargement   As Chapter 4 stated in the context of job design, *job enlargement* involves adding challenges or new responsibilities to employees' current jobs.

LO 9-4 Explain how job experiences can be used for developing skills.

Job Experiences
The combination of relationships, problems, demands, tasks, and other features of an employee's jobs.

Best Practices

Leadership Development Gets Better at Brooks Rehabilitation

Patients recovering from surgery or an injury in southeastern Georgia and northeastern Florida can seek care from one of the top U.S. hospitals according to rankings by *U.S. News & World Report,* Brooks Rehabilitation. The nonprofit operates a 127-bed rehabilitation hospital in Jacksonville, Florida, as well as more than two dozen outpatient rehabilitation clinics, a skilled nursing facility, a research center, and a physician practice specializing in rehabilitation.

With so many facilities to operate at a time when health care costs have been soaring and the pressure to bring costs down is intensifying, Brooks more than ever needs managers who are able to make complex decisions based on careful evaluation of the evidence. The effort requires not only training but creation of an environment where everyone is committed to sharing knowledge and embracing change. This need became the aim of leadership development at Brooks.

Brook's training and development specialists selected a leadership development program by James M. Kouzes and Barry Z. Posner. Their program, called the Leadership Challenge, had research supporting its effectiveness—a quality consistent with Brooks' own commitment to evidence-based decision making. Brooks' development team also believed the program would be well received because it focuses on day-to-day behaviors. The program is available to employees who want to pursue careers in management and leadership at Brooks.

The program begins with assessments, goal setting, and classwork focused on teaching basic concepts. Then participants move on to the main part of the program, what it calls "change projects." Through their assessments, participants in the development program have identified a process or function in the organization that they passionately want to change. They work with their own manager or a senior manager to settle on how they will pursue that change. Researching best practices used at other organizations, they craft an action plan for how to carry out the change. For example, the manager of an orthopedic clinic wanted to make research easily available to any therapist at Brooks so they can offer their patients options for care based on solid evidence. That manager worked with a colleague in information technology to set up a program they named the Scholarly Resource Center.

Before they launch the change effort, participants meet in groups to share their ideas. They offer feedback for one another's ideas, which not only can improve the plans and participants' skill in communicating their vision, but also helps participants learn to give and receive feedback. After this preparation, the participants implement their change projects.

Brooks quickly began seeing practical payoffs from using the Leadership Challenge. For instance, one participant set up a system for viewing payroll information online, saving the company $50,000. Brooks has also measured better staff retention and improved quality.

SOURCES: Brooks Rehabilitation, "Why Brooks? About Brooks," http://www.brookshealth.org, accessed March 29, 2012; Brooks Rehabilitation, "Why Work for Us?" https://brookshealth careers.silkroad.com, accessed March 29, 2012; "Best Hospitals: Brooks Rehabilitation Hospital," *U.S. News & World Report,* http://health.usnews.com, accessed March 29, 2012; Terri Armstrong Welch, "Evidence-Based Leadership for Evidence-Based Healthcare," *T + D,* December 2011, p. 68–70.

Examples include completing a special project, switching roles within a work team, or researching new ways to serve customers. An engineering employee might join a task force developing new career paths for technical employees. The work on the project could give the engineer a leadership role through which the engineer learns about the company's career development system while also practicing leadership skills to help the task force reach its goals. In this way, job enlargement not only makes a job more interesting, but also creates an opportunity for employees to develop new skills.

Job Rotation   Another job design technique that can be applied to employee development is *job rotation*, moving employees through a series of job assignments in one or more functional areas. Cummins uses job rotations as the major element

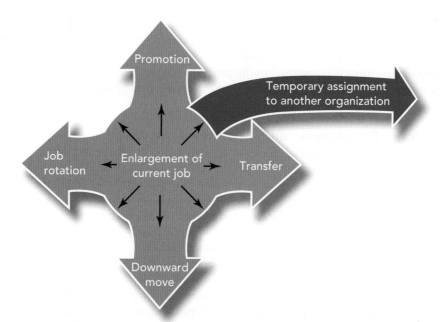

Figure 9.2
How Job Experiences
Are Used for Employee
Development

of its Engineering Development Program for newly hired engineers with leadership potential. During the five-year program, engineers spend 18 months each in two rotations where they develop basic skills in areas of engineering that are related to the manufacturing company's processes, including electronics and design for applied mechanics. Next is a 12-month rotation into a position that involves working with customer concerns. The final rotation is a 12-month job emphasizing product development. Throughout the program, the engineers are guided by mentors assigned by the company.[29]

Job rotation helps employees gain an appreciation for the company's goals, increases their understanding of different company functions, develops a network of contacts, and improves problem-solving and decision-making skills.[30] Job rotation also helps employees increase their salary and earn promotions faster. However, job rotation poses some problems for employees and the organization. Knowing they will be rotated to another job may give the employees a short-term perspective on problems and their solutions. Employees may feel less satisfied and motivated because they have difficulty developing specialized skills and leave the position too soon to fulfill any challenging assignments. The rotation of employees through a department may hurt productivity and increase the workload of those who remain after employees are rotated out. Job rotation is most likely to succeed when it meets certain conditions:[31]

- The organization establishes and communicates clear policies about which positions are eligible for job rotation. Job rotation for nonmanagement employees as well as managers can be beneficial, depending on the program's objectives.
- Employees and their managers understand and agree on the expectations for the job rotation, including which skills are to be developed.
- Goals for the program support business goals. These might include exposing high-potential employees to a variety of business units, customers, or geographic areas in preparation for management positions or rotating an experienced, talented employee through several business units to mentor or coach employees.

- The rotation schedule is realistic, taking into account how long employees will need to become familiar with their new position, as well as how much time is needed for employees to complete the assignments.
- Top management is committed to the program's success.
- Someone is responsible for measuring whether the program is meeting its goals.

Transfers, Promotions, and Downward Moves   Most companies use upward, downward, and lateral moves as an option for employee development. In a **transfer,** the organization assigns an employee to a position in a different area of the company. Transfers do not necessarily increase job responsibilities or compensation. They are usually lateral moves, that is, moves to a job with a similar level of responsibility. They may involve relocation to another part of the country or even to another country.

Relocation can be stressful because of the demands of moving, especially when family members are affected. People have to find new housing, shopping, health care, and leisure facilities, and they often lack the support of nearby friends and family. These stresses come at the same time the employee must learn the expectations and responsibilities associated with the new position. Because transfers can provoke anxiety, many companies have difficulty getting employees to accept them. Employees most willing to accept transfers tend to be those with high career ambitions and beliefs that the organization offers a promising future and that accepting the transfer will help the company succeed.[32]

A **downward move** occurs when an employee is given less responsibility and authority. The organization may demote an employee because of poor performance or move the employee to a lower-level position in another function so that the employee can develop different skills. The temporary cross-functional move is the most common way to use downward moves for employee development. For example, engineers who want to move into management often take lower-level positions, such as shift supervisor, to develop their management skills.

Many employees have difficulty associating transfers and downward moves with development; these changes may feel more like forms of punishment. Employees often decide to leave an organization rather than accept such a change, and then the organization must bear the costs of replacing those employees. Employees will be more likely to accept transfers and downward moves as development opportunities if the organization provides information about the change and its possible benefits and involves the employee in planning the change. Employees are also more likely to be positive about such a recommendation if the organization provides clear performance objectives and frequent feedback. Employers can encourage an employee to relocate by providing financial assistance with the move, information about the new location and job, and help for family members, such as identifying schools, child care and elder care options, and job search assistance for the employee's spouse.[33]

Transfer
Assignment of an employee to a position in a different area of the company, usually in a lateral move.

Downward Move
Assignment of an employee to a position with less responsibility and authority.

Working outside one's home country is the most important job experience that can develop an employee for a career in the global economy.

A **promotion** involves moving an employee into a position with greater challenges, more responsibility, and more authority than in the previous job. Usually promotions include pay increases. Because promotions improve the person's pay, status, and feelings of accomplishment, employees are more willing to accept promotions than lateral or downward moves. Even so, employers can increase the likelihood that employees will accept promotions by providing the same kind of information and assistance that are used to support transfers and downward moves. Organizations can more easily offer promotions if they are profitable and growing. In other conditions, opportunities for promoting employees may be limited.

Promotion
Assignment of an employee to a position with greater challenges, more responsibility, and more authority than in the previous job, usually accompanied by a pay increase.

Temporary Assignments with Other Organizations In some cases, an employer may benefit from the skills an employee can learn at another organization. The employer may encourage the employee to participate in an **externship**—a full-time temporary position at another organization. Externships are an attractive option for employees in analytical positions, who otherwise might solve the same kinds of problems over and over, becoming bored as they miss out on exposure to challenging new ideas and techniques. In a sign that this type of activity is gaining traction among businesses, an organization called World Action Teams recently formed to set up development programs in emerging markets in Asia, Africa, and Latin America. For client firms that want to provide their executives with firsthand experiences in these locales, World Action Teams will arrange a 4- to 28-day work project and provide the executives with information about how to lead people in the culture where they will be working.[34]

Externship
Employee development through a full-time temporary position at another organization.

Temporary assignments can include a **sabbatical**—a leave of absence from an organization to renew or develop skills. Employees on sabbatical often receive full pay and benefits. Sabbaticals let employees get away from the day-to-day stresses of their jobs and acquire new skills and perspectives. Sabbaticals also allow employees more time for personal pursuits such as writing a book or spending more time with family members. Universities often give sabbaticals to faculty members; some offer these development opportunities to staff members as well. After Shenandoah University in Winchester, Virginia, made sabbaticals available to employees who had worked there for at least 10 years, a staff member took time off and spent it interviewing alumni. The resulting stories will provide a valuable resource for creating the school's marketing materials. Jenny Lynne Semenza, a librarian at Idaho State University, used a six-month sabbatical to travel between Arizona and Alaska, visiting academic libraries along the way. Semenza gathered ideas for improving ISU's library when she returned to her job.[35] How employees spend their sabbaticals varies from company to company. Some employees may work for a nonprofit service agency; others may study at a college or university or travel and work on special projects in non-U.S. subsidiaries of the company.

Sabbatical
A leave of absence from an organization to renew or develop skills.

Interpersonal Relationships

Employees can also develop skills and increase their knowledge about the organization and its customers by interacting with a more experienced organization member. Two types of relationships used for employee development are mentoring and coaching.

LO 9-5 Summarize principles of successful mentoring programs.

Mentors

A **mentor** is an experienced, productive senior employee who helps develop a less experienced employee, called the *protégé*. Most mentoring relationships develop informally as a result of interests or values shared by the mentor and protégé. According to research, the employees most likely to seek and attract a mentor have certain personality characteristics: emotional stability, ability to adapt their behavior to the

Mentor
An experienced, productive senior employee who helps develop a less-experienced employee (a protégé).

situation, and high needs for power and achievement.[36] Mentoring relationships also can develop as part of the organization's planned effort to bring together successful senior employees with less-experienced employees.

One major advantage of formal mentoring programs is that they ensure access to mentors for all employees, regardless of gender or race. A mentoring program also can ensure that high-potential employees are matched with wise, experienced mentors in key areas—and that mentors are hearing the challenges facing employees who have less authority, work directly with customers, or hold positions in other parts of the organization.[37] However, in an artificially created relationship, mentors may have difficulty providing counseling and coaching.[38] One practical way employees can address this shortcoming is to look for more than one mentor, including informal relationships with interested people outside the organization. Employees also should accept the limits of mentoring relationships. Mentoring is not, for example, a substitute for therapy: a mentor might offer tips for navigating a business presentation, whereas a therapist is a better choice for someone who needs help with persistent anxiety.[39]

Mentoring programs tend to be most successful when they are voluntary and participants understand the details of the program. Rewarding managers for employee development is also important because it signals that mentoring and other development activities are worthwhile. In addition, the organization should carefully select mentors based on their interpersonal and technical skills, train them for the role, and evaluate whether the program has met its objectives.[40]

Mentors and protégés can both benefit from a mentoring relationship. Protégés receive career support, including coaching, protection, sponsorship, challenging assignments, and visibility among the organization's managers. They also receive benefits of a positive relationship—a friend and role model who accepts them, has a positive opinion toward them, and gives them a chance to talk about their worries. Employees with mentors are also more likely to be promoted, earn higher salaries, and have more influence within their organization.[41] Acting as a mentor gives managers a chance to develop their interpersonal skills and increase their feelings that they are contributing something important to the organization. Working with a technically trained protégé on matters such as new research in the field may also increase the mentor's technical knowledge.

So that more employees can benefit from mentoring, some organizations use *group mentoring programs*, which assign four to six protégés to a successful senior employee. A potential advantage of group mentoring is that protégés can learn from each other as well as from the mentor. The leader helps protégés understand the organization, guides them in analyzing their experiences, and helps them clarify career directions. Each member of the group may complete specific assignments, or the group may work together on a problem or issue.

LO 9-6 Tell how managers and peers develop employees through coaching.

Coach
A peer or manager who works with an employee to motivate the employee, help him or her develop skills, and provide reinforcement and feedback.

Coaching

A **coach** is a peer or manager who works with an employee to motivate the employee, help him or her develop skills, and provide reinforcement and feedback. Coaches may play one or more of three roles:[42]

1. Working one-on-one with an employee, as when giving feedback. For an example of how social media could support this coaching role, see "HRM Social."
2. Helping employees learn for themselves—for example, helping them find experts and teaching them to obtain feedback from others.
3. Providing resources such as mentors, courses, or job experiences.

Change Anything: Can a Website Make You Great?

Many employees arrive at a point where they know they need to change something about how they work. Assessments, feedback, and personal experience unite to tell them they need to listen more carefully, or give their staff clearer directions, or stop procrastinating on sales reports, or take time to thank employees for a job well done. Even if they see these problems, however, employees often get stuck, unable to see how they can change deeply ingrained work habits. At that point, what the employees need to propel their development forward is a coach—someone who is aware of their goals, pays attention to their progress, prods them along, and offers suggestions when they get stuck.

Researchers at an organization called VitalSmarts had an idea that this kind of coaching could be made available online, using social-media tools. They created a website called Change Anything, where people can set personal and professional goals for themselves and arrange to be coached both by the software and

by peers or managers they invite to fill that role.

An employee using Change Anything sets a measurable goal to improve in a particular performance area by a specific date. The site helps the employee identify the behaviors that will have the most significant impact on achieving those results. It then leads the employee through a process of identifying tactics for motivating employees to carry out those behaviors. Those tactics look at the employee's own motivation and ability by directing them to visualize their future selves and identify the skills they need to add. Employees also delve into social and structural influences, such as reminders, coaches, scorecards, and rewards. The plan can be set up to deliver e-mail reminders to the employee and to display the employee's progress each day—perhaps compared with the progress of the employee's peers.

VitalSmarts found that Change Anything is most successful when people's plans include coaching. The employees and their coaches

can send one another messages at the Change Anything website so coaches can offer encouragement or advice, along with simply being a person the employee knows is checking up on him or her. Change Anything users can volunteer to be coaches for other users. The employee can choose one of those volunteers from a list or can e-mail an invitation to another employee at his or her organization or someone else the employee knows and respects.

As of this writing, the system is still new, without a large body of results to report. But individuals can try out a change plan for no charge. If you're curious, visit **www .changeanything.com** and set a goal for yourself.

SOURCES: Change Anything, "Change Plan: Advance My Career," http://www .changeanything.com, accessed March 29, 2012; David Maxfield, "How to Promote Behavioral Change," *Chief Learning Officer*, October 2011, pp. 44–47; Joseph Grenny and Vincent Han, "The Upside to Social Networking," *Chief Learning Officer*, April 2011, pp. 30–33.

When ConAgra Foods selected lawyer Colleen Batcheler to be its general counsel, the company's human resource department offered her executive coaching to help prepare for this high-level role. Batcheler met several times with the coaching team, using the assessments and homework they gave her to draw up goals for what she wanted to achieve. For accountability, she met with ConAgra's chief executive and with her staff to review her goals with them. One of Batcheler's goals was to spend more time learning about the strengths of each person on the legal team so she could apply team members' unique qualities in a way that would get the best results for the team overall. Learning to look for personal qualities was difficult at first, but she practiced the behavior until it became second nature. As a result, she is a more effective leader, and her team members are more committed and productive.[43]

Research suggests that coaching helps managers improve by identifying areas for improvement and setting goals.[44] Getting results from a coaching relationship can take at least six months of weekly or monthly meetings. To be effective, a coach generally conducts an assessment, asks questions that challenge the employee to think deeply about his or her goals and motives, helps the employee create an action plan, and follows up regularly to help the employee stay on track. Employees contribute to the success of coaching when they persevere in practicing the behaviors identified in the action plan.[45]

LO 9-7 Identify the steps in the process of career management.

Systems for Career Management

Employee development is most likely to meet the organization's needs if it is part of a human resource system of career management. In practice, organizations' career management systems vary. Some rely heavily on informal relationships, while others are sophisticated programs. As shown in Figure 9.3, a basic career management system involves four steps: data gathering, feedback, goal setting, and action planning and follow-up. Human resource professionals can contribute to the system's success by ensuring that it is linked to other HR practices such as performance management, training, and recruiting. Two divisions of Walgreens created a career management program that is both relevant and popular by inviting divisional employees to take charge of creating the program themselves. The employee volunteers identified career paths, defined competencies required for each step of each path, developed training tools for acquiring the necessary competencies, and even designed the website that provides access to these materials.[46]

Data Gathering

Self-Assessment
The use of information by employees to determine their career interests, values, aptitudes, behavioral tendencies, and development needs.

In discussing the methods of employee development, we highlighted several assessment tools. Such tools may be applied to data gathering, the first step in the career management process. **Self-assessment** refers to the use of information by employees to determine their career interests, values, aptitudes, and behavioral tendencies. The employee's responsibility is to identify opportunities and personal areas needing improvement. The organization's responsibility is to provide assessment information for identifying strengths, weaknesses, interests, and values.

Figure 9.3
Steps in the Career Management Process

Criteria for success	**Data gathering**	**Feedback**	**Goal setting**	**Action planning & Follow-up**
	Focus on competencies needed for career success.	Maintain confidentiality.	Involve management and coaches/mentors.	Involve management and coaches/mentors.
	Include a variety of measures.	Focus on specific success factors, strengths, and improvement areas.	Specify competencies and knowledge to be developed.	Measure success and adjust plans as needed.
			Specify developmental methods.	Verify that pace of development is realistic.

Self-assessment tools often include psychological tests such as the Myers-Briggs Type Indicator (described earlier in the chapter), the Strong-Campbell Interest Inventory, and the Self-Directed Search. The Strong-Campbell inventory helps employees identify their occupational and job interests. The Self-Directed Search identifies employees' preferences for working in different kinds of environments—sales, counseling, and so on. Tests may also help employees identify the relative values they place on work and leisure activities. Self-assessment tools can include exercises such as the one in Figure 9.4. This type of exercise helps an employee consider his or her current career status, future plans, and the fit between the career and the employee's current situation and resources. Some organizations provide counselors to help employees in the self-assessment process and to interpret the results of psychological tests. Completing the self-assessment can help employees identify a development need. Such a need can result from gaps between current skills or interests and the type of work or position the employee has or wants.

Self-assessments play an important role in career development of employees being developed for leadership roles at Tyson Foods, a major processor of chicken, beef, and

Figure 9.4
Sample Self-Assessment Exercise

Step 1: Where am I?
Examine current position of life and career.
Think about your life from past and present to the future. Draw a time line to represent important events.

Step 2: Who am I?
Examine different roles.
Using 3" × 5" cards, write down one answer per card to the question "Who am I?"

Step 3: Where would I like to be, and what would I like to happen?
Begin setting goals.
Consider your life from present to future. Write an autobiography answering these questions:
• What do you want to have accomplished?
• What milestones do you want to achieve?
• What do you want to be remembered for?

Step 4: An ideal year in the future
Identify resources needed.
Consider a one-year period in the future. Answer these questions:
• If you had unlimited resources, what would you do?
• What would the ideal environment look like?
• Does the ideal environment match Step 3?

Step 5: An ideal job
Create current goal.
In the present, think about an ideal job for you with your available resources. Describe your role, resources, and type of training or education needed.

Step 6: Career by objective inventory
Summarize current situation.
• What gets you excited each day?
• What do you do well? What are you known for?
• What do you need to achieve your goals?
• What could interfere with reaching your goals?
• What should you do now to move toward reaching your goals?
• What is your long-term career objective?

SOURCE: Based on J. E. McMahon and S. K. Merman, "Career Development," in *The ASTD Training and Development Handbook,* 4e, edited by R. L. Craig (New York: McGraw-Hill, 1996), pp. 679–697. Reproduced with permission.

pork. These employees begin the development process by reading a book called *The Organization Champion* and completing an assessment that measures their skills in being an organization champion. The assessment helps the employees identify their strengths and areas for improvement. Next, the employees participate in a two-day event that includes time to identify their perspectives on life, their skills, what inspires them, and the unique contributions they make to the company. All of these efforts deliver information the Tyson employees can apply to setting goals for their career development.[47]

Feedback

Feedback
Information employers give employees about their skills and knowledge and where these assets fit into the organization's plans.

In the next step of career management, **feedback,** employees receive information about their skills and knowledge and where these assets fit into the organization's plans. The employee's responsibility is to identify what skills she or he could realistically develop in light of the opportunities available. The organization's responsibility is to communicate the performance evaluation and the opportunities available to the employee, given the organization's long-range plans. Opportunities might include promotions and transfers.

Usually the employer conducts the reality check as part of a performance appraisal or as the feedback stage of performance management. In well-developed career management systems, the manager may hold separate discussions for performance feedback and career development.

Managers at Vistaprint, an online seller of business cards, stationery, postcards, and other printed products, rely on 360-degree feedback to guide their career development. During years of rapid growth, the expanding company promoted its top-performing employees into management positions, but soon discovered that only some of them were succeeding. An investigation showed a need for the new managers to learn skills such as delegating, planning, coaching, and motivating. Now Vistaprint offers managers a training program in which they receive three separate 360-degree assessments that show them where they need to develop management skills and then track their progress in acquiring those skills. Since the program began, managers before, during, and after the training have continually raised their scores on these assessments. Apparently, knowledge about what to do differently has been an extremely powerful tool for management development at Vistaprint.[48]

Goal Setting

Based on the information from the self-assessment and reality check, the employee sets short- and long-term career objectives. These goals usually involve one or more of the following categories:

- Desired positions, such as becoming sales manager within three years.
- Level of skill to apply—for example, to use one's budgeting skills to improve the unit's cash flow problems.
- Work setting—for example, to move to corporate marketing within two years.
- Skill acquisition, such as learning how to use the company's human resource information system.

As in these examples, the goals should be specific, and they should include a date by which the goal is to be achieved. It is the employee's responsibility to identify the goal and the method of determining her or his progress toward that goal.

Usually the employee discusses the goals with his or her manager. The organization's responsibilities are to ensure that the goal is specific, challenging, and attainable and to help the employee reach the goal. In the Patient Care and Clinical Informatics (PCCI) division of Philips Healthcare, employees take assessments and then engage in regular career discussions to establish goals for where they want to go in PCCI and how they will get there over the next one to five years. These personalized goals can involve lateral moves, enrichment of one's ability to contribute in a current position, or even an exploration of career possibilities, not simply advancement to the next job upward in the company hierarchy. Just six months after PCCI launched this career management program, employees reported feeling much more excited about working there.[49]

Indra Nooyi became the first woman CEO of PepsiCo in 2006. Her success at the company gives her the distinction of being one of the women to break through the glass ceiling.

Action Planning and Follow-Up

During the final step, employees prepare an action plan for how they will achieve their short- and long-term career goals. The employee is responsible for identifying the steps and timetable to reach the goals. The employer should identify resources needed, including courses, work experiences, and relationships. The employee and the manager should meet in the future to discuss progress toward career goals.

Action plans may involve any one or a combination of the development methods discussed earlier in the chapter—training, assessment, job experiences, or the help of a mentor or coach. The approach used depends on the particular developmental needs and career objectives. For example, suppose the program manager in an information systems department uses feedback from performance appraisals to determine that he needs greater knowledge of project management software. The manager plans to increase that knowledge by reading articles (formal education), meeting with software vendors, and contacting the vendors' customers to ask them about the software they have used (job experiences). The manager and his supervisor agree that six months will be the target date for achieving the higher level of knowledge through these activities.

The outcome of action planning often takes the form of a career development plan. Figure 9.5 is an example of a development plan for a product manager. Development plans usually include descriptions of strengths and weaknesses, career goals, and development activities for reaching each goal.

Development-Related Challenges

A well-designed system for employee development can help organizations face three widespread challenges: the glass ceiling, succession planning, and dysfunctional behavior by managers.

LO 9-8 Discuss how organizations are meeting the challenges of the "glass ceiling," succession planning, and dysfunctional managers.

The Glass Ceiling

As we mentioned in Chapter 1, women and minorities are rare in the top level of U.S. corporations. Observers of this situation have noted that it looks as if an invisible barrier is keeping women and minorities from reaching the top jobs, a barrier that has come to be known as the **glass ceiling.** For example, a recent census of board membership of Fortune 500 companies found that just 16% of the seats were held by women.[50] Outside the United States (except in Norway, Sweden, and Finland), women are an even smaller share. For more evidence of the glass ceiling, see "Did You Know?"

The glass ceiling is likely caused by a lack of access to training programs, to appropriate developmental job experiences, and to developmental relationships such as mentoring.[51] With regard to developmental relationships, women and minorities often have trouble finding mentors. They may not participate in the organization's,

Glass Ceiling
Circumstances resembling an invisible barrier that keep most women and minorities from attaining the top jobs in organizations.

Figure 9.5
Career Development Plan

Name:	**Title:** Project Manager	**Immediate Manager:**

Competencies
Please identify your three greatest strengths and areas for improvement.
Strengths
- Strategic thinking and execution (confidence, command skills, action orientation)
- Results orientation (competence, motivating others, perseverance)
- Spirit for winning (building team spirit, customer focus, respect colleagues)

Areas for Improvement
- Patience (tolerance of people or processes and sensitivity to pacing)
- Written communications (ability to write clearly and succinctly)
- Overly ambitious (too much focus on successful completion of projects rather than developing relationships with individuals involved in the projects)

Career Goals
Please describe your overall career goals.
- **Long-term:** Accept positions of increased responsibility to a level of general manager (or beyond). The areas of specific interest include, but are not limited to, product and brand management, technology and development, strategic planning, and marketing.
- **Short-term:** Continue to improve my skills in marketing and brand management while utilizing my skills in product management, strategic planning, and global relations.

Next Assignments
Identify potential next assignments (including timing) that would help you develop toward your career goals.
- Manager or director level in planning, development, product, or brand management. Timing estimated to be Spring 2014.

Training and Development Needs
List both training and development activities that will either help you develop in your current assignment or provide overall career development.
- Master's degree classes will allow me to practice and improve my written communications skills. The dynamics of my current position, teamwork, and reliance on other individuals allow me to practice patience and to focus on individual team members' needs along with the success of the projects.

Employee _____ **Date** _____
Immediate Manager _____ **Date** _____
Mentor _____ **Date** _____

profession's, or community's "old boys' network." Also, recent evidence finds differences in how women and men pursue advancement and in how executives perceive women's and men's qualifications and ambitions. Female managers tend to find more mentors, but primarily mentors who give advice; their male counterparts find, on average, mentors who are more senior and will sponsor them for key positions. Patterns of promotion suggest that companies are more willing to select men from outside the organization based on their potential, while women do better when they stay with the same company where they can demonstrate a track record of achievements. Consistent with this difference, women who actively promote their achievements tend

Today's Directors Look a Lot Like Yesterday's Directors

As companies look for current and retired chief executive officers and chief financial officers to serve on their boards of directors, they are getting a lot of experience but not a lot of diversity. Since mainly white men have been CEOs and CFOs in the past, most boards of large U.S. corporations continue to be dominated by white men today.

Question

If populating a board of directors with current and former CEOs and CFOs does not increase the board's diversity, should a big corporation look for different sources of talent to serve on its board? Why or why not?

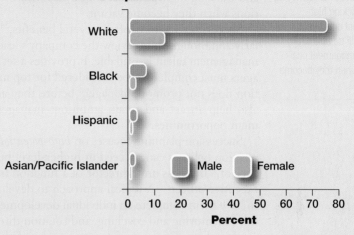

Race/Ethnic Group and Sex of Board Members, Fortune 500 Companies

SOURCES: Catalyst, "Women on Boards," *Quick Takes,* March 27, 2012, http://www.catalyst.org; "Female Directors: Why So Few?" *The Wall Street Journal,* December 27, 2011, http://online.wsj.com; "Corporate Boards: Now and Then," *Harvard Business Review,* November 2011, pp. 38–39.

to advance further in an organization, whereas broadcasting their achievements does not make much difference in their male colleagues' advancement.[52]

Organizations can use development systems to help break through the glass ceiling. Managers making developmental assignments need to carefully consider whether stereotypes are influencing the types of assignments men and women receive. A formal process for regularly identifying development needs and creating action plans can make these decisions more objective.

An organization that is actively trying to eliminate the glass ceiling is Coca-Cola Company, where the effort is part of a commitment to corporate sustainability. The company's chairman, Muhtar Kent, points out that at least two-thirds of the customers who buy the company's products are women. Coca-Cola can best serve these customers, Kent suggests, if it is demographically more like them. Under a program called 2020, Coca-Cola set goals for identifying and developing talented female employees. In the program's first three and a half years, the percentage of women in Coca-Cola's management rose from less than one-quarter of all managers to 40%. The company has a program aimed at developing managers' ability to foster inclusiveness, as well as a Women in Leadership program that selects high-potential female managers for accelerated development.[53]

Succession Planning

Organizations have always had to prepare for the retirement of their leaders, but the need is more intense than ever. The aging of the workforce means that a greater share

Succession Planning
The process of identifying and tracking high-potential employees who will be able to fill top management positions when they become vacant.

of employees are reaching retirement age. Many organizations are fueling the trend by downsizing through early-retirement programs. As positions at the top of organizations become vacant, many organizations have determined that their middle managers are fewer and often unprepared for top-level responsibility. This situation has raised awareness of the need for **succession planning**—the process of identifying and tracking high-potential employees who will be able to fill top management positions when they become vacant.

Succession planning offers several benefits.[54] It forces senior management to regularly and thoughtfully review the company's leadership talent. It ensures that top-level management talent is available. It provides a set of development experiences that managers must complete to be considered for top management positions, so the organization does not promote managers before they are ready. Succession planning systems also help attract and retain ambitious managerial employees by providing development opportunities.

Succession planning focuses on *high-potential employees*, that is, employees the organization believes can succeed in higher-level business positions such as general manager of a business unit, director of a function (such as marketing or finance), or chief executive officer.[55] A typical approach to development of high-potential employees is to have them complete an individual development program including education, executive mentoring and coaching, and rotation through job assignments. Job assignments are based on the successful career paths of the managers whom the high-potential employees are preparing to replace. High-potential employees may also receive special assignments, such as making presentations and serving on committees and task forces.

Research shows that an effective program for developing high-potential employees has three stages:[56]

1. *Selection of high-potential employees*—Organizations may select outstanding performers and employees who have completed elite academic programs, such as earning a master's degree in business administration from a prestigious university. They may also use the results of psychological tests such as assessment centers. For tips on selecting high-potential employees, see "HR How To."
2. *Developmental experiences*—As employees participate in developmental experiences, the organization identifies those who succeed in the experiences. The organization looks for employees who continue to show qualities associated with success in top jobs, such as communication skills, leadership talent, and willingness to make sacrifices for the organization. In today's high-performance business environment, these assessments should measure whether participants in the program are demonstrating an ability to lead and delivering results that contribute to the company's success. Employees who display these qualities continue to be considered high-potential employees.
3. *Active involvement with the CEO*—High-potential employees seen by top management as fitting into the organization's culture and having personality characteristics necessary for representing the company become actively involved with the chief executive officer. The CEO exposes these employees to the organization's key people and gives them a greater understanding of the organization's culture. The development of high-potential employees is a slow process. Reaching stage 3 may take 15 to 20 years.

Figure 9.6 breaks this process into eight steps. It begins with identifying the positions to be planned for and the employees to be included in the plan. Planning should also include establishing position requirements and deciding how to measure employees' potential for being able to fill those requirements. The organization also needs to develop a process for reviewing the existing talent. The next step is to link succession planning with other human resource systems. Then the organization needs a way to provide employees with feedback about career paths available to them and how well they are progressing toward their goals. Finally, measuring the plan's effectiveness provides information for continuing or adjusting future succession plans.

A good example of succession planning is the effort at General Electric. GE insists that there be in place a plan identifying the top candidate to replace each executive in a key position, as well as two or three backup candidates in case something goes wrong with the plan for the top choice. During six-month reviews, GE's board of directors learns about these individuals, so that if someone quickly fills a vacancy, the board is already familiar with that person. For instance, when senior vice president Larry Johnston left GE to become chief executive of Albertsons, the company's board already knew who would replace him. GE was able to announce the new senior vice president at the same time it announced Johnston's departure—in fact, it could also announce other management changes as a series of promotions took place to fill each key vacancy that resulted.[57]

Figure 9.6

Process for Developing a Succession Plan

SOURCES: Based on B. Dowell, "Succession Planning," in *Implementing Organizational Interventions*, ed. J. Hedge and E. Pulakos (San Francisco: Jossey-Bass, 2002), pp. 78–109; R. Barnett and S. Davis, "Creating Greater Success in Succession Planning," *Advances in Developing Human Resources* 10 (2008): 721–39.

Dysfunctional Managers

A manager who is otherwise competent may engage in some behaviors that make him or her ineffective or even "toxic"—someone who stifles good ideas and drives away employees. These dysfunctional behaviors include insensitivity to others, inability to be a team player, arrogance, poor conflict-management skills, inability to meet business objectives, and inability to adapt to change.[58] For example, a manager who has strong technical knowledge but is abrasive and discourages employees from contributing their ideas is likely to have difficulty motivating employees and may alienate people inside and outside the organization.

When a manager is an otherwise valuable employee and is willing to improve, the organization may try to help him or her change the dysfunctional behavior. The usual ways to provide this type of development include assessment, training, and counseling. Development programs for managers with dysfunctional behavior may also include specialized programs such as one called Individual Coaching for Effectiveness (ICE).

HR How To

Identifying High-Potential Employees

It makes sense to invest development dollars and time in the employees with the most potential to succeed when given greater responsibility. But how does an organization know which employees have high potential? Here are some tips for making the right choices:

- **Distinguish *potential* from *experience*.** Potential refers to a person's ability to grow into something more than he or she is today. A high-potential candidate is one who can grow into handling greater responsibilities—a larger budget, a bigger staff, and more complex activities. Success on a smaller scale is just one sign of potential. A high potential candidate is also eager to assume greater responsibility, able to

learn quickly, and willing to work hard to meet new challenges. In an assessment of potential, an employee's strong drive to learn from experience could outweigh a lack of experience in a particular area.

- **Seek nominations.** Organizations that are committed to succession planning give their managers responsibility for identifying employees with high potential. Waiting for employees to volunteer is less effective because people tend to overrate their own potential. But for managers' recommendations to be valid, the organization should also train managers in how to spot the qualities the organization is seeking.
- **Use several measures.** Performance appraisals may focus too

much on specific experiences with a particular supervisor, and personality tests are sometimes easy for test takers to manipulate. Mix both measures with interviews, peer assessments, assessment centers, and intelligence testing for a fuller picture of the candidates for the program.

SOURCES: Len Karakowsky and Igor Kotlyar, "Do 'High-Potential' Leadership Programs Really Work?" *Globe and Mail (Toronto)*, January 1, 2012, http://www.theglobeandmail.com; Claudio Fernández-Aráoz, Boris Groysberg, and Nitin Nohria, "How to Hang On to Your High Potentials," *Harvard Business Review*, October 2011, pp. 76–83; Tom Fox, "Developing the Leadership Skills of High-Potential Employees," *The Washington Post*, August 15, 2011, http://www.washingtonpost.com.

The ICE program includes diagnosis, coaching, and support activities tailored to each manager's needs.[59] Psychologists conduct the diagnosis, coach and counsel the manager, and develop action plans for implementing new skills on the job. Research suggests that managers who participate in programs like ICE improve their skills and are less likely to be terminated.[60] One possible conclusion is that organizations can benefit from offering development opportunities to valuable employees with performance problems, not just to star performers.

THINKING ETHICALLY

WHO GAINS FROM EMPLOYEE DEVELOPMENT?

When Derek Christian wanted to run his own business, he bought a cleaning company called My Maid Service. The company had decent revenues but little growth, and Christian figure out why: employees were constantly quitting. With a turnover rate of 300%, Christian was filling the same job three times every year. The reason was simple. No one wanted a career

cleaning houses, so people worked for the service only until they could find something closer to their real goals. Higher pay didn't address the problem, so Christian accepted that no one would stay forever. He opted for an unusual kind of employee development: if an employee agreed to stay with My Maid Service for two years, the company would pay for training and development (including stretch assignments at the company) to help the employee toward the next step of his or her career plan. Christian determined that the costs of this program are far less than he was spending to constantly hire and train entry-level employees. Customers, too, are more satisfied and loyal because they prefer having the same people clean their homes each time.

Derek Christian's plan for employee development is clever, and because he is the business's owner, he didn't have to convince anyone but himself to try it. But imagine trying a similar program at a corporation that is owned by many stockholders. They might conclude that the cost is not in their best interests as investors in the business. Some employers even insist that employees pay for any training they receive because the employees are the ones who get the greatest benefit from what they learn.

One person who might not see a conflict is Wendy S. Becker, associate professor of management at John L. Grove College of Business. Becker advocates the idea that human resource practices should be sustainable. By acquiring, developing, and managing employees in a way that is socially responsible—concerned for their welfare and the welfare of their communities—organizations can, over the long term, be the places where the best people want to work. One way to do this, Becker says, is to hire people not just for their experience and accomplishments but also for their potential, even though these employees

will reach their full value after the company has invested in their development. There is a risk that employees will take their newly learned skills elsewhere for better pay, but there is also a perhaps greater likelihood that employees will be more committed and loyal after the company invests in them. Perhaps if employers treat development programs as an investment in employees' future value to the company, rather than as an expense to minimize, employees, too, will focus more on their value to the company.

Questions

1. When a company spends money on employee development, who should receive the benefit—investors, customers, employees, or someone else? What is the most ethical way to distribute the benefits?
2. Do employees who participate in an employee development program have an ethical obligation to remain with the employer afterward? Why or why not?

SOURCES: Jack Berry, "Transforming HRD into an Economic Value Add," *T + D,* September 2011, pp. 66–69; Wendy S. Becker, "Are You Leading a Socially Responsible and Sustainable Human Resource Function?" *People & Strategy,* March 2011, pp. 18–23; Gary M. Stern, "Training Workers to Leave for a Better Job," *CNNMoney,* June 1, 2010, http://money.cnn.com.

SUMMARY

LO 9-1 Discuss how development is related to training and careers.

Employee development is the combination of formal education, job experiences, relationships, and assessment of personality and abilities to help employees prepare for the future of their careers. Training is more focused on improving performance in the current job, but training programs may support employee development. In modern organizations, the concept of a career is fluid—a protean career that changes along with changes in a person's interests, abilities, and values and changes in the work environment. To plan and prepare for a protean career requires active career management, which includes planning for employee development.

LO 9-2 Identify the methods organizations use for employee development.

Organizations may use formal educational programs at the workplace or off-site, such as workshops, university courses and degree programs, company-sponsored training, or programs

offered by independent institutions. Organizations may use the assessment process to help employees identify strengths and areas requiring further development. Assessment can help the organization identify employees with managerial potential or identify areas in which teams need to develop. Job experiences help employees develop by stretching their skills as they meet new challenges. Interpersonal relationships with a more experienced member of the organization—often in the role of mentor or coach—can help employees develop their understanding of the organization and its customers.

LO 9-3 Describe how organizations use assessment of personality type, work behaviors, and job performance to plan employee development.

Organizations collect information and provide feedback to employees about their behavior, communication style, and skills. The information may come from the employees, their peers, managers, and customers. Many organizations use performance appraisals as a source of assessment information. Appraisals may take the form of 360-degree feedback. Some organizations use psychological tests designed for this purpose, including the Myers-Briggs Type Indicator and the Benchmarks assessment. Assessment centers combine a variety of methods to provide assessment information. Managers must share the assessments, along with suggestions for improvement.

LO 9-4 Explain how job experiences can be used for developing skills.

Job experiences contribute to development through a combination of relationships, problems, demands, tasks, and other features of an employee's jobs. The assumption is that development is most likely to occur when the employee's skills and experiences do not entirely match the skills required for the employee's current job, so employees must stretch to meet the demands of the new assignment. The impact varies according to whether the employee views the experience as a positive or negative source of stress. Job experiences that support employee development may include job enlargement, job rotations, transfers, promotions, downward moves, and temporary assignments with other organizations.

LO 9-5 Summarize principles of successful mentoring programs.

A mentor is an experienced, productive senior employee who helps develop a less-experienced employee. Although most mentoring relationships develop informally, organizations can link mentoring to development goals by establishing a formal mentoring program. A formal program also provides a basis for ensuring that all eligible employees are included. Mentoring programs tend to be most successful when they are voluntary and participants understand the details of the program. The organization should reward managers for employee development, carefully select mentors based on interpersonal and technical skills, train them for the role, and evaluate whether the program has met its objectives.

LO 9-6 Tell how managers and peers develop employees through coaching.

A coach is a peer or manager who works with an employee to motivate the employee, help him or her develop skills, and provide reinforcement and feedback. Coaches should be prepared to take on one or more of three roles: working one-on-one with an employee, helping employees learn for themselves, and providing resources, such as mentors, courses, or job experiences.

LO 9-7 Identify the steps in the process of career management.

First, during data gathering employees use information to determine their career interests, values, aptitudes, and behavioral tendencies, looking for opportunities and areas needing improvement. Data gathering tools often include psychological tests or exercises that ask about career status and plans. The second step is feedback, during which the organization communicates information about the employee's skills and knowledge and how these fit into the organization's plan. The employee then sets goals and discusses them with his or her manager, who ensures that the goals are specific, challenging, and attainable. Finally, the employee works with his or her manager to create an action plan and follow-up for development activities that will help the employee achieve the goals.

LO 9-8 Discuss how organizations are meeting the challenges of the "glass ceiling," succession planning, and dysfunctional managers.

The glass ceiling is a barrier that has been observed preventing women and other minorities from achieving top jobs in an organization. Development programs can ensure that these employees receive access to development resources, such as coaches, mentors, and developmental job assignments. Succession planning ensures that the organization prepares qualified employees to fill management jobs as managers retire. It focuses on applying employee development to high-potential employees. Effective succession planning includes methods for selecting these employees, providing them with developmental experiences, and getting the CEO actively involved with employees who display qualities associated with success as they participate in the developmental activities. For dysfunctional managers who have the potential to contribute to the organization, the organization may offer development targeted at correcting the areas of dysfunction. Typically, the process includes collecting information about the manager's personality, skills, and interests; providing feedback, training, and counseling; and ensuring that the manager can apply new, functional behaviors on the job.

KEY TERMS

assessment, 274

assessment center, 276

Benchmarks, 277

coach, 284

downward move, 282

employee development, 271

externship, 283

feedback, 288

glass ceiling, 289

job experiences, 279

leaderless group discussion, 276

mentor, 283

Myers-Briggs Type Indicator (MBTI), 275

promotion, 283

protean career, 272

sabbatical, 283

self-assessment, 286

succession planning, 292

transfer, 282

REVIEW AND DISCUSSION QUESTIONS

1. How does development differ from training? How does development support career management in modern organizations?

2. What are the four broad categories of development methods? Why might it be beneficial to combine all of these methods into a formal development program?

3. Recommend a development method for each of the following situations, and explain why you chose that method.
   a. An employee recently promoted to the job of plant supervisor is having difficulty motivating employees to meet quality standards.
   b. A sales manager annoys salespeople by dictating every detail of their work.
   c. An employee has excellent leadership skills but lacks knowledge of the financial side of business.
   d. An organization is planning to organize its production workers into teams for the first time.

4. A company that markets sophisticated business management software systems uses sales teams to help customers define needs and to create systems that meet those needs. The teams include programmers, salespeople who specialize in client industries, and software designers. Occasionally sales are lost as a result of conflict or communication problems among team members. The company wants to improve the effectiveness of these teams, and it wants to begin with assessment. How can the teams use 360-degree feedback and psychological tests to develop?

5. In an organization that wants to use work experiences as a method of employee development, what basic options are available? Which of these options would be most attractive to you as an employee? Why?

6. Many employees are unwilling to relocate because they like their current community and family members prefer not to move. Yet preparation for management requires that employees develop new skills, strengthen areas of weakness, and be exposed to new aspects of the organization's business. How can an organization change an employee's current job to develop management skills?

7. Many people feel that mentoring relationships should occur naturally, in situations where senior managers feel inclined to play that role. What are some advantages of setting up a formal mentoring program, rather than letting senior managers decide how and whom to help?

8. What are the three roles of a coach? How is a coach different from a mentor? What are some advantages of using someone outside the organization as a coach? Some disadvantages?

9. Why should organizations be interested in helping employees plan their careers? What benefits can companies gain? What are the risks?

10. What are the manager's roles in a career management system? Which role do you think is most difficult for the typical manager? Which is the easiest role? List reasons why managers might resist becoming involved in career management.

11. What is the glass ceiling? What are the possible consequences to an organization that has a glass ceiling? How can employee development break the glass ceiling? Can succession planning help? Explain.

12. Why might an organization benefit from giving employee development opportunities to a dysfunctional manager, rather than simply dismissing the manager? Do these reasons apply to nonmanagement employees as well?

EXPERIENCING HR

To get a sense of what it feels like to undergo an assessment, prepare a basic assessment of your performance and potential as a college student. Identify four people who have some idea of your personality, study (or work) habits, and performance so far in school—for example, parents or grandparents, other students, a teacher, and a past or present supervisor. Ask each person to summarize for you what they see as your major strengths and weaknesses as a student. Listen carefully and take notes. Focus on recording what they say, not on challenging their views.

Gather the notes from your interviews and your grade reports. If you have other performance feedback, such as graded essays or lab reports with comments,

gather these as well. Review the assessment information, looking for themes and patterns in the feedback. Write a one- to two-page summary of what you learned, including answers to the following questions:

- What do other people see as your strengths and weaknesses? How well do their views match what *you* consider to be your strengths and weaknesses?
- How well do your accomplishments reflect your strengths? What would you need to do differently in order to put your strengths to work more fully?
- Are you a "high-potential" student? Why or why not?
- How did it feel to be assessed by others? How can you learn from the experience?

TAKING RESPONSIBILITY: Mentoring the Next Generation of Financial Planners

Often, the people who choose financial planning as a career are attracted to the independence of a small practice where they can work more or less on their own in an office and see their own clients. At the same time, the combination of skills required for success—the financial knowhow coupled with the ability to have clear and motivational conversations with clients, not to mention marketing one's services—is challenging to master. Inexperienced financial planners could greatly benefit from having someone guide them, yet the independent work style does not provide an easy avenue to finding mentors.

Several companies are stepping forward to mentor financial planners in spite of the obstacles. One of the larger organizations is Ameriprise Financial, based in Minneapolis. When new advisers sign on with the company, it matches them with a mentor as part of its training program. Broker-dealers may decide to leave company offices to work independently as franchisees. Those who set this goal can ask for a mentor from the Advisors in Transition Mentor Council, who will prepare them to move out on their own.

Smaller firms, too, can mentor their new hires. At Searcy Financial, which serves clients in Overland Park, Kansas, mentoring is a personal commitment of the founder, Mike Searcy. A leadership conference prompted Searcy to reflect on what kind of legacy he would leave to the next generation. He concluded that the only way his firm would outlive him would be if he hired and developed the next generation of financial

advisers to serve his community. He started with his daughter, Jessica Maldonado, whose background is in marketing and communications. The two of them started a formal mentoring program in which Searcy assigned Maldonado readings, which they would meet to discuss. As she learned enough about the financial industry to become proficient, their conversations became more informal, swapping ideas about industry trends and business strategy. Searcy brought in another financial planner, Marc Shaffer, who after four years of mentoring was able to take on an ownership stake as a partner in Searcy's firm.

Besides establishing a company's future, mentoring might play a role in helping the industry develop a broader pool of talent. Today most financial planners are white men, and some industry leaders see this as limiting their ability to relate well to a large segment of the population. Ameritrade, for example, is aiming to have its workforce reflect its market for services. It hosted a women's leadership roundtable at a recent national conference to address that issue. Speakers noted that women tend to handle a majority of household money and tend to outlive men, so they are in great need of financial advice. In that context, Ameritrade's concern for the issue is an intensely practical one.

While women are underrepresented among financial planners, racial and ethnic minorities are even rarer. A recent survey by the Certified Financial Planning Board of Standards found that 93% of certified financial planners were white. Major companies that hire financial planners have stated that diversity is a concern for them in recruiting, but progress can be slow. Karen Pomicter, executive director of the Financial Planning Association of Western New York, says the lack of diversity "bothers us." In her five years as executive director, Pomicter could not recall seeing any minority-group members at the group's events. One of her ideas for encouraging diversity is to offer mentoring programs for new financial planners.

If her group moves ahead with that idea, one person she might recruit for that program is former adviser Lavon Stephens, who worked for four years at Prudential as its only black financial adviser in upstate New York. Stephens sees a need to develop financial literacy in the black community and instill an ambition to leave a legacy. Since leaving Prudential, Stephens has been preparing to obtain a designation as a Certified Financial Planner, with the aim of working as an estate planner and opening a private practice with a mission of teaching financial literacy. If he achieves those goals,

Stephens will almost certainly be a mentor to many, many clients—and perhaps to the next generation of financial planners.

Questions

1. What methods of employee development would be most effective with financial planners who like to work independently?
2. Where might a small financial-planning firm find mentors for its staff?
3. Do you think mentors could be effective in breaking the glass ceiling and increasing diversity in the field of financial planning? Why or why not?

SOURCES: Searcy Financial Services, "About Us," http://searcyfinancial .com, accessed March 29, 2012; Ilana Polyak, "Pass It On," *Financial Planning*, August 2011, pp. 32–38; "Ameriprise Financial: Training Powerhouse," *Financial Planning*, June 2011, p. 65; Emma Sapong, "Diversity Is Top Priority of Financial Services Industry," *Buffalo (NY) News*, June 9, 2011, Business & Company Resource Center, http://galenet.galegroup .com; Ruthie Ackerman, "Women Advisers See Role Growing," *American Banker*, February 8, 2011, EBSCOhost, http://web.ebscohost.com.

MANAGING TALENT: How General Electric Develops the Best

In the past, as General Electric entered a wide variety of industries, it emphasized the strong set of general management skills that could enable the company to outperform rivals in industries as diverse as jet engines and finance. That approach led to management development in which GE's top talent moved from one business unit to another so they would be familiar with many parts of the company. For example, before John Krenicki became vice chairman and the head of GE's energy business, he held leadership posts in units that made chemicals and materials, lighting, superabrasives, transportation equipment, plastics, and advanced materials. Lorenzo Simonelli, the executive in charge of GE Transportation, took that job after working in the consumer products unit for six years and on the audit staff for four.

Recently, however, under the leadership of CEO Jeffrey Immelt, GE has shifted its approach to management development. Now the company is more interested in deepening executives' knowledge of particular business units' products and customers. The strategy seems to be based on recognition that competition in some of its industries, such as medical equipment and power plants, has become too difficult for a general-purpose leader to master. Susan Peters, who is in charge of executive development at GE, expresses the need this way: "The world is so complex. We need people who are pretty deep."

GE takes leadership development very seriously. On its careers website, the company claims, "There is simply no other company in the world with such a diverse set of businesses in which to work, and such a development-focused culture in which to grow." GE spends about $1 billion a year to train managers. The company's John F. Welch Leadership Development Center in Crotonville, New York, is famous around the world as a center for learning to lead. GE has entry-level leadership programs in which recent college graduates combine classroom training with rotations through varied assignments over the course of two years. Leadership leadershi_____ professio_____ the deve_____ best prac_____ they iden_____

Where_____ a set of t_____ unit as ne_____ over a bu_____ manager_____ but likely_____ have been_____ a new ma_____ downturn_____ _ecisions. The newe_____ __, of a particular business u_____ _ny to make managers

more accountable for results. The new approach also may be more practical in recent years because the company has shed many of its businesses to focus on the core businesses of energy, aircraft engines, health care, and financial services.

For evidence that deeper knowledge is working, Immelt points to Anders Wold, the head of GE's ultrasound division in its imaging business (part of the health care sector). Relative to pricier equipment such as MRI machines, ultrasounds were a fairly small part of the imaging business, but Wold's in-depth knowledge of customers and products helped the company capture a big share of the market. He was determined to make GE the industry's specialist, as opposed to a maker of basic equipment. Wold's strategy built sales from $200 million to $2 billion in a single decade and made ultrasounds the biggest division in the imaging business.

With results such as these, it is easy to see why Susan Peters see GE's leadership development as a necessary investment in the company's future. Just as the company invests in research and development so it will be able to offer the products needed in the world of the future, it invests in leadership development so it will have the people who can drive innovation in their business units.

Questions

1. What is the role of job experiences in GE's leadership development? How has that role shifted?
2. Do you think GE's change in focus from broad development of executives to developing specialized knowledge of a business line will promote the company's success? Why or why not?
3. How can GE's development program meet the challenges of the glass ceiling and succession planning?

SOURCES: General Electric, "Why GE," http://www.ge.com/careers/, accessed March 29, 2012; Kate Linebaugh, "The New GE Way: Go Deep, Not Wide," *The Wall Street Journal*, March 7, 2012, http://online.wsj.com; Frank Kalman, "Follow the Leader," *Chief Learning Officer*, February 2012, pp. 20–24; Vijay Govindarajan and Susan Peters, "Embedding Innovation in Leadership," *Bloomberg Businessweek*, February 2, 2011, EBSCOhost, http://web.ebscohost.com.

 TWITTER FOCUS: Employee Sabbatical Benefits Others at Little Tokyo Service Center

Using Twitter, continue the conversation about employee development by reading the Little Tokyo Service Center case at **www.mhhe.com/noefund5e**. Engage with your classmates and instructor via Twitter to chat about employee sabbaticals using the case questions posted on the Noe website. Don't have a Twitter account yet? See the instructions for getting started on the Online Learning Center.

NOTES

1. Ed Finkel, "Cultivating a Team Culture," *Modern Healthcare*, October 24, 2011, Business & Company Resource Center, http://galenet.galegroup.com.
2. M. London, *Managing the Training Enterprise* (San Francisco: Jossey-Bass, 1989) and D. Day, *Developing Leadership Talent* (Alexandria, VA: SHRM Foundation, 2007).
3. R. W. Pace, P. C. Smith, and G. E. Mills, *Human Resource Development* (Englewood Cliffs, NJ: Prentice Hall, 1991); W. Fitzgerald, "Training versus Development," *Training and Development Journal*, May 1992, pp. 81–84; R. A. Noe, S. L. Wilk, E. J. Mullen, and J. E. Wanek, "Employee Development: Issues in Construct Definition and Investigation of Antecedents," in *Improving Training Effectiveness in Work Organizations*, ed. J. K. Ford (Mahwah, NJ: Lawrence Erlbaum, 1997), pp. 153–89.
4. J. H. Greenhaus and G. A. Callanan, *Career Management*, 2nd ed. (Fort Worth, TX: Dryden Press, 1994); and D. Hall, *Careers in and out of Organizations* (Thousand Oaks, CA: Sage, 2002).
5. M. B. Arthur, P. H. Claman, and R. J. DeFillippi, "Intelligent Enterprise, Intelligent Careers," *Academy of Management Executive* 9 (1995), pp. 7–20; M. Lazarova and S. Taylor, "Boundaryless Careers, Social Capital, and Knowledge Management: Implications for Organizational Performance," *Journal of Organizational Behavior* 30 (2009): 119–39; D. Feldman and T. Ng, "Careers: Mobility, Embeddedness, and Success," *Journal of Management* 33 (2007): 350–77.
6. R. Noe, *Employee Training and Development*, 5th ed. (New York: McGraw-Hill Irwin, 2010).
7. Pat Galagan, "90,000 Served: Hamburger University Turns 50," *T + D*, April 2011, pp. 46–51; Beth Kowitt, "Why McDonald's Wins in Any Economy," *Fortune*, September 5, 2011, EBSCOhost, http://web.ebscohost.com.

8. University of Virginia Darden School of Business, "MBA for Executives," http://www.darden.virginia .edu, accessed March 30, 2012.

9. Alicia Korney, "From Toys to Talent," *Chief Learning Officer*, September 2011, pp. 48–52.

10. A. Howard and D. W. Bray, *Managerial Lives in Transition: Advancing Age and Changing Times* (New York: Guilford, 1988); J. Bolt, *Executive Development* (New York: Harper Business, 1989); J. R. Hinrichs and G. P. Hollenbeck, "Leadership Development," in *Developing Human Resources* ed. K. N. Wexley (Washington, DC: BNA Books, 1991), pp. 5-221–5-237; and Day, *Developing Leadership Talent*.

11. Margery Weinstein, "The X Factor," *Training*, May/June 2011, pp. 65–67.

12. A. Thorne and H. Gough, *Portraits of Type* (Palo Alto, CA: Consulting Psychologists Press, 1993).

13. D. Druckman and R. A. Bjork, eds., *In the Mind's Eye: Enhancing Human Performance* (Washington, DC: National Academy Press, 1991); M. H. McCaulley, "The Myers-Briggs Type Indicator and Leadership," in *Measures of Leadership*, eds. K. E. Clark and M. B. Clark (West Orange, NJ: Leadership Library of America, 1990), pp. 381–418.

14. G. C. Thornton III and W. C. Byham, *Assessment Centers and Managerial Performance* (New York: Academic Press, 1982); L. F. Schoenfeldt and J. A. Steger, "Identification and Development of Management Talent," in *Research in Personnel and Human Resource Management*, eds. K. N. Rowland and G. Ferris (Greenwich, CT: JAI Press, 1989), vol. 7, pp. 151–81.

15. Thornton and Byham, *Assessment Centers and Managerial Performance*.

16. P. G. W. Jansen and B. A. M. Stoop, "The Dynamics of Assessment Center Validity: Results of a Seven-Year Study," *Journal of Applied Psychology* 86 (2001), pp. 741–53; and D. Chan, "Criterion and Construct Validation of an Assessment Centre," *Journal of Occupational and Organizational Psychology* 69 (1996), pp. 167–81.

17. R. G. Jones and M. D. Whitmore, "Evaluating Developmental Assessment Centers as Interventions," *Personnel Psychology* 48 (1995), pp. 377–88.

18. C. D. McCauley and M. M. Lombardo, "Benchmarks: An Instrument for Diagnosing Managerial Strengths and Weaknesses," in *Measures of Leadership*, pp. 535–45; and Center for Creative Leadership, "Benchmarks®—Overview," www.ccl.org, accessed March 28, 2006.

19. C. D. McCauley, M. M. Lombardo, and C. J. Usher, "Diagnosing Management Development Needs: An Instrument Based on How Managers Develop," *Journal of Management* 15 (1989), pp. 389–403.

20. S. B. Silverman, "Individual Development through Performance Appraisal," in *Developing Human Resources*, pp. 5-120–5-151.

21. J. F. Brett and L. E. Atwater, "360-Degree Feedback: Accuracy, Reactions, and Perceptions of Usefulness," *Journal of Applied Psychology* 86 (2001), pp. 930–42.

22. PepsiCo, "Associate Learning and Development," http://www.pepsico.com, accessed March 30, 2012.

23. L. Atwater, P. Roush, and A. Fischthal, "The Influence of Upward Feedback on Self- and Follower Ratings of Leadership," *Personnel Psychology* 48 (1995), pp. 35–59; J. F. Hazucha, S. A. Hezlett, and R. J. Schneider, "The Impact of 360-Degree Feedback on Management Skill Development," *Human Resource Management* 32 (1993), pp. 325–51; J. W. Smither, M. London, N. Vasilopoulos, R. R. Reilly, R. E. Millsap, and N. Salvemini, "An Examination of the Effects of an Upward Feedback Program over Time," *Personnel Psychology* 48 (1995), pp. 1–34; J. Smither and A. Walker, "Are the Characteristics of Narrative Comments Related to Improvements in Multirater Feedback Ratings over Time?" *Journal of Applied Psychology* 89 (2004), pp. 575–81; and J. Smither, M. London, and R. Reilly, "Does Performance Improve Following Multisource Feedback? A Theoretical Model, Meta-analysis, and Review of Empirical Findings," *Personnel Psychology* 58 (2005), pp. 33–66.

24. Center for Creative Leadership, "360-Degree Feedback: Best Practices to Ensure Impact," 2011, http://www.ccl.org, accessed March 30, 2012.

25. M. W. McCall Jr., *High Flyers* (Boston: Harvard Business School Press, 1998).

26. R. S. Snell, "Congenial Ways of Learning: So Near yet So Far," *Journal of Management Development* 9 (1990), pp. 17–23.

27. M. McCall, M. Lombardo, and A. Morrison, *Lessons of Experience* (Lexington, MA: Lexington Books, 1988); M. W. McCall, "Developing Executives through Work Experiences," *Human Resource Planning* 11 (1988), pp. 1–11; M. N. Ruderman, P. J. Ohlott, and C. D. McCauley, "Assessing Opportunities for Leadership Development," in *Measures of Leadership*, pp. 547–62; and C. D. McCauley, L. J. Estman, and P. J. Ohlott, "Linking Management Selection and Development through Stretch Assignments," *Human Resource Management* 34 (1995), pp. 93–115.

28. C. D. McCauley, M. N. Ruderman, P. J. Ohlott, and J. E. Morrow, "Assessing the Developmental Components of Managerial Jobs," *Journal of Applied Psychology* 79 (1994), pp. 544–60.

29. Jill Jusko, "Engineering Bench Strength," *Industry Week*, August 2011, p. 18.

30. M. London, *Developing Managers* (San Francisco: Jossey-Bass, 1985); M. A. Camion, L. Cheraskin, and M. J. Stevens, "Career-Related Antecedents and Outcomes of Job Rotation," *Academy of Management Journal* 37 (1994), pp. 1518–42; and London, *Managing the Training Enterprise*.

31. Margaret Fiester, "Job Rotation, Total Rewards, Measuring Value," *HR Magazine*, August 2008, Business & Company Resource Center, http://galenet.galegroup.com; and "Energize and Enhance Employee Value with Job Rotation," *HR Focus*, January 2008, OCLC FirstSearch, http://newfirstsearch.oclc.org.

32. R. A. Noe, B. D. Steffy, and A. E. Barber, "An Investigation of the Factors Influencing Employees' Willingness to Accept Mobility Opportunities," *Personnel Psychology* 41 (1988), pp. 559–80; S. Gould and L. E. Penley, "A Study of the Correlates of Willingness to Relocate," *Academy of Management Journal* 28 (1984), pp. 472–78; J. Landau and T. H. Hammer, "Clerical Employees' Perceptions of Intraorganizational Career Opportunities," *Academy of Management Journal* 29 (1986), pp. 385–405; and J. M. Brett and A. H. Reilly, "On the Road Again: Predicting the Job Transfer Decision," *Journal of Applied Psychology* 73 (1988), pp. 614–20.

33. J. M. Brett, "Job Transfer and Well-Being," *Journal of Applied Psychology* 67 (1992), pp. 450–63; F. J. Minor, L. A. Slade, and R. A. Myers, "Career Transitions in Changing Times," in *Contemporary Career Development Issues*, eds. R. F. Morrison and J. Adams (Hillsdale, NJ: Lawrence Erlbaum, 1991), pp. 109–20; C. C. Pinder and K. G. Schroeder, "Time to Proficiency Following Job Transfers," *Academy of Management Journal* 30 (1987), pp. 336–53; Beverly Kaye, "Up Is Not the Only Way . . . Really!" *T + D*, September 2011, pp. 40–45.

34. "Business and Leadership Development Meet Social Innovation," *T + D*, February 2012, p. 22.

35. Adrienne Fox, "Make a 'Deal,'" *HR Magazine*, January 2012, Business & Company Resource Center, http://galenet.galegroup.com; "Wandering Librarian," *Library Journal*, March 15, 2012, EBSCOhost, http://web.ebscohost.com.

36. D. B. Turban and T. W. Dougherty, "Role of Protégé Personality in Receipt of Mentoring and Career Success," *Academy of Management Journal* 37 (1994), pp. 688–702; and E. A. Fagenson, "Mentoring: Who Needs It? A Comparison of Protégés' and Nonprotégés' Needs for Power, Achievement, Affiliation, and Autonomy," *Journal of Vocational Behavior* 41 (1992), pp. 48–60.

37. A. H. Geiger, "Measures for Mentors," *Training and Development Journal*, February 1992, pp. 65–67; Lynnie Martin and Tyler Robinson, "Why You Should Get on Board the Mentor Ship," *Public Manager*, Winter 2011, pp. 42–45; "The Payoff," *California CPA*, October 2011, p. 12.

38. K. E. Kram, *Mentoring at Work: Developmental Relationships in Organizational Life* (Glenview, IL: Scott-Foresman, 1985); L. L. Phillips-Jones, "Establishing a Formalized Mentoring Program," *Training and Development Journal* 2 (1983), pp. 38–42; K. Kram, "Phases of the Mentoring Relationship," *Academy of Management Journal* 26 (1983), pp. 608–25; G. T. Chao, P. M. Walz, and P. D. Gardner, "Formal and Informal Mentorships: A Comparison of Mentoring Functions and Contrasts with Nonmentored Counterparts," *Personnel Psychology* 45 (1992), pp. 619–36; and C. Wanberg, E. Welsh, and S. Hezlett, "Mentoring Research: A Review and Dynamic Process Model," in *Research in Personnel and Human Resources Management*, eds. J. Martocchio and G. Ferris (New York: Elsevier Science, 2003), pp. 39–124.

39. Michele Lent Hirsch, "Mentor Makeover," *Psychology Today*, July/August 2011, EBSCOhost, http://web.ebscohost.com.

40. L. Eby, M. Butts, A. Lockwood, and A. Simon, "Protégés' Negative Mentoring Experiences: Construct Development and Nomological Validation," *Personnel Psychology* 57 (2004), pp. 411–47; R. Emelo, "Conversations with Mentoring Leaders," *T + D*, June 2011, pp. 32–37; M. Weinstein, "Please Don't Go," *Training*, May/June 2011, pp. 38–34; "Training Top 125," *Training*, January/February 2011, pp. 54–93.

41. R. A. Noe, D. B. Greenberger, and S. Wang, "Mentoring: What We Know and Where We Might Go," in *Research in Personnel and Human Resources Management*, eds. G. Ferris and J. Martocchio (New York: Elsevier Science, 2002), vol. 21, pp. 129–74; and T. D. Allen, L. T. Eby, M. L. Poteet, E. Lentz, and L. Lima, "Career Benefits Associated with Mentoring for Protégés: A Meta-Analysis," *Journal of Applied Psychology* 89 (2004), pp. 127–36.

42. D. B. Peterson and M. D. Hicks, *Leader as Coach* (Minneapolis: Personnel Decisions, 1996).

43. Alex Vorro, "Coaching Counsel," *InsideCounsel*, February 2012, Business & Company Resource Center, http://galenet.galegroup.com.

44. J. Smither, M. London, R. Flautt, Y. Vargas, and L. Kucine, "Can Working with an Executive Coach Improve Multisource Ratings over Time? A Quasi-experimental Field Study," *Personnel Psychology* 56 (2003), pp. 23–44.

45. Vorro, "Coaching Counsel."
46. Tara Shawel, "Homegrown Career Development," *HR Magazine*, April 2011, pp. 36–38.
47. M. Thompson, "What Makes Tyson's High-Potential Leadership Program Critical to Company Success?" *T + D*, April 2011, pp. 98–100.
48. Jennifer Remis, "Using Manager Development to Grow the Business," *Chief Learning Officer*, June 2011, pp. 74–75, 80.
49. "Ladder Not Required," *T + D*, March 2012, p. 80.
50. Catalyst, "Women on Boards," *Quick Takes*, March 27, 2012, http://www.catalyst.org.
51. P. J. Ohlott, M. N. Ruderman, and C. D. McCauley, "Gender Differences in Managers' Developmental Job Experiences," *Academy of Management Journal* 37 (1994), pp. 46–67; L. A. Mainiero, "Getting Anointed for Advancement: The Case of Executive Women," *Academy of Management Executive* 8 (1994), pp. 53–67; and P. Tharenov, S. Latimer, and D. Conroy, "How Do You Make It to the Top? An Examination of Influences on Women's and Men's Managerial Advancements," *Academy of Management Journal* 37 (1994), pp. 899–931.
52. R. A. Noe, "Women and Mentoring: A Review and Research Agenda," *Academy of Management Review* 13 (1988), pp. 65–78; B. R. Ragins and J. L. Cotton, "Easier Said than Done: Gender Differences in Perceived Barriers to Gaining a Mentor," *Academy of Management Journal* 34 (1991), pp. 939–51; Joann S. Lublin, "Female Directors: Why So Few?" *The Wall Street Journal*, December 27, 2011, http://online.wsj.com; Christine Silva and Nancy Carter, "New Research Busts Myths about the Gender Gap," *Harvard Business Review*, October 6, 2011, http://blogs.hbr.org; Catalyst, "Catalyst Study Explodes Myths about Why Women's Careers Lag Men's," news release, October 13, 2011, http://www.catalyst.org; "Too Many Suits," *The Economist*, November 26, 2011, EBSCOhost, http://web.ebscohost.com.
53. Josh Dzieza, "Coke CEO: Promoting Women Is Good Business," *The Daily Beast*, March 9, 2012, http://www.thedailybeast.com; Coca-Cola Company, *As Inclusive as Our Brands*, 2010 U.S. Diversity Stewardship Report, accessed at http://www.thecoca-colacompany.com; Coca-Cola Enterprises Ltd., "Corporate Responsibility Review, 2010/11," http://www.cokecorporateresponsibility.co.uk, accessed March 30, 2012.
54. W. J. Rothwell, *Effective Succession Planning*, 2nd ed. (New York: AMACOM, 2001).
55. B. E. Dowell, "Succession Planning," in *Implementing Organizational Interventions*, eds. J. Hedge and E. D. Pulakos (San Francisco: Jossey-Bass, 2002), pp. 78–109.
56. C. B. Derr, C. Jones, and E. L. Toomey, "Managing High-Potential Employees: Current Practices in Thirty-Three U.S. Corporations," *Human Resource Management* 27 (1988), pp. 273–90; K. M. Nowack, "The Secrets of Succession," *Training and Development* 48 (1994), pp. 49–54; W. J. Rothwell, *Effective Succession Planning*, 4th ed. (New York: AMACOM, 2010).
57. Robert J. Grossman, "Rough Road to Succession," *HR Magazine*, June 2011, pp. 47–51.
58. M. W. McCall Jr. and M. M. Lombardo, "Off the Track: Why and How Successful Executives Get Derailed," *Technical Report*, no. 21 (Greensboro, NC: Center for Creative Leadership, 1983); and E. V. Veslo and J. B. Leslie, "Why Executives Derail: Perspectives across Time and Cultures," *Academy of Management Executive* 9 (1995), pp. 62–72.
59. L. W. Hellervik, J. F. Hazucha, and R. J. Schneider, "Behavior Change: Models, Methods, and a Review of Evidence," in *Handbook of Industrial and Organizational Psychology*, 2nd ed., eds. M. D. Dunnette and L. M. Hough (Palo Alto, CA: Consulting Psychologists Press, 1992), vol. 3, pp. 823–99.
60. D. B. Peterson, "Measuring and Evaluating Change in Executive and Managerial Development," paper presented at the annual conference of the Society for Industrial and Organizational Psychology, Miami, 1990.

Separating and Retaining Employees

What Do I Need to Know?

After reading this chapter, you should be able to:

LO 10-1 Distinguish between involuntary and voluntary turnover, and describe their effects on an organization.

LO 10-2 Discuss how employees determine whether the organization treats them fairly.

LO 10-3 Identify legal requirements for employee discipline.

LO 10-4 Summarize ways in which organizations can fairly discipline employees.

LO 10-5 Explain how job dissatisfaction affects employee behavior.

LO 10-6 Describe how organizations contribute to employees' job satisfaction and retain key employees.

Introduction

USAA has plenty to brag about. The financial-services firm, which focuses on serving members of the military and their families, was recently ranked number 20 in *Fortune* magazine's list of the 100 Best Companies to Work For. It tops *Computerworld*'s list of the Best Places to Work in IT and *Military Spouse*'s list of employers that are friendly to spouses of service members. And USAA placed on the *GI Jobs* list of military-friendly employers and *Latina Style*'s list of the best employers for Latinas.

What is behind all that praise? One factor is generous employee compensation, including a competitive level of pay, bonuses, and child care benefits. USAA also supports work/life balance with flexible work arrangements. In addition, USAA scored high in *Fortune* surveys asking employees whether they experience trustworthy managers, positive relationships with co-workers, and satisfaction with their jobs. But USAA's chief executive, Army Major General Joe Robles, believes that something else makes the organization a great place to work: "Serving military families, helping them toward financial security and looking out for the membership's best interests—rather than next quarter's results or stock price." USAA backs up this commitment with training that dramatically brings home to employees the family and financial issues that arise with a deployment. Performance management stresses customer service above all other measures. Considering all these factors, it comes as no surprise that employee turnover at USAA is exceptionally low.[1]

Every organization recognizes that it needs satisfied, loyal customers. In addition, success requires satisfied, loyal employees. Research provides evidence that retaining employees helps retain customers and increase sales.[2] Organizations with low turnover and satisfied employees tend to perform better.[3] On the other side of the coin, organizations have to act when an employee's performance consistently falls short. Sometimes terminating a poor performer is the only way to show fairness, ensure quality, and maintain customer satisfaction.

This chapter explores the dual challenges of separating and retaining employees. We begin by distinguishing involuntary and voluntary turnover, describing how each affects the organization. Next we explore the separation process, including ways to manage this process fairly. Finally, we discuss measures the organization can take to encourage employees to stay. These topics provide a transition between Parts 3 and 4. The previous chapters in Part 3 considered how to assess and improve performance, and this chapter describes measures to take depending on whether performance is high or low. Part 4 discusses pay and benefits, both of which play an important role in employee retention.

Managing Voluntary and Involuntary Turnover

Organizations must try to ensure that good performers want to stay with the organization and that employees whose performance is chronically low are encouraged—or forced—to leave. Both of these challenges involve *employee turnover*; that is, employees leaving the organization. When the organization initiates the turnover (often with employees who would prefer to stay), the result is **involuntary turnover**. Examples include terminating an employee for drug use or laying off employees during a downturn. Most organizations use the word *termination* to refer only to a discharge related to a discipline problem, but some organizations call any involuntary turnover a termination. When the employees initiate the turnover (often when the organization would prefer to keep them), it is **voluntary turnover**. Employees may leave to retire or to take a job with a different organization. Typically, the employees who leave voluntarily are either the organization's worst performers, who quit before they are fired, or its best performers, who can most easily find attractive new opportunities.[4]

In general, organizations try to avoid the need for involuntary turnover and to minimize voluntary turnover, especially among top performers. Both kinds of turnover are costly, as summarized in Table 10.1. Replacing workers is expensive, and new employees need time to learn their jobs and build teamwork skills.[5] Employees who leave voluntarily out of anger and frustration may not be shy about generating unfavorable publicity (see "HR Oops!"). People who leave involuntarily are sometimes ready to sue a former employer if they feel they were unfairly discharged. The prospect of workplace violence also raises the risk associated with discharging employees. Effective human resource management can help the organization minimize both kinds of turnover, as well as carry it out effectively when necessary. Despite a company's best

LO 10-1 Distinguish between involuntary and voluntary turnover, and describe their effects on an organization.

Involuntary Turnover
Turnover initiated by an employer (often with employees who would prefer to stay).

Voluntary Turnover
Turnover initiated by employees (often when the organization would prefer to keep them).

INVOLUNTARY TURNOVER	VOLUNTARY TURNOVER
Recruiting, selecting, and training replacements	Recruiting, selecting, and training replacements
Lost productivity	Lost productivity
Lawsuits	Loss of talented employees
Workplace violence	

Table 10.1

Costs Associated with Turnover

HR Oops!

Embarrassed by an Executive Exodus

Usually, when executives leave an organization, they make polite statements about new opportunities and a desire to spend time with family. In that context, the statements made by some former executives of Pabst Brewing Company are startling. Within about the first year after the company was purchased by C. Dean Metropoulos and his two sons in 2010, more than two dozen of its executives quit. Former chief executive officer Kevin Kotecki told a reporter, "Just about everything that I'd been working on or trying to accomplish ended up not being part of the plan going forward." And Bryan Clarke, former vice president of marketing said this about the new owners' strategy: "I want it to fail."

What was behind this public embarrassment? The Metropouloses haven't commented publicly on the leadership situation, but some information offers clues. Former Pabst executives including Kotecki, Clarke, and former marketing director Kyle Wortham had for several years enjoyed a sense of mission as they resurrected tired beer brands by talking to former customers and researching old brewing methods. They restored beloved formulas for brands such as Pabst Blue Ribbon, Schlitz, and Old Style. As beer drinkers reacquainted themselves with the brands, sales and profits soared along with the brands' reputations.

Pabst Brewing became an enticing target for the Metropouloses. However, after the acquisition, as the new owners expressed their goals to the company's executives, they didn't talk about learning the tastes of the regions served by each brand. They instead laid out ideas for promoting the brands more vigorously through advertising and celebrity endorsements. In what some saw as a sign of lack of commitment to local communities, the new owners moved the corporate headquarters from Woodridge, Illinois, near Chicago, to Los Angeles. As they pushed forward, sales growth slowed, and executives say their past contributions were devalued. One by one, they began leaving the company, with the departures including the chief executive officer, chief operating officer, and a series of two chief marketing officers. Some were so frustrated they publicly aired their difficulties in dealing with their new bosses.

Questions

1. Based on the information available, could the new owners of Pabst Brewing have prevented this high level of turnover at the top? *Should* they have prevented this employee turnover? Why or why not?
2. What problems resulted from the way the company's leaders handled the turnover? How could they have prevented these problems?

SOURCES: Julie Wernau, "Bitter Aftertaste for Ex-Pabst Execs," *Chicago Tribune,* June 5, 2011, sec. 2, pp. 1–2; Chris Prentice, "It's Back to Beer for Pabst Brewing Company's New CMO," *FINS Sales & Marketing,* May 23, 2011, http://sales-jobs.fins.com; "Pabst Brewing Co. to Move Its HQ to Los Angeles, CA," *Modern Brewery Age,* May 13, 2011, FindArticles, http://findarticles.com.

---

efforts at personnel selection, training, and compensation, some employees will fail to meet performance requirements or will violate company policies. When this happens, organizations need to apply a discipline program that could ultimately lead to discharging the individual.

For a number of reasons, discharging employees can be very difficult. First, the decision has legal aspects that can affect the organization. Historically, if the organization and employee do not have a specific employment contract, the employer or employee may end the employment relationship at any time. This is the *employment-at-will doctrine*, described in Chapter 5. This doctrine has eroded significantly, however. Employees who have been terminated sometimes sue their employers for wrongful discharge. Some judges have considered that employment at will is limited where managers make statements that amount to an implied contract; a discharge also can be found illegal if it violates a law (such as antidiscrimination laws) or public policy (for example, firing an employee for refusing to do something illegal).[6] In a typical lawsuit for wrongful discharge, the former employee tries to establish that the discharge violated either an implied agreement or public policy. Most employers settle these claims out of court. Even though few former employees win wrongful-discharge suits, and employers usually win when they appeal, the cost of defending the lawsuit can be hundreds of thousands of dollars.[7]

Along with the financial risks of dismissing an employee, there are issues of personal safety. Distressing as it is that some former employees go to the courts, far worse are the employees who react to a termination decision with violence. Violence in the workplace has become a major organizational problem. Although any number of organizational actions or decisions may incite violence among employees, the "nothing else to lose" aspect of an employee's dismissal makes the situation dangerous, especially when the nature of the work adds other risk factors.[8]

Retaining top performers is not always easy either, and recent trends have made this more difficult than ever. Today's psychological contract, in which workers feel responsibility for their own careers rather than loyalty to a particular employer, makes voluntary turnover more likely. Also, competing organizations are constantly looking at each other's top performers. For high-demand positions, such as software engineers, "poaching talent" from other companies has become the norm.

Employee Separation

Because of the critical financial and personal risks associated with employee dismissal, it is easy to see why organizations must develop a standardized, systematic approach to discipline and discharge. These decisions should not be left solely to the discretion of individual managers or supervisors. Policies that can lead to employee separation should be based on principles of justice and law, and they should allow for various ways to intervene.

Principles of Justice

The sensitivity of a system for disciplining and possibly terminating employees is obvious, and it is critical that the system be seen as fair. Employees form conclusions about the system's fairness based on the system's outcomes and procedures and the way managers treat employees when carrying out those procedures. Figure 10.1 summarizes these principles as outcome fairness, procedural justice, and interactional justice. Outcome fairness involves the ends of a discipline process, while procedural and interactional justice focus on the means to those ends. Not only is behavior ethical that is in accord with these principles, but research has also linked the last two categories of justice with employee satisfaction and productivity.[9]

People's perception of **outcome fairness** depends on their judgment that the consequences of a decision to employees are just. As shown in Figure 10.1, one employee's consequences should be consistent with other employees' consequences. Suppose several employees went out to lunch, returned drunk, and were reprimanded. A few weeks later, another employee was fired for being drunk at work. Employees might well conclude that outcomes are not fair because they are inconsistent. Another basis for outcome fairness is that everyone should know what to expect. Organizations promote outcome fairness when they clearly communicate policies regarding the consequences of inappropriate behavior. Finally, the outcome should be proportionate to the behavior. Terminating an employee for being late to work, especially if this is the first time the employee is late, would seem out of proportion to the offense in most situations. Employees' sense of outcome fairness usually would reserve loss of a job for the most serious offenses.

LO 10-2 Discuss how employees determine whether the organization treats them fairly.

Outcome Fairness
A judgment that the consequences given to employees are just.

Figure 10.1
Principles of Justice

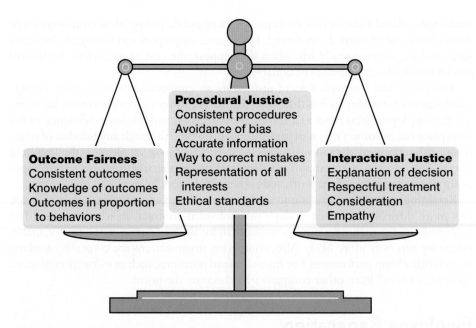

Procedural Justice
Consistent procedures
Avoidance of bias
Accurate information
Way to correct mistakes
Representation of all
  interests
Ethical standards

Outcome Fairness
Consistent outcomes
Knowledge of outcomes
Outcomes in proportion
  to behaviors

Interactional Justice
Explanation of decision
Respectful treatment
Consideration
Empathy

Procedural Justice
A judgment that fair methods were used to determine the consequences an employee receives.

People's perception of **procedural justice** is their judgment that fair methods were used to determine the consequences an employee receives. Figure 10.1 shows six principles that determine whether people perceive procedures as fair. The procedures should be consistent from one person to another, and the manager using them should suppress any personal biases. The procedures should be based on accurate information, not rumors or falsehoods. The procedures should also be correctable, meaning the system includes safeguards, such as channels for appealing a decision or correcting errors. The procedures should take into account the concerns of all the groups affected—for example, by gathering information from employees, customers, and managers. Finally, the procedures should be consistent with prevailing ethical standards, such as concerns for privacy and honesty.

Interactional Justice
A judgment that the organization carried out its actions in a way that took the employee's feelings into account.

A perception of **interactional justice** is a judgment that the organization carried out its actions in a way that took the employee's feelings into account. It is a judgment about the ways that managers interact with their employees. A disciplinary action meets the standards of interactional justice if the manager explains to the employee how the action is procedurally just. The manager should listen to the employee. The manager should also treat the employee with dignity and respect and should empathize with the employee's feelings. Even when a manager discharges an employee for doing something wrong, the manager can speak politely and state the reasons for the action. These efforts to achieve interactional justice are especially important when managing an employee who has a high level of hostility and is at greater risk of responding with violence.[10]

LO 10-3 Identify legal requirements for employee discipline.

Legal Requirements

The law gives employers wide latitude in hiring and firing, but employers must meet certain requirements. They must avoid wrongful discharge and illegal discrimination. They also must meet standards related to employees' privacy and adequate notice of layoffs.

Wrongful Discharge   As we noted earlier in the chapter, discipline practices must avoid the charge of wrongful discharge. First, this means the discharge may not violate an implied agreement. Terminating an employee may violate an implied agreement if the employer had promised the employee job security or if the action is inconsistent with company policies. An example might be that an organization has stated that an employee with an unexcused absence will receive a warning for the first violation, but an angry supervisor fires an employee for being absent on the day of an important meeting.

Another reason a discharge may be considered wrongful is that it violates public policy. Violations of public policy include terminating the employee for refusing to do something illegal, unethical, or unsafe. Suppose an employee refuses to dump chemicals into the sewer system; firing that employee could be a violation of public policy. It is also a violation of public policy to terminate an employee for doing what the law requires—for example, cooperating with a government investigation, reporting illegal behavior by the employer, or reporting for jury duty.

HR professionals can help organizations avoid (and defend against) charges of wrongful discharge by establishing and communicating policies for handling misbehavior. They should define unacceptable behaviors and identify how the organization will respond to them. Managers should follow these procedures consistently and document precisely the reasons for disciplinary action. In addition, the organization should train managers to avoid making promises that imply job security (for example, "As long as you keep up that level of performance, you'll have a job with us"). Finally, in writing and reviewing employee handbooks, HR professionals should avoid any statements that could be interpreted as employment contracts. When there is any doubt about a statement, the organization should seek legal advice.

Discrimination   Another benefit of a formal discipline policy is that it helps the organization comply with equal employment opportunity requirements. As in other employment matters, employers must make decisions without regard to individuals' age, sex, race, or other protected status. If two employees steal from the employer but one is disciplined more harshly than the other, the employee who receives the harsher punishment could look for the cause in his or her being of a particular race, country of origin, or some other group. Evenhanded, carefully documented discipline can avoid such claims.

Employees' Privacy   The courts also have long protected individuals' privacy in many situations. At the same time, employers have legitimate reasons for learning about some personal matters, especially when behavior outside the workplace can affect productivity, workplace safety, and employee morale. Employers therefore need to ensure that the information they gather and use is relevant to these matters. For example, safety and security make it legitimate to require drug testing of all employees holding jobs such as police officer, firefighter, and airline flight crew.[11] (Governments at the federal,

Organizations such as day care facilities and schools must protect employees' right to privacy in their lives and on the job while balancing the need to protect children from harm.

Table 10.2

Measures for Protecting Employees' Privacy

Ensure that information is relevant.
Publicize information-gathering policies and consequences.
Request consent before gathering information.
Treat employees consistently.
Conduct searches discreetly.
Share information only with those who need it.

state, and local levels have many laws affecting drug-testing programs, so it is wise to get legal advice before planning such tests.)

Privacy issues also surface when employers wish to search or monitor employees on the job. An employer that suspects theft, drug use, or other misdeeds on the job may wish to search employees for evidence. In general, random searches of areas such as desks, lockers, toolboxes, and communications such as e-mails are permissible, so long as the employer can justify that there is probable cause for the search and the organization has work rules that provide for searches.[12] Employers can act fairly and minimize the likelihood of a lawsuit by publicizing the search policy, applying it consistently, asking for the employee's consent before the search begins, and conducting the search discreetly. Also, when a search is a random check, it is important to clarify that no one has been accused of misdeeds.[13]

No matter how sensitively the organization gathers information leading to disciplinary actions, it should also consider privacy issues when deciding who will see the information.[14] In general, it is advisable to share the information only with people who have a business need to see it—for example, the employee's supervisor, union officials, and in some cases, co-workers. Letting outsiders know the reasons for terminating an employee can embarrass the employee, who might file a defamation lawsuit. HR professionals can help organizations avoid such lawsuits by working with managers to determine fact-based explanations and to decide who needs to see these explanations.

Table 10.2 summarizes these measures for protecting employees' privacy.

LO 10-4 Summarize ways in which organizations can fairly discipline employees.

Notification of Layoffs   Sometimes terminations are necessary not because of individuals' misdeeds, but because the organization determines that for economic reasons it must close a facility. An organization that plans such broad-scale layoffs may be subject to the Workers' Adjustment Retraining and Notification Act. This federal law requires that organizations with more than 100 employees give 60 days' notice before any closing or layoff that will affect at least 50 full-time employees. If employers covered by this law do not give notice to the employees (and their union, if applicable), they may have to provide back pay and fringe benefits and pay penalties as well. Several states and cities have similar laws, and the federal law contains a number of exemptions. Therefore, it is important to seek legal advice before implementing a plant closing.

Hot-Stove Rule
Principle of discipline that says discipline should be like a hot stove, giving clear warning and following up with consistent, objective, immediate consequences.

Progressive Discipline

Organizations look for methods of handling problem behavior that are fair, legal, and effective. A popular principle for responding effectively is the **hot-stove rule**. According to this principle, discipline should be like a hot stove: The glowing or burning stove gives warning not to touch. Anyone who ignores the warning will be burned. The stove has no feelings to influence which people it burns, and it delivers the same burn to any touch. Finally, the burn is immediate. Like the hot stove, an organization's discipline should give warning and have consequences that are consistent, objective, and immediate.

The principles of justice suggest that the organization prepare for problems by establishing a formal discipline process in which the consequences become more serious if the employee repeats the offense. Such a system is called **progressive discipline**. A typical progressive discipline system identifies and communicates unacceptable behaviors and responds to a series of offenses with the actions shown in Figure 10.2— spoken and then written warnings, temporary suspension, and finally, termination. This process fulfills the purpose of discipline by teaching employees what is expected of them and creating a situation in which employees must try to do what is expected. It seeks to prevent misbehavior (by publishing rules) and to correct, rather than merely punish, misbehavior.

> **Progressive Discipline**
> A formal discipline process in which the consequences become more serious if the employee repeats the offense.

Such procedures may seem exasperatingly slow, especially when the employee's misdeeds hurt the team's performance. In the end, however, if an employee must be discharged, careful use of the procedure increases other employees' belief that the organization is fair and reduces the likelihood that the problem employee will sue (or at least that the employee will win in court). For situations in which misbehavior is dangerous, the organization may establish a stricter policy, even terminating an employee for the first offense. In that case, it is especially important to communicate the procedure—not only to ensure fairness but also to prevent the dangerous misbehavior.

Creating a formal discipline process is a primary responsibility of the human resource department. The HR professional should consult with supervisors and managers to identify unacceptable behaviors and establish rules and consequences for violating the rules. The rules should cover disciplinary problems such as the following behaviors encountered in many organizations:

- Tardiness
- Absenteeism
- Unsafe work practices
- Poor quantity or quality of work
- Sexual harassment of co-workers
- Coming to work impaired by alcohol or drugs
- Theft of company property
- Cyberslacking (conducting personal business online during work hours)

For each infraction, the HR professional would identify a series of responses, such as those in Figure 10.2. In addition, the organization must communicate these rules and consequences in writing to every employee. Ways of publishing rules include

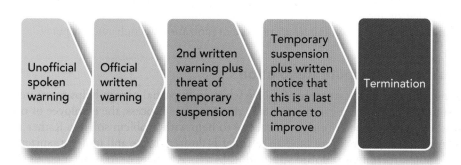

Figure 10.2
Progressive Discipline Responses

Unofficial spoken warning

Official written warning

2nd written warning plus threat of temporary suspension

Temporary suspension plus written notice that this is a last chance to improve

Termination

presenting them in an employee handbook, posting them on the company's intranet, and displaying them on a bulletin board. Supervisors should be familiar with the rules, so that they can discuss them with employees and apply them consistently.

Along with rules and a progression of consequences for violating the rules, a progressive discipline system should have requirements for documenting the rules, offenses, and responses. For issuing an unofficial warning about a less-serious offense, it may be enough to have a witness present. Even then, a written record would be helpful in case the employee repeats the offense in the future. The organization should provide a document for managers to file, recording the nature and date of the offense, the specific improvement expected, and the consequences of the offense. It is also helpful to indicate how the offense affects the performance of the individual employee, others in the group, or the organization as a whole. These documents are important for demonstrating to a problem employee why he or she has been suspended or terminated. They also back up the organization's actions if it should have to defend a lawsuit. Following the hot-stove rule, the supervisor should complete and discuss the documentation immediately after becoming aware of the offense. A copy of the records should be placed in the employee's personnel file. The organization may have a policy of removing records of warnings after a period such as six months, on the grounds that the employee has learned from the experience.

As we noted in the earlier discussion of procedural justice, the discipline system should provide an opportunity to hear every point of view and to correct errors. Before discussing and filing records of misbehavior, it is important for the supervisor to investigate the incident. The employee should be made aware of what he or she is said to have done wrong and should have an opportunity to present his or her version of events. Anyone who witnessed the misdeed also should have a chance to describe what happened. In general, employees who belong to a union have a right to the presence of a union representative during a formal investigation interview if they request representation. A method of gathering objective performance data also supports the fairness of the discipline system. The "HR How To" box provides additional ideas for handling discipline fairly.

Besides developing these policies, HR professionals have a role in carrying out progressive discipline.[15] In meetings to announce disciplinary actions, it is wise to include two representatives of the organization. Usually, the employee's supervisor presents the information, and a representative from the HR department acts as a witness. This person can help the meeting stay on track and, if necessary, can later confirm what happened during the meeting. Especially at the termination stage of the process, the employee may be angry, so it is helpful to be straightforward but polite. The supervisor should state the reason for the meeting, the nature of the problem behavior, and the consequences. Listening to the employee is important, but because an investigation was already conducted, there is no purpose to arguing. When an employee is suspended or terminated, the organization should designate a person to escort the employee from the building to protect the organization's people and property.

Alternative Dispute Resolution (ADR)
Methods of solving a problem by bringing in an impartial outsider but not using the court system.

Alternative Dispute Resolution

Sometimes problems are easier to solve when an impartial person helps to create the solution. Therefore, at various points in the discipline process, the employee or organization might want to bring in someone to help with problem solving. Rather than turning to the courts every time an outsider is desired, more and more organizations are using **alternative dispute resolution (ADR)**. A variety of ADR techniques show

Responding to Employee Misconduct

Whether the human resource professional is directly handling an employee with behavior problems or counseling a supervisor in how to handle the situation, the following guidelines should apply:

- **Be clear about performance standards from the outset—in selection interviews.** That information should include standards for human relations, such as that the organization requires employees to behave respectfully and unselfishly. If employees understand what is expected of them, the company can fairly discipline them for not meeting the standards.
- **Follow a consistent process of responding when employees are accused of serious misdeeds.** Never favor one employee over another in choosing complaints to investigate. Issues that require investigation are allegations that an employee violated a work rule, is not meeting performance standards, did something that could have harmed the employee or others, or engaged in incidents that disrupted the work environment.

- **Don't think you're smoothing over a situation or being nice by ignoring problem behavior.** One employee with a bad attitude can create an unpleasant work environment for all the group's best employees. Research on team performance found a performance decline of 30% or more when the team included just one person who slacked off or was anxious and irritable.
- **Investigate complaints as soon as possible.** That way, memories will be fresh, and people who have concerns will see that the company responds to concerns.
- **When investigating a complaint, record each person's statement in writing and have the statements signed and dated.** If any of the issues could lead to a lawsuit, consider having a company lawyer present, which may protect the confidentiality of the statement.
- **As much as possible, descriptions of problems should focus on behaviors, not personalities.** When the issue involves a violation of company rules, the statement should specify the rule and

indicate that the behavior was a violation of that rule.
- **Review the documentation to be sure it is clear and complete.** It should be clear enough to be understandable to someone who wasn't involved in the situation.
- **Be honest about the discipline.** If an employee is confused about whether or not rules were actually broken or what standards of performance are necessary, the employee could conclude that the supervisor won't actually follow through with discipline or that disciplinary measures result from discrimination.

SOURCES: Business & Legal Resources, "Employee Discipline: Properly Document Complaints and Investigations," *HR.BLR.com*, December 8, 2011, http://hr.blr.com; Robert Sutton, "How a Few Bad Apples Ruin Everything," *The Wall Street Journal,* October 24, 2011, http://online.wsj.com; Chris Frederick, "Effective Discipline without the Pain," *Motor Age,* March 2011, pp. 72–73; Michael S. Lavenant, "The Art of Employee Discipline: How to Retain Control and Increase Production," *Nonprofit World,* July/August 2010, pp. 22–23.

promise for resolving disputes in a timely, constructive, cost-effective manner (see Figure 10.3):

1. **Open-door policy**—Based on the expectation that two people in conflict should first try to arrive at a settlement together, the organization has a policy of making managers available to hear complaints. Typically, the first "open door" is that of the employee's immediate supervisor, and if the employee does not get a resolution from that person, the employee may appeal to managers at higher levels. This policy works only to the degree that employees trust management and managers who hear complaints listen and are able to act.
2. **Peer review**—The people in conflict take their conflict to a panel composed of representatives from the organization at the same levels as the people in the dispute.

Open-Door Policy
An organization's policy of making managers available to hear complaints.

Peer Review
Process for resolving disputes by taking them to a panel composed of representatives from the organization at the same levels as the people in the dispute.

Figure 10.3
Options for Alternative
Dispute Resolution

Mediation
Nonbinding process in
which a neutral party
from outside the orga-
nization hears the case
and tries to help the
people in conflict arrive
at a settlement.

Arbitration
Binding process in which
a professional arbitrator
from outside the organi-
zation (usually a lawyer
or judge) hears the case
and resolves it by mak-
ing a decision.

The panel hears the case and tries to help the parties arrive at a settlement. To set up a panel to hear disputes as they arise, the organization may assign managers to positions on the panel and have employees elect nonmanagement panel members.

3. **Mediation**—A neutral party from outside the organization hears the case and tries to help the people in conflict arrive at a settlement. The process is not binding, meaning the mediator cannot force a solution.

4. **Arbitration**—A professional arbitrator from outside the organization hears the case and resolves it by making a decision. Most arbitrators are experienced employment lawyers or retired judges. The employee and employer both have to accept this person's decision.

Typically, an organization's ADR process begins with an open-door policy, which is the simplest, most direct, and least expensive way to settle a dispute. When the parties to a dispute cannot resolve it themselves, the organization can move the dispute to peer review, mediation, or arbitration. At some organizations, if mediation fails, the process moves to arbitration as a third and final option. Although arbitration is a formal process involving an outsider, it tends to be much faster, simpler, and more private than a lawsuit.[16]

At Ford Motor Company, the introduction of a peer review process vastly improved the handling of employee complaints and disputes. Ford had an open-door policy for resolving disputes, but employees had come to distrust the process, believing that higher-level managers simply went along with whatever version of events they heard from the managers reporting to them. Ford created peer that use a panel of three randomly selected employee peers and two randomly selected managers, all of whom receive training. A facilitator runs a hearing of the issue, after which the panelists vote on whether the company's policies and practices were applied properly and consistently. The panel's decision is final and binding. In the year before the company tried peer reviews, it spent more than $8 million to defend itself against lawsuits filed by employees. In the six months after it began testing the use of peer reviews, it spent less than $100,000 to address a single discrimination charge that ultimately was sent to the peer review process. Employees were far less likely to turn to the courts because they saw the peer review process as consistently fair.[17]

Employee Assistance Programs

While ADR is effective in dealing with problems related to performance and disputes between people at work, many of the problems that lead an organization to want to terminate an employee involve drug or alcohol abuse. In these cases, the organization's discipline program should also incorporate an **employee assistance program (EAP)**. An EAP is a referral service that employees can use to seek professional treatment for emotional problems or substance abuse. EAPs began in the 1950s with a focus on treating alcoholism, and in the 1980s they expanded into drug treatment. Today, many are now fully integrated into employers' overall health benefits plans, where they refer employees to covered mental health services.

EAPs vary widely, but most share some basic elements. First, the programs are usually identified in official documents published by the employer, such as employee handbooks. Supervisors (and union representatives when workers belong to a union) are trained to use the referral service for employees whom they suspect of having health-related problems. The organization also trains employees to use the system to refer themselves when necessary. The organization regularly evaluates the costs and benefits of the program, usually once a year.

The variations among EAPs make evaluating these programs especially important. With many employees continuing to face pressures associated with the housing crisis and slow economic recovery, EAPs today are seeing signs of strains on mental and emotional health. Employees may be embarrassed to ask for mental health services, but when they call for help refinancing a mortgage or locating a divorce attorney, EAPs are identifying needs for counseling. Some EAPs will also train managers in how to talk to employees with behavior problems.[18] Reflecting back a decade after the 9/11 terrorist attacks, EAPs say employees then began to realize how valuable these services were for providing a variety of services, from grief counseling to financial advice to advice on legal issues. Building on these lessons, Verizon expanded its EAP to a 24-hour call center for counseling and referrals plus a menu of workshops on topics related to mental health (for example, financial planning and using humor to relieve stress).[19]

> **Employee Assistance Program (EAP)**
> A referral service that employees can use to seek professional treatment for emotional problems or substance abuse.

Outplacement Counseling

An employee who has been discharged is likely to feel angry and confused about what to do next. If the person feels there is nothing to lose and nowhere else to turn, the potential for violence or a lawsuit is greater than most organizations are willing to tolerate. This concern is one reason many organizations provide **outplacement counseling**, which tries to help dismissed employees manage the transition from one job to another. Organizations also may address ongoing poor performance with discussion about whether the employee is a good fit for the current job. Rather than simply firing the poor performer, the supervisor may encourage this person to think about leaving. In this situation, the availability of outplacement counseling may help the employee decide to look for another job. This approach may protect the dignity of the employee who leaves and promote a sense of fairness.

> **Outplacement Counseling**
> A service in which professionals try to help dismissed employees manage the transition from one job to another.

Some organizations have their own staff for conducting outplacement counseling. Other organizations have contracts with outside providers to help with individual cases. Either way, the goals for outplacement programs are to help the former employee address the psychological issues associated with losing a job—grief, depression, and fear—while at the same time helping the person find a new job.

The use of outplacement firms has become far more common since John Challenger witnessed IBM's first-ever round of major layoffs in 1993. Challenger's father, James, started the first outplacement firm in the United States, when downsizing was not yet a part of the business vocabulary. Today firms such as Challenger, Gray & Christmas, and Lee Hecht Harrison regularly dispatch counselors to help laid-off people recover from the shock of joblessness, polish their résumés, conduct job searches, and practice interviewing. Challenger's firm has even landed a contract to help with a new and increasingly common form of transition: moving from military service to employment in the civilian sector.[20]

Whatever the reason for downsizing, asking employees to leave is a setback for the employee and for the company. Retaining people who can contribute knowledge and talent is essential to business success. Therefore, the remainder of this chapter explores issues related to retaining employees.

Employee Engagement

Employee Engagement
The degree to which employees are fully involved in their work and the strength of their job and company commitment.

Employee engagement is the degree to which employees are fully involved in their work and the strength of their commitment to their job and company. Employees who are engaged in their work and committed to the company they work for provide a clear competitive advantage to that firm, including higher productivity, better customer service, and lower turnover.[21] Unfortunately, many companies have not given much attention to employee engagement in recent years, possibly due to the recession. Some survey results suggest that less than one-third of employees consider themselves as engaged. Still, some companies have managed to sustain and improve engagement levels during the recession by systematically gathering feedback from employees, analyzing their responses, and implementing changes. In these companies, engagement measures are considered as important as customer service or financial data.

Although the types of questions asked in employee engagement surveys may vary, some of the common themes generally measured include pride and satisfaction with employer; opportunity to perform challenging work; recognition and positive feedback from contributions; personal support from supervisor; and understanding of the link between one's job and the company's overall mission. At Pitney Bowes, about 80% of its employees complete an engagement survey each year, which gives them a chance to share their feelings and perceptions and help the company address problems.[22] The survey is also used to determine if the company is doing enough to help employees reach their career goals. Based on survey results, the company is trying out a program that is designed to help managers improve their skills in listening, change management, and problem solving. Pitney-Bowes managers are held accountable for helping employees with their careers, and this program ensures they have the skills necessary for success.

Another example of employee engagement happens at LifeGift, a Houston-based not-for-profit organization that recovers human organs and tissue from recently deceased donors and matches them to transplant recipients across the country. Engagement means having employees who never give up on finding a donor. LifeGift's CEO made employee engagement a priority and started measuring engagement annually in 2008. When engagement levels fell in the last survey, the CEO required company managers to hold quarterly one-on-one discussions with their employees, separate from annual evaluations. Results from the surveys and discussions ensure that employees receive the training, emotional support, and other resources needed to deal with the demands of the job. Most companies do not deal with life or death issues like LifeGift does, but focusing on employee engagement can ensure that employees are satisfied and productive.[23]

Job Withdrawal

Organizations need employees who are fully engaged and committed to their work. Therefore, retaining employees goes beyond preventing them from quitting. The organization needs to prevent a broader negative condition, called **job withdrawal**—or a

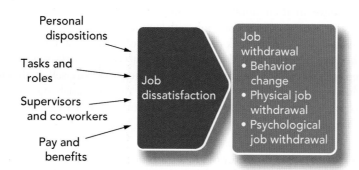

Figure 10.4
Job Withdrawal Process

set of behaviors with which employees try to avoid the work situation physically, mentally, or emotionally. Job withdrawal results when circumstances such as the nature of the job, supervisors and co-workers, pay levels, or the employee's own disposition cause the employee to become dissatisfied with the job. As shown in Figure 10.4, this job dissatisfaction produces job withdrawal. Job withdrawal may take the form of behavior change, physical job withdrawal, or psychological withdrawal. Some researchers believe employees engage in the three forms of withdrawal behavior in that order, while others think they select from these behaviors to address the particular sources of job dissatisfaction they experience.[24] Although the specifics of these models vary, the consensus is that withdrawal behaviors are related to one another and are at least partially caused by job dissatisfaction.[25]

Job Withdrawal
A set of behaviors with which employees try to avoid the work situation physically, mentally, or emotionally.

Job Dissatisfaction

Many aspects of people and organizations can cause job dissatisfaction, and managers and HR professionals need to be aware of them because correcting them can increase job satisfaction and prevent job withdrawal. Ideally, managers should catch and correct job dissatisfaction early because there is evidence linking changes in satisfaction levels to turnover: when satisfaction is falling, employees are far more likely to quit.[26] The causes of job dissatisfaction identified in Figure 10.4 fall into four categories: personal dispositions, tasks and roles, supervisors and co-workers, and pay and benefits.

LO 10-5 Explain how job dissatisfaction affects employee behavior.

Personal Dispositions   Job dissatisfaction is a feeling experienced by individuals, so it is not surprising that many researchers have studied individual personality differences to see if some kinds of people are more disposed to be dissatisfied with their jobs. In general, job turnover (and presumably dissatisfaction leading up to it) is higher among employees who are low in emotional stability, conscientiousness, and agreeableness.[27] In addition, two other personal qualities associated with job satisfaction are negative affectivity and negative self-evaluations.

Negative affectivity means pervasive low levels of satisfaction with all aspects of life, compared with other people's feelings. People with negative affectivity experience feelings such as anger, contempt, disgust, guilt, fear, and nervousness more than other people do, at work and away. They tend to focus on the negative aspects of themselves and others.[28] Not surprisingly, people with negative affectivity tend to be dissatisfied with their jobs, even after changing employers or occupations.[29]

Core self-evaluations are bottom-line opinions individuals have of themselves and may be positive or negative. People with a positive core self-evaluation have high

Role
The set of behaviors that people expect of a person in a particular job.

Role Ambiguity
Uncertainty about what the organization expects from the employee in terms of what to do or how to do it.

Role Conflict
An employee's recognition that demands of the job are incompatible or contradictory.

self-esteem, believe in their ability to accomplish their goals, and are emotionally stable. They also tend to experience job satisfaction.[30] Part of the reason for their satisfaction is that they tend to seek out and obtain jobs with desirable characteristics, and when they are in a situation they dislike, they are more likely to seek change in socially acceptable ways.[31] In contrast, people with negative core self-evaluations tend to blame other people for their problems, including their dissatisfying jobs. They are less likely to work toward change; they either do nothing or act aggressively toward the people they blame.[32]

Tasks and Roles   As a predictor of job dissatisfaction, nothing surpasses the nature of the task itself.[33] Many aspects of a task have been linked to dissatisfaction. Of particular significance are the complexity of the task, the degree of physical strain and exertion required, and the value the employee places on the task.[34] In general, employees (especially women) are bored and dissatisfied with simple, repetitive jobs.[35] People also are more dissatisfied with jobs requiring a great deal of physical strain and exertion. Because automation has removed much of the physical strain associated with jobs, employers often overlook this consideration. Still, many jobs remain physically demanding. Finally, employees feel dissatisfied if their work is not related to something they value.

Employees not only perform specific tasks but also have roles within the organization.[36] A person's **role** consists of the set of behaviors that people expect of a person in that job. These expected behaviors include the formally defined duties of the job but also much more. Sometimes things get complicated or confusing. Co-workers, supervisors, and customers have expectations for how the employee should behave often going far beyond a formal job description and having a large impact on the employee's work satisfaction. Several role-related sources of dissatisfaction are the following:

- **Role ambiguity** is uncertainty about what the organization and others expect from the employee in terms of what to do or how to do it. Employees suffer when they are unclear about work methods, scheduling, and performance criteria, perhaps because others hold different ideas about these. Employees particularly want to know how the organization will evaluate their performance. When they aren't sure, they become dissatisfied.[37]
- **Role conflict** is an employee's recognition that demands of the job are incompatible or contradictory; a person cannot meet all the demands. For example, a company might bring together employees from different functions to work on a team to develop a new product. Team members feel role conflict when they realize that their team leader and functional manager have conflicting expectations of them. Also, many employees may feel conflict between work roles and family roles. A role

Military reservists who are sent overseas often experience role conflict among *three* roles: soldier, family member, and civilian employee. Overseas assignments often intensify role conflicts.

conflict may be triggered by an organization's request that an employee take an assignment overseas. Foreign assignments can be highly disruptive to family members, and the resulting role conflict is the top reason that people quit overseas assignments.[38]

- **Role overload** results when too many expectations or demands are placed on a person. (The opposite situation is *role underload*.) After an organization downsizes, it may expect so much of the remaining employees that they experience role overload.

Role Overload
A state in which too many expectations or demands are placed on a person.

Supervisors and Co-workers Negative behavior by managers and peers in the workplace can produce tremendous dissatisfaction. Often much of the responsibility for positive relationships is placed on direct supervisors. For example, employees want regular performance feedback from their supervisors and want their ideas to be heard. They also have expectations from seniors, including honest communication and a workplace that enables high performance. Interestingly, employees are more engaged when their supervisors give negative feedback, focused on their weaknesses, than when supervisors give no feedback.[39] Employees want some evidence that the company's leaders care about them, so they are more likely to be dissatisfied if management is distant and unresponsive.

In other cases, conflicts between employees left unaddressed by management may cause job dissatisfaction severe enough to lead to withdrawal or departure. Research suggests that turnover is higher when employees do not feel that their values and beliefs fit with their work group's values and beliefs.[40] Furthermore uncivil behavior by co-workers generates unhappiness that manifests in a variety of ways, such as decreased commitment, effort, and performance.[41]

Pay and Benefits For all the concern with positive relationships and interesting work, it is important to keep in mind that employees definitely care about their earnings. A job is the primary source of income and financial security for most people. Pay also is an indicator of status within the organization and in society at large, so it contributes to some people's self-worth. For all these reasons, satisfaction with pay is significant for retaining employees. Decisions about pay and benefits are so important and complex that the chapters of the next part of this book are devoted to this topic.

With regard to job satisfaction, the pay level—that is, the amount of income associated with each job—is especially important. Employers seeking to lure away another organization's employees often do so by offering higher pay. Benefits, such as insurance and vacation time, are also important, but employees often have difficulty measuring their worth. Therefore, although benefits influence job satisfaction, employees may not always consider them as much as pay itself.

Behavior Change

A reasonable expectation is that an employee's first response to dissatisfaction would be to try to change the conditions that generate the dissatisfaction. As the employee tries to bring about changes in policy or personnel, the efforts may involve confrontation and conflict with the employee's supervisor. In an organization where employees are represented by a union, as we will discuss in Chapter 14, more grievances may be filed.

From the manager's point of view, the complaints, confrontations, and grievances may feel threatening. On closer inspection, however, this is an opportunity for the manager to learn about and solve a potentially important problem. Motivational writer and speaker Jon Gordon notes that employees who constantly complain can drain energy from the workplace, but the behavior can be channeled for good. Responding to complaints by requesting—and listening to—ideas for what would make the situation better develops a workforce of problem solvers.[42]

When employees cannot work with management to make changes, they may look for help from outside the organization. Some employees may engage in *whistle-blowing*, taking their charges to the media in the hope that if the public learns about the situation, the organization will be forced to change. From the organization's point of view, whistle-blowing is harmful because of the negative publicity.

Another way employees may go outside the organization for help is to file a lawsuit. This way to force change is available if the employee is disputing policies on the grounds that they violate state and federal laws, such as those forbidding employment discrimination or requiring safe working conditions. Defending a lawsuit is costly, both financially and in terms of the employer's image, whether the organization wins or loses. Most employers would prefer to avoid lawsuits and whistle-blowing. Keeping employees satisfied is one way to do this.

Physical Job Withdrawal

If behavior change has failed or seems impossible, a dissatisfied worker may physically withdraw from the job. Options for physically leaving a job range from arriving late to calling in sick, requesting a transfer, or leaving the organization altogether. Even while they are on the job, employees may withdraw by not actually working. All these options are costly to the employer.

Finding a new job is rarely easy and can take months, so employees often are cautious about quitting. Employees who would like to quit may be late for work. Tardiness is costly because late employees are not contributing for part of the day. Especially when work is done by teams, the tardiness creates difficulties that spill over and affect the entire team's ability to work. Absenteeism is even more of a problem. The U.S. Department of Labor has estimated that on the average workday, 3% to 5% of an employer's workforce is absent, costing the nation's employers perhaps $100 billion annually.[43]

An employee who is dissatisfied because of circumstances related to the specific job—for example, an unpleasant workplace or unfair supervisor—may be able to resolve that problem with a job transfer. If the source of the dissatisfaction is organizational policies or practices, such as low pay scales, the employee may leave the organization altogether. These forms of physical job withdrawal contribute to high turnover rates for the department or organization. As a result, the organization faces the costs of replacing the employees (often tens of thousands of dollars per employee), as well as lost productivity and sometimes lost sales until replacement employees learn the jobs.[44] And in today's world of social media, the costs of badly ended relationships with employees extend longer and farther than ever before (see "HRM Social").

Organizations need to be concerned with their overall turnover rates as well as the nature of the turnover in terms of who is staying and who is leaving. For example, younger workers, who are less likely to be tied down by a mortgage or children in local schools, are more ready to quit their jobs when they become disengaged. Failure to retain these workers can pose staffing problems at organizations with a large group of employees nearing retirement age.[45] Also, among managers, women and minorities often have higher turnover rates. Many leave because they see little opportunity for promotions. Chapter 9 discussed how organizations are addressing this problem through career management and efforts to break the glass ceiling.

Staying Connected to Former Employees

Part of the immense appeal of social media is the ability of these tools to connect us to more people than we could meet in our own physical communities. Online social networks include friends of friends, colleagues of colleagues, and members of shared-interest groups who may live anywhere on the globe. Increasingly, the people who interact with one another via social media are employers, their former (and future) employees, and others who have an interest in the employer's reputation.

This situation creates both challenges and opportunities. On the downside, an ugly departure can damage an employer's and/or former employee's reputation on a massive scale. In one recent incident, Joey DeFrancesco had himself filmed turning in his resignation at the hotel where he had worked and then marching out with a homemade marching band parading behind him. The clip was posted on YouTube, generating millions of views. Whether that did more damage to the hotel's reputation or DeFrancesco's ability to land future jobs is, of course, an open question.

The more positive view is that when employee departures are handled gracefully, social media can provide a way for valuable workers and their former employers to find each other in the future, should new opportunities arise. Entrepreneur Dave Balter admits that he didn't always pay enough attention to departing employees when he was focused on building up his company BzzAgent. But when he realized that his disregard for that stage of the employment process was creating hard feelings, he began to change his ways. He began to listen to the goals of departing workers and realized that they often were making changes that would lead to future relationships as supplier, customer, and collaborator on special projects—and perhaps, someday, returning employee.

In the past, maintaining those kinds of relationships might have been difficult. But today, employers and former employees can readily stay in touch by linking their profiles on LinkedIn or following one another on Twitter. The ease of building these relationships and the extent to which today's workers expect to be connected via social media are making it essential for employers to craft new policies. When employees create social-media accounts as representatives of their employer, what rights do they have to the relationships they have built with these accounts? What access should they have to the contact information? And how can employers ensure that their social-media relationships with outsiders protect confidential information? HR professionals will need to collaborate with legal and IT experts to craft workable answers so employers can realize the potential of relationships that outlive jobs.

SOURCES: Dave Balter, "How to Break Up with Employees," *Inc.,* November 2, 2011, http://www.inc.com; Emanuella Grinberg, "'Joey' Becomes Recession Hero after Using Marching Band to Quit Job," *CNN Wire,* October 24, 2011, Business & Company Resource Center, http://galenet.galegroup.com; Ed Frauenheim, "You Can't Take It with Yo . . . or Can You?" *Workforce Management,* June 2011, Business & Company Resource Center, http://galenet.galegroup.com.

Psychological Withdrawal

Employees need not leave the company in order to withdraw from their jobs. Especially if they have been unable to find another job, they may psychologically remove themselves. They are physically at work, but their minds are elsewhere.

Psychological withdrawal can take several forms. If an employee is primarily dissatisfied with the job itself, the employee may display a very low level of job involvement. **Job involvement** is the degree to which people identify themselves with their jobs. People with a high level of job involvement consider their work an important part of their life. Doing well at work contributes to their sense of who they are (their *self-concept*). For a dissatisfied employee with low job involvement, performing well or poorly does not affect the person's self-concept.

When an employee is dissatisfied with the organization as a whole, the person's organizational commitment may be low. **Organizational commitment** is the degree

Job Involvement
The degree to which people identify themselves with their jobs.

Organizational Commitment
The degree to which an employee identifies with the organization and is willing to put forth effort on its behalf.

to which an employee identifies with the organization and is willing to put forth effort on its behalf.[46] Employees with high organizational commitment will stretch themselves to help the organization through difficult times. Employees with low organizational commitment are likely to leave at the first opportunity for a better job. They have a strong intention to leave, so like employees with low job involvement, they are hard to motivate.

Job Satisfaction

Clearly, organizations want to prevent withdrawal behaviors. As we saw in Figure 10.4, the driving force behind job withdrawal is dissatisfaction. To prevent job withdrawal, organizations therefore need to promote **job satisfaction**, a pleasant feeling resulting from the perception that one's job fulfills or allows for the fulfillment of one's important job values.[47] This definition has three components:

- Job satisfaction is related to a person's *values*, defined as "what a person consciously or unconsciously desires to obtain."
- Different employees have different views of which values are *important*, so the same circumstances can produce different levels of job satisfaction.
- Job satisfaction is based on *perception*, not always on an objective and complete measurement of the situation. Each person compares the job situation to his or her values, and people are likely to differ in what they perceive.

In sum, people will be satisfied with their jobs as long as they perceive that their jobs meet their important values. As shown in Figure 10.5, organizations can contribute to job satisfaction by addressing the four sources of job dissatisfaction we identified earlier: personal dispositions, job tasks and roles, supervisors and co-workers, and pay and benefits.

Figure 10.5
Increasing Job Satisfaction

Monitoring job satisfaction

Hiring employees predisposed to being satisfied

Referring depressed employees for help

Designing complex, meaningful jobs

Establishing clear, appropriate roles

Reinforcing shared values

Encouraging social support

Helping employees pursue goals

Setting satisfactory pay levels

Communicating pay structure and policies

Personal Dispositions

In our discussion of job withdrawal, we noted that sometimes personal qualities of the employee, such as negative affectivity and negative core self-evaluation, are associated with job dissatisfaction. This linkage suggests employee selection in the first instance plays a role in raising overall levels of employee satisfaction. People making the selection decisions should look for evidence of whether employees are predisposed to being satisfied.[48] Interviews should explore employees' satisfaction with past jobs. If an applicant says he was dissatisfied with his past six jobs, what makes the employer think the person won't be dissatisfied with the organization's vacant position?

Employers also should recognize that dissatisfaction with other facets of life can spill over into the workplace. A worker who is having problems with a family member may attribute some of the negative feelings to the job or organization. Although the negative attitude may stem from outside causes, however, bad moods have been associated with productivity declines, and they can be contagious. Supervisors can respond most effectively by trying to shift the employee's attention away from the negative mood and onto work.[49] If a manager suspects an employee may have an ongoing issue, such as depression, burnout, or problems at home, the manager should suggest that the employee contact the organization's employee assistance program or his or her physician. As a reasonable accommodation under the Americans with Disabilities Act, the employer may need to grant a depressed employee time off or a flexible schedule to accommodate treatment.

Tasks and Roles

Organizations can improve job satisfaction by making jobs more complex and meaningful, as we discussed in Chapter 4. Some of the methods available for this approach to job design are job enrichment and job rotation. Organizations also can increase satisfaction by developing clear and appropriate job roles.

Job Complexity   Not only can job design add to enriching complexity, but employees themselves sometimes take measures to make their work more interesting. Some employees bring personal music players with headsets to work so they can listen to music or radio shows while they are working. Many supervisors disapprove, worrying that the headsets will interfere with the employees' ability to provide good customer service. However, in simple jobs with minimal customer contact (like processing paperwork or entering data into computers), research suggests that personal headsets can improve performance. One study examined the use of stereo headsets by workers in 32 jobs at a large retailing company. The stereo-using group outperformed the no-stereo group on simple jobs (like invoice processor), but performed worse than the stereo-free group on complex jobs (such as accountant).[50]

Meaningful Work   When it comes to generating satisfaction, the most important aspect of work is the degree to which it is meaningfully related to workers' core values. People sign

Appropriate tasks and roles include safety precautions, especially when work could involve risks to workers' health and safety.

on to help charitable causes for little or no pay simply because of the value they place on making a difference in the world. Royal DSM has shifted its business strategy from a focus on materials petrochemicals, plastics, and base chemicals—to emphasizing health-enhancing technologies and products such as nutritional supplements, pharmaceutical ingredients, and energy-efficient building materials. This sustainable strategy opens up opportunities for employees to use the organization's resources for good works. For example, Royal DSM partners with the World Food Programme to distribute vitamins and nutrient mixes free to poor people in Afghanistan, Bangladesh, Kenya, and Nepal. Furthering employee engagement, Royal DSM invites employees to nominate projects for the company to fund, and local managers include outreach and community engagement in their budgets.[51]

A similar kind of motivation can drive activities directly related to doing business. When Jeffrey Scott owned a landscaping business, he taught his foremen how each crew's output was related to the company's productivity. He also gave them authority to make spending decisions up to a certain dollar level so they could take action on the job to satisfy customers who had quality concerns. And Scott authorized them to "fire" clients if that seemed the best course of action. As a result, the foremen could see connections between their decisions, the company's well-being, and the customers' satisfaction. They were no longer just completing projects; they were building a business and pleasing customers. Their crews began to deliver better quality, and customers were happier as well, so the company was retaining clients, not firing them.[52]

Clear and Appropriate Roles   Organizations can do much to avoid role-related sources of dissatisfaction. They can define roles, clearly spelling out work methods, schedules, and performance measures. They can be realistic about the number of hours required to complete job requirements. When jobs require overtime hours, the employer must be prepared to comply with laws requiring overtime pay, as well as to help employees manage the conflict between work and family roles.

To help employees manage role conflict, employers have turned to a number of family-friendly policies. These policies may include provisions for child care, elder care, flexible work schedules, job sharing, telecommuting, and extended parental leaves. Although these programs create some headaches for managers in terms of scheduling work and reporting requirements, they increase employees' satisfaction (see "Did You Know?)" and commitment to the organization.[53] Organizations with family-friendly policies also have enjoyed improvements in performance, especially at companies that employ a large percentage of women.[54] Chapter 13 discusses such benefits in greater detail.

Organizations should also pay attention to the fit between job titles and roles, especially as more and more Americans feel overworked. One consequence of this perception is lawsuits seeking overtime pay. The Fair Labor Standards Act exempts managers and professionals from its requirement that the company pay overtime to employees who work more than a 40-hour week. Increasingly, employees are complaining that they have been misclassified as managers and should be treated as nonexempt workers. Their job titles sound like managerial jobs, but their day-to-day activities involve no supervision. Family Dollar Stores ran into trouble for classifying its store managers as exempt employees without first investigating what duties each of them performed. Two of its managers complained that they should have been paid overtime rates because they were misclassified. In the ensuing trial, which grew to include

Office Workers Appreciate Help Balancing Roles and Learning New Skills

Office workers who were asked which aspect of their job contributes most to their satisfaction were almost equally split in picking work-life balance or learning opportunities. This study by OfficeTeam did not offer "meaningful work" as one of the choices. In a separate, international study by Mercer, company representatives said the top three factors that keep their employees engaged are respectful treatment, work-life balance, and the type of work they do.

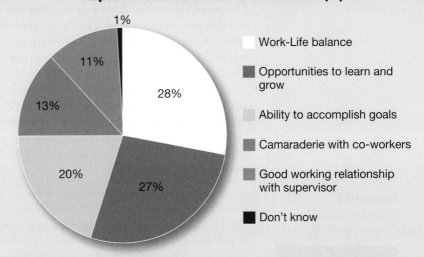

Aspect of Job Most Tied to Satisfaction (%)

- Work-Life balance
- Opportunities to learn and grow
- Ability to accomplish goals
- Camaraderie with co-workers
- Good working relationship with supervisor
- Don't know

Question

How would you predict the OfficeTeam responses would change if the available responses included meaningful work? Why?

SOURCES: Phaedra Brotherton, "Employee Loyalty Slipping Worldwide; Respect, Work-Life Balance Are Top Engagers," *T + D,* February 2012, p. 24; Ray Camma, "Work/Life Balance, Learning Opportunities Have Greatest Impact on Job Satisfaction," American Association of Finance and Accounting, January 27, 2012, http://aafa.com; OfficeTeam, "What Workers Want," news release, January 26, 2012, http://officeteam.rhi.mediaroom.com.

1,424 managers, the court learned that the store managers performed tasks of non-management employees (stocking shelves, ringing up sales, cleaning stores) and were forbidden from making decisions to hire assistants. The evidence of how the managers were spending their time and the limits on their authority did not support their classification as exempt employees. The fact that the store assigned them a title of "manager" was irrelevant.[55]

Because role problems rank just behind job problems in creating job dissatisfaction, some interventions aim directly at role elements. One of these is the **role analysis technique**, a process of formally identifying expectations associated with a role. The technique follows the steps shown in Figure 10.6. The *role occupant* (the person who fills a role) and each member of the person's *role set* (people who directly interact with this employee) each write down their expectations for the role. They meet to discuss their expectations and develop a preliminary list of the role's duties and behaviors, trying to resolve any conflicts among expectations. Next, the role occupant lists what he or she expects of others in the set, and the group meets again to reach a consensus on these expectations. Finally, the group modifies its preliminary list and reaches a consensus on the occupant's role. This process may uncover instances of overload and underload, and the group tries to trade off requirements to develop more balanced roles.

Role Analysis Technique
A process of formally identifying expectations associated with a role.

Supervisors and Co-Workers

The two primary sets of people in an organization who affect job satisfaction are co-workers and supervisors. A person may be satisfied with these people for one of three reasons:

1. The people share the same values, attitudes, and philosophies. Most individuals find this very important, and many organizations try to foster a culture of shared values. Even when this does not occur across the whole organization, values shared between workers and their supervisor can increase satisfaction.[56]
2. The co-workers and supervisor may provide social support, meaning they are sympathetic and caring. Social support greatly increases job satisfaction, whether the support comes from supervisors or co-workers.[57] Turnover is also lower among employees who experience support from other members of the organization.[58]
3. The co-workers or supervisor may help the person attain some valued outcome. For example, they can help a new employee figure out what goals to pursue and how to achieve them.[59]

Figure 10.6
Steps in the Role Analysis Technique

Members of role set write expectations for role

Members of role set discuss expectations

Preliminary list of role's duties and behaviors

Role occupant lists expectations for others in role set

Members of role set discuss expectations and reach consensus on occupant's role

Modified list of role's duties and behaviors

Because a supportive environment reduces dissatisfaction, many organizations foster team building both on and off the job (such as with softball or bowling leagues). The idea is that playing together as a team will strengthen ties among group members and develop relationships in which individuals feel supported by one another. Organizations also are developing their managers' mentoring skills and helping to set up these beneficial relationships.[60] (Mentoring was described in Chapter 9.) At Hayes Management Consulting, many employees work at client sites spread out across the United States. So that they feel connected and able to support one another, the company provides them with online collaboration tools and encourages them to share information and ideas on its database. The firm's senior managers also make a point of traveling around to the client sites to check in on their employees and offer support face-to-face. Hayes's marketing communications manager affirms these efforts: "People feel like they can reach out. They don't feel alone in the field."[61]

Pay and Benefits

Organizations recognize the importance of pay in their negotiations with job candidates. HR professionals can support their organizations in this area by repeatedly monitoring pay levels in their industry and for the professions or trades they employ. As we noted in Chapter 5 and will discuss further in Chapter 11, organizations make decisions about whether to match or exceed the industry averages. Also, HR professionals can increase job satisfaction by communicating to employees the value of their benefits. The "Best Practices" box describes how pay policy supports other methods of fostering employee engagement at NuStar Energy.

Two other aspects of pay satisfaction influence job satisfaction. One is satisfaction with pay structure—the way the organization assigns different pay levels to different levels and job categories. A manager of a sales force, for example, might be satisfied with her pay level until she discovers that some of the sales representatives she supervises are earning more than she is. The other important aspect of pay satisfaction is pay raises. People generally expect that their pay will increase over time. They will be satisfied if their expectations are met or dissatisfied if raises fall short of expectations. HR professionals

How NuStar Energy Keeps Employee Engagement Burning

NuStar Energy, based in San Antonio, Texas, refines and distributes asphalt and fuels. It operates three refineries, 89 storage facilities, and 8,420 miles of pipeline. The work can be stressful: asphalt is hot and smelly, and delivering gasoline, jet fuel, and heating oil is dangerous. Nevertheless, NuStar rated a spot on *Fortune* magazine's prestigious list of the 100 Best Companies to Work For.

One reason employees are satisfied is pay policy. NuStar pays well for its industry and has a generous health insurance plan. In addition to earning fair wage rates, all employees are eligible for an annual bonus, as well as pay increases for good performance. NuStar also pays eligible employees with grants of company stock. Of the $13.6 million stock grants in a recent year, $12 million went to employees below the executive level—reversing the pattern typical of most companies, where the most senior managers get the biggest stock payouts. And unlike most companies today, workers earn a pension (retirement income based on number of years worked).

But pay is far from the only advantage of working for NuStar.

Rather, it is only one expression of the company's belief that taking care of employees produces a culture in which employees will ensure that the company performs well. Concern for employees is an attitude practiced by NuStar's chairman, Bill Greehey, who is famous for having fired an executive who bullied the managers reporting to him.

NuStar's motto of "caring and sharing" is expressed in generous gifts to United Way and sponsoring volunteer work by its employees. The company's executives serve employees as well. They travel to NuStar's field locations, set up grills, and serve Texas-style barbecue to the workers there. In 2008, Hurricane Ike destroyed homes along the Texas Gulf Coast, where many of NuStar's facilities are located. NuStar employees traveled there from elsewhere in the country to cook, repair homes, and distribute free gasoline. In addition, concern for employees includes the practical and crucial issue of worker safety. Management is serious about enforcing a policy that if workers see a job is unsafe, they may decline to proceed without fear of punishment. NuStar's petroleum supply terminal in Colorado Springs recently won the Occupational Health and Safety Administration's top award for safety by meeting the standards of a voluntary program for exceeding safety requirements.

Perhaps most striking in these difficult economic times is that NuStar has never laid off workers. Instead, management asks employees to help the company figure out how to weather slowdowns. Recently, for example, orders for asphalt slowed. Rather than downsizing by 10%, the company asked workers for ideas in how to keep the company profitable. They came up with so many ideas to improve efficiency that profits actually increased.

SOURCES: NuStar Energy, "About NuStar Energy L.P.," http://www.nustarenergy.com, accessed April 5, 2012; "The 100 Best Companies to Work For," *Fortune*, February 6, 2012, EBSCOhost, http://web.ebscohost.com; Wayne Heilman, "Petroleum Terminal Operator Honored for Safety Record," *Gazette (Colorado Springs, CO)*, August 10, 2011, Business & Company Resource Center, http://galenet.galegroup.com; David A. Kaplan, "Undercover Employee: A Day on the Job at Three Best Companies," *Fortune*, January 20, 2011, http://features.blogs.fortune.cnn.com.

can contribute to these sources of job satisfaction by helping to communicate the reasoning behind the organization's pay structure and pay raises. For example, sometimes economic conditions force an organization to limit pay raises. If employees understand the circumstances (and recognize that the same conditions are likely to be affecting other employers), they may feel less dissatisfied.

Monitoring Job Satisfaction

Employers can better retain employees if they are aware of satisfaction levels, so they can make changes if employees are dissatisfied. The usual way to measure job satisfaction is with some kind of survey. A systematic, ongoing program of employee surveys should be part of the organization's human resource strategy. This program allows

Co-worker relationships can contribute to job satisfaction, and organizations therefore try to provide opportunities to build positive relationships. Would a strong sense of teamwork and friendship help you enjoy your work more?

the organization to monitor trends and prevent voluntary turnover. For example, if satisfaction with promotion opportunities has been falling over several years, the trend may signal a need for better career management (a topic of Chapter 9). An organizational change, such as a merger, also might have important consequences for job satisfaction. In addition, ongoing surveys give the organization a way to measure whether policies adopted to improve job satisfaction and employee retention are working. Organizations can also compare results from different departments to identify groups with successful practices that may apply elsewhere in the organization. Another benefit is that some scales provide data that organizations can use to compare themselves to others in the same industry. This information will be valuable for creating and reviewing human resource policies that enable organizations to attract and retain employees in a competitive job market. Finally, conducting surveys gives employees a chance to be heard, so the practice itself can contribute to employee satisfaction.

To obtain a survey instrument, an excellent place to begin is with one of the many established scales. The validity and reliability of many satisfaction scales have been tested, so it is possible to compare the survey instruments. The main reason for the organization to create its own scale would be that it wants to measure satisfaction with aspects of work that are specific to the organization (such as satisfaction with a particular health plan).

A widely used measure of job satisfaction is the Job Descriptive Index (JDI). The JDI emphasizes specific aspects of satisfaction—pay, the work itself, supervision, co-workers, and promotions. Figure 10.7 shows several items from the JDI scale. Other scales measure general satisfaction, using broad questions such as "All in all, how satisfied are you with your job?"[62] Some scales avoid language altogether, relying on pictures. The faces scale in Figure 10.8 is an example of this type of measure. Other scales exist for measuring more specific aspects of satisfaction. For example, the Pay

Figure 10.7

Example of Job Descriptive Index (JDI)

Instructions: Think of your present work. What is it like most of the time? In the blank beside each word given below, write

___Y___ for "Yes" if it describes your work
___N___ for "No" if it does NOT describe your work
___?___ if you cannot decide

Work Itself	**Pay**	**Promotion Opportunities**
_____ Routine	_____ Less than I deserve	_____ Dead-end job
_____ Satisfying	_____ Highly paid	_____ Unfair policies
_____ Good	_____ Insecure	_____ Based on ability

Supervision	**Co-workers**
_____ Impolite	_____ Intelligent
_____ Praises good work	_____ Responsible
_____ Doesn't supervise enough	_____ Boring

SOURCE: W. K. Balzar, D. C. Smith, D. E. Kravitz, S. E. Lovell, K. B. Paul, B. A. Reilly, and C. E. Reilly, *User's Manual for the Job Descriptive Index (JDI)* (Bowling Green, OH: Bowling Green State University, 1990).

Job Satisfaction from the Faces Scale
Consider all aspects of your job. Circle the face that
best describes your feelings about your job in general.

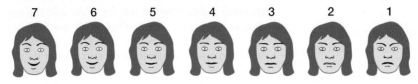

SOURCE: From R. B. Dunham and J. B. Herman, *Journal of Applied Psychology* 60 (1975), pp. 629–31. Reprinted
with permission.

Figure 10.8

Example of a Simplified,
Nonverbal Measure of
Job Satisfaction

Satisfaction Questionnaire (PSQ) measures satisfaction with specific aspects of pay, such as pay levels, structure, and raises.[63]

Along with administering surveys, more organizations are analyzing basic HR data to look for patterns in employee retention and turnover. The results may confirm expectations or generate surprises that merit further investigation. Either way, they can help HR departments and managers determine which efforts deliver the best return. Rosemont Center, a Columbus, Ohio, social-service agency analyzed turnover rates after government funding cutbacks contributed to stress and soaring employee turnover. The industry average turnover is 50% to 60%, but Rosemont Center's rate shot up from 41% in 2007 to 72% three years later. The agency's HR director reviewed annual turnover rates, exit interviews, and employee satisfaction surveys and determined that Rosemont was failing to retain employees because of a lack of career development, below-average benefits and compensation, a need for better support of managers, poor communication, and lack of support for work-life balance. The HR director studied how other agencies in the area were handling similar challenges, and she interviewed employees to learn which of those actions they thought would help. By implementing ideas from this process, Rosemont Center brought employee turnover down to 48% in a single year—again below the industry average.[64]

In spite of surveys and other efforts to retain employees, some employees inevitably will leave the organization. This presents another opportunity to gather information for retaining employees: the **exit interview**—a meeting of the departing employee with the employee's supervisor and/or a human resource specialist to discuss the employee's reasons for leaving. A well-conducted exit interview can uncover reasons why employees leave and perhaps set the stage for some of them to return. HR professionals can help make exit interviews more successful by arranging for the employee to talk to someone from the HR department (rather than the departing employee's supervisor) in a neutral location or over the phone.[65] Questions should start out open-ended and general, giving the employee a chance to name the source of the dissatisfaction or explain why leaving is attractive.

A recruiter armed with information about what caused a specific person to leave may be able to negotiate a return when the situation changes. And when several exiting employees give similar reasons for leaving, management should consider whether this indicates a need for change. In the war for talent, the best way to manage retention is to engage in a battle for every valued employee, even when it looks as if the battle has been lost.

Exit Interview
A meeting of a departing employee with the employee's supervisor and/or a human resource specialist to discuss the employee's reasons for leaving.

THINKING ETHICALLY

HOW CAN ETHICS PROMOTE JOB SATISFACTION?

Not only do most organizations want their people to behave ethically, there is some evidence that employees want their managers and employers to behave ethically as well. Thus, promoting ethical conduct is not only the moral thing for an organization to do, it also may support employee engagement.

In their research on leadership, for example, James Kouzes and Barry Posner have found that individuals around the world want their leaders to be honest. Evidently, if employees are going to follow someone's lead, they want to believe the person when he or she says where they all are going. Employees want to believe they can trust the people who are in charge.

One way managers provide this kind of leadership is to embrace the qualities of a "servant leader." Servant leadership involves leading with honesty, humility, integrity, and a focus on results. These qualities can be learned and developed. John Heer introduced the practice of servant leadership to North Mississippi Health Services, where he is chief executive. As managers at all levels learned to be servant leaders, employee satisfaction scores rose dramatically. So did patient and physician satisfaction—and financial performance as well.

Interestingly, there also seems to be some research showing satisfaction and ethics working in the opposite direction. That is, when employees are satisfied with their jobs and want to stay with the organization, they tend to make ethical decisions to a greater degree than employees who are not satisfied. The satisfied employees also tend to be more cooperative and more inclined to help out their co-workers.

Questions

1. Suppose you work in the HR department of an organization that wants to improve the job satisfaction of its employees. How might promoting ethical leadership contribute to this goal? How would you make the case for that effort?
2. At this same organization, what impact would you expect the promotion of ethical leadership to have on employee turnover? Why?

SOURCES: John Heer, "First Person," *Success,* January 2012, p. 37; Martha Perego, "Ethical Leaders," *Public Management,* September 2010, pp. 2–3; Network for Business Sustainability, "Satisfied Employees Behave More Ethically," *Research Insights: Business Sustainability,* September 2010, http://nbs.net.

SUMMARY

LO 10-1 Distinguish between involuntary and voluntary turnover, and describe their effects on an organization.

Involuntary turnover occurs when the organization requires employees to leave, often when they would prefer to stay. Voluntary turnover occurs when employees initiate the turnover, often when the organization would prefer to keep them. Both are costly because of the need to recruit, hire, and train replacements. Involuntary turnover can also result in lawsuits and even violence.

LO 10-2 Discuss how employees determine whether the organization treats them fairly.

Employees draw conclusions based on the outcomes of decisions regarding them, the procedures applied, and the way managers treat employees when carrying out those procedures. Outcome fairness is a judgment that the

consequences are just. The consequences should be consistent, expected, and in proportion to the significance of the behavior. Procedural justice is a judgment that fair methods were used to determine the consequences. The procedures should be consistent, unbiased, based on accurate information, and correctable. They should take into account the viewpoints of everyone involved, and they should be consistent with prevailing ethical standards. Interactional justice is a judgment that the organization carried out its actions in a way that took the employee's feelings into account— for example, by listening to the employee and treating the employee with dignity.

LO 10-3 Identify legal requirements for employee discipline.

Employee discipline should not result in wrongful discharge, such as a termination that violates an implied contract or public policy.

Discipline should be administered evenhandedly, without discrimination. Discipline should respect individual employees' privacy. Searches and surveillance should be for a legitimate business purpose, and employees should know about and consent to them. Reasons behind disciplinary actions should be shared only with those who need to know them. When termination is part of a plant closing, employees should receive the legally required notice, if applicable.

LO 10-4 Summarize ways in which organizations can fairly discipline employees.

Discipline should follow the principles of the hot-stove rule, meaning discipline should give warning and have consequences that are consistent, objective, and immediate. A system that can meet these requirements is called progressive discipline, in which rules are established and communicated, and increasingly severe consequences follow each violation of the rules. Usually, consequences range from a spoken warning through written warnings, suspension, and termination. These actions should be documented in writing. Organizations also may resolve problems through alternative dispute resolution, including an open-door policy, peer review, mediation, and arbitration. When performance problems seem to result from substance abuse or mental illness, the manager may refer the employee to an employee assistance program. When a manager terminates an employee or encourages an employee to leave, outplacement counseling may smooth the process.

LO 10-5 Explain how job dissatisfaction affects employee behavior.

Circumstances involving the nature of a job, supervisors and co-workers, pay levels, or the employee's own disposition may produce job dissatisfaction. When employees become dissatisfied, they may engage in job withdrawal. This may include behavior change, as employees try to bring about changes in policy and personnel through inside action or through whistle-blowing or lawsuits. Physical job withdrawal may range from tardiness and absenteeism to job transfer or leaving the organization altogether. Especially when employees cannot find another job, they may psychologically withdraw by displaying low levels of job involvement and organizational commitment.

LO 10-6 Describe how organizations contribute to employees' job satisfaction and retain key employees.

Organizations can try to identify and select employees who have personal dispositions associated with job satisfaction. They can make jobs more complex and meaningful—for example, through job enrichment and job rotation. They can use methods such as the role analysis technique to make roles clear and appropriate. They can reinforce shared values and encourage social support among employees. They can try to establish satisfactory pay levels and communicate with employees about pay structure and pay raises. Monitoring job satisfaction helps organizations identify which of these actions are likely to be most beneficial.

KEY TERMS

alternative dispute resolution (ADR), 312

arbitration, 314

employee assistance program (EAP), 315

employee engagement, 316

exit interview, 329

hot-stove rule, 310

interactional justice, 308

involuntary turnover, 305

job involvement, 321

job satisfaction, 322

job withdrawal, 317

mediation, 314

open-door policy, 313

organizational commitment, 321

outcome fairness, 307

outplacement counseling, 315

peer review, 313

procedural justice, 308

progressive discipline, 311

role, 318

role ambiguity, 318

role analysis technique, 325

role conflict, 318

role overload, 319

voluntary turnover, 305

REVIEW AND DISCUSSION QUESTIONS

1. Give an example of voluntary turnover and an example of involuntary turnover. Why should organizations try to reduce both kinds of turnover?

2. A member of a restaurant's serving staff is chronically late to work. From the organization's point of view, what fairness issues are involved in deciding how to handle this situation? In what ways might the employee's and other servers' ideas of fairness be different?

3. For the situation in Question 2, how would a formal discipline policy help the organization address issues of fairness?

4. The progressive discipline process described in this chapter is meant to be fair and understandable, but it tends to be slow. Try to think of two or three offenses that should result in immediate discharge, rather than follow all the steps of progressive discipline. Explain why you selected these offenses. If the dismissed employee sued, do you think the organization would be able to defend its action in court?

5. A risk of disciplining employees is that some employees retaliate. To avoid that risk, what organizational policies might encourage low-performing employees to leave while encouraging high-performing employees to stay? (Consider the sources of employee satisfaction and dissatisfaction discussed in this chapter.)

6. List forms of behavior that can signal job withdrawal. Choose one of the behaviors you listed, and describe how you would respond if an otherwise valuable employee whom you supervised engaged in this kind of behavior.

7. What are the four factors that influence an employee's job dissatisfaction (or satisfaction)? Which of these do you think an employer can most easily change? Which would be the most expensive to change?

8. The section on principles of justice used noncompete agreements as an example. How would you expect the use of noncompete agreements to affect voluntary turnover? How might the use of these agreements affect job withdrawal and job satisfaction? Besides requiring noncompete agreements, how could an organization reduce the likelihood of employees leaving to work for competitors? Would these other methods have a better effect on employee satisfaction?

9. Consider your current job or a job you recently held. Overall, were you satisfied or dissatisfied with that job? How did your level of satisfaction or dissatisfaction affect your behavior on the job? Is your own experience consistent with this chapter's models of job withdrawal and job satisfaction?

10. Suppose you are an HR professional who convinced your company's management to conduct a survey of employee satisfaction. Your budget was limited, and you could not afford a test that went into great detail. Rather, you investigated overall job satisfaction and learned that it is low, especially among employees in three departments. You know that management is concerned about spending a lot for HR programs because sales are in a slump, but you want to address the issue of low job satisfaction. Suggest some ways you might begin to make a difference, even with a small budget. How will you convince management to try your ideas?

11. Why are exit interviews important? Should an organization care about the opinions of people who are leaving? How are those opinions relevant to employee separation and retention?

EXPERIENCING HR

Divide into groups of about six students each. Visit the website for *Fortune*'s list of the 100 Best Companies to Work For (**http://money.cnn.com/magazines/fortune/**; click on Rankings or search for 100 Best Companies). Follow the link to the complete list of companies, and then choose a company that interests your group. Click the link for the company information. Read the reasons for selecting this company as one of the best, and take notes on what you learn.

Next, visit the Glassdoor website (**http://www.glassdoor.com**), and use its search function to look up company information for the company you selected. On the company page, use the Reviews link to read the information employees have posted about what it is like to work at this company. Look for patterns, and take notes on what you learn.

As a group, discuss what these two sources tell you about employee engagement at the company you selected. What criteria does the *Fortune* list use for predicting that employees will be satisfied? What criteria do the reviewers on Glassdoor use for reporting their satisfaction or dissatisfaction? What criteria from this chapter are not mentioned? Imagine you work in HR at the company you evaluated. What would you do to address any dissatisfaction you observe in the Glassdoor reviews? Be prepared to summarize your discussion in class (or, if your instructor directs, write a one-page summary of your discussion).

TAKING RESPONSIBILITY: Stryker's Striking Commitment to Employee Engagement

Stryker's 20,000 employees design, make, and sell medical and surgical equipment as varied as hospital beds, spinal implants, and power tools for use in surgery. The company runs 30 manufacturing and R&D locations in the United States, Europe, and China, and it sells products in 89 countries around the world. To run such complex operations and deliver products that must meet exacting standards to protect the patients who benefit from them, Stryker needs an extremely talented and dedicated workforce.

In one sign that the company has risen to the challenge, it recently landed a spot on *Fortune*'s list of the 100 Best Companies to Work For. Employees seeking help with work-life balance can take advantage of telecommuting, job sharing, and a compressed workweek. Career development is aided by 100 hours per year of training for hourly employees and 120 hours per year for salaried employees. The company's voluntary turnover rate is 8%.

But where Stryker stands out as an employer is its dedication to promoting employee engagement. Take the case of Stryker's product development and production facility in Freiburg, Germany, which specializes in navigation systems used in computer-assisted surgery. Stryker Navigation was preparing to tackle shortcomings in the production process and realized that teams in the facility were not cooperating. Stryker hired Gallup Management to conduct a survey of employee engagement and teamwork and compare the results for each team and the facility as a whole against standards developed by Gallup in its work with other organizations.

Gallup found that although Stryker Navigation had above-average employee engagement for Germany at that time, only 32% of its employees were engaged. Scores were low in the areas of employees knowing what was expected of them and having the resources they needed to do their jobs. Guided by the Gallup consultants, Stryker addressed those problems for each team. A year later, employees retook the engagement survey. This time, 64% of employees were engaged. To ensure that engagement remains important, Stryker Navigation holds monthly reviews of its action plans and shares the results with employees. It continues measuring engagement annually; so far, the improvement continues. At the same time, teams in Freiberg are

collaborating more effectively, and the facility's output and quality have risen.

Not long afterward, Stryker realized it needed to bring the lessons from Germany to the United States. At its orthopedics facility in Mahwah, New Jersey, employees were above average for a U.S. company: 48% of employees were engaged (versus 28% for the United States overall), 37% not engaged (versus 53%), and 15% actively disengaged (versus 19%). But above average is not good enough for Stryker; the company wanted a highly engaged workforce that can deliver exceptional results.

Stryker sent the Mahwah facility one of its experts: Sabine Krummel-Mihajlovic, senior human resources director for continental Europe. She learned that the managers in New Jersey administered the engagement surveys, but had not been acting on the results. Consequently, employees lacked trust in the process. Krummel-Mihajlovic trained the facility's leadership in the importance of employee engagement. Then, to demonstrate her deep commitment to the process, she announced that she would attend every team's meeting to review feedback from the survey and create an action plan. Her commitment would represent 55 planning meetings.

Krummel-Mihajlovic saw that some managers skillfully led the planning meetings. These managers tended to lead teams with high engagement scores. She targeted the managers with low scores and worked with them individually to help them interpret the scores and figure out what they needed so they could help their team improve. Often, these managers needed training in how to lead more effectively. Then, to keep the process moving forward without her direct involvement, Krummel-Mihajlovic gathered the names of informal leaders in each team and assembled them into a group that would meet monthly to discuss a driver of engagement and figure out how to improve in that area. Finally, she crafted ways to communicate how management was responding to all the ideas and action plans generated, and she arranged a dinner party to recognize those who had contributed to improving engagement.

Less than a year later, the employees retook the engagement survey. In that short time, scores improved to 57% engaged, 32% not engaged, and 11% actively disengaged. At that point, Krummel-Mihajlovic was offered a promotion in Europe, so the Mahwah plant's commitment to engagement would have to endure without her.

Questions

1. What impact would you expect Stryker's efforts to have on voluntary turnover? Why?
2. What should Stryker do about the workers who remain "actively disengaged"?

3. How can Stryker ensure that its progress on engagement continues in Mahwah?

SOURCES: Jennifer Robison, "Boosting Engagement at Stryker," *Gallup Management Journal*, January 5, 2012, Business & Company Resource Center, http://galenet.galegroup.com; Marco Nink and Klaus Welte, "Involving Employees in Change," *Gallup Management Journal*, December 6, 2011, Business & Company Resource Center, http://galenet.galegroup.com; Stryker, "Company Overview," version 1.3, September 2011, http://www.stryker.com; "100 Best Companies to Work For," *Fortune*, February 7, 2011, http://money.cnn.com.

MANAGING TALENT: A Termination Controversy at Jet Propulsion Laboratory

Occasionally, disputes in the workplace arise over matters that are controversial yet close to employees' hearts. In those situations, managers rely on human resource professionals to help them resolve the disputes constructively, with respect for the feelings of everyone involved. When efforts fail, the result can be extremely problematic, as a recent situation involving NASA's Jet Propulsion Laboratory illustrates.

JPL hires some of the top technical talent in the United States to create innovative designs for carrying out complex missions. One of those talented employees was David Coppedge, a systems administrator who for 15 years worked on NASA's Cassini mission to explore the solar system. He maintained computer networks and solved technical problems related to those networks. During part of that time, Coppedge served as team leader, a linking role between the managers and technicians involved with the mission. However, JPL demoted Coppedge in 2009, and two years later, the organization laid off Coppedge along with 200 other employees. After his demotion, Coppedge claimed he had been discriminated against on religious grounds. After the layoff, Coppedge added wrongful termination to his lawsuit against JPL on the grounds it had terminated him in retaliation for the discrimination complaint.

What went wrong? While the trial is still under way as this case is being written, enough facts are on record to identify issues relevant to human resource management. Coppedge, his managers, and co-workers agree that besides being a computer expert, he was known at JPL for his commitment to evangelical Christianity. In particular, he advocated his views favoring Intelligent Design, a religious understanding of the origins of the universe. In Coppedge's complaint, he charges that JPL harassed, demoted, and terminated him for expressing those views, yet the company did not punish other workers who disagreed with him. JPL's response to these charges was that Coppedge did not merely express a religious view. Rather, according to JPL, Coppedge engaged in disruptive behavior. More than a

dozen people had complained to Coppedge's supervisor that he was stubborn and unpleasant to interact with. However, Coppedge noted that co-worker complaints were that he was lending them DVDs on Intelligent Design and objecting to the name of the "holiday" potluck in December, complaints that Coppedge perceived as harassment of him based on religion.

JPL has insisted in court testimony that it focused on Coppedge's job-related behaviors, not on his beliefs. JPL's lawyer argued that Coppedge was told, "We have no problem with people discussing religion or politics in the office, as long as it's not unwelcome or disruptive." JPL also pointed out that when Coppedge was laid off, so were many others, following cuts in funding and as the Cassini project was nearing its end. Coppedge maintains that supervisors criticized him for "pushing religion" and told him not to discuss religion at all, or else he could be fired. He said JPL did not inform him that co-workers did not want to engage in religious discussions, but did tell him it was his duty to interpret their body language. Coppedge also said JPL told him he had violated the organization's policy against harassment as well as its policy related to ethics and business conduct. Personnel records show positive evaluations of Coppedge's work.

Questions

1. Imagine you were a human resource manager at JPL and were asked to address employee complaints about David Coppedge. How would you distinguish the relevant work-related behaviors from differences in religious views? What advice about behavior would you give to Coppedge? His co-workers? His supervisor?
2. How might alternative dispute resolution techniques have helped JPL resolve this dispute between Coppedge and his co-workers?
3. What else could JPL have done to maintain a productive work environment and prevent a discrimination lawsuit? (Consider, for example, the principles of justice and the factors associated with job satisfaction.)

SOURCES: Daniel Siegal, "Former JPL Employee Says He Was Fired, Lawyer Says He Was Laid Off," *Pasadena (CA) Sun*, March 17, 2012, http://articles.pasadenasun.com; Howard Law, "NASA's Jet Propulsion Lab Sued for Religious Discrimination, Wrongful Termination," *California Employment Lawyers Blog*, March 14, 2012, http://www .californiaemploymentlawyersblog.com; Daniel Siegal and Jason Wells, "JPL Employee Wasn't Fired over Religious Beliefs, Lawyer Says," *Glendale (CA) News-Press*, March 13, 2012, http://articles.glendalenewspress.com; "From the States," *Fair Employment Practices Guidelines*, January 2012, pp. 6–8.

 TWITTER FOCUS: Learning to Show Appreciation at Datotel

Using Twitter, continue the conversation about employee retention by reading the Datotel case at **www .mhhe.com/noefund5e.** Engage your classmates and instructor via Twitter to chat about Datotel's strategy for employee retention using the case questions posted on the Noe website. Don't have a Twitter account yet? See the instructions for getting started on the Online Learning Center.

NOTES

1. USAA, "Corporate Overview," https://www.usaa .com, accessed April 10, 2012; USAA, "USAA in Top 20 of *Fortune* '100 Best Companies' for Second Year," news release, January 19, 2012, https://www .usaa.com; Jena McGregor, "USAA's Battle Plan," *Bloomberg Businessweek*, February 18, 2010, http:// businessweek.com.

2. J. D. Shaw, M. K. Duffy, J. L. Johnson, and D. E. Lockhart, "Turnover, Social Capital Losses, and Performance," *Academy of Management Journal* 48 (2005), pp. 594–606; and R. Batt, "Managing Customer Services: Human Resource Practices, Quit Rates, and Sales Growth," *Academy of Management Journal* 45 (2002), pp. 587–97.

3. D. J. Koys, "The Effects of Employee Satisfaction, Organizational Citizenship Behavior, and Turnover on Organizational Effectiveness: A Unit-Level Longitudinal Study," *Personnel Psychology* 54 (2001), pp. 101–14; Batt, "Managing Customer Services"; and M. Boyle, "Happy People, Happy Returns," *Fortune*, January 22, 2007, p. 100.

4. W. J. Becker and R. Cropanzano, "Dynamic Aspects of Voluntary Turnover: An Integrated Approach to Curvilinearity in the Performance–Turnover Relationship," *Journal of Applied Psychology* 96 (2011): 233–46.

5. K. M. Kacmer, M. C. Andrews, D. L. Van Rooy, R. C. Steilberg, and S. Cerrone, "Sure Everyone Can Be Replaced . . . but at What Cost? Turnover as a Predictor of Unit-Level Performance," *Academy of Management Journal* 49 (2006), pp. 133–44; J. D. Shaw, N. Gupta, and J. E. Delery, "Alternative Conceptualizations of the Relationship between Voluntary Turnover and Organizational Performance," *Academy of Management Journal* 48 (2005),

pp. 50–68; and J. Lublin, "Keeping Clients by Keeping Workers," *Wall Street Journal*, November 20, 2006, p. B1.

6. The Lorrie Willey, "The Public Policy Exception to Employment at Will: Balancing Employer's Right and the Public Interest," *Journal of Legal, Ethical and Regulatory Issues* 12 no. 1 (2009), pp. 55–72; and Mitch Baker, "Commentary: 'At Will' Firing Shouldn't Lack a Reason," *Daily Journal of Commerce*, Portland, January 17, 2008, Business & Company Resource Center, http://galenet.galegroup.com.

7. Joel Brockner, "Why It's So Hard to Be Fair," *Harvard Business Review*, March 2006, http://hbr.org; Cynthia Barnes-Slater and John Ford, "Measuring Conflict: Both the Hidden Costs and Benefits of Conflict Management Interventions," *LawMemo*, http://www.lawmemo.com, accessed April 10, 2012.

8. M. M. Le Blanc and K. Kelloway, "Predictors and Outcomes of Workplace Violence and Aggression," *Journal of Applied Psychology*, 87, 2002, pp. 444–53.

9. B. J. Tepper, "Relationship among Supervisors' and Subordinates' Procedural Justice Perceptions and Organizational Citizenship Behaviors," *Academy of Management Journal* 46 (2003), pp. 97–105; T. Simons and Q. Roberson, "Why Managers Should Care about Fairness: The Effects of Aggregate Justice Perception on Organizational Outcomes," *Journal of Applied Psychology* 88 (2003), pp. 432–43; C. M. Holmvall and D. R. Bobocel, "What Fair Procedures Say about Me: Self-Construals and Reactions to Procedural Fairness," *Organizational Behavior and Human Decision Processes* 105 (2008), pp. 147–68.

10. T. A. Judge, B. A. Scott, and R. Ilies, "Hostility, Job Attitudes and Workplace Deviance: A Test of a

Multilevel Model," *Journal of Applied Psychology* 91 (2006), pp. 126–38.

11. *Harmon v. Thornburgh*, CA, DC No. 88-5265 (July 30, 1989); *Treasury Employees Union v. Von Raab*, U.S. Sup. Ct. No. 86-18796 (March 21, 1989); *City of Annapolis v. United Food & Commercial Workers Local 400*, Md. Ct. App. No. 38 (November 6, 1989); *Skinner v. Railway Labor Executives Association*, U.S. Sup. Ct. No. 87-1555 (March 21, 1989); and *Bluestein v. Skinner*, 908 F 451, 9th Cir. (1990).

12. D. J. Hoekstra, "Workplace Searches: A Legal Overview," *Labor Law Journal* 47, no. 2 (February 1996), pp. 127–38; "Workplace Searches and Interrogations," *FindLaw*, http://employment.findlaw.com, accessed April 6, 2012; "Workplace Searches: Dos and Don'ts," Nolo.com, http://www.nolo.com, accessed April 6, 2012.

13. G. Henshaw and K. Youmans, "Employee Privacy in the Workplace and an Employer's Right to Conduct Workplace Searches and Surveillance," *SHRM Legal Report*, Spring 1990, pp. 1–5; B. K. Repa, *Your Rights in the Workplace* (Berkeley, CA: Nolo Press, 1997).

14. M. Denis and J. Andes, "Defamation—Do You Tell Employees Why a Co-worker Was Discharged?" *Employee Relations Law Journal* 16, no. 4 (Spring 1991), pp. 469–79; R. S. Soderstrom and J. R. Murray, "Defamation in Employment: Suits by At-Will Employees," *FICC Quarterly*, Summer 1992, pp. 395–426; and "Keeping Pandora's Box Closed: Best Practices in Maintaining Personnel Records," *Mondaq Business Briefing*, June 8, 2009, Business & Company Resource Center, http://galenet.galegroup.com. "Your Rights in the Workplace: Privacy Rights," Nolo.com, http://www.nolo.com, accessed April 6, 2012.

15. K. Karl and C. Sutton, "A Review of Expert Advice on Employment Termination Practices: The Experts Don't Always Agree," in *Dysfunctional Behavior in Organizations*, eds. R. Griffin, A. O'Leary-Kelly, and J. Collins (Stanford, CT: JAI Press, 1998).

16. Resolution Systems Institute and Center for Conflict Resolution, "Why Do Courts Use ADR?" *Court ADR Pocket Guide*, http://courtadr.org, accessed April 6, 2012; Douglas Shontz, Fred Kipperman, and Vanessa Soma, *Business-to-Business Arbitration in the United States: Perceptions of Corporate Counsel* (Rand Institute for Civil Justice, 2011), http://www.rand.org.

17. Personal communication from Jonathan Tavalin, January 15, 2012.

18. Rebecca Vesely, "The Evolution of EAPs," *Workforce Management*, March 2012, Business & Company Resource Center, http://galenet.galegroup.com; Rita Pyrillis, "EAPs: First Responders in a 'Work-More Economy,'" *Workforce Management*, January 2012, Business & Company Resource Center, http://galenet.galegroup.com.

19. Kathleen Koster, "Hope Springs Eternal: EAPs Retain Relevance," *Employee Benefit News*, September 15, 2011, pp. 51–52.

20. Al Lewis, "Challenger Thrives in Challenging Economy," *Fox Business*, March 16, 2012, http://www.foxbusiness.com; Jim Doyle, "Five Questions: Getting Laid Off Workers Back on the Job," *St. Louis Post-Dispatch*, September 30, 2011, http://www.stltoday.com.

21. For examples see M. Huselid, "The Impact of Human Resource Management Practices on Turnover, Productivity, and Corporate Financial Performance," *Academy of Management Journal* 38 (1995), pp. 635–672; S. Payne and S. Webber, "Effects of Service Provider Attitudes and Employment Status on Citizenship Behaviors and Customers' Attitudes and Loyalty Behavior," *Journal of Applied Psychology* 91 (2006), pp. 365–368; J. Hartner, F. Schmidt, and T. Hayes, "Business-Unit Level Relationship between Employee Satisfaction, Employee Engagement, and Business Outcomes: A Meta-Analysis," *Journal of Applied Psychology* 87 (2002), pp. 268–279; I. Fulmer, B. Gerhart, and K. Scott, "Are the 100 Best Better? An Empirical Investigation of the Relationship between Being a 'Great Place to Work' and Firm Performance," *Performance Psychology* 56 (2003), pp. 965–993; "Working Today: Understanding What Drives Employee Engagement," *Towers Perrin Talent Report* (2003).

22. G. Kranz, "Losing Lifeblood," *Workforce Management*, June 2011, pp. 24–28; R. Vance, *Employee Engagement and Commitment* (Alexandria, VA: Society for Human Resource Management, 2006).

23. M. Ciccarelli, "Keeping the Keepers," *Human Resource Executive*, January/February 2011, pp. 1–20, 23.

24. D. W. Baruch, "Why They Terminate," *Journal of Consulting Psychology* 8 (1944), pp. 35–46; J. G. Rosse, "Relations among Lateness, Absence and Turnover: Is There a Progression of Withdrawal?" *Human Relations* 41 (1988), pp. 517–31; C. Hulin, "Adaptation, Persistence and Commitment in Organizations," in *Handbook of Industrial & Organizational Psychology*, 2nd ed., eds. M. D. Dunnette and L. M. Hough (Palo Alto, CA: Consulting Psychologists Press, 1991), pp. 443–50; and E. R. Burris, J. R. Detert, and D. S. Chiaburu, "Quitting before Leaving: The Mediating Effects of Psychological

Attachment and Detachment on Voice," *Journal of Applied Psychology* 93 (2008), pp. 912–22.

25. D. A. Harrison, D. A. Newman, and P. L. Roth, "How Important Are Job Attitudes? Meta-analytic Comparisons of Integrative Behavioral Outcomes and Time Sequences," *Academy of Management Journal* 49 (2006), pp. 305–25.

26. G. Chen, R. E. Ployhart, H. C. Thomas, N. Anderson, and P. D. Bliese, "The Power of Momentum: A New Model of Dynamic Relationships between Job Satisfaction Change and Turnover Intentions," *Academy of Management Journal*, 54 (2011): 159–81.

27. R. D. Zimmerman, "Understanding the Impact of Personality Traits on Individuals' Turnover Decisions: A Meta-analysis," *Personnel Psychology* 61 (2008), pp. 309–348.

28. T. A. Judge, E. A. Locke, C. C. Durham, and A. N. Kluger, "Dispositional Effects on Job and Life Satisfaction: The Role of Core Evaluations," *Journal of Applied Psychology* 83 (1998), pp. 17–34.

29. B. M. Staw, N. E. Bell, and J. A. Clausen, "The Dispositional Approach to Job Attitudes: A Lifetime Longitudinal Test," *Administrative Science Quarterly* 31 (1986), pp. 56–78; B. M. Staw and J. Ross, "Stability in the Midst of Change: A Dispositional Approach to Job Attitudes," *Journal of Applied Psychology* 70 (1985), pp. 469–80; and R. P. Steel and J. R. Rentsch, "The Dispositional Model of Job Attitudes Revisited: Findings of a 10-Year Study," *Journal of Applied Psychology* 82 (1997), pp. 873–79.

30. T. A. Judge and J. E. Bono, "Relationship of Core Self-Evaluation Traits—Self-Esteem, Generalized Self-Efficacy, Locus of Control, and Emotional Stability—with Job Satisfaction and Job Performance: A Meta-Analysis," *Journal of Applied Psychology* 86 (2001), pp. 80–92.

31. T. A. Judge, J. E. Bono, and E. A. Locke, "Personality and Job Satisfaction: The Mediating Role of Job Characteristics," *Journal of Applied Psychology* 85 (2000), pp. 237–49.

32. S. C. Douglas and M. J. Martinko, "Exploring the Role of Individual Differences in the Prediction of Workplace Aggression," *Journal of Applied Psychology* 86 (2001), pp. 547–59.

33. B. A. Gerhart, "How Important Are Dispositional Factors as Determinants of Job Satisfaction? Implications for Job Design and Other Personnel Programs," *Journal of Applied Psychology* 72 (1987), pp. 493–502.

34. E. F. Stone and H. G. Gueutal, "An Empirical Derivation of the Dimensions along Which Characteristics of Jobs Are Perceived," *Academy of Management Journal* 28 (1985), pp. 376–96.

35. L. W. Porter and R. M. Steers, "Organizational Work and Personal Factors in Employee Absenteeism and Turnover," *Psychological Bulletin* 80 (1973), pp. 151–76; and S. Melamed, I. Ben-Avi, J. Luz, and M. S. Green, "Objective and Subjective Work Monotony: Effects on Job Satisfaction, Psychological Distress, and Absenteeism in Blue Collar Workers," *Journal of Applied Psychology* 80 (1995), pp. 29–42.

36. D. R. Ilgen and J. R. Hollenbeck, "The Structure of Work: Job Design and Roles," in *Handbook of Industrial & Organizational Psychology*, 2nd ed.

37. J. A. Breaugh and J. P. Colihan, "Measuring Facets of Job Ambiguity: Construct Validity Evidence," *Journal of Applied Psychology* 79 (1994), pp. 191–201.

38. M. A. Shaffer and D. A. Harrison, "Expatriates' Psychological Withdrawal from Interpersonal Assignments: Work, Non-work, and Family Influences," *Personnel Psychology* 51 (1998), pp. 87–118.

39. Leslie Allan, "Gallup Study: Impact of Manager Feedback on Employee Engagement," *Toolbox.com*, January 6, 2011, http://hr.toolbox.com; Leslie Allan, "Manager Impact on Employee Engagement," *Leslie Allan Performance Blog*, April 27, 2011, http://leslieallan.blogspot.com.

40. J. M. Sacco and N. Schmitt, "A Dynamic Multilevel Model of Demographic Diversity and Misfit Effects," *Journal of Applied Psychology* 90 (2005), pp. 203–31; and R. E. Ployhart, J. A. Weekley, and K. Baughman, "The Structure and Function of Human Capital Emergence: A Multilevel Examination of the Attraction–Selection–Attrition Model," *Academy of Management Journal* 49 (2006), pp. 661–77.

41. S. Lim, L. M. Cortina, and V. J. Magley, "Personal and Work-Group Incivility: Impact on Work and Health Outcomes," *Journal of Applied Psychology* 93 (2008), pp. 95–107.

42. Comtex News, "Worn Out at Work? 12 Common Workplace Behaviors That Drain Everyone's Energy—and How to Purge Them in 2011," *Benzinga.com*, December 20, 2010, Business & Company Resource Center, http://galenet.galegroup.com.

43. Robert J. Grossman, "Gone but Not Forgotten," *HR Magazine*, September 2011, http://www.shrm.org.

44. Katherine Graham-Leviss, "The High Cost of Sales Team Turnover," *Entrepreneur*, September 15, 2011, http://www.entrepreneur.com; Gwen Moran, "The Hidden Costs of Employee Turnover," *Entrepreneur*, September 10, 2011, http://www.entrepreneur.com.

45. Devin Banerjee, "One in Three U.S. Workers Wants to Leave Job, Mercer Survey Says," *Bloomberg*, June 20, 2011, http://www.bloomberg.com/news/; Lisa

V. Gillespie, "Climbing the Corporate Lattice?" *Employee Benefit News*, January 2012, pp. 17–18.

46. R. T. Mowday, R. M. Steers, and L. W. Porter, "The Measurement of Organizational Commitment," *Journal of Vocational Behavior* 14 (1979), pp. 224–47.

47. E. A. Locke, "The Nature and Causes of Job Dissatisfaction," in *The Handbook of Industrial & Organizational Psychology*, ed. M. D. Dunnette (Chicago: Rand McNally, 1976), pp. 901–69.

48. N. A. Bowling, T. A. Beehr, S. H. Wagner, and T. M. Libkuman, "Adaptation-Level Theory, Opponent Process Theory, and Dispositions: An Integrated Approach to the Stability of Job Satisfaction," *Journal of Applied Psychology* 90 (2005), pp. 1044–53.

49. Sarah Morgan, "Ten Things Your Employees Won't Say," *SmartMoney.com*, March 19, 2012, http://www.smartmoney.com.

50. G. R. Oldham, A. Cummings, L. J. Mischel, J. M. Schmidtke, and J. Zhou, "Listen While You Work? Quasi-experimental Relations between Personal-Stereo Headset Use and Employee Work Responses," *Journal of Applied Psychology* 80 (1995), pp. 547–64.

51. Alison Beard and Richard Hornik, "It's Hard to Be Good," *Harvard Business Review*, November 2011, pp. 88–96.

52. Jeffrey Scott, "Give Employees Ownership Thinking," *Landscape Management*, October 2011, EBSCOhost, http://web.ebscohost.com.

53. Mary Shapiro, Cynthia Ingols, Stacy Blake-Beard, and Regina O'Neill, "Canaries in the Mine Shaft: Women Signaling a New Career Model," Alison Greco, "Corporate Culture: Culture Key to Work-Life Programs," *Employee Benefit News*, February 2012, Business & Company Resource Center, http://galenet.galegroup.com.

54. J. E. Perry-Smith, "Work Family Human Resource Bundles and Perceived Organizational Performance," *Academy of Management Journal* 43 (2000), pp. 801–15; and M. M. Arthur, "Share Price Reactions to Work-Family Initiatives: An Institutional Perspective," *Academy of Management Journal* 46 (2003), pp. 497–505.

55. Linda Bond Edwards, "Exempt Employees—What Do They Really Do?" *Mondaq Business Briefing*, February 23, 2012, Business & Company Resource Center, http://galenet.galegroup.com.

56. B. M. Meglino, E. C. Ravlin, and C. L. Adkins, "A Work Values Approach to Corporate Culture: A Field Test of the Value Congruence Process and Its Relationship to Individual Outcomes," *Journal of Applied Psychology* 74 (1989), pp. 424–33.

57. G. C. Ganster, M. R. Fusilier, and B. T. Mayes, "Role of Social Support in the Experience of Stress at Work," *Journal of Applied Psychology* 71 (1986), pp. 102–11.

58. R. Eisenberger, F. Stinghamber, C. Vandenberghe, I. L. Sucharski, and L. Rhoades, "Perceived Supervisor Support: Contributions to Perceived Organizational Support and Employee Retention," *Journal of Applied Psychology* 87 (2002), pp. 565–73.

59. R. T. Keller, "A Test of the Path-Goal Theory of Leadership with Need for Clarity as a Moderator in Research and Development Organizations," *Journal of Applied Psychology* 74 (1989), pp. 208–12.

60. S. C. Payne and A. H. Huffman, "A Longitudinal Examination of the Influence of Mentoring on Organizational Commitment and Turnover," *Academy of Management Journal* 48 (2005), pp. 158–68.

61. Ed Finkel, "Staying Connected," *Modern Healthcare*, October 19, 2011, http://www.modern healthcare.com.

62. R. P. Quinn and G. L. Staines, *The 1977 Quality of Employment Survey* (Ann Arbor, MI: Survey Research Center, Institute for Social Research, University of Michigan, 1979).

63. T. Judge and T. Welbourne, "A Confirmatory Investigation of the Dimensionality of the Pay Satisfaction Questionnaire," *Journal of Applied Psychology* 79 (1994), pp. 461–66.

64. Sonya M. Latta, "Save Your Staff, Improve Your Business," *HR Magazine*, January 2012, pp. 30–32.

65. Patricia M. Buhler, "The Exit Interview: A Goldmine of Information," *Supervision*, August 2011, pp. 11–13; Chuck Schwartau, "Exit Interviews Matter: Feedback to Enhance the Work Environment," *Top Producer*, February 2012, Business & Company Resource Center, http://galenet.galegroup.com; Robert Half Legal, "Exit Interviews," http://www .roberthalflegal.com, accessed April 6, 2012.

Compensating Human Resources

PART FOUR

11 Establishing a Pay Structure

What Do I Need to Know?

After reading this chapter, you should be able to:

LO 11-1 Identify the kinds of decisions involved in establishing a pay structure.

LO 11-2 Summarize legal requirements for pay policies.

LO 11-3 Discuss how economic forces influence decisions about pay.

LO 11-4 Describe how employees evaluate the fairness of a pay structure.

LO 11-5 Explain how organizations design pay structures related to jobs.

LO 11-6 Describe alternatives to job-based pay.

LO 11-7 Summarize how to ensure that pay is actually in line with the pay structure.

LO 11-8 Discuss issues related to paying employees serving in the military and paying executives.

Introduction

Getting started in a new career has always been challenging, but since the year 2000 it has also been less rewarding, at least in the financial sense. When adjusted for inflation, the hourly earnings of young college graduates ages 23 to 29 have been falling. According to the Economic Policy Institute, male graduates' wages fell by 11% to $21.68 per hour in the decade leading up to 2011, while female graduates' wages saw a decline of 7.6% to $18.80 per hour. (College graduates still earn significantly more than high school graduates, however.) One reason for the downward trend is high unemployment persisting since the recent recession. But wages paid to young workers began falling even before the recession started. Companies are not typically cutting wages for the workers already on their payroll; rather, they can reduce payroll costs by paying lower rates to their newly hired employees. The practice can boost the bottom line, but it leaves human resource managers with a significant challenge. A recent survey by MarketTools found that one-fifth of employees have been trying to find a new job, and their top reason for wanting to leave was dissatisfaction with their pay.[1]

From the employer's point of view, pay is a powerful tool for meeting the organization's goals. Pay has a large impact on employee attitudes and behaviors. It influences which kinds of employees are attracted to (and remain with) the organization. By rewarding certain behaviors, it can align employees' interests with the organization's goals. Employees care about policies affecting earnings because the policies affect the employees' income and standard of living. Besides the level of pay, employees care about the fairness of pay compared with what others earn. Also, employees consider pay a sign of status and success. They attach great importance to pay decisions when they evaluate their relationship with their employer. For these reasons, organizations must carefully manage and communicate decisions about pay.

At the same time, pay is a major cost. Its share of total costs varies widely from one industry or company to another. At the low end, the wholesaling industry spends over 5% of revenues on payroll expenses. At the other extreme, transportation, entertainment, and health care companies spend more than 25% to almost 40% of revenues on payroll.[2] Managers have to keep this cost reasonable.

This chapter describes how managers weigh the importance and costs of pay to arrive at a structure for compensation and levels of pay for different jobs. We first define the basic decisions in terms of pay structure and pay level. Next, we look at several considerations that influence these decisions: legal requirements related to pay, economic forces, the nature of the organization's jobs, and employees' judgments about the fairness of pay levels. We describe methods for evaluating jobs and market data to arrive at a pay structure. We then summarize alternatives to the usual focus on jobs. The chapter closes with a look at two issues of current importance—pay for employees on leave to serve in the military and pay for executives.

Decisions about Pay

Because pay is important both in its effect on employees and on account of its cost, organizations need to plan what they will pay employees in each job. An unplanned approach, in which each employee's pay is independently negotiated, will likely result in unfairness, dissatisfaction, and rates that are either overly expensive or so low that positions are hard to fill. Organizations therefore make decisions about two aspects of pay structure: job structure and pay level. **Job structure** consists of the relative pay for different jobs within the organization. It establishes relative pay among different functions and different levels of responsibility. For example, job structure defines the difference in pay between an entry-level accountant and an entry-level assembler, as well as the difference between an entry-level accountant, the accounting department manager, and the organization's comptroller. **Pay level** is the average amount (including wages, salaries, and bonuses) the organization pays for a particular job. Together, job structure and pay levels establish a **pay structure** that helps the organization achieve goals related to employee motivation, cost control, and the ability to attract and retain talented human resources.

The organization's job structure and pay levels are policies of the organization rather than the amount a particular employee earns. For example, an organization's pay structure could include the range of pay that a person may earn in the job of entry-level accountant. An individual accountant could be earning an amount anywhere within that range. Typically, the amount a person earns depends on the individual's qualifications, accomplishments, and experience. The individual's pay may also depend partly on how well the organization performs. This chapter focuses on the organization's decisions about pay structure, and the next chapter will explore decisions that affect the amount of pay an individual earns.

Especially in an organization with hundreds or thousands of employees, it would be impractical for managers and the human resource department to make an entirely unique decision about each employee's pay. The decision would have to weigh so many factors that this approach would be expensive, difficult, and often unsatisfactory.

LO 11-1 Identify the kinds of decisions involved in establishing a pay structure.

Job Structure
The relative pay for different jobs within the organization.

Pay Level
The average amount (including wages, salaries, and bonuses) the organization pays for a particular job.

Pay Structure
The pay policy resulting from job structure and pay-level decisions.

Figure 11.1

Issues in Developing a Pay Structure

Legal Requirements
- Equal pay for equal work
- Minimum wage
- Overtime pay
- Restrictions on child labor

Market Forces
- Product markets
- Labor markets

Organization's Goals
- High-quality workforce
- Cost control
- Equity and fairness
- Legal compliance

Pay Level Decision
Job Structure Decision
Pay Structure Decisions
- Pay rates
- Pay grades
- Pay ranges
- Pay differentials

Establishing a pay structure simplifies the process of making decisions about individual employees' pay by grouping together employees with similar jobs. As shown in Figure 11.1, human resource professionals develop this pay structure based on legal requirements, market forces, and the organization's goals, such as attracting a high-quality workforce and meeting principles of fairness.

LO 11-2 Summarize legal requirements for pay policies.

Legal Requirements for Pay

Pay policies and practices in the United States are subject to government laws and regulations. For example, just as competing businesses may not conspire to set prices, they may not conspire to set wage rates (see "HR Oops!"). In addition, government regulation affects pay structure in the areas of equal employment opportunity, minimum wages, pay for overtime, and prevailing wages for federal contractors. All of an organization's decisions about pay should comply with the applicable laws.

Equal Employment Opportunity

Under the laws governing Equal Employment Opportunity, described in Chapter 3, employers may not base differences in pay on an employee's age, sex, race, or other protected status. Any differences in pay must instead be tied to such business-related considerations as job responsibilities or performance. The goal is for employers to provide *equal pay for equal work*. Job descriptions, job structures, and pay structures can help organizations demonstrate that they are upholding these laws.

These laws do not guarantee equal pay for men and women, whites and minorities, or any other groups, because so many legitimate factors, from education to choice of occupation, affect a person's earnings. In fact, numbers show that women and racial minorities in the United States tend to earn less than white men. Among full-time workers in 2011, women on average earned 82 cents for every dollar earned by men. Among male employees, black workers earned 76 cents for every dollar earned by white workers, and Hispanic workers earned just 65 cents (a racial gap among black and Hispanic female employees also exists, at 85 and 72 cents per dollar, respectively).[3] Even

Sued for Fixing Pay Rates

Just two years after settling a probe by the U.S. Department of Justice, several giants of the high-tech industry again found themselves in court, defending claims that they were interfering with competition in the labor market. The latest charges found their way to a federal district court after five software engineers filed a complaint that five companies had agreed not to try to recruit away talent from one another. The impact, said the engineers, was that companies would keep pay lower by conspiring rather than competing in the labor market.

The companies charged in this lawsuit—Apple, Adobe Systems, Google, Intel, Intuit, and Pixar—had previously settled an investigation into their hiring practices. The Justice Department said promises not to cold-call one another's employees amounted to restraints on competition, and the companies agreed to stop.

Evidence filed with the court included an e-mail from Steve Jobs at Apple to Eric Schmidt of Google, complaining about an HR staffer trying to lure away an Apple engineer. Subsequent correspondence within Google tells Schmidt that the offending HR staffer would be terminated. In an early ruling in the case, the judge determined that the five engineers' complaint could not proceed as a single lawsuit against all the companies, but that it could be broken up into cases alleging specific misconduct.

The companies have denied they did anything wrong, but as of this writing, future litigation appears likely. Potentially, hundreds of millions of dollars in damages are at stake.

Questions

1. Why do you think high-tech companies might be tempted to recruit talent away from one another? What impact would this practice have on overall pay rates?

2. If companies may not prevent their competitors from trying to recruit away employees, what options do they have to keep from losing talent? Must they pay higher and higher salaries?

SOURCES: I.B. Times, "Apple, Google Face Suit over Alleged Workers' Salary Poaching Deal," *Fox Business,* January 30, 2012, http://www.foxbusiness.com; Alex Vorro, "Seven Major Tech Companies Accused in Anti-Poaching Lawsuit," *Inside Counsel,* January 27, 2012, http://www.insidecounsel.com; Reuters, "Jobs Told Google to Stop Poaching Workers: Filing," MSNBC.com, January 27, 2012, http://www.msnbc.msn.com; Reuters, "Poaching Lawsuit Against Tech Companies Will Proceed—Judge," *Thomson Reuters News & Insight,* January 26, 2012, http://newsandinsight.thomsonreuters.com.

---

when these figures are adjusted to take into account education, experience, and occupation, the earnings gap does not completely close.[4] Among executives, one cause of lower pay for women appears to be that less of their pay is tied to performance (for example, bonuses and stock, described in the next chapter).[5]

One explanation for historical lower pay for women has been that employers have undervalued work performed by women—in particular, placing a lower value on occupations traditionally dominated by women. Some policy makers have proposed a remedy for this called equal pay for *comparable worth*. This policy uses job evaluation (described later in the chapter) to establish the worth of an organization's jobs in terms of such criteria as their difficulty and their importance to the organization. The employer then compares the evaluation points awarded to each job with the pay for each job. If jobs have the same number of evaluation points, they should be paid equally. If they are not, pay of the lower-paid job is raised to meet the goal of comparable worth.

Comparable-worth policies are controversial. From an economic standpoint, the obvious drawback of such a policy is that raising pay for some jobs places the employer at an economic disadvantage relative to employers that pay the market rate.

Two employees who do the same job cannot be paid different wages because of gender, race, or age. It would be illegal to pay these two employees differently because one is male and the other is female. Only if there are differences in their experience, skills, seniority, or job performance are there legal reasons why their pay might be different.

In addition, a free-market economy assumes people will take differences in pay into account when they choose a career. The courts allow organizations to defend themselves against claims of discrimination by showing that they pay the going market rate.[6] Businesses are reluctant to place themselves at an economic disadvantage, but many state governments adjust pay to achieve equal pay for comparable worth. Also, at both private and government organizations, policies designed to shatter the "glass ceiling" (discussed in Chapter 9) can help to address the problem of unequal pay.

Minimum Wage

Minimum Wage
The lowest amount that employers may pay under federal or state law, stated as an amount of pay per hour.

Fair Labor Standards Act (FLSA)
Federal law that establishes a minimum wage and requirements for overtime pay and child labor.

In the United States, employers must pay at least the **minimum wage** established by law. (A *wage* is the rate of pay per hour.) At the federal level, the 1938 **Fair Labor Standards Act (FLSA)** establishes a minimum wage that is now $7.25 per hour. The FLSA also permits a lower "training wage," which employers may pay to workers under the age of 20 for a period of up to 90 days. This subminimum wage is approximately 85% of the minimum wage. Some states have laws specifying minimum wages; in these states, employers must pay whichever rate is higher.

From the standpoint of social policy, an issue related to the minimum wage is that it tends to be lower than the earnings required for a full-time worker to rise above the poverty level. A number of cities have therefore passed laws requiring a so-called *living wage*, essentially a minimum wage based on the cost of living in a particular region.

Overtime Pay

Another requirement of the FLSA is that employers must pay higher wages for overtime, defined as hours worked beyond 40 hours per week. The overtime rate under the FLSA is one and a half times the employee's usual hourly rate, including any bonuses and piece-rate payments (amounts paid per item produced). The overtime rate applies to the hours worked beyond 40 in one week. Time worked includes not only hours spent on production or sales but also time on such activities as attending required classes, cleaning up the work site, or traveling between work sites. Figure 11.2 shows

Figure 11.2
Computing Overtime Pay

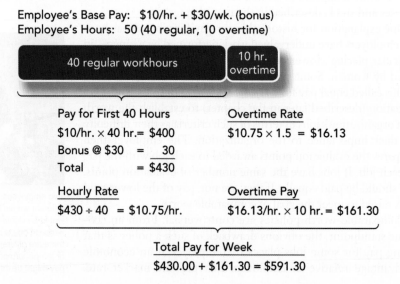

Employee's Base Pay: $10/hr. + $30/wk. (bonus)
Employee's Hours: 50 (40 regular, 10 overtime)

40 regular workhours | 10 hr. overtime

Pay for First 40 Hours
$10/hr. × 40 hr.= $400
Bonus @ $30   =   30
Total   = $430

Overtime Rate
$10.75 × 1.5 = $16.13

Hourly Rate
$430 ÷ 40 = $10.75/hr.

Overtime Pay
$16.13/hr. × 10 hr. = $161.30

Total Pay for Week
$430.00 + $161.30 = $591.30

how this applies to an employee who works 50 hours to earn a base rate of $10 per hour plus a weekly bonus of $30. The overtime pay is based on the base pay ($400) plus the bonus ($30), for a rate of $10.75 per hour. For each of the 10 hours of overtime, the employee would earn $16.13, so the overtime pay is $161.30 ($16.13 times 10). When employees are paid per unit produced or when they receive a monthly or quarterly bonus, those payments must be converted into wages per hour, so that the employer can include these amounts when figuring the correct overtime rate.

Overtime pay is required, whether or not the employer specifically asked or expected the employee to work more than 40 hours. In other words, if the employer knows the employee is working overtime but does not pay time and a half, the employer may be violating the FLSA.

Not everyone is eligible for overtime pay. Under the FLSA, executive, professional, administrative, and highly compensated white-collar employees are considered **exempt employees**, meaning employers need not pay them one and a half times their regular pay for working more than 40 hours per week. Exempt status depends on the employee's job responsibilities, salary level (at least $455 per week), and "salary basis," meaning that the employee is paid a given amount regardless of the number of hours worked or quality of the work.[7] Paying an employee on a salary basis means the organization expects that this person can manage his or her own time to get the work done, so the employer may deduct from the employee's pay only in certain limited circumstances, such as disciplinary action or for unpaid leave for personal reasons. Additional exceptions apply to certain occupations, including outside salespersons, teachers, and computer professionals (if they earn at least $27.63 per hour). Thus, the standards are fairly complicated. For more details about the standards for exempt employees, contact the Labor Department's Wage and Hour Division or refer to its website at **www.dol.gov/whd**.

Any employee who is not in one of the exempt categories is called a **nonexempt employee**. Most workers paid on an hourly basis are nonexempt and therefore subject to the laws governing overtime pay. However, paying a salary does not necessarily mean a job is exempt.

Exempt Employees
Managers, outside sales-people, and any other employees not covered by the FLSA requirement for overtime pay.

Nonexempt Employees
Employees covered by the FLSA requirements for overtime pay.

Child Labor

In the early years of the Industrial Revolution, employers could pay low wages by hiring children. The FLSA now sharply restricts the use of child labor, with the aim of protecting children's health, safety, and educational opportunities.[8] The restrictions apply to children younger than 18. Under the FLSA, children aged 16 and 17 may not be employed in hazardous occupations defined by the Department of Labor, such as mining, meatpacking, and certain kinds of manufacturing using heavy machinery. Children aged 14 and 15 may work only outside school hours in jobs defined as non-hazardous and for limited time periods. A child under age 14 may not be employed in any work associated with interstate commerce, except work performed in a nonhazardous job for a business entirely owned by the child's parent or guardian. A few additional exemptions from this ban include acting, babysitting, and delivering newspapers to consumers.

Besides the FLSA, state laws also restrict the use of child labor. Many states have laws requiring working papers or work permits for minors, and many states restrict the number of hours or times of day that minors aged 16 and older may work. Before hiring any workers under the age of 18, employers must ensure they are complying with the child labor laws of their state, as well as the FLSA requirements for their industry.

Prevailing Wages

Two additional federal laws, the Davis-Bacon Act of 1931 and the Walsh-Healy Public Contracts Act of 1936, govern pay policies of federal contractors. Under these laws, federal contractors must pay their employees at rates at least equal to the prevailing wages in the area. The calculation of prevailing rates must be based on 30% of the local labor force. Typically, the rates are based on relevant union contracts. Pay earned by union members tends to be higher than the pay of nonunion workers in similar jobs, so the effect of these laws is to raise the lower limit of pay an employer can offer.

These laws do not cover all companies. Davis-Bacon covers construction contractors that receive more than $2,000 in federal money. Walsh-Healy covers all government contractors receiving $10,000 or more in federal funds.

LO 11-3 Discuss how economic forces influence decisions about pay.

Economic Influences on Pay

An organization cannot make spending decisions independent of the economy. Organizations must keep costs low enough that they can sell their products profitably, yet they must be able to attract workers in a competitive labor market. Decisions about how to respond to the economic forces of product markets and labor markets limit an organization's choices about pay structure.

Product Markets

The organization's *product market* includes organizations that offer competing goods and services. In other words, the organizations in a product market are competing to serve the same customers. To succeed in their product markets, organizations must be able to sell their goods and services at a quantity and price that will bring them a sufficient profit. They may try to win customers by being superior in a number of areas, including quality, customer service, and price. An important influence on price is the cost to produce the goods and services for sale. As we mentioned earlier, the cost of labor is a significant part of an organization's costs.

If an organization's labor costs are higher than those of its competitors, it will be under pressure to charge more than competitors charge for similar products. If one company spends $50 in labor costs to make a product and its competitor spends only $35, the second company will be more profitable unless the first company can justify a higher price to customers. This is one reason U.S. automakers have had difficulty competing against Japanese companies. The labor-related expenses per vehicle for a U.S. company have been $700 higher than for Japanese carmakers operating in the United States. Recently, U.S. automakers have been able to reduce labor costs, partly by hiring new workers at lower wages, down to an average of $58 per hour. This is still somewhat above Toyota and Honda's $52 per hour and far above the average $27 per hour that Volkswagen is paying workers to build Volkswagen Passats at its new plant in Tennessee.[9]

Product markets place an upper limit on the pay an organization will offer. This upper limit is most important when labor costs are a large part of an organization's total costs and when the organization's customers place great importance on price. Organizations that want to lure top-quality employees by offering generous salaries therefore have to find ways to automate routine activities (so that labor is a smaller part of total costs) or to persuade customers that high quality is worth a premium price. Organizations under pressure to cut labor costs may respond by reducing staff levels, freezing pay levels, postponing hiring decisions, or requiring employees to bear more of the cost of benefits such as insurance premiums.

Labor Markets

Besides competing to sell their products, organizations must compete to obtain human resources in *labor markets*. In general, workers prefer higher-paying jobs and avoid employers that offer less money for the same type of job. In this way, competition for labor establishes the minimum an organization must pay to hire an employee for a particular job. If an organization pays less than the minimum, employees will look for jobs with other organizations.

An organization's competitors in labor markets typically include companies with similar products and companies in other industries that hire similar employees. For example, a truck transportation firm would want to know the pay earned by truck drivers at competing firms as well as truck drivers

There is a strong demand for nurses in the labor market. What this means for hospitals is that they have to pay competitive wages and other perks to attract and retain staff. How does this differ from the airline industry's current labor market?

for manufacturers that do their own shipping, drivers for moving and storage companies, and drivers for stores that provide delivery services. In setting pay levels for its bookkeepers and administrative assistants, the company would probably define its labor market differently because bookkeepers and administrative assistants work for most kinds of businesses. The company would likely look for data on the earnings of bookkeepers and administrative assistants in the region. For all these jobs, the company wants to know what others are paying so that it will pay enough to attract and keep qualified employees. The "Did You Know?" box compares average pay levels for some broad occupational categories in the United States.

Another influence on labor markets is the *cost of living*—the cost of a household's typical expenses, such as house payments, groceries, medical care, and gasoline. In some parts of the country, the cost of living is higher than in others, so the local labor markets there will likely demand higher pay. Also, over time, the cost of living tends to rise. When the cost of living is rising rapidly, labor markets demand pay increases. The federal government tracks trends in the nation's cost of living with a measure called the Consumer Price Index (CPI). Following and studying changes in the CPI can help employers prepare for changes in the demands of the labor market.

Pay Level: Deciding What to Pay

Although labor and product markets limit organizations' choices about pay levels, there is a range within which organizations can make decisions.[10] The size of this range depends on the details of the organization's competitive environment. If many workers are competing for a few jobs, employers will have more choice. Similarly, employers can be more flexible about pay policies if they use technology and work design to get better results from employees than their competitors do.

When organizations have a broad range in which to make decisions about pay, they can choose to pay at, above, or below the rate set by market forces. Economic theory holds that the most profitable level, all things being equal, would be at the market rate. Often, however, all things are not equal from one employer to another. For instance, an organization may gain an advantage by paying above the market rate if it uses the higher pay as one means to attract top talent and then uses these excellent employees' knowledge to be more innovative, produce higher quality, or work more efficiently.

Management, Professional, Technical Occupations Are the Highest Paid

Looking at broad occupational categories, the highest pay goes to managers, followed by members of the legal profession and experts in computers, mathematics, architecture, and engineering. The lowest-paid occupational groups involve providing services such as food preparation, personal care, and building maintenance.

The pay rates shown in the graph are for the *median* worker in each category (half the workers earn more, and half earn less). However, keep in mind that the range of earnings for an occupational category may be great. In sales, for example, median earnings range as low as $18,670 for models and $18,820 for cashiers and as high as $89,330 for sales engineers. The overall median is low because there are many more cashiers than sales engineers.

Question

If a company were to hire a new human resource manager, would the $92,880 figure shown here for management be an appropriate rate of pay? Why or why not?

SOURCE: Bureau of Labor Statistics, "Occupational Employment Statistics: May 2011 Occupational Employment and Wage Estimates," last modified March 27, 2012, http://www.bls.gov, accessed April 11, 2012.

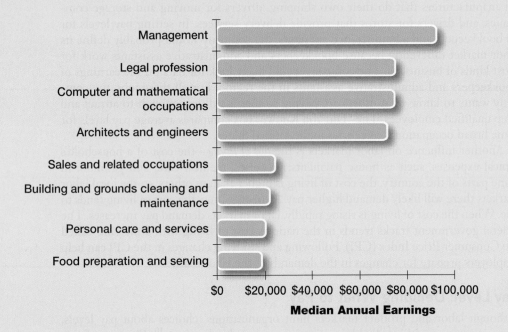

For example, in the highly competitive world of information technology, Google, Amazon, Microsoft, and Apple try to get and keep the best people by paying salaries far above market rates.[11] This pay policy leaves smaller high-tech companies with less cash to offer at a disadvantage in the competition for talent.

This approach is based on the view of employees as resources. Higher pay may be an investment in superior human resources. Having higher labor costs than your competitors is not necessarily bad if you also have the best and most effective workforce, which produces more products of better quality. Pay policies are one of the most important human resource tools for encouraging desired employee behaviors and discouraging undesired behaviors. Therefore, organizations must evaluate pay as more than a cost—it is an investment that can generate returns in attracting, retaining, and motivating a high-quality workforce. For this reason, paying above the going rate may be advantageous for an organization that empowers employees or that cannot closely watch employees (as with repair technicians who travel to customers). Those employers might use high pay to attract and retain top candidates and to motivate them to do their best because they want to keep their high-paying jobs.[12]

Gathering Information about Market Pay

To compete for talent, organizations use **benchmarking**, a procedure in which an organization compares its own practices against those of successful competitors. In terms of compensation, benchmarking involves the use of pay surveys. These provide information about the going rates of pay at competitors in the organization's product and labor markets. An organization can conduct its own surveys, but the federal government and other organizations make a great deal of data available already.

Pay surveys are available for many kinds of industries (product markets) and jobs (labor markets). The primary collector of this kind of data in the United States is the Bureau of Labor Statistics, which conducts an ongoing National Compensation Survey measuring wages, salaries, and benefits paid to the nation's employees. The "HR How To" box provides guidelines for using the BLS website as a source of wage data. Besides the BLS, the most widely used sources of compensation information include HR organizations such as WorldatWork and the Society for Human Resource Management.[13] In addition, many organizations, especially large ones, purchase data from consulting groups such as Mercer, Towers Watson, and Hewitt. Consulting firms charge for the service but can tailor data to their clients' needs. Employers also should investigate what compensation surveys are available from any industry or trade groups their company belongs to.

Human resource professionals need to determine whether to gather data focusing on particular industries or on job categories. Industry-specific data are especially relevant for jobs with skills that are specific to the type of product. For jobs with skills that can be transferred to companies in other industries, surveys of job classifications will be more relevant.

> **Benchmarking**
> A procedure in which an organization compares its own practices against those of successful competitors.

Employee Judgments about Pay Fairness

> **LO 11-4** Describe how employees evaluate the fairness of a pay structure.

In developing a pay structure, it is important to keep in mind employees' opinions about fairness. After all, one of the purposes of pay is to motivate employees, and they will not be motivated by pay if they think it is unfair.

Judging Fairness

Employees evaluate their pay relative to the pay of other employees. Social scientists have studied this kind of comparison and developed *equity theory* to describe how people make judgments about fairness.[14] According to equity theory, people measure outcomes such as pay in terms of their inputs. For example, an employee might think of her pay in terms of her master's degree, her 12 years of experience, and her 60-hour workweeks. To decide whether a level of pay is equitable, the person compares her ratio of outcomes and inputs with other people's outcome/input ratios, as shown in

Gathering Wage Data at the BLS Website

A convenient source of data on hourly wages is the wage query system of the Bureau of Labor Statistics (BLS). This federal agency makes data available at its website on an interactive basis. The data come from the BLS's National Compensation Survey. The user specifies the category of data desired, and the BLS provides tables of data almost instantly. Here's how to use the BLS system.

Visit the Databases and Tools page of the BLS website (**www.bls .gov/data/**), and click on the link to Pay and Benefits. Find the options offered for the National Compensation Survey (NCS). The multiscreen search asks you to specify one search category at a time, then click to open the next screen.

After you select Multi-Screen Data Search for NCS, the system presents you with a window in which to select either the entire United States or a single state. Click to highlight your choice and then click on Next Form. If you choose United States, your next choice is a Census region of the country; if you choose a state, the next option is a metropolitan region of the state.

On the next screen, select the occupation you wish to research. The survey data cover hundreds of occupations, grouped into more general categories. For example, at the most specific level, you could look at civil engineers. More broadly, you could look at all engineers, or at the larger grouping of architecture and engineering occupations.

You should select the most specific grouping that covers the occupation you want to investigate.

After selecting an occupation, select a work level. This describes the level of such work features as knowledge required and the scope, complexity, and demands of the job. For instance, you could look only at data for entry-level or senior accountants, rather than all accountants. Some occupations, including artists, athletes, and announcers, are not classified by work level.

Click on the Retrieve Data link to submit the request to the BLS. The system immediately processes the request and presents the table (or tables) on your computer screen.

SOURCE: Bureau of Labor Statistics website, www.bls.gov, accessed April 11, 2012.

Figure 11.3. The person in the previous example might notice that an employee with less education or experience is earning more than she is (unfair) or that an employee who works 80 hours a week is earning more (fair). In general, employees compare their pay and contributions against several yardsticks:

- What they think employees in other organizations earn for doing the same job.
- What they think other employees holding different jobs within the organization earn for doing work at the same or different levels.
- What they think other employees in the organization earn for doing the same job as theirs.

Figure 11.3

Opinions about Fairness: Pay Equity

Equity: Pay Seems Fair

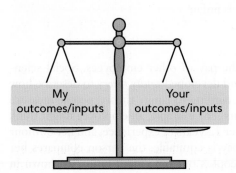

Inequity: Pay Seems Unfair

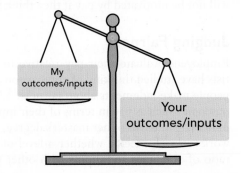

350

Employees' conclusions about equity depend on what they choose as a standard of comparison. The results can be surprising. For example, some organizations have set up two-tier wage systems as a way to cut labor costs without cutting employees' existing salaries. Typically, employers announce these programs as a way to avoid moving jobs out of the country or closing down altogether. In a two-tier wage system, existing employees continue on at their current (upper-tier) pay rate while new employees sign on for less pay (the lower tier). One might expect reaction among employees in the lower tier that the pay structure is unfair. But a study of these employees found that they were *more* satisfied than the top-tier employees.[15] The lower-tier employees were not comparing their pay with that of the upper-tier employees but with the other alternatives they saw for themselves: lower-paying jobs or unemployment.

The ways employees respond to their impressions about equity can have a great impact on the organization. Typically, if employees see their pay as equitable, their attitudes and behavior continue unchanged. If employees see themselves as receiving an advantage, they usually rethink the situation to see it as merely equitable. But if employees conclude that they are underrewarded, they are likely to make up the difference in one of three ways. They might put forth less effort (reducing their inputs), find a way to increase their outcomes (for example, stealing), or withdraw by leaving the organization or refusing to cooperate. Employees' beliefs about fairness also influence their willingness to accept transfers or promotions. For example, if a job change involves more work, employees will expect higher pay.

Communicating Fairness

Equity theory tells organizations that employees care about their pay relative to what others are earning and that these feelings are based on what the employees *perceive* (what they notice and form judgments about). As the "Best Practices" example of Google illustrates, an organization can do much to contribute to what employees know and, as a result, what they perceive. If the organization researches salary levels and concludes that it is paying its employees generously, it should communicate this. If the employees do not know what the organization learned from its research, they may reach an entirely different conclusion about their pay. Employees have accepted General Electric's use of two-tier wage plans to make U.S. factories competitive in a global marketplace. At GE's appliance facility in Louisville, Kentucky, new employees earn $12 to $19 per hour, versus $21 to $32 for workers covered by previous contracts. Similarly, at GE's plant in Salem, Virginia, new workers can earn $15 to $24 per hour making wind turbine controls; workers on the older pay scale earn $26 to $35 per hour. Employees are not enthusiastic about the lower pay scale, but they compare the lower-paid GE jobs with unemployment and are glad to have work.[16]

Employers must also recognize that employees know much more about what other employers pay now than they did before the Internet became popular. In the past, when gathering wage and salary data was expensive and difficult, employers had more leeway in negotiating with individual employees. Today's employees can go to websites like jobstar.org or salary.com to find hundreds of links to wage and salary data. For a fee, executive search firms such as Korn/Ferry provide data. Resources like these give employees information about what other workers are earning, along with the expectation that information will be shared. This means employers will face increased pressure to clearly explain their pay policies.

Managers play the most significant role in communication because they interact with their employees each day. The HR department should prepare them to explain

How Google Gets a Good Return on Payroll

Pay levels at Google are tied to the company's business strategy. According to Google's compensation director, Frank Wagner, the company sets pay levels to achieve three goals: (1) recruit and keep the best talent; (2) motivate superior performance, including innovation; and (3) link rewards to the company's success. Given the stiff competition for programmers and software engineers, Google tackled this project by applying one of its greatest strengths: expertise in gathering and interpreting data.

Google surveyed its employees to find out what kinds of pay plans they would value the most. Of course, Google employees, like any other human, want more of everything valuable, so the company used a statistical method called conjoint analysis. In this approach, the survey presents pairs of hypothetical compensation plans, and for each pair, employees have to choose the plan they value more. In addition, the survey asked employees questions about the value they place on a dollar's worth of compensation delivered in different ways. For example, they chose whether

they would place a higher value on an additional $1 bonus or an additional $1 of salary. Conjoint analysis takes all of these responses and finds patterns.

In the case of Google's compensation survey, a key lesson was that employees value an additional dollar most when it comes in the form of a higher salary. An equal increase in the size of employees' bonus is less desirable, and an extra dollar's worth of stock options has even less of an impact on employees' satisfaction with their pay. (The next chapter will describe bonuses and stock options as part of a compensation package.) The preference for extra money to come as part of the base salary was strongest among Google's top performers.

Based on the results of the survey, Google's compensation team persuaded the board of directors that the most effective way to continue retaining the best talent and sharing the company's success with employees was to increase pay levels for all employees through a 10% increase in salaries. With the board's approval, the team developed communications materials to announce

the raise, explain its timing, and describe how it would affect each employee. Every employee received an e-mailed invitation to a company meeting, where the news was delivered to all of them at once.

The across-the-board raise generated a wave of publicity. In the months following the announcement, Google saw a decline in its employee turnover, and the percentage of job candidates who accepted offers increased. At the same time, Google's stock price took a hit in the following quarter, because the greater payroll expense cut into the company's earnings per share. Nevertheless, as an analyst at *Fortune* magazine approvingly noted, putting employee happiness ahead of one quarter's stock price could position the company for long-term success.

SOURCES: Google, "Jobs: Life at Google," http://www.google.com, accessed April 11, 2012; "Highly Planned Pay Raise Reaps Rewards at Google," *Report on Salary Surveys,* July 2011, pp. 12–13; Seth Weintraub, "Google's Choice: Employees or Wall Street," *Fortune Tech,* April 18, 2011, http://tech.fortune.cnn.com.

why the organization's pay structure is designed as it is and to judge whether employee concerns about the structure indicate a need for change. A common issue is whether to reclassify a job because its content has changed. If an employee takes on more responsibility, the employee will often ask the manager for help in seeking more pay for the job.

LO 11-5 Explain how organizations design pay structures related to jobs.

Job Structure: Relative Value of Jobs

Along with market forces and principles of fairness, organizations consider the relative contribution each job should make to the organization's overall performance. In general, an organization's top executives have a great impact on the organization's performance, so they tend to be paid much more than entry-level workers. Executives at the same level of the organization—for example, the vice president of marketing and

	COMPENSABLE FACTORS			
JOB TITLE	**EXPERIENCE**	**EDUCATION**	**COMPLEXITY**	**TOTAL**
Computer operator	40	30	40	110
Computer programmer	40	50	65	155
Systems analyst	65	60	85	210

Table 11.1

Job Evaluation of Three Jobs with Three Factors

the vice president of information systems—tend to be paid similar amounts. Creation of a pay structure requires that the organization develop an internal structure showing the relative contribution of its various jobs.

One typical way of doing this is with a **job evaluation**, an administrative procedure for measuring the relative worth of the organization's jobs. Usually, the organization does this by assembling and training a job evaluation committee, consisting of people familiar with the jobs to be evaluated. The committee often includes a human resource specialist and, if its budget permits, may hire an outside consultant.

Job Evaluation
An administrative procedure for measuring the relative internal worth of the organization's jobs.

To conduct a job evaluation, the committee identifies each job's *compensable factors*, meaning the characteristics of a job that the organization values and chooses to pay for. As shown in Table 11.1, an organization might value the experience and education of people performing computer-related jobs, as well as the complexity of those jobs. Other compensable factors might include working conditions and responsibility. Based on the job attributes defined by job analysis (discussed in Chapter 4), the jobs are rated for each factor. The rater assigns each factor a certain number of points, giving more points to factors when they are considered more important and when the job requires a high level of that factor. Often the number of points comes from one of the *point manuals* published by trade groups and management consultants. If necessary, the organization can adapt the scores in the point manual to the organization's situation or even develop its own point manual. As in the example in Table 11.1, the scores for each factor are totaled to arrive at an overall evaluation for each job.

Job evaluations provide the basis for decisions about relative internal worth. According to the sample assessments in Table 11.1, the job of systems analyst is worth almost twice as much to this organization as the job of computer operator. Therefore, the organization would be willing to pay almost twice as much for the work of a systems analyst as it would for the work of a computer operator.

The organization may limit its pay survey to jobs evaluated as *key jobs*. These are jobs that have relatively stable content and are common among many organizations, so it is possible to obtain survey data about what people earn in these jobs. Organizations can make the process of creating a pay structure more practical by defining key jobs. Research for creating the pay structure is limited to the key jobs that play a significant role in the organization. Pay for the key jobs can be based on survey data, and pay for the organization's other jobs can be based on the organization's job structure. A job with a higher evaluation score than a particular key job would receive higher pay than that key job.

Popular actors, such as Leonardo DiCaprio, are evaluated by their impact on box office receipts and other revenues and then compensated based on these evaluations.

Pay Structure: Putting It All Together

As we described in the first section of this chapter, the pay structure reflects decisions about how much to pay (pay level) and the relative value of each job (job structure). The organization's pay structure should reflect what the organization knows about market forces, as well as its own unique goals and the relative contribution of each job to achieving the goals. By balancing this external and internal information, the organization's goal is to set levels of pay that employees will consider equitable and motivating. For an example of what employees find equitable and motivating today, see "HRM Social."

Hourly Wage
Rate of pay for each hour worked.

Piecework Rate
Rate of pay for each unit produced.

Salary
Rate of pay for each week, month, or year worked.

Organizations typically apply the information by establishing some combination of pay rates, pay grades, and pay ranges. Within this structure, they may state the pay in terms of a rate per hour, commonly called an **hourly wage**; a rate of pay for each unit produced, known as a **piecework rate**; or a rate of pay per month or year, called a **salary**.

Pay Rates

If the organization's main concern is to match what people are earning in comparable jobs, the organization can base pay directly on market research of as many of its key jobs as possible. To do this, the organization looks for survey data for each job title. If it finds data from more than one survey, it must weight the results based on their quality and relevance. The final number represents what the competition pays. In light of that knowledge, the organization decides what it will pay for the job.

Pay Policy Line
A graphed line showing the mathematical relationship between job evaluation points and pay rate.

The next step is to determine salaries for the nonkey jobs, for which the organization has no survey data. Instead, the person developing the pay structure creates a graph like the one in Figure 11.4. The vertical axis shows a range of possible pay rates, and the horizontal axis measures the points from the job evaluation. The analyst plots points according to the job evaluation and pay rate for each key job. Finally, the analyst fits a line, called a **pay policy line**, to the points plotted. (This can be done statistically

Figure 11.4
Pay Policy Lines

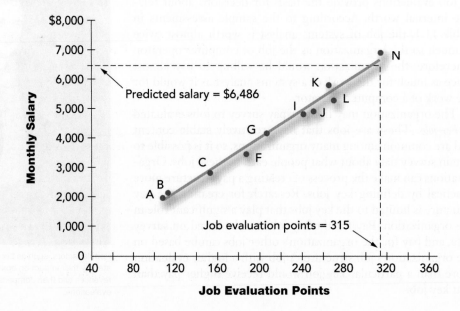

Pay Me Less if You Must—Just Don't Cut Me Off from Twitter

There is nothing new about employees being satisfied with lower-paying jobs, especially when employers offer some other benefit, such as a chance to do work people have a passion for, accomplish something important, or use flexible hours to meet other needs. But one kind of trade-off is relatively new: In a survey of college students and young college-educated employees in 14 countries, many of them placed access to social media on a par with salary levels in decisions about what job offers they would accept.

In the survey, conducted by computer-networking company Cisco,

one-third of students said access to social media and their electronic devices at work was more important to them than salary levels. Forty percent of college students and 45% of the young employees said they would accept lower pay in exchange for no limits on social-media access. Over half (56%) of college students said that if a company offering them a job had a policy of blocking access to social media at work, they either would turn down the offer or try to get around the rule.

Consultant John Paul Engel says employers and employees should be realistic about the trade-off.

Engel told a reporter that where an employer allows access to social media during the workday, the employer should offer lower pay rates because "there would be a loss of productivity as a result."

SOURCES: Cisco, "Cisco Connected World Technology Report," http://www.cisco.com, accessed April 11, 2012; Ryan Lytle, "Social Media Means More than Salary to Some College Students," *U.S. News and World Report,* December 6, 2011, http://www.usnews.com; Cisco, "The New Workplace Currency: It's Not Just Salary Anymore," news release, November 2, 2011, http://www.cisco.com.

on a computer, using a procedure called regression analysis.) Mathematically, this line shows the relationship between job evaluation and rate of pay. Thus, the line slopes upward from left to right, and if higher-level jobs are especially valuable to the organization, the line may curve upward to indicate even greater pay for high-level jobs. Using this line, the analyst can estimate the market pay level for a given job evaluation. Looking at the graph will give approximate numbers, or the regression analysis will provide an equation for calculating the rate of pay. For example, using the pay policy line in Figure 11.4, a job with 315 evaluation points would have a predicted salary of $6,486 per month.

The pay policy line reflects the pay structure in the market, which does not always match rates in the organization (see key job F in Figure 11.4). Survey data may show that people in certain jobs are actually earning significantly more or less than the amount shown on the pay policy line. For example, some kinds of expertise are in short supply. People with that expertise can command higher salaries because they can easily leave one employer to get higher pay somewhere else. Suppose, in contrast, that local businesses have laid off many warehouse employees. Because so many of these workers are looking for jobs, organizations may be able to pay them less than the rate that job evaluation points would suggest.

When job structure and market data conflict in these ways, organizations have to decide on a way to resolve the two. One approach is to stick to the job evaluations and pay according to the employees' worth to the organization. Organizations that do so will be paying more or less than they have to, so they will likely have more difficulty competing for customers or employees. A way to moderate this approach is to consider the importance of each position to the organization's goals.[17] If a position is critical for meeting the organization's goals, paying more than competitors pay may be worthwhile.

At the other extreme, the organization could base pay entirely on market forces. However, this approach also has some practical drawbacks. One is that employees may conclude that pay rates are unfair. Two vice presidents or two supervisors will expect to receive similar pay because their responsibilities are similar. If the differences between their pay are large, because of different market rates, the lower-paid employee will likely be dissatisfied. Also, if the organization's development plans include rotating managers through different assignments, the managers will be reluctant to participate if managers in some departments receive lower pay. Organizations therefore must weigh all the objectives of their pay structure to arrive at suitable rates.

Pay Grades

Pay Grades
Sets of jobs having similar worth or content, grouped together to establish rates of pay.

A large organization could have hundreds or even thousands of different jobs. Setting a pay rate for each job would be extremely complex. Therefore, many organizations group jobs into **pay grades**—sets of jobs having similar worth or content, grouped together to establish rates of pay. For example, the organization could establish five pay grades, with the same pay available to employees holding any job within the same grade.

A drawback of pay grades is that grouping jobs will result in rates of pay for individual jobs that do not precisely match the levels specified by the market and the organization's job structure. Suppose, for example, that the organization groups together its senior accountants (with a job evaluation of 255 points) and its senior systems analysts (with a job evaluation of 270 points). Surveys might show that the market rate of pay for systems analysts is higher than that for accountants. In addition, the job evaluations give more points to systems analysts. Even so, for simplicity's sake, the organization pays the same rate for the two jobs because they are in the same pay grade. The organization would have to pay more than the market requires for accountants or pay less than the market rate for systems analysts (so it would probably have difficulty recruiting and retaining them).

Pay Ranges

Pay Range
A set of possible pay rates defined by a minimum, maximum, and midpoint of pay for employees holding a particular job or a job within a particular pay grade.

Usually, organizations want some flexibility in setting pay for individual jobs. They want to be able to pay the most valuable employees the highest amounts and to give rewards for performance, as described in the next chapter. Flexibility also helps the organization balance conflicting information from market surveys and job evaluations. Therefore, pay structure usually includes a **pay range** for each job or pay grade. In other words, the organization establishes a minimum, maximum, and midpoint of pay for employees holding a particular job or a job within a particular pay grade. Employees holding the same job may receive somewhat different pay, depending on where their pay falls within the range.

A typical approach is to use the market rate or the pay policy line as the midpoint of a range for the job or pay grade. The minimum and maximum values for the range may also be based on market surveys of those amounts. Pay ranges are most common for white-collar jobs and for jobs that are not covered by union contracts. Figure 11.5 shows an example of pay ranges based on the pay policy line in Figure 11.4. Notice that the jobs are grouped into five pay grades, each with its own pay range. In this example, the range is widest for employees who are at higher levels in terms of their job evaluation points. That is because the performance of these higher-level employees will likely have more effect on the organization's performance, so the organization

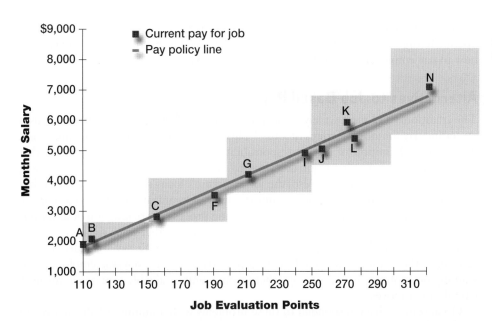

Figure 11.5
Sample Pay Grade Structure

needs more latitude to reward them. For instance, as discussed earlier, the organization may want to select a higher point in the range to attract an employee who is more critical to achieving the organization's goals.

Usually pay ranges overlap somewhat, so that the highest pay in one grade is somewhat higher than the lowest pay in the next grade. Overlapping ranges gives the organization more flexibility in transferring employees among jobs, because transfers need not always involve a change in pay. On the other hand, the less overlap, the more important it is to earn promotions in order to keep getting raises. Assuming the organization wants to motivate employees through promotions (and assuming enough opportunities for promotion are available), the organization will want to limit the overlap from one level to the next.

Pay Differentials

In some situations organizations adjust pay to reflect differences in working conditions or labor markets. For example, an organization may pay extra to employees who work the night shift because night hours are less desirable for most workers. Similarly, organizations may pay extra to employees in locations where living expenses are higher. These adjustments are called **pay differentials**.

Pay Differential
Adjustment to a pay rate to reflect differences in working conditions or labor markets.

A survey of businesses in the United States found that almost three-quarters have a policy of providing pay differentials based on geographic location.[18] These differentials are intended as a way to treat employees fairly without regard to where they work. The most common approach is to move an employee higher in the pay structure to compensate for higher living costs. For instance, according to the ACCRA Cost of Living Index (published by the Council for Community and Economic Research), the cost of living in New York City is more than twice that of the average metropolitan area. An organization with employees in New York City and in an average U.S. city might pay its New York office manager substantially more than its office manager

Night hours are less desirable for most workers. Therefore, some companies pay a differential for night work to compensate them.

in the average city. This pay policy can become expensive for organizations that must operate in high-cost locations. Also, organizations need to handle the delicate issue of how to pay employees transferred to lower-cost areas.

Alternatives to Job-Based Pay

LO 11-6   Describe alternatives to job-based pay.

The traditional and most widely used approach to developing a pay structure focuses on setting pay for jobs or groups of jobs.[19] This emphasis on jobs has some limitations. The precise definition of a job's responsibilities can contribute to an attitude that some activities "are not in my job description," at the expense of flexibility, innovation, quality, and customer service. Also, the job structure's focus on higher pay for higher status can work against an effort at empowerment. Organizations may avoid change because it requires repeating the time-consuming process of creating job descriptions and related paperwork. Another change-related problem is that when the organization needs a new set of knowledge, skills, and abilities, the existing pay structure may be rewarding the wrong behaviors. Finally, a pay structure that rewards employees for winning promotions may discourage them from gaining valuable experience through lateral career moves.

Delayering

Reducing the number of levels in the organization's job structure.

Organizations have responded to these problems with a number of alternatives to job-based pay structures. Some organizations have found greater flexibility through **delayering**, or reducing the number of levels in the organization's job structure. By combining more assignments into a single layer, organizations give managers more flexibility in making assignments and awarding pay increases. These broader groupings often are called *broad bands*. In the 1990s, IBM changed from a pay structure with 5,000 job titles and 24 salary grades to one with 1,200 jobs and 10 bands. When IBM began using broad bands, it replaced its point-factor job evaluation system with an approach based on matching jobs to descriptions. Figure 11.6 shows descriptions of several job characteristics used by IBM. Job descriptions are assigned to the band whose characteristics best match those in the job description. Broad bands reduce the opportunities for promoting employees, so organizations that eliminate layers in their job descriptions must find other ways to reward employees.

Skill-Based Pay Systems

Pay structures that set pay according to the employees' levels of skill or knowledge and what they are capable of doing.

Another way organizations have responded to the limitations of job-based pay has been to move away from the link to jobs and toward pay structures that reward employees based on their knowledge and skills.[20] **Skill-based pay systems** are pay structures that set pay according to the employees' level of skill or knowledge and what they are capable of doing. Paying for skills makes sense at organizations where changing technology requires employees to continually widen and deepen their knowledge. For example, modern machinery often requires that operators know how to program and monitor computers to perform a variety of tasks. Skill-based pay also supports efforts to empower employees and enrich jobs because it encourages employees to add to their knowledge so they can make decisions in many areas. In this way, skill-based pay helps organizations become more flexible and innovative. More generally, skill-based pay can encourage a climate of learning and adaptability and give employees a broader view of how the organization functions. These changes should help employees use their knowledge and ideas more productively. A field study of a manufacturing plant found that changing to a skill-based pay structure led to better quality and lower labor costs.[21]

Of course, skill-based pay has its own disadvantages.[22] It rewards employees for acquiring skills but does not provide a way to ensure that employees can use their new skills. The result may be that the organization is paying employees more for learning

Figure 11.6

IBM's New Job Evaluation Approach

Below is an abbreviated schematic illustration of the new—and simple—IBM job evaluation approach:

POSITION REFERENCE GUIDE

Band	Skills Required	Leadership/Contribution	Scope/Impact
1			
2			
3			
4			
5			
6			
7			
8			
9			
10			

Factors: Leadership/Contribution

Band 06: Understand the mission of the professional group and vision in own area of competence.

Band 07: Understand the departmental mission and vision.

Band 08: Understand departmental/functional mission and vision.

Band 09: Has vision of functional or unit mission.

Band 10: Has vision of overall strategies.

Both the bands and the approach are global. In the U.S., bands 1–5 are nonexempt; bands 6–10 are exempt. Each cell in the table contains descriptive language about key job characteristics. Position descriptions are compared to the chart and assigned to bands on a "best fit" basis. There are no points or scoring mechanisms. Managers assign employees to bands by selecting a position description that most closely resembles the work being done by an employee using an online position description library.

That's it!

SOURCE: From A. S. Richter, "Paying the People in Black at Big Blue," *Compensation and Benefits Review,* May–June 1998, pp. 51–59. Reprinted with permission of Sage Publications, Inc., via Copyright Clearance Center.

skills that the employer is not benefiting from. The challenge for HRM is to design work so that the work design and pay structure support one another. Also, if employees learn skills very quickly, they may reach the maximum pay level so quickly that it will become difficult to reward them appropriately. Skill-based pay does not necessarily provide an alternative to the bureaucracy and paperwork of traditional pay structures because it requires records related to skills, training, and knowledge acquired. Finally, gathering market data about skill-based pay is difficult because most wage and salary surveys are job-based.

Pay Structure and Actual Pay

Usually, the human resource department is responsible for establishing the organization's pay structure. But building a structure is not the end of the organization's decisions about pay structure. The structure represents the organization's policy, but what the organization actually does may be different. As part of its management responsibility, the HR department therefore should compare actual pay to the pay structure, making sure that policies and practices match.

LO 11-7 Summarize how to ensure that pay is actually in line with the pay structure.

Figure 11.7
Finding a Compa-Ratio

Pay Grade: 1
Midpoint of Range: $2,175 per month

Salaries of Employees in Pay Grade

Employee 1	$2,306
Employee 2	$2,066
Employee 3	$2,523
Employee 4	$2,414

Compa-Ratio

$$\frac{\text{Average}}{\text{Midpoint}} = \frac{\$2,327.25}{\$2,175.00} = 1.07$$

Average Salary of Employees
$2,306 + $2,066 + $2,523 + $2,414 = $9,309
$9,309 ÷ 4 = $2,327.25

A common way to do this is to measure a *compa-ratio*, the ratio of average pay to the midpoint of the pay range. Figure 11.7 shows an example. Assuming the organization has pay grades, the organization would find a compa-ratio for each pay grade: the average paid to all employees in the pay grade divided by the midpoint for the pay grade. If the average equals the midpoint, the compa-ratio is 1. More often, the compa-ratio is somewhat above 1 (meaning the average pay is above the midpoint for the pay grade) or below 1 (meaning the average pay is below the midpoint).

Assuming that the pay structure is well planned to support the organization's goals, the compa-ratios should be close to 1. A compa-ratio greater than 1 suggests that the organization is paying more than planned for human resources and may have difficulty keeping costs under control. A compa-ratio less than 1 suggests that the organization is underpaying for human resources relative to its target and may have difficulty attracting and keeping qualified employees. When compa-ratios are more or less than 1, the numbers signal a need for the HR department to work with managers to identify whether to adjust the pay structure or the organization's pay practices. The compa-ratios may indicate that the pay structure no longer reflects market rates of pay. Or maybe performance appraisals need to be more accurate, as discussed in Chapter 8.

LO 11-8 Discuss issues related to paying employees serving in the military and paying executives.

Current Issues Involving Pay Structure

An organization's policies regarding pay structure greatly influence employees' and even the general public's opinions about the organization. Issues affecting pay structure therefore can hurt or help the organization's reputation and ability to recruit, motivate, and keep employees. Recent issues related to pay structure include decisions about paying employees on active military duty and decisions about how much to pay the organization's top executives.

Pay during Military Duty

As we noted in Chapter 3, the Uniformed Services Employment and Reemployment Rights Act (USERRA) requires employers to make jobs available to their workers when they return after fulfilling military duties for up to five years. During the time these employees are performing their military service, the employer faces decisions related to paying these people. The armed services pay service members during their time of duty, but military pay often falls short of what they would earn in their civilian jobs. Some employers have chosen to support their employees by paying the difference between their military and civilian earnings for extended periods. Sears Holdings provides a pay differential for up to 60 months and also makes reservists on active duty eligible for annual raises and bonuses. In addition, these employees have the option to continue their medical, dental, and life insurance benefits while on duty.[23]

Policies to make up the difference between military pay and civilian pay are costly. The employer is paying employees while they are not working for the organization, and it may have to hire temporary employees as well. This challenge has posed a significant hardship on some employers since 2002, as hundreds of thousands of Reservists and National Guard members have been mobilized. Even so, as the nation copes with this challenge, hundreds of employers have decided that maintaining positive relations with employees—and the goodwill of the American public—makes the expense worthwhile.

Pay for Executives

The media have drawn public attention to the issue of executive pay. The issue attracts notice because of the very high pay that the top executives of major U.S. companies have received in recent years. For example, recent reviews of executive compensation at the largest publicly owned companies in the United States found that median compensation of chief executive offices was near $9 million. However, most CEOs do not run a Fortune 500 or S&P 500 company, and broader studies have found more modest—though still high—executive pay. A study by Chief Executive Group found that CEOs at private companies earning at least $5 million received median compensation of $405,000.[24] Notice also that as shown in Figure 11.8, only a small share of the average compensation paid to CEOs is in the form of a salary. Most CEO compensation takes the form of performance-related pay, such as bonuses and stock. This variable pay, discussed in the next chapter, causes the pay of executives to vary much more widely than other employees' earnings.

Although these high amounts apply to only a small proportion of the total workforce, the issue of executive pay is relevant to pay structure in terms of equity theory. As we discussed earlier in the chapter, employees draw conclusions about the fairness of pay by making comparisons among employees' inputs and outcomes. By many comparisons, U.S. CEOs' pay is high. Data from the Economic Policy Institute compare average CEO compensation with the compensation of the average U.S. worker. According to the EPI data, CEO pay surpassed 100 times average worker compensation in the 1990s, soared to 299 times the average in 2000, and stood at 243 to 1 in 2010.

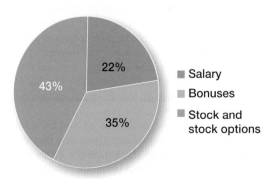

Figure 11.8
Average CEO Pay at 100 Large U.S. Companies

22%
43%
35%

- Salary
- Bonuses
- Stock and stock options

SOURCE: "Pay for Performance Is Working," *Corporate Board,* May/June 2011, p. 27.

Other comparisons have place the ratio even higher in the United States but lower in other developed nations.[25] To assess the fairness of this ratio, equity theory would consider not only the size of executive pay relative to pay for other employees but also the amount the CEOs contribute. An organization's executives potentially have a much greater effect on the organization's performance than its lowest-paid employees have. But if they do not seem to contribute 243 times more, employees will see the compensation as unfair. Likewise, if CEOs in the United States don't contribute more to their organization than CEOs in other countries do, the difference would be perceived as unfair.

Top executives help to set the tone or culture of the organization, and employees at all levels are affected by behavior at the top. As a result, the equity of executive pay can affect more employees than, say, equity among warehouse workers or sales-clerks. Recognizing this issue, Whole Foods Market limits the cash compensation of top executives to 19 times the average pay of the company's full-time workers. John Mackey, the founder and CEO, takes a salary of just $1. In 2011, that brought his total compensation to just $78,451. Even high-earning CEOs find justification for their pay when it is linked to performance. Meg Whitman in her new post as chief executive of Hewlett-Packard received 2011 compensation of $16.5 million. However, her salary, like Mackey's, was just $1. Most of her earnings came in the form of stock options allowing her to purchase HP stock over the course of three years—but only if HP's stock price meets certain targets along the way.[26]

One study that investigated this issue compared the pay of rank-and-file employees and executives in various business units.[27] In business units where the difference in pay was greater, customer satisfaction was lower. The researchers speculated that employees thought pay was inequitable and adjusted their behavior to provide lower inputs by putting forth less effort to satisfy customers. To avoid this type of situation, organizations need to plan not only *how much* to pay managers and executives, but also *how* to pay them. In the next chapter, we will explore many of the options available.

THINKING ETHICALLY

HOW DOES COMPENSATION FAIRNESS AFFECT EMPLOYEES' MOTIVATION?

Research into ethical behavior shows that employees are more likely to conduct themselves with honesty and integrity when they believe their organization values and rewards ethical conduct. For example, employees seek fairness. If they doubt that they and their peers get fair rewards for their efforts, they are apt to find ways—even unethical ways—to even the score. Conversely, if managers reward ethical conduct, employees are more likely to behave ethically.

In the context of pay policy, this means employees are looking for fair policies, both for themselves and for their co-workers. Compensation decisions that employees perceive as fair contribute to an overall ethical climate. If employees' pay differs from what they could make at another organization, or if one employee's pay differs from the pay of a colleague in a similar position, employees won't perceive fairness unless they understand and accept the reasons for the differences.

Communicating fairness is especially important but tricky during bad economic times, when it may be impossible to pay everyone generously. Some companies have even tried "rewarding" employees with a raise that carries no pay increase. Presumably the honor of a higher title and the potential for future raises would outweigh the downside of taking on more responsibility for the same pay.

The emphasis on communicating fairness suggests a policy of disclosing pay decisions. However, a recent study at the University of California raises some concerns. A few years ago, California's government allowed the publication of state workers' salaries, and the *Sacramento Bee* published the information on its website. A few days after notifying UC workers about the information, the researchers contacted them again. In that survey, most of the university employees indicated that they had looked up salary information. Those who were paid below the median salaries were dissatisfied and more likely to be looking for new jobs. Those who earned above the median had no significant change in their satisfaction; apparently, they just assumed they were above-average employees.

Questions

1. Do you think employees can be objective enough in measuring their own worth to reach accurate conclusions about the fairness of their pay? How can

an employer address biases in employees' perceptions about pay?
2. If you worked for a small business that wanted to promote a valued employee but had no more money in the payroll budget, how would you address the issue of fairness in this situation? How would you expect the employee to respond?

SOURCES: Paul O. Lopez, "The Risks of Promoting without Giving Raises," *The Wall Street Journal,* March 2, 2012, http://online.wsj.com; Christian Mastilak, Linda Matuszewski, Fabienne Miller, and Alexander Woods, "Designing Honesty into Your Organization," *Strategic Finance,* December 2011, pp. 35–40; Jack Hough, "Why Companies Keep Pay a Secret," *SmartMoney,* October 15, 2010, http://www.smartmoney.com.

SUMMARY

LO 11-1 Identify the kinds of decisions involved in establishing a pay structure.

Organizations make decisions to define a job structure, or relative pay for different jobs within the organization. They establish relative pay for different functions and different levels of responsibility for each function. Organizations also must establish pay levels, or the average paid for the different jobs. These decisions are based on the organization's goals, market data, legal requirements, and principles of fairness. Together, job structure and pay level establish a pay structure policy.

LO 11-2 Summarize legal requirements for pay policies.

To meet the standard of equal employment opportunity, employers must provide equal pay for equal work, regardless of an employee's age, race, sex, or other protected status. Differences in pay must relate to factors such as a person's qualifications or market levels of pay. Under the Fair Labor Standards Act (FLSA), the employer must pay at least the minimum wage established by law. Some state and local governments have established higher minimum wages. The FLSA also requires overtime pay—at one and a half times the employee's regular pay rate, including bonuses—for hours worked beyond 40 in each week. Managers, professionals, and outside salespersons are exempt from the overtime pay requirement. Employers must meet FLSA requirements concerning child labor. Federal contractors also must meet requirements to pay at least the prevailing wage in the area where their employees work.

LO 11-3 Discuss how economic forces influence decisions about pay.

To remain competitive, employers must meet the demands of product and labor markets. Product markets seek to buy at the lowest price, so organizations must limit their costs as much as possible. In this way, product markets place an upper limit on the pay an employer can afford to offer. Labor markets consist of workers who want to earn as much as possible. To attract and keep workers, employers must pay at least the going rate in their labor markets. Organizations make decisions about whether to pay at, above, or below the pay rate set by these market forces. Paying above the market rate may make the organization less competitive in product markets but give it an advantage in labor markets. The organization benefits only if it can attract the best candidates and provide the systems that motivate and enable them to do their best work. Organizations that pay below the market rate need creative practices for recruiting and training workers so that they can find and keep enough qualified people.

LO 11-4 Describe how employees evaluate the fairness of a pay structure.

According to equity theory, employees think of their pay relative to their inputs, such as training, experience, and effort. To decide whether their pay is equitable, they compare their outcome (pay)/input ratio with other people's outcome/input ratios. Employees make these comparisons with people doing the same job in other organizations and with people doing the same or different jobs in the same organization. If employees conclude that their outcome/input ratio is less than the comparison person's, they conclude that their pay is unfair and may engage in behaviors to create a situation they think is fair.

LO 11-5 Explain how organizations design pay structures related to jobs.

Organizations typically begin with a job evaluation to measure the relative worth of their jobs. A job evaluation committee identifies each job's compensable factors and rates each factor. The committee may use a point manual to assign an appropriate number of points to each job. The committee can research market pay levels for key jobs, then identify appropriate rates of pay for other jobs based on their number of points relative to the key jobs. The organization can do this with a pay policy line, which plots a salary for each job. The organization can combine jobs into several groups, called pay grades. For each pay grade or job, the organization typically establishes a pay range, using the market rate or pay policy line as the midpoint. Differences in working conditions or labor markets sometimes call for the use of pay differentials to adjust pay levels.

LO 11-6 Describe alternatives to job-based pay.

To obtain more flexibility, organizations may reduce the levels in the organization's job structure. This process of delayering creates broad bands of jobs with a pay range for each. Other organizations reward employees according to their knowledge and skills. They establish skill-based pay systems, or structures that set pay according to the employees' level of knowledge and what they are capable of doing. This encourages employees to be more flexible and adapt to changing technology. However, if the organization does not also provide systems in which employees can apply new skills, it may be paying them for skills they do not actually use.

LO 11-7 Summarize how to ensure that pay is actually in line with the pay structure.

The human resource department should routinely compare actual pay with the pay structure to see that policies and practices match. A common way to do this is to measure a compa-ratio for each job or pay grade. The compa-ratio is the ratio of average pay to the midpoint of the pay range. Assuming the pay structure supports the organization's goals, the compa-ratios should be close to 1. When compa-ratios are more or less than 1, the HR department should work with managers to identify whether to adjust the pay structure or the organization's pay practices.

LO 11-8 Discuss issues related to paying employees serving in the military and paying executives.

The Uniformed Services Employment and Reemployment Rights Act requires employers to make jobs available to any of their employees who leave to fulfill military duties for up to five years. While these employees are performing their military service, many are earning far less. To demonstrate their commitment to these employees and to earn the public's goodwill, many companies pay the difference between their military and civilian earnings, even though this policy is costly. Executive pay has drawn public scrutiny because top executive pay is much higher than average workers' pay. The great difference is an issue in terms of equity theory. Chief executive officers have an extremely large impact on the organization's performance, but critics complain that when performance falters, executive pay does not decline as fast as the organization's profits or stock price. Top executives help to set the organization's tone or culture, and employees at all levels are affected by the behavior of the people at the top. Therefore, employees' opinions about the equity of executive pay can have a large effect on the organization's performance.

KEY TERMS

benchmarking, 349

delayering, 358

exempt employees, 345

Fair Labor Standards Act (FLSA), 344

hourly wage, 354

job evaluation, 353

job structure, 341

minimum wage, 344

nonexempt employees, 345

pay differential, 357

pay grades, 356

pay level, 341

pay policy line, 354

pay range, 356

pay structure, 341

piecework rate, 354

salary, 354

skill-based pay systems, 358

REVIEW AND DISCUSSION QUESTIONS

1. In setting up a pay structure, what legal requirements must an organization meet? Which of these do you think would be most challenging for a small start-up business? Why?

2. In gathering data for its pay policies, what product markets would a city's hospital want to use as a basis for comparison? What labor markets would be relevant? How might the labor markets for surgeons be different from the labor markets for nursing aides?

3. Why might an organization choose to pay employees more than the market rate? Why might it choose to pay less? What are the consequences of paying more or less than the market rate?

4. Suppose you work in the HR department of a manufacturing company that is planning to enrich jobs by having production workers work in teams and rotate through various jobs. The pay structure will have to be adjusted to fit this new work design. How would you expect the employees to evaluate the fairness of their pay in their redesigned jobs? In terms of equity theory, what comparisons would they be likely to make?

5. Summarize the way organizations use information about jobs as a basis for a pay structure.

6. Imagine that you manage human resources for a small business. You have recently prepared a report on the market rate of pay for salespeople, and the company's owner says the market rate is too high. The company cannot afford this level of pay, and furthermore, paying that much would cause salespeople to earn more than most of the company's managers. Suggest three possible measures the company might take to help resolve this conflict.

7. What are the advantages of establishing pay ranges, rather than specific pay levels, for each job? What are the drawbacks of this approach?

8. Suppose the company in Question 1 wants to establish a skills-based pay structure. What would be some advantages of this approach? List the issues the company should be prepared to address in setting up this system. Consider the kinds of information you will need and the ways employees may react to the new pay structure.

9. Why do some employers subsidize the pay of military reserve members called up to active duty? If the military instead paid these people the wage they command in the civilian market (that is, the salary they earn at their regular jobs), who would bear the cost? When neither the reserve members' employers nor the military pays reserve members their civilian wage, reserve members and their families bear the cost. In your opinion, who *should* bear this cost—employers, taxpayers, or service members (or someone else)?

10. Do you think U.S. companies pay their chief executives too much? Why or why not?

EXPERIENCING HR

Divide into groups of three. (Or, if your instructor directs, students may complete the research independently and then discuss their results in class.) Imagine you work for a small company near your school. It has assembled your team to research salaries for a new marketing manager. Use the following public resources to look up average earnings for that position in your area:

- Following the directions in "HR How To" (p. 350), look up data from the National Compensation Survey.
- Starting at the BLS Databases and Tools page (**www.bls.gov/data/**), scroll down the options under Pay and Benefits to find the multiscreen search for Employment and Wages from the Occupational Employment Statistics (OES) survey. Use this tool to look up earnings data.
- Visit Salary.com, and use the salary search tool.

Discuss the results you found from these three sources, and try to come up with a range of salaries to recommend for this position. Did all three sources provide the same information? What do you think would account for any differences? What assumptions did you make with each source? What additional information would you need to specify for the results to be relevant to your specific situation?

For credit on the assignment, turn in the results of your research and the salary you recommend.

TAKING RESPONSIBILITY: Harris County Housing Authority's Unsustainable Pay

Based in Houston, Texas, the Harris County Housing Authority (HCHA) is a governmental nonprofit corporation with a mission to provide affordable housing to its community. It manages housing for senior citizens, is developing housing options for veterans, and administers about 4,000 federal vouchers that poor families use to help pay their rent. Most of HCHA's funding comes from the U.S. Department of Housing and Urban Development. It also collects fees from private builders when it enters arrangements to develop mixed-income housing with them. Thus, to operate sustainably, HCHA must have a positive impact on its community, treat its employees fairly, and use its federal funding efficiently.

HCHA notes that the Department of Housing and Urban Development (HUD) has for several years running been named the highest-performing housing agency in its region. Despite this acknowledgment from the federal government, however, the agency recently came under fire for being too generous with its employees.

The *Houston Chronicle* investigated the salaries paid to HCHA executives and ran a report saying they have been paid more than executives at other housing agencies, including those in New York, Chicago, Boston, Dallas, Los Angeles County, and Cook County, Illinois (where Chicago is located). Most of those agencies administer at least three times as many vouchers and manage thousands more housing units. For salaries at HCHA to reach their high levels, they rose rapidly between 2004 and 2008.

Reacting to the outcry that followed the story, Iowa's senator Charles Grassley wrote to HUD to ask for an investigation. In his letter, Senator Grassley noted that a recently passed federal law limits the pay of housing authority employees to a pay grade of Level IV federal executive, which at the time topped out at $155,500. HCHA's chief executive, Guy Rankin, was earning $242,008, a salary the senator termed "outrageous." The agency's chief administrative officer, David Gunter, also had earnings above the new ceiling, with a salary of $220,001. Both executives had enjoyed rapid pay increases. When Rankin because CEO in 2004, he earned $99,507, and at that time, Gunter was a senior accountant earning $74,256. One reason compensation rose so fast was that employees were earning bonuses. Executives could earn bonuses as large as $84,000. Most of the agency's lower-level employees also received annual bonuses, ranging from $1,000 to more than $10,000.

The chairman of HCHA's five-member board of directors noted that HUD audits the agency's books annually and has never objected to the agency's pay scales. The agency also noted that pay levels were established after the agency conducted two salary surveys of private-sector data. According to the surveys, HCHA was paying its employees 8% to 40% below the labor market rates for their occupations. Surveys also investigated pay at other housing agencies, with the goal that HCHA would pay its own employees "slightly above" the other agencies. Sympathetic observers noted that HCHA's increasing involvement with property developers is an effective way to stretch agency dollars but requires significant financial and negotiation skills. However, Houston Representative Gene Green expressed the view that pay comparisons should have been limited to government workers. Green worried that the pay raises, coming at a time when federal employees had been doing without cost-of-living pay raises for several years, would incite budget cutting.

In an effort to improve future salary planning at local agencies, HUD has asked all the housing agencies it funds to provide it with the salaries of their five highest-paid employees. HUD plans to post job titles (without names) and associated salaries on its website. Agency boards would then have easy access to salary data, at least at the executive level. Meanwhile, the HCHA's board asked CEO Rankin to resign, and then one week later admitted that it lacked sufficient funds to pay the agreed-upon severance pay.

Questions

1. Based on the information given, what were the goals of the pay levels set for the Harris County Housing Authority? Which of those goals did it meet?
2. Evaluate the fairness of the HCHA's pay levels from the perspective of (a) an HCHA employee; (b) a HUD employee; and (c) a taxpayer.
3. Imagine you are on HCHA's board of directors, so you need to balance concern for taxpayers, the community, the agency's mission, and its employees. How would you improve the agency's pay structure?

SOURCES: Mike Morris, "Housing Agency Is Too Broke to Pay Up," *Houston Chronicle*, March 29, 2012, Business & Company Resource Center, http://galenet.galegroup.com; Mike Morris, "Housing Authority Axes CEO," *Houston Chronicle*, March 22, 2012, Business & Company Resource Center, http://galenet.galegroup.com; Mike Morris, "Housing Authority Salaries under Fire," *Houston Chronicle*, November 22, 2011, Business & Company Resource Center, http://galenet.galegroup.com; Mike Morris, "Salaries Soar at Housing Agency," *Houston Chronicle*, November 20, 2011, Business & Company Resource Center, http://galenet.galegroup.com.

MANAGING TALENT: Why Pay Is Growing Slowly at ProLawnPlus

ProLawnPlus provides lawn and tree care to homeowners in Maryland. The current owner, Mark Schlossberg, became interested in environmental issues when he started working there, and he has developed his employees' skill in building healthy lawns with minimal use of pesticides and fertilizers. Along with Schlossberg's focus on naturally healthy lawns, he emphasizes training in customer service to build long-term client relationships. When customers sign up for service, they get the cell phone numbers of Schlossberg and his managers, so they can call anytime if they have questions or concerns.

This concern for quality has helped the company weather the recent recession. In the year following the 2008 financial crisis and collapsing housing market, homeowners looked to cut costs and lawn care services were an easy target. ProLawnPlus saw its sales dip 10%. Still, half the customers were back a year later. In addition, a deal to buy accounts from another company in an adjoining region helped the company grow ahead of the economic recovery. The customer retention and growth from the acquisition enabled the company to stay afloat without major price increases. That ability is especially important for a high-quality firm such as Schlossberg's, which tends to charge near the upper end of prices in the industry.

The economic downturn and its impact on the lawn care industry provide a difficult context for making decisions about pay. Schlossberg found that when the recession was hurting sales, employees understood the situation and did not expect their pay to rise. As ProLawnPlus begins taking on more clients and sales

volume grows, employees anticipate that the improved business environment will translate into higher pay. At the same time, recent increases in fuel costs are requiring some difficult choices in managing higher expenses for both fuel and payroll. Schlossberg's initial response is to find ways to pay employees more without raising pay rates. For example, employees have begun putting in more overtime. ProLawnPlus has also offered incentive pay for meeting specific goals. Still, Schlossberg expects that within months, employees who are not already at the top of their pay range will get a raise.

Questions

1. What general policies concerning pay would best support ProLawnPlus's business strategy?
2. How can ProLawnPlus ensure that it is meeting legal requirements for its pay policies?
3. What impact should product and labor markets have on pay levels at ProLawnPlus?

SOURCES: ProLawnPlus, "About ProLawnPlus," http://www.prolawnplus .com, accessed April 12, 2012; Gregg Wartgow, "Slow but Steady," *Green Industry Pro*, March 2012, Business & Company Resource Center, http:// galenet.galegroup.com; "Falling Back," *Pro Magazine*, September 2010, Business & Company Resource Center, http://galenet.galegroup.com.

 TWITTER FOCUS: Changing the Pay Level at Eight Crossings

Using Twitter, continue the conversation about pay structure by reading the Eight Crossings case at **www .mhhe.com/noefund5e**. Engage with your classmates and instructor via Twitter to chat about pay structure

decisions at Eight Crossings using the case questions posted on the Noe website. Don't have a Twitter account yet? See the instructions for getting started on the Online Learning Center.

NOTES

1. James R. Hagerty, "Young Adults See Their Pay Decline," *The Wall Street Journal*, March 6, 2012, http://online.wsj.com; Bonnie Easton, "Career Reality Check," *Library Journal*, January 2012, EBSCOhost, http://web.ebscohost.com; Market-Tools, "According to a New MarketTools Study, Only One-Third of U.S. Employees 'Very Satisfied' with Their Jobs," *PR Newswire*, March 2, 2011, http://www.prnewswire.com.
2. U.S. Census Bureau, American FactFinder, "Geographic Area Series: Economywide Key Statistics, 2007," 2007 Economic Census, release date April 13, 2010, http://factfinder.census.gov.
3. Bureau of Labor Statistics, "Usual Weekly Earnings of Wage and Salary Workers, Fourth Quarter 2011," news release, January 24, 2012, http://www.bls.gov.
4. B. Gerhart, "Gender Differences in Current and Starting Salaries: The Role of Performance, College Major, and Job Title," *Industrial and Labor Relations Review* 43 (1990), pp. 418–33; G. G. Cain, "The Economic Analysis of Labor Market Discrimination: A Survey," in *Handbook of Labor Economics*, eds. O. Ashenfelter and R. Layard (New York: North-Holland, 1986), pp. 694–785; and F. D. Blau and L. M. Kahn, "The Gender Pay Gap: Have Women Gone as Far as They Can?" *Academy of Management Perspectives*, February 2007, pp. 7–23.
5. C. Kulich, G. Trojanowski, M. K. Ryan, S. A. Haslam, and L. R. R. Renneboog, "Who Gets the Carrot and Who Gets the Stick? Evidence of Gender Disparities in Executive Remuneration," *Strategic Management Journal* 32 (2011): 301–321; F. Muñoz-Bullón,

"Gender-Level Differences among High-Level Executives," *Industrial Relations* 49 (2010): 346–70.

6. S. L. Rynes and G. T. Milkovich, "Wage Surveys: Dispelling Some Myths about the 'Market Wage,'" *Personnel Psychology* 39 (1986), pp. 71–90; and G. T. Milkovich, J. M. Newman, and B. Gerhart, *Compensation*, 10th ed. (New York: McGraw-Hill/Irwin, 2010).

7. U.S. Department of Labor, *eLaws: FLSA Overtime Security Advisor*, http://www.dol.gov/elaws/overtime.htm, accessed April 11, 2012.

8. U.S. Department of Labor (DOL), "Youth and Labor: Hazardous Jobs," http://www.dol.gov, accessed April 11, 2012; DOL, "When and How Many Hours Can Youth Work?" *eLaws: Fair Labor Standards Act Advisor*, http://www.dol.gov/elaws/faq/esa/flsa/toc.htm, accessed April 11, 2012; DOL, "What Jobs Can Youth Do?" *Youth Rules!*, http://youthrules.dol.gov, accessed April 11, 2012.

9. Mike Ramsey, "VW Chops Labor Costs in U.S.," *The Wall Street Journal*, May 23, 2011, http://online.wsj.com; Bill Poovey, "Volkswagen's New Passat Makes Hometown Debut," *Yahoo Finance*, January 13, 2011, http://finance.yahoo.com.

10. B. Gerhart and G. T. Milkovich, "Organizational Differences in Managerial Compensation and Financial Performance," *Academy of Management Journal* 33 (1990), pp. 663–91; and E. L. Groshen, "Why Do Wages Vary among Employers?" *Economic Review* 24 (1988), pp. 19–38.

11. Nathan Eddy, "IT Management: Google, Intel, Microsoft among Top-Paying IT Firms," *eWeek*, June 9, 2011, http://www.eweek.com.

12. G. A. Akerlof, "Gift Exchange and Efficiency-Wage Theory: Four Views," *American Economic Review* 74 (1984), pp. 79–83; and J. L. Yellen, "Efficiency Wage Models of Unemployment," *American Economic Review* 74 (1984), pp. 200–5.

13. IOMA, "Salary Data Sources Critical to Compensation Planning," *Report on Salary Surveys*, January 2012, pp. 11–13.

14. J. S. Adams, "Inequity in Social Exchange," in *Advances in Experimental Social Psychology*, ed. L. Berkowitz (New York: Academic Press, 1965); P. S. Goodman, "An Examination of Referents Used in the Evaluation of Pay," *Organizational Behavior and Human Performance* 12 (1974), pp. 170–95; C. O. Trevor and D. L. Wazeter, "A Contingent View of Reactions to Objective Pay Conditions: Interdependence among Pay Structure Characteristics and Pay Relative to Internal and External Referents," *Journal of Applied Psychology* 91 (2006): 1260–75; M. M. Harris, F. Anseel, and F. Lievens, "Keeping Up with the Joneses: A Field Study of the Relationships among Upward,

Lateral, and Downward Comparisons and Pay Level Satisfaction," *Journal of Applied Psychology* 93, no. 3 (May 2008), pp. 665–73; and Gordon D. A. Brown, Jonathan Gardner, Andrew J. Oswald, and Jing Qian, "Does Wage Rank Affect Employees' Well-Being?" *Industrial Relations* 47, no. 3 (July 2008), p. 355.

15. P. Capelli and P. D. Sherer, "Assessing Worker Attitudes under a Two-Tier Wage Plan," *Industrial and Labor Relations Review* 43 (1990), pp. 225–44.

16. Louis Uchitelle, "Factory Jobs Gain, but Wages Retreat," *The New York Times*, December 30, 2011, Business & Company Resource Center, http://galenet.galegroup.com; Dan Casey, "Labor of Love for City, America," *Roanoke (VA) Times*, February 26, 2012, http://www.roanoke.com.

17. J. P. Pfeffer and A. Davis-Blake, "Understanding Organizational Wage Structures: A Resource Dependence Approach," *Academy of Management Journal* 30 (1987), pp. 437–55.

18. Culpepper, "Geographic Pay Differentials: Practices in Managing Pay between Locations," *Culpepper eBulletin*, March 2011, http://www.culpepper.com.

19. This section draws freely on B. Gerhart and R. D. Bretz, "Employee Compensation," in *Organization and Management of Advanced Manufacturing*, eds. W. Karwowski and G. Salvendy (New York: Wiley, 1994), pp. 81–101.

20. E. E. Lawler III, *Strategic Pay* (San Francisco: Jossey-Bass, 1990); G. E. Ledford, "Paying for the Skills, Knowledge, Competencies of Knowledge Workers," *Compensation and Benefits Review*, July–August 1995, p. 55; G. Ledford, "Factors Affecting the Long-Term Success of Skill-Based Pay," *WorldatWork Journal*, First Quarter 2008, pp. 6–18; and E. C. Dierdorff and E. A. Surface, "If You Pay for Skills, Will They Learn? Skill Change and Maintenance under a Skill-Based Pay System," *Journal of Management* 34 (2008), pp. 721–43.

21. B. C. Murray and B. Gerhart, "An Empirical Analysis of a Skill-Based Pay Program and Plant Performance Outcomes," *Academy of Management Journal* 41, no. 1 (1998), pp. 68–78.

22. Ibid.; N. Gupta, D. Jenkins, and W. Curington, "Paying for Knowledge: Myths and Realities," *National Productivity Review*, Spring 1986, pp. 107–23; and J. D. Shaw, N. Gupta, A. Mitra, and G. E. Ledford, "Success and Survival of Skill-Based Pay Plans," *Journal of Management* 31 (2005), pp. 28–49.

23. Sears Holdings Corporation, "Sears Holdings Increases Commitment to Providing Jobs and Support to Military Personnel," *PR Newswire*, December 1, 2011, http://www.prnewswire.com; Sears Holdings, "Community Relations: Military

Support," http://www.searsholdings.com, accessed April 12, 2012.

24. Scott Thurm, "For CEOs, Pay Lags behind Results," *The Wall Street Journal*, March 26, 2012, http://online.wsj.com; Zoran Basich, "As Bonus Bonanza Recedes, CEOs Expect Pay to Decline in 2012," *The Wall Street Journal*, April 10, 2012, http://blogs.wsj.com; "Media Wrong about CEO Compensation," *Chief Executive*, September 19, 2011, http://chiefexecutive.net.

25. Josh Bivens, "CEOs Distance Themselves from the Average Worker," *Economic Snapshot*, November 9, 2011, http://www.epi.org; Jeremy Hobson, "New Rule Could Disclose CEO-to-Employee Pay Ratio," *Marketplace Morning Report*, December 14, 2011, http://www.marketplace.org (interview with David Brancaccio); "Bosses under Fire," *The Economist*, January 14, 2012, http://www.economist.com.

26. Scott DeCarlo, "America's Highest Paid CEOs," *Forbes*, April 4, 2012, http://www.forbes.com; Natasha Singer, "In Executive Pay, a Rich Game of Thrones," *The New York Times*, April 7, 2012, http://www.nytimes.com; Evan Nin, "Does It Pay to Be Amazon.com's CEO?" *Daily Finance*, April 17, 2012, http://www.dailyfinance.com; Whole Foods Market, "Values in Action," http://www.wholefoodsmarket.com, accessed April 17, 2012.

27. D. M. Cowherd and D. I. Levine, "Product Quality and Pay Equity between Lower-Level Employees and Top Management: An Investigation of Distributive Justice Theory," *Administrative Science Quarterly* 37 (1992), pp. 302–20.

12

Recognizing Employee Contributions with Pay

What Do I Need to Know?

After reading this chapter, you should be able to:

LO 12-1 Discuss the connection between incentive pay and employee performance.

LO 12-2 Describe how organizations recognize individual performance.

LO 12-3 Identify ways to recognize group performance.

LO 12-4 Explain how organizations link pay to their overall performance.

LO 12-5 Describe how organizations combine incentive plans in a "balanced scorecard."

LO 12-6 Summarize processes that can contribute to the success of incentive programs.

LO 12-7 Discuss issues related to performance-based pay for executives.

Introduction

In Massachusetts, two hospitals affiliated with Harvard University faced a challenge that has been common in the U.S. health care system: it is difficult to find enough primary-care physicians to fill the need for this type of medical care. The problem is expected to intensify as aging baby boomers need more health services and if government efforts at health care reform expand the pool of patients with health insurance. So the hospitals—Massachusetts General Hospital (MGH) and Brigham and Women's Hospital—looked for a solution in the way they pay the physicians on their staffs. The hospitals are paying the doctors extra to take on more patients. Along with the basic salary, the hospitals will pay each doctor 10% more based on the size of his or her practice (that is, the number of patients of that physician).[1]

At MGH and at Brigham and Women's, doctors not only are paid a basic salary, as described in the previous chapter, but also are rewarded according to the volume of work they take on. In this chapter we focus on using pay to recognize and reward employees' contributions to the organization's success. Employees' pay does not depend solely on the jobs they hold. Instead, organizations vary the amount paid according to differences in performance of the individual, group, or whole organization, as well as differences in employee qualities such as seniority and skills.[2]

In contrast to decisions about pay structure, organizations have wide discretion in setting performance-related pay, called **incentive pay.** Organizations can tie incentive pay to individual performance, profits, or many other measures of success. They select incentives based on their costs, expected influence on performance, and fit with the organization's broader HR and company policies and goals. These decisions are significant. A study of 150 organizations found that the way organizations paid employees was strongly associated with their level of profitability.[3]

This chapter explores the choices available to organizations with regard to incentive pay. First, the chapter describes the link between pay and employee performance. Next, we discuss ways organizations provide a variety of pay incentives to individuals. The following two sections describe pay related to group and organizational performance. We then explore the organization's processes that can support the use of incentive pay. Finally, we discuss incentive pay for the organization's executives.

Incentive Pay

> **Incentive Pay**
> Forms of pay linked to an employee's performance as an individual, group member, or organization member.

> **LO 12-1** Discuss the connection between incentive pay and employee performance.

Along with wages and salaries, many organizations offer *incentive pay*—that is, pay specifically designed to energize, direct, or control employees' behavior. Incentive pay is influential because the amount paid is linked to certain predefined behaviors or outcomes. For example, as we will see in this chapter, an organization can pay a salesperson a *commission* for closing a sale, or the members of a production department can earn a *bonus* for meeting a monthly production goal. Usually, these payments are in addition to wages and salaries. Knowing they can earn extra money for closing sales or meeting departmental goals, the employees often try harder or get more creative than they might without the incentive pay. In addition, the policy of offering higher pay for higher performance may make an organization attractive to high performers when it is trying to recruit and retain these valuable employees.[4] For reasons such as these, the share of companies offering variable pay rose from 78% of employers in 2005 to 92% in 2011.[5]

For incentive pay to motivate employees to contribute to the organization's success, the pay plans must be well designed. In particular, effective plans meet the following requirements:

- Performance measures are linked to the organization's goals.
- Employees believe they can meet performance standards.
- The organization gives employees the resources they need to meet their goals.
- Employees value the rewards given.
- Employees believe the reward system is fair.
- The pay plan takes into account that employees may ignore any goals that are not rewarded.

The "HR How To" box provides some additional ideas for creating and implementing an effective incentive-pay plan that is aligned with a company's strategy.

Since incentive pay is linked to particular outcomes or behaviors, the organization is encouraging employees to demonstrate those chosen outcomes and behaviors. As obvious as that may sound, the implications are more complicated. If incentive pay is extremely rewarding, employees may focus on only the performance measures rewarded under the plan and ignore measures that are not rewarded. Suppose an organization pays managers a bonus when employees are satisfied; this policy may interfere with other management goals. A manager who doesn't quite know how to inspire employees to do their best might be tempted to fall back on overly positive performance

HR How To

Aligning Incentive Programs with Company Strategy

Here are some measures organizations can take to can enhance the link between incentive pay and the organization's strategy:

- Identify the top performers who contribute to the organization's success. That requires knowing what kinds of accomplishments actually translate into sustainable profitability, as well as measuring who is responsible for those achievements. These people need to know that incentive pay is available and know what they must accomplish to earn it.
- Customize incentive plans rather than copy the competition. Salary surveys provide important baseline data, but incentive pay should reflect the company's own values, performance criteria, and employee characteristics.
- When the organization has a set budget to use for performance-related pay, consider all the measures of past and future performance that are relevant for allocating the budget. For

example, an organization could direct pay increases to people who have specific skills it will need in the future or who have skills and attitudes that suggest they may contribute a great deal to the organization over the long term. In other situations, a history of consistently meeting goals, such as sales targets, may be most relevant to the company's success.
- Acknowledge that when incentives are linked to performance, low performers will not receive the incentives. It can feel uncomfortable to tell employees that they will not get a raise or their team will not get a bonus this quarter. However, assuming the organization provides employees with the training and resources they need to meet performance targets, the consequences of failure can either spur employees to try harder or create an environment where unmotivated employees leave and make room for motivated ones.

- Recognize the limits of pay as a reward. If the company already compensates its most valuable employees at above-market rates, then that employee, at least in theory, is not likely to leave for a higher-paying job (the labor market is actually paying less). In that situation, more money will not likely improve employee retention; the company should look for other ways to show the employee that he or she is appreciated. The employee might appreciate more time off, a more flexible schedule, or a chance to mentor others.

SOURCES: Lori Wisper and Ken Abosch, "Does Merit Pay Still Have Merit in the New Economic Reality?" WorldatWork, http://www.worldatwork.org, accessed April 19, 2012; "Aligning Incentive Pay Programs with Business Goals," *Report on Salary Surveys,* February 2012, pp. 9– 10; Stephen Miller, "Pay for Performance: Make It More than a Catchphrase," *SHRM Online* Compensation Discipline, May 30, 2011, http://www.shrm.org.

appraisals, letting work slide to keep everyone happy. Similarly, many call centers pay employees based on how many calls they handle, as an incentive to work quickly and efficiently. However, speedy call handling does not necessarily foster good customer relationships. As we will see in this chapter, organizations may combine a number of incentives so employees do not focus on one measure to the exclusion of others.

Attitudes that influence the success of incentive pay include whether employees value the rewards and think the pay plan is fair. One idea for promoting a sense of fairness is to give employees a say in allocating incentives. Often, co-workers are in the best position to see individuals' performances. Four times a year, Coffee & Power, a San Francisco start-up company, gives each of its employees the authority to distribute stock options among their co-workers. Only a few restrictions apply: employees may not reward themselves or give the options to the company's founders. In one quarter, workers had 1,200 apiece to distribute. That quarter, the largest bonus was 2,530 shares, and the smallest was 855. One of the biggest rewards went to a developer who works in a remote location and devotes much of her time to helping her colleagues—someone the founders did not know well and might have neglected with a traditional reward system.[6]

Although most, if not all, employees value pay, it is important to remember that earning money is not the only reason people try to do a good job. As we discuss in other chapters (see Chapters 4, 8, and 13), people also want interesting work, appreciation for their efforts, flexibility, and a sense of belonging to the work group—not to mention the inner satisfaction of work well done. Therefore, a complete plan for motivating and compensating employees has many components, from pay to work design to developing managers so they can exercise positive leadership.

With regard to the fairness of incentive pay, the preceding chapter described equity theory, which explains how employees form judgments about the fairness of a pay structure. The same process applies to judgments about incentive pay. In general, employees compare their efforts and rewards with those of other employees, considering a plan to be fair when the rewards are distributed according to what the employees contribute.

The remainder of this chapter identifies elements of incentive pay systems. We consider each option's strengths and limitations with regard to these principles. The many kinds of incentive pay fall into three broad categories: incentives linked to individual, group, or organizational performance. Choices from these categories should consider not only their strengths and weaknesses, but also their fit with the organization's goals. The choice of incentive pay may affect not only the level of motivation but also the kinds of employees who are attracted to and stay with the organization. For example, there is some evidence that organizations with team-based rewards will tend to attract employees who are more team-oriented, while rewards tied to individual performance make an organization more attractive to those who think and act independently, as individuals.[7] Given the potential impact, organizations not only should weigh the strengths and weaknesses in selecting types of incentive pay but also should measure the results of these programs.

Pay for Individual Performance

LO 12-2 Describe how organizations recognize individual performance.

Organizations may reward individual performance with a variety of incentives:

- Piecework rates
- Standard hour plans
- Merit pay
- Individual bonuses
- Sales commissions

Piecework Rates

As an incentive to work efficiently, some organizations pay production workers a **piecework rate,** a wage based on the amount they produce. The amount paid per unit is set at a level that rewards employees for above-average production volume. For example, suppose that, on average, assemblers can finish 10 components in an hour. If the organization wants to pay its average assemblers $8 per hour, it can pay a piecework rate of $8/hour divided by 10 components/hour, or $.80 per component. An assembler who produces the average of 10 components per hour earns an amount equal to $8 per hour. An assembler who produces 12 components in an hour would earn $.80 × 12, or $9.60 each hour. This is an example of a **straight piecework plan** because the employer pays the same rate per piece no matter how much the worker produces.

Piecework Rate
A wage based on the amount workers produce.

Straight Piecework Plan
Incentive pay in which the employer pays the same rate per piece, no matter how much the worker produces.

Figure 12.1
How Incentives Sometimes "Work"

Differential Piece Rates
Incentive pay in which the piece rate is higher when a greater amount is produced.

A variation on straight piecework is **differential piece rates** (also called *rising* and *falling differentials*), in which the piece rate depends on the amount produced. If the worker produces more than the standard output, the piece rate is higher. If the worker produces at or below the standard, the amount paid per piece is lower. In the preceding example, the differential piece rate could be $1 per component for components exceeding 12 per hour and $.80 per component for up to 12 components per hour.

In one study, the use of piece rates increased production output by 30%—more than any other motivational device evaluated.[8] An obvious advantage of piece rates is the direct link between how much work the employee does and the amount the employee earns. This type of pay is easy to understand and seems fair to many people, if they think the production standard is reasonable. In spite of their advantages, piece rates are relatively rare for several reasons.[9] Most jobs, including those of managers, have no physical output, so it is hard to develop an appropriate performance measure. This type of incentive is most suited for very routine, standardized jobs with output that is easy to measure. For complex jobs or jobs with hard-to-measure outputs, piecework plans do not apply very well. Also, unless a plan is well designed to include performance standards, it may not reward employees for focusing on quality or customer satisfaction if it interferes with the day's output. In Figure 12.1, the employees quickly realize they can earn huge bonuses by writing software "bugs" and then fixing them, while writing bug-free software affords no chance to earn bonuses. More seriously, a bonus based on number of faucets produced gives production workers no incentive to stop a manufacturing line to correct a quality-control problem. Production-oriented goals may do nothing to encourage employees to learn new skills or cooperate with others. Therefore, individual incentives such as these may be a poor incentive in an organization that wants to encourage teamwork. They may not be helpful in an organization with complex jobs, employee empowerment, and team-based problem solving.

Standard Hour Plan
An incentive plan that pays workers extra for work done in less than a preset "standard time."

Standard Hour Plans

Another quantity-oriented incentive for production workers is the **standard hour plan,** an incentive plan that pays workers extra for work done in less than a preset "standard time." The organization determines a standard time to complete a task,

	COMPA-RATIO[a]		
PERFORMANCE RATING	**80%–90%**	**91%–110%**	**111%–120%**
Exceeds expectations	7%	5%	3%
Meets expectations	4%	3%	2%
Below expectations	2%	—	—

Table 12.1

Sample Merit Increase Grid: Recommended Salary Increase

[a]Compa-ratio is the employee's salary divided by the midpoint of his or her salary range.

such as tuning up a car engine. If the mechanic completes the work in less than the standard time, the mechanic receives an amount of pay equal to the wage for the full standard time. Suppose the standard time for tuning up an engine is 2 hours. If the mechanic finishes a tune-up in 1½ hours, the mechanic earns 2 hours' worth of pay in 1½ hours. Working that fast over the course of a week could add significantly to the mechanic's pay.

In terms of their pros and cons, standard hour plans are much like piecework plans. They encourage employees to work as fast as they can, but not necessarily to care about quality or customer service. Also, they only succeed if employees want the extra money more than they want to work at a pace that feels comfortable.

Merit Pay

Almost all organizations have established some program of **merit pay**—a system of linking pay increases to ratings on performance appraisals. (Chapter 8 described the content and use of performance appraisals.) To make the merit increases consistent, so they will be seen as fair, many merit pay programs use a *merit increase grid*, such as the sample in Table 12.1. As the table shows, the decisions about merit pay are based on two factors: the individual's performance rating and the individual's compa-ratio (pay relative to average pay, as defined in Chapter 11). This system gives the biggest pay increases to the best performers and to those whose pay is relatively low for their job. At the highest extreme, an exceptional employee earning 80% of the average pay for his job could receive a 7% merit raise. An employee rated as "below expectations" would receive a raise only if that employee was earning relatively low pay for the job (compa-ratio of 90% or less).

Merit Pay
A system of linking pay increases to ratings on performance appraisals.

Organizations establish and revise merit increase grids in light of changing economic conditions. When organizations revise pay ranges, employees have new compa-ratios. A higher pay range would result in lower compa-ratios, causing employees to become eligible for bigger merit increases. An advantage of merit pay is therefore that it makes the reward more valuable by relating it to economic conditions.

A drawback is that conditions can shrink the available range of increases. During recent years, budgets for merit pay increases were about 3% to 5% of pay, so average performers could receive a 4% raise, and top performers perhaps as much as 6%. The 2-percentage-point difference, after taxes and other deductions, would amount to only a few dollars a week on a salary of $40,000 per year. Over an entire career, the bigger increases for top performers can grow into a major change, but viewed on a year-by-year basis, they are not much of an incentive to excel.[10] As Figure 12.2 shows, companies typically spread merit raises fairly evenly across all employees. However, experts advise making pay increases far greater for top performers than for average employees—and not rewarding the poor performers with a raise at all.[11] Imagine if

Figure 12.2

Ratings and Raises: Underrewarding the Best

Worker Performance

SOURCE: BNA, "Mercer Report: Pay Levels Differentiate Workers," *Report on Salary Surveys,* September 2011, pp. 3–5.

the raises given to the bottom two categories in Figure 12.2 instead went toward 6% raises for the top performers. This type of decision signals that excellence is rewarded.

Another advantage of merit pay is that it provides a method for rewarding performance in all of the dimensions measured in the organization's performance management system. If that system is appropriately designed to measure all the important job behaviors, then the merit pay is linked to the behaviors the organization desires. This link seems logical, although so far there is little research showing the effectiveness of merit pay.[12]

A drawback of merit pay, from the employer's standpoint, is that it can quickly become expensive. Managers at a majority of organizations rate most employees' performance in the top two categories (out of four or five).[13] Therefore, the majority of employees are eligible for the biggest merit increases, and their pay rises rapidly. This cost is one reason that some organizations have established guidelines about the percentage of employees that may receive the top rating, as discussed in Chapter 8. Another correction might be to use 360-degree performance feedback (discussed in Chapter 9), but so far, organizations have not used multisource data for pay decisions.[14]

Another drawback of merit pay is that it makes assumptions that may be misleading. Rewarding employees for superior performance ratings assumes that those ratings depend on employees' ability and motivation. But performance may actually depend on forces outside the employee's control, such as managers' rating biases, the level of cooperation from co-workers, or the degree to which the organization gives employees the authority, training, and resources they need. Under these conditions, employees will likely conclude that the merit pay system is unfair. For an example, see the "HR Oops!" box.

Quality guru W. Edwards Deming also criticizes merit pay for discouraging teamwork. In Deming's words, "Everyone propels himself forward, or tries to, for his own good, on his own life preserver. The organization is the loser."[15] For example, if employees in the purchasing department are evaluated based on the number or cost of contracts they negotiate, they may have little interest in the quality of the materials they buy, even when the manufacturing department is having quality problems. In reaction to such problems, Deming advocated the use of group incentives. Another alternative is for merit pay to include ratings of teamwork and cooperation. Some employers ask co-workers to provide such ratings.

Where Merit Pay Has a Failing Grade

In recent years, communities looking to improve the quality of education in public schools have sought to motivate better teaching with performance-related pay. To supplement the past practice of giving teachers raises linked mainly to work experience and education levels, some districts have introduced various forms of merit pay.

Some of those efforts, however, have been a disappointment. New York City conducted an experiment in which participating teachers at "high-needs schools" were eligible to earn up to $3,000 for meeting a set of performance targets. However, at the end of three years, students' test scores, the schools' annual yearly progress, and the teachers' attitudes and instructional practices were no better at the schools selected to be eligible for bonuses than at schools not eligible. Similarly, a university-sponsored program in Nashville offered middle-school math teachers bonuses up to $15,000 if their students made exceptional progress on standardized math tests. There, too, students of the teachers who were eligible for the bonuses did not perform better than students of the teachers without the incentive. Worse, in Atlanta, bonuses paid for high test scores were blamed as an incentive for teachers and administers to cheat.

Why didn't the performance-based pay spur higher performance? One possibility is that teachers don't know how to teach more effectively or lack resources they need to use more effective teaching methods. They might need mentoring more than a pay incentive. Another possibility is that teachers are already under a lot of pressure to demonstrate adequate yearly progress on test scores, so a pay incentive is not going to further motivate them. Or perhaps people who choose a teaching career are motivated less by money and more by something else. Teachers also may not believe that their behavior is what will improve student performance the most. In the Nashville experiment with merit pay, the teachers rated themselves as effective, and they reported making no changes in their teaching methods to earn the bonus.

Recently, Chicago announced it would try merit pay to improve teaching. The Chicago school system hopes to improve on earlier efforts by directing the payments to principals and by providing them with training aimed at helping them meet the performance standards.

Questions

1. Why do you think merit pay has so far failed to lead to improvements in student performance?
2. What changes would you suggest for incentive pay for teachers and/or principals?

SOURCES: Azure Gilman, "Will Rahm Emanuel's Merit-Pay System Work Where Others Haven't?" *Freakonomics,* August 22, 2011, http://www.freakonomics.com; Rand Corporation, "What New York City's Experiment with Schoolwide Performance Bonuses Tells Us about Pay for Performance," Research Brief, 2011, http://www.rand.org; ChristopherConnell, "Merit Pay Study: Teacher Bonuses Don't Raise Student Test Scores," *USA Today,* September 21, 2010, http://www.usatoday.com.

Performance Bonuses

Like merit pay, performance bonuses reward individual performance, but bonuses are not rolled into base pay. The employee must re-earn them during each performance period. In some cases, the bonus is a one-time reward. Bonuses may also be linked to objective performance measures, rather than subjective ratings.

Bonuses for individual performance can be extremely effective and give the organization great flexibility in deciding what kinds of behavior to reward. An example is Continental Airlines, which pays employees a quarterly bonus for ranking in the top three airlines for on-time arrivals, a measure of service quality. In many cases, employees receive bonuses for meeting such routine targets as sales or production numbers. Such bonuses encourage hard work. But an organization that focuses on growth and innovation may get better results from rewarding employees for learning new skills than from linking bonuses to mastery of existing jobs. In the transportation business, companies need drivers who have learned and adhere to practices for driving safely

Fewer Companies Awarding Spot Bonuses

A decade ago, a majority of companies were paying *spot bonuses*—bonuses delivered on the spot for special recognition, to reward performance above and beyond expectations, or upon the completion of a project. More recently, the use of spot bonuses has been declining. In organizations that still award these bonuses, maximum payments to managers, supervisors, and professionals are typically in the range of $2,500 to $5,000.

Question

From the perspective of an employer, how could you determine whether the decline in use of spot bonuses makes good business sense?

SOURCES: BNA, "Survey Finds Fewer Companies Use Bonus Programs," *Report on Salary Surveys,* June 2011, pp. 9–10; WorldatWork, "WorldatWork: Employee Bonus Program Offerings Decline," news release, May 4, 2011, http://www.prweb.com; WorldatWork, "Bonus Programs and Practices," April 2011, http://www.worldatwork.org.

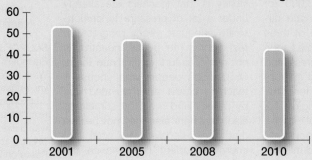

Percent of Companies with Spot Bonus Programs

and conserving fuel. Britain's Eddie Stobart trucking firm rewards drivers with a daily bonus. Each driver starts the day with 400 points, and electronics in the truck gather data on performance measures such as acceleration, braking, use of cruise control, and idling time. If they jam on the brakes or leave their vehicle idling, the system subtracts points. Drivers who end the day with at least 300 points earn a bonus of 5 pounds (equivalent to about $8).[16] Based on the success of these and other bonus programs, employers believe bonuses improve employee engagement and satisfaction, but as shown in the "Did You Know?" box, the use of bonuses has declined somewhat in recent years.

Adding to this flexibility, organizations also may motivate employees with one-time bonuses. For example, when one organization acquires another, it usually wants to retain certain valuable employees in the organization it is buying. Therefore, it is common for organizations involved in an acquisition to pay *retention bonuses*—one-time incentives paid in exchange for remaining with the company—to top managers, engineers, top-performing salespeople, and information technology specialists. When Raymond James Financial Corporation acquired Morgan Keegan & Company, it offered retention bonuses to Morgan Keegan's financial planners who generated fees of more than $300,000 per year. When the deal closed, Raymond James reported that 98% of the advisers who had been offered the bonus said they would stay with the merged firm.[17]

Sales Commissions

A variation on piece rates and bonuses is the payment of **commissions,** or pay calculated as a percentage of sales. For instance, a furniture salesperson might earn commissions equaling 6% times the price of the furniture the person sells during the period. Selling a $2,000 couch would add $120 to the salesperson's commissions for the period. Commission rates vary tremendously from one industry and company to another. Examples reported include an average rate between 5.0% and 5.5% for real estate, 15% to 20% of the annual premium for car insurance (paid to an independent insurance agent), and 22% to 30% of *profits* for auto sales.[18]

Many car salespeople earn a straight commission, meaning that 100% of their pay comes from commission instead of a salary. What type of individual might enjoy a job like this?

Some salespeople earn a commission in addition to a base salary; others earn only commissions—a pay arrangement called a *straight commission plan.* Straight commissions are common among insurance and real estate agents and car salespeople. Other salespeople earn no commissions at all, but a straight salary. Paying most or all of a salesperson's compensation in the form of salary frees the salesperson to focus on developing customer goodwill. Paying most or all of a salesperson's compensation in the form of commissions encourages the salesperson to focus on closing sales. In this way, differences in salespeople's compensation directly influence how they spend their time, how they treat customers, and how much the organization sells.

Commissions
Incentive pay calculated as a percentage of sales.

The nature of salespeople's compensation also affects the kinds of people who will want to take and keep sales jobs with the organization. Hard-driving, ambitious, risk-taking salespeople might enjoy the potential rewards of a straight commission plan. An organization that wants salespeople to concentrate on listening to customers and building relationships might want to attract a different kind of salesperson by offering more of the pay in the form of a salary. Basing part or all of a salesperson's pay on commissions assumes that the organization wants to attract people with some willingness to take risks—probably a reasonable assumption about people whose job includes talking to strangers and encouraging them to spend money.

Pay for Group Performance

Employers may address the drawbacks of individual incentives by including group incentives in the organization's compensation plan. To win group incentives, employees must cooperate and share knowledge so that the entire group can meet its performance targets. Common group incentives include gainsharing, bonuses, and team awards.

LO 12-3 Identify ways to recognize group performance.

Gainsharing

Organizations that want employees to focus on efficiency may adopt a **gainsharing** program, which measures increases in productivity and effectiveness and distributes a portion of each gain to employees. For example, if a factory enjoys a productivity gain worth $30,000, half the gain might be the company's share. The other $15,000 would be distributed among the employees in the factory. Knowing that they can enjoy a financial benefit from helping the company be more productive, employees supposedly will look for ways to work more efficiently and improve the way the factory operates.

Gainsharing
Group incentive program that measures improvements in productivity and effectiveness and distributes a portion of each gain to employees.

Gainsharing addresses the challenge of identifying appropriate performance measures for complex jobs. For example, how would a hospital measure the production of its nurses—in terms of satisfying patients, keeping costs down, or completing a number of tasks? Each of these measures oversimplifies the complex responsibilities involved in nursing care. Even for simpler jobs, setting acceptable standards and measuring performance can be complicated. Gainsharing frees employees to determine how to improve their own and their group's performance. It also broadens employees' focus beyond their individual interests. But in contrast to profit sharing, discussed later, it keeps the performance measures within a range of activity that most employees believe they can influence. Organizations can enhance the likelihood of a gain by providing a means for employees to share knowledge and make suggestions, as we will discuss in the last section of this chapter.

Gainsharing is most likely to succeed when organizations provide the right conditions. Among the conditions identified, the following are among the most common:[19]

- Management commitment.
- Need for change or strong commitment to continuous improvement.
- Management acceptance and encouragement of employee input.
- High levels of cooperation and interaction.
- Employment security.
- Information sharing on productivity and costs.
- Goal setting.
- Commitment of all involved parties to the process of change and improvement.
- Performance standard and calculation that employees understand and consider fair and that is closely related to managerial objectives.
- Employees who value working in groups.

Scanlon Plan

A gainsharing program in which employees receive a bonus if the ratio of labor costs to the sales value of production is below a set standard.

A popular form of gainsharing is the **Scanlon plan,** developed in the 1930s by Joseph N. Scanlon, president of a union local at Empire Steel and Tin Plant in Mansfield, Ohio. The Scanlon plan gives employees a bonus if the ratio of labor costs to the sales value of production is below a set standard. To keep this ratio low enough to earn the bonus, workers have to keep labor costs to a minimum and produce as much as possible with that amount of labor. Figure 12.3 provides an example. In this example, the standard is a ratio of 20/100, or 20% and the workers produced parts worth $1.2 million. To meet the standard, the labor costs should be less than 20% of $1.2 million, or $240,000. Since the actual labor costs were $210,000, the workers will get a gainsharing bonus based on the $30,000 difference between the $240,000 target and the actual cost.

Figure 12.3

Finding the Gain in a Scanlon Plan

$$\text{Target Ratio:} \quad \frac{\text{Labor Costs}}{\text{Sales Value of Production}} = \frac{20}{100}$$

Sales Value of Production: $1,200,000

Goal: $\frac{20}{100} \times \$1,200,000 = \$240,000$

Actual: $210,000

Gain: $240,000 − $210,000 = $30,000

SOURCE: Example adapted from B. Graham-Moore and Timothy L. Ross, *Gainsharing: Plans for Improving Performance* (Washington, DC: Bureau of National Affairs, 1990), p. 57.

Typically, an organization does not pay workers all of the gain immediately. First, the organization keeps a share of the gain to improve its own bottom line. A portion of the remainder goes into a reserve account. This account offsets losses in any months when the gain is negative (that is, when costs rise or production falls). At the end of the year, the organization closes out the account and distributes any remaining surplus. If there were a loss at the end of the year, the organization would absorb it.

Group Bonuses and Team Awards

In contrast to gainsharing plans, which typically reward the performance of all employees at a facility, bonuses for group performance tend to be for smaller work groups.[20] These bonuses reward the members of a group for attaining a specific goal, usually measured in terms of physical output. Team awards are similar to group bonuses, but they are more likely to use a broad range of performance measures, such as cost savings, successful completion of a project, or even meeting deadlines.

Both types of incentives have the advantage that they encourage group or team members to cooperate so that they can achieve their goal. However, depending on the reward system, competition among individuals may be replaced by competition among groups. Competition may be healthy in some situations, as when groups try to outdo one another in satisfying customers. On the downside, competition may also prevent necessary cooperation among groups. To avoid this, the organization should carefully set the performance goals for these incentives so that concern for costs or sales does not obscure other objectives, such as quality, customer service, and ethical behavior.

Group members that meet a sales goal or a product development team that meets a deadline or successfully launches a product may be rewarded with a bonus for group performance. What are some advantages and disadvantages of group bonuses?

Pay for Organizational Performance

LO 12-4 Explain how organizations link pay to their overall performance.

Two important ways organizations measure their performance are in terms of their profits and their stock price. In a competitive marketplace, profits result when an organization is efficiently providing products that customers want at a price they are willing to pay. Stock is the owners' investment in a corporation; when the stock price is rising, the value of that investment is growing. Rather than trying to figure out what performance measures will motivate employees to do the things that generate high profits and a rising stock price, many organizations offer incentive pay tied to those organizational performance measures. The expectation is that employees will focus on what is best for the organization.

These organization-level incentives can motivate employees to align their activities with the organization's goals. At the same time, linking incentives to the organization's profits or stock price exposes employees to a high degree of risk. Profits and stock price can soar very high very fast, but they can also fall. The result is a great deal of uncertainty about the amount of incentive pay each employee will receive in each period. Therefore, these kinds of incentive pay are likely to be most effective in organizations that emphasize growth and innovation, which tend to need employees who thrive in a risk-taking environment.[21]

Profit Sharing

Under **profit sharing,** payments are a percentage of the organization's profits and do not become part of the employees' base salary. For example, General Motors provides for profit sharing in its contract with its workers' union, the United Auto Workers. Depending on how large GM's profits are in relation to its total sales for the year, at least 6% of the company's profits are divided among the workers according to how many hours they worked during the year.[22] The formula for computing and dividing the profit-sharing bonus is included in the union contract.

Profit Sharing
Incentive pay in which payments are a percentage of the organization's profits and do not become part of the employees' base salary.

Organizations use profit sharing for a number of reasons. It may encourage employees to think more like owners, taking a broad view of what they need to do in order to make the organization more effective. They are more likely to cooperate and less likely to focus on narrow self-interests. Also, profit sharing has the practical advantage of costing less when the organization is experiencing financial difficulties. If the organization has little or no profit, this incentive pay is small or nonexistent, so employers may not need to rely as much on layoffs to reduce costs.[23]

Does profit sharing help organizations perform better? The evidence is not yet clear. Although research supports a link between profit-sharing payments and profits, researchers have questioned which of these causes the other.[24] For example, Ford, Chrysler, and GM have similar profit-sharing plans in their contracts with the United Auto Workers, but the payouts are not always similar. In one year, the average worker received $4,000 from Ford, $550 from GM, and $8,000 from Chrysler. Since the plans are similar, something other than the profit sharing must have made Ford and Chrysler more profitable than GM.

Differences in payouts, as in the preceding example, raise questions not only about the effectiveness of the plans, but about equity. Assuming workers at Ford, Chrysler, and GM have similar jobs, they would expect to receive similar profit-sharing checks. In the year of this example, GM workers might have seen their incentive pay as highly inequitable unless GM could show how Chrysler workers did more to earn their big checks. Employees also may feel that small profit-sharing checks are unfair because they have little control over profits. If profit sharing is offered to all employees but most employees think only management decisions about products, price, and marketing have much impact on profits, they will conclude that there is little connection between their actions and their rewards. In that case, profit-sharing plans will have little impact on employee behavior. This problem is even greater when employees have to wait months before profits are distributed. The time lag between high-performance behavior and financial rewards is simply too long to be motivating.

Adequate communication is essential for addressing issues related to equity, especially since profits can shrivel for reasons beyond employees' control. At CEA Technologies, a Colorado maker of medical devices, employees understand their profit-sharing amounts because the company also educates them in the finances behind the business. At monthly meetings, employees are given all the data on revenues and spending (except individuals' salaries) and shown how these numbers contribute to the company's profits before taxes. Every three months, if the company meets performance goals for the quarter, employees receive a profit-sharing payment. Because of the monthly meetings, the quarterly payments—or lack of payments—do not come as a surprise, and employees know the reasons.[25]

Given the limitations of profit-sharing plans, one strategy is to use them as a component of a pay system that includes other kinds of pay more directly linked to individual behavior. This increases employees' commitment to organizational goals while addressing concerns about fairness.

Stock Ownership

While profit-sharing plans are intended to encourage employees to "think like owners," a stock ownership plan actually makes employees part owners of the organization. Like profit sharing, employee ownership is intended as a way to encourage employees to focus on the success of the organization as a whole. The drawbacks of stock ownership as a form of incentive pay are similar to those of profit sharing. Specifically, it may not have a strong effect on individuals' motivation. Employees may not see a strong link between their actions and the company's stock price, especially in larger organizations. The link between pay and performance is even harder

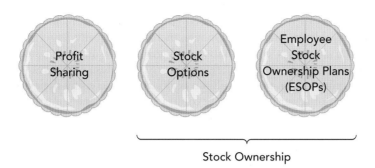

Figure 12.4
Types of Pay for
Organizational
Performance

to appreciate because the financial benefits mostly come when the stock is sold—
typically when the employee leaves the organization.

Ownership programs usually take the form of *stock options* or *employee stock ownership
plans*. These are illustrated in Figure 12.4.

Stock Options One way to distribute stock to employees is to grant them **stock
options**—the right to buy a certain number of shares of stock at a specified price.
(Purchasing the stock is called *exercising* the option.) Suppose that in 2010 a company's
employees received options to purchase the company's stock at $10 per share. The
employees will benefit if the stock price rises above $10 per share because they can pay
$10 for something (a share of stock) that is worth more than $10. If in 2015 the stock
is worth $30, they can exercise their options and buy stock for $10 a share. If they want
to, they can sell their stock for the market price of $30, receiving a gain of $20 for each
share of stock. Of course, stock prices can also fall. If the 2015 stock price is only $8,
the employees would not bother to exercise the options.

Traditionally, organizations have granted stock options to their executives. During
the 1990s, many organizations pushed eligibility for options further down in the organization's structure. Walmart and PepsiCo are among the large companies that have
granted stock options to employees at all levels. Stock values were rising so fast during
the 1990s that options were extremely rewarding for a time.

Some studies suggest that organizations perform better when a large percentage of
top and middle managers are eligible for long-term incentives such as stock options.
This evidence is consistent with the idea of encouraging employees to think like owners.[26] It is not clear whether these findings would hold up for lower-level employees.
They may see much less opportunity to influence the company's performance in the
stock market.

Recent scandals have drawn attention to another challenge of using stock options
as incentive pay. As with other performance measures, employees may focus so much
on stock price that they lose sight of other goals, including ethical behavior. Ideally,
managers would bring about an increase in stock price by adding value in terms of
efficiency, innovation, and customer satisfaction. But there are other, unethical ways to
increase stock price by tricking investors into thinking the organization is more valuable and more profitable than it actually is. Hiding losses and inflating the recorded
value of revenues are just two of the ways some companies have boosted stock prices,
enriching managers until these misdeeds come to light. Several years ago, when stock
prices tended to be high, some companies "backdated" options, meaning they changed
the date or price in the option agreement so that the option holder could buy shares at
a bargain price (this practice may be illegal if done secretly). More recently, after the

Stock Options
Rights to buy a certain
number of shares of
stock at a specified
price.

financial market collapsed in 2008, several large corporations, including Ford, General Electric, Goldman Sachs, and Google, included unusually large grants of stock options in their executives' compensation packages. Following a crash, stock prices are almost certain to rise. Sure enough, several years later, these executives were looking at the opportunity to earn tens of millions of dollars by exercising their options. Critics say this kind of reward has nothing to do with their actual contribution to their organizations.[27]

Employee Stock Ownership Plans   While stock options are most often used with top management, a broader arrangement is the **employee stock ownership plan (ESOP).** In an ESOP, the organization distributes shares of stock to its employees by placing the stock into a trust managed on the employees' behalf. Employees receive regular reports on the value of their stock, and when they leave the organization, they may sell the stock to the organization or (if it is a publicly traded company) on the open market.

Employee Stock Ownership Plan (ESOP)
An arrangement in which the organization distributes shares of stock to all its employees by placing it in a trust.

ESOPs are the most common form of employee ownership, with the number of employees in such plans increasing from over 3 million in 1980 to more than 10 million in the past few years in the United States.[28] Figure 12.5 shows the growth in the number of ESOPs in the United States. One reason for ESOPs' popularity is that earnings of the trust holdings are exempt from income taxes.

ESOPs raise a number of issues. On the negative side, they carry a significant risk for employees. By law, an ESOP must invest at least 51% of its assets in the company's own stock (in contrast to other kinds of stock funds that hold a wide diversity of companies). Problems with the company's performance therefore can take away significant value from the ESOP. Many companies set up ESOPs to hold retirement funds, so these risks directly affect employees' retirement income. Adding to the risk, funds in an ESOP are not guaranteed by the Pension Benefit Guarantee Corporation (described in Chapter 13). Sometimes employees use an ESOP to buy their company when it is experiencing financial problems; this is a highly risky investment.

Still, ESOPs can be attractive to employers. Along with tax and financing advantages, ESOPs give employers a way to build pride in and commitment to the

Figure 12.5
Number of Companies with ESOPs

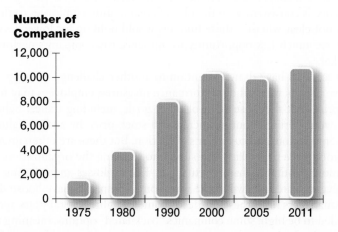

SOURCE: National Center for Employee Ownership, "A Statistical Profile of Employee Ownership," NCEO website, updated February 2012, www.nceo.org.

Employee Ownership Promotes Efficiency at Rable Machine

Rable Machine, a machine shop located in Mansfield, Ohio, has been employee owned since 1992. The rapidly growing company, which specializes in custom work, has seen its value of sales per employee grow an impressive 50% over the past few years. How do Rable's people manage to turn out more and more value? The answer, according to CEO Scott Carter, lies not so much in the millions of dollars of new equipment as it does in the commitment of its employee-owners.

All of Rable's 72 employees own stock in the company through its employee stock ownership plan. The company introduced the ESOP when its owner Rick Rupp was ready to retire but had no buyer in mind. So Rupp consulted with the Ohio Employee Ownership Center and created an ESOP to be his successor.

To support the sense of empowerment that can result from an ESOP, Rable organized an employee participation group. The EPG includes employee representatives from each department and shift. It develops ideas for projects and procedures and plays a role in establishing company policies. Ultimately, managers at Rable make strategy and policy decisions, but employees appreciate having an advisory role. Continuing the employee involvement informally, management also has a policy that whenever the company is considering the purchase of new equipment, it first consults with the employees who would use the equipment. Because employees enjoy rewards for improving efficiency, they are open-minded about ways that automated equipment can improve performance.

The ESOP is only one of Rable's incentives for group performance. Employees also participate in a gainsharing plan that pays bonuses for meeting objectives tied to manufacturing costs. Employees who submit successful ideas for cost reduction also may earn cash awards. A profit-sharing program pays an annual bonus. And as the company's stock value rises, there are annual distributions of additional company stock.

SOURCES: Rable Machine, "About Us," http://www.rablemachineinc.com, accessed April 19, 2012; Derek Korn, "The Employee-Owned Advantage," *Modern Machine Shop*, January 2011, EBSCOhost, http://web.ebscohost.com; Derek Korn, "Is an ESOP Your Answer?" *Modern Machine Shop*, January 2011, EBSCOhost, http://web.ebscohost.com.

organization. Employees have a right to participate in votes by shareholders (if the stock is registered on a national exchange, such as the New York Stock Exchange).[29] This means employees participate somewhat in corporate-level decision making. Still, the overall level of participation in decisions appears to vary significantly among organizations with ESOPs. Some research suggests that the benefits of ESOPs are greatest when employee participation is greatest.[30] The "Best Practices" box describes how an employee participation group reinforces the value of ESOPs at an Ohio machine shop.

Balanced Scorecard

As the preceding descriptions indicate, any form of incentive pay has advantages and disadvantages. For example, relying exclusively on merit pay or other individual incentives may produce a workforce that cares greatly about meeting those objectives but competes to achieve them at the expense of cooperating to achieve organizational goals. Relying heavily on profit sharing or stock ownership may increase cooperation but do little to motivate day-to-day effort or to attract and retain top individual performers. Because of this, many organizations design a mix of pay programs. The aim is to balance the disadvantages of one type of incentive pay with the advantages of another type.

LO 12-5 Describe how organizations combine incentive plans in a "balanced scorecard."

Tellabs is one company that uses a balanced scorecard. The company conducts quarterly meetings at which employees learn how their performance will be evaluated according to the scorecard. The company also makes this information available on its intranet.

SOURCE: Reprinted with permission of Tellabs.

Balanced Scorecard
A combination of performance measures directed toward the company's long- and short-term goals and used as the basis for awarding incentive pay.

One way of accomplishing this goal is to design a **balanced scorecard**—a combination of performance measures directed toward the company's long- and short-term goals and used as the basis for awarding incentive pay. A corporation would have financial goals to satisfy its stockholders (owners), quality- and price-related goals to satisfy its customers, efficiency goals to ensure better operations, and goals related to acquiring skills and knowledge for the future to fully tap into employees' potential. Different jobs would contribute to those goals in different ways. For example, an engineer could develop products that better meet customer needs and can be produced more efficiently. The engineer could also develop knowledge of new technologies in order to contribute more to the organization in the future. A salesperson's goals would include measures related to sales volume, customer service, and learning about product markets and customer needs. Organizations customize their balanced scorecards according to their markets, products, and objectives. The scorecards of a company that is emphasizing low costs and prices would be different from the scorecards of a company emphasizing innovative use of new technology. Table 12.2 shows the kinds of information that go into a balanced scorecard.

Not only does the balanced scorecard combine the advantages of different incentive-pay plans, it helps employees understand the organization's goals. By communicating the balanced scorecard to employees, the organization shows employees information about what its goals are and what it expects employees to accomplish. At ConocoPhillips, top executives have a scorecard that includes costs, health and safety, production, and resource replacement. In addition, the energy company has developed scorecards for operations-level activities such as safety measures. At Johnson & Johnson, bonuses are adjusted for performance on a variety of measures. J&J recently lowered management bonuses after it met targets for controlling costs but failed to meet goals for growth and maintaining the company's reputation.[31] In Table 12.2, the organization indicates not only that the manager should meet the four performance objectives but also that it is especially concerned with the financial target because half the incentive is based on this one target.

Table 12.2

Sample Balanced Scorecard for an Electric Cooperative

PERFORMANCE CATEGORY	CRITICAL SUCCESS FACTORS	GOALS		
		BASE (2%)	TARGET (3%)	STRETCH (5%)
Member service (40% of incentive pay)	Reliability (average interruption duration)	140 min.	130 min.	120 min.
	Customer satisfaction (index from quarterly survey)	9.0	9.1	9.2
Financial performance (25% of incentive pay)	Total operating expenses (¢/kilowatt-hour)	4.03¢	3.99¢	3.95¢
	Cash flow (% of investment)	75%	80%	85%
Internal processes (20% of incentive pay)	Safety (safety index based on injury rate and severity)	4.6	3.6	2.6
Innovation and learning (15% of incentive pay)	Member value (revenue/kWh sold)	Budget	−10% state median	−13% state median
	Efficiency and effectiveness (total margins/no. employees)	$534,400	$37,200	$40,000

SOURCE: Adapted from Tim Sullivan and Henry Cano, "Introducing a Balanced Scorecard for Electric Cooperatives: A Tool for Measuring and Improving Results," *Management Quarterly,* Winter 2009, Business & Company Resource Center, http://galenet.galegroup.com.

Processes That Make Incentives Work

LO 12-6 Summarize processes that can contribute to the success of incentive programs.

As we explained in Chapter 11, communication and employee participation can contribute to a belief that the organization's pay structure is fair. In the same way, the process by which the organization creates and administers incentive pay can help it use incentives to achieve the goal of motivating employees. The monetary rewards of gainsharing, for example, can substantially improve productivity,[32] but the organization can set up the process to be even more effective. In a study of an automotive parts plant, productivity rose when the gainsharing plan added employee participation in the form of monthly meetings with managers to discuss the gainsharing plan and ways to increase productivity. A related study asked employees what motivated them to participate actively in the plan (for example, by making suggestions for improvement). According to employees, other factors besides the pay itself were important—especially the ability to influence and control the way their work was done.[33]

Participation in Decisions

Employee participation in pay-related decisions can be part of a general move toward employee empowerment. If employees are involved in decisions about incentive pay plans and employees' eligibility for incentives, the process of creating and administering these plans can be more complex.[34] There is also a risk that employees will make decisions that are in their interests at the expense of the organization's interests. However, employees have hands-on knowledge about the kinds of behavior that can help the organization perform well, and they can see whether individuals are displaying that behavior.[35] Therefore, in spite of the potential risks, employee participation can contribute to the success of an incentive plan. This is especially true when monetary incentives encourage the monitoring of performance and when the organization fosters a spirit of trust and cooperation.

Communication

Along with empowerment, communicating with employees is important. It demonstrates to employees that the pay plan is fair. Also, when employees understand the requirements of the incentive pay plan, the plan is more likely to influence their behavior as desired.

It is particularly important to communicate with employees when changing the plan. Employees tend to feel concerned about changes. Pay is a frequent topic of rumors and assumptions based on incomplete information, partly because of pay's importance to employees. When making any changes, the human resource department should determine the best ways to communicate the reasons for the change. Some organizations rely heavily on videotaped messages from the chief executive officer. Other means of communication include brochures that show examples of how employees will be affected. The human resource department may also conduct small-group interviews to learn about employees' concerns, then address those concerns in the communications effort. The "HRM Social" box discusses ideas for using social media to reinforce the impact of incentive pay.

Incentive Pay for Executives

LO 12-7 Discuss issues related to performance-based pay for executives.

Because executives have a much stronger influence over the organization's performance than other employees do, incentive pay for executives warrants special attention. Assuming that incentives influence performance, decisions about incentives for executives should have a great impact on how well the executives and the organization perform. Along with overall pay levels for executives (discussed in Chapter 11), organizations need to create incentive plans for this small but important group of employees.

To encourage executives to develop a commitment to the organization's long-term success, executive compensation often combines short-term and long-term incentives. *Short-term incentives* include bonuses based on the year's profits, return on investment, or other measures related to the organization's goals. Sometimes, to gain tax advantages, the actual payment of the bonus is deferred (for example, by making it part of a retirement plan). *Long-term incentives* include stock options and stock purchase plans. The rationale for these long-term incentives is that executives will want to do what is best for the organization because that will cause the value of their stock to grow.

Each year *Bloomberg Businessweek* publishes a list of top executives who did the most for their pay (that is, their organizations performed best) and those who did the least. The performance of the latter group has prompted much of the negative attention that executive pay has received. The problem seems to be that in some organizations, the chief executive's pay is high every year, regardless of the organization's profitability or performance in the stock market. In terms of people's judgments about equity, it seems fairer if high-paid executives must show results to justify their pay levels.

A corporation's shareholders—its owners—want the corporation to encourage managers to act in the owners' best interests. They want managers to care about

Broadcasting Bonuses

The traditional approach to compensation is to keep it a confidential matter between the employer and each employee. However, in today's world of social media, some employers are finding there are many messages they want employees to spread, at least within the organization. For those messages, private, limited-access versions of social media can be an effective tool.

For example, rewards for meeting sales targets can be most effective when employees are excited about earning them. So at companies offering these incentives, it can be helpful to set up a web page similar to Facebook, open to all the salespeople and off limits to outsiders. There, the employer can post news and reminders related to the incentive, and salespeople can share comments, selling tips, and encouragement to egg one another on toward the prize.

Some sales-oriented social media include fun rewards linked to game-style features. For example, as a salesperson achieves higher and higher levels of sales, the site can award badges and titles for achieving each level. It can display these as part of the salesperson's online identity, and it can publish "leader boards" of its top performers at each level. This kind of recognition is highly motivating for many salespeople. A similar kind of recognition comes from tools such as Globoforce's Social Recognition software, which employees use to post appreciation for their co-workers' actions and accomplishments.

This approach can be motivating to employees beyond the sales force. Employers can set up pages for achieving any kind of business goal. Employees could, for example, post photos of improved work processes or creative marketing displays. Especially at an organization where employees work in different facilities, these pictures can give employees ideas to try in their own locations. This builds enthusiasm and increases the likelihood employees can earn the bonus, gainsharing, or other rewards tied to the performance improvement.

The data collection features of social media also can support incentive programs. Employers can keep track of which employees are receiving the most recognition from their colleagues or posting ideas for improvement. The organization may reward those kinds of activity as well as employees' offline contributions. If you can imagine the power of a workforce that is all fired up about sharing and commending one another's best practices, you may be envisioning the incentive plan of the near future.

SOURCES: Globoforce, "How We Do It: Recognition Solutions," http://www.globoforce.com, accessed April 19, 2012; Leo Jakobson, "Social Media Cometh," *Incentive,* October 2011, EBSCOhost, http://web.ebscohost.com; Peter Hart, "Benefits of Employee Recognition in the Workplace: Reduced Risk and Raised Revenues," *EHS Today,* February 2011, pp. 49–52.

---

the company's profits and stock price, and incentive pay can encourage this interest. One study has found that relying on such long-term incentives is associated with greater profitability.[36]

Performance Measures for Executives

The balanced-scorecard approach is useful in designing executive pay. Whirlpool, for example, has used a balanced scorecard that combines measures of whether the organization is delivering value to shareholders, customers, and employees. These measures are listed in Table 12.3. Rewarding achievement of a variety of goals in a balanced scorecard reduces the temptation to win bonuses by manipulating financial data.

Regulators and shareholders have pressured companies to do a better job of linking executive pay and performance. The Securities and Exchange Commission (SEC) has required companies to more clearly report executive compensation levels and the company's performance relative to that of competitors. These reporting requirements shine a light on situations where executives of poorly performing companies receive high pay, so companies feel more pressure to link pay to performance. The Dodd-Frank Wall Street Reform and Consumer Protection Act, passed in 2010, requires that

Warren Buffett must be doing something right. The billionaire once was ranked by *Bloomberg Businessweek* magazine as being the top executive who gave shareholders the most for their pay.

public companies report the ratio of median compensation of all its employees to the CEO's total compensation. Dodd-Frank also gives shareholders a "say on pay," meaning shareholders may vote to indicate their approval or disapproval of the company's executive pay plans.

Ethical Issues

Incentive pay for executives lays the groundwork for significant ethical issues. When an organization links pay to its stock performance, executives need the ethical backbone to be honest about their company's performance even when dishonesty or clever shading of the truth offers the tempting potential for large earnings. As scandals involving WorldCom, Enron, Global Crossing, and other companies have shown, the results can be disastrous when unethical behavior comes to light.

Among these issues is one we have already touched on in this chapter: the difficulty of setting performance measures that encourage precisely the behavior desired. In the case of incentives tied to stock performance, executives may be tempted to inflate the stock price in order to enjoy bonuses and valuable stock options. The intent is for the executive to boost stock value through efficient operations, technological innovation, effective leadership, and so on. Unfortunately, individuals at some companies determined that they could obtain faster results through accounting practices that stretched the norms in order to present the company's performance in the best light. When such practices are discovered to be misleading, stock prices plunge and the company's reputation is damaged, sometimes beyond repair.

A related issue when executive pay includes stock or stock options is insider trading. When executives are stockholders, they have a dual role as owners and managers. This places them at an advantage over others who want to invest in the company. An individual, a pension fund, or other investors have less information about the company than its managers do—for example, whether product development is proceeding on schedule, whether a financing deal is in the works, and so on. An executive who knows about these activities could therefore reap a windfall in the stock market by buying or

Table 12.3

Balanced Scorecard for Whirlpool Executives

TYPE OF VALUE CREATION	MEASURES
Shareholder value	Economic value added
	Earnings per share
	Cash flow
	Total cost productivity
Customer value	Quality
	Market share
	Customer satisfaction
Employee value	High-performance culture index
	High-performance culture deployment
	Training and development diversity

SOURCE: E. L. Gubman, *The Talent Solution* (New York: McGraw-Hill, 1998).

selling stock based on knowledge about the company's future. The SEC places strict limits on this "insider trading," but some executives have violated these limits. In the worst cases executives have sold stock, secretly knowing their company was failing, before the stock price collapsed. The losers are the employees, retirees, and other investors who hold the now-worthless stock.

As recent news stories have reminded us, linking pay to stock price can reward unethical behavior, at least in the short term and at least in the minds of a handful of executives. Yet, given the motivational power of incentive pay, organizations cannot afford to abandon incentives for their executives. These temptations are among the reasons that executive positions demand individuals who maintain the highest ethical standards.

THINKING ETHICALLY

CAN INCENTIVES PROMOTE ETHICS?

Pharmaceutical company GlaxoSmithKline (GSK) has recently been in legal hot water related to its marketing practices. In 2011, the company spent billions of dollars to settle a lawsuit in which the U.S. government charged GSK with using illegal marketing practices and defrauding the Medicaid program. The marketing allegations included claims that GSK's sales reps had been promoting certain drugs, such as Paxil and Wellbutrin, for uses that had not been approved by the Food and Drug Administration and that they had downplayed certain side effects.

GSK's top management concluded that this trouble arose not simply because sales reps violated legal requirements, but rather because the company had lost its focus on what should have been its fundamental values. To provide a clearer direction for the future, GSK defined and published four core values, stated in terms of how to put the values into practice: (1) focus on the patient; (2) be transparent about working relationships; (3) operate with integrity; and (4) respect those whom the company works with and serves.

So that its sales representatives would see a connection between their conduct and the core values, GSK revised the way it pays them. Instead of paying bonuses based on sales volume in each representative's territory, the company will use several measures for assessing eligibility for a bonus. These measures include the reps' scientific and business knowledge (including adherence to company values), the results of surveys from physicians (the reps' customers), and the sales performance of the reps' business unit as a whole. The goal is to improve the sales force so that when representatives call on doctors, they are focused more on helping the doctors improve the health of their patients and less on meeting sales quotas.

Questions

1. How could basing bonuses on an individual salesperson's sales volume promote unethical conduct?
2. How well do think the new incentive plan at GlaxoSmithKline will promote ethical conduct? Why?
3. What other ideas for incentive pay, if any, could promote ethical conduct by GSK's sales reps?

SOURCES: Jeanne Whalen, "Glaxo to Pay U.S. $3 Billion to Settle," *The Wall Street Journal,* November 4, 2011, http://online.wsj.com; Matthew Arnold, "GSK Shakes Up Sales Rep Pay Scale," *Medical Marketing & Media,* August 2011, p. 17; Matthew Arnold, "GSK Values Drive Flips Sales Rep Bonus Incentives," *Medical Marketing & Media,* March 2011, p. 8.

SUMMARY

LO 12-1 Discuss the connection between incentive pay and employee performance.

Incentive pay is pay tied to individual performance, profits, or other measures of success. Organizations select forms of incentive pay to energize, direct, or control employees' behavior.

It is influential because the amount paid is linked to predefined behaviors or outcomes. To be effective, incentive pay should encourage the kinds of behavior that are most needed, and employees must believe they have the ability to meet the performance standards. Employees must value the rewards, have the resources they need to meet the standards, and believe the pay plan is fair.

LO 12-2 Describe how organizations recognize individual performance.

Organizations may recognize individual performance through such incentives as piecework rates, standard hour plans, merit pay, sales commissions, and bonuses for meeting individual performance objectives. Piecework rates pay employees according to the amount they produce. Standard hour plans pay workers extra for work done in less than a preset "standard time." Merit pay links increases in wages or salaries to ratings on performance appraisals. Bonuses are similar to merit pay, because they are paid for meeting individual goals, but they are not rolled into base pay, and they usually are based on achieving a specific output rather than subjective performance ratings. A sales commission is incentive pay calculated as a percentage of sales closed by a salesperson.

LO 12-3 Identify ways to recognize group performance.

Common group incentives include gainsharing, bonuses, and team awards. Gainsharing programs, such as Scanlon plans, measure increases in productivity and distribute a portion of each gain to employees. Group bonuses reward the members of a group for attaining a specific goal, usually measured in terms of physical output. Team awards are more likely to use a broad range of performance measures, such as cost savings, successful completion of a project, or meeting a deadline.

LO 12-4 Explain how organizations link pay to their overall performance.

Incentives for meeting organizational objectives include profit sharing and stock ownership. Profit-sharing plans pay workers a percentage of the organization's profits; these payments do not become part of the employees' base salary. Stock ownership incentives may take the form of stock options or employee stock ownership plans. A stock option is the right to buy a certain number of shares at a specified price. The employee benefits by exercising the option at a price lower than the market price, so the employee benefits when the company's stock price rises. An employee stock ownership plan (ESOP) is an arrangement in which the organization distributes shares of its stock to employees by placing the stock in a trust managed on the employees'

behalf. When employees leave the organization, they may sell their shares of the stock.

LO 12-5 Describe how organizations combine incentive plans in a "balanced scorecard."

A balanced scorecard is a combination of performance measures directed toward the company's long- and short-term goals and used as the basis for awarding incentive pay. Typically, it includes financial goals to satisfy stockholders, quality- and price-related goals for customer satisfaction, efficiency goals for improved operations, and goals related to acquiring skills and knowledge for the future. The mix of pay programs is intended to balance the disadvantages of one type of incentive with the advantages of another type. The balanced scorecard also helps employees to understand and care about the organization's goals.

LO 12-6 Summarize processes that can contribute to the success of incentive programs.

Communication and participation in decisions can contribute to employees' feeling that the organization's incentive pay plans are fair. Employee participation in pay-related decisions can be part of a general move toward employee empowerment. Employees may put their own interests first in developing the plan, but they also have firsthand insight into the kinds of behavior that can contribute to organizational goals. Communicating with employees is important because it demonstrates that the pay plan is fair and helps them understand what is expected of them. Communication is especially important when the organization is changing its pay plan.

LO 12-7 Discuss issues related to performance-based pay for executives.

Because executives have such a strong influence over the organization's performance, incentive pay for them receives special attention. Executive pay usually combines long-term and short-term incentives. By motivating executives, these incentives can significantly affect the organization's performance. The size of incentives should be motivating but also meet standards for equity. Performance measures should encourage behavior that is in the organization's best interests, including ethical behavior. Executives need ethical standards that keep them from insider trading or deceptive practices designed to manipulate the organization's stock price.

KEY TERMS

balanced scorecard, 386
commissions, 379
differential piece rates, 374
employee stock ownership plan
    (ESOP), 384

gainsharing, 379
incentive pay, 371
merit pay, 375
piecework rate, 373
profit sharing, 381

Scanlon plan, 380
standard hour plan, 374
stock options, 383
straight piecework plan, 373

REVIEW AND DISCUSSION QUESTIONS

1. With some organizations and jobs, pay is primarily wages or salaries, and with others, incentive pay is more important. For each of the following jobs, state whether you think the pay should emphasize base pay (wages and salaries) or incentive pay (bonuses, profit sharing, and so on). Give a reason for each.
    a. An accountant at a manufacturing company.
    b. A salesperson for a software company.
    c. A chief executive officer.
    d. A physician in a health clinic.
2. Consider your current job or a job that you have recently held. Would you be most motivated in response to incentives based on your individual performance, your group's performance, or the organization's overall performance (profits or stock price)? Why?
3. What are the pros and cons of linking incentive pay to individual performance? How can organizations address the negatives?
4. Suppose you are a human resource professional at a company that is setting up work teams for production and sales. What group incentives would you recommend to support this new work arrangement?
5. Why do some organizations link incentive pay to the organization's overall performance? Is it appropriate to use stock performance as an incentive for employees at all levels? Why or why not?
6. Stock options have been called the pay program that "built Silicon Valley" because of their key role as incentive pay for employees in high-tech companies. They were popular during the 1990s, when

the stock market was rising rapidly. Since then, stock prices have fallen.
    a. How would you expect this change to affect employees' attitudes toward stock options as incentive pay?
    b. How would you expect this change to affect the effectiveness of stock options as an incentive?
7. Based on the balanced scorecard in Table 12.2, find the incentive pay for an employee earning a salary of $4,000 a month in each of the following situations.
    a. The company met all of its target goals for the year. (Multiply the percentage at the top of the table by the employee's salary.)
    b. The company met only its target goals for financial performance (25% of the total incentive pay) but none of the other goals.
    c. The company met its stretch goals for financial performance and its base goals in the other areas. (For each category of goals, multiply the percentages by the employee's salary, and then add the amounts together.)
8. Why might a balanced scorecard like the one in Question 7 be more effective than simply using merit pay for a manager?
9. How can the way an organization creates and carries out its incentive plan improve the effectiveness of that plan?
10. In a typical large corporation, the majority of the chief executive's pay is tied to the company's stock price. What are some benefits of this pay strategy? Some risks? How can organizations address the risks?

EXPERIENCING HR

Divide into groups of about six students. In each group, consider this scenario: You are managers at a small manufacturing company where an engineer (whose salary is $75,000) had an idea for improving how you make a product line. In the first year of using this idea, the

company has reduced manufacturing costs by $100,000. You agree that this contribution deserves some kind of reward, but you don't have an incentive pay system in place to cover it. The following ideas have been suggested:

- Give the engineer a higher-than-usual merit pay increase of 6%.
- Give the engineer a one-time $5,000 bonus.
- Give the engineer company stock currently worth $5,000. (The company is privately owned, so the engineer can't sell it on the stock market, but it could grow in value and be sold when the engineer retires.)
- Divide a $10,000 gainsharing bonus among the entire team that implemented the change.

Decide which of these rewards would be most effective from the company's standpoint. Then consider how the engineer might react to each of the rewards: which would seem fairest and most valuable? Choose someone to be the engineer and someone to be the engineer's supervisor, and role-play how the company should give the reward. How well did the supervisor communicate the value of the reward?

Write a one-paragraph summary of what type of performance-based pay you chose, why you chose it, and whether, after watching the role-play, you would change anything about your group's decisions.

TAKING RESPONSIBILITY: Continuum Health Partners Link Pay to Costs, Quality of Care

Continuum Health Partners started in 1997 when three New York hospitals—Beth Israel Medical Center, St. Luke's Hospital, and Roosevelt Hospital—formed a partnership. It has since grown into a larger health network that includes seven health care facilities as well as private-practice offices and ambulatory-care centers. Like other health care organizations, Continuum has seen its costs soar even as insurance companies and government payers have pressured the organization to charge less. In providing health care, however, it is not acceptable to compromise patients' well-being in order to save money.

To resolve this dilemma, Continuum has tried linking pay to performance. It recently participated in research that tested the impact of pay-for-performance on costs and patient outcomes. In the study, the Continuum hospitals set up a gainsharing program for participating physicians. The hospitals undertook a set of cost reduction efforts that included performance standards for dictating medical records in a timely fashion and prescribing certain medications associated with optimal patient outcomes for the eight commonly performed surgical procedures included in the study. The hospital measured its costs before and after the standards went into place. The physicians were paid a share of the savings generated during the study's four years.

Continuum found that the hospital saved about $18 million during the study's time period. At the same time, the rates of complications did not change significantly. In addition, there was no evidence that doctors avoided taking on sicker patients during the study period (which might have benefited them financially).

Gainsharing is an innovation in the health care industry. Doctors are highly trained professionals who have not traditionally appreciated being told standards they must meet. Hospitals are understandably concerned that emphasizing costs may compromise patient quality. Federal law also has made some of these arrangements legally questionable. However, one of the provisions of the Affordable Care Act allowed the use of gainsharing if it does not compromise the quality of care and if it includes mechanisms to prevent waste, fraud, and abuse. Also, physicians' participation in these pay-for-performance programs must be voluntary, and the gainsharing bonuses may not exceed 50% of the amount normally paid to physicians for handling the same number of patients.

These changes come at a challenging time for Continuum. In an effort to drive quality improvement even as it pushes down costs, the government's Centers for Medicare and Medicaid Services is planning to cut the basic rates it pays by 1% unless hospitals "earn back" the higher rates by meeting targets for clinical results and patient satisfaction or by showing major improvement in those measures. The hospital industry expects that the 1% at risk will grow and extend to private payers as frustration with the high cost of health care continues to be a public-policy issue. Serving a densely populated and multicultural community, Continuum and other New York City hospitals have found that they tend to lag the nation in patient satisfaction. So along with its experiment in pay for performance, Continuum has addressed the patient satisfaction piece of the equation by setting up a website where it reports its progress in quality and patient safety, hoping to increase awareness of its commitment to patients' well-being.

Questions

1. Discuss how well you think incentive pay was tied to relevant performance measures in Continuum's experiment with pay for performance.
2. Would the gainsharing program be appropriate for Continuum's nonmedical support staff, such as the employees who check in patients and clean rooms? Why or why not?

3. What kinds of performance measures would you include in a balanced scorecard for Continuum's top executives? To which measures do you think most of their compensation should be tied?

SOURCES: Continuum Health Partners, "About Us," http://www.chpnyc .org, accessed April 19, 2012; Continuum Health Partners, "Patient Qual- ity: Quality and Excellence, Our Shared Vision," http://www.chpnyc.org, accessed April 19, 2012; "New Data Show Pay-for-Performance Programs

Do Not Negatively Impact Patient Outcomes When Quality Variables Are Implemented," *Managed Care Outlook*, December 15, 2011, pp. 9–11; "What's Mine Is Yours: Gainsharing Arrangements in the Bundled Pay- ments for Care Improvement Initiative," *Mondaq Business Briefing*, October 10, 2011, Business & Company Resource Center, http://galenet.galegroup .com; Judith Messina, "Payment for Performance: City Hospitals Could Lose in a Program That Weighs Patient Options," *Crain's New York Busi- ness*, March 21, 2011, Business & Company Resource Center, http:// galenet.galegroup.com.

MANAGING TALENT: How Wal-Mart Is Setting Pay at the Top . . . and Bottom

By any measure, the chief executive officer of Wal-Mart Stores, Mike Duke, has a huge job. In the highly com- petitive retail industry, Wal-Mart operates more than 10,000 stores in more than two dozen countries, gener- ating sales in the hundreds of billions of dollars. For that responsibility, Duke is highly paid. In 2011, he received a base salary of $1.3 million, stock awards valued at $13.1 million, and a cash bonus of $2.9 million. Duke's salary and stock awards were each 3% larger than in the previous year, but his bonus was 25% smaller because the company failed to meet goals for operating income. His total compensation of $18.1 million made Duke the 82nd-highest paid chief executive in the United States, according to *Forbes* magazine.

Another change that took place in Duke's compen- sation was in the measures used for setting his incen- tive pay. In the past, Wal-Mart used a metric common to retailers: same-store sales, meaning sales volume at stores that have been open for one year or longer. By looking at same-stores sales, a company can determine whether its activities are making its stores more suc- cessful over time. Wal-Mart, however, decided to base Duke's incentive pay on the total sales for the entire company. The change came after Wal-Mart's same- store sales had been falling for two years as recession- strained consumers switched to dollar stores or put off purchases altogether. In its official explanation of the change, Wal-Mart said it would "align our performance share goals more closely with our evolving business strategy, which emphasizes productive growth, leverage and returns." Several years earlier, in contrast, Wal-Mart had said it measured same-store sales because that met- ric "is a key driver of shareholder returns" and investors view it "as an important measure of performance in the retail industry."

The change from same-stores sales to total sales as the basis for incentive pay followed another change in performance targets. Two years earlier, the company switched the time frame for measuring performance. In the past, Wal-Mart executives had to meet three-year goals before receiving incentives. Beginning in 2009, they began receiving their incentive pay for meeting one-year goals. The company said the change would make the goals more current and realistic.

Lower in the corporate hierarchy, Wal-Mart has made very different decisions about compensation. The average wage for an hourly Wal-Mart employee in the United $12.40 per hour. An average employee with a full-time schedule (many work part-time) would earn about $25,800 per year. Like Duke, wage earners at Wal-Mart are eligible for incentive pay, but the scale of the incentive pay is far smaller.

Under the company's founder, Sam Walton, Wal- Mart set up a profit-sharing program, which Walton in his autobiography called "the carrot that's kept Walmart headed forward" These payments have rep- resented up to 4% of employees' pay. The money was deposited in a fund that employees could cash in when they retired. In 2010, Wal-Mart paid its employ- ees $1.1 billion in profit sharing and contributions to employees' 401(k) retirement funds. However, that was the last year for the program. After 39 years, begin- ning in 2011, lower-level employees are no longer eligible for profit sharing. The company will instead increase its spending on quarterly and annual bonuses and medical insurance, and it will continue matching employees' contributions to their 401(k) plans, up to 6% of their pay. A company spokesperson noted that employees would be able to spend their bonuses imme- diately, rather than waiting for their retirement, as they did with the profit sharing.

Questions

1. Compare the impact of incentive pay on the total compensation of Wal-Mart's CEO and the compa- ny's average workers. Does the difference in the way pay is structured at these two levels make business sense? Why or why not?
2. How do you think Wal-Mart's store workers would judge the equity of the difference between their total compensation and Mike Duke's total compensation? Do you think the difference would motivate them to work hard to move into management positions? Why or why not?

3. What, if any, changes would you recommend that Wal-Mart make to its policies for incentive pay so that its compensation better supports its strategy?

SOURCES: Wal-Mart Stores, "About Us," http://www.walmartstores .com, accessed April 24, 2012; Anne D'Innocenzio, "Wal-Mart's CEO Paid

$18.1 Million in 2011," *Bloomberg Businessweek*, April 16, 2012, http://www .businessweek.com; Susanna Kim, "Pressure on SEC to Implement Rule Disclosing CEO to Median Worker Pay," *ABC News*, March 13, 2012, http://abcnews.go.com; Gretchen Morgenson, "Moving the Goal Posts on Pay," *The New York Times*, May 7, 2011; "Wal-Mart to End Profit-Sharing in Benefits Switch," Reuters, October 8, 2010, http://www.reuters.com.

 TWITTER FOCUS: Employees Own Bob's Red Mill

Using Twitter, continue the conversation about recognizing employee contributions with pay by reading the Bob's Red Mill case at **www.mhhe.com/noefund5e**. Engage with your classmates and instructor via Twitter to chat about Bob Moore's decision using the case questions posted on the Noe website. Don't have a Twitter account yet? See the instructions for getting started on the Online Learning Center.

NOTES

1. Armaghan N. Behlum, "HMS Revises Pay Structure," *Harvard Crimson*, March 8, 2012, http:// www.thecrimson.com.
2. This chapter draws freely on several literature reviews: B. Gerhart and G. T. Milkovich, "Employee Compensation: Research and Practice," in *Handbook of Industrial and Organizational Psychology*, 2nd ed., eds. M. D. Dunnette and L. M. Hough (Palo Alto, CA: Consulting Psychologists Press, 1992), vol. 3; B. Gerhart and S. L. Rynes, *Compensation: Theory, Evidence, and Strategic Implications* (Thousand Oaks, CA: Sage, 2003); B. Gerhart, "Compensation Strategy and Organization Performance," in *Compensation in Organizations: Current Research and Practice*, eds. S. L. Rynes and B. Gerhart (San Francisco: Jossey-Bass, 2000), pp. 151–94; and B. Gerhart, S. L. Rynes, and I. S. Fulmer, "Compensation," *Academy of Management Annals* 3 (2009).
3. B. Gerhart and G. T. Milkovich, "Organizational Differences in Managerial Compensation and Financial Performance," *Academy of Management Journal* 33 (1990), pp. 663–91.
4. G. T. Milkovich and A. K. Wigdor, *Pay for Performance* (Washington, DC: National Academy Press, 1991); Gerhart and Milkovich, "Employee Compensation"; Gerhart and Rynes, *Compensation*; A. Nyberg, "Retaining Your High Performers: Moderators of the Performance–Job Satisfaction–Voluntary Turnover Relationship," *Journal of Applied Psychology* 95, no. 3 (2010): 440–53; C. O. Trevor, G. Reilly, and B. Gerhart, "Reconsidering Pay Dispersion's Effect on the Performance of Interdependent Work: Reconciling Sorting and Pay Inequality," *Academy of Management Journal* (forthcoming).
5. Aon Corporation, "Salary Increases Stay Consistent with Recent Trends, as the Focus Remains on Variable Pay, according to Aon Hewitt," news release, September 1, 2011, http://aon.mediaroom .com.
6. Rachel Emma Silverman, "My Colleague, My Paymaster," *The Wall Street Journal*, April 3, 2012, http://online.wsj.com.
7. R. D. Bretz, R. A. Ash, and G. F. Dreher, "Do People Make the Place? An Examination of the Attraction-Selection-Attrition Hypothesis," *Personnel Psychology* 42 (1989), pp. 561–81; T. A. Judge and R. D. Bretz, "Effect of Values on Job Choice Decisions," *Journal of Applied Psychology* 77 (1992), pp. 261–71; and D. M. Cable and T. A. Judge, "Pay Performance and Job Search Decisions: A Person-Organization Fit Perspective," *Personnel Psychology* 47 (1994), pp. 317–48.
8. E. A. Locke, D. B. Feren, V. M. McCaleb, K. N. Shaw, and A. T. Denny, "The Relative Effectiveness of Four Methods of Motivating Employee Performance," in *Changes in Working Life*, eds. K. D. Duncan, M. M. Gruenberg, and D. Wallis (New York: Wiley, 1980), pp. 363–88.
9. Gerhart and Milkovich, "Employee Compensation."
10. E. E. Lawler III, "Pay for Performance: A Strategic Analysis," in *Compensation and Benefits*, ed. L. R. Gomez-Mejia (Washington, DC: Bureau of National Affairs, 1989); A. M. Konrad and J. Pfeffer, "Do You Get What You Deserve? Factors Affecting the Relationship between Productivity and Pay," *Administrative Science Quarterly* 35 (1990), pp. 258–85; J. L. Medoff and K. G. Abraham, "Are Those Paid More Really More Productive? The Case of Experience," *Journal of Human Resources*

16 (1981), pp. 186–216; and K. S. Teel, "Are Merit Raises Really Based on Merit?" *Personnel Journal* 65, no. 3 (1986), pp. 88–95.

11. Lyle Leritz, "Principles of Merit Pay," Economic Research Institute, 2012, http://www.erieri.com; Joanne Dahm and Pete Sanborn, "Addressing Talent and Rewards in 'The New Normal,'" Aon Hewitt, 2010, http://aonhewitt.com; Stephen Miller, "Pay for Performance: Make It More than a Catchphrase," *SHRM Online* Compensation Discipline, May 30, 2011, http://www.shrm.org.

12. R. D. Bretz, G. T. Milkovich, and W. Read, "The Current State of Performance Appraisal Research and Practice," *Journal of Management* 18 (1992), pp. 321–52; R. L. Heneman, "Merit Pay Research," Research in *Personnel and Human Resource Management* 8 (1990), pp. 203–63; and Milkovich and Wigdor, *Pay for Performance.*

13. Bretz et al., "Current State of Performance Appraisal Research."

14. S. L. Rynes, B. Gerhart, and L. Parks, "Personnel Psychology: Performance Evaluation and Compensation," *Annual Review of Psychology* (2005).

15. W. E. Deming, *Out of the Crisis* (Cambridge, MA: Center for Advanced Engineering Study, Massachusetts Institute of Technology, 1986), p. 110.

16. Guy Sheppard, "Finishing School," *Commercial Motor*, December 22, 2011, pp. 24–26.

17. Ted Evanoff, "Raymond James Outlines Retention Bonus Offers for Some Morgan Keegan Employees," *Commercial Appeal (Memphis, TN)*, January 27, 2012, Business & Company Resource Center, http://galenet.galegroup.com; Andrew Osterland, "Raymond James Closes on Morgan Keegan Deal," *Investment News*, April 9, 2012, Business & Company Resource Center, http://galenet.galegroup.com.

18. U.S. Department of Justice, Antitrust Division, "Competition and Real Estate: Home Prices and Commissions over Time," http://www.justice.gov, accessed April 19, 2012; Leslie Scism, "Insurance Fees, Revealed," *The Wall Street Journal*, March 30, 2012, http://online.wsj.com; Anonymous, "Confessions of a Car Salesman," *Popular Mechanics*, May 4, 2011, http://www.popularmechanics.com.

19. T. L. Ross and R. A. Ross, "Gainsharing: Sharing Improved Performance," in *The Compensation Handbook*, 3rd ed., eds. M. L. Rock and L. A. Berger (New York: McGraw-Hill, 1991).

20. T. M. Welbourne and L. R. Gomez-Mejia, "Team Incentives in the Workplace," in *The Compensation Handbook*, 3rd ed.

21. L. R. Gomez-Mejia and D. B. Balkin, *Compensation, Organizational Strategy, and Firm Performance* (Cincinnati: South-Western, 1992).

22. J. A. Fossum, *Labor Relations* (New York: McGraw-Hill, 2002).

23. This idea has been referred to as the "share economy." See M. L. Weitzman, "The Simple Macroeconomics of Profit Sharing," *American Economic Review* 75 (1985), pp. 937–53. For supportive research, see the following studies: J. Chelius and R. S. Smith, "Profit Sharing and Employment Stability," *Industrial and Labor Relations Review* 43 (1990), pp. 256S–73S; B. Gerhart and L. O. Trevor, "Employment Stability under Different Managerial Compensation Systems," working paper (Cornell University Center for Advanced Human Resource Studies, 1995); D. L. Kruse, "Profit Sharing and Employment Variability: Microeconomic Evidence on the Weitzman Theory," *Industrial and Labor Relations Review* 44 (1991), pp. 437–53.

24. Gerhart and Milkovich, "Employee Compensation"; M. L. Weitzman and D. L. Kruse, "Profit Sharing and Productivity," in *Paying for Productivity*, ed. A. S. Blinder (Washington, DC: Brookings Institution, 1990); D. L. Kruse, *Profit Sharing: Does It Make a Difference?* (Kalamazoo, MI: Upjohn Institute, 1993); and M. Magnan and S. St.-Onge, "The Impact of Profit Sharing on the Performance of Financial Services Firms," *Journal of Management Studies* 42 (2005), pp. 761–91.

25. Wayne Heilman, "Q&A with Marcus Boggs: Practicing Open-Book Management," *Colorado Springs Gazette*, March 29, 2012, http://www.gazette.com.

26. Gerhart and Milkovich, "Organizational Differences in Managerial Compensation."

27. David Kocieniewski, "Tax Benefits from Options as Windfall for Businesses," *The New York Times*, December 30, 2011, Business & Company Resource Center, http://galenet.galegroup.com. See also Alex Edmans, "How to Fix Executive Compensation," *The Wall Street Journal*, February 27, 2012, http://online.wsj.com.

28. National Center for Employee Ownership, "A Statistical Profile of Employee Ownership," updated February 2012, http://www.nceo.org.

29. M. A. Conte and J. Svejnar, "The Performance Effects of Employee Ownership Plans," in *Paying for Productivity*, pp. 245–94.

30. Ibid.; T. H. Hammer, "New Developments in Profit Sharing, Gainsharing, and Employee Ownership," in *Productivity in Organizations*, eds. J. P. Campbell, R. J. Campbell, et al. (San Francisco: Jossey-Bass, 1988); and K. J. Klein, "Employee Stock Ownership and Employee Attitudes: A Test of Three Models," *Journal of Applied Psychology* 72 (1987), pp. 319–32.

31. SAS Institute, "SAS Helps ConocoPhillips Norway Fucus on Performance and Control Costs," Customer Success, http://www.sas.com, accessed April 24, 2012; Jonathan D. Rockoff, "J&J Won't Give Full Bonuses to Employees," *The Wall Street Journal*, January 19, 2011, http://online.wsj.com.

32. R. T. Kaufman, "The Effects of Improshare on Productivity," *Industrial and Labor Relations Review* 45 (1992), pp. 311–22; M. H. Schuster, "The Scanlon Plan: A Longitudinal Analysis," *Journal of Applied Behavioral Science* 20 (1984), pp. 23–28; and J. A. Wagner III, P. Rubin, and T. J. Callahan, "Incentive Payment and Nonmanagerial Productivity: An Interrupted Time Series Analysis of Magnitude and Trend," *Organizational Behavior and Human Decision Processes* 42 (1988), pp. 47–74.

33. C. R. Gowen III and S. A. Jennings, "The Effects of Changes in Participation and Group Size on Gainsharing Success: A Case Study," *Journal of Organizational Behavior Management* 11 (1991), pp. 147–69.

34. D. I. Levine and L. D. Tyson, "Participation, Productivity, and the Firm's Environment," in *Paying for Productivity*.

35. T. Welbourne, D. Balkin, and L. Gomez-Mejia, "Gainsharing and Mutual Monitoring: A Combined Agency–Organizational Justice Interpretation," *Academy of Management Journal* 38 (1995), pp. 881–99.

36. Gerhart and Milkovich, "Organizational Differences in Managerial Compensation"; B. Gerhart, S. L. Rynes, and I. S. Fulmer, "Pay and Performance: Individuals, Groups, and Executives," *Academy of Management Annals* 3 (2009): 251–315.

13

Providing Employee Benefits

What Do I Need to Know?

After reading this chapter, you should be able to:

LO 13-1 Discuss the importance of benefits as a part of employee compensation.

LO 13-2 Summarize the types of employee benefits required by law.

LO 13-3 Describe the most common forms of paid leave.

LO 13-4 Identify the kinds of insurance benefits offered by employers.

LO 13-5 Define the types of retirement plans offered by employers.

LO 13-6 Describe how organizations use other benefits to match employees' wants and needs.

LO 13-7 Explain how to choose the contents of an employee benefits package.

LO 13-8 Summarize the regulations affecting how employers design and administer benefits programs.

LO 13-9 Discuss the importance of effectively communicating the nature and value of benefits to employees.

Introduction

To succeed with a low-price strategy, Wal-Mart Stores must control all of its costs, including wages paid to employees working in its stores and distribution centers. Critics of the company complained for years that many of those wage-earning employees lacked health insurance and earned so little that they qualified for Medicaid. In their view, Wal-Mart was not a socially responsible corporation because its compensation practices made many of its workers a burden on the state. In response, Wal-Mart a few years ago expanded the number of employees who were eligible for company-provided health insurance. Full- and part-time employees who opted to pay about $250 a year could obtain a health plan after one year of employment.

But that policy has been difficult to maintain because the cost of providing health insurance has climbed year after year. Wal-Mart's management, looking for ways to restrain the added compensation costs, recently announced some cuts in health insurance coverage. Employees who work less than 24 hours per week will no longer qualify for health insurance, and those who work 24 to 33 hours per week will no longer be able to include a spouse on their health insurance plan (children will be covered). In addition, the portion of the premium paid by employees will increase—in some cases, by more than 40%. The company noted that employees pay lower premiums than employees at other companies. However, one reason for the lower premiums is that the plans have high deductibles of as much as $5,000 a year. To help employees with the challenge of medical bills, Wal-Mart also contributes to savings plans in which workers set aside money for that purpose. In the past, it contributed $1,000 to these accounts, an amount it is reducing to $500 as part of its effort to economize. Wal-Mart's decision to cut back on health insurance spending makes it typical; over half of employers do not provide health insurance to part-time workers.[1]

Like Wal-Mart's full-time employees, employees at almost every organization receive more than dollars and cents in exchange for their efforts. They also receive a package of **employee benefits**—compensation in forms other than cash. Besides employer-paid health insurance, examples include paid vacation time and pension plans, among a wide range of possibilities.

Employee Benefits
Compensation in forms other than cash.

This chapter describes the contents of an employee benefits package and the way organizations administer employee benefits. We begin by discussing the important role of benefits as a part of employee compensation. The following sections define major types of employee benefits: benefits required by law, paid leave, insurance policies, retirement plans, and other benefits. We then discuss how to choose which of these alternatives to include in an employee benefits package so that it contributes to meeting the organization's goals. The next section summarizes the regulations affecting how employers design and administer benefits programs. Finally, we explain why and how organizations should effectively communicate with employees about their benefits.

LO 13-1 Discuss the importance of benefits as a part of employee compensation.

The Role of Employee Benefits

As a part of the total compensation paid to employees, benefits serve functions similar to pay. Benefits contribute to attracting, retaining, and motivating employees. The variety of possible benefits also helps employers tailor their compensation to the kinds of employees they need. Different employees look for different types of benefits. Employers need to examine their benefits package regularly to see whether they meet the needs of today. At the same time, benefits packages are more complex than pay structures, so benefits are harder for employees to understand and appreciate. Even if employers spend large sums on benefits, if employees do not understand how to use them or why they are valuable, the cost of the benefits will be largely wasted.[2] Employers need to communicate effectively so that the benefits succeed in motivating employees.

Employees have come to expect that benefits will help them maintain economic security. Social Security contributions, pensions, and retirement savings plans help employees prepare for their retirement. Insurance plans help to protect employees from unexpected costs such as hospital bills. This important role of benefits is one reason that benefits are subject to government regulation. Some benefits, such as Social Security, are required by law. Other regulations establish requirements that benefits must meet to obtain the most favorable tax treatment. Later in the chapter, we will describe some of the most significant regulations affecting benefits.

Even though many kinds of benefits are not required by law, they have become so common that today's employees expect them. Many employers find that attracting qualified workers requires them to provide medical and retirement benefits of some sort. A large employer without such benefits would be highly unusual and would have difficulty competing in the labor market. Still, the nature of the benefits package changes over time, as we will discuss at various points throughout the chapter.

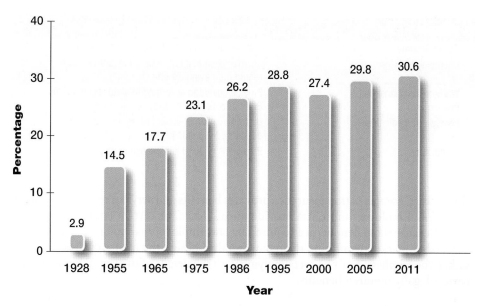

Figure 13.1

Benefits as a Percentage of Total Compensation

SOURCE: Bureau of Labor Statistics, "Employer Costs for Employee Compensation," http://data.bls.gov, accessed April 25, 2012.

Like other forms of compensation, benefits impose significant costs. On average, out of every dollar spent on compensation, more than 30 cents goes to benefits. As Figure 13.1 shows, this share has grown over the past decades. These numbers indicate that an organization managing its labor costs must pay careful attention to the cost of its employee benefits.

Why do organizations pay a growing share of compensation in the form of benefits? It would be simpler to pay all compensation in cash and let employees buy their own insurance and contribute to their own savings plans. That arrangement would also give employees greater control over what their compensation buys. However, several forces have made benefits a significant part of compensation packages. One is that laws require employers to provide certain benefits, such as contributions to Social Security and unemployment insurance. Also, tax laws can make benefits favorable to employees. For example, employees do not pay income taxes on most benefits they receive, but they pay income taxes on cash compensation. Therefore, an employee who receives a $1,000 raise "takes home" less than the full $1,000, but an employee who receives an additional $1,000 worth of benefits receives the full benefits. Another cost advantage of paying benefits is that employers, especially large ones, often can get a better deal on insurance or other programs than employees can obtain on their own. Finally, some employers assemble creative benefits packages that set them apart in the competition for talent. For example, Netflix lets people take off as much time as they want and doesn't keep track. This policy is in keeping with its HR strategy of "hiring adults"—experts who already have a history of success, love movies, and can manage their time. Since the company's success comes from people driven by a passion for what they do and what they can accomplish, offering freedom as a benefit contributes to attracting and keeping the right talent.[3]

Benefits Required by Law

The federal and state governments require various forms of social insurance to protect workers from the financial hardships of being out of work. In general, Social Security provides support for retired workers, unemployment insurance assists laid-off workers,

LO 13-2 Summarize the types of employee benefits required by law.

Table 13.1

Benefits Required by Law

BENEFIT	EMPLOYER REQUIREMENT
Social Security	Flat payroll tax on employees and employers
Unemployment insurance	Payroll tax on employers that depends on state requirements and experience rating
Workers' compensation insurance	Provide coverage according to state requirements Premiums depend on experience rating
Family and medical leave	Up to 12 weeks of unpaid leave for childbirth, adoption, or serious illness
Health care	Provisions of 2010 law phased in through 2014

and workers' compensation insurance provides benefits and services to workers injured on the job. Employers must also provide unpaid leave for certain family and medical needs. Because these benefits are required by law, employers cannot gain an advantage in the labor market by offering them, nor can they design the nature of these benefits. Rather, the emphasis must be on complying with the details of the law. Table 13.1 summarizes legally required benefits.

Social Security

In 1935 the federal Social Security Act established old-age insurance and unemployment insurance. Congress later amended the act to add survivor's insurance (1939), disability insurance (1956), hospital insurance (Medicare Part A, 1965), and supplementary medical insurance (Medicare Part B, 1965) for the elderly. Together, the law and its amendments created what is now the Old Age, Survivors, Disability, and Health Insurance (OASDHI) program, informally known as **Social Security.** This program covers over 90% of U.S. employees. The main exceptions are railroad and federal, state, and local government employees, who often have their own plans.

Workers who meet eligibility requirements receive the retirement benefits according to their age and earnings history. If they elect to begin receiving benefits at full retirement age, they can receive full benefits, or if they elect to begin receiving benefits at age 62, they receive benefits at a permanently reduced level. The full retirement age rises with birth year: a person born in 1940 reaches full retirement age at 65 years and 6 months, and a person born in 1960 or later reaches full retirement age at 67. The benefit amount rises with the person's past earnings, but the level goes up very little after a certain level. In 2012, the maximum benefit for a worker who retires at age 65 is more than $2,300, and it is above $3,200 for a worker who delays retirement until age 70. The government increases the payments each year according to the growth in the consumer price index. Also, spouses of covered earners receive benefits, even if they have no covered earnings. They receive either the benefit associated with their own earnings or one-half of the amount received by the covered earner, whichever is greater.

Benefits may be reduced if the worker is still earning wages above a maximum, called the *exempt amount*. In 2012, the exempt amount was $14,640 for beneficiaries under the full retirement age. A beneficiary in that age range who earns more than the exempt amount sees a reduction in his or her benefit. The amount of the reduction is $1 for every $2 the person earns above the exempt amount. For example a 63-year-old who earned $16,660 would have earned $2,000 above the exempt amount, so the person's Social Security benefits would be reduced by $1,000. During the year a worker reaches full retirement age, the maximum untaxed earnings are $38,880

Social Security
The federal Old Age, Survivors, Disability, and Health Insurance (OASDHI) program, which combines old age (retirement) insurance, survivor's insurance, disability insurance, hospital insurance (Medicare Part A), and supplementary medical insurance (Medicare Part B) for the elderly.

(in 2012), and benefits are reduced $1 for every $3 in earnings. Beginning in the month they reach full retirement age, workers face no reduction in benefits for earning above the exempt amount. For workers below that age, the penalty increases the incentive to retire or at least reduce the number of hours worked. Adding to this incentive, Social Security benefits are free from federal income taxes and free from state taxes in about half the states.

Employers and employees share the cost of Social Security through a payroll tax. The percentage is set by law and has changed from time to time. In 2012, employers paid a tax of 6.2% and employees paid 4.2% on the first $110,100 of the employee's earnings. Of that, the majority goes to OASDI, and 2.9% of earnings go to Medicare (Part A). For earnings above $110,100, only the 2.9% for Medicare is assessed, with half paid by the employer and half paid by the employee.

Unemployment Insurance

Along with OASDHI, the Social Security Act of 1935 established a program of **unemployment insurance.** This program has four objectives related to minimizing the hardships of unemployment. It provides payments to offset lost income during involuntary unemployment, and it helps unemployed workers find new jobs. The payment of unemployment insurance taxes gives employers an incentive to stabilize employment. And providing workers with income during short-term layoffs preserves investments in worker skills because workers can afford to wait to return to their employer, rather than start over with another organization. Technically, the federal government left it to each state's discretion to establish an unemployment insurance program. At the same time, the Social Security Act created a tax incentive structure that quickly led every state to establish the program.

Most of the funding for unemployment insurance comes from federal and state taxes on employers. Employers who pay their state taxes currently pay a federal tax of 0.8% of the first $7,000 of each employee's wages. The state tax rate varies from less than 1% to more than 15%, and the taxable wage base ranges from $7,000 to $38,800, so the amount paid depends a great deal on where the company is located.[4] Also, some states charge new employers whatever rate is the average for their industry, so the amount of tax paid in those states also depends on the type of business. In the severe recession of 2008–2009, layoffs were so widespread that unemployment insurance funds were drained and many states dramatically hiked premiums for unemployment insurance. Companies have therefore redoubled efforts to improve their experience ratings and control future costs for unemployment insurance. For example, helping laid-off workers find a new job can shorten the time in which they are receiving benefits. Some states allow sharedwork arrangements, in which companies reduce wages and hours, and employees receive partial unemployment benefits, rather than laying off workers.[5]

No state imposes the same tax rate on every employer in the state. The size of the unemployment insurance tax imposed on each employer depends on the employer's **experience rating**—the number of employees the company laid off in the past and the cost of providing them with unemployment benefits. Employers with a history of laying off a large share of their workforces pay higher taxes than those with few layoffs. In some states, an employer with very few layoffs may pay no state tax.

Unemployment Insurance
A federally mandated program to minimize the hardships of unemployment through payments to unemployed workers, help in finding new jobs, and incentives to stabilize employment.

Experience Rating
The number of employees a company has laid off in the past and the cost of providing them with unemployment benefits.

The U.S. economic recession that began in 2008 put quite a strain on the country's unemployment insurance system. Although the economy seems to be on the rebound, unemployment levels have been slow to recede.

In contrast, an employer with a poor experience rating could pay a tax as high as 5.4% to 15.4%, depending on the state. The use of experience ratings gives employers some control over the cost of unemployment insurance. Careful human resource planning can minimize layoffs and keep their experience rating favorable.

To receive benefits, workers must meet four conditions:

1. They meet requirements demonstrating they had been employed (often 52 weeks or four quarters of work at a minimum level of pay).
2. They are available for work.
3. They are actively seeking work. This requirement includes registering at the local unemployment office.
4. They were not discharged for cause (such as willful misconduct), did not quit voluntarily, and are not out of work because of a labor dispute (such as a union member on strike).

Workers who meet these conditions receive benefits at the level set by the state—typically about half the person's previous earnings—for a period of 26 weeks. States with a sustained unemployment rate above a particular threshold or significantly above recent levels also offer extended benefits for up to 13 weeks. Sometimes Congress funds emergency extended benefits. All states have minimum and maximum weekly benefit levels.

Workers' Compensation

Workers' Compensation
State programs that provide benefits to workers who suffer work-related injuries or illnesses, or to their survivors.

Decades ago, workers who suffered work-related injury or illness had to bear the cost unless they won a lawsuit against their employer. Those who sued often lost the case because of the defenses available to employers. Today, the states have passed **workers' compensation** laws, which help workers with the expenses resulting from job-related accidents and illnesses.[6] These laws operate under a principle of *no-fault liability*, meaning that an employee does not need to show that the employer was grossly negligent in order to receive compensation, and the employer is protected from lawsuits. The employer loses this protection if it intentionally contributes to a dangerous workplace. Employees are not eligible if their injuries are self-inflicted or if they result from intoxication or "willful disregard of safety rules."[7]

About 9 out of 10 U.S. workers are covered by state workers' compensation laws, with the level of coverage varying from state to state. The benefits fall into four major categories: (1) disability income, (2) medical care, (3) death benefits, and (4) rehabilitative services. The amount of income varies from state to state but is typically two-thirds of the worker's earnings before the disability. The benefits are tax free.

The states differ in terms of how they fund workers' compensation insurance. Some states have a single state fund. Most states allow employers to purchase coverage from private insurance companies. Most also permit self-funding by employers. The cost of the workers' compensation insurance depends on the kinds of occupations involved, the state where the company is located, and the employer's experience rating. Premiums for low-risk occupations may be less than 1% of payroll. For some of the most hazardous occupations, the cost may be as high as 100% of payroll. Costs also vary from state to state, so that one state's program requires higher premiums than another state's program. As with unemployment insurance, unfavorable experience ratings lead to higher premiums. Organizations can minimize the cost of this benefit by keeping workplaces safe and making employees and their managers conscious of safety issues, as discussed in Chapter 3.

Unpaid Family and Medical Leave

In the United States, unpaid leave is required by law for certain family needs. Specifically, the **Family and Medical Leave Act (FMLA)** of 1993 requires organizations with 50 or more employees within a 75-mile radius to provide as much as 12 weeks of unpaid leave after childbirth or adoption; to care for a seriously ill child, spouse, or parent, for an employee's own serious illness; or to take care of urgent needs that arise when a spouse, child, or parent in the National Guard or Reserve is called to active duty. In addition, if a family member (child, spouse, parent, or next of kin) is injured while serving on active military duty, the employee may take up to 26 weeks of unpaid leave under FMLA. Employers must also guarantee these employees the same or a comparable job when they return to work. The law does not cover employees who have less than one year of service, work fewer than 25 hours per week, or are among the organization's 10% highest paid. The 12 weeks of unpaid leave amount to a smaller benefit than is typical of Japan and most countries in Western Europe. Japan and West European nations typically require paid family leave.

Experience with the Family and Medical Leave Act suggests that a majority of those opting for this benefit fail to take the full 12 weeks. According to one report, about half took 10 days or fewer, and 80% took no more than 40 days of leave. The most common reason for taking a leave was the employee's own serious illness.[8] An obvious reason for not taking the full 12 weeks is that not everyone can afford three months without pay, especially when responsible for the expenses that accompany childbirth, adoption, or serious illness. Nevertheless, employers do need to keep track of leave requests to prevent abuse of the policy. In a recent case, the court upheld a Ford Motor Company decision to fire an employee for excessive absences. Ford had approved 68 workdays of medical leave, but on 10 occasions, the employee failed to meet the company's stated policies for providing documentation of her need for time off.[9]

When employees experience pregnancy and childbirth, employers must also comply with the Pregnancy Discrimination Act, described in Chapter 3. If an employee is temporarily unable to perform her job due to pregnancy, the employer must treat her in the same way as any other temporarily disabled employee. For example, the employer may provide modified tasks, alternative assignments, disability leave, or leave without pay.

Family and Medical Leave Act (FMLA)
Federal law requiring organizations with 50 or more employees to provide up to 12 weeks of unpaid leave after childbirth or adoption; to care for a seriously ill family member or for an employee's own serious illness; or to take care of urgent needs that arise when a spouse, child, or parent in the National Guard or Reserve is called to active duty.

Health Care Benefits

In 2010, Congress passed the **Patient Protection and Affordable Care Act,** a complex package of changes in how health care is to be paid for, including requirements for insurance companies, incentives and penalties for employers providing health insurance as a benefit, expansion of public funding, and creation of health insurance exchanges as an option for the sale of health insurance. Provisions of the law are being phased in between 2010 and 2014.

The first provisions of the law that took effect mainly involve requirements for insurance companies—for example, that they must cover children with pre-existing conditions and dependent children through age 26 and may not impose lifetime limits on coverage or end coverage for people when they get sick. Small-business employers (up to 25 employees) are affected by one change that took effect in 2010: a tax credit equal to half the cost of providing health insurance benefits. In 2014, automatic enrollment in health insurance is required at companies with over 200 employees. Companies with more than 50 employees that do not provide health insurance will have to pay a penalty.

Patient Protection and Affordable Care Act
Health care reform law passed in 2010 that includes incentives and penalties for employers providing health insurance as a benefit.

How Pearson Is Using Social Media to Get Employees Moving

For messages that are about building a spirit of teamwork, social media provide just the right tone. Consequently, some employers are using social media to get employees engaged with wellness programs, which aim to promote healthy behaviors in an effort to lower absenteeism and the cost of caring for lifestyle-related illnesses. Adam Wootton of the Towers Watson human resource consulting firm says the greatest barrier to the success of wellness programs is a lack of employee engagement. That means this advantage of social media is significant.

One firm applying this advantage is Pearson, which launched a software platform called Neo to keep its global workforce connected. The publishing company determined that Neo could persuade employees to get involved with a wellness program it was launching. The company signed on with the Global Corporate Challenge, which is a campaign to get employees walking. In the Global Health Challenge, teams of seven employees sign up to walk enough miles to equal a hike around the world. Every day, the teams wear pedometers and record their mileage—ideally, at least 10,000 steps per day—as they progress toward the goal.

Motivation to walk comes from several features of the program. First is the peer pressure of the team format; when the team says it is time to walk, it is harder to be "too busy" than when individuals walk alone. In addition, entry fees paid by the participants go to charity (a program that teaches children to adopt active lifestyles). And social media deliver reminders, praise, and encouragement. Participants can see not only how far they have trekked, but also the mileage covered by other teams. They can help others by sharing ideas that have worked for their team. The social-media format is ideal for this kind of communication because it is brief, timely, personal, and frequent.

In the first year that Pearson participated in the Global Corporate Challenge, more than 5,300 employees signed up, surpassing the company's enrollment goal by 35%. According to the Global Corporate Challenge organizers, their participation should have a real payoff for the employer: participating companies report higher morale, more teamwork, and noticeably healthier employees.

SOURCES: Global Corporate Challenge, "What Is the GCC?" http://www.gettheworldmoving.com, accessed April 27, 2012; Karen Pallarito, "Employee Benefits Communications See Technological Advances," *Business Insurance,* February 13, 2012, Business & Company Resource Center, http://galenet.galegroup.com; Pearson, "National Health and Fitness Week Will Feature Global Corporate Challenge," *For Your Benefit,* Winter 2011, p. 5, accessed at http://usaemployees.pearson.com; Kathleen Koster, "There's an App for That," *Employee Benefit News,* April 15, 2011, pp. 21–23.

The Affordable Care Act was challenged by 26 states, and in June 2012, the U.S. Supreme Court upheld the constitutionality of major portions of the legislation. Given this decision, employers should continue to administer group health care plans in accordance with the upheld legislation. They should also continue to prepare for upcoming requirements that will become effective over the next several years. For example, employers of a certain size are required to report the value of health care benefits on employees' W-2 forms, and employers must provide summaries of benefits and coverage to employees at the beginning of open enrollment periods for health care coverage starting in September 2012.

Because the law is complex, HR professionals must continue to educate themselves about the requirements and communicate often with employees, many of whom may be worried about how the law affects their health care benefits. A useful source of information continues to be the government's health reform website at **www.healthreform.gov**. Still, with the potential for employers to purchase insurance for more employees than ever, more companies are looking at ways to lower the cost of this employee benefit. The "HRM Social" box describes how Pearson, a global publishing company, is using social media applications to help lower insurance costs by promoting employees' health.

Optional Benefits Programs

Other types of benefits are optional. These include various kinds of insurance, retirement plans, and paid leave. Figure 13.2 shows the percentage of full-time workers having access to the most common employee benefits. (Part-time workers often have access to and receive fewer benefits.) The most widely offered benefits are paid leave for vacations and holidays, life and medical insurance, and retirement plans. In general, benefits packages at smaller companies tend to be more limited than at larger companies.

Benefits such as health insurance often extend to employees' dependents. Traditionally, these benefits have covered employees, their spouses, and dependent children. Today, many employers also cover *domestic partners*, defined either by local law or by the companies themselves. Typically, a domestic partner is an adult nonrelative who lives with the employee in a relationship defined as permanent and financially interdependent. Some local governments provide for registration of domestic partners. Organizations offering coverage to domestic partners generally require that the partners sign a document stating they meet the requirements for a domestic partnership. Benefits provided to domestic partners do not have the same tax advantages as benefits provided to spouses. The partner's benefits are taxed as wages of the employee receiving the benefits.

Paid Leave

The major categories of paid leave are vacations, holidays, and sick leave. Employers also should establish policies for other situations that may require time off. Organizations often provide for paid leave for jury duty, funerals of family members, and military duty. Some organizations provide for other paid leave, such as time off to vote or to donate blood. Establishing policies communicates the organization's values, clarifies what employees can expect, and prevents situations in which unequal treatment leads to claims of unfairness.

LO 13-3 Describe the most common forms of paid leave.

Type of Benefit

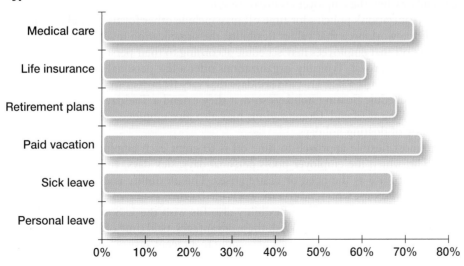

Figure 13.2
Percentage of Full-Time Workers with Access to Selected Benefit Programs

SOURCE: Bureau of Labor Statistics, "Employee Benefits in the United States, March 2011," news release, July 26, 2011, http://www.bls.gov.

Paid time off is a way for employees to enjoy time with their families and to refresh their bodies and spirits. Is paid time off an important factor for you when accepting a position?

At first blush, paid vacation, holidays, sick leave, and other paid leave may not seem to make economic sense. The employer pays the employee for time spent not working, so the employer receives nothing in return for the pay. Some employers may see little direct advantage. This may be the reason that Western European countries require a minimum number of paid vacation days, with new employees receiving 30 days off in many countries. The United States, in contrast, has no such legal requirement. It is up to U.S. employers to decide whether paid leave has a payoff in recruiting and retaining employees. At U.S. companies, paid vacation is typically two weeks or less a year for the first few years. To receive as much vacation as European employees, U.S. workers must typically stay with an employer for 15 or 20 years.[10]

Paid holidays are time off on specified days in addition to vacation time. In Western Europe and the United States, employees typically have about 10 paid holidays each year, regardless of length of service. The most common paid holidays in the United States are New Year's Day, Memorial Day, Independence Day, Labor Day, Thanksgiving Day, and Christmas Day.

Sick leave programs pay employees for days not worked because of illness. The amount of sick leave is often based on length of service, so that it accumulates over time—for example, one day added to sick leave for each month of service. Employers must decide how many sick days to grant and whether to let them continue accumulating year after year. If sick days accumulate without limit, employees can "save" them in case of disability. If an employee becomes disabled, the employee can use up the accumulated sick days, receiving full pay rather than smaller payments from disability insurance, discussed later. Some employers let sick days accumulate for only a year, and unused sick days "disappear" at year-end. This may provide an unintended incentive to use up sick days. Some healthy employees may call in sick near the end of the year so that they can obtain the benefit of the paid leave before it disappears. Employers may counter this tendency by paying employees for some or all of their unused sick days at year-end or when the employees retire or resign.

An organization's policies for time off may include other forms of paid and unpaid leave. For a workforce that values flexibility, the organization may offer paid *personal days*, days off that employees may schedule according to their personal needs, with the supervisor's approval. Typically, organizations offer a few personal days in addition to sick leave. *Floating holidays* are paid holidays that vary from year to year. The organization may schedule floating holidays so that they extend a Tuesday or Thursday holiday into a long weekend. Organizations may also give employees discretion over the scheduling of floating holidays.

The most flexible approach to time off is to grant each employee a bank of *paid time off*, in which the employer pools personal days, sick days, and vacation days for employees to use as the need or desire arises. This flexibility is especially attractive to younger workers, who tend to rate work/life balance as one of the most important sources of job satisfaction. The flexibility also fits with the U.S. trend toward more frequent but shorter vacations. With these advantages, paid time off has become available at a sizable share of companies, according to a recent survey.[11]

Employers should also establish policies for leaves without pay—for example, leaves of absence to pursue nonwork goals or to meet family needs. Unpaid leave is an employee benefit because the employee usually retains seniority and benefits during the leave.

Group Insurance

As we noted earlier, rates for group insurance are typically lower than for individual policies. Also, insurance benefits are not subject to income tax, unlike wages and salaries. When employees receive insurance as a benefit, rather than higher pay so they can buy their own insurance, employees can get more for their money. Because of this, most employees value group insurance. The most common types of insurance offered as employee benefits are medical, life, and disability insurance. As noted in the earlier discussion of benefits required under law, the U.S. government will require medium-sized and large businesses to offer health insurance or pay a penalty beginning in 2014; but until then, medical insurance is an optional benefit, and businesses continue to have many choices in the types of coverage they offer.

Medical Insurance   Although few employees fully appreciate what health insurance costs the employer, most value this benefit and look for it when they are contemplating a job offer.[12] As Figure 13.2 shows, almost three-quarters of full-time employees receive medical benefits. The policies typically cover three basic types of medical expenses: hospital expenses, surgical expenses, and visits to physicians. Some employers offer additional coverage, such as dental care, vision care, birthing centers, and prescription drug programs. Under the Mental Health Parity and Addiction Equity Act of 2008, if health insurance plans for employees include coverage for mental health care, that care must include the same scope of financial and treatment coverage as treatment for other illnesses. That means deductibles, copayments, coinsurance, and the number of covered days for hospitalization must be the same for treating mental illness and other illnesses. This law exempts companies with fewer than 50 employees. Companies in states with stricter requirements must also meet the state requirements. In the past, many health insurance policies limited payments for treating mental illness, so the law could have the effect of making health insurance a more expensive benefit. However, a recent survey of employers found that most companies providing health insurance included coverage for mental illness.[13]

Employers that offer medical insurance must meet the requirements of the **Consolidated Omnibus Budget Reconciliation Act (COBRA)** of 1985. This federal law requires employers to permit employees to extend their health insurance coverage at group rates for up to 36 months following a "qualifying event." Qualifying events include termination (except for gross misconduct), a reduction in hours that leads to loss of health insurance, and the employee's death (in which case the surviving spouse or dependent child would extend the coverage). To extend the coverage, the employee or the surviving spouse or dependent must pay for the insurance, but the payments are at the group rate. These employees and their families must have access to the same services as those who did not lose their health insurance.

As we will discuss later in the chapter, health insurance is a significant and fast-growing share of benefits costs at U.S. organizations, far outpacing the inflation rate.[14] Figure 13.3 shows that the United States spends much more of its total wealth on health care than other countries do. Most Western European countries have nationalized health systems, but the majority of Americans with coverage for health care expenses get it through their own or a family member's employer. As a result, a growing number of employees whose employers cannot afford this benefit are left without insurance to cover health care expenses.

LO 13-4 Identify the kinds of insurance benefits offered by employers.

Consolidated Omnibus Budget Reconciliation Act (COBRA)
Federal law that requires employers to permit employees or their dependents to extend their health insurance coverage at group rates for up to 36 months following a qualifying event, such as a layoff, reduction in hours, or the employee's death.

Figure 13.3

Health Care Costs in
Various Countries

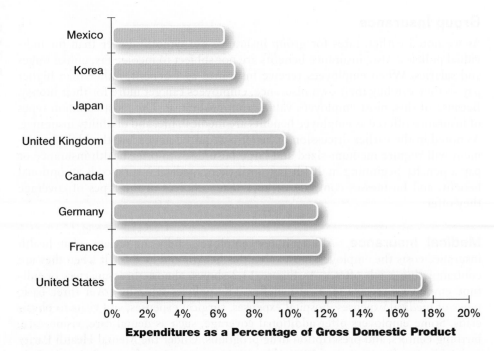

SOURCE: Organisation for Economic Co-operation and Development, "Health Expenditures and Financing," *OECD StatExtracts,* http://stats.oecd.org, accessed April 25, 2012.

Employers have looked for ways to control the cost of health care coverage while keeping this valuable benefit. They have used variations of managed care, employee-driven savings, and promotion of employee wellness:

Health Maintenance Organization (HMO)
A health care plan that requires patients to receive their medical care from the HMO's health care professionals, who are often paid a flat salary, and provides all services on a prepaid basis.

Preferred Provider Organization (PPO)
A health care plan that contracts with health care professionals to provide services at a reduced fee and gives patients financial incentives to use network providers.

- With *managed care*, the insurer plays a role in decisions about health care, aimed at avoiding unnecessary procedures. The insurer may conduct claims review, studying claims to determine whether procedures are effective for the type of illness or injury. Patients may be required to obtain approval before hospital admissions, and the insurer may require alternatives to hospital stays—for example, outpatient surgery or home health care.

- A **health maintenance organization (HMO)** is a health care plan that requires patients to receive their medical care from the HMO's health care professionals, who are often paid a flat salary, and provides all services on a prepaid basis. In other words, the premiums paid for the HMO cover all the patient's visits and procedures, without an additional payment from the patient. By paying physicians a salary, rather than a fee for each service, the HMO hopes to remove any incentive to provide more services than the patients really need. HMO coverage tends to cost less than traditional health insurance. The downside is that employees sometimes complain cost-control incentives work so well that they are denied access to services they actually need.

- A **preferred provider organization (PPO)** is a health care plan that contracts with health care professionals to provide services at a reduced fee. Often, the PPO does not require employees to use providers in the network, but it pays a larger share of the cost of services from PPO providers. For example, the employee might pay 10% of the cost of a test by an in-network provider and 20% if the employee goes out of the PPO network. PPOs have quickly grown to become the most widely used health plan among U.S. employers. A recent survey by the Society for Human

Resource Management found that 84% of employers were offering PPOs, but only 33% included HMOs as an option in their benefit plans.[15]

- With a **flexible spending account,** employees set aside a portion of pretax earnings to pay for eligible expenses. In particular, a *medical savings account* lets employees use their pretax savings to pay for qualified health care expenses (for example, payment of premiums). To avoid taxation, the money in the account must meet IRS requirements. Contributions to this account may not exceed $5,000 per year and must be designated in advance. The money in the account may be spent on health care expenses of the employee and employee's dependents during the plan year. At the end of the year, any remaining funds in the account revert to the employer. The major advantage of flexible spending accounts is that the money in the account is not taxed, so employees will have more take-home pay. But if they do not use all the money in the flexible spending account, they lose the amount they do not spend. Therefore, employees are most likely to benefit from a flexible spending account if they have predictable health care expenses, such as insurance premiums.

Flexible Spending Account
Employee-controlled pretax earnings set aside to pay for certain eligible expenses, such as health care expenses, during the same year.

- *Consumer-driven health plans* (CDHPs) are intended to provide health coverage in a way that gets employees involved as consumers making decisions to lower costs. A CDHP typically brings together three elements: insurance with a high deductible, a medical savings account in which the employer contributes to employee-controlled accounts for paying expenses below the deductible, and health education aimed at helping employees improve their health and thus lower their need for health care. The insurance described in the example of Wal-Mart at the beginning of this chapter has characteristics of a CDHP: high deductibles coupled with a savings plan. Surveys of insured workers have found slow but steady growth in the share of employees who enroll in these plans. Compared with employees who have traditional insurance coverage, CDHP enrollees are more likely to be unmarried, to have a college education, and to rate their health as excellent or very good.[16] Perhaps these workers feel more confident in their ability to limit their own health care costs.

- An **employee wellness program (EWP)** is a set of communications, activities, and facilities designed to change health-related behaviors in ways that reduce health risks. Typically, an EWP aims at specific health risks, such as high blood pressure, high cholesterol levels, smoking, and obesity, by encouraging preventive measures such as exercise and good nutrition. *Passive* programs provide information and services, but no formal support or motivation to use the program. Examples include health education (such as lunchtime courses) and fitness facilities. *Active* wellness programs assume that behavior change requires support and reinforcement along with awareness and opportunity. Such a program may include counselors who tailor programs to individual employees' needs, take baseline measurements (for example, blood pressure and weight), and take follow-up measures for comparison to the baseline. In general, passive health education programs cost less than fitness facilities and active wellness programs.[17] All these variations have had success in reducing risk factors associated with cardiovascular disease (obesity, high blood pressure, smoking, lack of exercise), but the follow-up method is most successful.

Employee Wellness Program (EWP)
A set of communications, activities, and facilities designed to change health-related behaviors in ways that reduce health risks.

Tom Johnson runs on a treadmill at the Western & Southern Financial Group headquarters building in Cincinnati. The company is encouraging employees to reduce their health risks as insurance costs climb. Can you think of firms that offer other unique benefits to reduce health risks?

The "Best Practices" box describes how companies are using wellness programs and other methods to slow the increases in their cost for health insurance benefits.

Best Practices

Reining In Rising Health Care Costs

In a recent study of wellness programs, researchers at Harvard concluded that employers are saving $3 for every dollar they spend on those programs. When employees take better care of themselves, they don't need as much care from their doctors and pharmacists. With savings like that, it is no surprise that some companies want to spread out the returns to employees' families covered by health insurance benefits. At Dell, when employees' spouses participate in wellness programs, the company applies a discount to employees' health insurance premiums. And at JPMorgan Chase, family members as well as the employees themselves have access to health coaches.

Other companies are saving money by limiting who is covered when employees are married. In two-career couples, a company could be paying for a family plan when an employee's spouse already has a full health care plan through his or her own employer. In such cases, the employer could

be paying a great deal of money for benefits that have little practical value to the employees receiving the coverage. Therefore, some employers are establishing policies that either exclude spouses with their own insurance or else require the employee to pay a surcharge for covering a spouse who has insurance already through his or her employer. Other employers are letting prices, rather than rules, guide employees to cost-effective choices. These employers charge higher premiums for a spouse's coverage than for an employee's coverage. This gives employees an incentive to get spousal coverage from the spouse's employer. Xerox Corporation is one of the companies using a surcharge; it expects to cut the cost of health benefits by 2%—a substantial sum at a large organization.

In an effort that exemplifies the company's culture of relying on data and analytics, Google is approaching health care costs by finding ways to nudge employees into healthy behavior—and measuring to make

sure that those nudges are actually delivering results. For example, Google moved its cafeteria salad bar to a spot just inside the entrance and shifted the dessert selection to an out-of-the-way location because it found that whatever employees see first is most likely to go on their plates. And by the plates, the company posted a sign saying that people who use bigger dishes tend to eat more. After the sign went up, the use of small plates rose by 50%. Measuring plate usage is a lot less intrusive than tracking employees' weight, and the company hopes such efforts will result in trimmer, healthier workers, who presumably will cost less to insure.

SOURCES: Cliff Kuang, "In the Cafeteria, Google Gets Healthy," *Fast Company,* March 2, 2012, http://www .fastcompany.com; David Tobenkin, "Spousal Exclusions on the Rise," *HR Magazine,* November 2011, pp. 55–58; Michelle Conlin, "Health Care: Human Resources Targets Your Family," *Bloomberg Businessweek,* January 21, 2010, http://www.businessweek.com.

Short-Term Disability Insurance
Insurance that pays a percentage of a disabled employee's salary as benefits to the employee for six months or less.

Long-Term Disability Insurance
Insurance that pays a percentage of a disabled employee's salary after an initial period and potentially for the rest of the employee's life.

Life Insurance   Employers may provide life insurance to employees or offer the opportunity to buy coverage at low group rates. With a *term life insurance* policy, if the employee dies during the term of the policy, the employee's beneficiaries receive a payment called the death benefit. In policies purchased as an employee benefit, the usual death benefit is twice the employee's yearly pay. The policies may provide additional benefits for accidental death and dismemberment (loss of a body part such as a hand or foot). Along with a basic policy, the employer may give employees the option of purchasing additional coverage, usually at a nominal cost.

Disability Insurance   Employees risk losing their incomes if a disability makes them unable to work. Disability insurance provides protection against this loss of income. Typically, **short-term disability insurance** provides benefits for six months or less. **Long-term disability insurance** provides benefits after that initial period, potentially for the rest of the disabled employee's life. Disability payments are a percentage of the employee's salary—typically 50% to 70%. Payments under short-term plans may be higher. Often the policy sets a maximum amount that may be paid each month. Because its limits make it more affordable, short-term disability coverage is offered by more employers. Fewer than half of employers offer long-term plans.

In planning an employee benefits package, the organization should keep in mind that Social Security includes some long-term disability benefits. To manage benefits costs, the employer should ensure that the disability insurance is coordinated with Social Security and any other programs that help workers who become disabled.

Long-Term Care Insurance   The cost of long-term care, such as care in a nursing home, can be devastating. Today, with more people living to an advanced age, many people are concerned about affording long-term care. Some employers address this concern by offering long-term care insurance. These policies provide benefits toward the cost of long-term care and related medical expenses.

Retirement Plans

Despite the image of retired people living on their Social Security checks, Figure 13.4 shows that those checks amount to less than half of a retired person's income. Among persons over age 65, pensions provided a significant share of income in 2010. Employers have no obligation to offer retirement plans beyond the protection of Social Security, but most offer some form of pension or retirement savings plan. About half of employees working for private businesses (that is, nongovernment jobs) have employer-sponsored retirement plans. These plans are most common for higher-earning employees. Among employees earning the top one-fourth of incomes, 80% participate in a retirement plan, and almost one out of four employees in the bottom one-fourth have such plans.[18] Retirement plans may be **contributory plans,** meaning they are funded by contributions from the employer and employee, or **noncontributory plans,** meaning all the contributions come from the employer.

Defined-Benefit Plans   Employers have a choice of using retirement plans that define the amount to be paid out after retirement or plans that define the amount the employer will invest each year. A **defined-benefit plan** guarantees a specified level of retirement income. Usually the amount of this defined benefit is calculated for each employee based on the employee's years of service, age, and earnings level (for example, the average of the employee's five highest-earnings years). These calculations typically result in pension payments that range from 20% of final salary for an employee who is relatively young and has few years of service to 35% of the final salary of an older employee who has spent many years with the organization. Using years of service as part of the basis for calculating benefits gives employees an incentive to stay with the organization as long as they can, so it can help to reduce voluntary turnover.

Defined-benefit plans must meet the funding requirements of the **Employee Retirement Income Security Act (ERISA)** of 1974. This law increased the responsibility of pension plan trustees to protect retirees, established certain rights related to vesting (earning a right to receive the pension) and *portability* (being able to move retirement savings when changing employers), and created the **Pension**

LO 13-5 Define the types of retirement plans offered by employers.

Contributory Plan
Retirement plan funded by contributions from the employer and employee.

Noncontributory Plan
Retirement plan funded entirely by contributions from the employer.

Defined-Benefit Plan
Pension plan that guarantees a specified level of retirement income.

Employee Retirement Income Security Act (ERISA)
Federal law that increased the responsibility of pension plan trustees to protect retirees, established certain rights related to vesting and portability, and created the Pension Benefit Guarantee Corporation.

Figure 13.4
Sources of Income for Persons 65 and Older

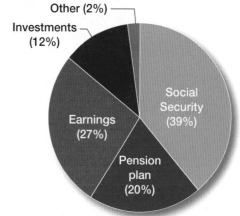

SOURCE: Based on Employee Benefit Research Institute, "Sources of Income for Persons Aged 55 and Over," Chapter 7, *EBRI Databook on Employee Benefits,* Chart 7.1b, updated November 2011, www.ebri.org.

Pension Benefit Guarantee Corporation (PBGC)
Federal agency that insures retirement benefits and guarantees retirees a basic benefit if the employer experiences financial difficulties.

Benefit Guarantee Corporation (PBGC). The PBGC is the federal agency that insures retirement benefits and guarantees retirees a basic benefit if the employer experiences financial difficulties. To fund the PBGC, employers must make annual contributions of $35 per fund participant. Plans that are *underfunded*—meaning the employer does not contribute enough to the plan each year to meet future obligations—must pay an additional premium tied to the amount by which the plan is underfunded.[19] The PBGC's protection applies to the pensions of more than 44 million workers.

With a defined-benefit plan, the employer sets up a pension fund to invest the contributions. As required by ERISA, the employer must contribute enough for the plan to cover all the benefits to be paid out to retirees. Defined-benefit plans protect employees from the risk that the pension fund will not earn as much as expected. If the pension fund earns less than expected, the employer makes up the difference from other sources. If the employer experiences financial difficulties so that it must end or reduce employee pension benefits, the PBGC provides a basic benefit, which does not necessarily cover the full amount promised by the employer's pension plan. The PBGC establishes a maximum, which varies with the age of retirement (those who retire later get larger maximum benefits). In 2012, the maximum PBGC benefit for someone who retired at age 65 was $4,653 per month. As discussed in the "HR Oops!" box, the inability to fully fund pension plans has been a problem for both business and government in recent years.

Defined-Contribution Plan
Retirement plan in which the employer sets up an individual account for each employee and specifies the size of the investment into that account.

Defined-Contribution Plans   An alternative to defined benefits is a **defined-contribution plan,** which sets up an individual account for each employee and specifies the size of the investment into that account, rather than the amount to be paid out upon retirement. The amount the retiree receives will depend on the account's performance. Many kinds of defined-contribution plans are available, including the following:

- *Money purchase plan*—The employer specifies a level of annual contributions (for example, 10% of salary). The contributions are invested, and when the employee retires, he or she is entitled to receive the amount of the contributions plus the investment earnings. ("Money purchase" refers to the fact that when employees retire, they often buy an annuity with the money, rather than taking it as a lump sum.)
- *Profit-sharing and employee stock ownership plans*—As we saw in Chapter 12, incentive pay may take the form of profit sharing and employee stock ownership plans (ESOPs). These payments may be set up so that the money goes into retirement plans. By defining its contributions in terms of stock or a share of profits, the organization has more flexibility to contribute less dollar value in lean years and more in good years.
- *Section 401(k) plans*—Employees contribute a percentage of their earnings, and employers may make matching contributions. The amount employees contribute is not taxed as part of their income until they receive it from the plan. The federal government limits the amount that may be contributed each year. The limit is $17,000 in 2012 and is subject to cost-of-living increases in years after 2012. The contribution limits are higher for persons 50 and older.[20]

These plans free employers from the risks that investments will not perform as well as expected. They put the responsibility for wise investing squarely on the shoulders of each employee. A defined-contribution plan is also easier to administer. The employer need not calculate payments based on age and service, and payments to the PBGC are not required. Considering the advantages to employers, it is not surprising that a

HR Oops!

Out of Money to Pay Pension Obligations

In what is expected to be the biggest default of a defined-benefit pension plan, American Airlines recently declared that as it entered bankruptcy, it would be unable to pay the pensions of 130,000 pilots, flight attendants, agents, and ground crews. The airline asked for permission to terminate the plans and replace them with defined-contribution plans called 401(k) plans. The money it had set aside in its defined-benefit plans—$8.3 billion to cover $18.5 billion worth of benefits—would be transferred to the Pension Benefit Guarantee Corporation.

American is hardly the only company struggling to fund its pension plans. In a recent survey of large companies with pension plans, the plans were only 78% funded.

Some governments have worse track records. State and local governments have a history of setting up pension plans for their employees, and many of these have been chronically underfunded. Often, the pension benefits for government workers—especially for police and fire fighters, whose physically demanding jobs are cited as a reason for retiring young—are generous compared with private-sector benefits. In San Diego, for example, the city government's future pension liability costs 11 cents of every payroll dollar. But because in the past San Diego underfunded its pensions, it actually needs to set aside 41 cents of every dollar if it is to catch up. Among state governments, the worst offender is West Virginia, which has funded only 43% of its pensions.

Why are government pensions so underfunded? One reason is that recent market returns have been poor. A bigger reason is that when governments are looking for ways to balance their budgets, they often find it easiest to make the cuts in pension contributions, on the grounds that they will make up the difference later, when the state's economy is stronger. But those later boom times seem to remain in the future.

Questions

1. Why do you think some businesses and governments don't fully fund their defined benefit pension plans? What are the consequences?
2. Which is the best solution to underfunding of pension plans: a better process for funding them or a switch to defined-contribution plans? Does your answer depend on whether you are thinking of businesses or governments?

SOURCES: Roger Lowenstein, "Pension, or Ponzi Scheme?" *Bloomberg Businessweek,* April 4, 2012, EBSCOhost, http://web.ebscohost.com; Mark Miller, "American Airlines Pension Default Q&A," *Reuters,* February 8, 2012, http://www.reuters.com; Susan Carey, Gina Chon, and Mike Spector, "AMR in Pension-Plan Spat," *The Wall Street Journal,* January 14, 2012, http://online.wsj.com.

growing share of retirement plans are defined-contribution plans. Since the 1980s, the share of employees participating in defined-benefit plans has been steadily falling, and the share participating in defined-contribution plans has risen. In medium and large establishments, less than one-third of employees are enrolled in defined-benefit plans, while over half participate in a defined-contribution plan.[21]

When retirement plans make individual employees responsible for investment decisions, the employees need information about retirement planning. Retirement savings plans often give employees much control over decisions about when and how much to invest. Many employees do not appreciate the importance of beginning to save early in their careers. As Figure 13.5 shows, an employee who invests $3,000 a year ($250 a month) between the ages of 21 and 29 will have far more at age 65 than an employee who invests the same amount between ages 31 and 39. Another important lesson is to diversify investments. Based on investment performance between 1946 and 1990, stocks earned an average of 11.4% per year, bonds earned 5.1%, and bank savings accounts earned 5.3%. But in any given year, one of these types of investments might outperform the other. And within the categories of stocks and bonds, it is important to invest in a wide variety of companies. If one company performs poorly, the investments in other companies might perform better. However, studies of investment decisions by

Figure 13.5
Value of Retirement Savings Invested at Different Ages

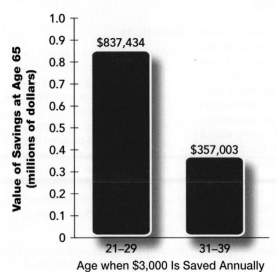

Note: Investment portfolio consists of 60% stocks, 30% bonds, and 10% cash (e.g., money-market funds, bank savings accounts), assuming average rates of return based on historical rates from 1946 to 1990.

Cash Balance Plan
Retirement plan in which the employer sets up an individual account for each employee and contributes a percentage of the employee's salary; the account earns interest at a predefined rate.

employees have found that few employees have followed basic guidelines for diversifying investments among stocks, bonds, and savings accounts according to their age and investment needs.[22] To help employees handle such risks, some organizations provide financial planning as a separate benefit, offer an option to have a professional invest the funds in a 401(k) plan, or direct funds into default investments called target date funds (TDFs), which are geared toward the needs of employees at different life stages. In the years after investment firm Vanguard began offering TDFs, the share of employees who allocated their investments into extremely concentrated positions fell from 35% to 18%.

In spite of these challenges, defined-contribution plans also offer an advantage to employees in today's highly mobile workforce. They do not penalize employees for changing jobs. With these plans, retirement earnings are less related to the number of years an employee stays with a company.

Cash Balance Plans   An increasingly popular way to combine the advantages of defined-benefit plans and defined-contribution plans is to use a **cash balance plan.** This type of retirement plan consists of individual accounts, as in a 401(k) plan. But in contrast to a 401(k), all the contributions come from the employer. Usually, the employer contributes a percentage of the employee's salary, say, 4% or 5%. The money in the cash balance plan earns interest according to a predetermined rate, such as the rate paid on U.S. Treasury bills. Employers guarantee this rate as in a defined-benefit plan. This arrangement helps employers plan their contributions and helps employees predict their retirement benefits. If employees change jobs, they generally can roll over the balance into an individual retirement account.

A switch from traditional defined-benefit plans to cash balance plans, like any major change, requires employers to consider the effects on employees as well as on the organization's bottom line. Defined-benefit plans are most generous to older employees with many years of service, and cash balance plans are most generous to young employees who will have many years ahead in which to earn interest. For an organization with many experienced employees, switching from a defined-benefit plan can produce great savings in pension benefits. In that case, the older workers are the greatest losers, unless the organization adjusts the program to retain their benefits. After IBM switched to a cash-benefit plan, a group of employees filed an age discrimination lawsuit. IBM won the lawsuit on appeal, and the Pension Protection Act of 2006 seeks to clarify the legal requirements of such plans. As a result, some companies may renew their interest in cash balance plans, but IBM has decided to focus on its 401(k) plan.

Government Requirementsl for Vesting and Communication   Along with requirements for funding defined-benefit plans, ERISA specifies a number of requirements related to eligibility for benefits and communication with employees. ERISA guarantees employees that when they become participants in a pension plan and work a specified number of years, they earn a right to a pension upon retirement. These rights are called **vesting rights.** Employees whose contributions are *vested* have met the requirements (enrolling and length of service) to receive a pension at retirement age, regardless of whether they remained with the employer until that time. Employees' own contributions to their pension plans are always completely vested. In most cases, the vesting of employer-funded pension benefits must take place under one of two schedules selected by the employer:

1. The employer may vest employees after five years and may provide zero vesting until that time.
2. The employer may vest employees over a three- to seven-year period, with at least 20% vesting in the third year and at least an additional 20% in each year after the third year.

These two schedules represent minimum requirements. Employers may vest employees more quickly if they wish. Two less-common situations have different vesting requirements. One is a "top-heavy" pension plan, meaning pension benefits for *key employees* (such as highly paid top managers) exceed a government-specified share of total pension benefits. A top-heavy plan requires faster vesting for nonkey employees. Another exception from the usual schedule involves multiemployer pension plans. These plans need not provide vesting until after 10 years of employment.

The intent of vesting requirements is to protect employees by preventing employers from terminating them before they meet retirement age in order to avoid paying pension benefits. In addition, it is illegal for employers to transfer or lay off employees as a way to avoid pension obligations, even if these changes are motivated partly by business need.[23] One way employers may legally try to minimize pension costs is in choosing a vesting schedule. For example, if many employees leave after three or four years of employment, the five-year vesting schedule would minimize pension costs.

ERISA's reporting and disclosure requirements involve the Internal Revenue Service, the Department of Labor, and employees.[24] Within 90 days after employees enter a plan, they must receive a **summary plan description (SPD),** a report that describes the plan's funding, eligibility requirements, risks, and other details. If the employee requests one, the employer must also make available an individual benefit statement, which describes the employee's vested and unvested benefits. Many employers provide such information regularly, without waiting for employee requests. This type of communication helps employees understand and value their retirement benefits.

"Family-Friendly" Benefits

As employers have recognized the significance of employees' need to manage conflicts between their work and family roles, many have added "family-friendly" benefits to their employee benefits. These benefits include family leave policies and child care. The programs discussed here apply directly to the subset of employees with family responsibilities. However, family-friendly benefits often have spillover effects in the form of loyalty because employees see the benefits as evidence that the organization cares about its people.[25] The following types of benefits are typical:

- *Family leave*—Family or parental leave grants employees time off to care for children and other dependents. As discussed earlier in the chapter, federal law requires 12 weeks of unpaid leave. Companies may choose to offer more generous leave policies, and California requires 6 weeks of leave at up to 55% of pay. Recent data from the Census Bureau show roughly half of U.S. women receiving some form of

---

Vesting Rights
Guarantee that when employees become participants in a pension plan and work a specified number of years, they will receive a pension at retirement age, regardless of whether they remained with the employer.

Summary Plan Description (SPD)
Report that describes a pension plan's funding, eligibility requirements, risks, and other details.

LO 13-6 Describe how organizations use other benefits to match employees' wants and needs.

Child Care Assistance Is Usually Cash Assistance

According to a recent survey of employed mothers by Care.com, child care benefits are uncommon. But among companies offering such benefits, the most common way employers give employees child care assistance is with flexible spending accounts that may be used for that purpose. Less-common forms of child care benefits include on-site child care, emergency backup care, and subsidies to help employees pay for child care.

Question

In your opinion, why are flexible spending accounts the most common way that companies provide child care benefits?

SOURCES: Laura Walter, "Survey: Employed Moms Enjoy Working, but Workplaces Fall Short on Childcare Benefits," *EHS Today,* March 29, 2012, http://www.ehstoday.com; Care.com, "Working Mothers Feel Empowered at Work and Supported at Home, but Few Have Support in the Workplace according to a New Survey from Care.com," news release, February 21, 2012, http://www.care.com; BLR, "Three-Quarters of Companies Where Working Moms Are Employed Don't Offer Child Care Benefits," *HR and Employment Law News,* February 21, 2012, http://hr.blr.com.

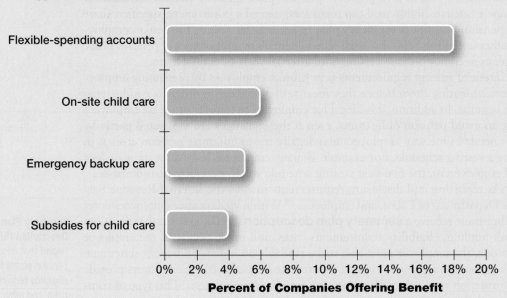

Type of Child Care Benefit

Flexible-spending accounts
On-site child care
Emergency backup care
Subsidies for child care

0% 2% 4% 6% 8% 10% 12% 14% 16% 18% 20%

Percent of Companies Offering Benefit

paid leave (maternity leave, vacation, or sick time) after they have a child. First-time mothers who received paid leave were more likely to be at least 25 years old, to work full-time, and to be college graduates. In contrast, most industrialized nations provide paid maternal leave and often paternal leave as well. The norm in Western Europe is at least three to four months' maternity leave at 80% to 100% of pay, plus additional (often unpaid) parental leave for both parents.[26]

- *Child care*—Child care benefits may take several forms, requiring different levels of organizational involvement (see "Did You Know?"). The lowest level of involvement is for the organization to supply and help employees collect information about the cost and quality of available child care. At the next level, organizations provide vouchers or discounts for employees to use at existing child care facilities. At the highest level of involvement, the employer provides child care at or near the work site. Staffing a child care facility is costly and involves important liability concerns.

At the same time, the results of this type of benefit, in terms of reducing absenteeism and enhancing productivity, have been mixed.[27] At AOL's offices in Virginia, setting up an on-site child care center made sense because many of the employees there have young children. The company sees an increase in employee loyalty and retention as a result. However, AOL recognizes that this type of benefit is not valued by all employees, so it also offers other programs aimed at employees with different needs.[28]

- *College savings*—As workers' children grow up, their needs shift from maternity leave and child care to college tuition. Some organizations have supported this concern by sponsoring tax-favored *529 savings plans*. These plans, named after the section of the Internal Revenue Code that regulates them, let parents and other family members defer taxes on the earnings of their deposits into the 529 account. Some states also provide a (limited) tax deduction for these contributions. As an employee benefit, organizations can arrange with a broker to offer direct deposit of a portion of employees' paychecks into their accounts. Besides offering the convenience of direct deposit, employers can negotiate lower management fees. At Johns Hopkins Bayview Medical Center, all employees are eligible to participate in a college savings plan that deducts contributions from employees' paychecks. This benefit is part of a compensation package designed to promote employees' personal and professional growth; related benefits include tuition reimbursement for employees (up to full tuition) and their dependent children (up to 50% reimbursement).[29]

- *Elder care*—As the population of the nation's elderly grows, so do the demands on adult children to care for elderly parents, aunts, and uncles. When these people become ill or disabled, they rely on family or professional caregivers. Responsibilities such as providing assistance, paying for professional caregivers, and locating services can be expensive, time consuming, and exhausting, often distracting employees from their work roles. In response, many employers have added elder care benefits. These programs often started by offering employees information and referrals; today these resources are often made available online. More recent enhancements of elder care benefits include referrals to decision support from experts in geriatric care, insurance, and the law, as well as flexible hours and paid time off. Employees at Johnson & Johnson have free use of a service that assesses elderly relatives' needs, helps the employee plan and coordinate services, reviews care facilities, helps employees select caregivers, assists with paperwork, and provides referrals to community services.[30] Even companies that cannot afford to offer counseling or referral services can use intranets to provide links to helpful websites such as the National Alliance for Caregiving (**www.caregiving.org**), the National Council on Aging (**www.benefitscheckup.org**), and the federal government's benefits information site (**www.benefits.gov**).

Other Benefits

The scope of possible employee benefits is limited only by the imagination of the organization's decision makers. Organizations have developed a wide variety of benefits to meet the needs of employees and to attract and keep the kinds of workers who will be of value to the organization. Traditional extras include subsidized cafeterias, on-site health care for minor injuries or illnesses, and moving expenses for newly hired or relocating employees. Stores and manufacturers may offer employee discounts on their products.

To encourage learning and attract the kinds of employees who wish to develop their knowledge and skills, many organizations offer *tuition reimbursement* programs.

In order to provide a relaxed environment for their employees, one of the perks at Neversoft Entertainment is allowing employees to bring their pets to work. What other unique benefits do companies offer their employees?

A typical program covers tuition and related expenses for courses that are relevant to the employee's current job or future career at the organization. Employees are reimbursed for these expenses after they demonstrate they have completed an approved course.

Especially for demanding, high-stress jobs, organizations may look for benefits that help employees put in the necessary long hours and alleviate stress. Recreational activities such as on-site basketball courts or company-sponsored softball teams provide for social interaction as well as physical activity. Employers may reward hard-working groups or individuals with a trip for a weekend, a meal, or any activity employees are likely to enjoy. Employees at Yelp, which runs the user review website of the same name, can visit the company's pub, and at Etsy, which runs an online marketplace, employees get special weekly meals created from locally sourced ingredients. Busy employees of S. C. Johnson can take advantage of a concierge service, which will run errands for them.[31]

LO 13-7 Explain how to choose the contents of an employee benefits package.

Selecting Employee Benefits

Although the government requires certain benefits, employers have wide latitude in creating the total benefits package they offer employees.[32] Decisions about which benefits to include should take into account the organization's goals, its budget, and the expectations of the organization's current employees and those it wishes to recruit in the future. Employees have come to expect certain things from employers. An organization that does not offer the expected benefits will have more difficulty attracting and keeping talented workers. Also, if employees believe their employer feels no commitment to their welfare, they are less likely to feel committed to their employer.

The Organization's Objectives

A logical place to begin selecting employee benefits is to establish objectives for the benefits package. This helps an organization select the most effective benefits and

Table 13.2

An Organization's Benefits Objectives

- To establish and maintain an employee benefit program that is based primarily on the employees' needs for leisure time and on protection against the risks of old age, loss of health, and loss of life.
- To establish and maintain an employee benefit program that complements the efforts of employees on their own behalf.
- To evaluate the employee benefit plan annually for its effect on employee morale and productivity, giving consideration to turnover, unfilled positions, attendance, employees' complaints, and employees' opinions.
- To compare the employee benefit plan annually with that of other leading companies in the same field and to maintain a benefit plan with an overall level of benefits based on cost per employee that falls within the second quintile of these companies.
- To maintain a level of benefits for nonunion employees that represents the same level of expenditures per employee as for union employees.
- To determine annually the costs of new, changed, and existing programs as percentages of salaries and wages and to maintain these percentages as much as possible.
- To self-fund benefits to the extent that a long-run cost savings can be expected for the firm and catastrophic losses can be avoided.
- To coordinate all benefits with social insurance programs to which the company makes payments.
- To provide benefits on a noncontributory basis except for dependent coverage, for which employees should pay a portion of the cost.
- To maintain continual communications with all employees concerning benefit programs.

SOURCE: Adapted from B. T. Beam Jr. and J. J. McFadden, *Employee Benefits,* 3rd ed. Copyright © 1992 by Dearborn Financial Publishing, Inc. Published by Dearborn Financial Publishing, Inc., Chicago. All rights reserved.

monitor whether the benefits are doing what they should. Table 13.2 is an example of one organization's benefits objectives. Unfortunately, research suggests that most organizations do not have written benefits objectives.

Among companies that do set goals, common objectives include controlling the cost of health care benefits and retaining employees.[33] The first goal explains the growing use of wellness programs and consumer-directed health plans. For the second goal, employees do say that valued benefits keep them from walking away, but employers need to learn what employees care about. To find out what its young, predominately male workforce values, British mobile-phone service Three got its staff involved in designing the benefits package. The result was a set of flexible benefits that is heavy on communication and personal control. Employees can "buy" or "sell" time off if the basic package is too little or too much, and they can buy into health benefits over and above those provided through the government. An online pension calculator shows them how their retirement savings are expected to grow, given their current or possible rates of contribution to the plan.[34]

Employees' Expectations and Values

Employees expect to receive benefits that are legally required and widely available, and they value benefits they are likely to use. To meet employee expectations about benefits, it can be helpful to see what other organizations offer. Employers can purchase survey information about benefits packages from private consultants. In addition, the Bureau of Labor Statistics gathers benefits data. The BLS website (**www.bls.gov**) is therefore a good place to check for free information about employee benefits in the United States. With regard to value, medical insurance is a high-value benefit because employees usually realize that surgery or a major illness can be financially devastating. Vision and dental care tend to be much less expensive, but many employees appreciate this type of coverage because so many people receive dental or vision care in the course of a year. Therefore, in contrast to the example of Wal-Mart at the beginning of this chapter, employers tend to try to maintain basic health insurance coverage, and if they must cut benefits to save money, they more often eliminate long-term care insurance and health coverage for retirees.[35]

Employers should also consider that the value employees place on various benefits is likely to differ from one employee to another. At a broad level, basic demographic factors such as age and sex can influence the kinds of benefits employees want. An older workforce is more likely to be concerned about (and use) medical coverage, life insurance, and pensions. A workforce with a high percentage of women of childbearing age may care more about disability or family leave. Young, unmarried men and women often place more value on pay than on benefits. However, these are only general observations; organizations should check which considerations apply to their own employees and identify more specific needs and differences. One approach is to use surveys to ask employees about the kinds of benefits they value. The survey should be carefully worded so as not to raise employees' expectations by seeming to promise all the benefits asked about at no cost to the employee.

The choice of benefits may influence current employees' satisfaction and may also affect the organization's recruiting, in terms of both the ease of recruiting and the kinds of employees attracted to the organization. For example, a benefits package that has strong medical benefits and pensions may be particularly attractive to older people or to those with many dependents. Such benefits may attract people with extensive experience and those who wish to make a long-term commitment to the organization. This strategy may be especially beneficial when turnover costs are very high. On the other hand, offering generous health care benefits may attract and retain people with high health care costs. Thus, organizations need to consider the signals sent by their benefits package as they set goals for benefits and select benefits to offer.

Organizations can address differences in employees' needs and empower their employees by offering flexible benefits plans in place of a single benefits package for all employees. These plans, often called **cafeteria-style plans,** offer employees a set of alternatives from which they can choose the types and amounts of benefits they want. The plans vary. Some impose minimum levels for certain benefits, such as health care coverage; some allow better employees to receive money in exchange for choosing a "light" package; and some let employees pay extra for the privilege of receiving more benefits. For example, some plans let employees give up vacation days for more pay or to purchase extra vacation days in exchange for a reduction in pay.

Cafeteria-Style Plan
A benefits plan that offers employees a set of alternatives from which they can choose the types and amounts of benefits they want.

Cafeteria-style plans have a number of advantages.[36] The selection process can make employees more aware of the value of the benefits, particularly when the plan assigns each employee a sum of money to allocate to benefits. Also, the individual choice in a cafeteria plan enables each employee to match his or her needs to the company's benefits, increasing the plan's actual value to the employee. And because employees would not select benefits they don't want, the company avoids the cost of providing employees with benefits they don't value. Another way to control costs is to give employees incentives to choose lower-cost options. For example, the employee's deductible on a higher-cost health plan could be larger than on a relatively low-cost HMO.

A drawback of cafeteria-style plans is that they have a higher administrative cost, especially in the design and start-up stages. Organizations can avoid some of the higher cost, however, by using software packages and standardized plans that have been developed for employers wishing to offer cafeteria-style benefits. Another possible drawback is that employee selection of benefits will increase rather than decrease costs because employees will select the kinds of benefits they expect to need the most. For example, an employee expecting to need a lot of dental work is more likely to sign up for a dental plan. The heavy use of the dental coverage would then drive up the employer's premiums for that coverage. Costs can also be difficult to estimate when employees select their benefits.

Benefits' Costs

Employers also need to consider benefits costs. One place to start is with general information about the average costs of various benefits types. Widely used sources of cost data include the Bureau of Labor Statistics (BLS), Employee Benefit Research Institute, and U.S. Chamber of Commerce. Annual surveys by the Chamber of Commerce state the cost of benefits as a percentage of total payroll costs and in dollar terms.

Employers can use data about costs to help them select the kinds of benefits to offer. But in balancing these decisions against organizational goals and employee benefits, the organization may decide to offer certain high-cost benefits while also looking for ways to control the cost of those benefits. The highest-cost items tend to offer the most room for savings, but only if the items permit choice or negotiation. Also, as we noted earlier, organizations can control certain costs such as workers' compensation by improving their experience ratings. Cost control is especially important—and difficult—when economic growth slows or declines.

In recent years, benefits related to health care have attracted particular attention because these costs have risen very rapidly and because employers have a number of options. Concern over costs has prompted many employers to shift from traditional health insurance to PPOs and CDHPs. Some employers shift more of the cost to employees. They may lower the employer's payments by increasing the amounts employees pay for deductibles and coinsurance (the employee's share of the payment for services). Or they may require employees to pay some or all of the difference in cost between traditional insurance and a lower-cost plan. Excluding or limiting coverage for certain types of claims also can slow the increase in health insurance costs. Employee wellness programs, especially when they are targeted to employees with risk factors and include follow-up and encouragement, can reduce risk factors for disease.[37]

Legal Requirements for Employee Benefits

LO 13-8 Summarize the regulations affecting how employers design and administer benefits programs.

As we discussed earlier in this chapter, some benefits are required by law. This requirement adds to the cost of compensating employees. Organizations looking for ways to control staffing costs may look for ways to structure the workforce so as to minimize the expense of benefits. They may require overtime rather than adding new employees, hire part-time rather than full-time workers (because part-time employees generally receive much smaller benefits packages), and use independent contractors rather than hire employees. Some of these choices are limited by legal requirements, however. For example, the Fair Labor Standards Act requires overtime pay for nonexempt workers, as discussed in Chapter 11. Also, the Internal Revenue Service strictly limits the definition of "independent contractors," so that employees cannot avoid legal obligations by classifying workers as self-employed when the organization receives the benefits of a permanent employee. Other legal requirements involve tax treatment of benefits, antidiscrimination laws, and accounting for benefits.

Tax Treatment of Benefits

The IRS provides more favorable tax treatment of benefits classified as *qualified plans.* The details vary from one type of benefit to another. In the case of retirement plans, the advantages include the ability for employees to immediately take a tax deduction for the funds they contribute to the plans, no immediate tax on employees for the amount the employer contributes, and tax-free earnings on the money in the retirement fund.[38]

To obtain status as a qualified plan, a benefit plan must meet certain requirements.[39] In the case of pensions, these involve vesting and nondiscrimination rules. The nondiscrimination rules provide tax benefits to plans that do not discriminate in favor of the organization's "highly compensated employees." To receive the benefits, the organization cannot set up a retirement plan that provides benefits exclusively to the organization's owners and top managers. The requirements encourage employers to provide important benefits such as pensions to a broad spectrum of employees. Before offering pension plans and other benefits, organizations should have them reviewed by an expert who can advise on whether the benefits are qualified plans.

Antidiscrimination Laws

As we discussed in Chapter 3, a number of laws are intended to provide equal employment opportunity without regard to race, sex, age, disability, and several other protected categories. Some of these laws apply to the organization's benefits policies.

Legal treatment of men and women includes equal access to benefits, so the organization may not use the employee's gender as the basis for providing more limited benefits. That is the rationale for the Pregnancy Discrimination Act, which requires that employers treat pregnancy as it treats any disability. If an employee needs time off for conditions related to pregnancy or childbirth, the employee would receive whatever disability benefits the organization offers to employees who take disability leave for other reasons. Another area of concern in the treatment of male and female employees is pension benefits. On average, women live longer than men, so on average, pension benefits for female employees are more expensive (because the organization pays the pension longer), other things being equal. Some organizations have used this difference as a basis for requiring that female employees contribute more than male employees to defined benefit plans. The Supreme Court in 1978 determined that such a requirement is illegal.[40] According to the Supreme Court, the law is intended to protect individuals, and when women are considered on an individual basis (not as averages), not every woman outlives every man.

Age discrimination is also relevant to benefits policies. Two major issues have received attention under the Age Discrimination in Employment Act (ADEA) and amendments. First, employers must take care not to discriminate against workers over age 40 in providing pay or benefits. For example, employers may not set an age at which retirement benefits stop growing as a way to pressure older workers to retire.[41] Also, early-retirement incentive programs need to meet certain standards. The programs may not coerce employees to retire, they must provide accurate information about the options available, and they must give employees enough time to make a decision. In effect, employees must really have a choice about whether they retire.

When employers offer early retirement, they often ask employees to sign waivers saying they will not pursue claims under the ADEA. The Older Workers Benefit Protection Act of 1990 set guidelines for using these waivers. The waivers must be voluntary and understandable to the employee and employer, and they must spell out the employee's rights under the ADEA. Also, in exchange for signing the waiver, the employee must receive "compensation," that is, greater benefits than he or she would otherwise receive upon retirement. The employer must inform employees that they may consult a lawyer before signing, and employees must have time to make a decision about signing—21 days before signing plus 7 days afterward in which they can revoke the agreement.

The Americans with Disabilities Act imposes requirements related to health insurance. Under the ADA, employees with disabilities must have "equal access to whatever health insurance coverage the employer provides other employees." Even so, the terms and conditions of health insurance may be based on risk factors—as long as the employer does not use this basis as a way to escape offering health insurance to someone with a disability. From the standpoint of avoiding legal challenges, an employer who has risk-based insurance and then hires an employee with a disability is in a stronger position than an employer who switches to a risk-based policy after hiring a disabled employee.[42]

Accounting Requirements

Companies' financial statements must meet the many requirements of the Financial Accounting Standards Board (FASB). These accounting requirements are intended to ensure that financial statements are a true picture of the company's financial status and that outsiders, including potential lenders and investors, can understand and compare financial statements. Under FASB standards, employers must set aside the funds they expect to need for benefits to be paid after retirement, rather than funding those benefits on a pay-as-you-go basis. On financial statements, those funds must appear as future cost obligations. For companies with substantial retirement benefits, reporting those benefits as future cost obligations greatly lowers income each year. Along with rising benefits costs, this reporting requirement has encouraged many companies to scale back benefits to retirees.

Communicating Benefits to Employees

LO 13-9 Discuss the importance of effectively communicating the nature and value of benefits to employees.

Organizations must communicate benefits information to employees so that they will appreciate the value of their benefits. This is essential so that benefits can achieve their objective of attracting, motivating, and retaining employees. Employees are interested in their benefits, and they need a great deal of detailed information to take advantage of benefits such as health insurance and 401(k) plans. It follows that electronic technology such as the Internet and supporting databases can play a significant role in modern benefit systems. Many companies are putting benefits information on their intranets. The "HR How To" box provides suggestions for using Internet technology to communicate effectively the value of the organization's benefits.

In actuality, employees and job applicants often have a poor idea of what benefits they have and what the market value of their benefits is. Research asking employees about their benefits has shown that employees significantly underestimate the cost

Using the Internet to Communicate Benefits

The Internet gives employers powerful capabilities for keeping information about the value of employee benefits at the forefront of workers' minds and for helping workers understand how to get the most out of their benefits. Here are some ideas for communicating about benefits online:

- Post a *total rewards statement* on the company's intranet (a website set up for employees only). These statements display for each employee a personalized accounting of the employee's pay plus the value of each benefit he or she is receiving.
- Enable employee actions at the total rewards statement website or on a site to which the statement links. Some possible actions include enrolling in programs, looking up a history of the growth in the value of the employee's retirement savings plan, and plotting a graph demonstrating the money lost by not taking advantage of employer-matching contributions to retirement savings.
- Post online surveys to find out what employees already know about their benefits, and identify areas in which employees need more information. Surveys also can identify which benefits are associated with the greatest employee satisfaction.
- Send out frequent messages through a variety of channels. Many employees hear about their benefits only when it is time for annual enrollment, and they wish they received more frequent communication. Online channels offer an inexpensive way to deliver short, easily digestible messages sent via e-mail, text messages, tweets (for those with a Twitter account), and links to an online newsletter. These short messages are easier for employees to absorb than the annual presentation of an entire benefits package.
- For employees with mobile devices, the company can provide apps that help employees understand and use their benefits. For example, employees using an app called Limeade enter daily wellness goals. The app tracks the goals and includes a tool that employees can use to compete with their co-workers toward achieving their goals first. GEICO offers federal government employees an app that lets them access the totals in their accounts for vacation and sick leave so they can learn their remaining time off wherever they are.

SOURCES: Aon Corporation, "Total Rewards Statements Enhance Employee Understanding and Appreciation of Value of Benefit Programs, according to Aon Hewitt Research," news release, November 16, 2011, http://aon.mediaroom.com; Thomas Giddens, "Five Tips for Clearly Communicating Employee Benefits," *American City and County,* October 2011, Business & Company Resource Center, http://galenet.galegroup.com; Kathleen Koster, "There's an App for That," *Employee Benefit News,* April 15, 2011, pp. 21–23.

and value of their benefits.[43] Probably a major reason for their lack of knowledge is a lack of communications from employers. Employees don't know what employers are spending for benefits, so many of them doubt employers' complaints about soaring costs and their impact on the company's future.[44] In one study, employees said their company neglected to tell them how to be better consumers of health care, and they would be willing to make changes in their lifestyle if they had a financial incentive to do so. Such research suggests to employers that better communication, coupled with well-designed benefits plans, will pay off in practical terms.

Employers have many options for communicating information about benefits. To increase the likelihood that employees will receive and understand the messages, employers can combine several media, such as brochures, question-and-answer meetings, intranet pages, memos, and e-mail. Some other possible media include paycheck inserts, retirement or health coaching, training programs, and benefits fairs. An investment of creativity in communications to employees can reap great returns in the form of committed, satisfied employees.

THINKING ETHICALLY

THE ETHICS OF SICK LEAVE

Ethical issues arise with paid time off for illness, from both the employer's and employee's perspectives. On the employer's side, decisions about sick leave are generally influenced by costs. The employer is paying the employee while the employee is not working. In a large corporation, it may be relatively simple for the many well employees to keep projects moving ahead while some employees are ill. But in a small organization, the absence of a few employees—or even just one or two—can create significant backlogs, especially if some of those employees have no colleagues qualified to do their work.

This challenge came to the fore recently when Connecticut became the first state to require that all businesses with at least 50 workers offer wage-earning service workers at least five days of paid sick leave. Cities including Seattle, San Francisco, and Washington, DC, have enacted similar requirements. Some business owners worry that they cannot afford such requirements. Others note that when a sick employee comes to work, the spread of infection and the worker's inability to concentrate can cause greater problems than the absence of that employee. Proponents of sick-time rules sometimes maintain that it is a matter of justice and compassion to encourage people to rest when they are ill.

From the employees' perspective, ethical questions involve their impact on others at work and their needs for time to take care of themselves and their dependents. Going to work when sick takes a personal toll and can spread the illness to one's co-workers and customers. Staying home can leave co-workers without support they need to carry out their work. In cases where the company does not pay for sick time, staying home to rest also may create a financial hardship. Low-wage workers are the least likely to have jobs that pay for sick leave.

These decisions are complicated for employees who have dependents. Typically, sick leave is meant for a worker's own illness, but as a practical matter, parents with sick children use this time when a child is ill. This may be seen as an abuse of the policy—or as the employee's only recourse for fulfilling personal duties when a policy does not recognize the realities of family life. But even employees without dependents feel tempted sometimes to take a "mental health" day when they are not actually sick but are mentally or physically worn out.

Questions

1. For an employee, what is the ethical choice to make about going to work when he or she has the flu? How does your answer depend on whether the employee is paid for the time off? How does your answer change, if at all, when the sick person is the employee's young child?
2. For an employer, does ethical conduct require providing employees with paid time off for illness? Why or why not?

SOURCES: Sarah E. Needleman, "Sick-Time Rules Re-emerge," *The Wall Street Journal,* February 29, 2012, http://online.wsj.com; Madeleine Gecht, "Should Every Worker Have Paid Sick Leave? The Ethics of Employee Benefits and Rights," *Ethical Inquiry* (International Center for Ethics, Justice, and Public Life, Brandeis University), August 2011, http://www/brandeis.edu; Peter Applebome, "In Connecticut, Paid Sick Leave for Service Workers Is Approved," *The New York Times,* June 4, 2011, http://www.nytimes.com.

SUMMARY

LO 13-1 Discuss the importance of benefits as a part of employee compensation.

Like pay, benefits help employers attract, retain, and motivate employees. The variety of possible benefits also helps employers tailor their compensation packages to attract the right kinds of employees. Employees expect at least a minimum level of benefits, and providing more than the minimum helps an organization compete in the labor market. Benefits are also a significant expense, but employers provide benefits because employees value them and many benefits are required by law.

LO 13-2 Summarize the types of employee benefits required by law.

Employers must contribute to the Old Age, Survivors, Disability, and Health Insurance program known as Social Security through a payroll tax shared by employers and employees. Employers must also pay federal and state taxes for unemployment insurance, based on each employer's experience rating, or percentage of employees a company has laid off in the past. State laws require that employers purchase workers' compensation insurance. Under the Family and Medical Leave Act, employees who need to care for a baby following birth or adoption or for an ill family member must be granted unpaid leave of up to 12 weeks. Under the Patient Protection and Affordable Care Act, employers need to prepare for future requirements to provide all employees with health insurance, as well as to educate themselves about other provisions such as insurance exchanges, tax rebates for small businesses, and broadened coverage from health insurers.

LO 13-3 Describe the most common forms of paid leave.

The major categories of paid leave are vacations, holidays, and sick leave. Paid time off may seem uneconomical, which may be the reason U.S. employers tend to offer much less vacation time than is common in Western Europe. At large U.S. companies, paid vacation is typically 10 days. The typical number of paid holidays is 10 in both Western Europe and the United States. Sick leave programs often provide full salary replacement for a limited period of time, with the amount of sick leave usually based on length of service. Policies are needed to determine how the organization will handle unused sick days at the end of each year. Some organizations let employees roll over some or all of the unused sick days into the next year, and others let unused days expire at the end of the year. Other forms of paid leave include personal days and floating holidays.

LO 13-4 Identify the kinds of insurance benefits offered by employers.

Medical insurance is one of the most valued employee benefits. Such policies typically cover hospital expenses, surgical expenses, and visits to physicians. Some employers offer additional coverage, such as dental care, vision care, birthing centers, and prescription drug programs. Under the Consolidated Omnibus Budget Reconciliation Act of 1985, employees must be permitted to extend their health insurance coverage at group rates for up to 36 months after they leave the organization. To manage the costs of health insurance, many organizations offer coverage through a health maintenance organization or preferred provider organization, or they may offer flexible spending accounts. Some encourage healthy behaviors through an employee wellness program. Life insurance usually takes the form of group term life insurance, with the usual benefit being two times the employee's yearly pay. Employers may also offer short-term and/or long-term disability insurance, with disability payments being a percentage of the employee's salary. Some employers provide long-term care insurance to pay the costs associated with long-term care such as nursing home care.

LO 13-5 Define the types of retirement plans offered by employers.

Retirement plans may be contributory, meaning funded by contributions from employer and employee, or noncontributory, meaning funded only by the employer. These plans may be defined-benefit plans, which guarantee a specified level of retirement income, usually based on the employee's years of service, age, and earnings level. Benefits under these plans are protected by the Pension Benefit Guarantee Corporation. An alternative is to set up a defined-contribution plan, such as a 401(k) plan. The employer sets up an individual account for each employee and guarantees the size of the investment into that account, rather than the amount to be paid out on retirement. Because employees have control over investment decisions, the organization may also offer financial planning services as an employee benefit. A cash balance plan combines some advantages of defined-benefit plans and defined-contribution plans. The employer sets up individual accounts and contributes a percentage of each employee's salary. The account earns interest at a predetermined rate, so the contributions and benefits are easier to predict.

LO 13-6 Describe how organizations use other benefits to match employees' wants and needs.

Employers have responded to work-family role conflicts by offering family-friendly benefits, including paid family leave, child care services or referrals, college savings plans, and elder care information and support. Other employee benefits have traditionally included subsidized cafeterias, on-site health clinics, and reimbursement of moving expenses. Stores and manufacturers may offer discounts on their products. Tuition reimbursement encourages employees to continue learning. Recreational services and employee outings provide social interaction as well as stress relief.

LO 13-7 Explain how to choose the contents of an employee benefits package.

A logical place to begin is to establish organizational objectives and select benefits that support those objectives. Organizations should also consider employees' expectations and values.

At a minimum, organizations offer the benefits employees have come to view as basic; some organizations go so far as to match extra benefits to individual employees' needs and interests. Cafeteria-style plans are an intermediate step that gives employees control over the benefits they receive. Employers must also weigh the costs of benefits, which are significant.

LO 13-8 Summarize the regulations affecting how employers design and administer benefits programs.

Employers must provide the benefits that are required by law, and they may not improperly classify employees as "independent contractors" to avoid paying benefits. Tax treatment of qualified plans is favorable, so organizations need to learn the requirements for setting up benefits as qualified plans—for example, ensuring that pension plans do not discriminate in favor of the organization's highly compensated employees. Employers may not use employees' gender as the basis for discriminating against anyone, as in pension benefits on the basis that women as a group may live longer. Nor may employers discriminate against workers over age 40 in providing pay or benefits, such as pressuring older workers to retire by limiting retirement benefits. When employers offer early retirement, they must meet the requirements of the Older Workers Benefit Protection Act of 1990. Under the Americans with Disabilities Act, employers must give disabled employees equal access to health insurance. To meet the requirements of the Financial Accounting Standards Board, employers must set aside the funds they expect to need for retirement benefits ahead of time, rather than funding the benefits on a pay-as-you-go basis.

LO 13-9 Discuss the importance of effectively communicating the nature and value of benefits to employees.

Communicating information about benefits is important so that employees will appreciate the value of their benefits. Communicating their value is the main way benefits attract, motivate, and retain employees. Employers have many options for communicating information about benefits, such as brochures, meetings, intranets, memos, and e-mail. Using a combination of such methods increases employees' understanding.

KEY TERMS

cafeteria-style plan, 422

cash balance plan, 416

Consolidated Omnibus Budget Reconciliation Act (COBRA), 409

contributory plan, 413

defined-benefit plan, 413

defined-contribution plan, 414

employee benefits, 400

Employee Retirement Income Security Act (ERISA), 413

employee wellness program (EWP), 411

experience rating, 403

Family and Medical Leave Act (FMLA), 405

flexible spending account, 411

health maintenance organization (HMO), 410

long-term disability insurance, 412

noncontributory plan, 413

Patient Protection and Affordable Care Act, 405

Pension Benefit Guarantee Corporation (PBGC), 414

preferred provider organization (PPO), 410

short-term disability insurance, 412

Social Security, 402

summary plan description (SPD), 417

unemployment insurance, 403

vesting rights, 417

workers' compensation, 404

REVIEW AND DISCUSSION QUESTIONS

1. Why do employers provide employee benefits, rather than providing all compensation in the form of pay and letting employees buy the services they want?
2. Of the benefits discussed in this chapter, list the ones you consider essential—that is, the benefits you would require in any job offer. Why are these benefits important to you?
3. Define the types of benefits required by law. How can organizations minimize the cost of these benefits while complying with the relevant laws?

4. What are some advantages of offering a generous package of insurance benefits? What are some drawbacks of generous insurance benefits?

5. Imagine that you are the human resource manager of a small architectural firm. You learn that the monthly premiums for the company's existing health insurance policy will rise by 15% next year. What can you suggest to help your company manage this rising cost?

6. In principle, health insurance would be most attractive to employees with large medical expenses, and retirement benefits would be most attractive to older employees. What else might a company include in its benefits package to appeal to young, healthy employees? How might the company structure its benefits so these employees can take advantage of the benefits they care about most?

7. What issues should an organization consider in selecting a package of employee benefits? How should an employer manage the trade-offs among these considerations?

8. How do tax laws and accounting regulations affect benefits packages?

9. What legal requirements might apply to a family leave policy? Suggest how this type of policy should be set up to meet those requirements.

10. Why is it important to communicate information about employee benefits? Suppose you work in the HR department of a company that has decided to add new benefits—dental and vision insurance plus an additional two days of paid time off for "personal days." How would you recommend communicating this change? What information should your messages include?

EXPERIENCING HR

Imagine that you work at a company where management is concerned about employee turnover. The human resource department has made a convincing case that spending an additional $200 per month on employee benefits would improve employee morale and retention. You have done some research and obtained the following ideas for additional benefits, with their associated average cost per employee:

- Better health insurance (lowering the deductible from $1,000 to $500 and increasing the benefit level from 80% of the provider's charge to 90%): $150 per month
- Dental insurance: $50 per month
- Vision care discount plan: $50 per month

- Increase employer's contribution to retirement savings: $200 per month
- Tuition reimbursement: Up to $200 per month
- Subsidy for child care or elder care: $100 per month

Which of these do you think employees would value the most? Test your assumptions by conducting a survey of five people (preferably people who are currently employed): ask them to choose up to $200 worth of additional benefits they would value most if their current employer did not already offer them. What surprises did you discover in the results?

Write a one-paragraph report summarizing your recommended benefits package for the imaginary company, assuming that the people in your survey work there.

TAKING RESPONSIBILITY: Are Phoenix Workers Overpaid?

Recently, the *Arizona Republic* published the results of an investigation that found a 277% increase over 10 years in the cost of funding pensions for city employees in newspaper report caused an outcry, so the city government promised to investigate. The government commissioned a compensation study that compared the total compensation of Phoenix employees with the total compensation of other government employees in Arizona and with employees holding similar kinds of positions in the private sector.

The study, carried out by the Segal Group, found that base salaries for Phoenix government workers are modest. However, the cost of benefits drives total compensation above what is paid by many of the organizations in the comparison groups. What drove up compensation costs the most were the costs for retirement benefits.

Phoenix offers its workers a variety of benefits. It pays part of their health insurance premiums and offers dental coverage as well. Employees also are automatically enrolled in life insurance policies and may purchase additional insurance for their spouse and dependent children. Employers and employees both make payments to the city's pension plan, and they may contribute a portion of their earnings to a retirement savings plan. They also may have a portion of their pretax earnings deposited in a flexible spending account for health care or day care. For paid time off, employees accrue 8 to 15 hours per month of vacation and 10 hours of sick leave each month they work for the city. There are 11 paid holidays each year as well. The city offers the use of an employee assistance program, elder care services (information and referrals), and a wellness program that includes classes on weight control, stress management, and smoking cessation, among other topics. A nearby child care center offers an employee discount, and low-wage workers may be eligible for subsidies on other dependent care. Other optional benefits include legal insurance, discounts on public transportation, and career counseling.

According to the Segal Group's study, base salaries for Phoenix employees are about equal to those of other government employees in Arizona. Compared with employees who work for private businesses, Phoenix employees earn 19% less. But when the cost of benefits are added in, the compensation expense for Phoenix workers is slightly above the top of the range for comparable jobs. For public-safety workers such as police and firefighters, the pay advantage is greater.

The benefits that gave Phoenix employees the biggest edge over the rest of the labor market were the employees' pension plans.

Other benefits do, however, play a role in keep Phoenix employees' total compensation high. Tuition reimbursement comes to about $9,200 per employee, while other employers typically cap this benefit at $5,000. Paid time off for sick leave, vacation, and holidays tends to be somewhat greater than the combined leave offered by other employers. However, the city's human resource director, Janet Smith, noted that sick pay is not as generous as it seems, because employees use it if they need time off for a short-term disability, and other employees offer separate benefits for a disability. The sick leave policy is nevertheless expensive, because employees may save up their unused sick days and convert them to cash when they retire. The *Arizona Republic* report claimed that this practice—which is common for state and city government employees but rare in the private sector—cost an average of $11,419 per retiring employee.

Compensation of government employees is an important and sensitive issue because their pay comes from citizens' taxes. Government decision makers have a responsibility to ensure that tax dollars are not wasted and that the government is able to hire and retain qualified workers who deliver important services such as police protection, teaching, and management of public resources. Many of these jobs require a high level of education and training. Even so, at a time when citizens are seeing their own buying power shrink, they are especially concerned that compensation policies meet these objectives without any waste, so questions like the ones that arose in Phoenix are likely to be a feature of public debate in every state and city.

Questions

1. Based on the information given, which of Phoenix's policies for pay and benefits seem reasonable, and which seem unreasonable?
2. What changes, if any, would you recommend to the city's benefits package? Why?
3. How might the city of Phoenix use online communication to build trust among its employees and citizens that its compensation practices are equitable and reasonable?

SOURCES: City of Phoenix, "Benefits Program," http://phoenix.gov, accessed April 27, 2012; Lynh Bui, "Benefits, Pay of Workers Studied," *USA Today*, January 24, 2012, http://www.usatoday.com; Craig Harris, "Retiring Arizona Public Employees Get to Cash In Years of Unused Sick Days," *Arizona Republic*, December 20, 2011, http://www.azcentral.com; Rollie Waters and T. L. Cox, "Public Sector Compensation: Panacea or Pandora's Box?" *Public Management*, November 2011, pp. 12–15.

MANAGING TALENT: Airbus Benefits Aim for Topflight Performance

"We aspire to be top in class for everything we do," Stephen Dumbleton told a reporter. The reward manager at Airbus UK was explaining the company's benefits package, and he was explaining how it is intended to support the company's strategy. Airbus is one of the world's large aircraft makers, and making jetliners and military aircraft requires excellence in product design, manufacturing, sales, and service. To support efforts at recruiting and keeping employees who will deliver on the company's exacting standards, Airbus wants to provide benefits that make the company an attractive employer.

Adding a further layer of complexity to this challenge, Airbus has operations in several countries and customers around the world. Most workers are located at the headquarters in France and in the United Kingdom, Germany, and Spain, so benefits packages must meet European requirements for employers. And even just in the United Kingdom, Airbus UK's 10,000 employees represent 60 nationalities. The average age is 41, and most employees are men, although the company is striving to attract more female employees, especially in engineering.

Airbus UK compared its total compensation with that of other companies and determined that other employers offered better compensation packages for management-level employees. In contrast, for nonmanagement employees, Airbus was at an acceptable level. But addressing dissatisfaction with compensation packages in Britain by boosting pay was impractical, because pay would be compared across geographic regions, and the company would have to raise pay levels worldwide. Instead, Airbus addressed the weak management compensation package with a flexible approach to benefits.

To design a benefits package for this diverse workforce, Airbus conducted focus groups of high-performing managers in Britain. The groups generated a variety of ideas suggesting a desire for a flexible benefits package. The greatest desire was for private medical insurance (individuals in Britain can use the public health care system but also have the option to purchase coverage from private insurers). Working from a budget starting at 150 British pounds (about $240) per manager per month, the benefits team selected a menu of benefits that started with private medical insurance and added choices from a set of other benefits, which included the choice to opt out of the medical insurance. A company called Vebnet contracted with Airbus to set up an interactive web portal where managers select the benefits they wish to receive within the budgeted amount for their position. The portal presents the choices in three categories: health, security, and lifestyle. Some of the choices are unusual, including a will-writing service and discounts on wine.

One advantage of offering this attractive benefits package to managers is that it creates an additional incentive for employees to develop their careers at Airbus and move into the management ranks. The company identifies high-potential employees and communicates with them to be sure they know a generous benefits package awaits them when they are promoted into their first management position. Dumbleton explains, "We try to make it clear that even though it may be a while before someone is promoted to the next grade, it will be worth the wait."

Still, some of Airbus's creative benefits are available to nonmanagement employees, too. In Britain, for example, one of the most popular benefits is participation in the bikes for work program, which helps people pay for bicycles they can ride to work. Employee participation has risen year after year as employees have signed up to cut their transportation costs, stay fit, and reduce their carbon footprint.

Airbus uses multiple channels to communicate about its benefits. Some messages go out through traditional media such as e-mail and notices on bulletin boards. Television screens in the company play Airbus's corporate channel, including news and background information about various benefits. The company occasionally mails information about the flexible-benefits scheme to employees at their homes—but not often, to avoid intrusiveness. The company also prepares total reward statements so that employees can readily review the value of their benefits package. Since it introduced My Flex to managers, company surveys indicate that their satisfaction with their total compensation has improved, and enrollment levels in the various options provide confirmation that the employees do indeed desire the choices made available to them. Dumbleton hopes that the success of this effort at the management level will lead to an expansion of similar benefits packages tailored to other levels of the organization.

Questions

1. How does the My Flex benefits package support Airbus's strategy?
2. Why do you think Airbus first offered flexible benefits just to managers in Britain? What would have been the pros and cons of launching it to all employees worldwide instead?
3. Airbus UK says it wants to attract more female employees, especially female engineers. How could it use its benefits package to help meet the goal of attracting and retaining female engineers?

SOURCES: Vebnet, "Vebnet Working in Partnership with Airbus Operations Ltd.," Research and Insight: Case Studies, January 2012, http://www .vebnet.com; Tynan Barton, "Reach for the Sky," Employee Benefits, February 2011, pp. 40–44; "Interview with Stephen Dumbleton, Reward Manager at Airbus Operations," Employee Benefits, November 1, 2010, http://www.emplyeebenefits.co.uk.

 TWITTER FOCUS: Babies Welcomed at T3

Using Twitter, continue the conversation about employee benefits by reading the T3 Ad Agency case at **www.mhhe.com/noefund5e**. Engage with your classmates and instructor via Twitter to chat about T3's employee benefits using the case questions posted on the Noe website. Don't have a Twitter account yet? See the instructions for getting started on the Online Learning Center.

NOTES

1. Steven Greenhouse and Reed Abelson, "Wal-Mart Cuts Some Health Care Benefits," *The New York Times*, October 21, 2011, Business & Company Resource Center, http://galenet.galegroup.com.

2. B. Gerhart and G. T. Milkovich, "Employee Compensation: Research and Practice," in *Handbook of Industrial and Organizational Psychology*, 2nd ed., eds. M. D. Dunnette and L. M. Hough (Palo Alto, CA: Consulting Psychologists Press, 1992), vol. 3; and J. Swist, "Benefits Communications: Measuring Impact and Values," *Employee Benefit Plan Review*, September 2002, pp. 24–26.

3. Erik Sherman, "Four Perks Employees Love," *Inc.*, April 11, 2012, http://www.inc.com; Robert J. Grossman, "Tough Love at Netflix," *HR Magazine*, April 2010, http://www.shrm.org.

4. U.S. Department of Labor, Employment and Training Administration, "Unemployment Insurance Tax Topic," updated January 9, 2012, http://workforcesecurity.doleta.gov; Robert J. Grossman, "Hidden Costs of Layoffs," *HR Magazine*, February 2012, Business & Company Resource Center, http://galenet.galegroup.com.

5. Grossman, "Hidden Costs of Layoffs."

6. J. V. Nackley, *Primer on Workers' Compensation* (Washington, DC: Bureau of National Affairs, 1989); and T. Thomason, T. P. Schmidle, and J. F. Burton, *Workers' Compensation* (Kalamazoo, MI: Upjohn Institute, 2001).

7. B. T. Beam Jr. and J. J. McFadden, *Employee Benefits*, 6th ed. (Chicago: Dearborn Financial Publishing, 2000).

8. AAUW, "The Family and Medical Leave Act: Facts and Statistics," http://www.aauw.org, accessed April 27, 2012.

9. Scott M. Wich, "With FMLA Leave Claims, Attention to Detail—Not Timing—Counts," *HR Magazine*, February 2012, p. 77.

10. A. Pawlowski, "Why Is America the 'No-Vacation Nation'?" *CNNTravel*, May 23, 2011, http://articles.cnn.com.

11. "Survey: Formal Paid Time-Off Programs Gaining Steam," *Talent Management*, July 6, 2011, http://talentmgt.com.

12. LIMRA, "Employees across All Generations Value Employer-Sponsored Benefits—but Most Don't Understand the Actual Costs," news release, April 18, 2011, http://www.limra.com.

13. U.S. Government Accountability Office, "Mental Health and Substance Abuse: Employers' Insurance Coverage Maintained or Enhanced Since Parity Act," *Medical Benefits*, January 15, 2012, pp. 6, 8; National Conference of State Legislatures, "State Laws Mandating or Regulating Mental Health Benefits," Issues and Research: Health, updated December 2011, http://www.ncsl.org.

14. Reed Abelson, "Health Insurance Costs Rising Sharply This Year, Study Shows," *The New York Times*, September 27, 2011, http://www.nytimes.com; Deborah Brunswick, "Health Insurance Costs to Rise Again Next Year," *CNNMoney*, September 22, 2011, http://money.cnn.com.

15. "SHRM Report Says Economy Forced Benefit Cuts, Changes," *HR Focus*, August 2011, Business & Company Resource Center, http://galenet.galegroup.com.

16. Paul Fronstin, "Characteristics of the Population with Consumer-Driven and High-Deductible Health Plans, 2005–2011," *Notes* (Employee Benefit Research Institute), April 2012, pp. 2–9.

17. J. C. Erfurt, A. Foote, and M. A. Heirich, "The Cost-Effectiveness of Worksite Wellness Programs for Hypertension Control, Weight Loss, Smoking Cessation and Exercise," *Personnel Psychology* 45 (1992), pp. 5–27.

18. Bureau of Labor Statistics, "Employee Benefits in the United States, March 2011," news release, July 26, 2011, http://www.bls.gov.

19. Pension Benefit Guaranty Corporation, "Pension Insurance Premiums Fact Sheet," Resources: Fact Sheets, http://www.pbgc.gov, accessed April 26, 2012.

20. Internal Revenue Service, "401(k) Resource Guide: Plan Sponsors—Limitation on Elective Deferrals," updated April 23, 2012, http://www.irs.gov.

21. Employee Benefit Research Institute, "Aggregate Trends in Defined Benefit and Defined Contribution Retirement Plan Sponsorship, Participation, and Vesting," *EBRI Databook on Employee Benefits*, chap. 10, updated May 2011, http://www.ebri.org.

22. BNA, "Employers Offer Too Much Information, Too Little Guidance about 401(k) Options," *Managing 401(k) Plans*, December 2011, pp. 1–4; Janet Levaux, "Target-Date Funds Dominate 401(k) Plans," *Research*, April 25, 2012, http://www.advisorone.com.

23. "Supreme Court Lets Stand Third Circuit Ruling That Pension Avoidance Scheme Is ERISA Violation," *Daily Labor Report*, no. 234 (December 8, 1987), p. A-14, summarizing *Continental Can Company v. Gavalik*.

24. Beam and McFadden, *Employee Benefits.*

25. S. L. Grover and K. J. Crooker, "Who Appreciates Family Responsive Human Resource Policies: The Impact of Family-Friendly Policies on the Organizational Attachment of Parents and Non-parents," *Personnel Psychology* 48 (1995), pp. 271–88; M. A. Arthur, "Share Price Reactions to Work-Family Initiatives: An Institutional Perspective," *Academy of Management Journal* 46 (2003), p. 497; and J. E. Perry-Smith and T. Blum, "Work-Family Human Resource Bundles and Perceived Organizational Performance," *Academy of Management Journal* 43 (2000), pp. 1107–17.

26. Catalyst, "Family Leave," Quick Takes, March 28, 2011, http://www.catalyst.org; Census Bureau, "Half of First-Time Mothers Receive Paid Leave, Census Bureau Reports," news release, November 10, 2011, http://www.census.gov.

27. E. E. Kossek, "Diversity in Child Care Assistance Needs: Employee Problems, Preferences, and Work-Related Outcomes," *Personnel Psychology* 43 (1990), pp. 769–91.

28. Alison Greco, "Corporate Culture," *Employee Benefit News*, February 2012, Business & Company Resource Center, http://galenet.galegroup.com.

29. Johns Hopkins Medicine, "Employee Benefits: Tuition Reimbursement/College Savings Plan," Bayview Jobs, http://www.bayviewjobs.org, accessed April 27, 2012.

30. National Alliance for Caregiving, *Best Practices in Workplace Eldercare*, March 2012, http://www.caregiving.org.

31. Colleen Kane, "Outrageous Workplace Perks," CNBC.com, August 4, 2011, http://www.cnbc.com; Sherman, "Four Perks Employees Love."

32. R. Broderick and B. Gerhart, "Nonwage Compensation," in *The Human Resource Management Handbook*, eds. D. Lewin, D. J. B. Mitchell, and M. A. Zadi (San Francisco: JAI Press, 1996).

33. Lauren Weber, "Benefits Matter," *The Wall Street Journal*, April 3, 2012, http://online.wsj.com.

34. Tynan Barton, "Sociable Network," *Employee Benefits*, September 2011, pp. 50–53.

35. "SHRM Report Says Economy Forced Benefit Cuts."

36. Beam and McFadden, *Employee Benefits.*

37. D. A. Harrison and L. Z. Liska, "Promoting Regular Exercise in Organizational Fitness Programs: Health-Related Differences in Motivational Building Blocks," *Personnel Psychology* 47 (1994), pp. 47–71; Erfurt et al., "The Cost-Effectiveness of Worksite Wellness Programs."

38. Beam and McFadden, *Employee Benefits*, p. 359.

39. For a description of these rules, see M. M. Sarli, "Nondiscrimination Rules for Qualified Plans: The General Test," *Compensation and Benefits Review* 23, no. 5 (September–October 1991), pp. 56–67.

40. *Los Angeles Department of Water & Power v. Manhart*, 435 U.S. S. Ct. 702 (1978), 16 E.P.D. 8250.

41. S. K. Hoffman, "Discrimination Litigation Relating to Employee Benefits," *Labor Law Journal*, June 1992, pp. 362–81.

42. Ibid., P. 375.

43. M. Wilson, G. B. Northcraft, and M. A. Neale, "The Perceived Value of Fringe Benefits," *Personnel Psychology* 38 (1985), pp. 309–20; H. W. Hennessey, P. L. Perrewe, and W. A. Hochwarter, "Impact of Benefit Awareness on Employee and Organizational Outcomes: A Longitudinal Field Experiment," *Benefits Quarterly* 8, no. 2 (1992), pp. 90–96; and MetLife, *Employee Benefits Benchmarking Report*, www.metlife.com, accessed June 24, 2007.

44. M. C. Giallourakis and G. S. Taylor, "An Evaluation of Benefit Communication Strategy," *Employee Benefits Journal* 15, no. 4 (1991), pp. 14–18; and Employee Benefit Research Institute, "How Readable Are Summary Plan Descriptions for Health Care Plans?" *EBRI Notes*, October 2006, www.ebri.org.

Meeting Other HR Goals

PART FIVE

14 Collective Bargaining and Labor Relations

What Do I Need to Know?

After reading this chapter, you should be able to:

LO 14-1   Define unions and labor relations and their role in organizations.

LO 14-2   Identify the labor relations goals of management, labor unions, and society.

LO 14-3   Summarize laws and regulations that affect labor relations.

LO 14-4   Describe the union organizing process.

LO 14-5   Explain how management and unions negotiate contracts.

LO 14-6   Summarize the practice of contract administration.

LO 14-7   Describe more cooperative approaches to labor-management relations.

Introduction

Dick Davis, a member of the Kansas City, Missouri, city council, called it the council's "most impressive achievement of the first year." That achievement was the successful negotiation of a three-year labor contract with the city's firefighters union. From the government's perspective, the new agreement would contribute to the city manager's goal to reduce the budget, including a cut of $7.6 million in the fire department's spending. To meet that goal, the city manager proposed eliminating the jobs of 107 firefighters. Under union rules, the most recently hired firefighters would be first to go, even though they would include many who had received cross-training to serve as paramedics and experts in fire suppression.

Local 42 of the International Association of Fire Fighters, which represents the Kansas City firefighters, objected to the layoffs. However, the union representatives acknowledged that cost cutting was inevitable. The union helped to come up with a revised plan in which 33 positions would be eliminated through attrition (employees choosing to leave) and early-retirement incentives aimed at firefighters who had been with the department for more than 25 years. Those measures were expected to save $3.3 million, and the firefighters agreed to accept changes in overtime rules that would save another $3.5 million. Finally, the negotiators identified management, civilian, and other positions that could be eliminated to save the remaining $800,000. Parties on both sides of the negotiation stated that they were pleased to arrive at a contract that saved money while avoiding layoffs of firefighters.[1]

The presence of unions in a government agency or business changes some aspects of human resource management by directing more attention to the interests of employees as a group. In general, employees and employers share the same interests. They both benefit when the organization is strong and growing, providing employees with jobs and employers with profits. But although the interests of employers and employees overlap, they obviously are not identical. In the case of pay, workers benefit from higher pay, but high pay cuts into the organization's profits, unless pay increases are associated with higher productivity or better customer service. Workers may negotiate differences with their employers individually, or they may form unions to negotiate on their behalf. This chapter explores human resource activities in organizations where employees belong to unions or where employees are seeking to organize unions.

We begin by formally defining unions and labor relations, and then describe the scope and impact of union activity. We next summarize government laws and regulations affecting unions and labor relations. The following three sections detail types of activities involving unions: union organizing, contract negotiation, and contract administration. Finally, we identify ways in which unions and management are working together in arrangements that are more cooperative than the traditional labor-management relationship.

Role of Unions and Labor Relations

In the United States today, most workers act as individuals to select jobs that are acceptable to them and to negotiate pay, benefits, flexible hours, and other work conditions. Especially when there is stiff competition for labor and employees have hard-to-replace skills, this arrangement produces satisfactory results for most employees. At times, however, workers have believed their needs and interests do not receive enough consideration from management. One response by workers is to act collectively by forming and joining labor **unions,** organizations formed for the purpose of representing their members' interests and resolving conflicts with employers.

Unions have a role because some degree of conflict is inevitable between workers and management.[2] As we commented earlier, for example, managers can increase profits by lowering workers' pay, but workers benefit in the short term if lower profits result because their pay is higher. Still, this type of conflict is more complex than a simple trade-off, such as wages versus profits. Rising profits can help employees by driving up profit sharing or other benefits, and falling profits can result in layoffs and a lack of investment. Although employers can use programs like profit sharing to help align employee interests with their own, some remaining divergence of interests is inevitable. Labor unions represent worker interests and the collective bargaining process provides a way to manage the conflict. In other words, through systems for hearing complaints and negotiating labor contracts, unions and managers resolve conflicts between employers and employees.

As unionization of workers became more common, universities developed training in how to manage union-management interactions. This specialty, called **labor relations,** emphasizes skills that managers and union leaders can use to foster effective labor-management cooperation, minimize costly forms of conflict (such as strikes), and seek win-win solutions to disagreements. Labor relations involves three levels of decisions:[3]

LO 14-1 Define unions and labor relations and their role in organizations.

Unions
Organizations formed for the purpose of representing their members' interests in dealing with employers.

Labor Relations
Field that emphasizes skills that managers and union leaders can use to minimize costly forms of conflict (such as strikes) and seek win-win solutions to disagreements.

Dennis Van Roekel is president of the National Education Association, the nation's largest labor union with 3.2 million members.

1. *Labor relations strategy*—For management, the decision involves whether the organization will work with unions or develop (or maintain) nonunion operations. This decision is influenced by outside forces such as public opinion and competition. For unions, the decision involves whether to fight changes in how unions relate to the organization or accept new kinds of labor-management relationships.

2. *Negotiating contracts*—As we will describe later in the chapter, contract negotiations in a union setting involve decisions about pay structure, job security, work rules, workplace safety, and many other issues. These decisions affect workers' and the employer's situation for the term of the contract.

3. *Administering contracts*—These decisions involve day-to-day activities in which union members and the organization's managers may have disagreements. Issues include complaints of work rules being violated or workers being treated unfairly in particular situations. A formal grievance procedure is typically used to resolve these issues.

Later sections in this chapter describe how managers and unions carry out the activities connected with these levels of decisions, as well as the goals and legal constraints affecting these activities.

National and International Unions

Most union members belong to a national or international union. Figure 14.1 shows the membership of the 10 largest national unions in the United States. Half of these have memberships of over a million workers.

These unions may be either craft or industrial unions. The members of a **craft union** all have a particular skill or occupation. Examples include the International Brotherhood of Electrical Workers for electricians and the United Brotherhood of Carpenters and Joiners of America for carpenters. Craft unions are often responsible for training their members through apprenticeships and for supplying craft workers to employers. For example, an employer would send requests for carpenters to the union hiring hall, which would decide which carpenters to send out. In this way, craft workers may work for many employers over time but have a constant link to the union. A craft union's bargaining power depends greatly on its control over the supply of its workers.

In contrast, **industrial unions** consist of members who are linked by their work in a particular industry. Examples include the United Steelworkers of America and the Communication Workers of America. Typically, an industrial union represents many different occupations. Membership in the union is the result of working for a particular employer in the industry. Changing employers is less common than it is among craft workers, and employees who change employers remain members of the same union only if they happen to move to other employers covered by that union. Another difference is that whereas a craft union may restrict the number of skilled craftsmen—say, carpenters—to maintain higher wages, industrial unions try to organize as many employees in as wide a range of skills as possible.

Most national unions are affiliated with the **American Federation of Labor and Congress of Industrial Organizations (AFL-CIO).** The AFL-CIO is not a labor

Craft Union
Labor union whose members all have a particular skill or occupation.

Industrial Union
Labor union whose members are linked by their work in a particular industry.

American Federation of Labor and Congress of Industrial Organizations (AFL-CIO)
An association that seeks to advance the shared interests of its member unions at the national level.

Figure 14.1
10 Largest Unions in the United States

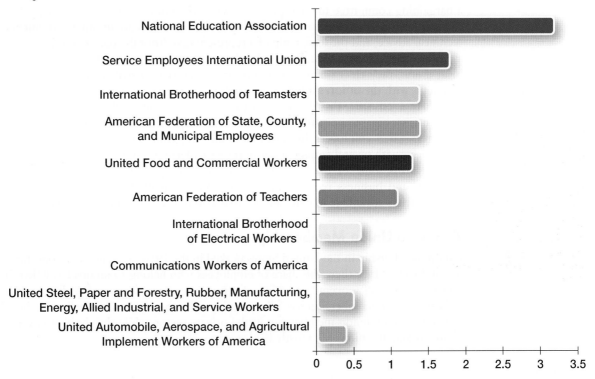

SOURCE: C. D. Gifford, *Directory of U.S. Labor Organizations* (Washington, DC: Bureau of National Affairs, 2010).

union but an association that seeks to advance the shared interests of its member unions at the national level, much as the Chamber of Commerce and the National Association of Manufacturers do for their member employers. Approximately 55 national and international unions are affiliated with the AFL-CIO. An important responsibility of the AFL-CIO is to represent labor's interests in public policy issues, such as labor law, economic policy, and occupational safety and health. The organization also provides information and analysis that member unions can use in their activities. In 2005, several unions broke away from the AFL-CIO to form an alliance called Change to Win, which is focused on innovative organizing campaigns. This group includes four unions representing a membership of about 5 million workers.[4]

Local Unions

Most national unions consist of multiple local units. Even when a national union plays the most critical role in negotiating the terms of a collective bargaining contract, negotiation occurs at the local level for work rules and other issues that are locally determined. In addition, administration of the contract largely takes place at the local union level. As a result, most day-to-day interaction between labor and management involves the local union.

Membership in the local union depends on the type of union. For an industrial union, the local may correspond to a single large facility or to a number of small facilities. In a craft union, the local may cover a city or a region.

Typically, the local union elects officers, such as president, vice president, and treasurer. The officers may be responsible for contract negotiation, or the local may form a bargaining committee for that purpose. When the union is engaged in bargaining, the national union provides help, including background data about other settlements, technical advice, and the leadership of a representative from the national office.

Individual members participate in local unions in various ways. At meetings of the local union, they elect officials and vote on resolutions to strike. Most of workers' contact is with the **union steward,** an employee elected by union members to represent them in ensuring that the terms of the contract are enforced. The union steward helps to investigate complaints and represents employees to supervisors and other managers when employees file grievances alleging contract violations.[5] When the union deals with several employers, as in the case of a craft union, a *business representative* performs some of the same functions as a union steward. Because of union stewards' and business representatives' close involvement with employees, it is to management's advantage to cultivate positive working relationships with them.

Union Steward
An employee elected by union members to represent them in ensuring that the terms of the labor contract are enforced.

Trends in Union Membership

Union membership in the United States peaked in the 1950s, reaching over one-third of employees. Since then, the share of employees who belong to unions has fallen. It now stands at 11.8% overall and 6.9% of private-sector employment.[6] As Figure 14.2 indicates, union membership has fallen steadily since the 1980s. The decline has been driven by falling union membership in the private sector, while the share of government workers in unions has mostly held steady.

Figure 14.2

Union Membership Density among U.S. Wage and Salary Workers, 1973–2011

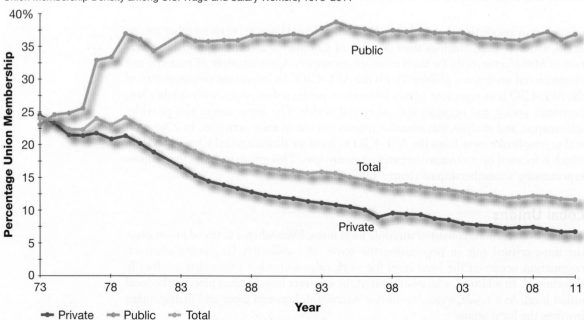

[a] Percentage of total, private-sector, and public-sector wage and salary workers who are union members. Beginning in 1977, workers belonging to "an employee association similar to a union" are included as members.

SOURCE: Data for 1973–2001 from B. T. Hirsch and D. A. MacPherson, *Union Membership and Earnings Data Book 2001* (Washington, DC: Bureau of National Affairs, 2002), using data from U.S. Current Population Surveys. Data for 2002 through 2011 from Bureau of Labor Statistics, "Union Affiliation Data from the Current Population Survey," http://data.bls.gov, accessed May 3, 2012.

The decline in union membership has been attributed to several factors:[7]

- *Change in the structure of the economy*—Much recent job growth has occurred among women and older workers in the service sector of the economy, while union strength has traditionally been among urban blue-collar workers, especially middle-aged workers. Women have been less likely than men to belong to unions, and services industries such as finance, insurance, and real estate have lower union representation than manufacturing. Also, much business growth has been in the South, where workers are less likely to join unions.[8]

- *Management efforts to control costs*—On average, unionized workers receive higher pay than their nonunionized counterparts, and the pressure is greater because of international competition. In the past, union membership across an industry such as automobiles or steel resulted in similar wages and work requirements for all competitors. Today, U.S. producers must compete with companies that have entirely different pay scales and work rules, often placing the U.S. companies at a disadvantage.

- *Human resource practices*—Competition for scarce human resources can lead employers to offer much of what employees traditionally sought through union membership.

- *Government regulation*—Stricter regulation in such areas as workplace safety and equal employment opportunity leaves fewer areas in which unions can show an advantage over what employers must already offer.

As Figure 14.3 indicates, the percentage of U.S. workers who belong to unions is lower than in many other countries. More dramatic is the difference in "coverage"—the percentage of employees whose terms and conditions of employment are governed by a union contract, whether or not the employees are technically union members. In Western Europe, it is common to have coverage rates of 80% to 90%, so the influence of labor unions far outstrips what membership levels would imply.[9] Also, employees in Western

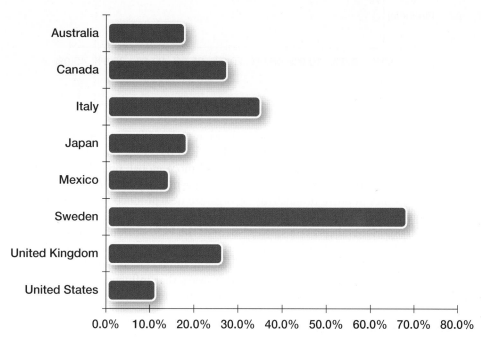

Figure 14.3
Union Membership Rates in Selected Countries

Note: Data for 2007, except U.S. coverage rate for 2005.

SOURCE: Organisation for Economic Co-operation and Development, StatExtracts, http://stats.oecd.org, accessed May 3, 2012.

Did You Know?

Sketch of a Union Worker

In the United States today, a union worker is most likely to be older than 54 and to hold a job in government, a transportation company, or a utility. Workers younger than 25 and in the financial or business services industries are least likely to be union members. Today's union members are both men and women.

Question

How well do these data fit your picture of a typical union worker?

SOURCE: U.S. Census Bureau, *Statistical Abstract of the United States: 2012,* table 665, p. 429, accessed at http://www.census.gov/compendia/statab/2012/tables/12s0665.pdf.

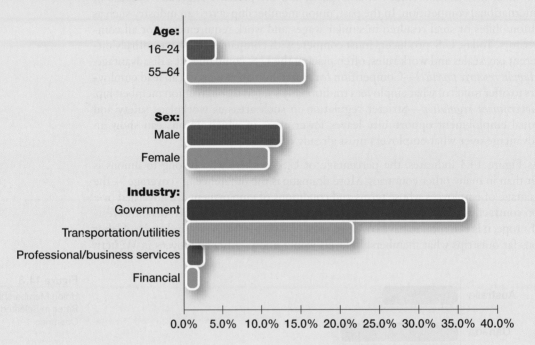

Europe tend to have a larger formal role in decision making than in the United States. This role, including worker representatives on boards of directors, is often mandated by the government. But as markets become more and more global, pressure to cut labor costs and increase productivity is likely to be stronger in every country. Unless unions can help companies improve productivity or organize new production facilities opened in lower-wage countries, union influence may decline in countries where it is now strong.

Although union members are a smaller share of the U.S. workforce, they are a significant part of many industries' labor markets. Along with strength in numbers, large unions have strength in dollars. Union retirement funds, taken together, are huge. Unions try to use their investment decisions in ways that influence businesses. The "Did You Know?" box presents some statistics on union members.

Unions in Government

Unlike union membership for workers in businesses, union membership among government workers has remained strong. Union membership in the public sector grew during the 1960s and 1970s and has remained steady ever since. Over one-third of government employees are union members, and a larger share are covered by collective bargaining agreements. One reason for this strength is that government regulations and laws support the right of government workers to organize. In 1962 Executive Order 10988 established collective bargaining rights for federal employees. By the end of the 1960s, most states had passed similar laws.

An interesting aspect of union growth among government workers is that much of it has occurred in the service industry and among white-collar employees—groups that have been viewed as difficult to organize. The American Federation of State, County and Municipal Employees (AFSCME) has about 1.6 million members. Among them are nurses, park rangers, school librarians, corrections officers, and many workers in clerical and other white-collar occupations.[10]

Labor relations with government workers is different in some respects, such as regarding the right to strike. Strikes are illegal for federal workers and for state workers in most states. At the local level, all states prohibit strikes by police (Hawaii being a partial exception) and firefighters (Idaho being the exception). Teachers and state employees are somewhat more likely to have the right to strike, depending on the state. Legal or not, strikes by government workers do occur. Of the 30 strikes involving 1,000 or more workers in 2010–2011, five involved workers in state and local government.

Impact of Unions on Company Performance

Organizations are concerned about whether union organizing and bargaining will hurt their performance, in particular, unions' impact on productivity, profits, and stock performance. Researchers have studied the general relationship between unionization and these performance measures. Through skillful labor relations, organizations can positively influence outcomes.

There has been much debate regarding the effects of unions on productivity.[11] One view is that unions decrease productivity because of work rules and limits on workloads set by union contracts and production lost to such union actions as strikes and work slowdowns. At the same time, unions can have positive effects on productivity.[12] They can reduce turnover by giving employees a route for resolving problems.[13] Unions emphasize pay systems based on seniority, which remove incentives for employees to compete rather than cooperate. The introduction of a union also may force an employer to improve its management practices and pay greater attention to employee ideas.

Although there is evidence that unions have both positive and negative effects on productivity, most studies have found that union workers are more productive than nonunion workers. Still, questions remain. Are highly productive workers more likely to form unions, or does a union make workers more productive? The answer is unclear. In theory, if unions caused greater productivity, we would expect union membership to be rising, not falling as it has been.[14]

Even if unions do raise productivity, a company's profits and stock performance may still suffer if unions raise wage and benefits costs by more than the productivity gain. On average, union members receive higher wages and more generous benefits than nonunion workers, and evidence shows that unions have a large negative effect on profits. Also, union coverage

Harley-Davidson and the International Association of Machinists and Aerospace Workers have cooperated to produce good results. In general, though, companies wishing to become more competitive need to continually monitor their labor relations strategies.

tends to decline faster in companies with a lower return to shareholders.[15] In summary, companies wishing to become more competitive must continually monitor their labor relations strategy.

The studies tend to look at the average effects of unions, not at individual companies or innovative labor relations. Some organizations excel at labor relations, and some have worked with unions to meet business needs. For example, even when the economy has slowed in recent years, manufacturers have reported that it is difficult to find enough skilled labor. Many companies depend on unions to recruit and train new workers through apprenticeship programs. In Alaska, more than half of the registered apprenticeship programs are partnerships between employers and unions or employee associations. For example, construction businesses, unions, and government organizations banded together to form the Construction Education Foundation, which sponsors training programs that prepare workers to enter the construction industry.[16]

LO 14-2 Identify the labor relations goals of management, labor unions, and society.

Goals of Management, Labor Unions, and Society

Resolving conflicts in a positive way is usually easiest when the parties involved understand each other's goals. Although individual cases vary, we can draw some general conclusions about the goals of labor unions and management. Society, too, has goals for labor and business, given form in the laws regulating labor relations.

Management Goals

Management goals are to increase the organization's profits. Managers tend to prefer options that lower costs and raise output. When deciding whether to discourage employees from forming a union, a concern is that a union will create higher costs in wages and benefits, as well as raise the risk of work stoppages. Managers may also fear that a union will make managers and workers into adversaries or limit management's discretion in making business and employment decisions.

When an employer has recognized a union, management's goals continue to emphasize restraining costs and improving output. Managers continue to prefer to keep the organization's operations flexible, so they can adjust activities to meet competitive challenges and customer demands. Therefore, in their labor relations managers prefer to limit increases in wages and benefits and to retain as much control as they can over work rules and schedules.

Labor Union Goals

In general, labor unions have the goals of obtaining pay and working conditions that satisfy their members and of giving members a voice in decisions that affect them. Traditionally, they obtain these goals by gaining power in numbers. The more workers who belong to a union, the greater the union's power. More members translates into greater ability to halt or disrupt production. Larger unions also have greater financial resources for continuing a strike; the union can help to make up for the wages the workers lose during a strike. The threat of a long strike—stated or implied—can make an employer more willing to meet the union's demands.

As we noted earlier, union membership is indeed linked to better compensation. In 2011, private-sector unionized workers received, on average, wages 16% higher than nonunion workers.[17] In addition, the impact of unionization on benefits packages was dramatic: Employer costs for benefits granted to union workers were nearly double the average benefits costs for nonunion workers. Taking into account other influences, such as the greater ease with which unions are able to organize relatively highly paid, productive workers, researchers estimate that the total "union effect" on wages is about 10% to 15%.[18] In other words, a union worker would earn $1.10 to $1.15 for every dollar earned by a nonunion worker.

Unions typically want to influence the *way* pay and promotions are determined. Unlike management, which tries to consider employees as individuals so that pay and promotion decisions relate to performance differences, unions try to build group solidarity and avoid possible arbitrary treatment of employees. To do so, unions focus on equal pay for equal work. They try to have any pay differences based on seniority, on the grounds that this measure is more objective than performance evaluations. As a result, where workers are represented by a union, it is common for all employees in a particular job classification to be paid at the same rate.

The survival and security of a union depend on its ability to ensure a regular flow of new members and member dues to support the services it provides. Therefore, unions typically place high priority on negotiating two types of contract provisions with an employer that are critical to a union's security and viability: checkoff provisions and provisions relating to union membership or contribution.

Under a **checkoff provision,** the employer, on behalf of the union, automatically deducts union dues from employees' paychecks. Security provisions related to union membership are *closed shop, union shop, agency shop,* and *maintenance of membership.*

The strongest union security arrangement is a **closed shop,** under which a person must be a union member before being hired. Under the National Labor Relations Act, discussed later in this chapter, closed shops are illegal. A legal membership arrangement that supports the goals of labor unions is the **union shop,** an arrangement that requires an employee to join the union within a certain time (30 days) after beginning employment. A similar alternative is the **agency shop,** which requires the payment of union dues but not union membership. **Maintenance of membership** rules do not require union membership but do require that employees who join the union remain members for a certain period of time, such as the length of the contract. As we will discuss later in the chapter, some states forbid union shops, agency shops, and maintenance of membership.

All these provisions are ways to address unions' concern about "free riders"—employees who benefit from union activities without belonging to a union. By law, all members of a bargaining unit, whether union members or not, must be represented by the union. If the union must offer services to all bargaining unit members but some of them are not dues-paying union members, the union may not have enough financial resources to operate successfully.

Societal Goals

The activities of unions and management take place within the context of society, with society's values driving the laws and regulations that affect labor relations. As long ago as the late 1800s and early 1900s, industrial relations scholars saw unions as a way to make up for individual employees' limited bargaining power.[19] At that time, clashes between workers and management could be violent, and many people hoped that unions would replace the violence with negotiation. Since then, observers have expressed concern that unions in certain industries have become too strong, achieving their goals at the expense of employers' ability to compete or meet other objectives.

Checkoff Provision
Contract provision under which the employer, on behalf of the union, automatically deducts union dues from employees' paychecks.

Closed Shop
Union security arrangement under which a person must be a union member before being hired; illegal for those covered by the National Labor Relations Act.

Union Shop
Union security arrangement that requires employees to join the union within a certain amount of time (30 days) after beginning employment.

Agency Shop
Union security arrangement that requires the payment of union dues but not union membership.

Maintenance of Membership
Union security rules not requiring union membership but requiring that employees who join the union remain members for a certain period of time.

But even former Senator Orrin Hatch, described by *BusinessWeek* as "labor's archrival on Capitol Hill," has spoken of a need for unions:

> There are always going to be people who take advantage of workers. Unions even that out, to their credit. We need them to level the field between labor and management. If you didn't have unions, it would be very difficult for even enlightened employers not to take advantage of workers on wages and working conditions, because of [competition from less-enlightened] rivals. I'm among the first to say I believe in unions.[20]

Senator Hatch's statement implies that society's goal for unions is to ensure that workers have a voice in how they are treated by their employers. As we will see in the next section, this view has produced a set of laws and regulations intended to give workers the right to join unions if they so wish.

LO 14-3 Summarize laws and regulations that affect labor relations.

Laws and Regulations Affecting Labor Relations

The laws and regulations pertaining to labor relations affect unions' size and bargaining power, so they significantly affect the degree to which unions, management, and society achieve their varied goals. These laws and regulations set limits on union structure and administration and the ways in which unions and management interact.

National Labor Relations Act (NLRA)

National Labor Relations Act (NLRA) Federal law that supports collective bargaining and sets out the rights of employees to form unions.

Perhaps the most dramatic example of labor laws' influence is the 1935 passage of the Wagner Act (also known as the **National Labor Relations Act,** or **NLRA**), which actively supported collective bargaining. After Congress passed the NLRA, union membership in the United States nearly tripled, from 3 million in 1933 to 8.8 million (19.2% of employment) in 1939.[21]

Before the 1930s, the U.S. legal system was generally hostile to unions. The courts tended to view unions as coercive organizations that hindered free trade. Unions' focus on collective voice and collective action (such as strikes and boycotts) did not fit well with the U.S. emphasis on capitalism, individualism, freedom of contract, and property rights.[22] Then the Great Depression of the 1930s shifted public attitudes toward business and the free-enterprise system. Unemployment rates as high as 25% and a steep fall in production between 1929 and 1933 focused attention on employee rights and the shortcomings of the economic system of the time. The nation was in crisis, and President Franklin Roosevelt responded dramatically with the New Deal. On the labor front, the 1935 NLRA ushered in an era of public policy for labor unions, enshrining collective bargaining as the preferred way to settle labor-management disputes.

Section 7 of the NLRA sets out the rights of employees, including the "right to self-organization, to form, join, or assist labor organizations, to bargain collectively through representatives of their own choosing, and to engage in other concerted activities for the purpose of collective bargaining."[23] Employees also have the right to refrain from these activities, unless union membership is a condition of employment. The following activities are among those protected under the NLRA:

- Union organizing.
- Joining a union, whether recognized by the employer or not.
- Going out on strike to secure better working conditions.
- Refraining from activity on behalf of the union.

Most employees in the private sector are covered by the NLRA. However, workers employed under the following conditions are not covered:[24]

- Employed as a supervisor.
- Employed by a parent or spouse.
- Employed as an independent contractor.
- Employed in the domestic service of any person or family in a home.
- Employed as agricultural laborers.
- Employed by an employer subject to the Railway Labor Act.
- Employed by a federal, state, or local government.
- Employed by any other person who is not an employer as defined in the NLRA.

State or local laws may provide additional coverage. For example, California's 1975 Agricultural Labor Relations Act covers agricultural workers in that state.

In Section 8(a), the NLRA prohibits certain activities by employers as unfair labor practices. In general, employers may not interfere with, restrain, or coerce employees in exercising their rights to join or assist a labor organization or to refrain from such activities. Employers may not dominate or interfere with the formation or activities of a labor union. They may not discriminate in any aspect of employment that attempts to encourage or discourage union activity, nor may they discriminate against employees for providing testimony related to enforcement of the NLRA. Finally, employers may not refuse to bargain collectively with a labor organization that has standing under the act. For more guidance in complying with the NLRA, see the examples in the "HR How To" box.

When employers or unions violate the NLRA, remedies typically include ordering that unfair labor practices stop. Employers may be required to rehire workers, with or without back pay. The NLRA is not a criminal law, and violators may not be assigned punitive damages (fines to punish rather than merely make up for the harm done).

Laws Amending the NLRA

Originally, the NLRA did not list any unfair labor practices by unions. In later amendments to the NLRA—the Taft-Hartley Act of 1947 and the Landrum-Griffin Act of 1959—Congress established some restrictions on union practices deemed unfair to employers and union members.

Under the Taft-Hartley Act, unions may not restrain employers through actions such as the following:[25]

- Mass picketing in such numbers that nonstriking employees physically cannot enter the workplace.
- Engaging in violent acts in connection with a strike.
- Threatening employees with physical injury or job loss if they do not support union activities.
- During contract negotiations, insisting on illegal provisions, provisions that the employer may hire only workers who are union members or "satisfactory" to the union, or working conditions to be determined by a group to which the employer does not belong.
- Terminating an existing contract and striking for a new one without notifying the employer, the Federal Mediation and Conciliation Service, and the state mediation service (where one exists).

HR How To

Avoiding Unfair Labor Practices

The National Labor Relations Act prohibits employers and unions from engaging in unfair labor practices. For employers, this means they must not interfere with employees' decisions about whether to join a union and engage in union-related activities. Employers may not discriminate against employees for being involved in union activities or testifying in court about actions under the NLRA. Here are some specific examples of unfair labor practices that *employers must avoid:*

- Threatening employees with loss of their jobs or benefits if they join or vote for a union.
- Threatening to close down a plant if it is organized by a union.
- Questioning employees about their union membership or activities in a way that restrains or coerces them.
- Spying or pretending to spy on union meetings.
- Taking an active part in organizing a union or committee to represent employees.

- Discharging employees for urging other employees to join a union.
- Refusing to reinstate workers when job openings occur, on the grounds that the workers participated in a lawful strike.
- Threatening changes to company procedures—for example, that supervisors will no longer be flexible in scheduling employees—if employees vote for a union.
- Stating that it would be futile to vote for a union—for example, that the company would never negotiate with a union.
- Forbidding employees from posting messages about unions on the company bulletin board if the company lets employees post messages about other topics.
- Forbidding employees from wearing union buttons or shirts with union logos, unless there is a valid business reason for the dress restrictions.
- Refusing to meet with employees' representatives because the employees are on strike.

- Refusing to supply the employees' representative with cost and other data concerning a group insurance plan covering employees.
- Announcing a wage increase without consulting the employees' representative.
- Failing to bargain about the effects of a decision to close one of the employer's facilities.

SOURCES: National Labor Relations Board, "Employer/Union Rights and Obligations," http://www.nlrb.gov, accessed May 3, 2012; Karen Morris, "Union Representation Elections: Tread Knowledgeably," *Hotel Management,* January 2012, Business & Company Resource Center, http://galenet .galegroup.com; Karen R. Harned, "Union Issues for Non-Union Employers," National Federation of Independent Business, http://www.nfib.com, accessed May 3, 2012.

Right-to-Work Laws
State laws that make union shops, maintenance of membership, and agency shops illegal.

The Taft-Hartley Act also allows the states to pass so-called **right-to-work laws,** which make union shops, maintenance of membership, and agency shops illegal. The idea behind such laws is that requiring union membership or the payment of union dues restricts the employees' right to freedom of association. In other words, employees should be free to choose whether they join a union or other group. Of course, unions have a different point of view. The union perspective is that unions provide services to all members of a bargaining unit (such as all of a company's workers), and all members who receive the benefits of a union should pay union dues. Figure 14.4 indicates which states currently have right-to-work laws.

The Landrum-Griffin Act regulates unions' actions with regard to their members, including financial disclosure and the conduct of elections. This law establishes and protects rights of union members. These include the right to nominate candidates for union office, participate in union meetings and secret-ballot elections, and examine unions' financial records.

Figure 14.4
States with Right-to-Work Laws

SOURCE: National Right to Work Legal Defense Foundation, "Right to Work States," www.nrtw.org, accessed May 3, 2012.

National Labor Relations Board (NLRB)

Enforcement of the NLRA rests with the **National Labor Relations Board (NLRB).** This federal government agency consists of a five-member board, the general counsel, and 52 regional and other field offices. Because the NLRB is a federal agency, its enforcement actions are limited to companies that have an impact on interstate commerce, but as a practical matter, this extends to all but purely local businesses. For federal government workers under the Civil Service Reform Act of 1978, Title VII, the Federal Labor Relations Authority has a role similar to that of the NLRB. Many states have similar agencies to administer their laws governing state and local government workers.

> **National Labor Relations Board (NLRB)**
> Federal government agency that enforces the NLRA by conducting and certifying representation elections and investigating unfair labor practices.

The NLRB has two major functions: to conduct and certify representation elections and to prevent unfair labor practices. It does not initiate either of these actions but responds to requests for action.

Representation Elections   The NLRB is responsible for ensuring that the organizing process follows certain steps, described in the next section. Depending on the response to organizing efforts, the NLRB conducts elections. When a majority of workers vote in favor of a union, the NLRB certifies it as the exclusive representative of a group of employees. The NLRB also conducts elections to decertify unions, following the same process as for representation elections.

The NLRB is also responsible for determining the appropriate bargaining unit and the employees who are eligible to participate in organizing activities. As we stated earlier, bargaining units may not include certain types of employees, such as agricultural laborers, independent contractors, supervisors, and managers. Beyond this, the NLRB attempts to group together employees who have a community of interest in their wages, hours, and working conditions. A unit may cover employees in one facility or multiple facilities within a single employer, or the unit may cover multiple employers. In general, employees on the payroll just before the ordering of an election are eligible to vote, although this rule is modified in some cases, for example, when employment in the industry is irregular. Most employees who are on strike and who have been replaced by other employees are eligible to vote in an election (such as a decertification election) that occurs within 12 months of the onset of the strike.

Prevention of Unfair Labor Practices   The NLRB prevents unfair labor practices by educating employers and employees about their rights and responsibilities under the National Labor Relations Act and by responding to complaints. In an extension of its education of employees, the NLRB recently issued a rule that employers must display a poster summarizing employee rights. However, at the time this is written, that requirement was suspended because of a legal challenge by employers. Check the NLRB's website (**www.nlrb.gov**) to find out whether the poster is now required.

The handling of complaints regarding unfair labor practices begins when someone files a charge. The deadline for filing a charge is six months after the alleged unfair practice. All parties must be served with a copy of the charge. (Registered mail is recommended.) The charge is investigated by a regional office. If, after investigating, the NLRB finds the charge has merit and issues a complaint, two actions are possible. The NLRB may defer to a grievance procedure agreed on by the employer and the union; grievances are discussed later in this chapter. Or a hearing may be held before an administrative law judge. The judge makes a recommendation, which either party may appeal. As the "HRM Social" box describes, the NLRB recently summarized decisions that guide employers in determining how much they may restrict employees' comments on social media.

The NLRB has the authority to issue cease-and-desist orders to halt unfair labor practices. It also can order the employer to reinstate workers, with or without back pay. The NLRB can set aside the results of an election if it believes either the union or the employer has created "an atmosphere of confusion or fear of reprisals."[26] If an employer or union refuses to comply with an NLRB order, the board has the authority to petition the U.S. Court of Appeals. The court may enforce the order, recommend it to the NLRB for modification, change the order itself, or set it aside altogether.

Union Organizing

LO 14-4 Describe the union organizing process.

Unions begin their involvement with an organization's employees by conducting an organizing campaign. To meet its objectives, a union needs to convince a majority of workers that they should receive better pay or other employment conditions and that the union will help them do so. The employer's objectives will depend on its strategy—whether it seeks to work with a union or convince employees that they are better off without union representation.

The Process of Organizing

The organizing process begins with authorization cards, such as the example shown in Figure 14.5. Union representatives make contact with employees, present their message about the union, and invite them to sign an authorization card. For the organization process to continue, at least 30% of the employees must sign an authorization card.

HRM Social

NLRB Protects Some Online Rants—But Not All

Employers know they must not interfere with employees' right to complain to one another about working conditions, because these complaints can be part of an effort at mutual aid or collective bargaining, protected by the National Labor Relations Act. But what if the employees are complaining on social media, where the comments can be seen by everyone in their social networks—perhaps anyone online? The NLRB has considered such cases and maintains that the basic protection of employees extends to social media, within limits.

For example, if employees call their supervisor nasty names on Facebook, those comments may be protected under the labor relations act—if the employee who is posting such comments is engaging his or her co-workers about the terms and conditions of employment. The same applies to rude comments about the company's customers and products. An employer may not protect itself from negative publicity by banning all negative comments by employees. The employer could, however, create a more specific policy that bans inappropriate comments in situations outside the scope of the labor relations act and permits negative remarks in the context of protected activity by employees.

In situations where an employee directed inappropriate comments specifically toward individuals who were not co-workers, the NLRB found that the employer could lawfully discipline the employees. In one such case, an employee was engaged in a Facebook conversation with two friends who were not co-workers, and in another, an employee replied on Facebook to a question posted by a friend who was not a co-worker. In both cases, the employees could not show that the company was punishing them for organizing or engaging in union activities. Rather, the employees were acting as individuals airing personal gripes.

Another situation in which employers have a right to discipline employees is when employers are making the comments as part of their jobs. In one such case, a newspaper dismissed a reporter who made inappropriate comments related to local news and media stories on his work-related Twitter account. These tweets were not covered by the labor relations act because they had nothing to do with working conditions or other issues related to the reporter's employment.

SOURCES: BNA, "NLRB's Solomon Issues Update, Covers Employer Dos and Don'ts," *HR Focus,* March 2012, pp. 7–8; Michael Pepperman, "The NLRB Offers Guidance on Social Media Policies and Practices," *Supervision,* January 2012, pp. 16–17; "New NLRB Guidance on Disciplining for Facebook Postings, Twitter Tweets and Blogs," *Mondaq Business Briefing,* September 13, 2011, Business & Company Resource Center, http://galenet.galegroup.com; BNA, "NLRB Memo Finds No Unfair Labor Practice in Firing Reporter for Offensive Twitter Posts," *HR Focus,* June 2011, p. 9.

YES, I WANT THE IAM

I, the undersigned employee of

(Company) _____

authorize the International Association of Machinists and Aerospace Workers (IAM) to act as my collective bargaining agent for wages, hours and working conditions. I agree that this card may be used either to support a demand for recognition or an NLRB election, at the discretion of the union.

Name (print)_____ Date _____

Home Address_____ Phone_____

City_____ State_____ Zip_____

Job Title_____ Dept. _____ Shift _____

Sign Here X _____

Note: This authorization to be SIGNED and DATED in employee's own handwriting. YOUR RIGHT TO SIGN THIS CARD IS PROTECTED BY FEDERAL LAW.

RECEIVED BY (Initial)_____

Figure 14.5
Authorization Card

SOURCE: From John A. Fossum, *Labor Relations: Development, Structure and Process, 2002.* Reprinted with permission of the McGraw-Hill Companies, Inc.

HR Oops!

The Case of the Misguided Supervisors

Recently, when a union sought to organize the nurses at a California hospital, the nursing supervisors, called charge nurses, didn't understand their proper role in the process. While the union was distributing cards for the nurses to indicate their desire for a representation election, several of the charge nurses participated in the union's meetings and decided they wanted to join. Some of these charge nurses also encouraged nurses who reported to them to support the union as well.

One month before the election, the hospital discovered that charge nurses had supported the union even though their positions in the organization qualified them as supervisors. The charge nurses stopped advocating for the union, and some even encouraged nonsupervisory nurses to vote against representation. The election went ahead, and the union won representation.

The hospital challenged the election because of the pro-union activity by the nurses. However, the NLRB and the court both upheld the union.

Questions

1. Why would an organization care whether its supervisors speak in favor of or against union representation?

2. How could the hospital in this example have prepared its supervisors so they would have understood their proper role during the organizing campaign?

SOURCES: National Labor Relations Boards, "The NLRB Process," http://www.nlrb.gov, accessed May 3, 2012; National Labor Relations Board, "NLRB Representation Case Amendments Take Effect Today," news release, April 30, 2012, http://www.nlrb.gov; Duane Morris LLP, "Two NLRB Rules Effective April 30 Affect Most Private-Sector Employers," *Mondaq Business Briefing,* April 20, 2012, http://galenet.galegroup.com.

If over half the employees sign an authorization card, the union may request that the employer voluntarily recognize the union. If the employer agrees, the NLRB certifies the union as the exclusive representative of employees. If the employer refuses, or if only 30% to 50% of employees signed cards, the NLRB conducts a secret-ballot election. The arrangements are made in one of two ways:

1. For a *consent election*, the employer and the union seeking representation arrive at an agreement stating the time and place of the election, the choices included on the ballot, and a way to determine who is eligible to vote.

2. For a *stipulation election*, the parties cannot agree on all of these terms, so the NLRB dictates the time and place, ballot choices, and method of determining eligibility. The NLRB has recently made changes streamlining this process, so employers have little time to make course corrections once an organizing effort is under way. Therefore, organizations—with or without unions—need to ensure supervisors are prepared to behave appropriately and avoid situations such as the one described in "HR Oops!"

On the ballot, workers vote for or against union representation, and they may also have a choice from among more than one union. If the union (or one of the unions on the ballot) wins a majority of votes, the NLRB certifies the union. If the ballot includes more than one union and neither gains a simple majority, the NLRB holds a runoff election.

As noted earlier, if the NLRB finds the election was not conducted fairly, it may set aside the results and call for a new election. Conduct that may lead to an election result's being set aside includes the following examples:[27]

- Threats of loss of jobs or benefits by an employer or union to influence votes or organizing activities.
- A grant of benefits or a promise of benefits as a means of influencing votes or organizing activities.

- Campaign speeches by management or union representatives to assembled groups of employees on company time less than 24 hours before an election.
- The actual use or threat of physical force or violence to influence votes or organizing activities.

After certification, there are limits on future elections. Once the NLRB has certified a union as the exclusive representative of a group of employees, it will not permit additional elections for one year. Also, after the union and employer have finished negotiating a contract, an election cannot be held for the time of the contract period or for three years, whichever comes first. The parties to the contract may agree not to hold an election for longer than three years, but an outside party (another union) cannot be barred for more than three years. Note that both union certifications and union elections can be conducted online.

Management Strategies

Sometimes an employer will recognize a union after a majority of employees have signed authorization cards. More often, there is a hotly contested election campaign. During the campaign, unions try to persuade employees that their wages, benefits, treatment by employers, and chances to influence workplace decisions are too poor or small and that the union will be able to obtain improvements in these areas. Management typically responds with its own messages providing an opposite point of view. Management messages say the organization has provided a valuable package of wages and benefits and has treated employees well. Management also argues that the union will not be able to keep its promises but will instead create costs for employees, such as union dues and lost income during strikes.

Employers use a variety of methods to oppose unions in organizing campaigns.[28] Their efforts range from hiring consultants to distributing leaflets and letters to presenting the company's viewpoint at meetings of employees. Some management efforts go beyond what the law permits, especially in the eyes of union organizers. Why would employers break the law? One explanation is that the consequences, such as reinstating workers with back pay, are small compared to the benefits.[29] If coercing workers away from joining a union saves the company the higher wages, benefits, and other costs of a unionized workforce, management may feel an incentive to accept costs like back pay.

Supervisors have the most direct contact with employees. Thus, as Table 14.1 indicates, it is critical that they establish good relationships with employees even before there is any attempt at union organizing. Supervisors also must know what *not* to do if a union drive takes place. They should be trained in the legal principles discussed earlier in this chapter.

Union Strategies

The traditional union organizing strategy has been for organizers to call or visit employees at home, when possible, to talk about issues like pay and job security. Local 130 UA of the Chicago Journeymen Plumbers Association forms a committee of volunteers to comb through lists of journeyman plumbers within the local's jurisdiction. The committee members cross off the names of union members to create a list of plumbers who are not represented by a union. The local mails organizing kits to these individuals, and then the volunteers follow up to arrange visits with interested individuals in their homes.[30]

Table 14.1

What Supervisors Should and Should Not Do to Discourage Unions

WHAT TO DO:
Report any direct or indirect signs of union activity to a core management group.
Deal with employees by carefully stating the company's response to pro-union arguments. These responses should be coordinated by the company to maintain consistency and to avoid threats or promises. Take away union issues by following effective management practices all the time:
Deliver recognition and appreciation.
Solve employee problems.
Protect employees from harassment or humiliation.
Provide business-related information.
Be consistent in treatment of different employees.
Accommodate special circumstances where appropriate.
Ensure due process in performance management.
Treat all employees with dignity and respect.

WHAT TO AVOID:
Threatening employees with harsher terms and conditions of employment or employment loss if they engage in union activity.
Interrogating employees about pro-union or anti-union sentiments that they or others may have or reviewing union authorization cards or pro-union petitions.
Promising employees that they will receive favorable terms or conditions of employment if they forgo union activity.
Spying on employees known to be, or suspected of being, engaged in pro-union activities.

SOURCE: Excerpted from J. A. Segal, "Unshackle Your Supervisors to Stay Union Free," in *HR Magazine*, June 1998. Copyright © 1998, Society for Human Resource Management, Alexandria, VA. Used with permission. All rights reserved.

Associate Union Membership
Alternative form of union membership in which members receive discounts on insurance and credit cards rather than representation in collective bargaining.

Corporate Campaigns
Bringing public, financial, or political pressure on employers during union organization and contract negotiation.

Beyond encouraging workers to sign authorization cards and vote for the union, organizers use some creative alternatives to traditional organizing activities. They sometimes offer workers **associate union membership,** which is not linked to an employee's workplace and does not provide representation in collective bargaining. Rather, an associate member receives other services, such as discounts on health and life insurance or credit cards.[31] In return for these benefits, the union receives membership dues and a broader base of support for its activities. Associate membership may be attractive to employees who wish to join a union but cannot because their workplace is not organized by a union.

Another alternative to traditional organizing is to conduct **corporate campaigns**—bringing public, financial, or political pressure on employers during union organization and contract negotiation.[32] The Amalgamated Clothing and Textile Workers Union (ACTWU) corporate campaign against textile maker J. P. Stevens during the late 1970s was one of the first successful corporate campaigns and served as a model for those that followed. The ACTWU organized a boycott of J. P. Stevens products and threatened to withdraw its pension funds from financial institutions where J. P. Stevens officers acted as directors. The company eventually agreed to a contract with ACTWU.[33]

Another winning union organizing strategy is to negotiate employer neutrality and card-check provisions into a contract. Under a *neutrality provision*, the employer pledges not to oppose organizing attempts elsewhere in the company. A *card-check provision* is an agreement that if a certain percentage—by law, at least a majority—of employees sign an authorization card, the employer will recognize their union representation. An impartial outside agency, such as the American Arbitration Association, counts the cards. Evidence suggests that this strategy can be very effective for unions.[34]

Decertifying a Union

The Taft-Hartley Act expanded union members' right to be represented by leaders of their own choosing to include the right to vote out an existing union. This action is called *decertifying* the union. Decertification follows the same process as a representation election. An election to decertify a union may not take place when a contract is in effect.

The number of decertification elections has increased from about 5% of all elections in the 1950s and 1960s to more than double that rate in recent years. In fiscal year 2011, the NLRB reported that 15% of elections were decertification elections. However, unions won a strong majority of those elections (more than 73%).[35]

Collective Bargaining

When the NLRB has certified a union, that union represents employees during contract negotiations. In **collective bargaining,** a union negotiates on behalf of its members with management representatives to arrive at a contract defining conditions of employment for the term of the contract and to resolve differences in the way they interpret the contract. Typical contracts include provisions for pay, benefits, work rules, and resolution of workers' grievances. Table 14.2 shows typical provisions negotiated in collective bargaining contracts.

Collective bargaining differs from one situation to another in terms of *bargaining structure*—that is, the range of employees and employers covered by the contract. A contract may involve a narrow group of employees in a craft union or a broad group in an industrial union. Contracts may cover one or several facilities of the same employer, or the bargaining structure may involve several employers. Many more interests must be considered in collective bargaining for an industrial union with a bargaining structure that includes several employers than in collective bargaining for a craft union in a single facility.

The majority of contract negotiations take place between unions and employers that have been through the process before. In the typical situation, management has come to accept the union as an organization it must work with. The situation can be very different when a union has just been certified and is negotiating its first contract. In over one-fourth of negotiations for a first contract, the parties are unable to reach an agreement.[36]

Bargaining over New Contracts

Clearly, the outcome of contract negotiations can have important consequences for labor costs, productivity, and the organization's ability to compete. Therefore, unions and management need to prepare carefully for collective bargaining. Preparation includes establishing objectives for the contract, reviewing the old contract, gathering data (such as compensation paid by competitors and the company's ability to survive a strike), predicting the likely demands to be made, and establishing the cost of meeting the demands.[37] This preparation can help negotiators develop a plan for how to negotiate. Different situations and goals call for different approaches to bargaining, such as the following alternatives proposed by Richard Walton and Robert McKersie:[38]

- *Distributive bargaining* divides an economic "pie" between two sides—for example, a wage increase means giving the union a larger share of the pie.
- *Integrative bargaining* looks for win-win solutions, or outcomes in which both sides benefit. If the organization's labor costs hurt its performance, integrative bargaining might seek to avoid layoffs in exchange for work rules that improve productivity.

LO 14-5 Explain how management and unions negotiate contracts.

Collective Bargaining Negotiation between union representatives and management representatives to arrive at a contract defining conditions of employment for the term of the contract and to administer that contract.

Table 14.2

Typical Provisions in Collective Bargaining Contracts

Establishment and administration of the agreement	Bargaining unit and plant supplements
	Contract duration and reopening and renegotiation provisions
	Union security and the checkoff
	Special bargaining committees
	Grievance procedures
	Arbitration and mediation
	Strikes and lockouts
	Contract enforcement
Functions, rights, and responsibilities	Management rights clauses
	Plant removal
	Subcontracting
	Union activities on company time and premises
	Union–management cooperation
	Regulation of technological change
	Advance notice and consultation
Wage determination and administration	General provisions
	Rate structure and wage differentials
	Allowances
	Incentive systems and production bonus plans
	Production standards and time studies
	Job classification and job evaluation
	Individual wage adjustments
	General wage adjustments during the contract period
Job or income security	Hiring and transfer arrangements
	Employment and income guarantees
	Reporting and call-in pay
	Supplemental unemployment benefit plans
	Regulation of overtime, shift work, etc.
	Reduction of hours to forestall layoffs
	Layoff procedures; seniority; recall
	Worksharing in lieu of layoff
	Attrition arrangements
	Promotion practices
	Training and retraining
	Relocation allowances
	Severance pay and layoff benefit plans
	Special funds and study committees
Plant operations	Work and shop rules
	Rest periods and other in-plant time allowances
	Safety and health
	Plant committees
	Hours of work and premium pay practices
	Shift operations
	Hazardous work
	Discipline and discharge
Paid and unpaid leave	Vacations and holidays
	Sick leave
	Funeral and personal leave
	Military leave and jury duty

(Continued)

Employee benefit plans	Health and insurance plans
	Pension plans
	Profit-sharing, stock purchase, and thrift plans
	Bonus plans
Special groups	Apprentices and learners
	Workers with disabilities and older workers
	Women
	Veterans
	Union representatives
	Nondiscrimination clauses

SOURCE: T. A. Kochan, *Collective Bargaining and Industrial Relations* (Homewood, IL: Richard D. Irwin, 1980), p. 29. Original data from J. W. Bloch, "Union Contracts—A New Series of Studies," *Monthly Labor Review 87* (October 1964), pp. 1184–85.

- *Attitudinal structuring* focuses on establishing a relationship of trust. The parties are concerned about ensuring that the other side will keep its part of any bargain.
- *Intraorganizational bargaining* addresses conflicts within union or management groups or objectives, such as between new employees and workers with high seniority or between cost control and reduction of turnover.

The collective bargaining process may involve any combination of these alternatives.

Negotiations go through various stages.[39] In the earliest stages, many more people are often present than in later stages. On the union side, this may give all the various internal interest groups a chance to participate and voice their goals. Their input helps communicate to management what will satisfy union members and may help the union achieve greater solidarity. At this stage, union negotiators often present a long list of proposals, partly to satisfy members and partly to introduce enough issues that they will have flexibility later in the process. Management may or may not present proposals of its own. Sometimes management prefers to react to the union's proposals.

During the middle stages of the process, each side must make a series of decisions, even though the outcome is uncertain. How important is each issue to the other side? How likely is it that disagreement on particular issues will result in a strike? When and to what extent should one side signal its willingness to compromise?

In the final stage of negotiations, pressure for an agreement increases. Public negotiations may be only part of the process. Negotiators from each side may hold one-on-one meetings or small-group meetings where they escape some public relations pressures. A neutral third party may act as a go-between or facilitator. In some cases, bargaining breaks down as the two sides find they cannot reach a mutually acceptable agreement. The outcome depends partly on the relative bargaining power of each party. That power, in turn, depends on each party's ability to withstand a strike, which costs the workers their pay during the strike and costs the employer lost production and possibly lost customers.

When Bargaining Breaks Down

The intended outcome of collective bargaining is a contract with terms acceptable to both parties. If one or both sides determine that negotiation alone will not produce such an agreement, bargaining breaks down. To bring this impasse to an end, the union may strike, or the parties may bring in outside help to resolve their differences.

Union members demonstrate outside of San Francisco General Hospital to protest cuts to hospital workers' benefits and salaries.

Strike

A collective decision by union members not to work until certain demands or conditions are met.

Strikes   A **strike** is a collective decision of the union members not to work until certain demands or conditions are met. The union members vote, and if the majority favors a strike, they all go on strike at that time or when union leaders believe the time is right. Strikes are typically accompanied by *picketing*—the union stations members near the worksite with signs indicating the union is on strike. During the strike, the union members do not receive pay from their employer, but the union may be able to make up for some of the lost pay. The employer loses production unless it can hire replacement workers, and even then, productivity may be reduced. Often, other unions support striking workers by refusing to cross their picket line—for example, refusing to make deliveries to a company during a strike.

The vast majority of labor-management negotiations do not result in a strike, and the number of strikes has plunged since the 1950s, as shown in Figure 14.6. In every year since 2000, the percentage of total working time lost to strikes each year has been 0.01%—that is, one-hundredth of 1% of working time—or even less.

A primary reason strikes are rare is that a strike is seldom in the best interests of either party. Not only do workers lose wages and employers lose production, but the negative experience of a strike can make future interactions more difficult. When 500

Figure 14.6

Strikes Involving 1,000 or More Workers

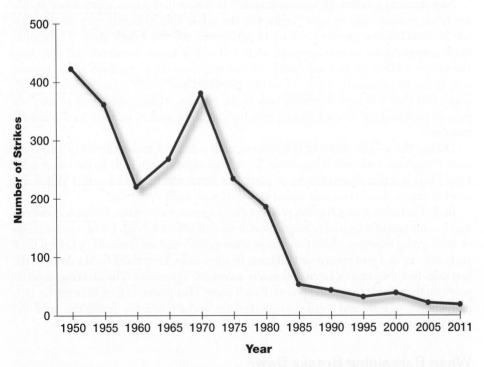

Note: Because strikes are most likely in large bargaining units, these numbers represent most lost working time in the United States.

SOURCE: Bureau of Labor Statistics, "Major Work Stoppages in 2011," news release, February 8, 2012, http://www.bls.gov.

members of the International Association of Machinists and Aerospace Workers went on strike against Caterpillar in Joliet, Illinois, they expressed some hope that they could persuade the company not to freeze wages and reduce benefits. But looking at the surrounding economic climate, they also admitted to many doubts that they could have much of a future continuing to work for Caterpillar. One of the striking workers told a reporter, "It's a good wage here, but if you take it away, why work here?"[40] When strikes do occur, the conduct of each party during the strike can do lasting harm to labor-management relations. Violence by either side or threats of job loss or actual job loss because jobs went to replacement workers can make future relations difficult. Finally, many government employees do not have a right to strike, and their percentage among unionized employees overall has risen in recent decades, as we discussed earlier.

Strikes such as this one between machinists and management at a Caterpillar plant are costly. Both unions and employees generally prefer to resolve contract conflicts in other ways.

Alternatives to Strikes   Because strikes are so costly and risky, unions and employers generally prefer other methods for resolving conflicts. Three common alternatives rely on a neutral third party, usually provided by the Federal Mediation and Conciliation Service (FMCS):

- **Mediation** is the least formal and most widely used of these procedures. A mediator hears the views of both sides and facilitates the negotiation process. The mediator has no formal authority to dictate a resolution, so a strike remains a possibility. In a survey studying negotiations between unions and large businesses, mediation was used in almost 4 out of 10 negotiation efforts.[41]
- A **fact finder,** most often used for negotiations with governmental bodies, typically reports on the reasons for the dispute, the views and arguments of both sides, and (sometimes) a recommended settlement, which the parties may decline. The public nature of these recommendations may pressure the parties to settle. Even if they do not accept the fact finder's recommended settlement, the fact finder may identify or frame issues in a way that makes agreement easier. Sometimes merely devoting time to this process gives the parties a chance to reach an agreement. However, there is no guarantee that a strike will be avoided.
- Under **arbitration,** the most formal type of outside intervention, an arbitrator or arbitration board determines a settlement that is *binding*, meaning the parties have to accept it. In conventional arbitration, the arbitrator fashions the solution. In "final-offer arbitration," the arbitrator must choose either management's or the union's final offer for each issue or for the contract as a whole. "Rights arbitration" focuses on enforcing or interpreting contract terms. Arbitration in the writing of contracts or setting of contract terms has traditionally been reserved for special circumstances such as negotiations between unions and government agencies, where strikes may be illegal or especially costly. Occasionally, arbitration has been used with businesses in situations where strikes have been extremely damaging. See the "Best Practices" box for an example of an industry that uses arbitration as a means to avoid costly strikes and litigation. However, the general opinion is that union and management representatives are in the best position to resolve conflicts themselves, because they are closer to the situation than an arbitrator can be.

Mediation
Conflict resolution procedure in which a mediator hears the views of both sides and facilitates the negotiation process but has no formal authority to dictate a resolution.

Fact Finder
Third party to collective bargaining who reports the reasons for a dispute, the views and arguments of both sides, and possibly a recommended settlement, which the parties may decline.

Arbitration
Conflict resolution procedure in which an arbitrator or arbitration board determines a binding settlement.

Best Practices

CIR Keeps Electricians and Contractors Humming

The Council on Industrial Relations (CIR) has a mission of creating "harmony and prosperity in the electrical industry through arbitration." In 1920, when the CIR was formed, harmony was far from the normal relationship of worker and unions. Following World War I, workers literally fought for the right to form unions. Several electrical contractors met regularly as a social club, and they decided to try working with the International Brotherhood of Electrical Workers (IBEW) to form a joint organization that would arbitrate disputes peacefully.

The CIR conducts arbitration by forming a panel of 12 members. Half are representatives from the IBEW, and half are representatives of the contractors, now united in a group called the National Electrical Contractors Association (NECA). The IBEW and NECA each select one of the representatives to be cochairman. All the panel members serve without compensation from the council, as a service to the industry. The objective of including equal numbers from both groups is to ensure that the panel fully understands both the concerns of workers and the impact of its decisions on companies in the electrical industry. The panel meets four times a year to hear issues the parties have not been able to resolve on their own—employee grievances, interpretation of contracts, and contract negotiations. The panel members must arrive at a unanimous decision, and then they announce the official decision in writing.

All decisions by the CIR are legally binding. Members of NECA whose workers are represented by the IBEW have in their collective bargaining agreements a "CIR clause." This clause says all disputes that the parties can settle on their own will go to CIR for arbitration. In the beginning, the CIR heard only a handful of cases each year. But as the fairness of the decisions gave the arbitrators more credibility, the CIR began to hear many more cases. Over the decades since 1920, the CIR has issued more than 8,000 decisions. Resolving differences with arbitration instead of strikes has preserved millions of dollars in wages to electrical workers and protected millions of dollars' worth of business for contractors.

Perhaps best of all, the very existence and use of the CIR make it more likely the parties to a labor-management dispute can arrive at a decision on their own. Knowing that the arbitration panel's decision will be final gives the parties an incentive to arrive at a mutually agreeable solution when they are in control of the outcome. Further, the history of CIR decisions gives union and management negotiators a body of past decisions to use as a model for future agreements.

SOURCES: Council on Industrial Relations, "About CIR," http://www.thecir.org, accessed May 7, 2012; CIR, "Basic Principles," http://www.thecir.org, accessed May 7, 2012; National Electrical Contractors Association, "Council on Industrial Relations," http://www.necanet.org, accessed May 7, 2012; International Brotherhood of Electrical Workers, "CIR/Bylaws and Appeals," http://www.ibew.org, accessed May 7, 2012.

LO 14-6 Summarize the practice of contract administration.

Contract Administration

Although the process of negotiating a labor agreement (including the occasional strike) receives the most publicity, other union-management activities occur far more often. Bargaining over a new contract typically occurs only about every three years, but administering labor contracts goes on day after day, year after year. The two activities are linked, of course. Vague or inconsistent language in the contract can make administering the contract more difficult. The difficulties can create conflict that spills over into the next round of negotiations.[42] Events during negotiations—strikes, the use of replacement workers, or violence by either side—also can lead to difficulties in working successfully under a conflict.

Contract administration includes carrying out the terms of the agreement and resolving conflicts over interpretation or violation of the agreement. Under a labor contract, the process for resolving these conflicts is called a **grievance procedure.**

Grievance Procedure
The process for resolving union-management conflicts over interpretation or violation of a collective bargaining agreement.

This procedure has a key influence on success in contract administration. A grievance procedure may be started by an employee or discharged employee who believes the employer violated the contract or by a union representative on behalf of a group of workers or union representatives.

For grievances launched by an employee, a typical grievance procedure follows the steps shown in Figure 14.7. The grievance may be settled during any of the four steps. In the first step, the employee talks to his or her supervisor about the problem. If this conversation is unsatisfactory, the employee may involve the union steward in further discussion. The union steward and employee decide whether the problem has been resolved and, if not, whether it is a contract violation. If the problem was not resolved and does seem to be a contract violation, the union moves to step 2, putting the grievance in writing and submitting it to a line manager. The union steward meets with a management representative to try to resolve the problem. Management consults with the industrial relations staff and puts its response

Figure 14.7

Steps in an Employee-Initiated Grievance Procedure

Step 1
- Employee (and union steward) discusses problem with supervisor.
- Union steward and employee decide whether problem was resolved.
- Union steward and employee decide whether contract was violated.

Step 2
- Written grievance is submitted to production superintendent, another line manager, or industrial relations representative.
- Steward and manager discuss grievance.
- Management puts response in writing.

Step 3
- Union appeals grievance to top line management and senior industrial relations staff.
- Additional local or international union officers may be involved.
- Decision resulting from appeal is put into writing.

Step 4
- Union decides whether to appeal unresolved grievance to arbitration.
- Union appeals grievance to arbitration for binding decision.

SOURCES: Adapted from T. A. Kochan, *Collective Bargaining and Industrial Relations* (Homewood, IL: Richard D. Irwin, 1980), p. 395; and J. A. Fossum, *Labor Relations* (Boston: McGraw-Hill/Irwin, 2002), pp. 448–52.

in writing too at this second stage. If step 2 fails to resolve the problem, the union appeals the grievance to top line management and representatives of the industrial relations staff. The union may involve more local or international officers in discussions at this stage (see step 3 in Figure 14.7). The decision resulting from the appeal is put into writing. If the grievance is still not resolved, the union may decide (step 4) to appeal the grievance to an arbitrator. If the grievance involves a discharged employee, the process may begin at step 2 or 3, however, and the time limits between steps may be shorter. Grievances filed by the union on behalf of a group may begin at step 1 or step 2.

The majority of grievances are settled during the earlier steps of the process. This reduces delays and avoids the costs of arbitration. If a grievance does reach arbitration, the arbitrator makes the final ruling in the matter. Based on a series of Supreme Court decisions, courts generally avoid reviewing arbitrators' decisions and focus only on whether the grievance involved an issue that is subject to arbitration under the contract.[43]

Employers can judge a grievance procedure in terms of various criteria.[44] One consideration is effectiveness: how well the procedure resolves day-to-day contract questions. A second basic consideration is efficiency: whether it resolves issues at a reasonable cost and without major delays. The company also should consider how well the grievance procedure adapts to changing circumstances. For example, if sales drop off and the company needs to cut costs, how clear are the provisions related to layoffs and subcontracting of work? In the case of contracts covering multiple business units, the procedure should allow for resolving local contract issues, such as work rules at a particular facility. Companies also should consider whether the grievance procedure is fair—whether it treats employees equitably and gives them a voice in the process.

From the point of view of employees, the grievance procedure is an important means of getting fair treatment in the workplace. Its success depends on whether it provides for all the kinds of problems that are likely to arise (such as how to handle a business slowdown), whether employees feel they can file a grievance without being punished for it, and whether employees believe their union representatives will follow through. Under the National Labor Relations Act, the union has a *duty of fair representation*, which means the union must give equal representation to all members of the bargaining unit, whether or not they actually belong to the union. Too many grievances may indicate a problem—for example, the union members or line supervisors do not understand how to uphold the contract or have no desire to do so. At the same time, a very small number of grievances may also signal a problem. A very low grievance rate may suggest a fear of filing a grievance, a belief that the system does not work, or a belief that employees are poorly represented by their union.

What types of issues most commonly reach arbitration? According to data from the Federal Mediation and Conciliation Service, the largest share of arbitration cases involved discharge or other disciplinary actions.[45] Other issues that often reach arbitration involve wages, benefits, layoffs, work schedules, and management's rights. In reaching decisions about these and other issues, arbitrators consider a number of criteria, such as employees' understanding of the rules, the employer's consistency and fairness, and the employees' chance to present a defense and appeal a decision.[46]

Labor-Management Cooperation

LO 14-7 Describe more cooperative approaches to labor-management relations.

The traditional understanding of union-management relations is that the two parties are adversaries, meaning each side is competing to win at the expense of the other. There have always been exceptions to this approach. And since at least the 1980s, there seems to be wider acceptance of the view that greater cooperation can increase employee commitment and motivation while making the workplace more flexible.[47] Also, evidence suggests that employees who worked under traditional labor relations systems and then under the new, more cooperative systems prefer the cooperative approach.[48]

Cooperation between labor and management may feature employee involvement in decision making, self-managing employee teams, labor-management problem-solving teams, broadly defined jobs, and sharing of financial gains and business information with employees.[49] The search for a win-win solution requires that unions and their members understand the limits on what an employer can afford in a competitive marketplace.

Without the union's support, efforts at employee empowerment are less likely to survive and less likely to be effective if they do survive.[50] Unions have often resisted employee empowerment programs, precisely because the programs try to change workplace relations and the role that unions play. Union leaders have feared that such programs will weaken unions' role as independent representatives of employee interests. Indeed, the National Labor Relations Act makes it an unfair labor practice for an employer to "dominate or interfere with the formation or administration of any labor organization or contribute financial or other support to it."

Although employers must be careful to meet legal requirements, the NLRB has clearly supported employee involvement in work teams and decision making. For example, in a 2001 ruling, the NLRB found that employee participation committees at Crown Cork & Seal's aluminum-can factory did not violate federal labor law.[51] Those committees make and carry out decisions regarding a wide range of issues, including production, quality, training, safety, and certain types of discipline. The NLRB determined that the committees were not employer dominated. Instead of "dealing with" management, where employees make proposals for management to accept or reject, the committees exercise authority within boundaries set by management, similar to the authority of a first-line supervisor. In spite of the legal concerns, cooperative approaches to labor relations likely contribute to an organization's success.[52]

Beyond avoiding any taint of misuse of employee empowerment, employers build cooperative relationships by the way they treat employees—with respect and fairness, in the knowledge that attracting talent and minimizing turnover are in the employer's best interests. One organization that does this is Black & Veatch, a global engineering, consulting, and construction company. The firm is committed to employee safety, and its senior vice president of construction and labor negotiator Richard King has a background in workplace health and safety. King's commitment to keeping workers safe aligns well with the concerns of the unions representing Black & Veatch construction workers, which hire their own safety and environmental experts. Cooperation on safety also helps the company manage the cost of workers' compensation insurance and satisfy its large clients, which typically give contracts only to construction firms with exceptional safety records.[53] For Black & Veatch, then, good labor relations directly contributes to business sustainability.

THINKING ETHICALLY

IS IT FAIR TO FAVOR UNIONIZED FACILITIES?

As General Motors has rebounded from its near-bankruptcy following the financial crisis and recession of a few years ago, it has been adding shifts, reopening factories, and calling back workers. All of those moves are potentially good news for the United Auto Workers union, which represents many—but not all—GM factory workers. So the union is trying to make sure that its members benefit from the company's renewed prosperity.

At GM's factory in Lordstown, Ohio, employees are working around the clock to assemble the Chevrolet Cruze. At the assembly plant in Moraine, Ohio, however, the doors have remained closed. The workers in Moraine were not UAW members, and when the union negotiated with GM, it demanded that its members be given priority for rehiring. Non-UAW workers are not allowed to transfer to unionized plants. A UAW negotiator explained to a reporter that it was unfortunate some workers would be shut out of the recovery, but "we had to take care of our own members." If the company needs more workers than the union can provide, GM can hire workers from Moraine, but they will be considered new employees, and their wage rate will be lower. On the current pay scale, a newly hired UAW worker earns on average $14 per hour; experienced workers earn about twice as much. Under the current contract, workers can earn a series of raises over time, eventually reaching $19 per hour.

These decisions are part of a complicated history in response to years of global expansion and stiff competition. GM almost closed the unionized Lordstown plant in 2007 and moved the assembly of small cars to Mexico. But UAW and GM negotiated an agreement aimed at making the Lordstown plant more competitive. One important area of concessions in 2007 was that GM began allowing a two-tier pay scale in which newly hired workers earn much less than workers on the prior pay scale. Then when the U.S. government provided a financial rescue to GM in 2009, it negotiated concessions from the UAW, including no cost-of-living pay increases and a contract clause forbidding strikes. The UAW hoped members would accept those concessions in exchange for their priority place in line when GM began to grow again. The union emphasizes that its priority is job creation for its members.

Questions

1. In its negotiations with GM management, whose well-being has the UAW sought to protect? Whose well-being *should* the UAW be protecting? Why?
2. In its negotiations with the UAW, whose well-being has GM sought to protect? Whose wellbeing *should* GM negotiators be concerned about? Why?

SOURCES: Sharon Terlep, "UAW Freezes Rival out of Rebound," *The Wall Street Journal,* April 29, 2012, http://online.wsj.com; "Detroit Three Automakers to Hire Thousands in Coming Years," *Quality,* February 2012, pp. 13–14; Nick Bunkley, "UAW Open to More Jobs at a Second-Tier Pay Level," *The New York Times,* March 29, 2011.

SUMMARY

LO 14-1 Define unions and labor relations and their role in organizations.

A union is an organization formed for the purpose of representing its members in resolving conflicts with employers. Labor relations is the management specialty emphasizing skills that managers and union leaders can use to minimize costly forms of conflict and to seek win-win solutions to disagreements. Unions—often locals belonging to national and international organizations—engage in organizing, collective bargaining, and contract administration with businesses and government organizations. In the United States, union membership has been declining among businesses but has held steady with government employees. Unionization is associated with more generous compensation and higher productivity but lower profits. Unions may reduce a business's flexibility and economic performance.

LO 14-2 Identify the labor relations goals of management, labor unions, and society.

Management goals are to increase the organization's profits. Managers generally expect that unions will make these goals harder to achieve. Labor unions have the goal of obtaining pay and working conditions that satisfy their members. They obtain these results by gaining power in numbers. Society's values have included the hope that the existence of unions will replace conflict or violence between workers and employers with fruitful negotiation.

LO 14-3 Summarize laws and regulations that affect labor relations.

The National Labor Relations Act supports the use of collective bargaining and sets out the rights of employees, including the right to organize, join a union, and go on strike. The NLRA prohibits unfair labor practices by employers, including interference with efforts to form a labor union and discrimination against employees who engage in union activities. The Taft-Hartley Act and Landrum-Griffin Act establish restrictions on union practices that restrain workers, such as their preventing employees from working during a strike or determining who an employer may hire. The Taft-Hartley Act also permits state right-to-work laws.

LO 14-4 Describe the union organizing process.

Organizing begins when union representatives contact employees and invite them to sign an authorization card. If over half the employees sign a card, the union may request that the employer voluntarily recognize the union. If the employer refuses or if 30% to 50% of employees signed authorization cards, the NLRB conducts a secret-ballot election. If the union wins, the NLRB certifies the union. If the union loses but the NLRB finds that the election was not conducted fairly, it may set aside the results and call a new election.

LO 14-5 Explain how management and unions negotiate contracts.

Negotiations take place between representatives of the union and the management bargaining unit. The majority of negotiations involve parties that have been through the process before. The process begins with preparation, including research into the other side's strengths and demands. In the early stages of negotiation, many more people are present than at later stages. The union presents its demands, and management sometimes presents demands as well. Then the sides evaluate the demands and the likelihood of a strike. In the final stages, pressure for an agreement increases, and a neutral third party may be called on to help reach a resolution. If bargaining breaks down, the impasse may be broken with a strike, mediation, fact finder, or arbitration.

LO 14-6 Summarize the practice of contract administration.

Contract administration is a daily activity under the labor agreement. It includes carrying out the terms of the agreement and resolving conflicts over interpretation or violation of the contract. Conflicts are resolved through a grievance procedure. Typically, the grievance procedure begins with an employee talking to his or her supervisor about the problem and possibly involving the union steward in the discussion. If this does not resolve the conflict, the union files a written grievance with a line manager, and union and management representatives meet to discuss the problem. If this effort fails, the union appeals the grievance to top line management and the industrial relations staff. If the appeal fails, the union may appeal the grievance to an arbitrator.

LO 14-7 Describe more cooperative approaches to labor-management relations.

In contrast to the traditional view that labor and management are adversaries, some organizations and unions work more cooperatively. Cooperation may feature employee involvement in decision making, self-managing employee teams, labor-management problem-solving teams, broadly defined jobs, and sharing of financial gains and business information with employees. If such cooperation is tainted by attempts of the employer to dominate or interfere with labor organizations, however, such as by dealing with wages, grievances, or working conditions, it may be illegal under the NLRA. In spite of such legal concerns, cooperative labor relations seem to contribute to an organization's success.

KEY TERMS

agency shop, 445

American Federation of Labor and Congress of Industrial Organizations (AFL-CIO), 438

arbitration, 459

associate union membership, 454

checkoff provision, 445

closed shop, 445

collective bargaining, 455

corporate campaigns, 454

craft union, 438

fact finder, 459

REVIEW AND DISCUSSION QUESTIONS

1. Why do employees join labor unions? Did you ever belong to a labor union? If you did, do you think union membership benefited you? If you did not, do you think a union would have benefited you? Why or why not?

2. Why do managers at most companies prefer that unions not represent their employees? Can unions provide benefits to an employer? Explain.

3. How has union membership in the United States changed over the past few decades? How does union membership in the United States compare with union membership in other countries? How might these patterns in union membership affect the HR decisions of an international company?

4. What legal responsibilities do employers have regarding unions? What are the legal requirements affecting unions?

5. Suppose you are the HR manager for a chain of clothing stores. You learn that union representatives have been encouraging the stores' employees to sign authorization cards. What events can follow in this process of organizing? Suggest some ways that you might respond in your role as HR manager.

6. If the parties negotiating a labor contract are unable to reach an agreement, what actions can resolve the situation?

7. Why are strikes uncommon? Under what conditions might management choose to accept a strike?

8. What are the usual steps in a grievance procedure? What are the advantages of resolving a grievance in the first step? What skills would a supervisor need so grievances can be resolved in the first step?

9. The Black & Veatch example at the end of the chapter describes union-management cooperation. What does the company gain from this effort? What do workers gain?

10. What are the legal restrictions on labor-management cooperation?

EXPERIENCING HR

Divide into groups of six students each. List your names in order of your birthdates (month and day). The first half of the students on the list will be the management team in this exercise, and the second half of the students will be the union team. (If the class size results in a group with an odd number of members, the last person on the list in that group can choose which team to join.)

Imagine that you work for a manufacturing company whose machinists belong to a union. As international competition for your products has increased, management is concerned that it needs to rein in personnel costs and is considering changes to employees' insurance and pension plans. Management has been proud of what it sees as the company's history of innovation and a positive working environment. The union has been proud of what it sees as its role in promoting fair and safe working conditions, as well as job opportunities that have built a strong community. The machinists' labor agreement is set to expire next year, so management and union representatives have agreed to meet and begin discussing the issue of compensation costs.

Spend 5 minutes in your separate teams deciding what positions you want to take. Then spend 15 minutes together, trying to find a way forward that takes into account the interests of labor and management. After this discussion, work independently to write your own assessment: Do you think your company and union can arrive at an agreement that is fair to both sides? Why or why not?

TAKING RESPONSIBILITY: High-Flying Labor Relations at Southwest Airlines

Even at a time when air travel has become associated with long lines, cramped seats, and invasive security, Southwest Airlines has maintained its reputation for keeping customers happy. To accomplish this, Southwest does not merely deliver passengers from one point to the next, it also tries to keep up their spirits by hiring and motivating employees to deliver a sense of fun. And it has managed to do that—and stay consistently profitable—with a unionized workforce. At the heart of this success is the company's principle that "well-treated employees translate to well-treated customers." The company's stated objective for labor relationships is to develop "solid relationships" through "communication, transparency, and consistency."

Southwest has called itself "the most unionized airline," reporting that more than 80% of its employees are union members. The airline's 6,000-plus pilots have been represented by the Southwest Airlines Pilots' Association (SWAPA) since 1978. Its flight attendants have been represented by Local 556 of the Transport Workers Union since 1975. At the time, the company had just 54 flight attendants, and the motivating issue was to establish written work rules. Under Texas law, employees could choose whether or not to join. Only about one-third signed up until some of the members tackled what was for them a nagging problem: the required uniform of hot pants, which constantly drew unpleasant, unwanted attention. With that engaging issue to back, most of the rest of the attendants joined the union, and they successfully pushed through this fundamental change in working conditions.

Joe Harris, Southwest's senior labor relations counsel, has represented the company in negotiations since the 1970s. He says the company's history of constructive labor relations is a reflection of attitudes at the top. According to Harris, Southwest's founder, Lamar Muse, and the CEO who succeeded him, Herb Kelleher, both took the attitude that union representation was a reasonable option for employees, who "needed an effective voice," so the company would work with them. That tone is echoed by SWAPA, which notes that before it began representing Southwest's pilots, the pilots and management cooperatively developed work rules promoting safety and efficiency. SWAPA adds, "That cooperative spirit has continued through the negotiation of eight labor contracts." Likewise, a historical note published by the flight attendants union says that at Southwest, "we have some of the best working conditions in the industry."

That attitude hardly means that unions and management see eye to eye on everything. Negotiations can be adversarial. But once a contract is in place, both sides again turn their focus to the company's long-term well-being and the customers' satisfaction. That shared focus can pay off for employees in practical ways. During the severe recession that began in 2008, the company avoided layoffs, and by 2010, it was actually hiring.

Southwest's latest labor relations challenge will follow its acquisition of AirTran Airways. With employees at both companies coming from different unions, the parties have to agree on who will represent the employees of the combined company and what level of seniority each employee will have relative to the others. In terms of flight attendants, for example, 10,000 Southwest employees are represented by the Transport Workers Union, while 2,400 AirTran employees are represented by the Association of Flight Attendants. Expectations are that with Southwest being the larger, acquiring business, the TWU will represent all the flight attendants, and that AirTran's wages and benefits will be increased to match those of the relatively generous Southwest.

Questions

1. Contrast the general labor relations goals of Southwest's management, its employees' unions, and the society in which it operates. Where are those goals in conflict, and where are they consistent?
2. Would you say that Southwest's labor relations help promote the company's sustainability (ability to make a profit without sacrificing the resources of its employees, community, and environment)? Why or why not?
3. What advice would you give Southwest for its labor relations following the acquisition of AirTran?

SOURCES: Southwest Airlines Pilots' Association, home page, http://www.swapa.org, accessed May 3, 2012; Mary (Ravella) Longobardi, "The History of Our Union," TWU Local 556, http://twu556.org, accessed May 3, 2012; Southwest Airlines, *2010 Southwest Airlines One Report*, http://www.southwestonereport.com, accessed May 3, 2012; Susan Carey, "Southwest, AirTran Unions Agree on Seniority," *The Wall Street Journal*, December 26, 2011, http://online.wsj.com; Alison Beard and Richard Hornik, "It's Hard to Be Good," *Harvard Business Review*, November 2011, pp. 88–96; Will McDonald, "The Secret to Southwest's Success? Putting Workers First," *American Rights at Work*, June 13, 2011, http://www.americanrightsatwork.org.

MANAGING TALENT: The SEIU Takes On the California Hospital Association

Hospitals in California recently experienced firsthand that employers may find themselves negotiating with unions even when their employees are not represented by a union. The California Hospital Association, representing the state's private hospitals, signed an agreement with the Service Employees International Union (SEIU), whose members include nurses, respiratory therapists, maintenance workers, and other hospital workers. In the agreement, titled the Partnership for a Healthy California, the hospital association promised to facilitate meetings between the SEIU and the chief executives of its hospitals and health systems. The parties also acknowledged that the agreement does not require the hospitals to sign union-organizing agreements.

In announcing the agreement, both sides described it as an effort to partner in improving health care costs and quality, as well as access to health care. Dave Regan, president of SEIU-United Healthcare Workers West, insisted that the agreement is "not a labor relations agreement" but a commitment to making "durable, lasting, meaningful change" in the health care system. Both sides described the agreement as "groundbreaking."

However, the events leading up to the agreement suggest that it was about more than a shared desire to improve the health care system. During the months before the agreement was reached, the SEIU had been gathering signatures to have a measure placed before the state's voters. That measure would have forbidden private hospitals from setting fees at more than 25% above the cost to provide care, and it would have required nonprofit hospitals to spend at least 5% of patient revenue on free health care services for the poor. (Government-run hospitals were excluded because most of their patients are poor.) The SEIU promoted the measure as a way to make health care more widely available to poor people while reining in excessive charges. State law requires nonprofit hospitals to provide charity care, but does not specify an amount or type of care that must be provided.

Coincidentally or not, the measure was written with wording that exempts two health care chains where the employees are SEIU members: Dignity Health (the largest hospital chain in California) and Kaiser Permanente (the largest HMO in California). The SEIU represents about 60,000 employees at those two organizations. In contrast, it applies mainly to organizations where the SEIU does not represent the workers. Critics complained that the charitable-sounding ballot measure was a way to give a competitive advantage to companies where employees were organized by the union. They noted that the collection of signatures was launched at Sacramento's Sutter General Hospital, where the SEIU had long been trying to organize workers. The SEIU's Regan responded that the initiative was a broad one that would address practices at three-quarters of the state's hospitals, that Dignity already provides a substantial amount of charity care, and that Kaiser has its own insurance company and reports different financial data to the state.

When the signature-gathering campaign began outside Sutter, SEIU workers were spreading the message that the hospital, on average, overcharged patients by more than 400%, even though it had $3.2 billion in reserves. At that point in the campaign, Sutter's spokesperson merely pointed out that the numbers were wrong and that although the current business model for healthcare "is not sustainable," the ballot initiative was not the way to solve the problem. Whether or not he continued to feel that way, a few months later, the hospital association had agreed to be a problem-solving partner with the SEIU.

Questions

1. What impact could a political campaign such as the SEIU's ballot initiative have on a hospital's ability to carry out its strategy?
2. Why do you think the hospital association signed an agreement with the SEIU when most of its members did not have collective bargaining agreements with the union?
3. Do you think the SEIU can (or will) help California hospitals reduce costs and increase quality and access to care? Why or why not? What would be the most advantageous relationship for a California hospital to have with the union?

SOURCES: David Goll, "California Hospital Labor Groups Drop November Ballot Plans," *Los Angeles Business*, May 3, 2012, http://www.bizjournals.com/losangeles/; Michael J. Mishak, "SEIU Drops Initiatives as Part of California Hospital Accord," *Los Angeles Times*, May 2, 2012, http://latimesblogs.latimes.com; Michael J. Mishak, "Union Seeks to Cut California Hospital Billings, Boost Care for Poor," *Los Angeles Times*, March 10, 2012, http://articles.latimes.com.

TWITTER FOCUS: Republic Gets Serious

Using Twitter, continue the conversation about collective bargaining and labor relations by reading the Serious Materials case at **www.mhhe.com/noefund5e**. Engage with your classmates and instructor via Twitter to chat about Serious Materials' actions using the case questions posted on the Noe website. Don't have a Twitter account yet? See the instructions for getting started on the Online Learning Center.

NOTES

1. Mike Hendricks, "Fire Union Agreement Called 'Most Impressive Achievement' of KC Council," *Kansas City Star*, May 2, 2012, http://www.kansascity.com.

2. J. T. Dunlop, *Industrial Relations Systems* (New York: Holt, 1958); and C. Kerr, "Industrial Conflict and Its Mediation," *American Journal of Sociology* 60 (1954), pp. 230–45.

3. T. A. Kochan, *Collective Bargaining and Industrial Relations* (Homewood, IL: Richard D. Irwin, 1980), p. 25; and H. C. Katz and T. A. Kochan, *An Introduction to Collective Bargaining and Industrial Relations*, 3rd ed. (New York: McGraw-Hill, 2004).

4. Change to Win, "About Us," http://www.changetowin.org, accessed May 4, 2012.

5. Whether the time the union steward spends on union business is paid for by the employer, the union, or a combination is a matter of negotiation between the employer and the union.

6. Bureau of Labor Statistics, "Union Members—2011," news release, January 27, 2012, http://www.bls.gov.

7. Katz and Kochan, *An Introduction to Collective Bargaining*, building on J. Fiorito and C. L. Maranto, "The Contemporary Decline of Union Strength," *Contemporary Policy Issues* 3 (1987), pp. 12–27; and G. N. Chaison and J. Rose, "The Macrodeterminants of Union Growth and Decline," in *The State of the Unions*, ed. G. Strauss et al. (Madison, WI: Industrial Relations Research Association, 1991).

8. Bureau of Labor Statistics, "Union Members—2011."

9. C. Brewster, "Levels of Analysis in Strategic HRM: Questions Raised by Comparative Research," Conference on Research and Theory in HRM, Cornell University, October 1997.

10. American Federation of State, County and Municipal Employees, "Jobs We Do," www.afscme.org, accessed May 4, 2012.

11. J. T. Addison and B. T. Hirsch, "Union Effects on Productivity, Profits, and Growth: Has the Long Run Arrived?" *Journal of Labor Economics* 7 (1989), pp. 72–105; and R. B. Freeman and J. L. Medoff, "The Two Faces of Unionism," *Public Interest* 57 (Fall 1979), pp. 69–93.

12. L. Mishel and P. Voos, *Unions and Economic Competitiveness* (Armonk, NY: M. E. Sharpe, 1991); Freeman and Medoff, "Two Faces"; and S. Slichter, J. Healy, and E. R. Livernash, *The Impact of Collective Bargaining on Management* (Washington, DC: Brookings Institution, 1960).

13. A. O. Hirschman, *Exit, Voice, and Loyalty* (Cambridge, MA: Harvard University Press, 1970); and R. Batt, A. J. S. Colvin, and J. Keefe, "Employee Voice, Human Resource Practices, and Quit Rates: Evidence from the Telecommunications Industry," *Industrial and Labor Relations Review* 55 (1970), pp. 573–94.

14. R. B. Freeman and J. L. Medoff, *What Do Unions Do?* (New York: Basic Books, 1984); Addison and Hirsch, "Union Effects on Productivity"; M. Ash and J. A. Seago, "The Effect of Registered Nurses' Unions on Heart-Attack Mortality," *Industrial and Labor Relations Review* 57 (2004), p. 422; and C. Doucouliagos and P. Laroche, "What Do Unions Do to Productivity? A Meta-Analysis," *Industrial Relations* 42 (2003), pp. 650–91.

15. B. E. Becker and C. A. Olson, "Unions and Firm Profits," *Industrial Relations* 31, no. 3 (1992), pp. 395–415; B. T. Hirsch and B. A. Morgan, "Shareholder Risks and Returns in Union and Nonunion Firms," *Industrial and Labor Relations Review* 47, no. 2 (1994), pp. 302–18; and Hristos Doucouliagos and Patrice Laroche, "Unions and Profits: A Meta-Regression Analysis," *Industrial Relations* 48, no. 1 (January 2008), p. 146.

16. Nicole A. Bonham Colby, "Labor and Management: Working Together for a Stable Future," *Alaska Business Monthly*, October 2011, Business & Company Resource Center, http://galenet.galegroup.com.

17. Bureau of Labor Statistics, "Employer Costs for Employee Compensation—December 2011," news release, March 14, 2012, http://www.bls.gov.

18. S. B. Jarrell and T. D. Stanley, "A Meta-Analysis of the Union-Nonunion Wage Gap," *Industrial and Labor Relations Review* 44 (1990), pp. 54–67; L. Mishel and M. Walters, "How Unions Help

All Workers," *Economic Policy Institute Briefing Paper*, August 2003, www.epinet.org; and McKinley L. Blackburn, "Are Union Wage Differentials in the United States Falling?" *Industrial Relations* 47, no. 3 (July 2008), p. 390.

19. S. Webb and B. Webb, *Industrial Democracy* (London: Longmans, Green, 1897); and J. R. Commons, *Institutional Economics* (New York: Macmillan, 1934).

20. "Why America Needs Unions, but Not the Kind It Has Now," *Bloomberg Businessweek*, May 23, 1994, p. 70.

21. E. E. Herman, J. L. Schwatz, and A. Kuhn, *Collective Bargaining and Labor Relations* (Englewood Cliffs, NJ: Prentice Hall, 1992).

22. Kochan, *Collective Bargaining and Industrial Relations*, p. 61.

23. National Labor Relations Board, *Basic Guide to the National Labor Relations Act* (Washington, DC: U.S. Government Printing Office, 1997).

24. National Labor Relations Board, "Who Is Covered by the National Labor Relations Act?" Frequently Asked Questions, http://www.nlrb.gov, accessed May 4, 2012; U.S. Department of Labor, Office of Labor-Management Standards, "Employee Rights under the National Labor Relations Act," poster, http://www.dol.gov/olms/, accessed May 8, 2012.

25. National Labor Relations Board, *Basic Guide*.

26. Ibid.

27. Ibid.

28. R. B. Freeman and M. M. Kleiner, "Employer Behavior in the Face of Union Organizing Drives," *Industrial and Labor Relations Review* 43, no. 4 (April 1990), pp. 351–65.

29. J. A. Fossum, *Labor Relations*, 8th ed. (New York: McGraw-Hill, 2002), p. 149.

30. Local Union 130 UA, Chicago Journeymen Plumbers, "Organizing," http://www.plumberslu130ua.org, accessed May 4, 2012.

31. Herman et al., *Collective Bargaining*; and P. Jarley and J. Fiorito, "Associate Membership: Unionism or Consumerism?" *Industrial and Labor Relations Review* 43 (1990), pp. 209–24.

32. Katz and Kochan, *An Introduction to Collective Bargaining*.

33. Katz and Kochan, *An Introduction to Collective Bargaining*.

34. A. E. Eaton and J. Kriesky, "Union Organizing under Neutrality and Card Check Agreements," *Industrial and Labor Relations Review* 55 (2001), pp. 42–59.

35. National Labor Relations Board, "Election Data, FY 2011," Election Reports, http://www.nlrb.gov/election-reports, accessed May 7, 2012.

36. Chaison and Rose, "The Macrodeterminants of Union Growth and Decline."

37. Fossum, *Labor Relations*, p. 262.

38. R. E. Walton and R. B. McKersie, *A Behavioral Theory of Negotiations* (New York: McGraw-Hill, 1965).

39. C. M. Steven, *Strategy and Collective Bargaining Negotiations* (New York: McGraw-Hill, 1963); and Katz and Kochan, *An Introduction to Collective Bargaining*.

40. James R. Hagerty and Bob Tita, "Unions Confront Rising Tide," *The Wall Street Journal*, May 6, 2012, http://online.wsj.com.

41. Kochan, *Collective Bargaining and Industrial Relations*, p. 272.

42. Katz and Kochan, *An Introduction to Collective Bargaining*.

43. *United Steelworkers v. American Manufacturing Company*, 363 U.S. 564 (1960); *United Steelworkers v. Warrior Gulf and Navigation Company*, 363 U.S. 574 (1960); and *United Steelworkers v. Enterprise Wheel and Car Corporation*, 363 U.S. 593 (1960).

44. Kochan, *Collective Bargaining and Industrial Relations*, p. 386; and John W. Budd and Alexander J. S. Colvin, "Improved Metrics for Workplace Dispute Resolution Procedures: Efficiency, Equity, and Voice," *Industrial Relations* 47, no. 3 (July 2008), p. 460.

45. Federal Mediation and Conciliation Service, "What We Do: Arbitration; Arbitration Statistics," www.fmcs.gov, accessed May 4, 2012.

46. J. R. Redecker, *Employee Discipline: Policies and Practices* (Washington, DC: Bureau of National Affairs, 1989).

47. T. A. Kochan, H. C. Katz, and R. B. McKersie, *The Transformation of American Industrial Relations* (New York: Basic Books, 1986), chap. 6; and E. Appelbaum, T. Bailey, and P. Berg, *Manufacturing Advantage: Why High-Performance Work Systems Pay Off* (Ithaca, NY: Cornell University Press, 2000).

48. L. W. Hunter, J. P. MacDuffie, and L. Doucet, "What Makes Teams Take? Employee Reactions to Work Reforms," *Industrial and Labor Relations Review* 55 (2002), pp. 448–472.

49. J. B. Arthur, "The Link between Business Strategy and Industrial Relations Systems in American Steel Minimills," *Industrial and Labor Relations Review* 45 (1992), pp. 488–506; M. Schuster, "Union Management Cooperation," in *Employee and Labor Relations*, ed. J. A. Fossum (Washington, DC: Bureau of National Affairs, 1990); E. Cohen-Rosenthal and C. Burton, *Mutual Gains: A Guide to Union-Management Cooperation*, 2nd ed. (Ithaca, NY: ILR Press, 1993); T. A. Kochan and P. Osterman, *The Mutual Gains Enterprise* (Boston: Harvard Business School Press, 1994); and E. Applebaum and R. Batt, *The New American Workplace* (Ithaca, NY: ILR Press, 1994).

50. A. E. Eaton, "Factors Contributing to the Survival of Employee Participation Programs in Unionized Settings," *Industrial and Labor Relations Review* 47, no. 3 (1994), pp. 371–89.

51. "NLRB 4–0 Approves Crown Cork & Seal's Use of Seven Employee Participation Committees," *HR News*, September 3, 2001.

52. Kochan and Osterman, *The Mutual Gains Enterprise*; W. N. Cooke, "Employee Participation Programs, Group-Based Incentives, and Company Performance: A Union-Nonunion Comparison," *Industrial and Labor Relations Review* 47, no. 4 (1994), pp. 594–609; C. Doucouliagos, "Worker Participation and Productivity in Labor-Managed and Participatory Capitalist Firms: A Meta-Analysis," *Industrial and Labor Relations Review* 49, no. 1 (1995), pp. 58–77; S. J. Deery and R. D. Iverson, "Labor-Management Cooperation: Antecedents and Impact on Organizational Performance," *Industrial and Labor Relations Review* 58 (2005), pp. 588–609; James Combs, Yongmei Liu, Angela Hall, and David Ketchen, "How Much Do High-Performance Work Practices Matter? A Meta-analysis of Their Effects on Organizational Performance," *Personnel Psychology* 59, no. 3 (2006), pp. 501–28; Robert D. Mohr and Cindy Zoghi, "High-Involvement Work Design and Job Satisfaction," *Industrial and Labor Relations Review* 61, no. 3 (April 2008), pp. 275–96; T. Rabl, M. Jayasinghe, B. Gerhart, and T. M. Köhlmann, "How Much Does Country Matter? A Meta-analysis of the HPWP Systems–Business Performance Relationship," *Academy of Management Annual Meeting Proceedings*, August 2011.

53. Roberto Ceniceros, "Workplace Safety a Major Push for Unions," *Business Insurance*, February 12, 2012, http://www.businessinsurance.com; Black & Veatch, "Company," http://bv.com/Company, accessed May 4, 2012.

15 Managing Human Resources Globally

What Do I Need to Know?

After reading this chapter, you should be able to:

LO 15-1 Summarize how the growth in international business activity affects human resource management.

LO 15-2 Identify the factors that most strongly influence HRM in international markets.

LO 15-3 Discuss how differences among countries affect HR planning at organizations with international operations.

LO 15-4 Describe how companies select and train human resources in a global labor market.

LO 15-5 Discuss challenges related to managing performance and compensating employees from other countries.

LO 15-6 Explain how employers prepare managers for international assignments and for their return home.

Introduction

As China's middle class grows, so too does its appetite for dining out. The restaurant industry in China is still smaller than in the United States, but it is growing much faster—at 16% a year in China versus just 1% in the United States. That climate has been irresistible for entrepreneurs such as Scott Minoie, who left his native city of Boston to open Element Fresh in Shanghai. Minoie observed that Chinese shoppers visit the market every day to buy the freshest ingredients, so he applied that commitment to freshness in his restaurants. At the same time, he focused on training his staff to deliver American-style service with behaviors such as smiling at customers and asking them if they are enjoying their meals. The right mix of Chinese and American values has helped Minoie expand from one restaurant to a successful chain of 11, with plans to continue growing.

From Minoie's vantage point as a successful business operator in China, he has watched larger U.S. chains stumble in their early attempts to enter the Chinese market. Restaurants such as Outback Steakhouse and California Pizza Kitchen found that their brands did not readily translate. However, Yum Brands, which operates KFC and Pizza Hut, has a better track record. Part of the credit goes to the company's hiring of Asian executives to run the Asian operations. With local insights, they added menu items that would be more familiar to Chinese tastes, such as rice porridge and soy milk for breakfast at KFC and afternoon tea at Pizza Hut.[1]

In every industry today, established companies such as Yum Brands and start-ups like Element Fresh are setting up operations in foreign countries. Therefore, human resource management truly takes place on an international scale. This chapter discusses the HR issues that organizations must address in a world of global competition. We begin by describing how the global nature of business is affecting human resource management in modern organizations. Next, we identify how global differences among countries affect the organization's decisions about human resources. In the following sections we explore HR planning, selection, training, and compensation practices in international settings. Finally, we examine guidelines for managing employees sent on international assignments.

HRM in a Global Environment

LO 15-1 Summarize how the growth in international business activity affects human resource management.

The environment in which organizations operate is rapidly becoming a global one. More and more companies are entering international markets by exporting their products, building facilities in other countries, and entering into alliances with foreign companies. At the same time, companies based in other countries are investing and setting up operations in the United States. Indeed, most organizations now function in the global economy.

What is behind the trend toward expansion into global markets? Foreign countries can provide a business with new markets in which there are millions or billions of new customers; developing countries often provide such markets, but developed countries do so as well. In addition, companies set up operations overseas because they can operate with lower labor costs—for example, video game developers that pay $12,000 to $15,000 per month for U.S. employees can hire Indian workers at monthly pay scales in the range of $4,000 to $5,000.[2] Finally, thanks to advances in telecommunications and information technology, companies can more easily spread work around the globe, wherever they find the right mix of labor costs and abilities. Teams with members in different time zones can keep projects moving around the clock, or projects can be assigned according to regions with particular areas of expertise. Once organizations have taken advantage of these opportunities, they sometimes find themselves locked into overseas arrangements. In the consumer electronics industry, for example, so much of the manufacturing has shifted to China and other low-wage countries that U.S. companies no longer would have suppliers nearby if they tried to build a factory in North America.[3]

Global activities are simplified and encouraged by trade agreements among nations. For example, most countries in Western Europe belong to the European Union and share a common currency, the euro. Canada, Mexico, and the United States have encouraged trade among themselves with the

As companies in the United States and Britain cut software jobs and outsource to other countries in order to drive down costs, countries such as India continue to see employment rates rise.

North American Free Trade Agreement (NAFTA). The World Trade Organization (WTO) resolves trade disputes among more than 100 participating nations.

As these trends and arrangements encourage international trade, they increase and change the demands on human resource management. Organizations with customers or suppliers in other countries need employees who understand those customers or suppliers. Organizations that operate facilities in foreign countries need to understand the laws and customs that apply to employees in those countries. They may have to prepare managers and other personnel to take international assignments. They have to adapt their human resource plans and policies to different settings. Even if some practices are the same worldwide, the company now has to communicate them to its international workforce. A variety of international activities require managers to understand HRM principles and practices prevalent in global markets.

Employees in an International Workforce

When organizations operate globally, their employees are very likely to be citizens of more than one country. Employees may come from the employer's parent country, a host country, or a third country. The **parent country** is the country in which the organization's headquarters is located. For example, the United States is the parent country of General Motors, because GM's headquarters is in Michigan. A GM employee who was born in the United States and works at GM's headquarters or one of its U.S. factories is therefore a *parent-country national.*

A **host country** is a country (other than the parent country) in which an organization operates a facility. Great Britain is a host country of General Motors because GM has operations there. Any British workers hired to work at GM's British facility would be *host-country nationals,* that is, employees who are citizens of the host country.

A **third country** refers to a country that is neither the parent country nor the host country. (The organization may or may not have a facility in the third country.) In the example of GM's operations in Great Britain, the company could hire an Australian manager to work there. The Australian manager would be a *third-country national* because the manager is neither from the parent country (the United States) nor from the host country (Great Britain).

When organizations operate overseas, they must decide whether to hire parent-country nationals, host-country nationals, or third-country nationals for the overseas operations. Usually, they hire a combination of these. In general, employees assigned to work in another country are called **expatriates.** In the GM example, the U.S. and Australian managers working in Great Britain would be expatriates during those assignments.

The extent to which organizations use parent-country, host-country, or third-country nationals varies. Until recently, Western companies tended to use parent company nationals to manage operations in China, where employers found a shortage of management skills. Today, however, those skills are more widely available, and at multinational companies, three-fourths of senior executives are now host country nationals. Employers prefer these leaders because they understand the culture of their customers, governments, and business partners. Competition is stiffest for hiring Asian managers who lived in the host country but were educated in the United States or Europe. An example is Mei-Wei Cheng, who was born in China and educated at Cornell University. Siemens, based in Germany, hired Cheng to lead its Chinese operations, formerly headed by a European executive.[4] Nevertheless, some skill sets in China come primarily from employees in the West. A company that uses a network of direct salespeople to sell cosmetics door-to-door placed its Chinese operations under the control of a U.S. businessman familiar with how this type of marketing works. Although the manager knows the

Parent Country
The country in which an organization's headquarters is located.

Host Country
A country (other than the parent country) in which an organization operates a facility.

Third Country
A country that is neither the parent country nor the host country of an employer.

Expatriates
Employees assigned to work in another country.

ins-and-outs of personal selling, he is challenged to learn the politics, regulations, and values of an unfamiliar culture. For example, he tried recruiting salespeople among college students, only to ignite a furor among parents who evidently felt selling would distract their children. When the government joined in the criticism, the manager quickly pulled back from campuses.[5]

Employers in the Global Marketplace

Just as there are different ways for employees to participate in international business—as parent-country, host-country, or third-county nationals—so there are different ways for employers to do business globally, ranging from simply shipping products to customers in other countries to transforming the organization into a truly global one, with operations, employees, and customers in many countries. Figure 15.1 shows the major levels of global participation.

Most organizations begin by serving customers and clients within a domestic marketplace. Typically, a company's founder has an idea for serving a local, regional, or national market. The business must recruit, hire, train, and compensate employees to produce the product, and these people usually come from the business owner's local labor market. Selection and training focus on employees' technical abilities and, to some extent, on interpersonal skills. Pay levels reflect local labor conditions. If the product succeeds, the company might expand operations to other domestic locations, and HRM decisions become more complex as the organization draws from a larger labor market and needs systems for training and motivating employees in several locations. As the employer's workforce grows, it is also likely to become more diverse. Even in small domestic organizations, a significant share of workers may be immigrants. In this way, even domestic companies are affected by issues related to the global economy.

As organizations grow, they often begin to meet demand from customers in other countries. The usual way that a company begins to enter foreign markets is by *exporting*, or shipping domestically produced items to other countries to be sold there. Eventually, it may become economically desirable to set up operations in one or more foreign countries. An organization that does so becomes an **international organization.** The decision to participate in international activities raises a host of HR issues, including the basic question of whether a particular location provides an environment where the organization can successfully acquire and manage human resources.

International Organization
An organization that sets up one or a few facilities in one or a few foreign countries.

Figure 15.1
Levels of Global Participation

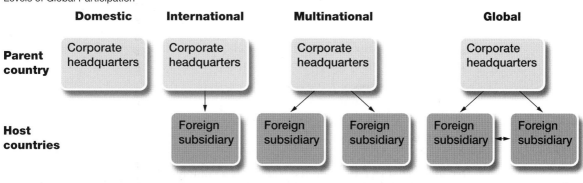

Multinational Company
An organization that builds facilities in a number of different countries in an effort to minimize production and distribution costs.

While international companies build one or a few facilities in another country, **multinational companies** go overseas on a broader scale. They build facilities in a number of different countries as a way to keep production and distribution costs to a minimum. In general, when organizations become multinationals, they move production facilities from relatively high-cost locations to lower-cost locations. The lower-cost locations may have lower average wage rates, or they may reduce distribution costs by being nearer to customers. The HRM challenges faced by a multinational company are similar to but larger than those of an international organization because more countries are involved. More than ever, the organization needs to hire managers who can function in a variety of settings, give them necessary training, and provide flexible compensation systems that take into account the different pay rates, tax systems, and costs of living from one country to another.

Global Organization
An organization that chooses to locate a facility based on the ability to effectively, efficiently, and flexibly produce a product or service, using cultural differences as an advantage.

At the highest level of involvement in the global marketplace are **global organizations.** These flexible organizations compete by offering top products tailored to segments of the market while keeping costs as low as possible. A global organization locates each facility based on the ability to effectively, efficiently, and flexibly produce a product or service, using cultural differences as an advantage. Rather than treating differences in other countries as a challenge to overcome, a global organization treats different cultures as equals. It may have multiple headquarters spread across the globe, so decisions are more decentralized. This type of organization needs HRM practices that encourage flexibility and are based on an in-depth knowledge of differences among countries. Global organizations must be able to recruit, develop, retain, and use managers who can get results across national boundaries. The "HRM Social" box describes how companies are using social media and other web-based tools to help them recruit a global workforce online.

Transnational HRM System
Type of HRM system that makes decisions from a global perspective, includes managers from many countries, and is based on ideas contributed by people representing a variety of cultures.

A global organization needs a **transnational HRM system**[6] that features decision making from a global perspective, managers from many countries, and ideas contributed by people from a variety of cultures. Decisions that are the outcome of a transnational HRM system balance uniformity (for fairness) with flexibility (to account for cultural and legal differences). This balance and the variety of perspectives should work together to improve the quality of decision making. The participants from various countries and cultures contribute ideas from a position of equality, rather than the parent country's culture dominating.

Factors Affecting HRM in International Markets

LO 15-2 Identify the factors that most strongly influence HRM in international markets.

Whatever their level of global participation, organizations that operate in more than one country must recognize that the countries are not identical and differ in terms of many factors. To simplify this discussion, we focus on four major factors:

- culture
- education
- economic systems
- political-legal systems

Culture

By far the most important influence on international HRM is the culture of the country in which a facility is located. *Culture* is a community's set of shared assumptions about how the world works and what ideals are worth striving for.[7] Cultural influences may be expressed through customs, languages, religions, and so on.

Inviting Job Hunters to Virtual Career Fairs

As we saw in Chapter 5, employers today are finding job candidates online. Motivated job seekers often learn about positions through their social networks—for example, by visiting and "liking" employers' Facebook pages, signing up for companies' Twitter feeds, and viewing announcements in interest groups they have joined on LinkedIn. These social-media activities provide low-cost opportunities for employers to reach workers anywhere in the world. But this raises a new challenge: how can employers and prospective employees get to know one another without high travel expenses?

The solution again comes from Internet applications with a social dimension—in this case, animated environments in which users control avatars for business purposes. Think of playing "The Sims," "Minecraft," or your favorite online role-playing game, only instead of furnishing a house or winning battles, your character is interviewing for a job at a virtual job fair. The character who is interviewing your avatar at the fair actually works for a real employer.

For example, when Procter and Gamble (P&G) wanted to reach qualified employees throughout Europe, it hosted a virtual career fair. The online environment was an exhibit hall dotted with booths at which P&G recruiters were prepared to talk about jobs in different functions and locations. About 900 job seekers visited the fair from their computers throughout western Europe, Turkey, Russia, and Romania. They could choose booths and visit them to learn about company culture and the specific jobs available. One candidate who logged in from Athens learned about job openings, obtained advice for applying, and decided he was interested enough to take a vacation day and visit a career fair in person. After several face-to-face interviews, he took a position as an assistant brand manager in Geneva, Switzerland.

As P&G has found, virtual career fairs help employers open up a wider pool of talent very efficiently.

Companies can contract with a service such as ON24 to create a virtual environment, which may resemble an exhibit hall or space at the company's own offices. The client tells ON24 what elements to include in order to create a customized environment, much as a "Sims" player decides whether to add a swimming pool or a "Minecraft" player decides to build and install a workbench. The virtual recruiting center can be a short-term live event or an ongoing static environment where visitors can watch video clips and learn about jobs and the work environment. Besides P&G, other companies that have created virtual job fairs include IBM and SAE International.

SOURCES: ON24, "Solutions: Virtual Job Fairs," http://www.on24.com, accessed May 11, 2012; Glenn Bischoff, "Enterprises Go 'Virtual' to Extend Reach, Serve Customers Better," *Urgent Communications,* May 3, 2012, http://urgentcomm.com; Emily Glazer, "Virtual Fairs Offer Real Jobs," *The Wall Street Journal,* October 31, 2011, http://online.wsj.com.

Culture is important to HRM for two reasons. First, it often determines the other three international influences. Culture can greatly affect a country's laws because laws often are based on the culture's definitions of right and wrong. Culture also influences what people value, so it affects people's economic systems and efforts to invest in education.

Even more important for understanding human resource management, culture often determines the effectiveness of various HRM practices. Practices that are effective in the United States, for example, may fail or even backfire in a country with different beliefs and values.[8] Consider the five dimensions of culture that Geert Hofstede identified in his classic study of culture:[9]

1. *Individualism/collectivism* describes the strength of the relation between an individual and other individuals in the society. In cultures that are high in individualism, such as the United States, Great Britain, and the Netherlands, people tend to think and act as individuals rather than as members of a group. People in these countries are expected to stand on their own two feet, rather than be protected by the group. In cultures that are high in collectivism, such as Colombia, Pakistan,

In Taiwan, a country that is high in collectivism, co-workers consider themselves more as group members instead of individuals.

and Taiwan, people think of themselves mainly as group members. They are expected to devote themselves to the interests of the community, and the community is expected to protect them when they are in trouble.

2. *Power distance* concerns the way the culture deals with unequal distribution of power and defines the amount of inequality that is normal. In countries with large power distances, including India and the Philippines, the culture defines it as normal to maintain large differences in power. In countries with small power distances, such as Denmark and Israel, people try to eliminate inequalities. One way to see differences in power distance is in the way people talk to one another. In the high-power-distance countries of Mexico and Japan, people address one another with titles (Señor Smith, Smith-san). At the other extreme, in the United States, in most situations people use one another's first names—behavior that would be disrespectful in other cultures.

3. *Uncertainty avoidance* describes how cultures handle the fact that the future is unpredictable. High uncertainty avoidance refers to a strong cultural preference for structured situations. In countries such as Greece and Portugal, people tend to rely heavily on religion, law, and technology to give them a degree of security and clear rules about how to behave. In countries with low uncertainty avoidance, including Singapore and Jamaica, people seem to take each day as it comes.

4. *Masculinity/femininity* is the emphasis a culture places on practices or qualities that have traditionally been considered masculine or feminine. A "masculine" culture is a culture that values achievement, money making, assertiveness, and competition. A "feminine" culture is one that places a high value on relationships, service, care for the weak, and preserving the environment. In this model, Germany and Japan are examples of masculine cultures, and Sweden and Norway are examples of feminine cultures.

5. *Long-term/short-term orientation* suggests whether the focus of cultural values is on the future (long term) or the past and present (short term). Cultures with a long-term orientation value saving and persistence, which tend to pay off in the future. Many Asian countries, including Japan and China, have a long-term orientation. Short-term orientations, as in the cultures of the United States, Russia, and West Africa, promote respect for past tradition and for fulfilling social obligations in the present.

Such cultural characteristics as these influence the ways members of an organization behave toward one another, as well as their attitudes toward various HRM practices. For instance, cultures differ strongly in their opinions about how managers should lead, how decisions should be handled, and what motivates employees. In Germany, managers achieve their status by demonstrating technical skills, and employees look to managers to assign tasks and resolve technical problems. In the Netherlands, managers focus on seeking agreement, exchanging views, and balancing the interests of the people affected by a decision.[10] Clearly, differences like these would affect how an organization selects and trains its managers and measures their performance.

Cultures strongly influence the appropriateness of HRM practices. For example, the extent to which a culture is individualist or collectivist will affect the success of a compensation program. Compensation tied to individual performance may be seen as fairer and more motivating by members of an individualist culture; a culture favoring individualism will be more accepting of great differences in pay between the organization's highest- and lowest-paid employees. Collectivist cultures tend to have much flatter pay structures.

The success of HRM decisions related to job design, benefits, performance management, and other systems related to employee motivation also will be shaped by culture. In an interesting study comparing call center workers in India (a collectivist culture) and the United States (an individualistic culture), researchers found that in the United States, employee turnover depended more on person—job fit than on person—organization fit. In the United States, employees were less likely to quit if they felt that they had the right skills, resources, and personality to succeed on the job. In India, what mattered more was for employees to feel they fit in well with the organization and were well connected to the organization and the community.[11]

Finally, cultural differences can affect how people communicate and how they coordinate their activities. In collectivist cultures, people tend to value group decision making, as in the previous example. When a person raised in an individualistic culture must work closely with people from a collectivist culture, communication problems and conflicts often occur. People from the collectivist culture tend to collaborate heavily and may evaluate the individualistic person as unwilling to cooperate and share information with them. Cultural differences in communication affected the way a North American agricultural company embarked on employee empowerment at its facilities in the United States and Brazil.[12] Empowerment requires information sharing, but in Brazil, high power distance leads employees to expect managers to make decisions, so they do not desire information that is appropriately held by managers. Empowering the Brazilian employees required involving managers directly in giving and sharing information to show that this practice was in keeping with the traditional chain of command. Also, because uncertainty avoidance is another aspect of Brazilian culture, managers explained that greater information sharing would reduce uncertainty about their work. At the same time, greater collectivism in Brazil made employees comfortable with the day-to-day communication of teamwork. The individualistic U.S. employees needed to be sold more on this aspect of empowerment.

Because of these challenges, organizations must prepare managers to recognize and handle cultural differences. They may recruit managers with knowledge of other cultures or provide training, as described later in the chapter. For expatriate assignments, organizations may need to conduct an extensive selection process to identify individuals who can adapt to new environments. At the same time, it is important to be wary of stereotypes and avoid exaggerating the importance of cultural differences. Recent research that examined Hofstede's model of cultural differences found that differences among organizations within a particular culture were sometimes larger than differences from country to country.[13] This finding suggests that it is important for an organization to match its HR practices to its values; individuals who share those values are likely to be interested in working for the organization.

Education and Skill Levels

Countries also differ in the degree to which their labor markets include people with education and skills of value to employers. As discussed in Chapter 1, the United States suffers from a shortage of skilled workers in many occupations, and the problem is expected to increase. For example, the need for knowledge workers (engineers, teachers, scientists, health care workers) is expected to grow almost twice as fast as the

Developing Talent in India

India represents a massive marketplace, and its businesses have been expanding at breakneck speed. Companies in the West are eager to hire Indian workers with computer skills and the ability to communicate in English. India's educational system is trying to keep pace with the demand; in engineering alone, 770,000 new graduates join the workforce each year.

As companies try to keep up with the demand for employees, they are finding that many of these new graduates are not really prepared to work. By one estimate, only about one-fourth of new engineering graduates have all the skills they need to handle an engineering job, and another one-fourth can do so with training. The others will have to fill less-skilled positions.

Infosys, a $6 billion provider of outsourced services, tackles the challenge with extensive training. The company aggressively recruits the best candidates from universities and then sends them to an eight-month training program. Infosys is not alone; research into Indian management practices found that India's leading businesses are deeply committed to employee development. Top executives named talent development, not cost cutting, as their company's highest priority for human resource management. In information technology, companies provide new hires with an average of 60 days of formal training. Even in industries with low-skill jobs, companies invest in training. At call centers, for example, new employees receive about 30 days of training. In contrast, the Census Bureau once estimated that U.S. companies provide an average of 13 *hours* of training to employees who had been on the job for two years or less.

In visits to India to explore the commitment to training, researchers from Harvard and Duke learned how Indian companies are making a talented workforce out of inconsistently educated professionals. These employers are treating their training programs as an essential driver of success. They have studied the Western companies that outsourced functions to India, and they selected and improved management and training practices that would be relevant. They started with basic skills and employee orientation then moved on to create management development programs. The companies built training centers and hired trainers—sometimes hundreds of them. Infosys operates its Global Education Center in the city of Mysore; the center has the capacity to train 13,500 employees in technical, communications, and management skills.

SOURCES: Raju Gopalakrishnan, "Bangalore Software Industry Trying to Avoid an Ironic Fate," *Chicago Tribune,* April 17, 2012, sec. 2, p. 3; Peter Cappelli, "India's Management Mind-Set," *HR Magazine,* August 2011, pp. 59–62; Vivek Wadhwa, "Why America Needs to Start Educating Its Workforce Again," *TechCrunch,* March 27, 2010, http://techcrunch.com.

overall rate of job growth in the United States.[14] On the other hand, the labor markets in many countries are very attractive because they offer high skills and low wages.

Educational opportunities also vary from one country to another. In general, spending on education is greater per pupil in high-income countries than in poorer countries.[15] Poverty, diseases such as AIDS, and political turmoil keep children away from school in some areas. A concerted international effort to provide universal access to primary education has dramatically reduced the number and proportion of children without access to schooling, especially in South Asia. However, the problem persists in sub-Saharan Africa.[16]

Companies with foreign operations locate in countries where they can find suitable employees. The education and skill levels of a country's labor force affect how and the extent to which companies want to operate there. In countries with a poorly educated population, companies will limit their activities to low-skill, low-wage jobs. In contrast, India's large pool of well-trained technical workers is one reason that the country has become a popular location for outsourcing computer programming jobs. But even there, companies are finding they need to invest heavily in training and development, as described in the "Best Practices" box.

Economic System

A country's economic system, whether capitalist or socialist, as well as the government's involvement in the economy through taxes or compensation, price controls, and other activities, influences human resource management practices in a number of ways.

As with all aspects of a region's or country's life, the economic system and culture are likely to be closely tied, providing many of the incentives or disincentives for developing the value of the labor force. Socialist economic systems provide ample opportunities for educational development because the education system is free to students. At the same time, socialism may not provide economic rewards (higher pay) for increasing one's education. In capitalist systems, students bear more of the cost of their education, but employers reward those who invest in education.

The health of an economic system affects human resource management. In developed countries with great wealth, labor costs are relatively high. Such differences show up in compensation systems and in recruiting and selection decisions.

In general, socialist systems take a higher percentage of each worker's income as the worker's income increases. Capitalist systems tend to let workers keep

Students at the University of Warsaw in Poland are provided with a government-supported education. In general, former Soviet bloc countries tend to be generous in funding education, so they tend to have highly educated and skilled labor forces. Capitalist countries such as the United States generally leave higher education up to individual students to pay for, but the labor market rewards students who earn a college degree.

more of their earnings. In this way, socialism redistributes wealth from high earners to the poor, while capitalism apparently rewards individual accomplishments. In any case, since the amount of take-home pay a worker receives after taxes may thus differ from country to country, in an organization that pays two managers in two countries $100,000 each, the manager in one country might take home more than the manager in the other country. Such differences make pay structures more complicated when they cross national boundaries, and they can affect recruiting of candidates from more than one country.

Political-Legal System

A country's political-legal system—its government, laws, and regulations—strongly impinges on human resource management. The country's laws often dictate the requirements for certain HRM practices, such as training, compensation, hiring, firing, and layoffs. As we noted in the discussion of culture, the political-legal system arises to a large degree from the culture in which it exists, so laws and regulations reflect cultural values.

For example, the United States has led the world in eliminating discrimination in the workplace. Because this value is important in U.S. culture, the nation has legal safeguards such as the equal employment opportunity laws discussed in Chapter 3, which affect hiring and other HRM decisions. As a society, the United States also has strong beliefs regarding the fairness of pay systems. Thus, the Fair Labor Standards Act (discussed in Chapter 11), among other laws and regulations, sets a minimum wage for a variety of jobs. Other laws and regulations dictate much of the process of negotiation between unions and management. All these are examples of laws and regulations that affect the practice of HRM in the United States.

Similarly, laws and regulations in other countries reflect the norms of their cultures. In Western Europe, where many countries have had strong socialist parties, some laws have been aimed at protecting the rights and benefits of workers. The European Union has agreed that employers in member nations must respect certain rights of workers, including workplace health and safety; equal opportunities for men and women; protection against discrimination based on sex, race, religion, age, disability, and sexual orientation; and labor laws that set standards for work hours and other conditions of work. Concerning work hours, the EU expects employers in member nations to schedule no more than 48 hours of work each week, 11 hours of rest in each 24-hour period, at least one day off each week, and at least four weeks of paid vacation each year, subject to the nation's practices and laws.[17]

An organization that expands internationally must gain expertise in the host country's legal requirements and ways of dealing with its legal system, often leading organizations to hire one or more host-country nationals to help in the process. Some countries have laws requiring that a certain percentage of the employees of any foreign-owned subsidiary be host-country nationals, and in the context of our discussion here, this legal challenge to an organization's HRM may hold an advantage if handled creatively.

Human Resource Planning in a Global Economy

LO 15-3 Discuss how differences among countries affect HR planning at organizations with international operations.

As economic and technological change creates a global environment for organizations, human resource planning is involved in decisions about participating as an exporter or as an international, multinational, or global company. Even purely domestic companies may draw talent from the international labor market. As organizations consider decisions about their level of international activity, HR professionals should provide information about the relevant human resource issues, such as local market pay rates and labor laws. When organizations decide to operate internationally or globally, human resource planning involves decisions about where and how many employees are needed for each international facility.

Decisions about where to locate include HR considerations such as the cost and availability of qualified workers. In addition, HR specialists must work with other members of the organization to weigh these considerations against financial and operational requirements. As discussed earlier, India and China have been popular locations because of low labor costs. But as the job creation has driven up living standards and demand for labor, it has driven up the price of labor in those countries. Cost-oriented call centers are looking to locations such as the Philippines and Eastern Europe. In response, Indian contractors have started up companies that offer more specialized skills, such as engineering, biotechnology, and computer animation. In China, where pay for factory workers has risen 69% over the past few years, the main advantage of continuing to operate there may become the greater buying power of the Chinese consumer.[18]

Other location decisions involve outsourcing, described in Chapter 2. Many companies have boosted efficiency by arranging to have specific functions performed by outside contractors. Many—but not all—of these arrangements involve workers outside the United States in lower-wage countries.

In Chapter 5, we saw that human resource planning includes decisions to hire and lay off workers to prepare for the organization's expected needs. Compared with other countries, the United States allows employers wide latitude in reducing their workforce, giving U.S. employers the option of hiring for peak needs, then laying off employees if needs decline. Other governments place more emphasis on protecting workers' jobs. European countries, and France in particular, tend to be very strict in this regard.

Selecting Employees in a Global Labor Market

LO 15-4 Describe how companies select and train human resources in a global labor market.

Many companies such as Microsoft have headquarters in the United States plus facilities in locations around the world. To be effective, employees in the Microsoft Mexico operations in Mexico City must understand that region's business and social culture. Organizations often meet this need by hiring host-country nationals to fill most of their foreign positions. A key reason is that a host-country national can more easily understand the values and customs of the local workforce than someone from another part of the world can. Also, training for and transporting families to foreign assignments is more expensive than hiring people in the foreign country. Employees may be reluctant to take a foreign assignment because of the difficulty of moving overseas. Sometimes the move requires the employee's spouse to quit a job, and some countries will not allow the employee's spouse to seek work, even if jobs might be available.

Even so, organizations fill many key foreign positions with parent-country or third-country nationals. Sometimes a person's technical and human relations skills outweigh the advantages of hiring locally. In other situations, the local labor market simply does not offer enough qualified people. For example, seafood processors and farmers in Alabama have reported difficulty in finding people willing to do demanding physical labor for long hours to gut catfish and pick tomatoes. Whether the problem is that Americans aren't willing to work that hard or that they expect higher pay and generous benefits in exchange for their efforts, these employers have for years turned to immigrant labor to fill the positions.[19] In recent years, immigrant workers in the United States have been most common in jobs where the demand for labor is highest—in the nation's fastest-growing occupations, both those at the low end of the pay scale, such as agriculture and food services, and in jobs requiring a technical education, such as high-tech manufacturing and information technology.[20] The ability to tap this labor supply is limited by government paperwork and delays, which deter some immigrant workers, as well as by expanding opportunities in fast-developing nations such as China and India. Recent surveys have found that Chinese and Indian professionals returning home to work are most likely to say their reason is that they see better opportunities in their home country. In addition, as described in Chapter 6, U.S. employers must take care to hire employees who are eligible to work in the United States. Recently, Immigration and Customers Enforcement has been auditing the eligibility status of workers at hundreds of companies.[21]

Whether the organization is hiring immigrants or selecting parent-country or third-country nationals for foreign assignments, some basic principles of selection apply. Selection of employees for foreign assignments should reflect criteria that have been associated with success in working overseas:

- Competency in the employee's area of expertise.
- Ability to communicate verbally and nonverbally in the foreign country.
- Flexibility, tolerance of ambiguity, and sensitivity to cultural differences.
- Motivation to succeed and enjoyment of challenges.
- Willingness to learn about the foreign country's culture, language, and customs.
- Support from family members.[22]

Qualities associated with success in foreign assignments are the ability to communicate in the foreign country, flexibility, enjoying a challenging situation, and support from family members. What would persuade you to take a foreign assignment?

Figure 15.2
Emotional Stages
Associated with a
Foreign Assignment

SOURCE: Adapted from Delia Flanja, "Culture Shock in Intercultural Communication," *Studia Europaea* (October 2009), Business & Company Resource Center, http://galenet.galegroup.com.

In research conducted a number of years ago, the factor most strongly influencing whether an employee completed a foreign assignment was the comfort of the employee's spouse and family.[23] Personality may also be important. Research has found successful completion of overseas assignments to be most likely among employees who are extroverted (outgoing), agreeable (cooperative and tolerant), and conscientious (dependable and achievement oriented).[24]

Qualities of flexibility, motivation, agreeableness, and conscientiousness are so important because of the challenges involved in entering another culture. The emotions that accompany an overseas assignment tend to follow stages like those in Figure 15.2.[25] For a month or so after arriving, the foreign worker enjoys a "honeymoon" of fascination and euphoria as the employee enjoys the novelty of the new culture and compares its interesting similarities to or differences from the employee's own culture. Before long, the employee's mood declines as he or she notices more unpleasant differences and experiences feelings of isolation, criticism, stereotyping, and even hostility. As the mood reaches bottom, the employee is experiencing **culture shock,** the disillusionment and discomfort that occur during the process of adjusting to a new culture and its norms, values, and perspectives. Eventually, if employees persist and continue learning about their host country's culture, they begin to recover from culture shock as they develop a greater understanding and a support network. As the employee's language skills and comfort increase, the employee's mood should improve as well. Eventually, the employee reaches a stage of adjustment in which he or she accepts and enjoys the host country's culture.

Culture Shock
Disillusionment and discomfort that occur during the process of adjusting to a new culture.

Training and Developing a Global Workforce

In an organization whose employees come from more than one country, some special challenges arise with regard to training and development: (1) Training and development programs should be effective for all participating employees, regardless of their country of origin; and (2) When organizations hire employees to work in a foreign country or transfer them to another country, the employer needs to provide the employees with training in how to handle the challenges associated with working in the foreign country.

Training Programs for an International Workforce

Developers of effective training programs for an international workforce must ask certain questions.[26] The first is to establish the objectives for the training and its content. Decisions about the training should support those objectives. The developers should next ask what training techniques, strategies, and media to use. Some will be more effective than others, depending on the learners' language and culture, as well as the content of the training. For example, in preparation U.S. employees might expect to discuss and ask questions about the training content, whereas employees from other

Table 15.1

Effects of Culture on Training Design

CULTURAL DIMENSION	IMPACT ON TRAINING
Individualism	Culture high in individualism expects participation in exercises and questioning to be determined by status in the company or culture.
Uncertainty avoidance	Culture high in uncertainty avoidance expects formal instructional environments. There is less tolerance for impromptu style.
Masculinity	Culture low in masculinity values relationships with fellow trainees. Female trainers are less likely to be resisted in low-masculinity cultures.
Power distance	Culture high in power distance expects trainers to be experts. Trainers are expected to be authoritarian and controlling of session.
Time orientation	Culture with a long-term orientation will have trainees who are likely to accept development plans and assignments.

SOURCE: Based on B. Filipczak, "Think Locally, Act Globally," *Training*, January 1997, pp. 41–48.

cultures might consider this level of participation to be disrespectful, so for them some additional support might be called for. Language differences will require translations and perhaps a translator at training activities. Next, the developers should identify any other interventions and conditions that must be in place for the training to meet its objectives. For example, training is more likely to meet its objectives if it is linked to performance management and has the full support of management. Finally, the developers of a training program should identify who in the organization should be involved in reviewing and approving the training program.

The plan for the training program must consider international differences among trainees. For example, economic and educational differences might influence employees' access to and ability to use web-based training. Cultural differences may influence whether they will consider it appropriate to ask questions and whether they expect the trainer to spend time becoming acquainted with employees or to get down to business immediately. Table 15.1 provides examples of how cultural characteristics can affect training design.

Cross-Cultural Preparation

When an organization selects an employee for a position in a foreign country, it must prepare the employee for the foreign assignment. This kind of training is called **cross-cultural preparation,** preparing employees to work across national and cultural boundaries, and it often includes family members who will accompany the employee on the assignment. The training is necessary for all three phases of an international assignment:

1. Preparation for *departure*—language instruction and an orientation to the foreign country's culture.
2. The *assignment* itself—some combination of a formal program and mentoring relationship to provide ongoing further information about the foreign country's culture.
3. Preparation for the *return* home—providing information about the employee's community and home-country workplace (from company newsletters, local newspapers, and so on).

Cross-Cultural Preparation
Training to prepare employees and their family members for an assignment in a foreign country.

Methods for providing this training may range from lectures for employees and their families to visits to culturally diverse communities.[27] Employees and their families may also spend time visiting a local family from the country where they will be working. In the later section on managing expatriates, we provide more detail about cross-cultural preparation.

Despite the importance of preparation, the 2011 Global Relocation Trends Survey Report found that only 74% of companies were providing this service—the lowest level in the history of the report, perhaps as an effort at cost cutting.[28] These companies typically offered self-service, often web-based sources of information as an alternative. However, most of the companies offered repatriation discussions for returning employees. It is important for employers to remember that returning home is also a challenge when employees have been away for months or years. Returning employees often find that life at home seems boring, relative to the excitement of learning a new culture, and family members and colleagues at home may find it hard to relate to their recent experiences. Employers should be ready for employees who want to share what they learned and put their recently acquired skills to work in new assignments.[29]

Global Employee Development

At global organizations, international assignments are a part of many career paths. The organization benefits most if it applies the principles of employee development in deciding which employees should be offered jobs in other countries. Career development helps expatriate and inpatriate employees make the transitions to and from their assignments and helps the organization apply the knowledge the employees obtain from these assignments.

LO 15-5 Discuss challenges related to managing performance and compensating employees from other countries.

Performance Management across National Boundaries

The general principles of performance management may apply in most countries, but the specific methods that work in one country may fail in another. Therefore, organizations have to consider legal requirements, local business practices, and national cultures when they establish performance management methods in other countries. Differences may include which behaviors are rated, how and the extent to which performance is measured, who performs the rating, and how feedback is provided.[30]

For example, National Rental Car uses a behaviorally based rating scale for customer service representatives. To measure the extent to which customer service representatives' behaviors contribute to the company's goal of improving customer service, the scale measures behaviors such as smiling, making eye contact, greeting customers, and solving customer problems. Depending on the country, different behaviors may be appropriate. In Japan, culturally defined standards for polite behavior include the angle of bowing as well as proper back alignment and eye contact. In Ghana and many other African nations, appropriate measures would include behaviors that reflect loyalty and repaying of obligations as well as behaviors related to following regulations and procedures.

The extent to which managers measure performance may also vary from one country to another. In rapidly changing regions, such as Southeast Asia, the organization may have to update its performance plans more often than once a year.

Feedback is another area in which differences can occur. Employees around the world appreciate positive feedback, but U.S. employees are much more used to direct feedback than are employees in other countries. In Mexico managers are expected to provide positive feedback before focusing the discussion on behaviors the employee needs to improve.[31] At the Thai office of Singapore Airlines, managers resisted giving negative feedback to employees because they feared this would cause them to have bad karma, contributing to their reincarnation at a lower level in their next life.[32] The airlines therefore allowed the managers to adapt their feedback process to fit local cultures.

Compensating an International Workforce

The chapters in Part 4 explained that compensation includes decisions about pay structure, incentive pay, and employee benefits. All these decisions become more complex when an organization has an international workforce. Johnson & Johnson meets the challenge by creating a global compensation strategy for its 250 pharmaceutical, consumer, and medical-device businesses with employees in 70 countries. J&J developed the strategy at its U.S. headquarters because compensation expertise at the company varied from one region to another. However, it had representatives from each region serve on the project teams so the company would be familiar with local issues, such as the need for frequent salary reviews in Venezuela and Argentina, where high inflation rates take a toll on buying power.[33]

Pay Structure

As Figure 15.3 shows, market pay structures can differ substantially across countries in terms of both pay level and the relative worth of jobs. For example, compared with the

Figure 15.3

Earnings in Selected Occupations in Three Countries

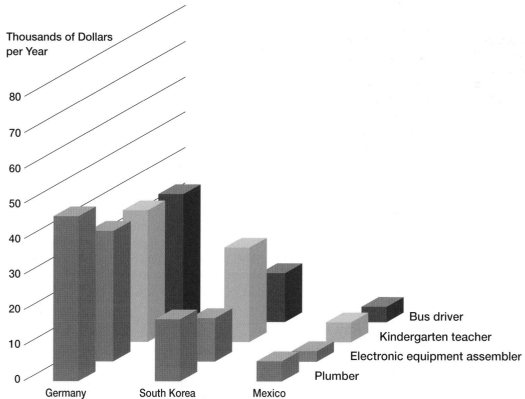

SOURCE: Wage and hour data from International Labour Organization, LABORSTA Internet, http://laborsta.ilo.org, accessed May 10, 2012.

labor market in Germany, the market in Mexico provides much lower pay levels overall. In Germany, bus drivers average higher pay than kindergarten teachers, while the relative pay of teachers is much greater in Mexico and South Korea. For all the types of jobs shown, the pay differences between jobs are much less dramatic in Germany than in the other two countries. One reason for big pay differences is a shortage of talent in local labor markets. In Brazil, for example, companies have trouble finding enough managers with technical expertise, because big construction projects and oil drilling are driving heavy demand for those positions. In addition, the fast-growing Brazilian economy has drawn many multinationals to locate facilities in Brazil, further increasing the demand for managers there. Finally, Brazilian managers tend to be loyal employees, so recruiters need to offer especially tempting compensation packages to lure them away.[34]

Differences such as these create a dilemma for global companies: Should pay levels and differences reflect what workers are used to in their own countries? Or should they reflect the earnings of colleagues in the country of the facility, or earnings at the company headquarters? For example, should a German engineer posted to Bombay be paid according to the standard in Frankfurt or the standard in Bombay? If the standard is Frankfurt, the engineers in Bombay will likely see the German engineer's pay as unfair. If the standard is Bombay, the company will likely find it impossible to persuade a German engineer to take an assignment in Bombay. Dilemmas such as these make a global compensation strategy important as a way to show employees that the pay structure is designed to be fair and related to the value that employees bring to the organization.

These decisions affect a company's costs and ability to compete. The average hourly labor costs in industrialized countries such as the United States, Germany, and Japan are far higher than these costs in newly industrialized countries such as Mexico, Brazil, and the Philippines.[35] As a result, we often hear that U.S. labor costs are too high to allow U.S. companies to compete effectively unless the companies shift operations to low-cost foreign subsidiaries. That conclusion oversimplifies the situation for many companies. Merely comparing wages ignores differences in education, skills, and productivity.[36] If an organization gets more or higher-quality output from a higher-wage workforce, the higher wages may be worth the cost. Besides this, if the organization has many positions requiring highly skilled workers, it may need to operate in (or hire immigrants from) a country with a strong educational system, regardless of labor costs. Finally, labor costs may be outweighed by other factors, such as transportation costs or access to resources or customers. When a production process is highly automated, differences in labor costs may not be significant.

Cultural and legal differences also can affect pay structure. Some countries, including Colombia, Greece, and Malaysia, require that companies provide salary increases to employees earning minimum wage. In Venezuela, employers must provide employees with a meal allowance. In Mexico and Puerto Rico, employers must pay holiday bonuses. Organizations with a global pay strategy must adjust the strategy to account for local requirements and determine how pay decisions for optional practices will affect their competitive standing in local labor markets.[37]

Incentive Pay

Besides setting a pay structure, the organization must make decisions with regard to incentive pay, such as bonuses and stock options. Although stock options became a common form of incentive pay in the United States during the 1990s, European businesses did not begin to embrace this type of compensation until the end of that decade.

HR How To

Tailoring Benefits to an International Workforce

As we saw in Chapter 13, to be motivating, employee benefits need to be valued. Therefore, organizations may need to tailor their benefits to the differences in values that may occur in one location or another.

One way to achieve this is to think of the organization's worldwide employees as a highly diverse workforce and offer flexible benefits. Informa is a media company with employees in 40 countries. Its benefits package is shaped by the needs of each group of employees. In Britain, for example, the employees are relatively young, so pension plans are hard for many of those employees to appreciate. So the company offers a set of short-term, medium-term, and long-term savings plans for employees to choose from. It increases their value by providing financial education to help employees appreciate the value of saving when they are young and when compound interest will have the greatest impact on their eventual wealth. Benefits choices such as these are communicated on the company website, in total-reward

statements, and in a booklet sent to employees' homes.

Companies can balance the focus on diversity with savings from pooling their purchases on a global scale. This can enable benefits budgets to deliver the greatest value. Businesses such as MetLife, ING, and Zurich Employee Benefits Network serve many countries and can set up insurance and other financial benefits that meet local governments' requirements. Life and health insurance plans may be priced more attractively if the employer purchases them from one company for all its employees worldwide.

Finally, companies can choose valued benefits by learning from leaders who are well acquainted with employees' local culture. Plantronics is headquartered in Santa Cruz, California, and makes wireless headsets and other communications equipment at its facility in Tijuana, Mexico. The company placed Alejandro Bustamente in charge of the plant more than a dozen years ago, and he immediately announced that his goal was to treat his employees

with respect. For Bustamente and his Mexican employees, respect meant investing in their careers and treating them as valued family members. Employee benefits support this vision with on-site health care facilities, presentations to employees and their families on topics such as parenting and drug abuse prevention, and even subsidized weddings at the company's facility. Indeed, over the past decade, hundreds of employees really have gotten married at their workplace.

SOURCES: MetLife, "Multination: Solutions for a Global Workforce," http://metlife.com, accessed May 11, 2012; MAXIS Global Benefits Network, "Employee Benefits Solutions for Multinational Companies," https://www.maxisnetowrk.com, accessed May 11, 2012; "Multinational Pooling," *Employee Benefits,* March 2012, Business & Company Resource Center, http://galenet.galegroup.com; "Informed Choice," *Employee Benefits,* December 2011, Business & Company Resource Center, http://galenet.galegroup.com; Steve Minter, "Respect Underpins Success of Mexican Plant," *Industry Week,* September 2011, p. 14.

However, the United States and Europe differ in the way they award stock options. European companies usually link the options to specific performance goals, such as the increase in a company's share price compared with that of its competitors.

Employee Benefits

As in the United States, compensation packages in other countries include benefits. Decisions about benefits must take into account the laws of each country involved, as well as employees' expectations and values in those countries (see "HR How To"). Some countries require paid maternity leave, and some countries have nationalized health care systems, which would affect the value of private health insurance in a compensation package. Pension plans are more widespread in parts of Western Europe than in the United States and Japan. Over 90% of workers in Switzerland have pension plans, as do all workers in France. Among workers with pension plans, U.S. workers are significantly less likely to have defined benefit plans than workers in Japan or Germany.

Figure 15.4
Average Hours Worked
in Selected Countries

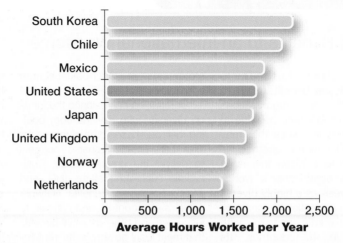

SOURCE: Organisation for Economic Co-operation and Development, "Average Annual Hours Actually Worked per Worker," OECD StatExtracts, http://stats.oecd.org, accessed May 10, 2012.

Paid vacation, discussed in Chapter 13, tends to be more generous in Western Europe than in the United States. Figure 15.4 compares the number of hours the average employee works in various countries. Of these countries, only in South Korea, Chile, and Mexico do workers put in more hours than U.S. workers. In the other countries, the norm is to work fewer hours than a U.S. worker over the course of a year.

International Labor Relations

Companies that operate across national boundaries often need to work with unions in more than one country. Organizations establish policies and goals for labor relations, for overseeing labor agreements, and for monitoring labor performance (for example, output and productivity).[38] The day-to-day decisions about labor relations are usually handled by each foreign subsidiary. The reason is that labor relations on an international scale involve differences in laws, attitudes, and economic systems, as well as differences in negotiation styles.

At least in comparison with European organizations, U.S. organizations exert more centralized control over labor relations in the various countries where they operate.[39] U.S. management therefore must recognize differences in how various countries understand and regulate labor relations. For example, in the United States, collective bargaining usually involves negotiations between a union local and an organization's management, but in Sweden and Germany, collective bargaining generally involves negotiations between an employer's organization and a union representing an entire industry's employees.[40] Legal differences range from who may form a union to how much latitude an organization is allowed in laying off workers. General Motors, in trying to pare back its Opel operations in Europe, has run into union requirements that forbid plant closings before 2014—a deal that the local governments say they will fight to retain. In an effort to demonstrate that the union workers were not expected to make all the sacrifices, GM eliminated bonuses for salaried workers, but the gesture was poorly received in the relatively labor-friendly environment of Europe.[41] In some situations, governments get involved to protect workers who immigrate to other countries. Many workers from Indonesia and the Philippines, for example, travel to the Middle East to find work and have complained about poor working conditions. The Philippines negotiated an agreement with Saudi Arabia setting minimum pay, and the Indonesian government negotiated with Malaysia to protect the rights of Indonesian maids, including the right to hold their own passports.[42]

International labor relations must also take into account that negotiations between labor and management take place in a different social context, not just different economic and legal contexts. Cultural differences that affect other interactions come into play in labor negotiations as well. Negotiators will approach the process differently depending on whether the culture views the process as primarily cooperative or competitive and whether it is local practice to negotiate a deal by starting with the specifics or agreeing on overall principles.[43] Working with host-country nationals can help organizations navigate such differences in negotiation style.

Boeing recently announced plans to open an Aerospace Research and Technology Center in Sao Paulo, Brazil. With a fast-growing Brazilian economy leading to a possible shortage of talent, Boeing may find it difficult to find enough local managers with technical expertise for the new center.

Managing Expatriates

At some point, most international and global organizations assign managers to foreign posts. These assignments give rise to significant human resource challenges, from selecting managers for these assignments to preparing them, compensating them, and helping them adjust to a return home. The same kinds of HRM principles that apply to domestic positions can help organizations avoid mistakes in managing expatriates: planning and goal setting, selection aimed at achieving the HR goals, and performance management that includes evaluation of whether the overseas assignment delivered value relative to the costs involved.[44] See what category of mistakes you think triggered the problem described in the "HR Oops!" box.

Selecting Expatriate Managers

The challenge of managing expatriate managers begins with determining which individuals in the organization are most capable of handling an assignment in another country. Expatriate managers need technical competence in the area of operations, in part to help them earn the respect of subordinates. Of course, many other skills are also necessary for success in any management job, especially one that involves working overseas. Depending on the nature of the assignment and the culture where it is located, the organization should consider each candidate's skills, learning style, and approach to problem solving. Each of these should be related to achievement of the organization's goals, such as solving a particular problem, transferring knowledge to host-country employees, or developing future leaders for the organization.[45]

A successful expatriate manager must be sensitive to the host country's cultural norms, flexible enough to adapt to those norms, and strong enough to survive the culture shock of living in another culture. In addition, if the manager has a family, the family members must be able to adapt to a new culture. Adaptation requires three kinds of skills:[46]

1. Ability to maintain a positive self-image and feeling of well-being.
2. Ability to foster relationships with the host-country nationals.
3. Ability to perceive and evaluate the host country's environment accurately.

How to Recruit a Public Outcry

British Prime Minister David Cameron learned the hard way that sometimes only a local candidate will do. The British police had been rocked by scandal and scathing criticism. The department had responded ineffectively to rioting in London in the summer of 2011, and the police department was mixed up in the scandal in which News Corporation reporters arranged to hack into the phones of public figures. Looking for someone to lead an overhaul of the police department, Cameron looked across the Atlantic and saw someone with major accomplishments: Bill Bratton.

Bratton headed the police departments in Boston, Los Angeles, and New York City. His accomplishments included leading those organizations as they restored morale and reduced crime in each city. Based on those successes, Cameron believed Bratton could help the department rein in gang violence and soothe racially based tensions as commissioner of the London Metropolitan Police. So praising Bratton's experience and knowledge, he invited the retired commissioner, now a security consultant, to come work for the British government.

Bratton was intrigued by the offer, but the British public was appalled, as were the British police unions. One detective was quoted calling the choice "a sad indictment of what the government thinks of our senior officers in this country." Britain's Home Secretary pointed out that the London police commissioner is also responsible for national security and there should be a British citizen in the position. Prime Minister Cameron opted to work with Bratton as a consultant instead.

Questions

1. Should recruiting always aim to find the person whose talents and experience are the best match for a position, or should some jobs be reserved for locals? Why?
2. How could Prime Minister Cameron have avoided the embarrassment of reversing his recruiting decision while considering the best options to fill the commissioner's position?

SOURCES: Kroll, "William J. Bratton," http://www.kroll.com, accessed May 11, 2012; "When Talent Stops at the Border," *Bloomberg Businessweek,* August 29, 2011, EBSCOhost, http://web.ebscohost.com; Alyssa Newcomb, "Bill Bratton: 'I Never Close Any Door before It's Opened," *ABC News,* August 13, 2011, http://abcnews.go.com; Janet Stobart, "Bratton as Advisor Doesn't Sit Well with Some British Police," *Los Angeles Times,* August 14, 2011, http://articles.latimes.com.

In a study that drew on the experience of people holding international assignments, expatriates told researchers that the most important qualities for an expatriate manager are, in order of importance, family situation, flexibility and adaptability, job knowledge and motivation, relational skills, and openness to other cultures.[47] To assess candidates' ability to adapt to a new environment, interviews should address topics such as the ones listed in Table 15.2. The interviewer should be certain to give candidates a clear and complete preview of the assignment and the host-country culture. This helps the candidate evaluate the assignment and consider it in terms of his or her family situation, so the employer does not violate the employee's privacy.[48]

LO 15-6 Explain how employers prepare managers for international assignments and for their return home.

Preparing Expatriates

Once the organization has selected a manager for an overseas assignment, it is necessary to prepare that person through training and development. Because expatriate success depends so much on the entire family's adjustment, the employee's spouse should be included in the preparation activities. Employees selected for expatriate assignments already have job-related skills, so preparation for expatriate assignments often focuses on cross-cultural training—that is, training in what to expect from the host country's culture. The general purpose of cross-cultural training is to create an

Table 15.2

Topics for Assessing Candidates for Overseas Assignments

Motivation
- Investigate reasons and degree of interest in wanting to be considered.
- Determine desire to work abroad, verified by previous concerns such as personal travel, language training, reading, and association with foreign employees or students.
- Determine whether the candidate has a realistic understanding of what working and living abroad require.
- Determine the basic attitudes of the spouse toward an overseas assignment.

Health
- Determine whether any medical problems of the candidate or his or her family might be critical to the success of the assignment.
- Determine whether he or she is in good physical and mental health, without any foreseeable change.

Language ability
- Determine potential for learning a new language.
- Determine any previous language(s) studied or oral ability (judge against language needed on the overseas assignment).
- Determine the ability of the spouse to meet the language requirements.

Family considerations
- How many moves has the family made in the past among different cities or parts of the United States?
- What problems were encountered?
- How recent was the last move?
- What is the spouse's goal in this move?
- What are the number of children and the ages of each?
- Has divorce or its potential, or death of a family member, weakened family solidarity?
- Will all the children move? Why or why not?
- What are the location, health, and living arrangements of grandparents and the number of trips normally made to their home each year?
- Are there any special adjustment problems that you would expect?
- How is each member of the family reacting to this possible move?
- Do special educational problems exist within the family?

Resourcefulness and initiative
- Is the candidate independent; can he make and stand by his decisions and judgments?
- Does she have the intellectual capacity to deal with several dimensions simultaneously?
- Is he able to reach objectives and produce results with whatever personnel and facilities are available, regardless of the limitations and barriers that might arise?
- Can the candidate operate without a clear definition of responsibility and authority on a foreign assignment?
- Will the candidate be able to explain the aims and company philosophy to the local managers and workers?
- Does she possess sufficient self-discipline and self-confidence to overcome difficulties or handle complex problems?
- Can the candidate work without supervision?
- Can the candidate operate effectively in a foreign environment without normal communications and supporting services?

Adaptability
- Is the candidate sensitive to others, open to the opinions of others, cooperative, and able to compromise?
- What are his reactions to new situations and efforts to understand and appreciate differences?
- Is she culturally sensitive, aware, and able to relate across the culture?
- Does the candidate understand his own culturally derived values?
- How does the candidate react to criticism?
- What is her understanding of the U.S. government system?
- Will he be able to make and develop contacts with peers in the foreign country?
- Does she have patience when dealing with problems?
- Is he resilient; can he bounce back after setbacks?

(Continued)

Table 15.2   Concluded

Career planning
- Does the candidate consider the assignment anything other than a temporary overseas trip?
- Is the move consistent with her progression and that planned by the company?
- Is his career planning realistic?
- What is the candidate's basic attitude toward the company?
- Is there any history or indication of interpersonal problems with this employee?

Financial
- Are there any current financial and/or legal considerations that might affect the assignment, such as house purchase, children and college expenses, car purchases?
- Are financial considerations negative factors? Will undue pressures be brought to bear on the employee or her family as a result of the assignment?

SOURCE: Reproduced with permission. Chapter 5, pages 55–57 from *"Multinational People Management: A Guide for Organizations and Employees,"* by David M. Noer. Copyright © 1975 by The Bureau of National Affairs, Inc., Arlington, VA 22202. For Bloomberg BNA Books publications call toll free 1-800-960-1220 or visit www.bnabook.com.

appreciation of the host country's culture so expatriates can behave appropriately.[49] Paradoxically, this requires developing a greater awareness of one's own culture so that the expatriate manager can recognize differences and similarities between the cultures and, perhaps, home-culture biases. Consider, for example, the statements in Figure 15.5, which are comments made by visitors to the United States. Do you think these observations accurately describe U.S. culture?

On a more specific level, cross-cultural training for foreign assignments includes the details of how to behave in business settings in another country—the ways people behave in meetings, how employees expect managers to treat them, and so on. As an example, Germans value promptness for meetings to a much greater extent than do Latin Americans—and so on. How should one behave when first meeting one's business counterparts in another culture? The "outgoing" personality style so valued in the United States may seem quite rude in other parts of the world.[50]

Employees preparing for a foreign assignment also need information about such practical matters as housing, schools, recreation, shopping, and health care facilities in the country where they will be living. This is a crucial part of the preparation.

Communication in another country often requires a determined attempt to learn a new language. Some employers try to select managers who speak the language of the host country, and a few provide language training. Most companies assume that employees in the host country will be able to speak the host country's language. Even if this is true, host country nationals are not likely to be fluent in the home country's language, so language barriers remain. When Diana Silva moved from PricewaterhouseCoopers' offices in Mexico to an assignment in Vancouver, British Columbia, she was able to speak English with her Canadian colleagues, but because it is her second language, it was tiring. But the biggest challenge in communicating went beyond knowing the words of English. Her manager told her that her writing style was too abrupt and unfriendly, so she had to learn how to express herself differently. Silva also had to learn to interpret the directions of her Canadian managers, who tend to give employees more latitude in how they carry out assignments than managers do in Mexico.[51]

Along with cross-cultural training, preparation of the expatriate should include career development activities. Before leaving for a foreign assignment, expatriates should discuss with their managers how the foreign assignment fits into their career

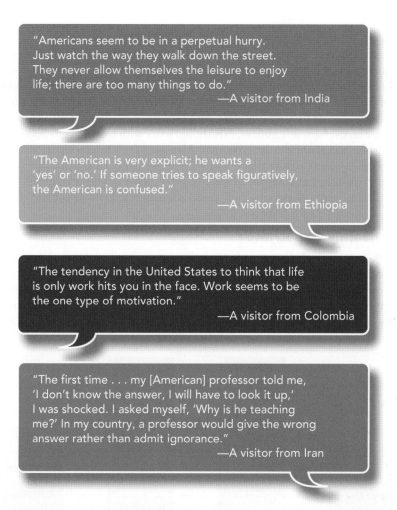

SOURCE: J. Feig and G. Blair, *There Is a Difference,* 2nd ed. (Washington, DC: Meridian House International, 1980), cited in N. Adler, *International Dimensions of Organizational Behavior,* 2nd ed. (Boston: PWS-Kent, 1991).

plans and what types of positions they can expect upon their return. This prepares the expatriate to develop valuable skills during the overseas assignment and eases the return home when the assignment is complete.

When the employee leaves for the assignment, the preparation process should continue. Expatriate colleagues, coaches, and mentors can help the employee learn to navigate challenges as they arise. For example, workers in a new culture sometimes experience internal conflict when the culture where they are working expects them to behave in a way that conflicts with values they learned from their own culture. For example, an Italian manager had difficulty motivating an Indian workforce because the employees were used to authoritarian leadership, and the manager felt as if that style was harsh and disempowering. By talking over the problem with experienced expatriates, the manager came to understand why the situation was so awkward and frustrating. He identified specific ways in which he could be more assertive without losing his temper, so that his Indian employees would better understand what was expected of them. Practicing a new style of leadership became more satisfying as the manager realized that the employees valued his style and that he was becoming a more capable cross-cultural leader.[52]

Managing Expatriates' Performance

Performance management of expatriates requires clear goals for the overseas assignment and frequent evaluation of whether the expatriate employee is on track to meet those goals. Communication technology including e-mail and teleconferencing provides a variety of ways for expats' managers to keep in touch with these employees to discuss and diagnose issues before they can interfere with performance. In addition, before employees leave for an overseas assignment, HR should work with managers to develop criteria measuring the success of the assignment.[53] Measures such as productivity should take into account any local factors that could make expected performance different in the host country than in the company's home country. For example, a country's labor laws or the reliability of the electrical supply could affect the facility's output and efficiency.

Compensating Expatriates

One of the greatest challenges of managing expatriates is determining the compensation package. Most organizations use a *balance sheet approach* to determine the total amount of the package. This approach adjusts the manager's compensation so that it gives the manager the same standard of living as in the home country plus extra pay for the inconvenience of locating overseas. As shown in Figure 15.6, the

Figure 15.6
The Balance Sheet for Determining Expatriate Compensation

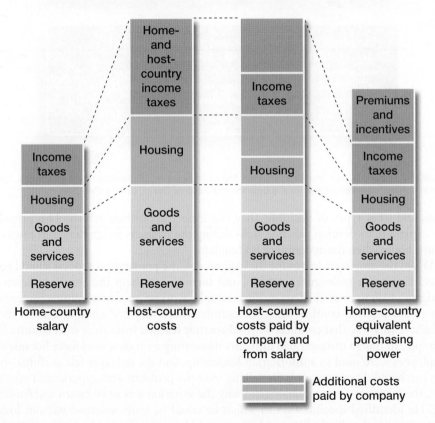

SOURCE: From C. Reynolds, "Compensation of Overseas Personnel," in *Handbook of Human Resource Administration,* 2nd ed., ed. by J. J. Famularo, McGraw-Hill, 1986, p. 51. Reprinted with permission of The McGraw-Hill Companies, Inc.

balance sheet approach begins by determining the purchasing power of compensation for the same type of job in the manager's own country—that is, how much a person can buy, after taxes, in terms of housing, goods and services, and a reserve for savings. Next, this amount is compared with the cost (in dollars, for a U.S. company) of these same expenses in the foreign country. In Figure 15.6, the greater size of the second column means the costs for a similar standard of living in the foreign country are much higher in every category except the reserve amount. This situation would be likely in one of the cities identified in the "Did You Know?" box. For the expatriate in this situation, the employer would pay the additional costs, as shown by the third column. Finally, the expatriate receives additional purchasing power from premiums and incentives. Because of these added incentives, the expatriate's purchasing power is more than what the manager could buy at home with the salary for an equivalent job. (Compare the fourth column with the first.) Expatriates sent to expensive destinations such as Singapore and Hong Kong can receive $200,000 a year in subsidies to cover the expenses of housing, transportation, and schools for their children—plus an additional $100,000 to cover the cost of taxes on these benefits. Adding in the costs to relocate the employee and his or her family can send the total bill for the assignment up to $1 million.[54] That high cost is one of the reasons employers are investing more in recruiting and training local talent.

After setting the total pay, the organization divides this amount into the four components of a total pay package:

1. *Base salary*—Determining the base salary is complex because different countries use different currencies (dollars, yen, euros, and so on). The exchange rate—the rate at which one currency may be exchanged for another—constantly shifts in response to a host of economic forces, so the real value of a salary in terms of dollars is constantly changing. Also, as discussed earlier, the base salary may be comparable to the pay of other managers at headquarters or comparable to other managers at the foreign subsidiary. Because many organizations pay a salary premium as an incentive to accept an overseas assignment, expatriates' salaries are often higher than pay for staying at headquarters.

2. *Tax equalization allowance*—Companies have different systems for taxing income, and in many countries, tax rates are much higher than in the United States. Usually, the employer of an expatriate withholds the amount of tax to be paid in the parent country, then pays all of the taxes due in the country where the expatriate is working.

3. *Benefits*—Most benefits issues have to do with whether an employee can use the same benefits in the foreign country. For example, if an expatriate has been contributing to a pension plan in the United States, does this person have a new pension in the foreign country? Or can the expatriate continue to contribute to the U.S. pension plan? Similarly, health benefits may involve receiving care at certain health facilities. While the person is abroad, does the same health plan cover services received in the foreign country? In one case, flying a manager back to the United States for certain procedures actually would have cost less than having the procedures done in the country where the person was working. But the company's health plans did not permit this alternative. An employer may offer expatriates additional benefits to address the problem of uprooting the spouse when assigning an employee overseas.

Priciest Cities Are Spread over Three Continents

Expatriates spend more for housing, transportation, food, clothing, and other living expenses in Luanda, Angola, than in any other major city, according to a survey by Mercer Human Resources Consulting. In recent years, Asian cities dominated the top five, but in the most recent survey, two of the most expensive cities are in Africa, and only two (counting Russia) are in Asia.

Rankings are influenced by the relative value of national currencies, as well as by political strife and natural disasters. The least expensive city among those studied was Karachi, Pakistan, where security concerns have reduced the demand for housing.

Mercer's list of the 50 most expensive cities includes only one city in North America: New York, ranked number 32.

Question

Why might an organization choose to locate a facility in one of the most expensive cities, in spite of the higher costs?

SOURCES: Mercer, "Mercer's 2011 Cost of Living Survey Highlights—Global," http://www.mercer.com, accessed May 10, 2012; Mercer, "Worldwide Cost of Living Survey 2011—City Rankings," news release, July 12, 2011, http://www.mercer.com; Blake Ellis, "World's Most Expensive Cities," *CNNMoney,* July 12, 2011, http://money.cnn.com.

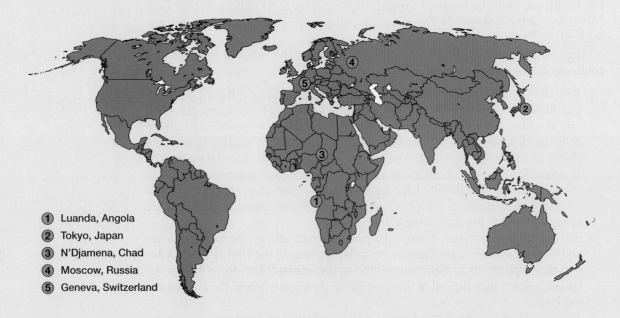

1. Luanda, Angola
2. Tokyo, Japan
3. N'Djamena, Chad
4. Moscow, Russia
5. Geneva, Switzerland

4. *Allowances to make a foreign assignment more attractive*—Cost-of-living allowances make up the differences in expenses for day-to-day needs. Housing allowances ensure that the expatriate can maintain the same standard of living as in the United States. Education allowances reimburse expatriates who pay tuition for their children to attend private English-speaking schools. Relocation allowances cover the expenses of making the move to the foreign country, including transportation, shipping or storage of possessions, and expenses for temporary housing until the employee can rent or purchase a home.

Figure 15.7 is an example of a summary sheet for an expatriate manager's compensation package, showing a variety of allowances.

John H. Doe _____   1 October 2012 _____
Name   **Effective date**

Singapore _____   Manager, SLS./Serv. AP/ME
Location of assignment   **Title**

Houston, Texas _____   1234   202   202
Home base   **Emp. no.**   **LCA code**   **Tax code**

Reason for Change: _____   International Assignment _____

	Old	New
Monthly base salary		$5,000.00
Living cost allowance		$1,291.00
Foreign service premium		$ 750.00
Area allowance		-0-
Gross monthly salary		$7,041.00
Housing deduction		$ 500.00
Hypothetical tax		$ 570.00
Other		
Net monthly salary		$5,971.00

_____   _____
Prepared by   **Date**

_____   _____
Vice President, Human Resources   **Date**

Figure 15.7
International Assignment
Allowance Form

Helping Expatriates Return Home

As the expatriate's assignment nears its end, the human resource department faces a final challenge: helping the expatriate make the transition back to his or her home country. The process of preparing expatriates to return home from a foreign assignment is called **repatriation.** Reentry is not as simple as it might sound. Culture shock takes place in reverse. The experience has changed the expatriate, and the company's and expatriate's home cultures have changed as well. Also, because of differences in economies and compensation levels, a returning expatriate may experience a decline in living standards. The standard of living for an expatriate in many countries includes maid service, a limousine, private schools, and clubs.

Companies are increasingly making efforts to help expatriates through this transition. Two activities help the process along: communication and validation.[55] Communication refers to the expatriate receiving information and recognizing changes while abroad. The more the organization keeps in contact with the expatriate, the

Repatriation
The process of preparing expatriates to return home from a foreign assignment.

more effective and satisfied the person will be upon return. The expatriate plays a role in this process as well. Expatriates should work at maintaining important contacts in the company and industry. Communication related to career development before and during the overseas assignment also should help the employee return to a position that is challenging and interesting. Validation means giving the expatriate recognition for the overseas service when this person returns home. Expatriates who receive praise and recognition from colleagues and top managers for their overseas service and future contribution have fewer troubles with reentry than those whose contributions are disregarded. Validation should also include planning for how the returning employee will contribute to the organization. What skills will this person bring back? What position will he or she fill?

Guardian Industries, a glass manufacturer based in Auburn Hills, Michigan, treats its returning expatriates as valuable employees who have made a sacrifice for the company. They are therefore placed first in line for key assignments. After Dana Partridge worked for Guardian in Saudi Arabia and Thailand for a total of 13 years, the company couldn't immediately give him the job he was prepared for, plant manager, but as soon as a position became available, Partridge was selected.[56]

THINKING ETHICALLY

CAN OFFSHORING BE DONE MORE ETHICALLY?

As we saw in Chapter 5, human resource planning involves several options to meet an organization's needs for talent. One option is to outsource activities that can be performed more effectively and efficiently by a contractor. In today's global marketplace, outsourcing decisions frequently involve offshoring activities to companies in lower-wage locations. However, the reasons why labor costs are lower in another country include lower standards for working conditions—even conditions that would be considered unethical in the parent country.

As a result, this kind of decision can open up a company to criticism, as Apple has faced with regard to its contractors in China. Apple's employees develop and market new products, but manufacturing of iPhones, iPads, and other products is done by contractors in China. The largest of these is Foxconn, a manufacturer of consumer electronics sold under other companies' brands. Foxconn has been criticized for permitting unsafe working conditions, including the accumulation of aluminum dust thought to have caused two serious explosions in its factories. Foxconn workers have reported working long shifts, as long as 12 hours a day, six days a week, some of them standing throughout their work shifts.

Apple is the customer, not the owner, of these facilities, but it tries to exert influence. It has developed a supplier code of conduct laying out standards that contractors must meet in order for Apple to continue buying from them. Suppliers are expected to provide safe working conditions, hire fairly, treat workers with dignity, and follow environmentally responsible practices. Apple sends auditors to visit the factories to check that suppliers are meeting the standards in the code of conduct. It publishes supplier responsibility reports that detail how well the suppliers are meeting the standards. Since Apple began keeping records in 2007, however, more than half of its suppliers have violated at least one requirement every year. Typical problems include employees working more than 60 hours per week; other problems have included using underage workers, paying less than minimum wage, and violating safety requirements. Apple insists that each violation be corrected, and it notes that contractors are showing improvement each year. But former managers of Apple and the China factories have claimed that Apple expresses far more interest in the cost, quality, and speedy delivery of its products than in the working conditions of the people making them. Apple insists that it meets and in some areas exceeds the standards for its industry.

Questions

1. In deciding whether to outsource functions, does an organization such as Apple have an ethical obligation to consider how workers will be treated by

the contractor that hires those workers? Why or why not?

2. What ethical standards for human resource management do you think a company should require from all its operations worldwide? In what areas of HRM, if any, should ethical standards be relaxed to match the prevailing norms of a particular country?

3. Based on the information given, how well has Apple met the standards you set for applying ethical principles internationally? How could the company improve?

SOURCES: Apple, "Supplier Responsibility," http://www.apple.com, accessed January 26, 2012; Charles Duhigg and David Barboza, "In China, Human Costs Are Built into an iPad," *The New York Times,* January 25, 2012, http://www.nytimes.com; Nick Wingfield and Charles Duhigg, "Apple Lists Its Suppliers for First Time," *The New York Times,* January 14, 2012, Business & Company Resource Center, http://galenet.galegroup.com.

SUMMARY

LO 15-1 Summarize how the growth in international business activity affects human resource management.

More and more companies are entering international markets by exporting and operating foreign facilities. Organizations therefore need employees who understand customers and suppliers in other countries. They need to understand local laws and customs and be able to adapt their plans to local situations. To do this organizations may hire a combination of parent-country, host-country, and third-country nationals. They may operate on the scale of an exporter or an international, global, or multinational organization. A global organization needs a transnational HRM system, which makes decisions from a global perspective, includes managers from many countries, and is based on ideas contributed by people representing a variety of cultures.

LO 15-2 Identify the factors that most strongly influence HRM in international markets.

By far the most important influence is the culture of each market—its set of shared assumptions about how the world works and what ideals are worth striving for. A culture has the dimensions of individualism/collectivism, high or low power distance, high or low uncertainty avoidance, masculinity/femininity, and long-term or short-term orientation. Countries also differ in the degree to which their labor markets include people with education and skills of value to employers. Another influence on international HRM is the foreign country's political-legal system—its government, laws, and regulations. Finally, a country's economic system, capitalist or socialist, as well as the government's involvement in the country's economy, such as through taxes and price controls, is a strong factor determining HRM practices.

LO 15-3 Discuss how differences among countries affect HR planning at organizations with international operations.

As organizations consider decisions about their level of international activity, HR professionals should provide information about the relevant human resource issues. When organizations decide to operate internationally or globally, HR planning involves decisions about where and how many employees are needed for each international facility. Some countries limit employers' ability to lay off workers, so organizations would be less likely to staff for peak periods. Other countries allow employers more flexibility in meeting human resource needs. HRM professionals need to be conversant with such differences.

LO 15-4 Describe how companies select and train human resources in a global labor market.

Many organizations with foreign operations fill most positions with host-country nationals. These employees can more easily understand the values and customs of the local workforce, and hiring locally tends to be less expensive than moving employees to new locations. Organizations also fill foreign positions with parent-country and third-country nationals who have human relations skills associated with success in foreign assignments. When sending employees on foreign assignments, organizations prepare the employees (and often their families) through cross-cultural training. Before the assignment, the training provides instruction in the foreign country's language and culture. During the assignment, there is communication with the home country and mentoring. For the return home the employer provides further training.

LO 15-5 Discuss challenges related to managing performance and compensating employees from other countries.

Pay structures can differ substantially among countries in terms of pay level and the relative worth of jobs. Organizations must decide whether to set pay levels and differences in terms of what workers are used to in their own countries or in terms of what employees' colleagues earn at headquarters. Typically, companies have resolved this dilemma by linking pay and benefits more closely to those of the employee's country, but this practice may be weakening so that it depends more on the nature and length of the foreign assignment. These decisions affect the organization's costs and ability to compete, so organizations consider local labor costs in their location decisions. Along with the basic pay structure, organizations must make decisions regarding incentive pay, such as bonuses and stock options. Laws may dictate differences in benefit packages, and the value of benefits will differ if a country requires them or makes them a government service.

LO 15-6 Explain how employers prepare managers for international assignments and for their return home.

When an organization has selected a manager for an overseas assignment, it must prepare the person for the experience. In cross-cultural training the soon-to-be expatriate learns about the foreign culture he or she is heading to, and studies her or his own home-country culture as well for insight. The trainee is given a detailed briefing on how to behave in business settings in the new country. Along with cross-cultural training, preparation of the expatriate should include career development activities to help the individual acquire valuable career skills during the foreign assignment and at the end of the assignment to handle repatriation successfully. Communication of changes at home and validation of a job well done abroad help the expatriate through the repatriation process.

KEY TERMS

cross-cultural preparation, 485
culture shock, 484
expatriates, 474
global organization, 476

host country, 474
international organization, 475
multinational company, 476
parent country, 474

repatriation, 499
third country, 474
transnational HRM system, 476

REVIEW AND DISCUSSION QUESTIONS

1. Identify the parent country, host country(ies), and third country(ies) in the following example: A global soft-drink company called Cold Cola has headquarters in Atlanta, Georgia. It operates production facilities in Athens, Greece, and in Jakarta, Indonesia. The company has assigned a manager from Boston to head the Athens facility and a manager from Hong Kong to manage the Jakarta facility.
2. What are some HRM challenges that arise when a U.S. company expands from domestic markets by exporting? When it changes from simply exporting to operating as an international company? When an international company becomes a global company?
3. In recent years, many U.S. companies have invested in Russia and sent U.S. managers there in an attempt to transplant U.S.-style management. According to Hofstede, U.S. culture has low power distance, uncertainty avoidance, and long-term orientation and high individuality and masculinity. Russia's culture has high power distance and uncertainty avoidance, low masculinity and long-term orientation, and moderate individuality. In light of what you know about cultural differences, how well do you think U.S. managers can succeed in each of the following U.S.-style HRM practices? (Explain your reasons.)
   a. Selection decisions based on extensive assessment of individual abilities.
   b. Appraisals based on individual performance.
   c. Systems for gathering suggestions from workers.
   d. Self-managing work teams.
4. Besides cultural differences, what other factors affect human resource management in an organization with international operations?

5. Suppose you work in the HR department of a company that is expanding into a country where the law and culture make it difficult to lay off employees. How should your knowledge of that difficulty affect human resource planning for the overseas operations?

6. Why do multinational organizations hire host-country nationals to fill most of their foreign positions, rather than sending expatriates for most jobs?

7. Suppose an organization decides to improve collaboration and knowledge sharing by developing an intranet to link its global workforce. It needs to train employees in several different countries to use this system. List the possible cultural issues you can think of that the training program should take into account.

8. For an organization with operations in three different countries, what are some advantages and disadvantages of setting compensation according to the labor markets in the countries where the employees live and work? What are some advantages and disadvantages of setting compensation according to the labor market in the company's headquarters? Would the best arrangement be different for the company's top executives and its production workers? Explain.

9. What abilities make a candidate more likely to succeed in an assignment as an expatriate? Which of these abilities do you have? How might a person acquire these abilities?

10. In the past, a large share of expatriate managers from the United States have returned home before successfully completing their foreign assignments. Suggest some possible reasons for the high failure rate. What can HR departments do to increase the success of expatriates?

EXPERIENCING HR

Imagine that you work in the human resources department of a small but growing company that runs a chain of clothing stores. The top managers believe that by next year, the company will be able to get financing to expand overseas, where consumer demand is growing. They are researching whether the next step should involve opening a few stores in Brazil or in China. Other members of your company are investigating the marketing and financial aspects of the expansion. You have been asked to learn more about the human resource issues the company would face in each country.

Review this chapter and do some research online or in your library to identify HR issues that are likely to be important in each country. Write a one- or two-page summary of what you learned about each country, what your company should investigate further before moving into either country, and which of the two countries you would recommend from a human resource perspective.

Some good places to get started with basic information about the countries include *The World Factbook* (published by the CIA at **https://www.cia.gov/library/ publications/the-world-factbook/**); the Bureau of Labor Statistics site "International Labor Comparisons: Country at a Glance" (**http://www.bls.gov/fls/ country.htm**); and the topics and statistics pages of the International Labor Organization (**www.ilo.org**). You could also use an Internet search engine to look for links to information about each country's culture.

TAKING RESPONSIBILITY: BP Australasia's Sustainable Workforce

Oil giant BP has more than 83,000 employees in 30 countries; 5,000 of those employees work in Australia. The Australian employees "work well together," notes their boss, Paul Waterman, the president of BP Australasia. Waterman, who is originally from Michigan and has held various positions with BP around the world, notes several distinctive qualities of the Australian workforce. Compared with Americans, the Australians are quicker to comply with requirements, but less driven by their work.

BP Australasia is growing, and it readily attracts new talent. However, retaining employees can be difficult because a strong mining industry in Australia competes for experienced workers. To keep employees, BP focuses on combining training, work assignments, and career management that will help employees see and follow an attractive career path. BP also tries to ensure that its compensation package is attractive relative to the competition.

BP Australasia seeks the broadest talent pool and excellent employee retention by valuing diversity. According to Waterman, ethnic and gender diversity is a newer concept to Australian culture than in the United States, so many employees are just grasping its importance. This is a significant challenge. Many companies are surprised when they roll out diversity training to their international operations and discover that the programs don't work because they are not speaking to the issues faced by employees in other cultures. For example, gender roles differ from one part of the world to another, and race is not a major issue in many parts of the world. Ethnic identity plays a role in most cultures, but its meaning differs in a homogeneous country such as Japan, a culture with much immigration such as the United States, and a country where immigration is seen by some people as compromising national identity, as in France. Sexual orientation is accepted as a concern for diversity training in much of the West, but is a sensitive issue elsewhere. The United States, in contrast, tends to downplay diversity in terms of social class, but in some parts of the world, that is a major component of diversity.

In Australia, one measure of which issues are important for valuing diversity is the legal environment. Laws in Australia promote employment opportunity for women. The Workplace Gender and Equality Act requires that companies with at least 100 employees create a workplace gender equity plan and prepare reports detailing the participation rates of men and women, as well as the availability of flexible work practices. Australian employers are required by law to consider employees' requests for flexible work arrangements if the employees are responsible for children under the age of 18 or with a disability. The Australian government also has created a plan for paid parental leave for primary caregivers of children born or adopted after January 1, 2011. Employees can receive up to 18 weeks of leave at the national minimum wage.

BP Australasia is committed to more than just meeting legal requirements. The company in 2009 established a five-year plan for ensuring an organization that is diverse and inclusive. The company conducts an annual analysis of its pay to ensure parity for male and female employees, and it sets targets for increasing the number of women in managerial and executive positions. In filling its leadership development program, it ensures that

at least half the participants are women. Benefits include generous maternity leave that offers half pay for up to eight months, as well as flexible work arrangements and an affinity network for part-time workers. With measures such as these, BP Australasia was recently named an Employer of Choice for Women for the second year in a row by an organization called Equal Employment for Women Australia. More significantly for the business, Waterman notes that the number of women applying for technical jobs at BP has been rising—a sign that efforts to be inclusive are attracting a wider pool of talent.

One woman who has risen through the ranks at BP Australasia is Brooke Miller, the company's chief financial officer. Before joining BP, Miller was a landscape architect who wanted a career in a major corporation. She was interested in how businesses make investment decisions, and she made a point to learn as much as she could as she took on management jobs. This, coupled with BP's formal training programs, enabled Miller to learn enough about financial structures and reporting to become CFO after 12 years.

Questions
1. What are some challenges Waterman faces as a Michigan-born executive leading an Australian company?
2. What differences do you see between HRM at BP Australasia and in a U.S. organization?
3. Which of BP Australasia's diversity initiatives would be effective in the United States?

SOURCES: BP Australia, "BP Wins Citation as Employer of Choice for Women," news release, March 13, 2012, http://www.bp.com; Louis White, "Oil Giant Tackles Challenge of Growth," *The Australian*, May 12, 2012, http://www.theaustralian.com.au; Neal Goodman, "Diversity Dimensions," *Training*, November/December 2011, EBSCOhost, http://web.ebscohost.com; Richard J. Charney, Madeleine L. S. Loewenberg, Karen Ainslie, et al., "Diversity Laws: A Global Overview," *Mondaq Business Briefing*, June 10, 2011, Business & Company Resource Center, http://galenet.galegroup.com.

MANAGING TALENT: Intel's Location Decisions

Unlike many electronics businesses, Intel, the world's largest semiconductor company, does most of its manufacturing in the United States. Nevertheless, Intel is an international business. The company fabricates microprocessors and chip sets in the United States (in Oregon, Arizona, Massachusetts, and New Mexico), Israel, China, and Ireland. Then employees complete the assembly of the microprocessors and test them at Intel's seven assembly test facilities in China, Malaysia, Vietnam, and Costa Rica. Intel also has sales and research facilities around the world, with locations in 46 countries.

Most companies that make microchips have located their manufacturing facilities outside the United States; only about 16% of the manufacturing capacity is within U.S. borders. The main reason is not the cost of labor, although overseas manufacturing is cheaper. Rather, lower tax rates, sophisticated distribution channels, and a large supply of skilled workers make overseas locations attractive.

Intel seeks an advantage by building exceptionally sophisticated plants and locating them near its research and development experts. Its most recent addition is Fab 42, a factory being built in Chandler, Arizona, expected to be the most advanced microchip fabrication plant ever built. Fabrication involves etching integrated circuits onto silicon wafers, which are then cut up into individual microchip. The larger the wafer the process starts with, the more efficient the manufacturing process. Several companies are making microprocessors from wafers that measure 300 millimeters on each side; Fab 42 will be one of only a few plants that work with 450-millimeter wafers. Intel will also gain an efficiency advantage by building Fab 42 as an expansion of an existing facility in Arizona, which is cheaper than starting up a new facility from scratch.

Since Intel also has facilities in China, Ireland, and Israel, future manufacturing expansion could occur there as well. Intel's managers say they would be more likely to keep building in the United States if the government would lower its corporate tax rates and speed up the approval process for new construction, and if U.S. colleges would prepare more engineers to feed the company's need for talent.

In contrast to manufacturing, research and development for microchips mainly takes place in the United States. However, industrywide, the share of R&D in the United States is declining relative to the R&D growth in Europe, Israel, and Singapore. The sharpest decline in the United States is R&D related to making the chips. Intel hires its R&D talent from around the world to stay at the forefront in its fast-changing industry.

One challenge with a global R&D workforce is how to get employees to share ideas and motivate one another. Intel recently tackled that problem by bringing together 1,000 of its researchers from 22 countries to attend a TechFest in the Oregon Convention Center, near Intel's most advanced operations. During the weeklong event, the researchers attended lectures as well as social events where they could build professional relationships and learn about one another's work.

Questions

1. In general, how can Intel's HRM professionals support the company's strategy of locating the majority of its fabrication plants in the United States?
2. How can they support the strategy of locating marketing and research employees around the world?
3. Intel's managers mentioned some challenges of expanding production within the United States. What HRM challenges would you expect the company to face if, instead, it expanded in China or Israel, where it also has facilities?

SOURCES: Noel Randewich, "Trying to Keep Chip-Making in U.S. No Small Job," *Chicago Tribune*, May 6, 2012, sec. 2, p. 3; Intel, "Jobs at Intel: Our Locations," http://www.intel.com, accessed May 6, 2012; Intel, "Intel Global Manufacturing Facts," http://newsroom.intel.com, accessed May 6, 2012; Mike Rogoway, "Intel Convenes Its Researchers in Portland for First Ever TechFest," *America's Intelligence Wire*, May 4, 2011, Business & Company Resource Center, http://galenet.galegroup.com.

 TWITTER FOCUS: Is Translating a Global Business?

Using Twitter, continue the conversation about managing HR globally by reading the Translations case at **www.mhhe.com/noe5e**. Engage with your classmates and instructor via Twitter to chat about translating languages as a global business using the case questions posted on the Noe website. Don't have a Twitter account yet? See the instructions for getting started on the Online Learning Center.

NOTES

1. Laurie Burkitt, "A Secret Recipe in China," *The Wall Street Journal*, October 25, 2011, http://online.wsj.com; Leslie Kwoh, "Asia's Endangered Species: The Expat," *The Wall Street Journal*, March 28, 2012, http://online.wsj.com.
2. Raju Gopalakrishnan, "Bangalore Software Industry Trying to Avoid an Ironic Fate," *Chicago Tribune*, April 17, 2012, sec. 2, p. 3.
3. "Moving Back to America," *The Economist*, May 14, 2011, EBSCOhost, http://web.ebscohost.com.
4. Kwoh, "Asia's Endangered Species."
5. "A Tale of Two Expats," *The Economist*, January 1, 2011, EBSCOhost, http://web.ebscohost.com.
6. N. Adler and S. Bartholomew, "Managing Globally Competent People," *The Executive* 6 (1992), pp. 52–65.
7. V. Sathe, *Culture and Related Corporate Realities* (Homewood, IL: Richard D. Irwin, 1985); and M. Rokeach, *Beliefs, Attitudes, and Values* (San Francisco: Jossey-Bass, 1968).
8. N. Adler, *International Dimensions of Organizational Behavior*, 2nd ed. (Boston: PWS-Kent, 1991).

9. G. Hofstede, "Dimensions of National Cultures in Fifty Countries and Three Regions," in *Expectations in Cross-Cultural Psychology*, eds. J. Deregowski, S. Dziurawiec, and R. C. Annis (Lisse, Netherlands: Swets and Zeitlinger, 1983); and G. Hofstede, "Cultural Constraints in Management Theories," *Academy of Management Executive* 7 (1993), pp. 81–90.

10. Hofstede, "Cultural Constraints in Management Theories."

11. A Ramesh and M. Gelfland, "Will They Stay or Will They Go? The Role of Job Embeddedness in Predicting Turnover in Individualistic and Collectivistic Cultures," *Journal of Applied Psychology* 95, no. 5 (2010): 807–823.

12. W. A. Randolph and M. Sashkin, "Can Organizational Empowerment Work in Multinational Settings?" *Academy of Management Executive* 16, no. 1 (2002), pp. 102–15.

13. B. Gerhart and M. Fang, "National Culture and Human Resource Management: Assumptions and Evidence," *International Journal of Human Resource Management* 16, no. 6 (June 2005): 971–86.

14. L. A. West Jr. and W. A. Bogumil Jr., "Foreign Knowledge Workers as a Strategic Staffing Option," *Academy of Management Executive* 14, no. 4 (2000), pp. 71–83.

15. Organisation for Economic Co-operation and Development, "Financial and Human Resources Invested in Education," in *Education at a Glance 2011: OECD Indicators*, 2011, http://www.oecd.org, accessed May 14, 2012.

16. World Bank, "The State of Education," *EdStats*, http://www.worldbank.org, accessed May 15, 2012.

17. European Commission, "Rights at Work," http://ec.europa.eu, accessed May 14, 2012; European Union, "Organisation of Working Time (Basic Directive)," http://europa.eu, accessed May 14, 2012.

18. Gopalakrishnan, "Bangalore Software Industry"; *The Economist*, "Moving Back to America."

19. Elizabeth Dwoskin, "Do You Want This Job?" *Bloomberg Businessweek*, November 14, 2011, EBSCOhost, http://web.ebscohost.com.

20. Brookings Institution, "Immigrant Workers in the U.S. Labor Force," research paper, March 15, 2012, http://www.brookings.edu.

21. Miriam Jordan, "Fresh Raids Target Illegal Hiring," *The Wall Street Journal*, May 2, 2012, http://online.wsj.com; Kevin Lashus, "Morton Announces Record Increase in Worksite Enforcement Activity," *Lawlogix.com*, October 13, 2011, http://www.lawlogix.com.

22. W. A. Arthur Jr. and W. Bennett Jr., "The International Assgnee: The Relative Importance of Factors Perceived to Contribute to Success," *Personnel Psychology* 48 (1995), pp. 99–114; and G. M. Spreitzer, M. W. McCall Jr., and J. D. Mahoney, "Early Identification of International Executive Potential," *Journal of Applied Psychology* 82 (1997), pp. 6–29.

23. J. S. Black and J. K. Stephens, "The Influence of the Spouse on American Expatriate Adjustment and Intent to Stay in Pacific Rim Overseas Assignments," *Journal of Management* 15 (1989), pp. 529–44.

24. P. Caligiuri, "The Big Five Personality Characteristics as Predictors of Expatriates' Desire to Terminate the Assignment and Supervisor-Rated Performance," *Personnel Psychology* 53 (2000), pp. 67–88.

25. Delia Flanja, "Culture Shock in Intercultural Communication," *Studia Europaea* (October 2009), Business & Company Resource Center, http://galenet.galegroup.com.

26. D. M. Gayeski, C. Sanchirico, and J. Anderson, "Designing Training for Global Environments: Knowing What Questions to Ask," *Performance Improvement Quarterly* 15, no. 2 (2002), pp. 15–31.

27. J. S. Black and M. Mendenhall, "A Practical but Theory-Based Framework for Selecting Cross-Cultural Training Methods," in *Readings and Cases in International Human Resource Management*, eds. M. Mendenhall and G. Oddou (Boston: PWS-Kent, 1991), pp. 177–204.

28. "Brookfield GRS 2011 Global Relocation Trends Survey Report," *Re:locate*, April 26, 2011, http://www.relocatemagazine.com; "Companies Prefer Age and Experience in International Assignees," *Expatica*, April 24, 2012, http://www.expatica.com.

29. Jordan Burchette, "Ultimate Checklist for Returning U.S. Expats," *CNNGo.com*, February 21, 2012, http://www.cnngo.com.

30. D. D. Davis, "International Performance Measurement and Management," in *Performance Appraisal: State of the Art in Practice*, ed. J. W. Smither (San Francisco: Jossey-Bass, 1998), pp. 95–131.

31. M. Gowan, S. Ibarreche, and C. Lackey, "Doing the Right Things in Mexico," *Academy of Management Executive* 10 (1996), pp. 74–81.

32. L. S. Chee, "Singapore Airlines: Strategic Human Resource Initiatives," in *International Human Resource Management: Think Globally, Act Locally*, ed. D. Torrington (Upper Saddle River, NJ: Prentice Hall, 1994), pp. 143–59.

33. "Johnson & Johnson Takes World View on Compensation," *Employee Benefits*, June 2011, p. 7.

34. "Top Whack: Big Country, Big Pay Cheques," *The Economist*, January 29, 2011, EBSCOhost, http://web.ebscohost.com.

35. Bureau of Labor Statistics, International Labor Comparisons, "Country at a Glance," http://www.bls.gov/fls/country.htm, last modified July 20, 2011.

36. See, for example, A. E. Cobet and G. A. Wilson, "Comparing 50 Years of Labor Productivity in U.S. and Foreign Manufacturing," *Monthly Labor Review*, June 2002, pp. 51–63; Bureau of Labor Statistics, "International Comparisons of Manufacturing Productivity and Labor Cost Trends, 2008," news release, October 22, 2009, www.bls.gov; and Daron Acemoglu and Melissa Dell, "Productivity Differences between and within Countries," *American Economic Journal: Macroeconomics 2010* 2, no. 1 (2010): 169–88.

37. Stephen Miller, "Grasp Country Difference to Manage Global Pay," Compensation Discipline, March 30, 2010, http://www.shrm.org.

38. P. J. Dowling, D. E. Welch, and R. S. Schuler, *International Human Resource Management*, 3rd ed. (Cincinnati: South-Western, 1999), pp. 235–36.

39. Ibid.; J. La Palombara and S. Blank, *Multinational Corporations and National Elites: A Study of Tensions* (New York: Conference Board, 1976); A. B. Sim, "Decentralized Management of Subsidiaries and Their Performance: A Comparative Study of American, British and Japanese Subsidiaries in Malaysia," *Management International Review* 17, no. 2 (1977), pp. 45–51; Y. K. Shetty, "Managing the Multinational Corporation: European and American Styles," *Management International Review* 19, no. 3 (1979), pp. 39–48; and J. Hamill, "Labor Relations Decision-Making within Multinational Corporations," *Industrial Relations Journal* 15, no. 2 (1984), pp. 30–34.

40. Dowling, Welch, and Schuler, *International Human Resource Management*, p. 231.

41. Sharon Terlep, "GM's Mr. Fix-It Tackles Opel Mess," *The Wall Street Journal*, April 15, 2012, http://online.wsj.com.

42. Eric Bellman, "Seeking Safeguards for Unskilled Workers Abroad," *The Wall Street Journal*, February 6, 2012, http://online.wsj.com.

43. J. K. Sebenius, "The Hidden Challenge of Cross-Border Negotiations," *Harvard Business Review*, March 2002, pp. 76–85.

44. E. Krell, "Evaluating Returns on Expatriates," *HRMagazine*, March 2005, downloaded from Infotrac at http://web5.infotrac.galegroup.com.

45. Ibid.; and M. Harvey and M. M. Novicevic, "Selecting Expatriates for Increasingly Complex Global Assignments," *Career Development International* 6, no. 2 (2001), pp. 69–86.

46. M. Mendenhall and G. Oddou, "The Dimensions of Expatriate Acculturation," *Academy of Management Review* 10 (1985), pp. 39–47.

47. Arthur and Bennett , "The International Assignee."

48. J. I. Sanchez, P. E. Spector, and C. L. Cooper, "Adapting to a Boundaryless World: A Developmental Expatriate Model," *Academy of Management Executive* 14, no. 2 (2000), pp. 96–106.

49. P. Dowling and R. Schuler, *International Dimensions of Human Resource Management* (Boston: PWS-Kent, 1990).

50. Sanchez, Spector, and Cooper, "Adapting to a Boundaryless World."

51. Mary Teresa Bitti, "Au Canada," *CA Magazine*, May 2012, pp. 31–37.

52. Andrew L. Molinsky, "Code Switching between Cultures," *Harvard Business Review*, January–February 2012, pp. 140–41.

53. "How Can a Company Manage an Expatriate Employee's Performance?" *SHRM India*, www.shrmindia.org, accessed May 6, 2010.

54. Kwoh, "Asia's Endangered Species."

55. Adler, *International Dimensions of Organizational Behavior*.

56. Alice Andors, "Happy Returns," *HR Magazine*, March 2010, Business & Company Resource Center, http://galenet.galegroup.com.

Creating and Maintaining High-Performance Organizations

What Do I Need to Know?

After reading this chapter, you should be able to:

LO 16-1 Define high-performance work systems, and identify the elements of such a system.

LO 16-2 Summarize the outcomes of a high-performance work system.

LO 16-3 Describe the conditions that create a high-performance work system.

LO 16-4 Explain how human resource management can contribute to high performance.

LO 16-5 Discuss the role of HRM technology in high-performance work systems.

LO 16-6 Summarize ways to measure the effectiveness of human resource management.

Introduction

Running a not-for-profit organization once meant finding people who were passionate about a cause and then assuming that passion alone would motivate them to work hard for the cause. No shareholders kept an eye on sales and profits; what mattered was that the organization was focused on doing good deeds. But today's donors insist on knowing that the organizations they support are using their resources effectively and efficiently. Managers of not-for-profits are expected to demonstrate careful use of their monetary and human resources.

In this environment, not-for-profit organizations today are adopting the HRM practices that have been helping businesses excel. The World Wildlife Fund no longer simply gives employees raises based on how long they have been with the organization. Rather, it has set up a performance management system, which in turn required the WWF to train its managers on how to measure performance and talk to employees about needs for improvement. At the Inter-American Development Bank (IADB), managers knew how to measure performance, but they struggled to keep employees motivated after a few years with the organization. The IADB doesn't have much money to give pay raises, so it looks for other rewards, including flexible schedules, sabbaticals, and career development through assignments in the offices of the countries it serves.[1]

The experience of these and other not-for-profit organizations shows that a compelling mission does not guarantee an organization's success. Someone in the organization has to recognize how its mission, activities, and funding levels will affect the organization's people. The organization must design work, compensation policies, and performance management systems so they bring out the best in the employees. These challenges are some of the most crucial responsibilities of human resource management.

This chapter summarizes the role of human resource management in creating an organization that achieves a high level of performance, measured in such terms as long-term profits, quality, and customer satisfaction. We begin with a definition of *high-performance work systems* and a description of these systems' elements and outcomes. Next, we identify the conditions that contribute to high performance. We explain how the various HRM functions can contribute to high performance. Finally, we introduce ways to measure the effectiveness of human resource management.

High-Performance Work Systems

The challenge facing managers today is how to make their organizations into **high-performance work systems,** with the right combination of people, technology, and organizational structure to make full use of resources and opportunities in achieving their organizations' goals. To function as a high-performance work system, each of these elements must fit well with the others in a smoothly functioning whole. Many manufacturers use the latest in processes including flexible manufacturing technology, total quality management, and just-in-time inventory control (meaning parts and supplies are automatically restocked as needed), but of course these processes do not work on their own; they must be run by qualified people. Organizations need to determine what kinds of people fit their needs, and then locate, train, and motivate those special people.[2] According to research, organizations that introduce integrated high-performance work practices usually experience increases in productivity and long-term financial performance.[3]

Creating a high-performance work system contrasts with traditional management practices. In the past, decisions about technology, organizational structure, and human resources were treated as if they were unrelated. An organization might acquire a new information system, restructure jobs, or add an office in another country without considering the impact on its people. More recently, managers have realized that success depends on how well all the elements work together. For instance, based on his experience running the customer contact center Vixicom, Luis Echevarria has determined that running a call center where agents reliably meet customers' needs is more than a matter of hiring experienced agents with positive attitudes. Rather, Echevarria says, the call center needs to keep abreast of the latest technology, which routes calls efficiently to minimize customer wait times. Managers need to learn how to select employees who not only speak cheerfully on the phone but also can quickly assess a situation and make decisions that go beyond what is on a script. For the agents to apply that skill requires job designs that empower the agents to some degree. Finally, the center needs a compensation plan with at least half of total compensation linked to positive behavior and goal achievement because incentive pay creates a motivating atmosphere for employees who excel at this type of work.[4]

Elements of a High-Performance Work System

As shown in Figure 16.1, in a high-performance work system, the elements that must work together include organizational structure, task design, people (the selection,

LO 16-1 Define high-performance work systems, and identify the elements of such a system.

High-Performance Work System
The right combination of people, technology, and organizational structure that makes full use of the organization's resources and opportunities in achieving its goals.

Figure 16.1
Elements of a
High-Performance
Work System

training, and development of employees), reward systems, and information systems, and human resource management plays an important role in establishing all these.

Organizational structure is the way the organization groups its people into useful divisions, departments, and reporting relationships. The organization's top management makes most decisions about structure, for instance, how many employees report to each supervisor and whether employees are grouped according to the functions they carry out or the customers they serve. Such decisions affect how well employees coordinate their activities and respond to change. In a high-performance work system, organizational structure promotes cooperation, learning, and continuous improvement.

Task design determines how the details of the organization's necessary activities will be grouped, whether into jobs or team responsibilities. In a high-performance work system, task design makes jobs efficient while encouraging high quality. In Chapter 4, we discussed how to carry out this HRM function through job analysis and job design.

The right *people* are a key element of high-performance work systems. HRM has a significant role in providing people who are well suited and well prepared for their jobs.

In a high-performance work system, all the elements—people, technology, and organizational structure—work together for success.

Human resource personnel help the organization recruit and select people with the needed qualifications. Training, development, and career management ensure that these people are able to perform their current and future jobs with the organization.

Reward systems contribute to high performance by encouraging people to strive for objectives that support the organization's overall goals. Reward systems include the performance measures by which employees are judged, the methods of measuring performance, and the incentive pay and other rewards linked to success. Human resource management plays an important role in developing and administering reward systems, as we saw in Chapters 8 through 12.

The final element of high-performance work systems is the organization's *information systems*. Managers make decisions about the types of information to gather and the sources of information. They also must decide who in the organization should have access to the information and how they will make the information available. Modern information systems, including the Internet, have enabled organizations to share information widely. HR departments take advantage of this technology to give employees access to information about benefits, training opportunities, job openings, and more, as we will describe later in this chapter.

Outcomes of a High-Performance Work System

Consider the practices of steel minimills in the United States. Some of these mills have strategies based on keeping their costs below competitors' costs; low costs let them operate at a profit while winning customers with low prices. Other steel minimills focus on "differentiation," meaning they set themselves apart in some way other than low price—for example, by offering higher quality or unusual product lines. Research has found that the minimills with cost-related goals tend to have highly centralized structures, so managers can focus on controlling through a tight line of command. These organizations have low employee participation in decisions, relatively low wages and benefits, and pay highly contingent on performance.[5] At minimills that focus on differentiation, structures are more complex and decentralized, so authority is more spread out. These minimills encourage employee participation and have higher wages and more generous benefits. They are high-performance work systems. In general, these differentiator mills enjoy higher productivity, lower scrap rates, and lower employee turnover than the mills that focus on low costs.

Outcomes of a high-performance work system thus include higher productivity and efficiency. These outcomes contribute to higher profits. A high-performance work system may have other outcomes, including high product quality, great customer satisfaction, and low employee turnover. Some of these outcomes meet intermediate goals that lead to higher profits (see Figure 16.2). For example, high quality contributes to

LO 16-2 Summarize the outcomes of a high-performance work system.

Figure 16.2
Outcomes of a High-Performance Work System

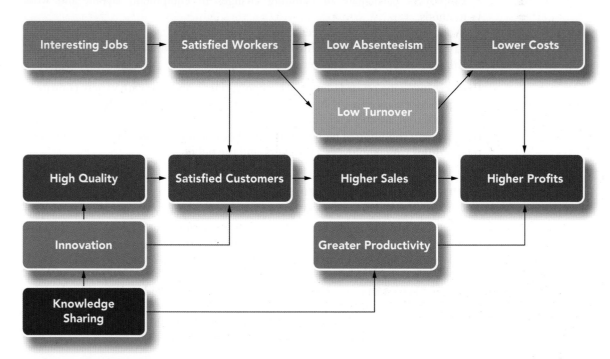

customer satisfaction, and customer satisfaction contributes to growth of the business. Likewise, improving productivity lets the organization do more with less, which satisfies price-conscious customers and may help the organization win over customers from its competitors. Other ways to lower cost and improve quality are to reduce absenteeism and turnover, providing the organization with a steady supply of experienced workers. In the previous example of minimills, some employers keep turnover and scrap rates low. Meeting those goals helps the minimills improve productivity, which helps them earn more profits.

In a high-performance work system, the outcomes of each employee and work group contribute to the system's overall high performance. The organization's individuals and groups work efficiently, provide high-quality goods and services, and so on, and in this way, they contribute to meeting the organization's goals. When the organization adds or changes goals, people are flexible and make changes as needed to meet the new goals.

Conditions That Contribute to High Performance

LO 16-3 Describe the conditions that create a high-performance work system.

Certain conditions underlie the formation of a high-performance work system:[6]

- Teams perform work.
- Employees participate in selection.
- Employees receive formal performance feedback and are actively involved in the performance improvement process.
- Ongoing training is emphasized and rewarded.
- Employees' rewards and compensation relate to the company's financial performance.
- Equipment and work processes are structured, and technology is used to encourage maximum flexibility and interaction among employees.
- Employees participate in planning changes in equipment, layout, and work methods.
- Work design allows employees to use a variety of skills.
- Employees understand how their jobs contribute to the finished product or service.
- Ethical behavior is encouraged.

Practices involving rewards, employee empowerment, and jobs with variety contribute to high performance by giving employees skills, incentives, knowledge, autonomy—and satisfaction, another condition associated with high performance. Ethical behavior is a necessary condition of high performance because it contributes to good long-term relationships with employees, customers, and the public.

Teamwork and Empowerment

As we discussed in Chapter 2, today's organizations empower employees. They expect employees to make more decisions about how they perform their jobs. One of the most popular ways to empower employees is to design work so that it is performed by teams. On a work team, employees bring together various skills and experiences to produce goods or provide services. The organization may charge the team with making decisions traditionally made by managers, such as hiring team members and planning work schedules. Teamwork and empowerment contribute to high performance when they improve job satisfaction and give the organization fuller use of employees' ideas and expertise.

At General Electric's Greenville Airfoils facility in Piedmont, South Carolina, production workers are cross-trained to work on teams. The production teams are involved in the employee selection process, interviewing job candidates and observing them as they participate in games where they work as a team to build a helicopter from blocks. In this way, they choose team members who work together effectively. In addition, the teams are empowered to design their own work processes. Teams have been so effective in improving efficiency that GE lets the teams carry out essentially the same processes in different ways, if that is how they design the work.[7]

It's important for companies to capture and share the knowledge of workers who have had years to learn their specialty.

For empowerment to succeed, managers must serve in linking and coordinating roles[8] and provide the team with the resources it needs to carry out its work. The manager should help the team and its members interact with employees from other departments or teams and should make sure communication flows in both directions—the manager keeps the team updated on important issues and ensures that the team shares information and resources with others who need them.

Knowledge Sharing

For more than a decade, managers have been interested in creating a **learning organization,** that is, an organization in which the culture values and supports lifelong learning by enabling all employees to continually acquire and share knowledge. The people in a learning organization have resources for training, and they are encouraged to share their knowledge with colleagues. Managers take an active role in identifying training needs and encouraging the sharing of ideas.[9] An organization's information systems, discussed later in this chapter, have an important role in making this learning activity possible. Information systems capture knowledge and make it available even after individual employees who provided the knowledge have left the organization. Ultimately, people are the essential ingredients in a learning organization. They must be committed to learning and willing to share what they have learned. For an example of an organization where people have a strong commitment to learning, see the "Best Practices" box.

A learning organization has several key features:[10]

Learning Organization
An organization that supports lifelong learning by enabling all employees to acquire and share knowledge.

- It engages in **continuous learning,** each employee's and each group's ongoing efforts to gather information and apply the information to their decisions. In many organizations, the process of continuous learning is aimed at improving quality. To engage in continuous learning, employees must understand the entire work system they participate in, the relationships among jobs, their work units, and the organization as a whole. Employees who continuously learn about their work system are adding to their ability to improve performance.

Continuous Learning
Each employee's and each group's ongoing efforts to gather information and apply the information to their decisions in a learning organization.

- Knowledge is *shared*. Therefore, to create a learning organization, one challenge is to shift the focus of training away from merely teaching skills and toward a broader focus on generating and sharing knowledge.[11] In this view, training is an investment in the organization's human resources; it increases employees' value to the organization. Also, training content should be related to the organization's goals. Human resource departments can support the creation of a learning organization by planning training programs that meet these criteria, and they can help to create both face-to-face and electronic systems for employee collaboration to create, capture, and share knowledge.

How Farmers Insurance Promotes Learning

In spite of the challenges that recently hit the economy's financial sector, one of the firms that has remained strong is Farmers Insurance Group. The organization's leaders give much of the credit to effective talent management and a commitment to training. Farmers hires individuals who display empathy and a desire to serve, with the assumption that the company can then use its award-winning training programs to teach them the basics of the insurance business and the details of Farmers' products.

A substantial part of learning at Farmers Insurance takes place in formal training programs delivered by 140 learning professionals to 26,000 employees, 36,000 independent agents, and 14,000 exclusive (Farmers-only) agents. The learning team, under the name University of Farmers, delivers thousands of courses to these people online and at two corporate campuses. The University of Farmers is divided into units that each focus on a particular business unit of the company—for example, commercial products or customer contact centers. Each training unit is responsible for identifying the kinds of knowledge needed by the business unit, and its performance is evaluated in terms of how well it helps the business unit accomplish its goals. For example, a recent training program for the call centers shaved three minutes off the time it takes agents to process transactions.

In the case of insurance agents, maintaining a commitment to learning is made more complex by the fact that the agents are not directly employed by Farmers; they are independent contractors. So Farmers makes a point of measuring and demonstrating the results of its training programs—how learning the material helps agents better interact with customers and meet customer needs, which translates into continuing sales growth. As agents see how learning more helps them build their business, they become enthusiastic about the training.

SOURCES: Tony Bingham and Pat Galagan, "Proud to Tout Their Talent," *T + D*, February 2012, pp. 33–37; Deanna Hartley, "Insuring Relevance," *Chief Learning Officer*, January 2012, pp. 22–25; Lorri Freifeld, "Farmers Insures Success," *Training*, January/February 2012, EBSCOhost, http://web.ebscohost.com.

- *Critical, systematic thinking* is widespread. This occurs when organizations encourage employees to see relationships among ideas and to test assumptions and observe the results of their actions. Reward systems can be set up to encourage employees and teams to think in new ways.
- The organization has a *learning culture*—a culture in which learning is rewarded, promoted, and supported by managers and organizational objectives. This culture may be reflected in performance management systems and pay structures that reward employees for gathering and sharing more knowledge. A learning culture creates the conditions in which managers encourage *flexibility* and *experimentation*. The organization should encourage employees to take risks and innovate, which means it cannot be quick to punish ideas that do not work out as intended.
- *Employees are valued*. The organization recognizes that employees are the source of its knowledge. It therefore focuses on ensuring the development and well-being of each employee.

Continuous learning and knowledge sharing can support an environment of employee empowerment. For example, some organizations are giving employees access to software that monitors their productivity on the assumption that if they know data about their performance, they can use the data to improve their own productivity. For example, a program called RescueTime measures how long computer users spend on each website and application, as well as their time away from the computer; TallyZoo lets users enter data—say, time spent on activities and amount of work completed—and create interactive graphs for measuring progress and spotting trends and other patterns. One employee who used tools such as these discovered that he was most productive when he switched tasks periodically, so he set up the software to remind him every 20 minutes to do something different. A programmer who assumed that chatting online was making him less productive tested that assumption and found that time chatting was associated with writing *more* lines of code. Armed with that information, the programmer gave a higher priority to networking with co-workers and customers. Notice in these examples that the workers had latitude to discover how they work best and to control how they applied what they learned.[12]

Job Satisfaction and Employee Engagement

A condition underpinning any high-performance organization is that employees be fully engaged with their work. This tends to require that they experience job satisfaction—they experience their jobs as fulfilling or allowing them to fulfill important values. Research supports the idea that employees' job satisfaction and job performance are related.[13] Higher performance at the individual level should contribute to higher performance for the organization as a whole. Consultants at Towers Watson have found that employee engagement is associated with greater profitability, especially when engagement is coupled with employee well-being and access to the necessary resources.[14] Aon Hewitt, another major HR consulting firm, has measured an association between employee engagement and companies' stock market performance. At companies studied by Aon Hewitt, those with the highest levels of employee engagement also experience lower turnover, better employee retention, and greater productivity.[15] And as the "Did You Know?" box suggests, many employees agree with the idea that the way they are treated at work affects their attitudes and effort on the job.

Chapter 10 described a number of ways organizations can promote job satisfaction and employee engagement. They include making jobs more interesting, setting clear and challenging goals, and providing valued rewards that are linked to performance in a performance management system that employees consider fair. Globally, Aon Hewitt has found that the practices that do most to promote employee engagement are opportunities for career progress, recognition for accomplishments, and brand alignment. **Brand alignment** is the process of ensuring that HR policies, practices, and programs support or are congruent with an organization's overall culture or brand, including its products and services. One way to ensure HR policies align with a company's strategic vision is to educate employees about the company's "brand" and their role in bringing that brand to life as part of everyday work activities. Some companies discuss brand alignment as part of employee orientation programs while others develop in-depth training programs about the company's brand and how each employee is an important contributor to the company's overall success. In North America, employers have the most impact on brand alignment by providing career opportunities, using effective performance management systems, and maintaining a positive reputation.[16]

Brand Alignment
The process of ensuring that HR policies, practices, and programs support or are congruent with an organization's overall culture (or brand), products, and services.

Some organizations are moving beyond concern with mere job satisfaction and are trying to foster employees' *passion* for their work. Passionate people are fully engaged with something so that it becomes part of their sense of who they are. Feeling this way about one's work has been called *occupational intimacy*.[17] People experience occupational intimacy when they love their work, when they and their co-workers care about one another, and when they find their work meaningful. Human resource managers have a significant role in creating these conditions. For example, they can select people who care about their work and customers, provide methods for sharing knowledge, design work to make jobs interesting, and establish policies and programs that show

Appreciation Drives Effort

In a recent survey, only about half of employees said they love their job and that their company cares about them. In spite of a slow economy, almost 4 in 10 said they intended to look for a new job. But whether or not they intend to stay, solid majorities said they would work harder if their employer better recognized and appreciated their efforts.

Question

How can employers demonstrate to employees that the organization values them and appreciates their efforts?

SOURCES: Globoforce, "Globoforce Workforce Mood Tracker: The Impact of Recognition on Employee Retention," September 2011, http://www.globoforce.com; Globoforce, "Thirty-Eight Percent of Workers Seek New Jobs, according to Globoforce Workforce Mood Tracker," news release, September 28, 2011, http://www.globoforce.com.

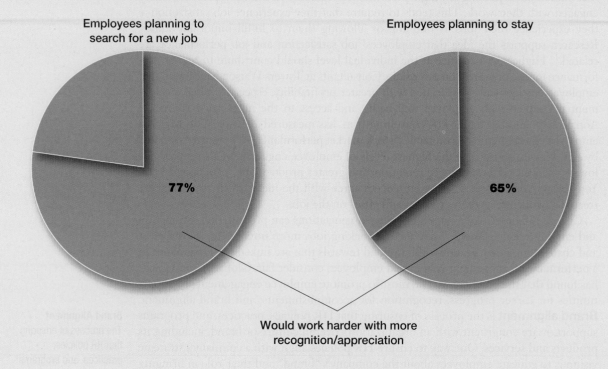

Employees planning to search for a new job

77%

Employees planning to stay

65%

Would work harder with more recognition/appreciation

concern for employees' needs. Such efforts may become increasingly important as the business world increasingly uses employee empowerment, teamwork, and knowledge sharing to build flexible organizations.[18]

Ethics

In the long run, a high-performance organization meets high ethical standards. Ethics, defined in Chapter 1, establishes fundamental principles for behavior, such as honesty and fairness. Organizations and their employees must meet these standards if they are to maintain positive long-term relationships with their customers and their community.

Ethical behavior is most likely to result from values held by the organization's leaders combined with systems that promote ethical behavior. At Arthur J. Gallagher & Company, an insurance brokerage and risk management firm, a vice president of corporate ethics and sustainability reports directly to the firm's CEO to ensure that ethical conduct is a priority. That vice president, Tom Tropp, travels to the firm's more than 100 offices to discuss its values and listen to employees tell about issues they face. Employees might not expect at first that the company really means what it says, but after Tropp takes employees' concerns back to headquarters and the employees see top management respond, they recognize that the concern for ethics is real. Often, the person in charge of ethics is a lawyer, but Tropp's training is in ethics and philosophy, which helps him think about ethical matters in a deeper way than mere compliance with the law.[19]

A number of organizational systems can promote ethical behavior.[20] These include a written code of ethics that the organization distributes to employees and expects them to use in decision making. This type of guidance can be especially effective if developed with input from employees about situations they encounter. However, standards alone are not enough—the organization should reinforce ethical behavior. For example, performance measures should include ethical standards, and misdeeds should receive swift discipline, as described in Chapter 10. The organization should provide channels employees can use to ask questions about ethical behavior or to seek help if they are expected to do something they believe is wrong. Organizations also can provide training in ethical decision making, including training for supervisors in how to handle employees' concerns about ethical matters.

As these examples suggest, ethical behavior is a human resource management concern. The systems that promote ethical behavior include such HRM functions as training, performance management, and discipline policies. A reputation for high ethical standards can also help a company attract workers—and customers—who share those high standards. CA Technologies, which develops management software, includes standards for maintaining an ethical culture among its criteria for managers to receive performance-based pay. The company also provides training to help managers guide their employees in how to handle situations ethically. A chief ethics officer in CA Technologies' legal department meets with managers and focus groups of employees to ensure they understand what the ethical standards are and how the company's legal and ethical resources can help them navigate difficult decisions.[21]

HRM's Contribution to High Performance

Management of human resources plays a critical role in determining companies' success in meeting the challenges of a rapidly changing, highly competitive environment.[22] Compensation, staffing, training and development, performance management, and other HRM practices are investments that directly affect employees' motivation and ability to provide products and services that are valued by customers. Table 16.1 lists examples of HRM practices that contribute to high performance.

Research suggests that it is more effective to improve HRM practices as a whole than to focus on one or two isolated practices, such as the organization's pay structure or selection system.[23] Also, to have the intended influence on performance, the HRM practices must fit well with one another and the organization as a whole.[24] For ideas on how HR professionals can strengthen the function's connection to the organization's mission, see "HR How To."

LO 16-4 Explain how human resource management can contribute to high performance.

Job Design

For the organization to benefit from teamwork and employee empowerment, jobs must be designed appropriately. Often, a high-performance work system places

• HRM practices match organization's goals.	• Performance management system measures customer satisfaction and quality.
• Individuals and groups share knowledge.	• Organization monitors employees' satisfaction.
• Work is performed by teams.	• Discipline system is progressive.
• Organization encourages continuous learning.	• Pay systems reward skills and accomplishments.
• Work design permits flexibility in where and when tasks are performed.	• Skills and values of a diverse workforce are valued and used.
• Selection system is job related and legal.	• Technology reduces time and costs of tasks while preserving quality.

employees in work teams where employees collaborate to make decisions and solve problems. Individual employees also may be empowered to serve on teams that design jobs and work processes.

Job design aimed at empowerment includes access to resources such as information technology. The Lowe's chain of home improvement stores wanted to empower its salespeople with more information they need to close sales. So it equipped the salespeople with iPhones that have apps for price scanning, locating items in the store, checking inventory, and looking up competitors' prices. Eventually, the phones also will be able to scan customers' credit cards to complete sales transactions.[25] Lowe's hopes this much access to information will enable its salespeople to initiate conversations with shoppers and walk them through the entire decision process to the closing of a sale.

Recruitment and Selection

At a high-performance organization, recruitment and selection aim at obtaining the kinds of employees who can thrive in this type of setting. These employees are enthusiastic about and able to contribute to teamwork, empowerment, and knowledge sharing. Qualities such as creativity and ability to cooperate as part of a team may play a large role in selection decisions. High-performance organizations need selection methods that identify more than technical skills like ability to perform accounting and engineering tasks. Employers may use group interviews, open-ended questions, and psychological tests to find employees who innovate, share ideas, and take initiative.

Training and Development

When organizations base hiring decisions on qualities like decision-making and teamwork skills, training may be required to teach employees the specific skills they need to perform the duties of their job. Extensive training and development also are part of a learning organization, described earlier in this chapter. And when organizations delegate many decisions to work teams, the members of those teams likely will benefit from participating in team development activities that prepare them for their roles as team members.

A call center in Charleston, South Carolina, called in a trainer from Ember Carriers, an organizational development firm, when its teamwork was suffering. The trainer, Mary Hladio, learned that the call center's director was having difficulty coaching her supervisors, who were engaged in constant conflict, divided by their areas of expertise and by whether they were new or longtime employees. Hladio arranged an off-site team-building session with the supervisors. Over two and a half days, the supervisors described their ideas of

HR How To

Supporting Line Management

Human resource management contributes most to building high-performance organizations when HR professionals understand the goals of the business and clearly demonstrate how they can help achieve those goals. Here are some ways that HR professionals can collaborate better with line managers and top executives:

- Learn about the organization's business. Whether the organization is a manufacturing corporation or a not-for-profit agency, it creates products or services and makes them available to customers or clients. HR professionals should have a basic understanding of the organization's production processes, markets, competitors, and technologies, as well as the major opportunities and threats facing the organization. Generally, this understanding will require some knowledge about finance, accounting, and other tools of business measurement.
- Follow and analyze the trends affecting the business. Anticipate where human resource

management can equip the organization to ride or drive the trends rather than merely react to laws, technology change, or market forces.
- Avoid using HRM jargon when talking to the organization's leaders. Especially at the highest levels, managers are likely to be annoyed by jargon such as *proactive, synergy,* and *value added.* At any level, managers will appreciate communication that avoids or defines technical terms and abbreviations of the HRM profession, such as PTO, FLSA, and FMLA.
- If HR professionals have not been included in strategy or planning meetings, identify specific contributions the profession can make to achieving strategic goals. Then visit the person organizing the meeting, and ask to be included in order to present the idea. Be ready to make a brief statement of how the idea will benefit the organization in terms of its business goals.
- Communicate honestly and respectfully. When line managers offer their perspectives,

listen carefully. If their attitudes or viewpoints are different from the HR perspective, take time to consider that the different viewpoint also might be important.
- Be assertive in expressing the value of effective human resource management. Know the research showing relationships between effective HR practices and organizational performance, and be ready to tell how HR programs support high performance. For example, in recent years, executives have been keenly aware of the need for talent management and succession planning.

SOURCES: Human Resources Professionals Association and Knightsbridge Human Capital Solutions, "The Role and Future of HR: The CEO's Perspective," 2011 Research Highlight, http://www.hrpa.ca, accessed May 21, 2012; Bureau of National Affairs, "Attorney Urges HR Professionals to Think Like the CEO," *HR Focus,* April 2012, p. 10; Sage (UK) Ltd., "Top 10 Tips for HR to Build Effective Relationships with Line Managers," *Sage Blog,* January 20, 2011, http://www.sage.co.uk.

a well-functioning call center, identified the issues that had triggered their conflict, and practiced communication and trust on a ropes course. They ended the program by noticing how their attitudes had shifted and by establishing mutually agreed-upon rules for how they would treat one another more constructively in the future. Six months after the training, Hladio followed up and found that the supervisors were continuing to communicate more effectively and were functioning as a cohesive team.[26]

Performance Management

In a high-performance organization, employees know the organization's goals and what they must do to help achieve those goals. HR departments can contribute to this ideal through the design of the organization's performance management system. As we discussed in Chapter 8, performance management should be related to the organization's goals. For example, banks today want tellers to do more than merely process transactions, much of which can be handled electronically. Tellers are now expected to identify customer needs and offer products, as well as to maintain positive relationships between customers and the bank. This calls for sophisticated goal setting and performance measurement—not merely numbers of transactions processed, for example, but numbers of customers retained by the branch, scores in customer satisfaction surveys, or value of certificates of deposit or other services sold.[27]

To set up a performance management system that supports the organization's goals, managers need to understand the process of employee performance. As shown in Figure 16.3, individual employees bring a set of skills and abilities to the job, and by applying a set of behaviors, they use those skills to achieve certain results. But success is more than the product of individual efforts. The organization's goals should influence each step of the process. The organization's culture and other factors influence the employees' abilities, behaviors, and results. It mustn't be forgotten that sometimes uncontrollable forces such as the current economic conditions enter the picture—for example, a salesperson can probably sell more during an economic expansion than during an economic slowdown.

This model suggests some guidelines for performance management. First, each aspect of performance management should be related to the organization's goals. Business goals should influence the kinds of employees selected and their training, the requirements of each job, and the measures used for evaluating results. Generally, this means the organization identifies what each department must do to achieve the desired results, then defines how individual employees should contribute to their department's goals. More specifically, the following guidelines describe how to make the performance management system support organizational goals:[28]

- *Define and measure performance in precise terms*—Focus on outcomes that can be defined in terms of how frequently certain behaviors occur. Include criteria that describe ways employees can add value to a product or service (such as through quantity, quality, or timeliness). Include behaviors that go beyond the minimum required to perform a job (such as helping co-workers).

Figure 16.3

Employee Performance as a Process

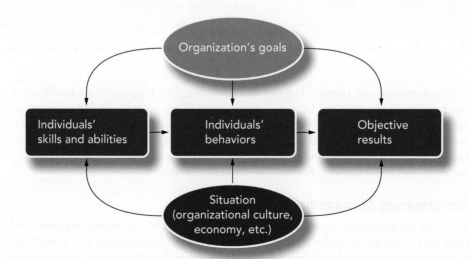

- *Link performance measures to meeting customer needs*—"Customers" may be the organization's external customers, or they may be internal customers (employees receiving services from a co-worker). Service goals for internal customers should be related to satisfying external customers.
- *Measure and correct for the effect of situational constraints*—Monitor economic conditions, the organization's culture, and other influences on performance. Measures of employees' performance should take these influences into account.

This approach gives employees the information they need to behave in ways that contribute to high performance. In addition, organizations should help employees identify and obtain the abilities they need to meet their performance goals.

Training magazine annually recognizes the top 125 organizations that excel at employee development. McDonald's Corporation ranked fifth, joining Verizon, Farmers Insurance, Miami Children's Hospital, and Mohawk Industries in the top spots.

Compensation

Organizations can reinforce the impact of this kind of performance management by linking compensation in part to performance measures. Chapter 12 described a number of methods for doing this, including merit pay, gainsharing, and profit sharing. At Intel, part of employees' variable pay (individual bonus and profit sharing) is tied to the achievement of corporate objectives, including specific objectives for operating sustainably—for example, reducing greenhouse gas emissions per chip manufactured, increasing the energy efficiency of notebook computers, and reducing the amount of chemical waste sent to landfills down to zero. The percentage of the bonus tied to meeting objectives is greater for employees near the top of the organization, where they have more control over whether the targets are met.[29] Compensation systems also can help to create the conditions that contribute to high performance, including teamwork, empowerment, and job satisfaction. For example, as discussed in Chapter 12, compensation can be linked to achievement of team objectives.

Organizations can increase empowerment and job satisfaction by including employees in decisions about compensation and by communicating the basis for decisions about pay. When the organization designs a pay structure, it can set up a task force that includes employees with direct experience in various types of jobs. Some organizations share financial information with their employees and invite them to recommend pay increases for themselves, based on their contributions. Employees also may participate in setting individual or group goals for which they can receive bonuses. Research has found that employee participation in decisions about pay policies is linked to greater satisfaction with the pay and the job.[30] And as we discussed in Chapter 11, when organizations explain their pay structures to employees, the communication can enhance employees' satisfaction and belief that the system is fair.

LO 16-5 Discuss the role of HRM technology in high-performance work systems.

HRM Technology

Human resource departments can improve their own and their organization's performance by appropriately using new technology. New technology usually involves *automation and collaboration*—that is, using equipment and information processing to perform activities that had been performed by people and facilitating electronic communication between people. Over the last few decades, automation has improved HRM efficiency by reducing the number of people needed to perform routine tasks. Using automation can free HRM experts to concentrate on ways to determine how human resource management can help the organization meet its goals so technology also can make this function more valuable.[31] For example, information technology provides ways to build and improve systems for knowledge generation and sharing, as part of a learning organization. Among the applications are databases or networking sites where employees can store and share their knowledge, online directories of employee skills and experiences, and online libraries of learning resources, such as technical manuals and employees' reports from seminars and training programs.

HRM Applications   As computers become ever more powerful, new technologies continue to be introduced. In fact, so many HRM applications are developed for use on personal computers that publications serving the profession (such as *HR Magazine* and *Workforce Management*) devote annual issues to reviewing this software. Some of the technologies that have been widely adopted are transaction processing, decision support systems, and expert systems.[32]

Transaction Processing
Computations and calculations involved in reviewing and documenting HRM decisions and practices.

Transaction processing refers to computations and calculations involved in reviewing and documenting HRM decisions and practices. It includes documenting decisions and actions associated with employee relocation, training expenses, and enrollments in courses and benefit plans. Transaction processing also includes the activities required to meet government reporting requirements, such as filling out EEO-1 reports, on which employers report information about employees' race and gender by job category. Computers enable companies to perform these tasks more efficiently. Employers can fill out computerized forms and store HRM information in databases (data stored electronically in user-specified categories), so that it is easier to find, sort, and report.

Decision Support Systems
Computer software systems designed to help managers solve problems by showing how results vary when the manager alters assumptions or data.

Decision support systems are computer software systems designed to help managers solve problems. They usually include a "what if?" feature that managers can use to enter different assumptions or data and see how the likely outcomes will change. By applying internal data or research results such as the study described in the "HR Oops!" box, this type of system can help managers make decisions for human resource planning. The manager can, for example, try out different assumptions about turnover rates to see how those assumptions affect the number of new employees needed. Or the manager can test a range of assumptions about the availability of a certain skill in the labor market, looking at the impact of the assumptions on the success of different recruiting plans. Possible applications for a decision support system include forecasting (discussed in Chapter 5) and succession planning (discussed in Chapter 9).

Expert Systems
Computer systems that support decision making by incorporating the decision rules used by people who are considered to have expertise in a certain area.

Expert systems are computer systems that incorporate the decision rules used by people who are considered to have expertise in a certain area. The systems help users make decisions by recommending actions based on the decision rules and the information provided by the users. An expert system is designed to recommend the same actions that a human expert would in a similar situation. For example, an expert

Paying More, Getting Less

Today's computing power lets employers crunch data about employees and their performance to find patterns that can help them make better predictions. In the academic world, researchers also are analyzing business data to detect patterns that may apply beyond a single organization. For example, at the University of Pennsylvania, Matthew Bidwell analyzed six years' worth of data from an investment bank to look for patterns in the pay and performance of its employees.

Bidwell found an unfavorable pattern in the bank's hiring and pay practices: When the organization brought in an outside person to fill a vacant position, it paid 18% to 20% more than when it filled a position internally (through a promotion or transfer). But compared with internal hires for that type of position, external hires got significantly lower performance evaluations during their first two years on the job.

Furthermore, the external hires were 61% more likely to leave involuntarily and 21% more likely to quit. Bidwell compared these results with pay and performance at another investment bank and at a publishing company, and he found similar patterns.

In an effort to explain the mismatch between performance and pay, Bidwell noted that the external hires tended to have more education and experience than employees who were promoted or transferred. Once on the job, they need time to build relationships within the organization, and this holds back their ability to perform well for the first couple of years. Even when jobs are filled by an internal hire, initial performance tends to suffer for a while if the person taking the job comes from a different department and therefore needs time to establish new working relationships.

Questions

1. How might a decision support system improve an organization's hiring and compensation decisions?
2. Suppose that the bank Matthew Bidwell studied is setting up a DSS for employment decisions. In general terms, how should Bidwell's data analysis shape the results provided by the DSS?

SOURCES: Rachel Emma Silverman, "Is It Better to Promote from Within?" *The Wall Street Journal,* April 3, 2012, http://online.wsj.com; "Why External Hires Get Paid More, and Perform Worse, than Internal Staff," *Knowledge@Wharton,* March 28, 2012, http://knowledge.wharton.upenn.edu; Matthew Bidwell, "Paying More to Get Less: The Effects of External Hiring versus Internal Mobility," *Administrative Science Quarterly* 56, no. 3 (2011): 369–407.

system could guide an interviewer during the selection process. Some organizations use expert systems to help employees decide how to allocate their money for benefits (as in a cafeteria plan) and help managers schedule the labor needed to complete projects. Expert systems can deliver both high quality and lower costs. By using the decision processes of experts, an expert system helps many people to arrive at decisions that reflect the expert's knowledge. An expert system helps avoid the errors that can result from fatigue and decision-making biases, such as biases in appraising employee performance, described in Chapter 8. An expert system can increase efficiency by enabling fewer or less-skilled employees to do work that otherwise would require many highly skilled employees.

In modern HR departments, transaction processing, decision support systems, and expert systems often are part of a human resource information system. Also, these technologies may be linked to employees through a network such as an intranet. Information systems and networks have been evolving rapidly; the following descriptions provide a basic introduction.

Human Resource Information Systems A standard feature of a modern HRIS is the use of *relational databases*, which store data in separate files that can be linked by common elements. These common elements are fields identifying the type of data. Commonly used fields for an HR database include name, Social Security number, job status (full- or part-time), hiring date, position, title, rate of pay, citizenship status, job history, job location, mailing address, birth date, and emergency contacts. A relational database lets a user sort the data by any of the fields. For example, depending on how the database is set up, the user might be able to look up tables listing employees by location, rates of pay for various jobs, or employees who have completed certain training courses. This system is far more sophisticated than the old-fashioned method of filing employee data by name, with one file per employee.

The ability to locate and combine many categories of data has a multitude of uses in human resource management. Databases have been developed to track employee benefit costs, training courses, and compensation. The system can meet the needs of line managers as well as the HR department. On an oil rig, for example, management might look up data listing employee names along with safety equipment issued and appropriate skill certification. HR managers at headquarters might look up data on the same employees to gather information about wage rates or training programs needed. Another popular use of an HRIS is applicant tracking, or maintaining and retrieving records of job applicants. This is much faster and easier than trying to sort through stacks of résumés. With relational databases, HR staff can retrieve information about specific applicants or obtain lists of applicants with specific skills, career goals, work history, and employment background. Such information is useful for HR planning, recruitment, succession planning, and career development. Taking the process a step further, the system could store information related to hiring and terminations. By analyzing such data, the HR department could measure the long-term success of its recruiting and selection processes.

HR Dashboard

A display of a series of HR measures, showing human resource goals and objectives and progress toward meeting them.

One of the most creative developments in HRIS technology is the **HR dashboard,** a display of a series of HR-related indicators, or measures, showing human resource goals and objectives and the progress toward meeting them. Managers with access to the HRIS can look at the HR dashboard for an easy-to-scan review of HR performance. For example, at Cisco Systems, employee development is a priority, so its HR dashboard includes a measure that tracks how many employees move and why.[33] By looking for divisions in which many employees make many lateral and upward moves, Cisco can identify divisions that are actively developing new talent.

Human Resource Management Online: E-HRM   During the last decade or so, organizations have seen the advantages of sharing information in computer networks. At the same time, the widespread adoption of the Internet has linked people around the globe. As we discussed in Chapter 2, more and more organizations are engaging in e-HRM, providing HR-related information over the Internet. Because much human resource information is confidential, organizations may do this with an intranet, which uses Internet technology but allows access only to authorized users (such as the organization's employees). For HR professionals, Internet access also offers a way to research new developments, post job openings, trade ideas with colleagues in other organizations, and obtain government documents. In this way, e-HRM combines company-specific information on a secure intranet with links to the resources on the broader Internet.

As Internet use has increasingly taken the form of social-media applications, e-HRM has moved in this direction as well. Generally speaking, social media bring networks of people together to collaborate on projects, solve problems, or socialize. Social-media applications for human resource management include YouTube access to instructional videos, Facebook-style networking sites where employees can share project updates and ideas for improvement, web pages where employees can praise

HRM Social

Communicating with Employees via Social Media

An essential part of the HR professional's job involves communicating with employees about company policies and benefits. Traditionally, those messages have been distributed in e-mail, displayed on posters, and presented in meetings. But more employers are also using social media to deliver messages aimed at building involvement and promoting collaboration. A recent survey found that about three-quarters of employers have a presence on social media, and 40% use it for communicating with employees.

Northrop Grumman uses social media to increase employee involvement in its wellness program. The aircraft and defense company uses Facebook posts and a Twitter feed to deliver messages every few days to its 73,000 employees, who are spread over more than two dozen countries. Messages include health tips and details about events such as blood pressure screenings and exercise classes. These messages are readily available to employees with mobile devices, whether they are at work, traveling, or at home.

In Britain, IBM uses social media to enhance the value of one of its employee benefits, a discount plan that gives employees a percentage off on purchases from participating sellers. IBM set up an employee blog called IBM Rewards Community, which features videos of interviews with employees telling how they used the rewards. To build participation, the company awards a prize to anyone who submits a story that is selected for publication on the blog. IBM also set up the IBM Rewards Twitter group to send daily messages about updates to company benefits.

Inchcape Retail UK also offers a discount plan as an employee benefit. Inchcape promotes it at a private (employees-only) Facebook page. Employees can visit the page to learn what offers are currently available and swap opinions about how to get the best value from the program. Features that build interest include lists of the most popular offers and retailers. Employees also can get customer support for the program through the Facebook page. A few months after the page

launched, employees were enthusiastic, and several had posted stories of their positive experience with the rewards program.

Employers that use social media for employee communications need to take some precautions, of course. One is to have a sign-up method that ensures participants are limited to current employees. Another is to reserve social media for messages that aren't personal. The collaborative nature of the media means that occasionally a user will post a negative message. The employer may handle this by appointing someone to act as the site's moderator, who responds constructively and tries to steer the conversation in a positive direction.

SOURCES: Jenny Keefe, "When to Tweet," *Employee Benefits,* December 2011, pp. 30–31; Alex Bailey, "Utilising Social Media in Benefits Communication," *Employee Benefits,* October 2011, pp. 4–5; Julie Gallant, "Companies Get the Message on Using Social Media In-House," *San Diego Business Journal,* October 31, 2011, Business & Company Resource Center, http://galenet.galegroup.com.

---

peers' accomplishments and deliver rewards, and crowdsourcing tools for performance appraisals. In terms of job design, social media can promote teamwork by providing an easy means of collaboration, and for recruiting over great distances social media allow virtual job fairs and/or selection interviews. The "HRM Social" box describes how organizations are using social media as a channel for communicating with employees. As the use of social media continues to expand, creative minds will devise many other applications that forward-thinking HR professionals can introduce as ways to get employees more fully engaged with the organization and one another.

A benefit of e-HRM is that employees can help themselves to the information they need when they need it, instead of contacting an HR staff person. For example, employees can go online to enroll in or select benefits, submit insurance claims, or fill out employee satisfaction surveys. This can be more convenient for the employees, as well as more economical for the HR department. Adding another kind of

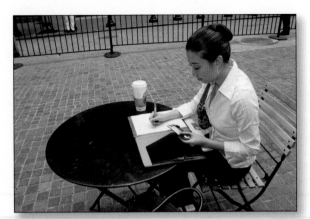

Many companies use social media applications as part of their e-HRM strategies to communicate, coach, and train employees.

convenience, some companies are offering access to online coaching. Employees can look up answers to common problems in databases, post questions for colleagues to answer, or contact a professional online. Thanks to the versatility and efficiency of this kind of coaching, employers can offer it to employees at all levels, not just executives or high-potential managers targeted for development.[34]

Most administrative and information-gathering activities in human resource management can be part of e-HRM. For example, online recruiting has become a significant part of the total recruiting effort, as candidates submit résumés online. Employers go online to retrieve suitable résumés from job search sites or retrieve information from forms they post at their own websites. For selection decisions, the organization may have candidates use one of the online testing services available; these services conduct the tests, process the results, and submit reports to employers. Companies can automate aspects of job design, such as schedules, delivery routes, and production layouts. Online appraisal or talent management systems provide data that can help managers spot high performers to reward or types of skills where additional training is a priority. After Comcast installed a computerized talent management system, supervisors caught up with a backlog of performance appraisals, and management became able to find the best employees to groom for promotions.[35] Many types of training can be conducted online, as we discussed in Chapter 7. Herman Miller, which makes office furniture, set up a performance support system that lets its salespeople use their mobile devices to learn about new product features whether they are in the office or out with clients.[36] Online surveys of employee satisfaction can be quick and easy to fill out. Besides providing a way to administer the survey, an intranet is an effective vehicle for communicating the results of the survey and management's planned response.

Not only does e-HRM provide efficient ways to carry out human resource functions, it also poses new challenges to employees and new issues for HR managers to address. The Internet's ability to link people anytime, anywhere has accelerated such trends as globalization, the importance of knowledge sharing, the need for flexibility, and cloud computing. Cloud computing is another recent advance in technology that has several implications for HR practices. **Cloud computing** involves using a network of remote servers hosted on the Internet to store, manage, and process data. These services are offered by data centers around the world (and not within an organization's offices) and are collectively called "the cloud." These services offer the ability to access information that's delivered on demand from any device, anywhere, at any time. Global giant Siemens is said to have the largest cloud computing system in the world for its more than 400,000 employees across 190 countries. In an effort to become more efficient, the company standardized its global recruitment and personal development processes into a single system via the cloud.[37]

Cloud Computing
The practice of using a network of remote servers hosted on the Internet to store, manage, and process data.

These trends change the work environment for employees. For example, employees in the Internet age are expected to be highly committed but flexible, able to move from job to job. Employees also may be connected to the organization 24/7. In the car, on vacation, in airports, and even in the bathroom, employees with handheld computers can be interrupted by work demands. Organizations depend on their human resource departments to help prepare employees for this changing work world through such activities as training, career development, performance management, and benefits packages that meet the need for flexibility and help employees manage stress.

Effectiveness of Human Resource Management

In recent years, human resource management at some organizations has responded to the quest for total quality management by taking a customer-oriented approach. For an organization's human resource division, "customers" are the organization as a whole and its other divisions. They are customers of HRM because they depend on HRM to provide a variety of services that result in a supply of talented, motivated employees. Taking this customer-oriented approach, human resource management defines its customer groups, customer needs, and the activities required to meet those needs, as shown in Table 16.2. These definitions give an organization a basis for defining goals and measures of success.

Depending on the situation, a number of techniques are available for measuring HRM's effectiveness in meeting its customers' needs. These techniques include reviewing a set of key indicators, measuring the outcomes of specific HRM activity, and measuring the economic value of HRM programs.

LO 16-6 Summarize ways to measure the effectiveness of human resource management.

Human Resource Management Audits

An **HRM audit** is a formal review of the outcomes of HRM functions. To conduct the audit, the HR department identifies key functions and the key measures of business performance and customer satisfaction that would indicate each function is succeeding. Table 16.3 lists examples of these measures for a variety of HRM functions: staffing, compensation, benefits, training, appraisal and development, and overall effectiveness. The audit may also look at any other measure associated with successful management of human resources—for instance, compliance with equal employment opportunity laws, succession planning, maintaining a safe workplace, and positive labor relations. An HRM audit using customer satisfaction measures supports the customer-oriented approach to human resource management.

HRM Audit
A formal review of the outcomes of HRM funcions, based on identifying key HRM functions and measures of business performance.

After identifying performance measures for the HRM audit, the staff carries out the audit by gathering information. The information for the key business indicators is usually available in the organization's documents. Sometimes the HR department has to create new documents for gathering specific types of data. The usual way to measure customer satisfaction is to conduct surveys. Employee attitude surveys, discussed in Chapter 10, provide information about the satisfaction of these internal customers. Many organizations conduct surveys of top line executives to get a better view of how

WHO ARE OUR CUSTOMERS?	WHAT DO OUR CUSTOMERS NEED?	HOW DO WE MEET CUSTOMER NEEDS?
Line managers	Committed employees	Qualified staffing
Strategic planners	Competent employees	Performance management
Employees		Rewards
		Training and development

Table 16.2

Customer-Oriented Perspective of Human Resource Management

Table 16.3

Key Measures of Success for an HRM Audit

BUSINESS INDICATORS	CUSTOMER SATISFACTION MEASURES
Staffing	
Average days taken to fill open requisitions	Anticipation of personnel needs
Ratio of acceptances to offers made	Timeliness of referring qualified workers to line supervisors
Ratio of minority/women applicants to representation in local labor market	Treatment of applicants
Per capita requirement costs	Skill in handling terminations
Average years of experience/education of hires per job family	Adaptability to changing labor market conditions
Compensation	
Per capita (average) merit increases	Fairness of existing job evaluation system in assigning grades and salaries
Ratio of recommendations for reclassification to number of employees	Competitiveness in local labor market
Percentage of overtime hours to straight time	Relationship between pay and performance
Ratio of average salary offers to average salary in community	Employee satisfaction with pay
Benefits	
Average unemployment compensation payment (UCP)	Promptness in handling claims
Average workers' compensation payment (WCP)	Fairness and consistency in the application of benefit policies
Benefit cost per payroll dollar	Communication of benefits to employees
Percentage of sick leave to total pay	Assistance provided to line managers in reducing potential for unnecessary claims
Training	
Percentage of employees participating in training programs per job family	Extent to which training programs meet the needs of employees and the company
Percentage of employees receiving tuition refunds	Communication to employees about available training opportunities
Training dollars per employee	Quality of introduction/orientation programs
Employee appraisal and development	
Distribution of performance appraisal ratings	Assistance in identifying management potential
Appropriate psychometric properties of appraisal forms	Organizational development activities provided by HRM department
Overall effectiveness	
Ratio of personnel staff to employee population	Accuracy and clarity of information provided to managers and employees
Turnover rate	Competence and expertise of staff
Absenteeism rate	Working relationship between organizations and HRM department
Ratio of per capita revenues to per capita cost	
Net income per employee	

SOURCE: From Chapter 1.5, "Evaluating Human Resource Effectiveness," by Anne S. Tsui and Luis R. Gomez-Mejia from *Human Resource Management: Evolving Roles & Responsibilities,* edited by Lee Dyer, 1988. Copyright 1988, Society for Human Resource Management, Alexandria, VA. Used with permission. All rights reserved.

HRM practices affect the organization's business success. To benefit from the HR profession's best practices, companies also may invite external auditing teams to audit specific HR functions. In New Hampshire, Claremont Savings Bank hired an outside specialist to conduct a comprehensive audit of its HRM practices, focusing on payroll. The auditor showed the bank's HR department how to ensure that its payroll contractor was submitting all the required taxes, and it verified that the correct amounts were being deducted for the benefits each employee had signed up for. Based on this positive experience, Claremont now conducts an external audit every three years, as well as yearly internal audits.[38]

Analyzing the Effect of HRM Programs

Another way to measure HRM effectiveness is the use of **HR analytics.** This process involves measuring a program's success in terms of whether it achieved its objectives and whether it delivered value in an economic sense. For example, if the organization sets up a training program, it should set up goals for that program, such as the training's effects on learning, behavior, and performance improvement (results). The analysis would then measure whether the training program achieved the preset goals. Wincanton, a trucking and logistics company in the United Kingdom, determined that it needed a more highly skilled workforce to continue winning the competition for customers. For warehouse workers, the company set three levels of learning objectives (two mandatory levels plus an optional level for employees seeking career development). It also let each warehouse set additional performance measures for serving its own set of customers. Two years after launching the training program, Wincanton measured its success in terms of 2,500 warehouse workers trained, a decline in time lost to accidents (down 7.5% in the first year and another 10.3% in the second year), and a 22% increase in the overall score for employee engagement.[39]

The analysis can take an economic approach that measures the dollar value of the program's costs and benefits. Successful programs should deliver value that is greater than the programs' costs. Costs include employees' compensation as well as the costs to administer HRM programs such as training, employee development, or satisfaction surveys. Benefits could include a reduction in the costs associated with employee absenteeism and turnover, as well as improved productivity associated with better selection and training programs.

In general, HR departments should be able to improve their performance through some combination of greater efficiency and greater effectiveness. Greater efficiency means the HR department uses fewer and less-costly resources to perform its functions. Greater effectiveness means that what the HR department does—for example, selecting employees or setting up a performance management system—has a more beneficial effect on employees' and the organization's performance. The computing power available to today's organizations, coupled with people who have skills in HR analytics, enables companies to find more ways than ever to identify practices associated with greater efficiency and effectiveness. For example, organizations can measure patterns in employees' social networks—who is talking to whom, how often—and combine that with performance data. One lesson from such research is that a recruiter's closest friends and colleagues are less useful as a source of leads to qualified job candidates than are people the recruiter communicates with only occasionally. These less-close associates are likelier to have acquaintances who aren't already familiar to the recruiter.[40]

HRM's potential to affect employees' well-being and the organization's performance makes human resource management an exciting field. As we have shown throughout the book, every HRM function calls for decisions that have the potential to help individuals and organizations achieve their goals. For HR managers to fulfill that potential, they must ensure that their decisions are well grounded. The field of human resource management provides tremendous opportunity to future researchers and managers who want to make a difference in many people's lives.

HR Analytics
Type of assessment of HRM effectiveness that involves determining the impact of, or the financial cost and benefits of, a program or practice.

THINKING ETHICALLY

HOW CAN HRM HELP MAINTAIN AN ETHICAL CULTURE?

On some level, the choice to behave ethically is always a personal choice. However, there are some measures that organizations can take to promote ethical conduct. And many of those efforts can start or be supported by human resource professionals.

One approach, for example, is to create a climate of trust. Businesspeople can readily see that trust provides a strong foundation for all kinds of business relationships, including purchase contracts, labor-management agreements, and employees' confidence in the fairness of supervisors' decisions. People are more likely to trust an organization, manager, or employee when they see evidence of competence, openness and honesty, concern for stakeholders including employees and the community, reliability in keeping commitments, and identification with the organization in the sense that an individual's values match up with the values expressed by the organization. HR professionals can provide performance feedback, training, coaching, and rewards to foster the development of many of these drivers of trust. Job design in which employees are empowered to deliver excellent customer care, make well-crafted products, or deliver other valued outcomes helps to align individual practices with an organization's highest values.

Another way to maintain an ethical culture is to define ethical conduct and ethical abuses and to respond appropriately when these are detected. Ethical conduct should be rewarded. Employee development programs should include goals for the trust-building ethical practices of leaders, and developmental work assignments should include opportunities to try out those kinds of behavior. Ethical abuses should be punished, not ignored or hidden. When ethical violations are tolerated, employees take away the message that the organization is not actually serious about ethics. HR professionals can support these objectives with performance measures and pay policies that reward ethical conduct, never ethical lapses.

Questions

1. Imagine that you work in the human resource department of a company that sells medical equipment. One of the salespeople, who has an enormous amount of student loans, is tempted to misrepresent the uses of the equipment in order to increase his sales and therefore the commissions he earns. As an HR professional, how much can you do to shape a salesperson's conduct so that it remains ethical (and legal)?
2. Would you prefer to work at a company where the human resource department has developed and established policies to promote ethical conduct, such as the ones described here? Why or why not?

SOURCES: Pamela Shockley-Zalabak, "A Matter of Trust," *Communication World*, May–June 2011, pp. 17–21; Ross Tartell, "Can Leadership Ethics Be Learned?" *Training*, May/June 2011, EBSCOhost, http://web.ebscohost.com; Christiane Krieger-Boden, "Ethics, Trust and Altruism in Society, Politics and Business," background paper to Global Economic Symposium 2011, August 8, 2011, accessed at http://www.global-economic-symposium.org.

SUMMARY

LO 16-1 Define high-performance work systems, and identify the elements of such a system.

A high-performance work system is the right combination of people, technology, and organizational structure that makes full use of the organization's resources and opportunities in achieving its goals. The elements of a high-performance work system are organizational structure, task design, people, reward systems, and information systems. These elements must work together in a smoothly functioning whole.

LO 16-2 Summarize the outcomes of a high-performance work system.

A high-performance work system achieves the organization's goals, typically including growth, productivity, and high profits. On the way to achieving these overall goals, the high-performance work system meets such intermediate goals as high quality, innovation, customer satisfaction, job satisfaction, and reduced absenteeism and turnover.

LO 16-3 Describe the conditions that create a high-performance work system.

Many conditions contribute to high-performance work systems by giving employees skills, incentives, knowledge, autonomy, and employee satisfaction. Teamwork and empowerment can make work more satisfying and provide a means for employees to improve quality and productivity. Organizations can improve performance by creating a learning organization in which people constantly learn and share knowledge so that they continually expand their capacity to achieve the results they desire. In a high-performance organization, employees experience job satisfaction or even "occupational intimacy." For long-run high performance, organizations and employees must be ethical as well.

LO 16-4 Explain how human resource management can contribute to high performance.

Jobs should be designed to foster teamwork and employee empowerment. Recruitment and selection should focus on obtaining employees who have the qualities necessary for teamwork, empowerment, and knowledge sharing. When the organization selects for teamwork and decision-making skills, it may have to provide training in specific job tasks. Training also is important because of its role in creating a learning organization. The performance management system should be related to the organization's goals, with a focus on meeting internal and external customers' needs. Compensation should include links to performance, and employees should be included in decisions about compensation. Research suggests that it is more effective to improve HRM practices as a whole than to focus on one or two isolated practices.

LO 16-5 Discuss the role of HRM technology in high-performance work systems.

Technology can improve the efficiency of the human resource management functions and support knowledge sharing. HRM applications involve transaction processing, decision support systems, and expert systems, often as part of a human resource information system using relational databases, which can improve the efficiency of routine tasks and the quality of decisions. With Internet technology, organizations can use e-HRM to let all the organization's employees help themselves to the HR information they need whenever they need it.

LO 16-6 Summarize ways to measure the effectiveness of human resource management.

Taking a customer-oriented approach, HRM can improve quality by defining the internal customers who use its services and determining whether it is meeting those customers' needs. One way to do this is with an HRM audit, a formal review of the outcomes of HRM functions. The audit may look at any measure associated with successful management of human resources. Audit information may come from the organization's documents and surveys of customer satisfaction. Another way to measure HRM effectiveness is to analyze specific programs or activities. The analysis can measure success in terms of whether a program met its objectives and whether it delivered value in an economic sense, such as by leading to productivity improvements.

KEY TERMS

brand alignment, 515
cloud computing, 526
continuous learning, 513
decision support systems, 522

expert systems, 522
high-performance work system, 509
HR analytics, 529
HR dashboard, 524

HRM audit, 527
learning organization, 513
transaction processing, 522

REVIEW AND DISCUSSION QUESTIONS

1. What is a high-performance work system? What are its elements? Which of these elements involve human resource management?
2. As it has become clear that HRM can help create and maintain high-performance work systems, it appears that organizations will need two kinds of human resource professionals. One kind focuses on identifying how HRM can contribute to high performance. The other kind develops expertise in particular HRM functions, such as how to administer a benefits program that complies with legal requirements. Which aspect of HRM is more interesting to you? Why?
3. How can teamwork, empowerment, knowledge sharing, and job satisfaction contribute to high performance?

4. If an organization can win customers, employees, or investors through deception, why would ethical behavior contribute to high performance?
5. How can an organization promote ethical behavior among its employees?
6. Summarize how each of the following HR functions can contribute to high performance.
   a. Job design
   b. Recruitment and selection
   c. Training and development
   d. Performance management
   e. Compensation
7. How can HRM technology make a human resource department more productive? How can technology improve the quality of HRM decisions?
8. Why should human resource departments measure their effectiveness? What are some ways they can go about measuring effectiveness?

EXPERIENCING HR

Divide into groups of about four students each. This exercise will give your group a chance to review concepts from this book while exploring the current state of HRM technology.

As a group, select one of the end-of-chapter cases that interests you. It can be a case from this chapter or any of the earlier chapters. Review the case, and list the issues that the organization in the case was facing. With your group members, discuss and create a list of the kinds of information from inside and outside the organization that would help the organization address the issues you listed.

Using an Internet search engine, search information on terms such as "human resource information system," "HR software," and "HRIS" to learn about the kinds of software available to support HR decision making. Identify types of software that could help the organization in the case you are considering. Discuss the ideas that each group member found, and seek a consensus on the products that would be most relevant to the case.

With your group, prepare a 5-minute presentation that summarizes the problem in the case and recommends technology that could help the organization solve that problem and/or prevent the problem from occurring in the future.

TAKING RESPONSIBILITY: Aon Hewitt Wants to Help Employers Manage Health Benefits

When companies around the world want help in designing HR programs or a qualified contractor for outsourcing HRM functions, many of them turn to one of the giants in the field, Aon Hewitt. For its part, Aon Hewitt is constantly scanning its business environment, looking for areas in which employers are likely to need more help. An obvious growth area in the United States in recent years is help with the cost of providing employees (and for some employers, retirees) with health insurance.

For the past few decades, the usual approach to providing this employee benefit is for employers to purchase group health insurance plans and enroll full-time employees and their dependents. Some employers offer a choice of several different insurance plans, and some extend coverage to employees after they retire. This benefit is highly valued, but offering it is becoming a burden. The employers in Aon Hewitt's database are beginning to spend more than $10,000 annually per person.

Aon Hewitt sees an opportunity that also plays into employees' desire for flexible benefits packages: the creation of health care exchanges for employers to offer. Aon Hewitt acts as a broker: it arranges for various insurers to make available different insurance plans with different costs and benefit levels. Aon Hewitt sets up an information site where participating employees can see choices arranged by insurance carrier, level of coverage (basic through premium), plan features, and prices. Individuals go to the exchange, review the options, and if they wish, get advice from an exchange employee. Then they select the plan they prefer, paid for with some combination of employer and employee dollars: presumably, the employer would pay up to some set level, and the employee would bear any additional cost. Because the exchange handles the enrollment and billing for the plans, the employer may pay less for administration. Also, employers' HR departments don't have to shop around for the best deals on insurance every year. Aon Hewitt's CEO, Kristi Savacool, sees a parallel with trends in retirement benefits: employers used to offer mainly defined-benefit plans, where the employer invested the funds and later made promised pension payments, but now most have switched to defined-contribution plans controlled largely by the employees themselves.

The firm first introduced the health care exchanges as a retiree benefit. Employers offering health insurance to retirees were enthusiastic, and more than 2.4 million retirees have signed up. As the demand for this service grew, Aon Hewitt decided to make it available for employers to offer their current employees. In spite of the growing costs, most of the large employers served by Aon Hewitt have expressed an intention to continue offering health coverage, so they are extremely interested in ways to do so more economically. Whether or not states create the health insurance exchanges called for under the recent health care reform law, the state exchanges are meant to serve individuals and medium-sized and small businesses, leaving large companies (those with at least 1,000 full-time employees) as a wide-open market for Aon Hewitt's exchanges. Among its current clients, Aon Hewitt expects that nearly half will include its exchange in their benefits packages.

Besides setting up health care exchanges, Aon Hewitt helps set up wellness programs aimed at lowering the need for expensive services. Aon Hewitt's services include designing the programs and preparing communications to employees aimed at promoting healthy behavior.

Questions

1. How compatible would Aon Hewitt's health insurance exchange be with the elements of a high-performance work system? Explain.
2. Suppose you work for the HR department of a large company that is planning to replace its traditional two choices of health insurance with access to the health insurance exchange. How would you communicate about this change in a way that maintains the company's high performance?
3. How could you use information technology (for example, e-HRM and social media) to implement a health insurance exchange at your company?

SOURCES: Russ Banham, "Private Exchanges Link Buyers, Sellers," *Business Insurance*, May 7, 2012, Business & Company Resource Center, http://galenet.galegroup.com; Elizabeth Galentine, "No Such Thing as 'Wait and See,'" *Employee Benefit Adviser*, March 2012, Business & Company Resource Center, http://galenet.galegroup.com (interview with Kristi Savacool); BNA, "Consulting Firm Aon Hewitt to Form National Exchange for Large Employers," *Managing Benefits Plans*, June 2011, p. 11; Dave Lindorff, "Early Health Exchange," *Treasury & Risk*, June 2011, p. 20.

MANAGING TALENT: How Mohawk Industries' HR Practices Empower Employees

Mohawk Industries produces and sells commercial and residential flooring, including carpet, wood, ceramic tile, vinyl, and more. The company started as a carpet manufacturer in the 1800s and now operates on three continents, with headquarters in Calhoun, Georgia. The company operates its own trucking fleet and distributes through its warehouses to stores and contractors.

Mohawk's corporate vision for sustainability includes a "people strategy" that emphasizes fair labor practices and supports employees' involvement in their communities. The company prides itself on its commitment to employee training and development. Four years in a row, it has been named to *Training* magazine's list of the top 125 organizations for training. In addition, its benefits package includes benefits that reflect a commitment to learning: tuition reimbursement for employees enrolled in college, as well as a college savings plan.

Mohawk has sought ways to give employees more control over their career growth at the company. It views self-service as one tool for that empowerment. The company set up a human resource information system, and to make it easily accessible to employees who aren't tied to their desks, Mohawk installed kiosks in manufacturing plants and created a version of the system for salespeople's mobile devices. With the HRIS, employees can go online anytime to update their personal information or find answers to questions about their benefits.

Mohawk's human resources department is also committed to using technology to communicate with employees and deliver training. For example, the home page on every employee's computer is a myMohawk page that serves as a portal to the company's intranet. The HR team posts information about training opportunities and other messages on myMohawk. It also posts polls as a way to get employees more actively engaged with the site. The company recently added blogs aimed at encouraging employees to share ideas. It also set up a social-media application that employees can use to find help from subject-matter experts, with the hope that this will contribute to the establishment of informal mentoring relationships. Mohawk hopes to improve its training delivery by expanding the offerings that use other languages and reflect the cultural differences of the locations where it operates.

To prepare employees for the choices they would be making during the annual enrollment in employee benefits, the company supplemented face-to-face meetings with e-mail reminders and links to podcasts. Most popular, though, was a company-produced nine-part video series in which actors portrayed characters making wise choices about their employee benefits to meet a variety of needs. That series, titled "Johnny's Diner," was available on the company's intranet, on YouTube, and on a DVD mailed to employees' homes. Mohawk's learning director, Amanda Arnwine, rated "Johnny's Diner" a success based on the number of employees who watched and the percentage of employees who chose their health care plan without further assistance.

In addition to its commitment to learning, Mohawk is committed to employee health, which not only can boost employees' well-being and engagement, but also can reduce costs of providing health benefits. Mohawk arranged for an organization called PictureWellness to deliver a wellness plan to employees. PictureWellness offers health risk assessments, exercise classes, nutrition seminars, and more. Mohawk estimates that it saved an average of $4,000 per employee on health care costs for employees who participated in the wellness program.

Questions

1. Based on the information given, what conditions at Mohawk Industries are those of a high-performance organization?
2. Besides the measures described here, what else could Mohawk do to increase employee empowerment and employee engagement?
3. Would you describe Mohawk as a learning organization? Why or why not? What else could it do to promote continuous learning and knowledge sharing?

SOURCES: Mohawk Industries, "Corporate Profile," http://mohawkind .com, accessed May 21, 2012; "Growing Obesity and Rising Healthcare Costs Plague Employers," *Times Union (Albany, NY)*, May 16, 2012, http:// www.timesunion.com; Margery Weinstein, "Mohawk Maximizes Learning," *Training*, January–February 2012, Business & Company Resource Center, http://galenet.galegroup.com.

 TWITTER FOCUS: Employees Make a Difference at Amy's Ice Creams

Using Twitter, continue the conversation about strategically managing the HRM function by reading the Amy's Ice Creams case at **www.mhhe.com/noefund5e**. Engage with your classmates and instructor via Twitter to chat about Amy's unique approach to HRM using the case questions posted on the Noe website. Don't have a Twitter account yet? See the instructions for getting started on the Online Learning Center.

NOTES

1. Sarah Murray, "Focus on Productivity Brings Use of Business Practices," *Financial Times*, March 24, 2011, Business & Company Resource Center, http://galenet.galegroup.com.
2. S. Snell and J. Dean, "Integrated Manufacturing and Human Resource Management: A Human Capital Perspective," *Academy of Management Journal* 35 (1992), pp. 467–504.
3. M. A. Huselid, "The Impact of Human Resource Management Practices on Turnover, Productivity, and Corporate Financial Performance," *Academy of Management Journal* 38 (1995), pp. 635–72; U.S. Department of Labor, *High-Performance Work Practices and Firm Performance* (Washington, DC: U.S. Government Printing Office, 1993); and J. Combs, Y. Liu, A. Hall, and D. Ketchen, "How Much Do High-Performance Work Practices Matter? A Meta-Analysis of Their Effects on Organizational Performance," *Personnel Psychology* 59 (2006), pp. 501–28.
4. R. N. Ashkenas, "Beyond the Fads: How Leaders Drive Change with Results," *Human Resource Planning* 17 (1994), pp. 25–44; Ronald M. Katz, "OPTimize Your Workforce," *HR Magazine*, October 2009, p. 85; and Luis Echevarria, "Creating Call Center Agents Who Think for Themselves," *Response*, June 2011, p. 45.
5. J. Arthur, "The Link between Business Strategy and Industrial Relations Systems in American Steel Minimills," *Industrial and Labor Relations Review* 45 (1992), pp. 488–506.
6. J. A. Neal and C. L. Tromley, "From Incremental Change to Retrofit: Creating High-Performance Work Systems," *Academy of Management Executive* 9 (1995), pp. 42–54; and M. A. Huselid, "The Impact of Human Resource Management Practices on Turnover, Productivity, and Corporate Financial Performance," *Academy of Management Journal* 38 (1995), pp. 635–72.

7. P. Coy, "A Renaissance in U.S. Manufacturing," *Bloomberg Businessweek*, May 9, 2011, pp. 11–12.

8. D. McCann and C. Margerison, "Managing High-Performance Teams," *Training and Development Journal*, November 1989, pp. 52–60.

9. D. Senge, "The Learning Organization Made Plain and Simple," *Training and Development Journal*, October 1991, pp. 37–44.

10. M. A. Gephart, V. J. Marsick, M. E. Van Buren, and M. S. Spiro, "Learning Organizations Come Alive," *Training and Development* 50 (1996), pp. 34–45.

11. T. T. Baldwin, C. Danielson, and W. Wiggenhorn, "The Evolution of Learning Strategies in Organizations: From Employee Development to Business Redefinition," *Academy of Management Executive* 11 (1997), pp. 47–58; J. J. Martocchio and T. T. Baldwin, "The Evolution of Strategic Organizational Training," in *Research in Personnel and Human Resource Management* 15, ed. G. R. Ferris (Greenwich, CT: JAI Press, 1997), pp. 1–46; and "Leveraging HR and Knowledge Management in a Challenging Economy," *HR Magazine*, June 2009, pp. S1–S9.

12. H. James Wilson, "Employees, Measure Yourselves," *The Wall Street Journal*, April 2, 2012, http://online.wsj.com.

13. T. A. Judge, C. J. Thoresen, J. E. Bono, and G. K. Patton, "The Job Satisfaction-Job Performance Relationship: A Qualitative and Quantitative Review," *Psychological Bulletin* 127 (2001), pp. 376–407; and R. A. Katzell, D. E. Thompson, and R. A. Guzzo, "How Job Satisfaction and Job Performance Are and Are Not Linked," *Job Satisfaction*, eds. C. J. Cranny, P. C. Smith, and E. F. Stone (New York: Lexington Books, 1992), pp. 195–217.

14. Towers Watson, "Employee Engagement to the Power of Three," *Viewpoints*, March 2011, http://www.towerswatson.com.

15. Aon Hewitt, "Trends in Global Employee Engagement," 2011, http://www.aon.com.

16. Kathleen Kindle, "Brand Alignment: Getting It Right," http://www.siegelgate.com/blog, accessed May 30, 2012; Aon Hewitt, "Trends in Global Employee Engagement," 2011, http://www.aon.com.

17. P. E. Boverie and M. Kroth, *Transforming Work: The Five Keys to Achieving Trust, Commitment, and Passion in the Workplace* (Cambridge, MA: Perseus, 2001), pp. 71–72, 79.

18. R. P. Gephart Jr., "Introduction to the Brave New Workplace: Organizational Behavior in the Electronic Age," *Journal of Organizational Behavior* 23 (2002), pp. 327–44.

19. Kristin Samuelson, "Secrets of Succeeding with Ethics," *Chicago Tribune*, April 15, 2012, sec. 2, p. 3.

20. Ibid.; Max H. Bazerman and Ann E. Tenbrunsel, "Ethical Breakdowns," *Harvard Business Review*, April 2011, http://hbr.org; and Ethics Resource Center, "Why Have a Code of Conduct," May 29, 2009, http://www.ethics.org.

21. Amy Fliegelman Olli, "Aligning Ethics and Compliance with Business Objectives," *Ethisphere*, March 31, 2011, http://ethisphere.com.

22. W. F. Cascio, *Costing Human Resources: The Financial Impact of Behavior in Organizations*, 3rd ed. (Boston: PWS-Kent, 1991); and Gergana Markova, "Can Human Resource Management Make a Big Difference in a Small Company?" *International Journal of Strategic Management* 9, no. 2 (2009), pp. 73–80.

23. B. Becker and M. A. Huselid, "High-Performance Work Systems and Firm Performance: A Synthesis of Research and Managerial Implications," in *Research in Personnel and Human Resource Management* 16, ed. G. R. Ferris (Stamford, CT: JAI Press, 1998), pp. 53–101.

24. B. Becker and B. Gerhart, "The Impact of Human Resource Management on Organizational Performance: Progress and Prospects," *Academy of Management Journal* 39 (1996), pp. 779–801.

25. David Hatch, "Can Apple Polish Lowe's Reputation?" *U.S. News & World Report*, May 15, 2012, http://money.usnews.com.

26. "Climbing to Higher Ground," *T + D*, September 2010, p. 80.

27. "The Evolving Teller Role: Measuring Performance, Creating Accountability," *TellerVision*, March 2012, pp. 1–3 (interview with Linda Eagle).

28. H. J. Bernardin, C. M. Hagan, J. S. Kane, and P. Villanova, "Effective Performance Management: A Focus on Precision, Customers, and Situational Constraints," in *Performance Appraisal: State of the Art in Practice*, ed. J. W. Smither (San Francisco: Jossey-Bass, 1998), p. 56.

29. Patrick Darling, "Intel Sets 2020 Environmental Goals," Intel newsroom blog, May 17, 2012, http://newsroom.intel.com; Intel, *2011 Corporate Responsibility Report*, http://www.intel.com, accessed May 18, 2012.

30. L. R. Gomez-Mejia and D. B. Balkin, *Compensation, Organizational Strategy, and Firm Performance* (Cincinnati: South-Western, 1992); and G. D. Jenkins and E. E. Lawler III, "Impact of Employee Participation in Pay Plan Development," *Organizational Behavior and Human Performance* 28 (1981), pp. 111–28.

31. S. Shrivastava and J. Shaw, "Liberating HR through Technology," *Human Resource Management* 42, no. 3 (2003), pp. 201–17.

32. R. Broderick and J. W. Boudreau, "Human Resource Management, Information Technology, and the Competitive Edge," *Academy of Management Executive* 6 (1992), pp. 7–17.

33. N. Lockwood, *Maximizing Human Capital: Demonstrating HR Value with Key Performance Indicators* (Alexandria, VA: SHRM Research Quarterly, 2006).

34. Grace Ahrend, Fred Diamond, and Pat Gill Webber, "Virtual Coaching: Using Technology to Boost Performance," *Chief Learning Officer*, July 2010, pp. 44–47.

35. Kim Girard, "A Talent for Talent," *CFO*, May 2011, pp. 27–28.

36. Bob Mosher and Jeremy Smith, "The Case for Performance Support," *Training*, November–December 2011, Business & Company Resource Center, http://galenet.galegroup.com.

37. Matt Charney, "Five Reasons Why Cloud Computing Matters for Recruiting and Hiring," *Monster.com*, http://hiring.monster.com/hr, accessed May 30, 2012; Daniel Shane, "A Human Giant," *Information Age*, http://www.information-age.com, accessed May 30, 2012.

38. Eric Krell, "Auditing Your HR Department," *HR Magazine*, September 2011, http://www.shrm.org.

39. Sean Cusack, "Train to Gain," *Transport and Logistics*, October 2011, pp. 53–56.

40. Steve Lohr, "The Age of Big Data," *The New York Times*, February 11, 2012, http://www.nytimes.com.

Glossary

Achievement Tests: Tests that measure a person's existing knowledge and skills.

Action Learning: Training in which teams get an actual problem, work on solving it and commit to an action plan, and are accountable for carrying it out.

Adventure Learning: A teamwork and leadership training program based on the use of challenging, structured outdoor activities.

Affirmative Action: An organization's active effort to find opportunities to hire or promote people in a particular group.

Agency Shop: Union security arrangement that requires the payment of union dues but not union membership.

Alternative Dispute Resolution (ADR): Methods of solving a problem by bringing in an impartial outsider but not using the court system.

Alternative Work Arrangements: Methods of staffing other than the traditional hiring of full-time employees (for example, use of independent contractors, on-call workers, temporary workers, and contract company workers).

American Federation of Labor and Congress of Industrial Organizations (AFL-CIO): An association that seeks to advance the shared interests of its member unions at the national level.

Apprenticeship: A work-study training method that teaches job skills through a combination of on-the-job training and classroom training.

Aptitude Tests: Tests that assess how well a person can learn or acquire skills and abilities.

Arbitration: Conflict resolution procedure in which an arbitrator or arbitration board determines a binding settlement.

Assessment: Collecting information and providing feedback to employees about their behavior, communication style, or skills.

Assessment Center: A wide variety of specific selection programs that use multiple selection methods to rate applicants or job incumbents on their management potential.

Associate Union Membership: Alternative form of union membership in which members receive discounts on insurance and credit cards rather than representation in collective bargaining.

Avatars: Computer depictions of trainees, which the trainees manipulate in an online role-play.

Balanced Scorecard: A combination of performance measures directed toward the company's long- and short-term goals and used as the basis for awarding incentive pay.

Behavior Description Interview (BDI): A structured interview in which the interviewer asks the candidate to describe how he or she handled a type of situation in the past.

Behavioral Observation Scale (BOS): A variation of a BARS which uses all behaviors necessary for effective performance to rate performance at a task.

Behaviorally Anchored Rating Scale (BARS): Method of performance measurement that rates behavior in terms of a scale showing specific statements of behavior that describe different levels of performance.

Benchmarking: A procedure in which an organization compares its own practices against those of successful competitors.

Benchmarks: A measurement tool that gathers ratings of a manager's use of skills associated with success in managing.

Bona Fide Occupational Qualification (BFOQ): A necessary (not merely preferred) qualification for performing a job.

Brand Alignment: The process of ensuring that HR policies, practices, and programs support or are congruent with an organization's overall culture (or brand), products, and services.

Cafeteria-Style Plan: A benefits plan that offers employees a set of alternatives from which they can choose the types and amounts of benefits they want.

Calibration Meeting: Meeting at which managers discuss employee performance ratings and provide evidence supporting their ratings with the goal of eliminating the influence of rating errors.

Cash Balance Plan: Retirement plan in which the employer sets up an individual account for each employee and contributes a percentage of the employee's salary; the account earns interest at a predefined rate.

Checkoff Provision: Contract provision under which the employer, on behalf of the union, automatically deducts union dues from employees' paychecks.

Closed Shop: Union security arrangement under which a person must be a union member before being hired; illegal for those covered by the National Labor Relations Act.

Cloud Computing: The practice of using a network of remote servers hosted on the Internet to store, manage, and process data.

Coach: A peer or manager who works with an employee to motivate the employee, help him or her develop skills, and provide reinforcement and feedback.

Cognitive Ability Tests: Tests designed to measure such mental abilities as verbal skills, quantitative skills, and reasoning ability.

Collective Bargaining: Negotiation between union representatives and management representatives to arrive at a contract defining conditions of employment for the term of the contract and to administer that contract.

Commissions: Incentive pay calculated as a percentage of sales.

Communities of Practice: Groups of employees who work together, learn from each other, and develop a common understanding of how to get work accomplished.

Compensatory Model: Process of arriving at a selection decision in which a very high score on one type of assessment can make up for a low score on another.

Competency: An area of personal capability that enables employees to perform their work successfully.

Concurrent Validation: Research that consists of administering a test to people who currently hold a job, then comparing their scores to existing measures of job performance.

Consolidated Omnibus Budget Reconciliation Act (COBRA): Federal law that requires employers to permit employees or their dependents to extend their health insurance coverage at group rates for up to 36 months following a qualifying event, such as a layoff, reduction in hours, or the employee's death.

Construct Validity: Consistency between a high score on a test and high level of a construct such as intelligence or leadership ability, as well as between

mastery of this construct and successful performance of the job.

Content Validity: Consistency between the test items or problems and the kinds of situations or problems that occur on the job.

Continuous Learning: Each employee's and each group's ongoing efforts to gather information and apply the information to their decisions in a learning organization.

Contributory Plan: Retirement plan funded by contributions from the employer and employee.

Coordination Training: Team training that teaches the team how to share information and make decisions to obtain the best team performance.

Core Competency: A set of knowledges and skills that make the organization superior to competitors and create value for customers.

Corporate Campaigns: Bringing public, financial, or political pressure on employers during union organization and contract negotiation.

Craft Union: Labor union whose members all have a particular skill or occupation.

Criterion-Related Validity: A measure of validity based on showing a substantial correlation between test scores and job performance scores.

Critical-Incident Method: Method of performance measurement based on managers' records of specific examples of the employee acting in ways that are either effective or ineffective.

Cross-Cultural Preparation: Training to prepare employees and their family members for an assignment in a foreign country.

Cross-Training: Team training in which team members understand and practice each other's skills so that they are prepared to step in and take another member's place.

Culture Shock: Disillusionment and discomfort that occur during the process of adjusting to a new culture.

Decision Support Systems: Computer software systems designed to help managers solve problems by showing how results vary when the manager alters assumptions or data.

Defined Benefit Plan: Pension plan that guarantees a specified level of retirement income.

Defined Contribution Plan: Retirement plan in which the employer sets up an individual account for each employee and specifies the size of the investment into that account.

Delayering: Reducing the number of levels in the organization's job structure.

Development: The acquisition of knowledge, skills, and behaviors that improve an employee's ability to meet changes in job requirements and in customer demands.

Differential Piece Rates: Incentive pay in which the piece rate is higher when a greater amount is produced.

Direct Applicants: People who apply for a vacancy without prompting from the organization.

Disability: Under the Americans with Disabilities Act, a physical or mental impairment that substantially limits one or more major life activities, a record of having such an impairment, or being regarded as having such an impairment.

Disparate Impact: A condition in which employment practices are seemingly neutral yet disproportionately exclude a protected group from employment opportunities.

Disparate Treatment: Differing treatment of individuals, where the differences are based on the individuals' race, color, religion, sex, national origin, age, or disability status.

Diversity Training: Training designed to change employee attitudes about diversity and/or develop skills needed to work with a diverse workforce.

Downsizing: The planned elimination of large numbers of personnel with the goal of enhancing the organization's competitiveness.

Downward Move: Assignment of an employee to a position with less responsibility and authority.

Due-Process Policies: Policies that formally lay out the steps an employee may take to appeal the employer's decision to terminate that employee.

EEO-1 Report: The EEOC's Employer Information Report, which details the number of women and minorities employed in nine different job categories.

E-Learning: Receiving training via the Internet or the organization's intranet.

Electronic Human Resource Management (e-HRM):   The processing and transmission of digitized HR information, especially using computer networking and the Internet.

Electronic Performance Support System (EPSS):   Computer application that provides access to skills training, information, and expert advice as needed.

Employee Assistance Program (EAP):   A referral service that employees can use to seek professional treatment for emotional problems or substance abuse.

Employee Benefits: Compensation in forms other than cash.

Employee Development: The combination of formal education, job experiences, relationships, and assessment of personality and abilities to help employees prepare for the future of their careers.

Employee Empowerment: Giving employees responsibility and authority to make decisions regarding all aspects of product development or customer service.

Employee Engagement: The degree to which employees are fully involved in their work and the strength of their job and company commitment.

Employee Retirement Income Security Act (ERISA):   Federal law that increased the responsibility of pension plan trustees to protect retirees, established certain rights related to vesting and portability, and created the Pension Benefit Guarantee Corporation.

Employee Stock Ownership Plan (ESOP):   An arrangement in which the organization distributes shares of stock to all its employees by placing it in a trust.

Employee Wellness Program (EWP):   A set of communications, activities, and facilities designed to change health-related behaviors in ways that reduce health risks.

Employment at Will: Employment principle that if there is no specific employment contract saying otherwise, the employer or employee may end an employment relationship at any time, regardless of cause.

Equal Employment Opportunity (EEO):   The condition in which all individuals have an equal chance for employment, regardless of their race, color, religion, sex, age, disability, or national origin.

Equal Employment Opportunity Commission (EEOC):   Agency of the Department of Justice charged with enforcing Title VII of the Civil Rights Act of 1964 and other antidiscrimination laws.

Ergonomics: The study of the interface between individuals' physiology and the characteristics of the physical work environment.

Ethics: The fundamental principles of right and wrong.

Evidence-Based HR: Collecting and using data to show that human resource practices have a positive influence on the company's bottom line or key stakeholders.

Exempt Employees: Managers, outside salespeople, and any other employees not covered by the FLSA requirement for overtime pay.

Exit Interview: A meeting of a departing employee with the employee's supervisor and/or a human resource specialist to discuss the employee's reasons for leaving.

Expatriates: Employees assigned to work in another country.

Experience Rating: The number of employees a company has laid off in the past and the cost of providing them with unemployment benefits.

Experiential Programs: Training programs in which participants learn concepts and apply them by simulating behaviors involved and analyzing the activity, connecting it with real-life situations.

Expert Systems: Computer systems that support decision making by incorporating the decision rules used by people who are considered to have expertise in a certain area.

External Labor Market: Individuals who are actively seeking employment.

Externship: Employee development through a full-time temporary position at another organization.

Fact Finder: Third party to collective bargaining who reports the reasons for a dispute, the views and arguments of both sides, and possibly a recommended settlement, which the parties may decline.

Fair Labor Standards Act (FLSA): Federal law that establishes a minimum wage and requirements for overtime pay and child labor.

Family and Medical Leave Act (FMLA): Federal law requiring organizations with 50 or more employees to provide up to 12 weeks of unpaid leave after childbirth or adoption, to care for a seriously ill family member, or for an employee's own serious illness.

Feedback: Information employers give employees about their skills and knowledge and where these assets fit into the organization's plans.

Fleishman Job Analysis System: Job analysis technique that asks subject-matter experts to evaluate a job in terms of the abilities required to perform the job.

Flexible Spending Account: Employee-controlled pretax earnings set aside to pay for certain eligible expenses, such as health care expenses, during the same year.

Flextime: A scheduling policy in which full-time employees may choose starting and ending times within guidelines specified by the organization.

Forced-Distribution Method: Method of performance measurement that assigns a certain percentage of employees to each category in a set of categories.

Forecasting: The attempts to determine the supply of and demand for various types of human resources to predict areas within the organization where there will be labor shortages or surpluses.

Four-Fifths Rule: Rule of thumb that finds evidence of potential discrimination if an organization's hiring rate for a minority group is less than four-fifths the hiring rate for the majority group.

Gainsharing: Group incentive program that measures improvements in productivity and effectiveness objectives and distributes a portion of each gain to employees.

Generalizable: Valid in other contexts beyond the context in which the selection method was developed.

Glass Ceiling: Circumstances resembling an invisible barrier that keep most women and minorities from attaining the top jobs in organizations.

Global Organization: An organization that chooses to locate a facility based on the ability to effectively, efficiently, and flexibly produce a product or service, using cultural differences as an advantage.

Graphic Rating Scale: Method of performance measurement that lists traits and provides a rating scale for each trait; the employer uses the scale to indicate the extent to which an employee displays each trait.

Grievance Procedure: The process for resolving union-management conflicts over interpretation or violation of a collective bargaining agreement.

Health Maintenance Organization (HMO): A health care plan that requires patients to receive their medical care from the HMO's health care professionals, who are often paid a flat salary, and provides all services on a prepaid basis.

High-Performance Work System: An organization in which technology, organizational structure, people, and processes work together seamlessly to give an organization an advantage in the competitive environment.

Host Country: A country (other than the parent country) in which an organization operates a facility.

Hot-Stove Rule: Principle of discipline that says discipline should be like a hot stove, giving clear warning and following up with consistent, objective, immediate consequences.

Hourly Wage: Rate of pay for each hour worked.

HR Analytics: Type of assessment of HRM effectiveness that involves determining the impact of, or the financial cost and benefits of, a program or practice.

HR Dashboard: A display of a series of HR measures, showing the measure and progress toward meeting it.

HRM Audit: A formal review of the outcomes of HRM functions, based on identifying key HRM functions and measures of business performance.

Human Capital: An organization's employees, described in terms of their training, experience, judgment, intelligence, relationships, and insight.

Human Resource Information System (HRIS): A computer system used to acquire, store, manipulate, analyze, retrieve, and distribute information related to an organization's human resources.

Human Resource Management (HRM): The policies, practices, and systems that influence employees' behavior, attitudes, and performance.

Human Resource Planning: Identifying the numbers and types of employees the organization will require in order to meet its objectives.

Immigration Reform and Control Act of 1986: Federal law requiring employers to verify and maintain records on applicants' legal rights to work in the United States.

Incentive pay: Forms of pay linked to an employee's performance as an individual, group member, or organization member.

Industrial Engineering: The study of jobs to find the simplest way to structure work in order to maximize efficiency.

Industrial Union: Labor union whose members are linked by their work in a particular industry.

Instructional Design: A process of systematically developing training to meet specified needs.

Interactional Justice: A judgment that the organization carried out its actions in a way that took the employee's feelings into account.

Internal Labor Force: An organization's workers (its employees and the people who have contracts to work at the organization).

International Organization: An organization that sets up one or a few facilities in one or a few foreign countries.

Internship: On-the-job learning sponsored by an educational institution as a component of an academic program.

Involuntary Turnover: Turnover initiated by an employer (often with employees who would prefer to stay).

Job: A set of related duties.

Job Analysis: The process of getting detailed information about jobs.

Job Description: A list of the tasks, duties, and responsibilities (TDRs) that a particular job entails.

Job Design: The process of defining how work will be performed and what tasks will be required in a given job.

Job Enlargement: Broadening the types of tasks performed in a job.

Job Enrichment: Empowering workers by adding more decision-making authority to jobs.

Job Evaluation: An administrative procedure for measuring the relative internal worth of the organization's jobs.

Job Experiences: The combination of relationships, problems, demands, tasks, and other features of an employee's job.

Job Extension: Enlarging jobs by combining several relatively simple jobs to form a job with a wider range of tasks.

Job Hazard Analysis Technique: Safety promotion technique that involves breaking down a job into basic elements, then rating each element for its potential for harm or injury.

Job Involvement: The degree to which people identify themselves with their jobs.

Job Posting: The process of communicating information about a job vacancy on company bulletin boards, in employee publications, on corporate intranets, and anywhere else the organization communicates with employees.

Job Rotation: Enlarging jobs by moving employees among several different jobs.

Job Satisfaction: A pleasant feeling resulting from the perception that one's job fulfills or allows for the fulfillment of one's important job values.

Job Sharing: A work option in which two part-time employees carry out the tasks associated with a single job.

Job Specification: A list of the knowledge, skills, abilities, and other characteristics (KSAOs) that an individual must have to perform a particular job.

Job Structure: The relative pay for different jobs within the organization.

Job Withdrawal: A set of behaviors with which employees try to avoid the work situation physically, mentally, or emotionally.

Knowledge Workers: Employees whose main contribution to the organization is specialized knowledge, such as knowledge of customers, a process, or a profession.

Labor Relations: Field that emphasizes skills that managers and union leaders can use to minimize costly forms of conflict (such as strikes) and seek win-win solutions to disagreements.

Leaderless Group Discussion: An assessment center exercise in which a team of five to seven employees is assigned a problem and must work together to solve it within a certain time period.

Leading Indicators: Objective measures that accurately predict future labor demand.

Learning Management System (LMS):   A computer application that automates the administration, development, and delivery of training programs.

Learning Organization: An organization that supports lifelong learning by enabling all employees to acquire and share knowledge.

Long-Term Disability Insurance: Insurance that pays a percentage of a disabled employee's salary after an initial period and potentially for the rest of the employee's life.

Maintenance of Membership: Union security rules not requiring union membership but requiring that employees who join the union remain members for a certain period of time.

Management by Objectives (MBO):   A system in which people at each level of the organization set goals in a process that flows from top to bottom, so employees at all levels are contributing to the organization's overall goals; these goals become the standards for evaluating each employee's performance.

Material Safety Data Sheets (MSDSs):   Forms on which chemical manufacturers and importers identify the hazards of their chemicals.

Mediation: Conflict resolution procedure in which a mediator hears the views of both sides and facilitates the negotiation process but has no formal authority to dictate a resolution.

Mentor: An experienced, productive senior employee who helps develop a less experienced employee (a protégé).

Merit Pay: A system of linking pay increases to ratings on performance appraisals.

Minimum Wage: The lowest amount that employers may pay under federal or state law, stated as an amount of pay per hour.

Mixed-Standard Scales: Method of performance measurement that uses several statements describing each trait to produce a final score for that trait.

Multinational Company: An organization that builds facilities in a number of different countries in an effort to minimize production and distribution costs.

Multiple-Hurdle Model: Process of arriving at a selection decision by eliminating some candidates at each stage of the selection process.

Myers-Briggs Type Indicator (MBTI):   Psychological inventory that identifies individuals' preferences for source of energy, means of information gathering, way of decision making, and lifestyle, providing information for team building and leadership development.

National Labor Relations Act (NLRA):   Federal law that supports collective bargaining and sets out the rights of employees to form unions.

National Labor Relations Board (NLRB):   Federal government agency that enforces the NLRA by conducting and certifying representation elections and investigating unfair labor practices.

Needs Assessment: The process of evaluating the organization, individual employees, and employees' tasks to determine what kinds of training, if any, are necessary.

Nepotism: The practice of hiring relatives.

Noncontributory Plan: Retirement plan funded entirely by contributions from the employer.

Nondirective Interview: A selection interview in which the interviewer has great discretion in choosing questions to ask each candidate.

Nonexempt Employees: Employees covered by the FLSA requirements for overtime pay.

Occupational Safety and Health Act (OSH Act):   U.S. law authorizing the federal government to establish and enforce occupational safety and health standards for all places of employment engaging in interstate commerce.

Occupational Safety and Health Administration (OSHA):   Labor Department agency responsible for inspecting employers, applying safety and health standards, and levying fines for violation.

Office of Federal Contract Compliance Programs (OFCCP):   The agency responsible for enforcing the executive orders that cover companies doing business with the federal government.

Offshoring: Moving operations from the country where a company is headquartered to a country where pay rates are lower but the necessary skills are available.

On-the-Job Training (OJT):   Training methods in which a person with job experience and skill guides trainees in practicing job skills at the workplace.

Open-Door Policy: An organization's policy of making managers available to hear complaints.

Organization Analysis: A process for determining the appropriateness of training by evaluating the characteristics of the organization.

Organizational Behavior Modification (OBM):   A plan for managing the behavior of employees through a formal system of feedback and reinforcement.

Organizational Commitment: The degree to which an employee identifies with the organization and is willing to put forth effort on its behalf.

Orientation: Training designed to prepare employees to perform their jobs effectively, learn about their organization, and establish work relationships.

Outcome Fairness: A judgment that the consequences given to employees are just.

Outplacement Counseling: A service in which professionals try to help dismissed employees manage the transition from one job to another.

Outsourcing: Contracting with another organization (vendor, third-party provider, or consultant) to provide services.

Paired-Comparison Method: Method of performance measurement that compares each employee with each other employee to establish rankings.

Panel Interview: Selection interview in which several members of the organization meet to interview each candidate.

Parent Country: The country in which an organization's headquarters is located.

Patient Protection and Affordable Care Act: Health care reform law passed in 2010 that includes incentives and penalties for employers providing health insurance as a benefit.

Pay Differential: Adjustment to a pay rate to reflect differences in working conditions or labor markets.

Pay Grades: Sets of jobs having similar worth or content, grouped together to establish rates of pay.

Pay Level: The average amount (including wages, salaries, and bonuses) the organization pays for a particular job.

Pay Policy Line: A graphed line showing the mathematical relationship between job evaluation points and pay rate.

Pay Ranges: A set of possible pay rates defined by a minimum, maximum, and midpoint of pay for employees holding a particular job or a job within a particular pay grade.

Pay Structure: The pay policy resulting from job structure and pay level decisions.

Peer Review: Process for resolving disputes by taking them to a panel composed of representatives from the organization at the same levels as the people in the dispute.

Pension Benefit Guarantee Corporation (PBGC):   Federal agency that insures retirement benefits and guarantees retirees a basic benefit if the employer experiences financial difficulties.

Performance Management: The process through which managers ensure that employees' activities and outputs contribute to the organization's goals.

Person Analysis: A process for determining individuals' needs and readiness for training.

Personnel Selection: The process through which organizations make decisions about who will or will not be allowed to join the organization.

Piecework Rate: Rate of pay for each unit produced.

Position: The set of duties (job) performed by a particular person.

Position Analysis Questionnaire (PAQ):   A standardized job analysis questionnaire containing 194 questions about work behaviors, work conditions, and job characteristics that apply to a wide variety of jobs.

Predictive Validation: Research that uses the test scores of all applicants and looks for a relationship between the scores and future performance of the applicants who were hired.

Preferred Provider Organization (PPO):   A health care plan that contracts with health care professionals to provide services at a reduced fee and gives patients financial incentives to use network providers.

Procedural Justice: A judgment that fair methods were used to determine the consequences an employee receives.

Profit Sharing: Incentive pay in which payments are a percentage of the organization's profits and do not become part of the employees' base salary.

Progressive Discipline: A formal discipline process in which the consequences become more serious if the employee repeats the offense.

Promotion: Assignment of an employee to a position with greater challenges, more responsibility, and more authority than in the previous job, usually accompanied by a pay increase.

Protean Career: A career that frequently changes based on changes in the person's interests, abilities, and values and in the work environment.

Psychological Contract: A description of what an employee expects to contribute in an employment relationship and what the employer will provide the employee in exchange for those contributions.

Readability: The difficulty level of written materials.

Readiness for Training: A combination of employee characteristics and positive work environment that permit training.

Realistic Job Preview: Background information about a job's positive and negative qualities.

Reasonable Accommodation: An employer's obligation to do something to enable an otherwise qualified person to perform a job.

Recruiting: Any activity carried on by the organization with the primary purpose of identifying and attracting potential employees.

Recruitment: The process through which the organization seeks applicants for potential employment.

Reengineering: A complete review of the organization's critical work processes to make them more efficient and able to deliver higher quality.

Referrals: People who apply for a vacancy because someone in the organization prompted them to do so.

Reliability: The extent to which a measurement is from random error.

Repatriation: The process of preparing expatriates to return home from a foreign assignment.

Right-to-Know Laws: State laws that require employers to provide employees with information about the health risks associated with exposure to substances considered hazardous.

Right-to-Work Laws: State laws that make union shops, maintenance of membership, and agency shops illegal.

Role: The set of behaviors that people expect of a person in a particular job.

Role Ambiguity: Uncertainty about what the organization expects from the employee in terms of what to do or how to do it.

Role Analysis Technique: A process of formally identifying expectations associated with a role.

Role Conflict: An employee's recognition that demands of the job are incompatible or contradictory.

Role Overload: A state in which too many expectations or demands are placed on a person.

Sabbatical: A leave of absence from an organization to renew or develop skills.

Salary: Rate of pay for each week, month, or year worked.

Scanlon Plan: A gainsharing program in which employees receive a bonus if the ratio of labor costs to the sales value of production is below a set standard.

Selection: The process by which the organization attempts to identify applicants with the necessary knowledge, skills, abilities, and other characteristics that will help the organization achieve its goals.

Self-Assessment: The use of information by employees to determine their career interests, values, aptitudes, and behavioral tendencies.

Self-Service: System in which employees have online access to information about HR issues and go online to enroll themselves in programs and provide feedback through surveys.

Sexual Harassment: Unwelcome sexual advances as defined by the EEOC.

Short-Term Disability Insurance: Insurance that pays a percentage of a disabled employee's salary as benefits to the employee for six months or less.

Simple Ranking: Method of performance measurement that requires managers to rank employees in their group from the highest performer to the poorest performer.

Simulation: A training method that represents a real-life situation, with trainees making decisions resulting in outcomes that mirror what would happen on the job.

Situational Interviews: A structured interview in which the interviewer describes a situation likely to arise on the job, then asks the candidate what he or she would do in that situation.

Skill-Based Pay Systems: Pay structures that set pay according to the employees' levels of skill or knowledge and what they are capable of doing.

Social Security: The federal Old Age, Survivors, Disability, and Health Insurance (OASDHI) program, which combines old age (retirement) insurance, survivor's insurance, disability insurance, hospital insurance (Medicare Part A), and supplementary medical insurance (Medicare Part B) for the elderly.

Stakeholders: The parties with an interest in the company's success (typically, shareholders, the community, customers, and employees).

Standard Hour Plan: An incentive plan that pays workers extra for work done in less than a preset "standard time."

Stock Options: Rights to buy a certain number of shares of stock at a specified price.

Straight Piecework Plan: Incentive pay in which the employer pays the same rate per piece, no matter how much the worker produces.

Strike: A collective decision by union members not to work until certain demands or conditions are met.

Structured Interview: A selection interview that consists of a predetermined set of questions for the interviewer to ask.

Succession Planning: The process of identifying and tracking high-potential employees who will be able to fill top management positions when they become vacant.

Summary Plan Description: Report that describes a pension plan's funding, eligibility requirements, risks, and other details.

Sustainability: An organization's ability to profit without depleting its resources, including employees, natural resources, and the support of the surrounding community.

Talent Management: A systematic, planned effort to attract, retain, develop, and motivate highly skilled employees and managers.

Task Analysis: The process of identifying and analyzing tasks to be trained for.

Team Leader Training: Training in the skills necessary for effectively leading the organization's teams.

Teamwork: The assignment of work to groups of employees with various skills who interact to assemble a product or provide a service.

Technic of Operations Review (TOR): Method of promoting safety by determining which specific element of a job led to a past accident.

Third Country: A country that is neither the parent country nor the host country of an employer.

360-Degree Performance Appraisal: Performance measurement that combines information from the employee's managers, peers, subordinates, self, and customers.

Total Quality Management (TQM): A company-wide effort to continuously improve the ways people, machines, and systems accomplish work.

Training: An organization's planned efforts to help employees acquire job-related knowledge, skills, abilities, and behaviors, with the goal of applying these on the job.

Transaction Processing: Computations and calculations involved in reviewing and documenting HRM decisions and practices.

Transfer: Assignment of an employee to a position in a different area of the company, usually in a lateral move.

Transfer of Training: On-the-job use of knowledge, skills, and behaviors learned in training.

Transitional Matrix: A chart that lists job categories held in one period and shows the proportion of employees in each of those job categories in a future period.

Transnational HRM System: Type of HRM system that makes decisions from a global perspective, includes managers from many countries, and is based on ideas contributed by people representing a variety of cultures.

Trend Analysis: Constructing and applying statistical models that predict labor demand for the next year, given relatively objective statistics from the previous year.

Unemployment Insurance: A federally mandated program to minimize the hardships of unemployment through payments to unemployed workers, help in finding new jobs, and incentives to stabilize employment.

Uniform Guidelines on Employee Selection Procedures: Guidelines issued by the EEOC and other agencies to identify how an organization should develop and administer its system for selecting employees so as not to violate antidiscrimination laws.

Union Shop: Union security arrangement that requires employees to join the union within a certain amount of time (30 days) after beginning employment.

Union Steward: An employee elected by union members to represent them in ensuring that the terms of the labor contract are enforced.

Unions: Organizations formed for the purpose of representing their members' interests in dealing with employers.

Utility: The extent to which something provides economic value greater than its cost.

Validity: The extent to which performance on a measure (such as a test score) is related to what the measure is designed to assess (such as job performance).

Vesting Rights: Guarantee that when employees become participants in a pension plan and work a specified number of years, they will receive a pension at retirement age, regardless of whether they remained with the employer.

Virtual Reality: A computer-based technology that provides an interactive, three-dimensional learning experience.

Voluntary Turnover: Turnover initiated by employees (often when the organization would prefer to keep them).

Work Flow Design: The process of analyzing the tasks necessary for the production of a product or service.

Workers' Compensation: State programs that provide benefits to workers who suffer work-related injuries or illnesses, or to their survivors.

Workforce Analytics: The use of quantitative tools and scientific methods to analyze data from human resource databases and other sources to make evidence-based decisions that support business goals.

Workforce Utilization Review: A comparison of the proportion of employees in protected groups with the proportion that each group represents in the relevant labor market.

Yield Ratio: A ratio that expresses the percentage of applicants who successfully move from one stage of the recruitment and selection process to the next.

Photo Credits

Name and Company Index

Subject Index